James D. Bulloch

James D. Bulloch

*Secret Agent and Mastermind
of the Confederate Navy*

WALTER E. WILSON *and*
GARY L. MCKAY

McFarland & Company, Inc., Publishers
Jefferson, North Carolina, and London

LIBRARY OF CONGRESS CATALOGUING-IN-PUBLICATION DATA

Wilson, Walter E., 1949–
James D. Bulloch : secret agent and mastermind of the
Confederate navy / Walter E. Wilson and Gary L. McKay.
p.   cm.

Includes bibliographical references and index.

ISBN 0-7864-6659-7
softcover : acid free paper ∞

1. Bulloch, James Dunwoody, 1823–1901.   2. United States — History — Civil War, 1861–1865 — Biography.   3. Spies — Confederate States of America — Biography.   4. Confederate States of America. Navy — Officials and employees — Biography.   5. United States — History — Civil War, 1861–1865 — Secret service.   6. United States — History — Civil War, 1861–1865 — Naval operations, Confederate.   7. Confederate States of America — Foreign relations — Great Britain.   8. Great Britain — Foreign relations — Confederate States of America.   I. McKay, Gary L.   II. Title.
E467.1.B85W55   2012   973.7'57092 — dc23   [B]   2012000884

BRITISH LIBRARY CATALOGUING DATA ARE AVAILABLE

© 2012 Walter E. Wilson and Gary L. McKay. All rights reserved

*No part of this book may be reproduced or transmitted in any form
or by any means, electronic or mechanical, including photocopying
or recording, or by any information storage and retrieval system,
without permission in writing from the publisher.*

Front cover: James Dunwoody Bulloch (by Henry Skinner, Liverpool,
c. late 1860s); cover design by David K. Landis (Shake It Loose Graphics)

Manufactured in the United States of America

*McFarland & Company, Inc., Publishers
Box 611, Jefferson, North Carolina 28640
www.mcfarlandpub.com*

Contents

Preface	1
1. In Connection with Great and Irresistible Events	3
2. Esteemed and Worthy	7
3. A Man of Amiable Character	18
4. Against Strong Northerly Winds and Head Seas — Prelude to War	31
5. Brains and Dash — Liverpool, 1861	44
6. Anglo-Rebel Pirates and Confederate Navy Cruisers — 1862	62
7. Of Incalculable Value — 1862	94
8. Grim Aspect and Formidable Equipment — 1863	111
9. Harassing Perplexity — 1863	135
10. Act Upon Your Own Judgment — 1864	155
11. I Know Not What Your Circumstances May Be — 1865	187
12. Under a New Flag	210
13. Once More	225
14. A President's Oracle	247
15. From Splendid Isolation	275
Appendix 1: Bulloch's Family, Friends, and Foes	287
Appendix 2: Bulloch's Fleet of Ships	295
Chapter Notes	301
Bibliography	339
Index	351

Preface

Imagine one morning, every major network interrupts its programming with the news that over 100 U.S. merchant ships have been captured and sunk in oceans around the world. At the same time, mysterious underwater explosions are sinking U.S. Navy ships as they attempt to enter or exit Norfolk Naval Base.

Imagine that the city of Washington, D.C., wakes the next day only to discover a fearsome warship looming out of the Potomac River fog. Incredibly, the vessel begins to bombard the city and proves to be impervious to all attacks. In a distinctly American accent, the captain of the ship vows to completely destroy the city unless the government pays a ransom — in gold. Imagine that the people turn to their president for answers and the nation is staggered: he has been kidnapped and spirited out of the country! Finally, imagine that one man was behind it all, and this man is the uncle of a future president of the United States of America.

While this scenario sounds more like Hollywood than history, the Confederate Navy planned or executed every one of the events just described during the American Civil War. For each of these operations, there was only one man who could make them possible: Commander James Dunwoody Bulloch. He was the Confederate Navy's secret agent and head of its covert shipbuilding and logistics program in Europe during the American Civil War. Bulloch acquired the Confederacy's most destructive commerce raiders, built "invulnerable" ocean-going ironclads, sustained Confederate logistics, and financed covert operations. He was President Theodore Roosevelt's favorite uncle and hero. The story of Bulloch's development into one of America's most admired maritime figures, his pivotal role as one of its most dangerous enemies, and his transformation into America's greatest forgotten naval hero is the subject of this book.

Despite the importance of James D. Bulloch to American and world history, there has never been a dedicated biography of his life and influence. This omission is largely due to the popular focus on his ships, particularly the *Alabama*, *Florida*, *Shenandoah*, and *Stonewall*. Other factors include Bulloch's penchant for secrecy and the difficulty in researching a person who spent equal parts of his life in the U.S. and Great Britain. This work was written by Gary McKay, Ph.D., based in Europe, who has tactical U.S. Navy and Army intelligence experience, and Captain Walter Wilson, U.S. Navy (retired), who is based in the U.S. and is the former senior U.S. naval intelligence officer in Europe.

A work of this magnitude could not have been completed without the encouragement and unselfish cooperation of myriad personal and professional associates. The authors owe a particular debt of gratitude to Gwen Koehler, the Bulloch Hall education coordinator. She not only provided invaluable family history and original source material, she spent many hours meticulously helping the authors review and refine the narrative. As a special treat, the authors met Gwen and the Bulloch Hall staff in Roswell, Georgia, where we composed and collaborated on portions of the text in the Bulloch family home. Equally important was the inspiration provided by Bob Jones and Roy Rawlinson, the preeminent local historians of the American Civil War in Liverpool. Roy also originated the informative "When Liverpool Was Dixie" website.

The authors also thank Gilly Little for her professional editorial assistance. Sharon Wilson provided moral support and invaluable assistance with the final editing of the text. James "Hal" Hardaway remained a constant source of encouragement. Andrew Choong Han Lin (curator of Historic Photographs and Ship Plans, National Maritime Museum, Greenwich, England) provided research assistance and helpful suggestions. Dr. Tom Sebrell provided invaluable insight based on his in-depth study of Charles K. Prioleau. The authors offer profound thanks to Richard Harris and appreciation to Robert Thorpe for permission to use information from his forthcoming book on W.C. Miller. Thanks are also due to Mr. Michael Higgins, retired commercial maritime captain, the foremost expert on the construction and operations of the *CSS Shenandoah* (ex–*Sea King*).

The following persons and archives were generous with their time and advice in offering access to their priceless resources. Teresa Roane (library manager, Museum of the Confederacy, Richmond, Virginia), Douglas J. Mayo (associate librarian, John D. Rockefeller, Jr., Library, Colonial Williamsburg Foundation), Amanda K. Hawk (special collections assistant, Seeley G. Mudd Manuscript Library, Princeton, New Jersey), and Robert B. Hitchings (Sargeant Memorial Room, Norfolk Main Library). Finally, special thanks are in order for Wallace Finley Dailey (curator, Theodore Roosevelt Collection, Harvard College Library), who patiently identified and retrieved invaluable materials during multiple visits to Cambridge.

1

In Connection with Great and Irresistible Events

In the latter days of October 1905, the Appalachian foothill town of Roswell, Georgia, was colored by the brilliant red and gold falling leaves of autumn, while its streets were festooned with flags and pennants of red, white and blue. Local ladies opined that it was by far the most festive occasion in the sleepy town's history since at least the early 1850s. That occasion witnessed the lavish marriage of a daughter of one of Roswell's founding families into a prominent New York family. Not even the scourge of Sherman's "March Through Georgia" was as monumental as this event. For the offspring of the union between Martha "Mittie" Bulloch and Theodore Roosevelt, Sr., was coming to Roswell to visit his mother's home, Bulloch Hall. The president of the United States of America, Theodore "Teddy" Roosevelt, was on tour through the cities and towns of the South to speak to the societies and organizations that had been most affected by the American Civil War. Though the war had been over for forty years, few areas of the American South had been as devastated as Georgia.

How could the Republican Roosevelt possibly empathize with what the Southerners had experienced? Mittie Bulloch Roosevelt lived in New York City during the Civil War, where she raised Teddy and his brother and sisters in comfort and safety. To salve Southern wounds and soothe Northern sensibilities Roosevelt had to speak softly and deliver a message of compassionate conciliation, for his every word would be reported and printed in the national press. When Teddy Roosevelt stood before the people of Roswell, his words had to ring true in the hearts and minds of all Americans — both North and South. Roosevelt needed a miracle — and as had happened so many times in the past, a Bulloch came to the rescue of a Roosevelt, even though this Bulloch had been dead for four years, was considered to be a traitor to the United States, and was even connected with the assassination of President Abraham Lincoln. Yet, this Bulloch was Teddy's hero who epitomized his idea of a real man.

When Teddy Roosevelt rose to speak at Roswell Town Square, he did so with a stern, knowing look on his face. He knew he had a real American naval hero on his shoulder when he began to speak:

> It has been my great fortune to have the right to claim that my blood is half-Southern and half-Northern, and I would deny the right of any man here to feel a greater pride in deeds of every Southern man than I feel. Of the children, the brothers and sisters of my mother who were

brought up in that house on the hill there, my two uncles afterwards entered the Confederate service and served in the Confederate Navy. One, the youngest man ... [was] my Uncle Irvine Bulloch [and the other was] James Dunwoody Bulloch.

Roosevelt had unleashed the name of James Dunwoody Bulloch like a naval broadside. The effect was electric to the rapt audience, for Roosevelt could veritably see backs straighten and eyes glow with pride. Bulloch, the man who tormented the United States Navy and State departments, who brought Northern maritime trade to a virtual halt through commerce raiding, sustained the Confederate Army's ability to fight for an additional two years, and personally made the greatest blockade run during the Civil War, had sailed forth again from the lips of the president of the United States of America. And this Yankee was *damn* proud of what his Uncle Jimmie had accomplished.

Men and women, don't you think I have the ancestral right to claim a proud kinship with those who showed their devotion to duty as they saw their duty, whether they wore the grey or whether they wore the blue? All Americans who are worthy of the name feel an equal pride in the valor of those who fought on one side or the other, provided only that each did with all his might and soul and strength and mind his duty as it was given him to see his duty.

James Dunwoody Bulloch, who faithfully served as the Confederate Navy's secret agent throughout the American Civil War from his base in Liverpool, England, never returned to America (except to visit) and even obtained British citizenship. He was vilified by American ship owners for the depredations of his commerce-raiding cruisers, yet lionized and studied by U.S. and international naval strategists for his brilliant logistical, tactical, and strategic operations. Bulloch had inspired Teddy Roosevelt's interest in all things maritime since childhood, and when Roosevelt took a serious interest in U.S. naval affairs at Harvard University, he continued to tutor and encourage Teddy during his frequent visits to Liverpool. The birth of modern U.S. naval strategy, with precepts and concepts that remain valid in the twenty-first century, began with the conversations between James Dunwoody Bulloch and a young Theodore Roosevelt. Before Alfred Thayer Mahan and before Corbett of Britain, Roosevelt recognized the naval genius of his uncle. The special genius of Roosevelt in adapting and advocating Bulloch's ideas to elevate American expectations and become a great nation is a profound milestone in the continuum of American and world history.

The story of the extraordinary life of James Dunwoody Bulloch, the man lost to American history, begins where it ended, in England.

On 8 January 1901, newspapers throughout the United Kingdom reported the death of a 77-year-old gentleman at No. 76 Canning Street, Liverpool. With universal approbation from journals such as *The Scotsman* of Edinburgh, *The Times* of London and of course, the *Liverpool Post* and *Liverpool Mercury*, his life was described as "remarkable" and "chivalrous." He was "a man of amiable character and engaging manners."[1] The gentleman was James Dunwoody Bulloch, a native of the state of Georgia in the United States of America, but a resident of Liverpool and Britain for the last 39 years of his life.

Within a few days of the first British reports of Bulloch's death, the relatively new technology of the telegraph relayed the information to American newspaper rooms. While Northern newspapers such as the *New York Times* commented rather negatively on Bulloch's life, Southern newspapers sang his praises as if he had been a heroic Greek warrior in a Homeric poem. Lavish in its appreciation of his endeavors in the American Civil War, the *Savannah Morning News* said that he was the "naval representative of the Confederate States in Europe, and under his direction the fleet of cruisers that swept the merchant marine of the United States from the seas was built, launched and started on its errand of destruction."[2]

Continuing in this same vein, the *Morning News* wrote, "Bulloch's high services to the Confederate government found their best recognition in the hearty anathemas of the Federal authorities, and in the fact that he was one of the few remaining Confederates, upon which the United States had no pardon to bestow."[3] In fact, it was largely due to his exertions that the United States Government forced Great Britain into the first-ever international arbitration on war-related damages. Through a process known as the "*Alabama Claims*" Bulloch's name remained in the news for over seven years after the war. Washington managed to extract *15.5 million dollars* in gold or almost a billion dollars in current U.S. dollars for punitive damages.[4] The Confederacy may have disappeared into the rubbish heap of history, but Bulloch's success had irrevocably damaged, and eventually cost the United States its position as the world's leading merchant fleet. The cost to Britain, at the height of its Victorian power, was humiliation and an enormous amount of money.

Yet, neither the American nor British government ever prosecuted James Dunwoody Bulloch for his activities on behalf of the Confederate States of America. Why? The answer is complex, somewhat owing to the contemporary cultural and legal situation, but mostly embodied within the character of the man. Bulloch's life spanned the midpoint in America's ascendancy from a former colony of the British Empire to its evolution into a world superpower.

His ancestors and relations were a microcosm of this development, starting with great-grandfather Archibald Bulloch and extending to his young nephew "Teedie." Archibald had been the first governor and president of the state of Georgia after the American Revolution. Teedie became better known as Theodore Roosevelt, the former assistant secretary of the United States Navy, governor of New York, and soon thereafter, president of the United States of America.

Many historians have commented on Bulloch's legacy to the world's navies, both past and present, but his contributions have never been analyzed or defined in detail. Other than his 1883 two-volume memoir about his Confederate Navy exploits, Bulloch never publicly commented about his actions.

Naval specialists of the era could only speculate on key aspects of the Confederacy's international naval strategy and tactics. Recent naval historians have been keen to describe the exploits of his famous commerce raiders, such as the CSS *Florida*, CSS *Alabama*, and CSS *Shenandoah*, but have been extraordinarily silent about the remarkable man who was responsible for both the vessels and their strategies. This omission reflects the difficulty of researching a life spent in equal parts on two continents. It also reflects an academic reluctance to be associated with historical and biographical studies of leaders from the stigmatized Confederate States of America.

The man whose stratagems were studied by the Germans before World War I, whose ideas on the strategic employment of naval forces directly influenced President Theodore Roosevelt, and whose ideas about fast raiding boats would be recognizable by today's special warfare naval units, is long overdue for a biographical examination. As an intelligence operative, he provides a case study of an overt agent who was able to conduct covert operations and maintain secrecy. The U.S. Central Intelligence Agency (CIA), even today, maintains an "open source" publication citing the example of James Dunwoody Bulloch.[5]

The story of this quiet gentleman who lived "in connection with great and irresistible events," will at times have the appearance of a penny book romance, but it is an epic story, played out on the oceans and diplomatic parlors of the world. Before Bulloch's extraordinary vision, only the gods of the ancient Greeks would have dared to presume that the world's oceans could be used as a board game for the designs and whims of global strategy.

The preeminent naval and geo-political strategist Alfred Thayer Mahan paid homage to his ideas by noting that if one nation could deny another nation the use of the sea, that nation's economy would collapse, thus leading to victory. Bulloch fostered that vision, and although wildly successful in his wartime efforts, it was a goal he could not achieve with the time and means at his disposal. More importantly for the history of the United States and the rest of the world, he influenced those who could and did.

2

Esteemed and Worthy

The story of James Dunwoody Bulloch's family in America begins with his great-great-grandfather James Bulloch. Born in 1701, he emigrated from Scotland to Charleston around 1728, where he met and married Jean Stobo, daughter of Reverend Archibald Stobo. Their son, Archibald Bulloch (1730–1777), practiced law in South Carolina, and by 1757 joined the South Carolina militia as a lieutenant.[1] A year later, the elder Bulloch established the family's roots in Savannah, Georgia. When Archibald Bulloch followed in 1762, he rapidly made his presence felt in Georgia's political, cultural, and social affairs.

On 9 October 1764, Archibald married Mary De Veaux. Archibald had not only landed well, financially speaking, but he had also married into a Georgia family with a multitude of social and political connections that rivaled his own.[2] In their first four years of marriage, Mary and Archibald had four children: James, Archibald Jr., Jane, and William.

In 1768, Archibald was elected to the Common's House of Georgia as a member of the Liberty Party. Already, the southern colonies were cooperating with their counterparts in the North to address the increasingly cloudy relations with the mother country, Great Britain. Archibald Bulloch soon headed a committee that corresponded with Benjamin Franklin about the American colonies' growing list of grievances. Although Archibald's rebellious political activism made him known to Crown authorities, he was elected speaker of the Royal Assembly for Georgia in 1772. By 1775, the divisiveness of the independence and loyalist issues meant that Archibald presided over Georgia's political descent into civil war. As a firm supporter of independence, he was elected as the Colony's delegate to the Constitutional Congress in 1775.[3] There, he was a member of the "Secret Committee" in charge of gathering war supplies.[4] Echoes of these duties are reflected in the tasks James Dunwoody Bulloch performed for the Confederate Navy 86 years later.[5]

Archibald's meteoric rise both politically and militarily, reached its zenith on 20 June 1776 when he was elected as president of Georgia.[6] On 22 February 1777, in response to the threat of a British invasion from Florida, Georgia's Council for Safety granted him "executive powers of government," authorizing him to direct military operations. Like Julius Caesar, he became the *de facto* military as well as political leader of Georgia. Two days later, he was dead. Speculation persisted that political opponents poisoned him, playing the role of Brutus. Despite his untimely death, Archibald Bulloch's political and military legacy had far reaching influences on his great-grandson and the nation.[7]

Archibald's eldest son, James, was the grandfather of James Dunwoody Bulloch and the most accomplished of Archibald's progeny.[8] Born in 1765, James, like his father, Archi-

The USS *Erie* was James D. Bulloch's first assignment as a passed midshipman (U.S. Naval Historical Center).

bald, lived a short, but eventful life. From 1778 to 1781 he rose to the rank of captain in the Virginia State Garrison, even though he was only 16! At the conclusion of the War of Independence, he returned to Georgia where he joined the militia. By 1790, he again attained the rank of captain and was a clerk of both the Superior and Inferior Courts of Georgia.[9]

Married in 1786 to Ann Irvine, James had two daughters (Jane and Ann) and two sons, John Irvine and James Stephens Bulloch. If Archibald had provided the resilient political and military genes of the Bulloch clan, it was James Stephens who developed the financial and maritime acumen that would come to fruition in his son James Dunwoody.

When he was just thirteen years of age, James Stephens Bulloch's father died in 1807. By necessity, he grew up quickly and obtained a post as the deputy collector for customs at the Port of Savannah, became a major of the Chatham Battalion militia (named for the county surrounding Savannah), and was an officer of the Savannah branch of the U.S. Bank. Among a substantial list of achievements, he served as one of the directors of the company that underwrote the construction of the first steamship to cross the Atlantic Ocean, the SS *Savannah*.[10]

As busy as James Stephens' professional life was, he followed the Bulloch tradition of marrying well. On 31 December 1817, he married twenty-year-old Hester ("Hettie") Amarintha Elliott, the daughter of John Elliott, a U.S. senator from Georgia. Sen. Elliott was a considerable force in Georgia's affairs and James Stephens Bulloch married into the family as John Elliott's star was still in the ascendant.[11]

The maze of relationships in the new Bulloch-Elliott household would rival the complexity of any twenty-first century blended family unit. It appears that Hettie had not been James Stephens' first choice for a wife. A few months prior to his marriage to Hettie, he had proposed to eighteen-year-old Martha Stewart. It was only after Martha declined his proposal that James Stephens married Senator Elliott's daughter Hettie. In turn, or perhaps in spite, it was only one week later that Martha Stewart became the second wife of Senator Elliott.[12]

James Stephens and Hettie were already related through marriage. James' sister (Jane) had married Hettie's uncle John Dunwody. James would later become Dunwody's law partner.[13] James and Hettie's first son was born about 12 months later and named after his grandfather. Unfortunately, young John Elliott Bulloch died in September 1821.[14] On 25 June 1823, James Dunwoody, their only child to survive into adulthood, was born. Less than five years later, on 4 August 1827, Senator Elliott died of dysentery while trying to treat an outbreak that had already claimed 12 of the slaves on his plantation in Liberty County.[15]

Despite the loss of his most important political, social, and financial patron, James Stephens continued an active political, business, and social life in Savannah. He served as a city alderman and had several directorships in addition to his law partnership with his brother-in-law John Dunwody. Like many well-to-do southerners, Hettie and James rented out their Savannah home and left the stifling and unhealthy Georgia summers for the cooler northeast. They spent the spring and summer of 1829 with their young son in New York, returning in October to Savannah by ship.[16] Accompanying them were the now-widowed Martha Elliott, her three young children, and her stepdaughter Corinne.[17] Martha, James' former sweetheart and stepmother-in-law, was about the same age (30) as his wife Hettie, who by now was in ill health.

The following spring, the Bulloch family repeated the annual trek to the North. If these trips were an attempt to improve his wife's condition, they failed. James Dunwoody's mother, Hettie, died in February 1831 at the age of 32 "after a protracted and painful illness."[18]

After Hettie's death, James Stephens is believed to have moved in with his stepmother-in-law, Martha Stewart Elliott and her children in Savannah.[19] The maternal care that Martha provided along with the companionship of her children may have mitigated the trauma young James Dunwoody felt at the loss of his mother. Martha's presence was also a comfort to his father.

It was on 8 May 1832, fourteen months after Hettie's death, that the feelings of "sisterly regard" that Martha originally had for her stepson-in-law was officially transformed into matrimony. James Stephens joined his 8-year-old son, James Dunwoody, with Martha's own three young children: Susan Ann (11), Georgia Amanda (9), and Daniel Stewart (3).[20] To this large family, James and Martha soon added their own daughter, Anna, in 1833.

In addition to the large family at home, James Stephens and Martha had to contend with the offended sensibilities of Savannah's society. Living in the same house or marrying one's stepmother-in-law might have been acceptable, but taken together, the situation enlivened many a parlor discussion. The "very much enraged" feelings of John Elliott's nineteen-year-old daughter, Corinne Louisa, exacerbated the situation.[21] She had been "devotedly attached to her Step Mother" Martha, who had raised her from the age of five. However, after the marriage, she would "refuse to have any intercourse with her or her

Brother-in-Law."[22] Despite these initial hard feelings, Corinne would eventually become reconciled to the union.

Ironically, Corinne's tragic demise in a shipwreck off the coast of North Carolina in 1838 would have a profound effect on young James Dunwoody's own love life.[23] It was through the second marriage of Corinne's husband, Robert Hutchison (to Mary Edmonia Caskie), that the family was introduced to the future Mrs. James Dunwoody Bulloch.

The sizable estate that John Elliott left to his widow may have relieved some of the social pressure on James Stephens and Martha. It included acreage, cash, and a number of slaves.[24] Through this inheritance, her share of her father's sizable estate, and the sale of annual cotton crops, Martha was financially secure.[25] James and Martha were able to continue their luxurious habit of spending summers in the North. In June 1835, the expanded Bulloch family and at least one slave traveled to Hartford, Connecticut. According to family history, the reason for going to Hartford was to enroll 12-year-old James Dunwoody in an academy, but schooling for the two Elliott girls was also a factor. Martha Bulloch arrived in Hartford just weeks before she delivered their daughter Martha ("Mittie") in July 1835. Martha and the children lived there through 1837.[26] While there, James Dunwoody attended a college preparatory school and had individual instruction in Spanish, French, and singing.[27]

During this period, his father split his time between the family residence in Hartford and business in Georgia.[28] James Stephens corresponded with other Georgia planters, conducted business as a cotton broker, and closely followed the 1837 currency crisis and cotton prices. That year, he decided to move his family back to Savannah.[29] His plans were delayed by a lawsuit filed by the freed slave James Mars in the spring of 1837. The Bullochs had violated the state's 1774 statute forbidding the importation of slaves when they brought their slave Nancy Jackson with them to Connecticut.[30] In a case widely publicized by the abolitionist press, the Supreme Court of Errors ruled that Nancy had to be freed.[31] By the spring of 1838, they left the legal problems of Connecticut and the social discomfort of Savannah behind them and settled in Roswell, Georgia, a new community just north of the rail terminus that became Atlanta.

As part of the move, James Stephens Bulloch and Roswell King formed a business partnership to construct a cotton mill in Roswell. Moving from Savannah in 1839, the Bullochs temporarily lived in an abandoned Cherokee farmhouse on 480 acres of land called Clifton farm. There, James raised cotton and speculated in mineral resources, including a search for gold in the Georgia Gold Belt. A contemporary sketch titled "Diggin Major Bulloch's Gold" shows two men panning for gold on his property.[32] Attending to practical matters, he soon constructed one of Georgia's most famous neo-classical homes, located just off the small town's square. Occupied by the family in the winter of 1839, the stunning ante-bellum home came to be known as Bulloch Hall. It is one of the South's finest examples of authentic temple-style Greek Revival architecture.[33]

With the exception of their eldest son, James Dunwoody, the Bullochs raised their young family in Roswell. Another son, Charles Irvine, was born in 1838, but died just three years later. James Stephens and Martha's grief would have been assuaged in 1842 with the birth of Irvine Stephens. Two of the daughters, Susan and Martha (known as "Mittie"), were married in the house. Mittie's marriage was the more notable for she wed Theodore Roosevelt, Sr., the father of the future president of the United States.

By the time Irvine Stephens was born, James Dunwoody was 19 and had already served

2. Esteemed and Worthy

Bulloch Hall in Roswell, Georgia (Harold Alan Photographers, courtesy Janice Metzler, Bulloch Hall).

in the United States Navy for three years, having entered service on 21 June 1839. On that day, the young sailor was just four days shy of his 16th birthday and stood 5 feet, 8 inches tall with dark, almost black eyes and brown hair. His brother-in-law Robert Hutchison described him as having a low, but broad forehead, a small round chin with a large nose and small thin lips framed by a round face.[34] As a midshipman-in-training, he was first posted to the frigate USS *United States*, based at Boston. The frigate cruised along the eastern United States coast and made port calls at New York and Norfolk. James Stephens closely followed the progress of his son through his influential friends, including Georgia's former governor and current senator, Wilson Lumpkin.[35]

While at Norfolk, Virginia, Midshipman Bulloch transferred to the USS *Potomac* on 31 March 1840 along with the entire officer staff and crew of the USS *United States*. The *Potomac* then set sail for "Brazil station" where it remained from 12 May 1840 to 31 July 1842.[36] There, Bulloch received his first indication of full acceptance into the naval fraternity. The commanding officer of the *Potomac* recommended him for his warrant as a midshipman in January 1841. The promotion became official on 1 March 1841 and reflected his date of rank as 21 June 1839. After a year on board the *Potomac*, he transferred to the new sloop-of-war USS *Decatur*.[37] His experiences off Brazil, and the rest of South America, would serve him well during and after the American Civil War.

Bulloch served aboard the USS *Decatur* until a few days before her departure for the United States in late 1842. During his stint on board the *Decatur*, he served under three different commanding officers, including Captain David Glasgow Farragut who would become the U.S. Navy's first admiral and its most celebrated naval hero.[38] Rather than return with his ship to the United States, Midshipman Bulloch requested and received a transfer to the battleship-of-the-line USS *Delaware*.[39] He remained with the USS *Delaware* through the remainder of her South American cruise and subsequent deployment to the Mediterranean in February 1843. The USS *Delaware* returned to the U.S. on 4 March 1844, and was decommissioned later that month. Bulloch gained friends and practical experience during these deployments that helped advance his military and civilian careers. Since Midshipman Bulloch had earned 90 days of leave, he used it to visit family at Roswell and await his next duty assignment.[40]

While at home in Roswell on June 18th, he wrote to the Navy Department requesting a new set of orders. Midshipman Bulloch promptly received orders to the "Receiving Ship" at Norfolk on 27 June 1844.[41] This ship was the 120-gun USS *Pennsylvania* that served as a naval school for midshipman. Shortly afterwards, in August of 1844, he went to the naval school at the Philadelphia Naval Shipyard. There, his intellect and keen ambition held him in good stead, for he graduated second in his class.[42] Official naval records list his date of warrant as a "Passed Midshipman" as 2 July 1845.[43]

Insofar as the United States Navy was concerned, James Dunwoody Bulloch was fully entered into the faith and body of the holy order of the sail. Though he was only a lowly acolyte, he had taken his first, exciting step up the ladder that could lead him to a career of adventure and more importantly, command of his own vessel. For a truly ambitious young naval officer, it was command at sea that mattered most.

His orders must have been a disappointment for he was sent to the aging USS *Erie*, built 32 years previously as a sloop-of-war during the War with Great Britain (1812–15). The USS *Erie* soon departed for Pacific Station, where she arrived on 18 November 1845.[44] He may have thought that his first cruise aboard a tired old sloop-of-war, now relegated to the status of a glorified supply scow, would be tedious. However, America's foreign policy and hunger for continental expansion were about to add a touch of excitement for every sea-going naval officer.

Scharf's *History of the Confederate States Navy* vaguely describes Bulloch's career with the Pacific squadron as one of "being transferred to several different ships as the necessities of the service required." Consequently, the first firm indication of his reappearance in historical records is his assignment to the USS *Shark* in the spring of 1846. The *Shark* was a small schooner, but at least she was a warship.

Bulloch served as acting master of the *Shark*, and this title alone indicated the smooth progression of his naval career. The position of acting master was granted only to those who had demonstrated particularly good shiphandling skills. The weapons aboard the *Shark* included two 9-pound "Long Tom" guns and ten 18-pound cannonades and a crew of 70 officers and ratings. When the schooner was launched at the Washington, D.C., naval yard in May 1821, her first commander was the renowned Lt. Matthew C. Perry.[45]

The *Shark* had been cruising off the coast of Peru for five years when she was ordered to Honolulu, Hawaii, on 1 April 1846. There, she was refit for a deployment to the coast of Oregon Territory and an exploratory cruise up the Columbia River. At that time, Great Britain and the United States both claimed the area north of the Columbia. The U.S. Navy was Washington's policy "stick" of choice to propagate and project "manifest destiny" policies on the far side of the North American continent.[46] As the *Shark* prepared for her mission, "Oregon Treaty" negotiations were underway in Washington to set the boundary between British North America (Canada) and the Northwestern United States. Despite the outbreak of the U.S.-Mexican War in April 1846, the USS *Shark* continued on its "exploration" mission to the Columbia River under the command of Lt. Neil Howison. The U.S. Navy needed to assert its claim and ascertain the intentions of its powerful neighbor that occupied much of what would become the state of Washington.

The USS *Shark* arrived off Fort Vancouver on the evening of 24 July 1846. Fort Vancouver was a fur trading post on the north side of the Columbia River. It was also the headquarters of the Hudson's Bay Company, the famous British trade firm that dominated the early history of Canada.[47] Located 100 miles up the Columbia River, the site was close to the mouth of the Willamette River on a wide flat plain. Consequently, ocean-going vessels faced a considerable challenge in negotiating the insidious river currents and shoals to reach the fort. For traders and the permanent inhabitants of the trade outpost, Fort Vancouver offered ready access to beaver-filled streams and fertile fields.

As the *Shark* approached the anchorage, Bulloch sighted another sailing ship lying before the fort. It was the sloop *Modeste* of Her Britannic Majesty's fleet. The commanding officer, Capt. Baillie, immediately sent over his "compliments and offer of services." The hospitable British had seen the *Shark* prowling off the mouth of the Columbia, but they had not expected her to come up river.[48] For the next thirty days, the *Shark* and her crew sailed up and down the navigable portions of the river visiting the small settlements. The British and Americans had frequent and friendly contact including a fully laid-on evening meal and a horse race for the officers of the *Shark* at the invitation of their British hosts.[49]

As acting master of the *Shark*, Bulloch was responsible for supervising the schooner's daily activities. Navigation was a considerable challenge since the waters of the Columbia River were virtually uncharted. In his official report, Howison says that the *Shark* briefly grounded on 26 July 1846 while making its way into the Willamette River. He sent off a boat to reconnoiter up the river and to visit Oregon City. His other objective was to gain intelligence about American settlers living in the area and to ascertain their relations with their British rulers.[50] Bulloch was probably left behind to get the vessel afloat and under weigh again.

On 20 August 1846, the American *Oregon Spectator* noted, "We have recently been honored with the presence of the officers of the U.S. schr. *Shark* amongst us, and heartily glad we were to see them. There appears to be an indefinable something about them different from officers of other nations." Bulloch, while busy with the routine tasks of ship management, was also keenly observing how Howison and the other officers handled their relations with the British. It was a practical education in localized international diplomacy that all U.S. naval officers of the era were expected to attain.

On 23 August 1846 after bidding his gracious hosts farewell, Howison turned the bow of the *Shark* westward to head down the Columbia River. The vessel made a slow and careful procession to the mouth of the Columbia. Their experience of grounding was foremost in their minds (and it likely occurred several times in the uncharted waters). The *Shark* didn't attempt the turbulent mouth of the Columbia River until 10 September 1846. In navigating the dramatic and dangerous collision of the waters of the Pacific Ocean and the Columbia River, the *Shark* made several attempts to plow through the towering waves and over the hidden sandbars. However, the ship was driven toward the southern side of the Columbia's mouth and wrecked on Clatsop Spit on the afternoon of September 10th.

While Howison's report is in the crisp style typical of a naval officer, his letter to Bulloch's father is more illuminating of the terrifying situation confronting the crew of the *Shark*. Howison had ordered "Abandon ship!" and detailed Bulloch to take command of the boats and remove the crew before they were lost. Howison praised Bulloch's conduct in this life-threatening situation and noted that the crew was "dependent for our lives on the good management and return of the boats under his charge ... an hour later or the least loss of time or mismanagement in his pull through darkness and breakers ... would have found us swept away." The men were saved but all of the ship's papers and property went down with her, possibly including some $4,000 in gold.[51]

Further testimony of his "gallantry, perseverance and skill" came from the ship's executive officer, Lieutenant Woodhull Smith Schenck, who told his brother James (who would be promoted to rear admiral) about Bulloch's heroism. Since Lt. Schenck was a married man, Bulloch volunteered to take his place on the wreck. He credited Bulloch with saving the lives of the seventeen men who were stranded onboard the wreck of the *Shark* overnight.[52]

Howison's official report said, "Cast on the shore as we were, with nothing besides the clothes we stood in, and those thoroughly saturated, no time was to be lost in seeking new supplies. I left the crew, indifferently sheltered, at Astoria, and ... pushed up the river to Vancouver; whither news of our disaster had preceded us, and elicited the sympathy of and prompt attentions of the factors [trade managers] of the Hudson's Bay Company and of Captain Baillie and the officers of her Britannic Majesty's ship *Modeste*."[53]

Howison and the crew of the *Shark* braved the winter weather trying to salvage the vessel until finally abandoning their efforts in mid–January 1847. On 16 January 1847, the entire crew boarded the *Cadboro* (a leased fur-trading vessel) bound for San Francisco and arrived there on 27 January 1847.[54]

For Bulloch, it had been an adventure and the severest instruction about the ultimate danger facing all seamen, shipwreck. It had also been a relevant lesson in foreign policy with the most powerful nation in the world, the British Empire. The kindnesses and pragmatism of the Royal Navy and British managers of the Hudson's Bay Company impressed upon him a different way of thinking and managing affairs, in both a personal and national sense.

While Bulloch and the *Shark* were guarding U.S. interests in the Northwest, the remainder of the U.S. Pacific Squadron was conducting offensive operations from San Francisco along the entirety of the California and Mexico coastline. After arriving in California, Bulloch soon rejoined the USS *Erie*, and participated in the naval brigade's occupation of Mazatlan on 11 November 1847.[55]

The *Erie* sailed for the East Coast shortly thereafter, but Bulloch stayed with the Pacific Squadron, transferring to the sloop USS *Warren* as part of the U.S. Coast Survey.[56] This assignment seemed perfectly to match the needs of the service with the skills of the individual. Given the ongoing war with Mexico, it is doubtful that the *Warren* had much time for surveying duties. But the idea of participating in more scientific pursuits must have intrigued him. The U.S. had just acquired a largely unexplored continental shelf and Bulloch possessed the navigational skills and practical experience to create new and accurate charts. The final phase of his U.S. Navy career would be spent with the U.S. Coast Survey on the West and East Coasts. However, before he departed the California coast, another seminal event occurred in the life of the nation.

The discovery of gold at Sutter's Mill, California, in January 1848 added impetus to America's expansion and financed the transformation of its economic, political, social, and military infrastructure. Overnight, America entered into the front rank of nations, though Washington may not have fully grasped the strategic shift until much later. The discovery of gold had an immediate, practical effect on Navy crewmen. By May 1848, able-bodied U.S. Army and Navy personnel either abandoned their posts, or refused to sign new enlistment contracts. They left to hunt for gold.

When the Pacific Squadron restricted shore leave in California to stem the tide of rampant desertions, Bulloch had time to think and assess. His thoughts must have returned to his own father's speculative ventures in Roswell during the Georgia gold rush.[57] As the California gold rush reached fever pitch, 25-year-old James Dunwoody Bulloch found himself a hero in the eyes of his shipmates, but demoted in the rigid estimation of the Navy. Due to the number of more senior passed midshipmen, Bulloch lost his appointment as master when he returned to the squadron. It was in this environment of supreme sacrifice and gluttonous opportunity that Bulloch received orders to return to the East Coast and remain with the Coast Survey.

In October 1848 while he was at Monterey, CA, Bulloch transferred to the store ship USS *Lexington* that was headed for San Francisco to take in gold. The *Lexington* left San Francisco on 28 November 1848 with Bulloch and $500,000 in gold on board. From there, the ship proceeded by way of the Sandwich Islands (Hawaii) and Valparaiso, Chile. Sailing around the horn, he did not reach Rio de Janeiro until 20 January 1849.[58]

While he was enjoying a Brazilian port call, events in Roswell would have profound effects for both Bulloch and the nation. At Bulloch Hall on 25 January 1849, Martha's daughter Susan Elliott married Hilborne West, a Philadelphia merchant who introduced the Bullochs to the Roosevelts. West's sister Mary had previously married Silas Weir Roosevelt, the older brother of Theodore Roosevelt, Sr. On a visit to Philadelphia in 1848, Susan and Hilborne had regaled the Roosevelts with tales of the beauty of Bulloch Hall—and of her sister "Mittie." Not surprisingly, Theodore Roosevelt, Sr., accepted Susan and Hilborne's invitation to attend their wedding at Bulloch Hall. Upon reaching Roswell, Roosevelt may well have appreciated the beauty of the South, but the stunningly beautiful 15-year-old "Mittie" Bulloch bowled him over. The future parents of the 26th president of the United States of America had met. Bulloch would become "Uncle Jimmie" to his future nephew and U.S. president; the two men would have intersecting influences that neither family could have imagined.[59]

As the *Lexington* slowly sailed back to New York City, Bulloch anticipated a joyous family reunion at Bulloch Hall. As evidenced by numerous affectionate letters, Bulloch had a close relationship with his stepmother and siblings. While there is little written evidence about his relationship with his father, they shared mutual respect and James Stephens was obviously interested in the wellbeing of his son. It was a shock for James Dunwoody to learn that his father died suddenly on 18 February 1849 at the Roswell Presbyterian Church as he taught a Sunday school class.[60]

On June 12th, just two days after the *Lexington* arrived at New York City, the Navy granted James Dunwoody 90 days leave to return home and visit his stepmother.[61] Despite taking the new steamer *Cherokee* that had just been placed in service from New York to Savannah, Midshipman Bulloch did not arrive in Roswell until June 28th. The elder Bulloch bequeathed Bulloch Hall and its lands to his wife Martha. Any assets James Dunwoody may have received are unrecorded.[62] Although frustrated with his lack of opportunity for advancement in the U.S. Navy, his inherited financial and family incentives were insufficient for him to resign his commission. Bulloch promptly requested and received orders to the U.S. Coast Survey, where he remained on active service for most of the next two and one-half years. The Coast Survey may not have been as glamorous as warship duty, but it increased the young midshipman's monthly pay by almost half.[63]

The U.S. Coast Survey was responsible for mapping all the bays, inlets, and other hydrographic features along the coast of the United States. It was independent of the U.S. Navy, a fact that rankled some in the naval hierarchy. When Bulloch rejoined the Coast Survey, a bruising political battle at the Congressional level had just ended. The careers of Navy officers who stayed too long on Coast Survey duty would be at risk; they needed to get back to the "real Navy."

While he was still on leave in Roswell on August 3rd, he wrote to the Navy Department with a specific request for orders to the U.S. Coast Survey schooner *Morris*.[64] Bulloch's first exposure to the U.S. Coast Survey had been with the USS *Warren* (June 1847 to October 1848) and he seemed to relish the scientific aspects of his profession.[65] The *Morris* had been transferred from the army and modified for hydrographic work by its supremely competent and engaging captain, John Newland Maffitt. The son of a famous Methodist preacher, Maffitt was a convivial and popular commander who would gain fame as one of the Confederacy's great cruiser commanders.[66] Later that same month, Bulloch received orders to join Maffitt off Nantucket, Massachusetts. Bulloch's home address was recorded as Saratoga Springs, NY, the resort town where his family spent their summers.[67]

Shortly after arriving onboard the *Morris*, Midshipman Bulloch requested orders to fill a sailing master vacancy occasioned by the transfer of Daniel Ammen. However, as winter closed in, Lieutenant Commanding Maffitt took both Ammen and Bulloch with him on the schooner *Gallatin*. The *Gallatin* had suffered damage in the shallow coastal waters of New England but after repairs at Wilmington, Delaware, they set sail for southern waters. The *Gallatin* conducted survey operations from the Virginia approaches of Chesapeake Bay, to Cape Fear, North Carolina, and Charleston.[68] The need for accurate coast maps for defensive measures became evident when the British burned Washington, D.C., during the War of 1812.[69] The infamous and deadly shifting sands of Cape Fear region, on the other hand, required frequent surveying for safety's sake.

During the winter lull in the *Gallatin's* operations, in late February 1850, James Dunwoody returned to Roswell for a family visit. It was during this hiatus that we have James' first recorded meeting with his future wife, Elizabeth (Lizzie) Euphemia Caskie. Lizzie's sister Mary had married the widowed Robert Hutchison. Hutchison's first wife had been James' stepsister Corinne who died at sea in the *Pulaski* disaster. Lizzie soon became a close friend of the Bulloch sisters and "Brother Jimmie" was charmed by her "gayety and vivacity of manner."[70] Lizzie's father, John Caskie, was a wealthy and well-connected Virginian who, like the Bulloch family, was of Scottish descent. He heartily approved the union.

James Dunwoody's matrimonial interest in Lizzie had an immediate impact on his waning interest in the U.S. Navy. Returning to duty on the *Gallatin*, he requested to be transferred from the Coast Survey and granted leave. Although the Navy granted his request for 90 days leave starting 2 December 1850, he found himself back onboard the *Gallatin* in March. At least he was on Coast Survey duty in the South, working the approaches to Charleston harbor where he had the opportunity for frequent contact with his love interest. Shortly after discovering and surveying a new entrance into Charleston, called "Maffitt's Channel," the *Gallatin* moved farther southward toward Bulloch's ancestral roots around Tybee Island, Georgia.

Any hopes he may have had for shore duty were dashed on 2 May 1851, when he received orders to the Coast Survey party under Lt. Charles N. McBlair in New England. Although Lt. McBlair was listed as his senior officer, Bulloch was actually assigned to the brig *Washington* under Lt. Commanding Samuel Swartwout. He finally had his promotion as acting master, but he was far from home, family, and loved ones. The *Washington* operated in Coast Survey Section 1, the Martha's Vineyard area.[71]

On 19 November 1851, he officially reported for shore duty at the Coast Survey office in Washington, D.C.[72] Those orders conveniently included shore leave. On that same day, James Dunwoody Bulloch married Elizabeth Euphemia Caskie in a ceremony at the Caskie home in Richmond, Virginia.[73]

His next career move re-established his connections with California and brought him onto the stage of international politics. In January 1852, he requested a transfer from the Navy Department and the Coast Survey to an even better paying position on the U.S. mail steamship, the SS *Georgia*. Lt. David Dixon Porter, the future Civil War admiral, had requested three midshipmen from the Navy Department. Bulloch made it clear that he made his request with the knowledge and at the suggestion of Lt. Porter. The next phase of Bulloch's career began on 22 March 1852, when the Navy Department ordered Passed Midshipman Bulloch to report to Lt. Porter via Commodore Kearny, who was in charge of the Navy's support to the U.S. mail steamship effort.[74]

3

A Man of Amiable Character

The settlement of the Oregon question in mid–1846 and the California gold rush of 1848–1849 crystallized the need for improved communications and mail service between the West Coast and East Coast of the United States.[1] Consequently, the U.S. Congress ordered the Navy to offer substantial contracts for carrying mail to and from the Pacific. Congress added the stipulation that U.S. Navy officers had to be in command of the commercially contracted steamships.[2] The SS *Georgia* was one of the U.S. Mail Steamship Company steamers that completed the Atlantic and Gulf leg of the mail, freight, and passenger service to and from California. Based in New York City, it called at Havana, Cuba, New Orleans, and Chagres in Panama and back again. The Pacific Mail Steamship Company (PMSC) made the final connection with California and Oregon Territory from the Pacific Coast side of the Isthmus.

On 24 March 1852, the *Georgia* left Manhattan Island loaded with cargo and passengers. As the most senior officer under Lieutenant David Dixon Porter, James Dunwoody Bulloch was responsible for the daily management of the ship, a side-wheel steamer of 3,300 tons. Although he would be at sea for long periods of time, he at least had a regular schedule and would be assured of several days each month at home, certainly an important consideration for newlyweds![3]

In addition to the normal hazards of the sea, even Bulloch's routine cruises on the *Georgia* had their own elements of drama. Newspaper articles note frequent groundings and various shenanigans of Captain Porter, including an incident in Cuba on another ship while the *Georgia* was being repaired. Porter's bravado helped his reputation in the popular press, but the secretary of the Navy thought otherwise and ordered Porter back to the *Georgia* when it returned to service.[4]

Like Porter, Bulloch also needed a change, but his issues were related to family concerns. In July 1852, he requested a year's furlough from naval service. According to a 1905 newspaper article, his wife Lizzie hated the frequent separations and begged him to leave the U.S. Navy. The Navy Department's approval of his request allowed him to continue serving in the merchant marine. Unfortunately for Lizzie, her sailor's change of sea-service uniforms did not alter the frequency or duration of their separations. By October 1852, the *Georgia* recommenced its monthly runs carrying passengers and freight to and from New Orleans and the California gold fields. While his flamboyant captain, David Dixon Porter, navigated turbulent political waters, the Navy recognized Bulloch's consistently high performance with his warrant as a ship's master on 10 February 1853, and a date of rank effective as of 7 January 1853.[5]

Bulloch continued to serve on the *Georgia* through June, when he assumed command of the ship from Porter. He was able to share the good news of his first command with his future brother-in-law, Theodore Roosevelt, Sr. By May 1853, Bulloch and Roosevelt had begun a lifelong friendship that extended well beyond obligatory familial relations. Theodore enthusiastically reported his frequent meetings with "Brother Jimmie" and Lizzie to his wife Mittie and the rest of the Roosevelt family.

"Captain" Bulloch should have felt supreme satisfaction and excitement at achieving the goal he had nurtured since he was a 16-year-old midshipman. He had command at sea before he turned 30 years of age, albeit via an unconventional route. However, Lizzie suffered from frequent bouts of excessive hemorrhaging and her health became increasingly fragile. He was concerned enough that Lizzie accompanied him on his first and only trip as captain of the SS *Georgia* when the ship cleared New York Harbor on 6 June 1853.[6] A New York newspaper, dated 30 June 1853, notes "Lt. Bulloch" in command of the SS *Georgia* as she returned to New York from Aspinwall (Panama) and Havana, Cuba, with over $2,000,000 of gold aboard.[7]

Captain Bulloch traveled with his ailing wife to her family's home in Richmond soon after they returned from this first voyage as a steamship commander.[8] On July 5th, while he was in Richmond, the SS *Georgia* sailed under a new captain, John McGowan. Bulloch had been relieved of his command. On July 9th, two days after he personally met with Secretary of the Navy James C. Dobbin, he officially requested another one-year furlough from the Navy.

His request was probably related to the health of his Lizzie. If he had been assigned to a U.S. Navy warship, James would have been deployed away from home for at least two years and probably longer. However, there were other contributing factors for his request. The first was financial. Steamship captains were paid considerably more than mere Navy midshipmen. The second was prestige and responsibility. If Bulloch returned to mainstream Navy duties, he was not senior enough to be an executive officer, much less the commanding officer of a warship.

His third motivation was the poor seaworthiness of the SS *Georgia* and the equally questionable character of its owner, George Law. Perhaps weakened by the damage it had sustained when it ran aground under Captain Porter, the side-wheel steamship developed a severe leak just two months after Bulloch relinquished command. It promptly sank in the coastal shallows of Hampton Roads near Norfolk. George Law was not the sort of person that Bulloch would have associated with, given a choice. Law was a New Yorker known for his inferior steamers that had lower fares and catered to the rough class of passengers that were flowing to the gold fields of California. It had been George Law's intransigence that precipitated the Cuban incident involving Captain David Dixon Porter in 1852.[9]

The Navy's response to Bulloch's request for an extended furlough from the regular Navy came in short order: "Request approved." Commodore Kearny assigned James D. Bulloch as captain of the U.S. mail steamship *Black Warrior*.[10] Launched in July 1852 at the New York shipyard of William Collyer, the *Black Warrior* cost $135,000, and was a first-rate vessel. The ship was propelled by both a fully rigged sail system as well as two flank-mounted steam engines, allowing her to economize on coal in favorable winds.[11] Not only was the *Black Warrior* a newer ship, it was more reliable. Not surprisingly, the proud builder (or perhaps the owners) commissioned a portrait of the ship by the accomplished artist James Bard that now hangs in the Mariner's Museum of Newport News, Virginia.

The *Black Warrior* was owned by the New York and Alabama Steamship Company, one of the new steamship companies that provided federal-government-sponsored transport and mail services. Bulloch had carefully orchestrated this career move in advance, making himself available exactly when the company needed him most, since the ship's previous captain, had just resigned. As a result, the *Black Warrior* was under weigh again from the company pier at the foot of Harrison Street and into the waters of the North River on its normal schedule on 23 July 1853.

Theodore Roosevelt, Sr., was Bulloch's lifelong friend (U.S. National Park Service).

The shipping agent, Livingston, Crocheron and Co., was a New York firm that had been operating the company's two well-designed steam vessels, *Black Warrior* and *Cahawba*, to Mobile, Alabama via Havana for two years.[12] Bulloch's first few months on the *Black Warrior* severely tested both his personal and his professional mettle. In what was soon to be bitter irony, Bulloch left the active naval service to placate and care for his wife and to achieve promotion opportunities that were not available in the Navy.

After his second voyage on the *Black Warrior*, Lizzie's health continued to decline and he became seriously ill as well. The gravity of Captain Bulloch's illness was not known until he returned from Havana on October 1st. He had contracted yellow fever during the voyage and the New York Port Authority placed him in quarantine. As his illness subsided, his wife, her sister Mary, and Theodore Roosevelt, Sr., all visited and helped nurse him back to health.[13] Despite this near-death experience and increasing concerns for Lizzie's well being, the *Black Warrior*'s captain cast off all lines precisely at noon on October 10th and exactly on schedule. It was the resilient James D. Bulloch who gave the order from the bridge, "Make your rudder amidships, all ahead standard."[14]

As a reminder of the military life that he had left behind, the Navy promoted him to the rank of lieutenant on 29 November 1853.[15] This important milestone should have been a gratifying affirmation of his 14 years of naval service. However, his current civilian employment had benefits that were not possible had he been on a warship. As a merchant captain, not only was he assured of seeing his wife every month, he could take her to sea with him.

3. A Man of Amiable Character

SS *Georgia*, c.1852 U.S. Mail ship, was commanded by David Dixon Porter and then by Bulloch (U.S. Naval Historical Center).

Shortly after assisting Brother Jimmie with his recovery from yellow fever, Theodore Roosevelt, Sr., traveled to Bulloch Hall in Roswell, GA, to marry James' sister Mittie on 22 December 1853. Although his presence is not confirmed, it is possible that Bulloch traveled to Roswell for the wedding celebrations as well. His ship, the *Black Warrior*, was in port at Mobile from the 17th to the 24th of December. He could have traveled by riverboat to Montgomery, AL, and then by rail to Marietta via Atlanta in less than five days.[16] Getting back downstream in less than two days would have been tight, but he could have left earlier on the 21st or 22nd, and then set sail from Mobile later on the 24th. He was the captain after all, and the ship wasn't leaving without him. Unless his ailing wife was aboard the *Black Warrior* and required his attentions, it is hard to imagine him not making the trip, even if he could not stay for the wedding ceremony. Even if he did not attend, Mittie may have set the date with the hope that her brother and his wife could be there.

As her health continued to decline, Lizzie continued to accompany her husband on the *Black Warrior* as she had on the *Georgia*. Having Lizzie with him on his ship was the only way he could care for her, hoping that the sea air might restore her health. Family history, as recounted in a newspaper article dated 23 October 1905, says that Elizabeth Caskie Bulloch died before James could reach her bedside.[17] However, the truth is far more poignant. As indicated on her headstone and in the 1905 Richmond newspaper article, Lizzie died on 23 January 1854. Contrary to family lore, her grieving husband was with her in Mobile, and most likely at her bedside when she died.

Reminiscent of his mother's demise, Bulloch would have recognized the symptoms of Lizzie's impending death when he began what was to have been a normal run aboard the *Black Warrior* from New York to Mobile via Havana on 8 January, 1854.[18] The trip began badly when heavy weather off Cape Hatteras required the *Black Warrior* to put into Charleston for engine repairs before continuing on to Havana.[19] Captain Bulloch finally arrived in Mobile on January 20th and did not depart until the 28th after Lizzie succumbed to her illness. He probably telegraphed Lizzie's family in Richmond and his company in

New York to help him make arrangements for his deceased wife. Upon his arrival at Havana, the reporter for the *New York Times*, bylined as "Occator," filed this report: "We have regretted to learn of the death of the lady of Captain Bullock [sic], of the *Black Warrior*, who died at Mobile. Her remains return by this steamer."

After returning to New York City on February 6th, he escorted his young wife's remains south to Richmond for burial in the Caskie family plot. A burial card from the Richmond cemetery authorities notes Elizabeth's final rest took place on 9 February 1854; the cause of death was "consumption," now known as tuberculosis.[20]

The loss of a loved one in the nineteenth century typically engendered a greater and longer formal grieving process than is generally observed today. In James Dunwoody Bulloch's case, his public grieving was necessarily brief. The demands of his nautical profession quickly took him back to sea and propelled him onto the stage of international politics. On 11 February 1854, only two days after burying his bride in Richmond, Captain Bulloch was under weigh with the *Black Warrior* on its normal run from New York to Havana, Mobile, and back.[21] He cleared Mobile harbor on 25 February 1854 aboard the *Black Warrior* and reached Havana two days later. When he steamed past Castle Morro and into Havana harbor, he sailed into the eye of an international maelstrom.[22]

The *Black Warrior* stopped in Havana to take on coal, a few passengers, and some light freight on its normally scheduled return from Mobile to New York. As required by Spanish customs authorities, Bulloch delivered a copy of the ship's cargo manifest upon arrival. As always, he listed his cargo as ballast only, even though he had a thousand bales of cotton aboard. Since the cotton bales were cargo that was in transit to another port, he only declared goods that were unloaded at their destination port. This had been the *modus operandi* in Havana for as long as he had been making his shipping runs there. But this time, things were different.

The Havana customs officer "discovered" that Bulloch had 1000 cotton bales aboard the *Black Warrior* and promptly seized the vessel, even though the captain had the right under Spanish law to make changes to his declared manifest up to 12 hours *after* arrival.[23] The *New York Times* reporter, dubbed Occator, promptly interviewed Bulloch who said that the customs officer had wanted him to produce a shorter manifest to avoid having to translate a lengthy document. This new requirement obviously annoyed Bulloch. Previous instructions required him to manifest every moveable object on the ship. According to the reporter, Bulloch's "dialogue was uttered with courtesy, but with a little piquant sauce in tone, that gave zest for the digestion of the Chief of Inspection."[24] This testy exchange prompted the Cuban Customs Official to find fault with the *Black Warrior's* cargo manifest and seize the ship.

Following his well-known propensity for protocol, Bulloch marched off to the U.S. consul general in Cuba, William H. Robertson. He alerted Robertson to the situation and sought his assistance in releasing the *Black Warrior*.[25] Bulloch, his officers, crew, and passengers received food and shelter aboard the side-wheel steamer warship USS *Fulton* that was in Havana when the affair began.[26]

U.S. Consul Robertson promptly petitioned the captain-general of Havana, the Marquis Juan de la Pezuela, to secure the ship's immediate release. The marquis refused, stating that the law must be followed.[27] The recalcitrance of the captain-general provided a convenient "outrage" that helped propel the prevailing sentiment in United States politics

Plaza de las Armas in Havana, Cuba (Bibliograph Institut in Hidlburghausen, 1854).

and foreign policy to the front page. The United States coveted Cuba, and many Southern Democrats saw the *Black Warrior* affair as just the excuse they needed to satisfy that desire. Spain was unfortunate in having the wrong man in the right place at the right time. Prior to the incident, newspapers in the North had praised Captain-General Pezuela for his antislavery actions, which only added to the tension and the political opportunity.

Word of the seizure of the *Black Warrior* reached America quickly and newspapers were eager to pounce on the incident to raise the political pressure on President Franklin Pierce. Southern Democrats wanted an immediate declaration of war, while cooler heads in the North merely wanted reparations. Although Cuba would not get its first undersea telegraphic connection to the United States until 1868, news of the growing anger of America reached the erstwhile Captain-General Pezuela in Havana quickly. The Marquis Juan de la Pezuela remained obstinate despite the American outrage.

Bulloch was sorely tempted to take the matter into his own hands and his temper was barely in control, for we have in his own words the anger he felt:

> I am convinced that we would not want volunteers to retake the good old ship by force, if such a course were proper ... I do not hesitate to say, that we have been subjected to the most villainous and outrageous treatment that has ever been inflicted upon a friendly power, and if we are not protected and redressed in this matter by our government, the American eagle had better fold its wings forever.... You may be sure that I am with you in sympathy and indignation in this affair, and that I shall henceforth devote all my energies to the realization of our just demands.[28]

In the face of these tensions and temptations, Bulloch repressed his anger, resisted the impulse to recapture his ship by force, and paid a $6,000 fine to the Cuban authorities.[29]

When Bulloch regained the *Black Warrior* on March 20th, his quartermaster pointed out that the entire ship's stores had been looted while in the "protective custody" of Cuban customs authorities. Bulloch again marched ashore and complained to the head of the customs house. A Spanish officer in charge of Havana harbor heard of this confrontation and thought that Bulloch had accused him as well as his dishonest underling. The Spanish officer stormed into the customs house and threatened the customs official with death and said he would deal with Bulloch as well. Aggressively cool and with impeccable manners, Bulloch faced the aggrieved officer and said that his complaint was with the customs official, not with him. However, he would be more than happy to accommodate a duel if the Spaniard felt his honor was not fully satisfied. Apparently, Bulloch's steely-eyed and calmly delivered statement of purpose fully assuaged the portly, and shaken, Spanish officer.[30]

American protestations over the affair continued to gain in their fury, even as Bulloch sailed the *Black Warrior* north to New York City on 24 March 1854. Bulloch's performance in the affair was roundly debated before he and the *Black Warrior* had even returned to New York City. As the *New York Times* comments in its 28 March 1854 issue (the day before *Black Warrior* docked), "It strikes us that Capt. Bullock [sic] and the owners of the ship should have acted with more discretion at the onset, or with more courage afterwards," implying that the issue could have been avoided or resolved by more forceful means. The commentator does not offer what those actions might have been.[31]

The main instigator in leveraging the crisis for political ends of the South was U.S. Minister to Spain Pierre Soulé. A pro-slavery Southern Democrat, Soulé had held the Madrid post since 1853, and was a "fire-eater" who coveted Cuba as a slave state.[32] Southern Democrats in the U.S. Congress had long feared that Spain would pursue an abolitionist agenda within Cuba that would make its acquisition more difficult, if not impossible. Other key Congressional players were Sen. John Slidell of Louisiana, the future Confederate representative to France, Sen. Jefferson Davis of Mississippi, the future president of the Confederacy, and Sen. Judah Benjamin of Louisiana, the future Confederate secretary of war and secretary of state (and *de facto* head of covert intelligence operations).

President Pierce, sensing a political quagmire, resorted to a half-measure. He ordered James Buchanan, U.S. minister to Great Britain (and a future U.S. president), John Mason, U.S. minister to France (and future Confederate commissioner to Great Britain) to meet with Pierre Soulé at Ostend, Belgium, and produce a resolution stating the U.S. position. Their resulting Ostend Manifesto suggested that America should take Cuba by force if Spain refused to sell the island. This provocative notion created political waves on both sides of the Atlantic when it was leaked to the press.

President Pierce's attempt to let events gently decide themselves had gone wildly awry. Pierce reined in Secretary of State William Marcy and instructed him to have Minister Soulé take a more diplomatic tone with the Spanish. The Spanish government eventually agreed to refund the *Black Warrior's* fine, plus $44,000 in further reparations for her owners.[33] The *Black Warrior* affair exposed America's expansionist impulses that would eventually catapult Bulloch's nephew up San Juan Hill and into the presidency.

For the time being, all matters regarding Cuba returned to the *status quo*. Bulloch and the *Black Warrior* resumed their runs to Havana via Mobile in April, returning to the Cuban port on the 28th before heading north for home. In contrast to the previous visit, newspapers commented that the Spanish-Cuban authorities received Bulloch with marked politeness.³⁴ The *Black Warrior* successfully returned to its important business of delivering mail, passengers, and cargo. Bulloch's schedule had him leaving New York from the pier at the foot of Beach Street on the North River on the ninth day of the month (except on Sundays). He transited to Havana (6 days) and stopped for coal (1 day or less). After reaching Mobile (2 days), he loaded the primary bulk cargo of cotton and passengers (7–8 days), and then retraced his route to New York via Havana. If the weather cooperated, the return trip was about a day shorter due to the helpful effect of the Gulf Stream. As reported in the daily newspapers, Bulloch docked his ship in New York City, usually on the second or third day of the month.

Shortly after his contretemps with the Cubans, Bulloch severed his last remaining regular link with Mobile. In its third year of operations, the owners of the *Black Warrior* and *Cahawba* shifted the final stop on their circuit from Mobile to New Orleans. One other link was cut forever in 1854. In August, Bulloch's one-year furlough from the regular Navy expired. When the *Black Warrior* returned to New York from its first run into New Orleans, he found a message from the Navy Department waiting for him. A letter dated 12 September 1854 ordered him to report to the frigate USS *John Adams* in Boston no later than October 1st.³⁵ Since the *Black Warrior* had left New York on September 9th and did not return until October 3rd, he was technically in violation of his orders.³⁶

Surprised by this unexpected but inevitable turn of events, he immediately submitted his letter of resignation. He expressed regret that "reasons of a purely private nature with which the Dept. need not be troubled, render it impossible for me to go on service at this time." He then went on to say that "if a warlike exigency should ever arise I would be happy and proud to hold again any position of usefulness."³⁷ On 5 October 1854, the U.S. Navy accepted Lieutenant James Dunwoody Bulloch's resignation, a celebrity event that merited a headline in the *New York Times*. He had served 15 years with the U.S. Navy, but he would never again serve under the Stars and Stripes.³⁸ Despite his resignation from the U.S. Navy, he was able to continue his career as the captain of the *Black Warrior*.

In New York City, Bulloch enjoyed the company of his sister Mittie and her husband Theodore Roosevelt. He frequently dined with Theodore and his older brother Silas Weir Roosevelt even when Mittie was out of town. Another brother-in-law, Robert Hutchinson, often joined the men for dinner and drinks and even recommended Bulloch for membership in one of New York's exclusive clubs.³⁹

In December 1855, Captain Bulloch took a short break from his busy sailing schedule. When the *Black Warrior* returned from its normal run on December 3rd, the New York and New Orleans Steamship Company (the new name of the ship's owner) assigned him to its newly constructed ship, the SS *Cahawba*, a 1643-ton side-wheel steamer. Like the *Black Warrior*, the *Cahawba* was named after a river in Alabama.⁴⁰

Bulloch's maritime career and history were impatient suitors, leaving little time for personal affairs, for he sailed on the day after Christmas. For the first six months of 1856, his new schedule had the *Cahawba* departing from Pier No. 27 on the North River at the foot of Robinson Street on or about the 26th or 27th of each month and returning about 23 days later. This routine changed abruptly in July.

The *Cahawba* did not sail from New York in July, possibly due to a yellow fever outbreak in Havana.⁴¹ More likely it was another kind of fever that had captured Bulloch's attention. On 11 August 1856, the *Cahawba* cleared for San Juan de Nicaragua, serving as a replacement for the SS *Orizaba*. The *Cahawba* carried a unique human cargo of over 250 mercenary soldiers and 10 artillerymen for General William Walker, the newly designated "President of Nicaragua."[42] Walker was one of the more successful of this almost forgotten aberration of American history, extremist Manifest Destiny ideologues called "filibusters." This Spanish term for pirate or buccaneer was revived in the 19th century to describe freelance military adventurers and operations intended to overthrow existing governments or start separarist movements.

This self-styled "general" of a small band of mercenaries (originally only 58), had managed to calm a civil-war-torn Nicaragua, rout an invasion force from Costa Rica, and by June 1856, he was proclaimed President.[43] The surrounding Central American countries refused to recognize the Walker government (considered a Yankee "puppet") and proceeded to invade from all sides. The British Royal Navy supported their actions against Walker by blockading the Nicaraguan ports. As an exception, the British granted mail packets such as the *Cahawba* passage through the blockade.

Taking advantage of the chaos, Cornelius Vanderbilt concluded a contract with the Nicaraguan government that gave him construction rights for a canal across the isthmus. Vanderbilt also obtained exclusive rights to all transport modes across the country between the Pacific and Atlantic for twelve years.[44] Vanderbilt's "Accessory Transit" company dramatically reduced the time to get to the California gold fields, turned a tidy profit — and upset the British. Washington also became alarmed and issued proclamations forbidding Americans from 'filibustering' in Nicaragua. Vanderbilt countered this move by diverting gold bullion to fund Walker's adventure and provided free tickets for men headed to Nicaragua from New York and California ports.[45]

By August 1856, Walker had fended off attacks from Costa Rica and dissident Nicaraguans. The U.S. first recognized and then repudiated the validity of his presidency. Walker became desperate for American support, leading him to set aside the constitutional ban of slavery, which sent pro-slavery politicians in the South into fits of joy. Walker's run of good luck was about to end, even before Bulloch and his reinforcements left New York.[46]

With a load of supplies and filibusters consigned to the shipping agent Charles A. Whitney, the *Cahawba* made Greytown, Nicaragua, in just seven days. Bulloch needed three days to offload the men and their cargo before he departed Greytown and returned to New York on August 30th.[47] There is no evidence that Bulloch was directly involved in the planning or approval of this expedition, but he certainly understood the risks of entering a war zone and he supported the political implications of his actions.[48]

After this single trip to Nicaragua, the *Cahawba* returned to its the normal route and shipping agent. The only change to the schedule was a shift in the departure date to about the eleventh of each month, with a return on or about the second of the following month. While seemingly routine, each of these voyages offered individual excitements. Among these were violent, life-threatening storms, deadly boiler explosions, collisions, virulent disease, and ... matrimony.

James' matrimonial excitement occurred during his first trip of the new year, 1857. He married Harriott Cross Foster during the *Cahawba*'s six-day port call to New Orleans (21–27 January). Harriott, the widow of a planter named Joseph Foster, was a tall, vivacious, 26-year-old, blue-eyed blonde who was fond of riding. Her usually serious sea captain husband, James, was 33 years old with a clear appreciation for beautiful women, congenial friends, and fine wines.[49]

Harriott's mother was the former Louise von Schaumburg, from a family in the New Orleans area descended from German nobility. Harriott's father was Osborne Cross, an officer in the U.S. Army.[50] At the time of his daughter's wedding, Major Cross was chief quartermaster of the Pacific Division in California, which placed him in charge of army supplies and contracts on the West Coast of the United States. One of Osborne's brothers was in the Navy and his other one was also in the Army. Major Cross would rise to the rank of brigadier general with the position of assistant quartermaster of the Union army during the Civil War. Bulloch had much in common with his new, extended family.[51]

The Cross family had another connection with the Roosevelt family via Harriott's sister Annette. Annette Cross had married Captain S. Grosvenor Porter whose sister Laura was married to Cornelius Van Schaack Roosevelt, Jr., an older brother of Theodore Roosevelt, Sr. Considering himself a full member of the Bulloch-Cross family, Theodore made the difficult winter journey from New York to the Louisiana countryside of Plaquamene, near New Orleans, to attend Brother Jimmie's wedding. Theodore was very impressed with Harriott, describing her as having, "light hair, blue eyes, and the ordinary peculiarities of a blond, but is dependent more on expression for her pleasant appearance than on anything else. Her figure is very tall but not awkward and she is what I think would be termed a fine looking woman by this casual observer ... and I think is one we will all learn to like exceedingly."[52]

On his return trip to Havana in February 1857, Bulloch felt the fingers of history upon his shoulders again. The *New York Times* reported him at the helm of the *Cahawba* as he carried the remains of Dr. Elisha Kent Kane from Havana to New Orleans.[53] Kane was, in a grand understatement, *the* contemporary American hero of his era. Born in 1820, Kane trained as a doctor and practiced independently until he joined the U.S. Navy and was physician to the U.S. legation to China in 1843. He was a hero of the Mexican War, participated in and led expeditions to rescue Sir John Franklin, the acclaimed Arctic explorer, and lectured on his experiences. James Dunwoody Bulloch, like any other young naval officer of the era, would have admired Kane's exploits. Until the death of Abraham Lincoln, the greatest and largest funeral procession was that of Dr. Kane.[54]

Returning to New York by May 1857, the Bullochs set up housekeeping in the New York area. If Liverpool was the heart of the British Empire's maritime trade and shipbuilding industry, then the same could be said of New York City for the rapidly growing American republic. There was no better place for a professional American mariner like Bulloch than New York City now that most of his closest family also lived nearby. Harriott became close to her Roosevelt in-laws and the rest of her husband's large and extended family in New York, New Jersey, Philadelphia, and Richmond. James' stepmother, Martha, his brother Irvine, and sister Anna had already made the move from Georgia in 1856.[55] Stepmother Martha spent considerable time with her daughter Susan and her husband, Dr. Hilborne West, in Philadelphia and in New York.

Bulloch spent the rest of 1857 at the helm of the *Cahawba* and he followed a settled routine with regular trips to Havana and New Orleans. The exception to these monthly departures was the now standard summer hiatus to avoid the ravages of cholera and yellow fever prevalent in the southern ports. As an affirmation of his status as a merchant captain, he was inducted as a member of the "Marine Society of the City of New York in the State of New York," on 9 November 1857.

On the Bulloch home front, the most important event of the following year was the April 1858 birth of their first son, James Dunwoody Bulloch, Jr. Harriott traveled back to Louisiana to her parent's home for the birth. She and baby James Junior returned to New York with her husband as unregistered passengers on the *Cahawba* in early October, and took up temporary residence on West 21st Street. By the time their daughter Jessie was born almost two years later, the Bullochs were living in Morristown, New Jersey. Morristown provided easy access to New York City, Philadelphia, and the resort areas of New Jersey. It was also a favorite summer retreat for wealthy New Yorkers, including the Roosevelts.[56]

For Dunwoody Bulloch, Sr., 1858 was the year he gained a modicum of fame in literary circles. Henry Howard Brownell dedicated a poem to Bulloch that Brownell wrote on board the *Cahawba* in January, titled "The Burial of the Dane."[57] Unaffected by the notoriety, Bulloch's busy cruising schedule had few changes. Contemporary newspapers reported that the *Cahawba*, with Bulloch (often misspelled as "Bullock") as captain, cleared New York harbor around the twelfth of each month and returned about the fourth of the following month, weather permitting. The exception to this schedule once again was July when there was no recorded sailing from New York. One last significant event occurred before the year was out as well. On 27 October 1858, Bulloch's sister Mittie gave birth to Theodore Roosevelt. Harriott was nearby and assisted in locating a doctor for the delivery of the Bullochs' to-become-famous nephew.[58]

It is within the first few months of 1859 that we get perhaps the best exposition of Bulloch through an extraordinary passage within Richard Henry Dana's book, *To Cuba and Back: A Vacation Voyage*. Dana's recounting of an evening conversation with James Dunwoody Bulloch took place on a voyage to Cuba that began on 12 February 1859 in New York City. As the *Cahawba* headed south, Dana, one of the great American authors of maritime literature, spoke with Captain Bulloch during an evening stroll around the deck. While poet Brownell alluded to Bulloch's qualities as a mariner, Dana's description is compelling.

> By night, I walk deck for a couple of hours with the young captain. After due enquiries about his family in Georgia, ... the fascinating topic of the navy, the frigates and the line-of-battle ships and little sloops, the storms, the wrecks, and the sea-fights fill up the time. He loves the navy still, and has left it with regret; but the navy does not love her sons as they love her. On the quarter-deck at fifteen, the first in rank of his year, favored by his commanders, with service in the best vessels, making the great fleet cruise [to the Mediterranean] under [Commodore Charles] Morris, taking part in the actions of the Naval Brigade on shore in California, serving on the Coast Survey, a man of science as well as a sailor — yet what is there before him, or those like him, in our navy? The best must continue as a subaltern, a lieutenant, until he is grey. At fifty, he may be entitled to his first command, and that of a class below a frigate. If he survives the African and Isthmus fevers and the perils of the sea, he may totter on the quarterdeck of a line-of-battle ship when his skill is out of date and his capacity for further command problematical. Whatever may be the gallantry or the merit of his service, though he may cut off his right hand or pluck out his eye for the country's honor, the navy can give him no promotion, not even a barren title of brevet, nor a badge of recognition of merit, though it be but a star, or a half yard of blue ribbon. The most meritorious officers receive large offers from civil life; and then, it is home, family, society, education of children, and pecuniary competency on the one side, and on the other, only the navy, less and less attractive as middle life draws on.[59]

Dana's passage not only draws upon Bulloch's personal pain at leaving the U.S. Navy, but it serves as a vehicle for the great American maritime writer to critique the professional conundrum of the nation's well-trained and motivated naval officers. Bulloch's memoirs would later echo these reasons for departing the U.S. Navy, but Dana's commentary pulls no punches on the professional sailor's predicament.

Another useful aspect of Dana's short travel monologue is its description of the *Cahawba's* arrival at Havana. Once again, we are as close as we will ever come to standing in Captain James Dunwoody Bulloch's shoes: "What a world of shipping! The masts make a belt of dense forest along the edge of the city, all the ships lying head in to the street, like horses at their mangers; while the vessels at anchor nearly choke up the passage-ways to the deeper bays beyond.... We thread our slow and careful way among these, pass under the broadside of a ship-of-the-line, and under the stern of a screw frigate, both bearing the Spanish flag, and cast our anchor in the Regla Bay, by the side of the steamer Karnac, which sailed from New York a few days before us."[60]

Richard Henry Dana was an American author who once described Bulloch on a cruise to Cuba.

Dana captured Bulloch on his favorite command at the right moment, for he only made three more runs aboard the *Cahawba*. After returning to New York on 4 June 1859, he attended the launching of his new command, the *DeSoto*, a 1675-ton, 253-foot long, side-wheel steamship. Bulloch made eleven monthly voyages aboard the *DeSoto* beginning with the ship's maiden cruise from New York on 27 August 1859.

In late October 1859, the New York newspapers trumpeted the fact that the *DeSoto*, under Bulloch's command, arrived with $243,000 in gold from the California gold fields. Although considerably less than the over $2,000,000 he carried during his runs on the SS *Georgia* from Panama, the continuing flow of gold from California and the associated risks and opportunities were evident in every voyage.[61] Based on what we know of his character, he was entirely satisfied with the more proven commercial route to financial security.

In 1860, he continued his steady schedule of runs to New Orleans via Havana. While life was relatively placid afloat, the political pressures that were threatening to tear America apart became increasingly turbulent. Even at this early stage, internal "migrants" were fleeing northward, or conversely, southward, depending on their loyalties. As a prominent commercial ship captain, many politicians in the South knew of Bulloch either by reputation or personally, as he transported them between New Orleans and Washington, via New York.

On 1 August 1860, the *New York Times* reported Bulloch at the helm of another new vessel, the *Bienville*, a side-wheel steamer and a sister-ship of the *DeSoto*. At the end of her first month of operation, the New York press proclaimed on 22 August 1860 that the *Bienville* had brought "the heaviest cargo ever shipped by steamer from Havana to this port." By this time, James Dunwoody Bulloch was one of the most famous commercial shipping captains in America.[62] He had successfully leveraged his maritime skills and family connections to become a respected and influential player at the heart of New York City's shipping industry. When he captained a steamer into or out of New York, his ship was usually the first one listed under the newspaper's daily "Marine Intelligence" column. The event often merited its own headline, with "Bulloch" (or "Bullock") prominently listed as its captain. He was in the full spring of life, but the winter of America's darkest discontent was fast approaching, which would dramatically change the rest of his days.

Most of the newspaper headlines were devoted to the titanic political campaign for the U.S. presidency. In the southern states, the Democratic Party was in meltdown after its tumultuous convention in Charleston broke up in May 1860 largely due to disagreements about slavery issues. Six candidates had been proposed during the convention, including the famous orator Sen. Stephen A. Douglas (IL) and Sen. Andrew Johnson (TN), but none of the candidates could achieve the required majority.

On 18 June 1860, the Democrats reconvened in Baltimore. This time, 110 Southern Democrats stormed out when the Northern Democrats failed to support a resolution to extend slavery into new territories. The remaining delegates nominated Sen. Stephen A. Douglas as their presidential candidate.[63] The Southern Democrats then decamped to Richmond, Virginia, where on 28 June 1860 they nominated Vice President John C. Breckinridge as their candidate.[64] In yet another contribution to the destabilization of the U.S. political landscape, former Whigs and "Know Nothings" formed a new political party known as the Constitutional Union Party. The Constitutionalists promptly nominated John Bell over Gov. Sam Houston of Texas.[65]

The Republican Party, whose members met after the dissolution of the Democratic convention in Charleston, were supremely confident of victory, if only they could overcome fractionalization as well! William H. Seward (NY) was initially regarded as the most likely winner, with Abraham Lincoln (IL) and Salmon P. Chase (OH) the next two in order of popularity. As the convention wore on, it became apparent that virtually all the candidates had incensed various factions of the party. In the end, the least offensive candidate was chosen. On 18 May 1860, Lincoln was nominated as the Republican presidential candidate, with Sen. Hannibal Hamlin (ME) as his vice presidential running mate.[66] When the U.S. presidential elections were held on 6 November 1860, Lincoln monitored the results via the telegraph office in Springfield, IL. Late that evening, he captured enough of the northern states to win the Electoral College vote. Southerners who didn't heave a sorrowful sigh, exploded with fury. To many, Lincoln's election signaled the final gasp of the American experiment.[67]

Four days later, the U.S. senators from South Carolina resigned from Congress. Lame-duck President Buchanan watched helplessly as the U.S. government disintegrated and Lincoln could do nothing officially until his inauguration in March 1861.[68] James Dunwoody Bulloch's own thoughts, written years later, reflected on this period of intractable differences: "Political parties had ceased to be divided upon principles and interests common to both sections of the country, and had come to be separated by a geographical line. Thus, had arisen a condition which the Fathers of the Republic foresaw might happen, and which they had predicted would be dangerous, if not destructive, to the Union."[69]

4

Against Strong Northerly Winds and Head Seas — Prelude to War

James Dunwoody Bulloch and the *Bienville* returned to New York City on 22 November 1860 after enduring a "strong northerly gale from Cape Hatteras up."[1] It had been a longer than normal return from Havana, but he and his ship were back in port, anchored in placid waters. The same could not be said for America.

With the resignation of the South Carolina senators, the nation plunged into an anxious period of frenzied "fire-eating" Southern rhetoric. On 20 December 1860 in a unanimous vote of 169–0, the State of South Carolina seceded, defiantly proclaiming that "the union ... between South Carolina and other States" had been broken.[2] As the remaining members of the U.S. Congress departed Washington for a very unsettled Christmas break, Bulloch made two more transits to Havana via New Orleans, returning home just before Christmas Eve.[3] Other notable sailors who were staying in New York City for that last Christmas of American peace included Commodore Josiah Tattnall of Savannah, Georgia, and Lt. Charles Manigault Morris of South Carolina.[4] Morris resigned from the U.S. Navy within a month, followed by Tattnall. Both men would soon meet Bulloch under drastically altered circumstances. At home, James and Harriott, with their new baby son, James Jr., were enjoying their last family Christmas in America.

On 2 January 1861, Bulloch got the *Bienville* under weigh, again destined for Havana.[5] By the time he returned to New York on 22 January 1861, Mississippi, Florida, Alabama and Georgia had all joined South Carolina as seceded states. He had literally sailed around the littoral of an American republic that was in the process of rapid political decomposition. With his sailing schedule strangely unaffected by political storms, he departed New York City in early February. When he arrived in New Orleans, it was as a visitor to a foreign country, for Louisiana had seceded on 26 January 1861. When he proceeded to Havana and back to the New York City, "against strong northerly winds and head seas," his passengers carried stories of Southerners in full-cry for war and in a near blood-lust should Lincoln dare invade the South to reassert the "Union."[6]

Southerners believed that they were on the morally and Constitutionally correct side of the "eternal struggle between liberty and power" envisioned by the Founding Fathers. On 7 February 1861, the seven seceded states agreed to their own constitution and united

SS *Bienville* in 1860 was Bulloch's last U.S. command and a future Union warship (U.S. Naval Historical Center).

as "The Confederate States of America." Montgomery, Alabama, was the new, but temporary, capital with Jefferson Davis as the provisional president.[7]

Back in New York, schedules had to be kept and duties had to be met, so the *Bienville* cleared for Havana and New Orleans on 1 March 1861. Abraham Lincoln was sworn in as president of the remaining United States while the *Bienville* sailed around the recently seceded state of Florida.[8] When Bulloch arrived in New Orleans, the man that Southerners hated and feared most was now in charge of an "oppressive" Union. In Havana, Bulloch met with Captain L.W. Smith who now commanded the *Cahawba*.[9] The two men discussed the ambiguous situation regarding port clearances and customs declarations. Since the Union did not recognize customs papers issued by the "rebels" in charge of Southern ports, routine business now became more complicated. Bulloch and the *Bienville* departed Havana on 20 March 1861 at 11:30 AM, and arrived in New York three days later.[10] United States Treasury authorities greeted him at the dock and immediately seized his ship for "irregular Confederate Custom House clearances."[11]

Bulloch's notoriety through the "*Black Warrior* Affair" may have made the *Bienville* and its captain a logical choice for a customs test case. Lincoln had decided to implement the customs enforcement policy he had formulated prior to his inauguration. Both Southern and Northern businessmen were keenly monitoring the seizure of the *Bienville*.[12] Bulloch's own commentary on the situation is illuminating: "By a law of the United States, a vessel sailing from one home port to another was required to have a regular Custom House clearance, under penalty of seizure and forfeiture. The authorities at Washington did not ... recognise those at Montgomery, and a certificate of clearance from New Orleans, verified by a Collector of Customs appointed by the Confederate Treasury Department, was not admissible at any port in the United States."[13]

Bulloch then described his predicament with the *Bienville* after noting that Washington had previously seized other vessels for the same infraction, but released them: "I was requested to go to Washington, where I had an official interview with the Secretary of the Treasury, the Hon. Salmon P. Chase, on the subject. I pointed out that there was no United

4. Against Strong Northerly Winds and Head Seas

States official of any kind at New Orleans, and that I was compelled to either take a clearance from the de facto authority or to remain at that port indefinitely."[14]

Sec. Chase understood the complexity of Bulloch's position, and absolved the *Bienville* (and the other greatly relieved owners) from any financial or legal penalty. But Chase, keen to advance Lincoln's doctrine, asked whether the owners Livingston and Crocheron intended to send the *Bienville* southwards again. Bulloch responded in the affirmative and his observations set the stage for what was to come: "He (Chase) then said that the right of the so-called Confederate government to assume control of the Custom Houses at the Southern ports could not be admitted even by implication; but still it was obvious that for the moment those who had usurped the legitimate authority had the power to enforce it against private persons, and he directed me on the next occasion of applying for a clearance to make a formal protest setting forth the precise circumstances."[15]

U.S. Secretary of the Treasury Salmon P. Chase (Library of Congress).

Chase's attempt to finesse the Confederate states into accepting the Union's governance authority was soon overtaken by violent events. His release of the *Bienville* on 29 March 1861 had Bulloch scurrying northward to meet his normal sailing schedule from New York. For the sake of convenience, he stayed at the nearby Astor House as he prepared the *Bienville* for another voyage south. A day later, U.S. customs cleared the *Bienville* to sail for Havana and New Orleans.[16] When he sailed out of New York, it was the last time Bulloch would leave the city as a loyal U.S. citizen.

Though he had resigned his commission as a lieutenant in the U.S. Navy in 1854, Bulloch commanded a mail steamer that had been built according to Navy specifications and could be readily converted into an auxiliary warship. Given this official connection with the federal government as well as his personal history as a U.S. Navy officer, any responses he uttered to Chase would have been relayed as first-person intelligence to Secretary of the Navy Gideon Welles.[17] Although Welles had been in office only since 7 March 1861, Bulloch would have been aware of his reputation as an ardent hater of slavery. However, he may not have fully appreciated Welles' concurrent distrust of all Southern-born U.S. naval officers that automatically placed Bulloch under suspicion.[18] On 13 April 1861, the *Bienville* was in New Orleans awaiting fuel and supplies before sailing the following day for Havana. At about 10 o'clock in the morning, news swept through the city that Brigadier General Pierre G.T. Beauregard of the newly created Confederate States Army had shelled a small Union garrison lodged in Ft. Sumter, South Carolina.[19] The arrival of Lincoln's rapidly organized naval rescue expedition off Charleston Harbor provided impetus for the Confederate shore batteries to open fire. With no hope of reinforcements or resupply, the Union forces surrendered.[20]

As he absorbed the meaning of the news through the excited cacophony in the streets, Bulloch considered what it meant for him personally. He had resigned from the U.S. Navy due to a lack of advancement opportunity and low pay. He mused that, though he had no business interests or property within the new Confederacy, he was Georgia born. Most of his personal interests and friends were in the North, but the soil of the South was where his roots lay. Even his Northern friends knew that when the time came, Bulloch would align his fate with the South.[21] Mid-morning of 13 April 1861, he penned a letter to the former senator from Louisiana and the new attorney general of the Confederate States of America, Judah P. Benjamin. He asked Benjamin to offer his professional maritime skills to the members of the newly formed Confederate cabinet. The "warlike exigency" he had foreseen in his letter of resignation from the Navy had become reality. He would be defending the constitution that he had sworn to uphold (a constitution that affirmed the right of states to base their economy on chattel slavery). However, by casting his lot with this new and uncertain nation, he would soon become the enemy of the president and officers he had sworn to obey.

While he could offer the Confederacy his skills, he could not offer the *Bienville* to the new Confederate Navy without violating his own sense of personal honor. He informed Benjamin that he would have to return north with his ship and place her in the hands of her New York owners. He earnestly added that he would be ready for any service after that point. After posting his letter, he raced to the *Bienville* to make ready for a rapid departure.[22] That afternoon, Bulloch confronted the first of many tense situations that he would face during the next four years. Two gentlemen from the Louisiana Board of War came aboard the *Bienville* and declared that they were authorized to buy the ship for the Confederate government. All he had to do was name his price and the governor of Louisiana would authorize payment. Bulloch replied with an emphatic, "No!" He explained that he could not place a value on her for sale, nor would he arrange for her conveyance into the arms of the Confederacy. The gentlemen continued to press the issue in friendly terms, implying a personal benefit if he succumbed to their offer, but Bulloch held firm. Informing him that they would be back, the two men scurried away to consult with the Louisiana governor.[23]

In his memoirs, Bulloch presents his conflicting thoughts about the propriety of his actions. He knew that the Confederacy needed ships, and that he had just offered his services to the Confederate government. He also realized that he had responsibilities to the owners. One detail that he purposely omitted in his memoirs was that he was a part-owner of the *Bienville*. A post–Civil War court case affirmed that the *Bienville* had several Southern co-owners that held shares in the vessel in 1861. One of those owners was James Dunwoody Bulloch.[24] His part-ownership of the *Bienville* adds to the questions of why he did not sell the ship then and there to the Louisiana Board of War.

On one hand, Bulloch was only a part-owner; the other owners, not to mention Livingston and Crocheron, had trusted him to do his duty. On the other hand, he had multiple reasons for selling the *Bienville*. First, as a part-owner, he could have bargained for the best deal possible as a representative of the other owners. He could have claimed duress (i.e., the visits by the Louisiana Board of War agents were intimidating). He was about to join a Confederate Navy that needed ships, and he could have literally commanded his "own" vessel in war. Selling her to the Louisiana Board of War would have ingratiated him to the Confederate government and would have kept the *Bienville* from the clutches of the rapidly expanding Union Navy.

In the end, Bulloch refused to sell despite the many justifications and temptations: he would return the ship to her rightful owners. He knew that the *Bienville* was liable under the "special conditions" laid down for ships constructed to carry the mail for the U.S. government. The U.S. Navy was certain to purchase the ship. He didn't know, however, that the federal government would be so vindictive in its treatment of "rebels." It would take decades after the war for him to retrieve his investment in the *Bienville* from the U.S. Navy.[25] Ever the pragmatic businessman, he never mentioned this unpaid bill or the helpful role of his brother-in-law Theodore Roosevelt, Sr., while the case was pending.

U.S. Secretary of the Navy Gideon Welles (U.S. Naval Historical Center).

On the afternoon of 13 April 1861, Bulloch felt varied and conflicting thoughts and emotions as he awaited the return of the Louisiana Board of War representatives. One of the men returned to the *Bienville* before sunset to tell him that the governor had telegraphed Montgomery and was awaiting instructions. The local mail steamship company agent, John Fox, reassured him that he had done the right thing by refusing to sell or surrender the vessel. Bulloch promptly ordered the engine room to make ready for getting under weigh and arranged the mooring lines so that they could be quickly let loose from aboard the ship. He was set to make a rapid departure.[26]

As the sun set, Bulloch and Fox discussed the dramatic events of the day, awaiting the word that would force him to run the *Bienville* past the forts guarding the mouth of the Mississippi River south of New Orleans. Even if he succeeded, such an attempt would have fouled his reputation with the Confederate government. In light of Bulloch's partial ownership of the *Bienville*, he was certainly in an interesting situation.[27] The representatives of the Louisiana Board of War finally solved his problem when they returned that evening at 10 P.M. with a message from the Louisiana governor. He was free to sail. President Jefferson Davis' reply to the governor's query cleared stated that the Confederacy did not wish to "interfere ... with private property." Davis undoubtedly consulted Attorney General Benjamin about his legal options concerning the *Bienville* and their mutual desire to avoid drawing attention to their prospective secret agent.²⁸

On 15 April 1861, the *Bienville* arrived in Havana carrying the city's first reports of the firing on Ft. Sumter. The incendiary news of war raced through Havana, electrifying both the shipping trade and Cubans alike. Spanish authorities would have sighed in relief. For the time being, "Manifest Destiny" would be put on the back burner of the United States' political agenda. The U.S. had to keep from imploding before thinking about expanding. Still, the Spaniards realized the dangerous implications of a successful Confederate government, as the most radical Manifest Destiny advocates and filibusters had all come from the South. A voracious wolf would be next door to Cuba and Mexico if the Confederacy endured as a nation.²⁹

Confederate Secretary of the Navy Stephen Mallory (U.S. Naval Historical Center).

While in Havana, Bulloch observed an entire regiment of U.S. cavalrymen aboard the SS *Corwin* en route to New York. Pulled out of their garrison when Texas seceded, state authorities forced them to abandon their posts. Hearing the news of war, the officers of the regiment visited Bulloch aboard the *Bienville* for details. Ship captains and officers, both commercial and military, also called. None were passionate about going to war; all were disconsolate at what had come to pass. As these were Northern officers, Bulloch kept his own counsel.³⁰

With his passengers ashore, customs cleared, and cargo stowed, Bulloch got the *Bienville* away from Havana on schedule and reached New York on the evening of 22 April 1861. On the way, he passed two steamships, both headed south. One "spoke" to the *Bienville* and said she was loaded with troops for Washington, D.C. Lincoln's government wasted no time protecting the Union capital.³¹

As he got the *Bienville* alongside her berth, a shipping company director raced across the gangway with more disturbing news. A riot had broken out in Baltimore between Southern sympathizers and volunteer soldiers of a Union regiment. There had been deaths and Washington wanted to get Maryland locked down before it could secede. The Livingston and Crocheron director then pointed to the *Empire State* lying off the head of the pier. The ship was full of Union troops from Rhode Island. As a final straw, he broke the news concerning the future of the *Bienville*. The Union government had chartered the ship to deploy immediately and convey the remainder of the Rhode Island Army regiment to Washington. Bulloch's fate was clearly defined in that moment. He told the shipping director that

4. Against Strong Northerly Winds and Head Seas

he could not captain any ship on such a venture. The Livingston and Crocheron managers quickly appointed another captain to navigate the *Bienville* into the Civil War. As Bulloch had surmised, the government soon purchased the *Bienville* and officially transferred it to the Union Navy. He would see his old command in the future, though under more extraordinary and ironic circumstances.[32]

Gathering his thoughts and his sea bag, he went to the shipping agent's offices the next morning and quickly checked to see if Attorney General Benjamin had replied to his letter. He had. Ripping open Benjamin's letter, he learned that Secretary of the Confederate States Navy Stephen Mallory wanted him in Montgomery, Alabama, "without delay." Bulloch immediately realized the danger in holding such a letter and destroyed it. His heart was in "Dixie" but everything else was under Union control including his former ship, worldly assets, family, and friends. He had orders for unspecified active service into a wartime navy. This was not the U.S. Navy he had sworn his loyalty to years before. For all practical purposes, it did not even exist. He would be sailing into the unknown.[33] It was 24 April 1861.

Bulloch said in his memoirs that he used the days between 24 April and 2 May 1861 to sever his relationship with Livingston and Crocheron, and attended to other "matters of business." He made no mention of his family situation, perhaps in deference to the undocumented assistance he received from the Roosevelts. One particular family concern was the pending birth of his third child. Harriott was in her ninth month of pregnancy and was due any day.

As a man bent on treason (at least in the eyes of the Union government), he needed to move carefully and avoid attracting the attention of "public authorities." For the next ten days, he quietly attended to personal affairs in New York and New Jersey, transferring bonds and property to his stepmother Martha. He entrusted the safety of his family to his sister Mittie and the Roosevelt clan. He had every reason to believe that his act of loyalty in returning the *Bienville* to its rightful owners, coupled with his innocuous activities, gave him the appearance of a normal citizen conducting routine business. Even when he published his memoirs in 1883, Bulloch did not suspect that U.S. government officials knew what he was doing, or was about to do.[34]

However, official U.S. government records prove that he was wrong. Just three days after he left New York City for Montgomery, AL, he had been betrayed by his own lack of operational security. Secretary Seward sent a report dated 5 May 1861 to U.S. Consul Freeman H. Morse in London warning him that "Capt. J.D. Bulloch" was headed to Liverpool, England, as a Confederate secret agent. The report originated from one of Secretary of the Treasury Stanton's special agents by the name of Hollis White.[35] Seward's intelligence report contradicts Bulloch's oft-quoted assertion that he had no idea that he would be asked to go abroad until he arrived in Montgomery and met with Confederate Attorney General Benjamin and Navy Secretary Mallory.

His reasons for proclaiming lack of foreknowledge reflected a desire to protect his extended family in New York and Philadelphia. If his Roosevelt, West, or Cross relatives had known that Bulloch was an agent of the South before he left for Montgomery, or even more damning, that they had helped him transfer assets, they would have been colored disloyal. When Bulloch wrote his memoirs in the early 1880s, his beloved nephew, Theodore Roosevelt, was a well-known political figure who could ill-afford another family scandal. Twenty-odd years after the American Civil War, Bulloch still needed to protect the reputation of his relatives.

Special Agent Hollis White's information indicates that Bulloch had *a priori* knowledge of his tasking from the Confederate government.[36] White was an officer of the company that managed the Niagara Falls suspension bridge connecting the New York Central Railroad with Canada. This rail line reached from Niagara Falls to Toronto and westward to Windsor, opposite Detroit.[37] White most likely discovered Bulloch's destination in early May while Bulloch was in New York making his travel arrangements for the Canadian portion of the journey to Liverpool. Those rail and steamship reservations required Bulloch to connect with a telegraph station at Niagara Falls. White probably saw, or got a copy of, that telegram soon after it was sent. He then passed the information on to Stanton and Seward, who was White's political patron. Seward was the former governor of New York who visited the suspension bridge with White as his host and had supported White's recent designation as a special agent to the U.S. Treasury on 26 March 1861.[38]

Bulloch also hints of previous conversations on the subject of sending a naval agent abroad in his memoirs, writing that "...as early as April, 1861, it was determined to send an agent to England to set on foot and direct such naval operations as it might be possible to organize beyond the limits of the Confederate States."[39]

As to his dealing with other "affairs" before leaving New York, we can assemble the pieces of Bulloch's carefully constructed puzzle. He explained that after closing down his life in New York City, he took a train to Philadelphia where he spent the night. Philadelphia would seem to be an inopportune place to stop, but his stepsister Susan ("Susy") lived there with her husband, Dr. Hilborne West, stepmother Martha, and adoring younger half-brother, Irvine Bulloch.[40] It would be hard to imagine that Brother Jimmie did not spend a last night with them. While his natural characteristic was to be tight-lipped about his activities, the family must have been aware of what was transpiring, especially since he was leaving behind his pregnant wife and two children under the age of four.

As he departed Philadelphia (most likely 3 May 1861) via Pittsburgh to Cincinnati, the discussions in the West household must have been heated. Both Hilborne West and his wife, Susy, had sisters who were married to Roosevelts (Silas Weir and Theodore Sr.) and had much to lose by assisting a Confederate agent. Harriott remained in New York City and was in frequent contact with Mittie and Theodore who must have known about Bulloch's "flitting" (a Scottish term for leaving in haste) by the first week in May 1861. They may have even helped with his family and property arrangements. Not all of the Roosevelt clan would be as charitable. The risk to the Roosevelts' social and financial position was too great to have it destroyed by a wayward in-law. In a time that tested the strength and even the definition of "loyalty," at least one of his relatives believed that the cloth of the Union flag was sewn with thread stronger than the ties of family.

As James Dunwoody Bulloch settled into his train seat on that early morning of May 1861 and headed west to Pittsburgh and Cincinnati, he had done as well as could be expected in covering his tracks. He did not suspect that his own family would turn on him with such vituperation, or that his personal communiqués (telegrams and letters) were in the hands of such people as Stanton and Seward. But this was the uncivil nature of the American Civil War.

Bulloch's luck held in his escape from the North, when he met a trusted gentleman in

4. Against Strong Northerly Winds and Head Seas

Pittsburgh with obvious Southern leanings who vouched for his integrity with the steamboat officials. They allowed him onboard for the voyage to Louisville, Kentucky, without a search or interrogation.[41] Union agents may have been looking for Bulloch, but they could not be sure if they were looking in the right direction.[42] Arriving in Louisville the morning of 5 May 1861, he rushed from the city's docks to its train station, leaping onto the first train headed to Nashville, Tennessee. Rolling into Nashville at noon on the same day, the harried Bulloch checked into a hotel, where he telegraphed Judah Benjamin that he was on his way to Montgomery.[43]

He arrived in Nashville while the Tennessee Secession Convention was meeting. Upon chance, he met General George Washington Barrow, a past political ally of Abraham Lincoln, but who now returned to public life as an ardent secessionist.[44] A flamboyant military man who had fought in the Seminole War (1836), Barrow urged him to tell President Jefferson Davis that Tennessee was sure to secede in a few more days.[45] After observing more of the secession fervor in the city, Bulloch retired to his hotel to rest and await the departure of his train. A few hours later, he was again on the move. On a fast train, he steamed through Chattanooga and Atlanta, and finally reached his destination, Montgomery, Alabama, the first home of the Confederacy. He was exhausted from travel and the nervous comportment of the people he met during the journey from New York. There was but one conversation on their lips: secession and war. He collapsed into his hotel bed near midnight on 7 May 1861.[46]

Rising at an early hour on 8 May 1861, he had a quick breakfast and hurried to the offices of the newly formed Confederate government, searching for Attorney General Benjamin.[47] Benjamin told Bulloch that Secretary of the Navy Mallory had been waiting impatiently for his arrival and that he would take him directly across to his office. By necessity, Mallory was the most creative man in the cabinet of the Confederate government. The Confederacy was blessed with army officers and former enlisted men with considerable experience who by and large had horses and some form of weapon. Naval men and material were an entirely different matter, for the Confederacy essentially had no sailors and nothing to sail.

The brevity of their meeting belied its long-term effect upon both American and world history. Naval strategists and historians around the world from the *Kaiserliche Marine* to the Imperial Japanese, Chinese, and U.S. would study the strategy that the two men discussed. Bulloch said he was astonished when Mallory greeted him by saying, "I am glad to see you: I want you to go to Europe. When can you start?"[48] In the light of what we now know, per the Hollis White report, Bulloch was primed and ready to go abroad. In fact, in his memoirs he said that he could leave immediately. This is a remarkable statement considering his claim that in only 10 days he had resigned his position as a merchant marine captain, found means to support his family, and settled his financial accounts; a difficult achievement in modern times, much less in the mid-nineteenth century.

Bulloch hinted at his awareness of the true assignment only after deftly introducing the subject of the meeting with Mallory. He spent nearly five full pages commenting about how he thought his naval expertise would be employed to improve the sea defenses of New Orleans. He then casually mentioned that he "unofficially discussed" military plans with the Louisiana Board of War in March 1861. This early date was before the *Bienville*'s fateful visit to New Orleans on 13 April 1861, when Bulloch first heard the news of Ft. Sumter's bombardment.[49] His attempt to obfuscate the extent of his involvement with Confederate officials prior to the start of the Civil War was akin to the clever moves of a magician, who redirects the audience's attention to distract them from his real moves. Bulloch's memoirs were part of that gentle deception, saying much, but not all.

Meanwhile, in Mallory's hectic office, he discussed the new Confederate Department of the Navy, its human and material resources, and efforts to contact Southern-born naval officers who were either still in the North or at sea. As of 8 May 1861, the Confederate Navy had only the *Habana*, which was purchased in New Orleans and not yet re-christened the *Sumter*, under the command of Raphael Semmes.[50] It was not an enviable starting position. The Confederate Navy would be the proverbial mosquito trying to afflict Lincoln's elephant.

Mallory moved on to describe Bulloch's mission: the South had an immediate need to get blue-water cruisers to sea to attack the Union's commerce. Mallory hoped to draw Union warships away from blockade duty, thus creating holes that would allow Southern commerce to flow in and out of the Confederacy. He also wanted to inflict enough economic pain on the "Yankee" mercantile class that the resulting hue and cry would create sufficient political pressure to stop the war and recognize the Confederacy. Mallory laid out the type, design, and source for the cruisers: they would come from Great Britain.[51]

There is no direct evidence that Bulloch discussed this naval strategy with anyone in the Confederate government beforehand, and in this instance, Mallory certainly deserves credit for the accuracy of his strategic vision. Having given Bulloch much to think about, Mallory told him to return to the hotel and write out a detailed operational plan. They could address any other questions on the naval program abroad when they met again the next day.[52]

Bulloch inferred that Mallory suggested that he travel via the western periphery of the Union into Canada, then on to Europe. This route avoided the already restrictive blockade, the possibility of search and seizure, and provided a more reliable and timely departure for Europe. He memorized all the details of the meeting and its points, but his memoir uses literary license concerning his travel arrangements. By the time he left Mallory's office, Hollis White's report on Bulloch's travel plan was already four days old.[53]

The following morning, Bulloch re-entered Mallory's office and they went over key points of the naval program they hoped to launch abroad. Justification for Mallory's proposed commerce-raiding strategy was straightforward and based on American successes in previous wars against a superior naval force (i.e., Great Britain). The operational approach for adjudicating the prizes captured by the commerce raiders would have to be learned under weigh. They reviewed the "Great European" powers' view of the Confederacy, their probable recognition of the new Southern republic, and the likelihood that they would grant belligerent status to Bulloch's cruisers. On the subject of recognition, Mallory predicted that only decisive military victories would prompt the Europeans to recognize the Confederacy as a rightful nation. The imposition of might, whether or not it was right, was still paramount in the European mindset of *realpolitik*.[54]

While fallible, Bulloch's memoirs were not prone to lapses of memory or the factual inaccuracies that were common to other Civil War diarists. Most of his narrative was purposeful in detail, particularly whether certain information is included or omitted. Once more, we come to an issue that is either a juxtaposition of events in his memoirs, written

4. Against Strong Northerly Winds and Head Seas   41

Montgomery, Alabama, was the capital of the Confederacy in 1861 (U.S. Naval Historical Center).

some twenty-odd years later, or another subtle effort to justify the Confederate Navy's commerce-raiding strategy. In this case, he related that during the 9 May 1861 meeting, Mallory advised him to become thoroughly familiar with Britain's Foreign Enlistment Act and Queen Victoria's Proclamation of Neutrality. The British Foreign Enlistment Act of 1819 was not re-issued until 6 May 1861 and Queen Victoria did not announce her Proclamation of Neutrality until 13 May 1861.[55] Since direct, reliable telegraph connections between Britain and North America would not occur until 1866, neither the Confederate government nor Bulloch could have known about either of these events while he was in Montgomery on 9 May 1861. Mallory may have instructed him to become familiar with and respect neutrality rights and British laws regarding ship acquisition, but he did not cite the specific proclamation (neutrality) or law (Foreign Enlistment) during this meeting.[56]

Yet, there is another possibility. On 19 April 1861, Abraham Lincoln proclaimed a naval blockade against the seven Southern states that had seceded. This action gave the Confederacy legitimacy as a *de facto* nation in the eyes of the international community. The nasty little incivility within the American Republic had now become a full-blown war between two recognized belligerents. The Union blockade announcement gave the Confederacy the rights of an actual nation-state in the eyes of the international community. The United States' failure to ratify the Treaty of Paris (1856) that prohibited privateering, and had been signed by virtually every maritime nation, now haunted Lincoln's wartime government.[57]

Attorney General Benjamin had significant experience in international law and was widely recognized as one of the North American continent's greatest legal minds.[58] It is possible that Benjamin recognized Lincoln's mistake and advised Davis and Mallory how the maritime powers would react to Lincoln's blockade. Lincoln proclaimed the Union blockade in retaliation for Jefferson Davis' issuance of letters of marquee and reprisal that authorized Southern privateers to attack Northern vessels.[59] Benjamin knew exactly how the privateer proclamation should be worded, i.e., in accordance with the stipulations of the Treaty of Paris. The end result was that the Confederacy gained a diplomatic victory. Without being officially recognized by any nation, it was accorded the status of a nation-at-war. Bulloch's assertions about the legal aspects of his 9 May 1861 meeting are most likely based on Benjamin's assumptions and interpretation of the Treaty of Paris.[60]

Bulloch wound up his meeting with Mallory by discussing the financial arrangements for purchasing the Confederacy's ships and naval material abroad, and contacts with the London-based Confederate commissioners, William Lowndes Yancey and Dudley Mann.[61] The Charleston-based firm of Fraser, Trenholm and Company would be the Confederacy's overseas banker, but in practice, the company became the Confederacy's offshore treasury. For the duration of the Civil War, the firm performed extraordinary feats of financial magic for the South.[62] Final admonishments by Mallory on how to deal with the myriad network of other Confederate agents and representatives must have left even the sanguine Bulloch reeling.

Although not recorded in his memoirs or letters, he obtained a copy of "Cobb's Miniature Lexicon" for the purpose of encoding sensitive communications. Using a simple word substitution, Mallory and Bulloch arranged to use Cobb's book for their ciphers. For example, the message "gratified to find *your ship progressing* so well" would read "gratified to find 817.17, 674.26, 599.22ing so well." The cipher "817.17" equated to the word "your" by turning to page number "817" and counting down to the 17th word on that page.[63] With Mallory's instructions and Cobb's Lexicon in hand, Bulloch dashed for the night train out of Montgomery and headed north through enemy territory, the United States of America.[64]

As he began his journey, he must have pondered how he had come to be selected for this daunting mission. It is a question that has perplexed maritime historians or caused them to offer a simplistic or inaccurate rationale. He was not a quartermaster or military supply/contracting officer, a senior navy officer, an experienced shipbuilder or financier, a successful business man or merchant, or a even a politician. He was not even a confidant of Mallory or Davis. He would later acquire these attributes, but at the time of his selection, he had none. The Confederacy sent several other agents to Europe who had far more impressive credentials, but were far less successful.

The qualities that Bulloch did have were honesty, leadership, broad merchant marine and naval experience, and an incredible network of personal, business, and family trust-relationships. Added to this mix were his unsurpassed energy, loyalty, courage, intelligence, and bold creativity. He had been born into an aristocratic Southern family with significant experience and lofty expectations that included transporting a valuable commodity (cotton) over vast distances. He also had extensive financial and political contacts in Europe and the United States. This combination of skills, experience, and ability to act unilaterally under extreme pressure made him a perfect choice for this critical mission.

After his brief sojourn to Montgomery, Bulloch was ready to commence his adventures as a Confederate secret agent. Retracing his steps to Louisville, he erased any evidence of papers or notes from his belongings before re-entering Union territory. He was able to

4. Against Strong Northerly Winds and Head Seas

leave the rebellious states without bother, implying that searches of individuals going north were not as thorough.[65]

While he merely relates that he traveled north to Detroit (about 13 May 1861) before crossing into Canada by way of Lake Erie, the information from Hollis White indicates his point of entry to Canada was Windsor, Ontario. Catching the Grand Trunk Railway to Montreal, he arrived about May 15th and remained there until his departure for Liverpool, England, two days later. To reach Liverpool, he first had to endure a 12-hour shipboard transit to Quebec and then, on the other side of the Atlantic, a stop in Londonderry, Ireland.[66] Assuming he had not crossed the Canadian-American border until 14 May 1861, there are two days in Canada that are unaccounted for prior to his departure early on 17 May 1861. So, what was he doing during this time? This is a question that has taxed Civil War historians and conspiracy theorists alike for a century and more.

Officially, Canada was neutral in relation to the American Civil War, but significant numbers of her people (both in official and unofficial capacity) assisted or turned a blind-eye to Confederate activities within her borders.[67] Canadians were aware that Confederates, whether government officials or businessmen, needed fast transport to Europe. They also needed sanctuary before and after venturing to Europe and they were willing to pay for it in cash.

Later in the war, the Confederacy took advantage of Canada's long, porous, and proximate border to conduct covert operations, gather intelligence, and launch attacks against Union military, political, and civil infrastructures. These activities all occurred after Bulloch's first and only wartime appearance in Montreal in May 1861. However, there are tantalizing bits of information that suggest that he may have had a role in nurturing the development of the Canadian Confederate secret service infrastructure.[68]

In August 1861, the U.S. consul reported the first blockade runner from the Confederacy (that he knew of) at Halifax Nova Scotia. By December 1861, he reported that Confederate couriers carrying secret dispatches regularly transited the city. By the end of 1861, there was so much covert Confederate activity in Canada, especially in cities with rail or maritime connections to the U.S. (e.g., Windsor, Toronto, Montreal, and Halifax), that the U.S. consul assigned to Quebec had to beg Washington, D.C., for additional personnel to carry out adequate surveillance.[69]

In addition to his travel itinerary, Bulloch probably made advance arrangements for temporary accommodation in Montreal before he left New York. It is possible that he received assistance from Confederate operatives in Canada, as it became a new theater of military, political, and intelligence confrontation. While in Montreal, it is likely that he sent news to his wife and family either by telegraph, or possibly by placing a coded personal advertisement in a New York City newspaper.[70] The important news from New York was that Harriott delivered their third child, Henry Dunwody Bulloch, on 17 May 1861. The child's mother was fine and his father was off to war.[71]

5

Brains and Dash — Liverpool, 1861

When Bulloch sailed on the *North American* from Quebec on 18 May 1861, he left the North American continent for the first time as a Confederate citizen. He was headed for Great Britain, a country that neither recognized nor refuted this new nation.[1] His memoirs give no hint of his thoughts at leaving; he only picked up the story upon his arrival in Liverpool, late on the afternoon of Tuesday, 4 June 1861.[2]

Early the next morning, he entered the offices of Fraser, Trenholm and Company for the first time. Pausing only long enough to introduce himself and obtain the address for the Confederate commissioners in London, Dudley Mann and William L. Yancey, Bulloch found his way to the train station for a trip to London to establish official contact and verify his *bona fides*.[3]

Upon his arrival in London, he quickly met with the two commissioners. Bulloch knew very little about the efforts by the two rather hapless Southern "diplomats" in the delicate arena of international relations. Mann had reached London via New York on 15 April 1861 while Bulloch was still a merchant steamship captain. Yancey arrived in London two weeks later after departing from New Orleans on 29 March 1861 while Bulloch was busy extricating the *Bienville* from the clutches of the U.S. Treasury's customs agents.[4]

If the Union had any doubts about Confederate intention to establish foreign relations, Mann alerted them fully to the fact by brazenly and stupidly visiting the U.S. legation at Portland Place in London on 18 April 1861. Slow to realize that the Confederacy and Union were at war, he collegially called on the departing U.S. minister, George M. Dallas, a long-time friend. It is hard to imagine that some form of surveillance over Mann did not begin immediately after that. As for Yancey, he was barely tolerable as a human being much less as a minister, even for the British.[5] Regarded as one of the most ardent pro-slavery Southerners, the long-time abolitionist British could barely stomach the idea of his presence, making him suspect to both British *and* Union governments.

Bulloch walked unknowingly into a web of agents observing the two Confederate commissioners. If Bulloch was not followed from Liverpool from the very outset, he certainly was after visiting Yancey and Mann.

Behind closed doors, the two Confederate commissioners gave Bulloch a hearty handshake and got down to business by explaining the current state-of-affairs. The results of their diplomatic entreaties to the British had been disappointing with neither an official reception by the British secretary of state for Foreign Affairs, nor any other form of acknowledgment. However, the Great Powers had recognized the *de facto* government of the Confederacy and granted belligerent rights. As expected, the diplomatic gaffe of Lincoln's early days proved providential to the South. The Confederate diplomats believed that the South, as a recognized belligerent, could procure the material of war they needed in Europe. After receiving a pat on his back and, ironically, a warning to maintain a low-key approach to his affairs, Bulloch returned to Liverpool with the commissioners' words of promised assistance ringing in his ears. What Bulloch thought of the two at that moment is not revealed; he was always circumspect in his memoirs: quick to praise, leaving criticisms unsaid.[6]

As the train carrying Bulloch back to Liverpool trundled through the English midlands, the first land forces of the struggling Confederacy were tentatively maneuvering against Union forces in a contest to control western Virginia. In naval affairs, the Confederacy discovered that the privateer policy of President Davis had achieved its political ends, but had little military or tactical value. In June, the Union brig USS *Perry* captured the privateer *Savannah* and threatened its crew with execution as pirates. With the onset of summer, the scorecard for 1861 showed a stalemate on land, a minor Union victory at sea, and a hopeful, but unrealized, Confederate political agenda.[7]

In Liverpool, Bulloch soon took up residence in the offices of Fraser, Trenholm and Company at 10 Rumford Place, becoming close to the resident manager, Charles K. Prioleau. While Bulloch made a point of his need to establish credibility and *bona fides*, it is highly doubtful that Fraser, Trenholm was not already well aware of his reputation and the expectations of the Confederate government. Prioleau already had experience with his emerging role as a wartime financier. Captain Caleb Huse of the Confederate States Army arrived ahead of Bulloch as the primary ordnance supply agent of the War Department. Huse, like Bulloch, had a Texas-sized wish list and a pauper's purse. Prioleau told Bulloch, as he told Huse, to go ahead and buy or contract for whatever he needed. The financial resources of Fraser, Trenholm and Co. were at the Confederacy's disposal, up to a point.[8]

Completing the obligatory official calls, Bulloch then availed himself of professional legal advice to discover what he could and could not do under the British Foreign Enlistment Act. He quickly obtained the services of Frederick S. Hull, a prominent Liverpool solicitor. Hull discovered that no legal case had ever been brought to court regarding the building of a ship for use by a declared belligerent nation. He brilliantly observed that it was necessary to determine if the mere *act* of building a ship for a belligerent for any reason and for any future use, made the builders and contractors liable for legal prosecution or seizure of the vessel and forfeiture of any associated funds.[9] A favorable legal opinion that excused potential contractors from liability would aide his progress. If a legal counsel's opinion was negative, however, the Confederate naval program would be stillborn.

Hull carefully composed a test case and placed it in the hands of two barristers. Since Hull submitted the case as a theoretical legal question, there was no specific connection with any particular individual or entity. The barristers returned their observations and legal opinion to Hull, who duly reported it to Bulloch:

1. It is no offence for British subjects to equip, etc., a ship at some country without [beyond] Her Majesty's dominions, though the intent be to cruise against a friendly State.

2. It is no offence for any person (subject or no subject) to equip a ship within her Majesty's dominions, if it be not done with the intent to cruise against a friendly State.
3. The mere building of a ship within her Majesty's dominions by any person (subject or no subject) is no offence, whatever may be the intent of the parties, because the offence is not the building, but the equipping. Therefore, any shipbuilder may build any ship in her Majesty's dominions, provided he does not equip her within Her Majesty's dominions, and has nothing to do with the acts of the purchasers done within Her Majesty's dominions without his concurrence, nor without Her Majesty's dominions with his concurrence.[10]

Bulloch was delighted with this piece of legal legerdemain, for he now had a chart to navigate his shipbuilding program through the vagaries of the British maritime contracting system. He would stringently avoid (a) informing the builder of the intended use of the vessel (or supplies), (b) supplying any ship with war material of any kind within Her Majesty's lands or waters, and finally, (c) allowing any builder or supplier for any Confederate vessel to participate in equipping the ship even when it was located beyond Her Majesty's realm.[11] Solicitor Hull remained on a legal retainer throughout Bulloch's endeavors in Liverpool.

Bulloch wasted no time in using his newfound legal standing, and his credit line with Fraser, Trenholm and Co. He purchased numerous naval supplies and signed a contract for the Confederacy's first purpose-built commerce raider, the CSS *Florida*. Originally christened under the *nom de guerre* of *Oreto*, her construction was well underway by the end of June 1861, with her ribs beginning to take form the next month.[12]

The *Florida* was a case of imitation being the sincerest form of flattery. Her design was lifted directly from the plans for the *Philomel* (or *Ranger*) class gunboats of the Royal Navy. The shipbuilder, William C. Miller & Sons, had just completed and commissioned the HMS *Steady* on 12 June 1861, so the plans were still warm when Bulloch arrived. With bit of tweaking with the hull lines, and a few adjustments of the sail plan, Bulloch had a faster, better sea-handling vessel. The firm of Fawcett, Preston and Co. handled the mechanicals, including the engines, without inquiry. Interestingly, the engineering firm was the main contractor for the *Florida*, and W.C. Miller was the sub-contractor as Fraser, Trenholm and Co. guaranteed timely payment.[13] The snap of Bulloch's case and the rapid tap of his heels on the street marching away from W.C. Miller's office could be heard across Liverpool's narrow streets.

Clearly, Bulloch understood the type of ships required for the Confederate Navy. He was not, however, a naval architect and he had little experience in ship construction.[14] As the naval agent, he needed only to understand and describe the suitable mission requirements, and he did that admirably. Bulloch's knowledge was operational, business, political, legal, and above all, practical—but not technical. To understand the basics of ship construction, Bulloch referred to James Peake's authoritative *Rudimentary Treatise of Ship Building*. For advice on technical matters involved with naval architecture, the shipyards of Liverpool and Glasgow were the best in the world; Bulloch had no need to worry when he was surrounded by nautical genius and artisanship at every turn.

It was exactly this nautical genius that Bulloch exploited in the creation of his greatest and most famous Confederate commerce raider, the vessel known to history as the CSS *Alabama*. While still negotiating the terms and specifications of the CSS *Florida*, he availed himself of the riches of choice shipbuilders, by visiting the Birkenhead Ironworks, owned by the Laird family. The Laird dynasty in shipbuilding began in 1824 when William Laird, a Scottish businessman and entrepreneur, moved to the Liverpool area to set up a boiler-making factory. By 1828, the elder Laird had been joined by his son John, who pushed his father into building iron-hulled ships. This was a bold move since iron-hull design lagged behind developments in steam propulsion. When James Dunwoody Bulloch arrived on the scene in the late spring of 1861, the company was in transition, as John Laird had retired, leaving the management of the company in the hands of his young and aggressive sons, Henry, John, and William.[15] Bulloch had entered shipbuilding heaven with fresh shipyards, engine fabrication works, and managers who were eager to turn his unique ideas into reality.

Bulloch's activities quickly attracted the attention of Union officials in Europe. Henry S. Sanford, the Union minister to Belgium, took charge of organizing the initial Union surveillance efforts in England. Sanford instructed his hired detectives and informants to pay particular attention to James D. Bulloch. By July 4th, just one month after Bulloch's arrival, Sanford doubled the surveillance force against him, considering Bulloch to be "the most dangerous man the South have here and fully up to his business."[16]

If there had been any question of Bulloch's purpose as a Confederate secret agent, it was answered in a remarkable letter to Secretary Seward from Hiram Barney, a U.S. customs official for New York. On 10 July 1861, Barney reported a meeting with James A. Roosevelt in New York. Roosevelt claimed that his in-law, James Dunwoody Bulloch, was in Britain with three-quarters of a million dollars at his disposal. Bulloch had purchased several ships that were to be converted into warships. Explosively, Roosevelt claimed that these Confederate ships would operate from Liverpool and would attack Union merchantmen and naval vessels. Barney pointed out that "J.A. Roosevelt" was a nephew of "Judge Roosevelt" and a family connection of "Mr. Bulloch," thus stressing the loyalty and reliability of his informant. Roosevelt stuck his knife further into his "family connection" by telling Barney that he had seen letters from Bulloch's own hand. These letters instructed Bulloch's associates to transfer his properties to others in order to escape confiscation by Union authorities. This action affirms that while Bulloch may have underestimated the loyalty of his more distant Roosevelt relatives, he understood the vindictiveness of Seward, Stanton, and Welles.[17]

Seward wrote to his emissaries in England 10 days later, warning them about Bulloch. By September 12th, Liverpool's acting consul Henry Wilding was able to report that his agents were following the Confederate agent. They knew where he lived and that he was building two steamers in partnership with Fraser, Trenholm. The agents shared this description: "Captain Bulloch ... is a very dark, sallow man with black hair and eyes, whiskers down each cheek but shaved clean off his chin and below, dark moustache, about 5'8" high."[18]

Unaware of his family betrayal but well aware of the ever-present surveillance, Bulloch adroitly met with the shipbuilding wizards within Lairds. Dazzled by the possibilities, Bulloch conjured up a vision of the perfect commerce-raiding warship. He began a conversation with the Lairds about a screw-propelled "despatch vessel," this time getting into the details of how he might get such a ship built. Could the Lairds' naval architects create a set of specifications, drawings, and plans to build a ship that matched Bulloch's vision? The Lairds responded in the affirmative and even promised a scale model of the proposed vessel if Bulloch could supply a financial deposit. Bulloch agreed to the Lairds' terms, and after ironing out a few niggling details, signed a contract on 1 August 1861.[19] Bulloch wondered how he was going to come up with the funds, but help arrived in the nick of time. On 27 July 1861, Fraser, Trenholm and Co. received £131,000 from the Confederate government, a portion of which was designated for Bulloch's use.[20]

While the Lairds' company was the mother of her invention, Bulloch has been regarded by naval historians as the *Alabama's* father, and rightly so. His affection for her is evident in his memoirs where he lovingly describes her measurements, weight, sails, hull lines, and the power of her engines. The quality of the *Alabama* would equal, if not exceed, any warship of Her Majesty's Royal Navy. Bulloch had reason to be proud of his creation. Attention to detail was everywhere. He included a mechanism to produce fresh water with a condenser and cooling tank (reducing the need for stops to get fresh water for the crew) and a copper-clad bottom (ensuring her wooden hull would foul much less quickly). She was Bulloch's sea-nymph, destined to be launched into Neptune's kingdom to sweep Yankee merchant ships — and naval vessels when necessary — from the world's oceans. Her total cost was £47,500 and she would return the Confederacy's investment in her construction many times.[21]

While events were proceeding at break-neck speed in Liverpool, across the Atlantic the Confederate Army achieved an early success in Virginia. Confederate forces under Gen. Beauregard routed Union troops led by Gen. McDowell at the "Battle of Bull Run" (or Manassas) on 21 July 1861. News of this shocking event reached Liverpool as Bulloch signed the contract for the *Alabama*. It was in the flush of excitement regarding that singular victory when Bulloch learned of another Fraser, Trenholm and Company initiative.[22]

Charles Prioleau, the principal manager of Fraser, Trenholm and Co., decided to send a steamship across the Atlantic to convince British and other European exporters that the Union blockade was more talk than reality. It was more than happenstance that the firm stood to make a tidy profit if this venture was successful. Prioleau brought Bulloch into his confidence, along with Captain (later Major) Caleb Huse. Did they have war material to send to the Confederacy? Bulloch and Huse needed no further inducement. In an example of Army — Navy cooperation seldom seen within the Confederacy, Bulloch agreed to manage the shipment of the material, while Huse handled the purchase. Huse promptly had it all shipped to West Hartlepool, a port 255 miles from London on the northeastern coast of England.[23] The ship that would perform this risky mission was the aptly named *Bermuda*. She was the first vessel that Bulloch would send into harm's way as an agent of the Confederate Navy, even though it technically belonged to a "private owner."

Bulloch paused just long enough on 13 August 1861 to report to Sec. Mallory on his success in getting two vessels under construction, the purchase of munitions, his paucity of funds, and problems with British neutrality. Most of all, he required a commission in the Confederate Navy; he desperately desired to command one of the two ships under construction. At the time, Bulloch was merely a Navy Department civil servant. The strain of dealing with Union spies and bureaucracy was already telling, but it would get much worse. He posted this letter without mentioning the *Bermuda* by name.[24]

Captain Eugene Tessier, a long-time commander of ships owned by the Charleston branch of the Fraser trade empire (John Fraser and Co.), and a pilot (Peck) who was familiar with the southeastern coast of the Confederacy, had been brought in to navigate the

CSS *Alabama*, Bulloch's most destructive raider, shown in a painting by RADM Schmidt (U.S. Naval Historical Center).

Bermuda across the Atlantic and into a Southern port. It is easy to picture Tessier and Peck directing the frenzied provisioning and loading of precious cargo. Bulloch was hurrying among Liverpool, London, and Hartlepool to ensure that the supplies he and Huse had ordered were delivered and paid for — all the while trying not to draw too much attention to their efforts.[25]

The *Bermuda* departed West Hartlepool on 18 August 1861 and stopped at the west coast port of Falmouth in Cornwall on 22 August 1861, where she filled her coalbunkers. She then departed for North America, claiming Cuba as their destination. Union agents were aware of the ship and cargo, but not her precise destination. She managed a relatively placid crossing of the Atlantic until just before her run into the Georgia coast, for a tremendous storm moved up the coast of the United States. The weather assisted the *Bermuda*, for the storm drove the Union blockade ship USS *Savannah* offshore. The Union frigate never saw the *Bermuda* make its run into the mouth of the winding Savannah River. The blockade runner defiantly docked beneath the high bluffs of Savannah's riverfront docks on 18 September 1861. The cargo she brought to the Confederacy was valued at $1,000,000 and news of her triumphant run was broadcast throughout Southern newspapers and grudgingly published in the North.

Union Secretary of the Navy Gideon Welles was furious over the Confederate success, for he saw the handiwork of James Dunwoody Bulloch, even though Bulloch only claimed a minor role in the event.[26] The British government, specifically Prime Minister Lord Palmerston, got direct after-action intelligence of the *Bermuda*'s arrival from former British Prime

Minister Lord Derby, who was in North America and reported that "the *Bermuda* ... reached Savannah bringing among other valuable stores, 25,550 rifles."[27] Bulloch and Captain Caleb Huse had done their jobs well.

One of Bulloch's army counterparts, Maj. Edward C. Anderson, was in Europe to investigate the "fidelity" of Capt. Caleb Huse concerning his handling of Confederate War Department funds. Relying on his own observations and placing particular credibility with Bulloch's unreserved endorsement, Anderson promptly assured Richmond of Huse's loyalty, energy, and effectiveness. Having no need to replace Huse, Anderson merely helped him acquire arms and armaments.[28]

While the American Civil War may have captured the attention of former and low-level British officials, at the highest levels the Empire operated as usual. On the day *Bermuda* departed West Hartlepool, Queen Victoria was much more concerned with the Prussian Empire's desire to conquer Denmark and Finland, along with the Polish and Hungarian Revolutions. The intrigues of its ancient enemy, France, were, as always, a top priority. When the *Bermuda* arrived in Savannah, Queen Victoria was lauding peaceful relations in India.[29] Meanwhile, the American Civil War moved into a vicious new phase. Washington would not condone British "interference" in their suppression of the rebellion. Any action that provided material or moral support to the "rebels" was considered an unfriendly act. American politicians would not admit that international legal standards, such as neutrality or belligerent rights, applied to the states in rebellion, the "so called" Confederate states. There would be no reasoning with the Lincoln government.

While maintaining a frenetic pace, Bulloch was not too busy for a bit of relaxation, including London theater-going. He took advantage of tickets provided courtesy of a Mr. Samuel Isaac in consideration of his large contract with Anderson. The Confederate Army had purchased a lot of Enfield rifles and 11,000 English muskets "of very good quality" that would be delivered via Bulloch's next blockade running adventure.[30]

After his first successes, it was time for James Dunwoody Bulloch to reflect and assess his situation. A point-by-point examination of the main issues contained in his 13 August 1861 letter to Mallory accurately sets the scene. Its forthright tone is subtly different from Bulloch's subsequent memoirs.

- Bulloch could not sign any contracts without funds in hand. Although he paints Fraser, Trenholm, and Co. as bankers extraordinaire for the Confederacy in his memoirs, at this early juncture they were doing very little beyond promising timely payments on the *Florida* project. They based that promise on the prerequisite that the Confederate government would pay quickly, and provide more *Bermuda*-like opportunities for profit.
- Northern agents and other Confederate agents were bidding against each other for the munitions and supplies they needed. In fact, Bulloch suffered from well-meaning "patriotic" Confederates trying to aid "The Cause." The Union and individual Northern states also had agents such as Consul Sanford bidding up prices and reducing the availability of essential arms and commissary supplies.
- The Queen's Proclamation of Neutrality frightened some British businesses away from dealing with Bulloch and other Confederates. Secrecy had been lost from the moment he had arrived, due to the "open" newspaper publication of his mission.

- He was forced to adapt British *wooden* gunboat plans (W.C. Miller's *Philomel*, for example). Contrary to public opinion and "informed" naval experts, the existing iron warships were "too thin in the plates, light in the deck frames and stanchions" to carry the necessary naval gun ordnance for commerce raiding (he needed long-range firing capability). He discovered that even naval artillery-firing tables and information on rifled guns were tightly held secrets within the Royal Navy.
- Bulloch reserved the last $40,000 of the funds sent on 27 July 1861 for himself, as he planned to join with Major Huse and Capt. Anderson to purchase more war material. He intended to buy a ship, load it, and then run her through the blockade with himself "in charge." Bulloch was stretching the discretionary options within his orders. In fact, his decision to return to the Confederacy implicitly contradicted Mallory's directive. In this instance, he carefully described how he had executed all of Mallory's orders and practically exhausted all of his funds. Almost as an afterthought, he announced his impending return to the Confederacy as a blockade runner. He knew that the lag-time in transatlantic communications would preclude any contrary directions from Mallory prior to his departure.
- He again pleaded with Mallory for an actual *commission* in the Confederate Navy. He only held a civilian position and had no military rank. This oversight, from the perspective of a man with past U.S. Navy experience and over eight years of command at sea, was already a problem in the person of Lt. James North, CSN. North arrived in England with Major Anderson and assumed that he superseded Bulloch's authority since he was a Navy officer. Not only was North a commissioned officer, he had been senior to Bulloch when they were both in the "old Navy." Mallory had sent North to Britain only for the purpose of acquiring or building an ironclad. However, Bulloch's broader authority and responsibility did not match his relative status with old-school Navy officers like North.
- Finally, Bulloch wanted command of either the *Florida* or the *Alabama*. He didn't care which one, but the aggravation he had already endured was telling. He was persisting as a one-man Navy Department against incredible odds.

Bulloch was temporarily at a loss about his best course of action. He needed a better mechanism for communications and a steady flow of funds. Family matters were also on his mind. Harriott, their three children, two maids, and a manservant left New York City on 28 August 1861 aboard the Cunard steamer SS *Persia*.[31] Bulloch needed to arrange for accommodation and ensure that he was present to greet them upon their arrival in Liverpool. Harriott would have to tend to the details of settling the family in England while Bulloch completed his frantic preparations for a perilous return to the Confederacy.

The memoirs of Bulloch and Anderson both cite a 2 September 1861 conclave with Huse, Prioleau, Andrew Low, and Charles Green, where they jointly decided to fund the purchase of a fast steamship. They would load her to the gunwales with war supplies, run the blockade, and then report directly to Richmond about the situation in Britain. Bulloch based his decision on the fact that all his funds were tied up in the *Florida* and *Alabama* projects and there was nothing he could contribute to their construction at the moment. He further justified his action by getting affirmation from Fraser, Trenholm and Co. in Liverpool and from Commissioner Dudley Mann in London. Mann assented because he trusted

Bulloch's knowledge and reputation on naval affairs, while Fraser, Trenholm and Co. were looking for fresh Confederate monies to recharge the corporate coffers. Bulloch had already made his decision to run the blockade weeks beforehand. As a part of that decision, he searched for a suitable "fast steamer" so that he was prepared to act quickly when the decision was official.[32]

In the Confederacy on 20 September 1861, Mallory received Bulloch's letter via the *Bermuda*. Six days later, he endorsed the blockade-running initiative and submitted the Navy Department's shopping list of items that he should bring with him. By then, Bulloch, Huse, and Anderson had long been in action.

Bulloch knew the type of hybrid vessel they needed. It first had to be capable of making a high-speed run into port past the Union blockade. Second, it had to have good seakeeping capabilities for a transatlantic crossing. Finally, it had to be of exceptional build and quality. At that time, the fastest and most durable steamships were in the island ferry trade of the Hebrides (Western Isles) of Scotland. These gale-ravaged seas and shallow coastal waters forced Glasgow builders to craft vessels for just such conditions and these were the characteristics that Bulloch knew they would need to complete their mission. Late September and October were notorious hurricane months in the North Atlantic.[33]

Exactly how Bulloch learned of the "Clyde-built" steamer *Fingal* is unclear. He departed Liverpool on the evening of 2 September 1861 and returned from Glasgow two days later. By the 11th of September, he had purchased the *Fingal* from its Scottish owners, indicating that Bulloch or his compatriots (most likely Andrew Low) already had well-established connections in Scotland.[34] Bulloch placed her alongside the quay in Greenock, on the west coast of Scotland (on the upper Firth of Clyde), where she was loaded.

In the midst of the meetings and financial dealings involved with buying the *Fingal*, on September 4th Bulloch hurried back to Liverpool from Greenock via Glasgow to greet his family after a four-month separation. Harriott, the children and three servants arrived in Liverpool two days later.[35] Although details are sparse, it is evident that Bulloch made arrangements for his family to join him in Liverpool before he left New York or shortly thereafter. The family set up household at 2 Marine Terrace in Liverpool, where they lived for about a month before moving to nearby 3 Wellington Street.[36] Although Harriott was accustomed to separations of three to four weeks as a sailor's wife, the relocation of her entire household, children, and servants across the ocean to a foreign country in wartime, without her spouse would have taxed anyone. At least she knew that her family would be safe in England, far removed from the raging battlefields of the U.S., or so she thought. Harriott could not have been pleased to learn that her husband would leave Liverpool in six weeks. He was not only leaving her alone in a foreign country, he was risking his life in a war zone where blockade runners were still considered pirates and faced summary execution.

Anderson and Huse, along with Bulloch, frenetically ordered, purchased, and shipped war material to the *Fingal* by rail and sea. Operating as secretly as possible, as they knew that Union agents were reporting their every move, Bulloch used "cut-outs" when possible to maintain distance from his ships.[37] He did have the advantage of a convenient back door from his Liverpool offices that allowed clandestine visitors to come and go unobserved.[38]

The cargo that filled the *Fingal*'s hold was a cornucopia of war supplies for both the Confederate Army and Navy. Thousands of rifles, ball cartridges, percussion caps, sabers,

5. Brains and Dash   53

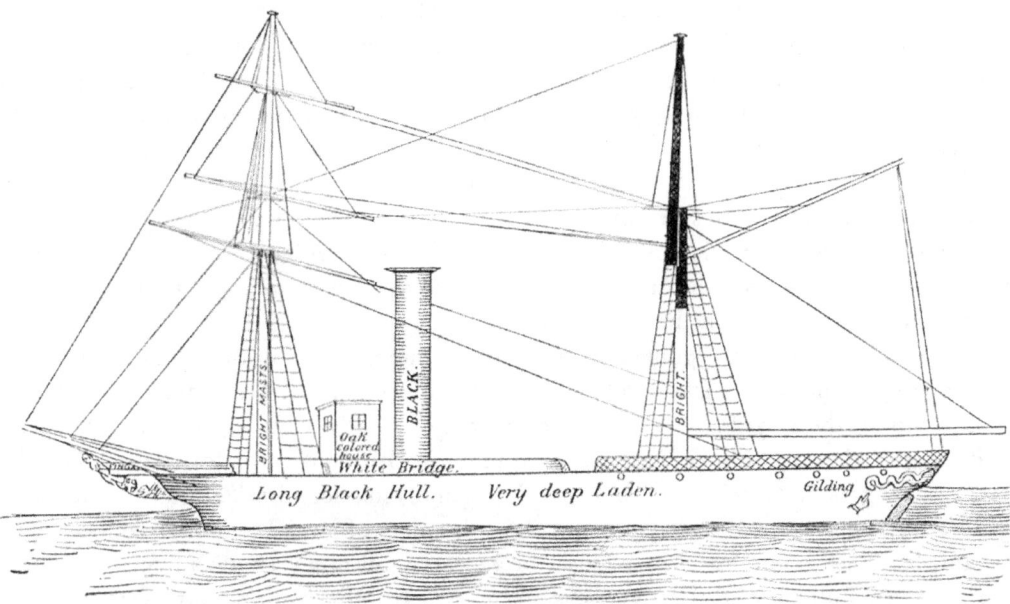

Union agent drawing of the blockade runner *Fingal* (*Official Records of the Union and Confederate Navies in the War of the Rebellion*).

bayonets, pistols, and muzzle-loading rifled guns (with carriages) filled the ship. It was the greatest single shipment of supplies solely for the Confederate military during the course of the Civil War. Realizing that Huse was fully up to the task, Anderson decided to return to the Confederacy on the *Fingal*, joining a cross-section of military men, adventurers, spies, and businessmen who filled the ship's meager berths.[39]

Bulloch was fortunate that a fellow Georgian with significant maritime experience arrived in England before the *Fingal* was ready to sail. John Low, born in Aberdeen, Scotland, in 1836, had gone to sea at age sixteen. After a life-threatening fever left him abandoned in Burma four years later, Low's Uncle Andrew easily convinced him to come to Savannah, Georgia, where he established his own cotton-shipping and naval supply business. He married the younger sister of Uncle Andrew's partner, Charles Green, and mixed with the well-connected society of Savannah. Like Bulloch, he had a successful life and career going when the war broke out. After joining the Confederate Army as part of the Georgia Hussars and serving in the front lines in Virginia, he transferred to the Confederate Navy where Sec. Mallory dispatched him to Britain for "secret service."[40] Bulloch not only gained a good sailor with invaluable experience and contacts, but also a life-long friend and business associate.

Time was critical for the *Fingal*. On 3 October 1861, Bulloch sat down in his Liverpool office and penned a message to Dudley Mann in London, taking full responsibility for the success or failure of the mission. He felt that he had to seize the initiative before the Union blockade sealed the major Southern ports. He asked Mann to reply by "next Wednesday," before the *Fingal* set sail on 9 October 1861.[41]

Ever careful on the legal tightrope he was walking, Bulloch found a captain who held a British Board of Trade certification to take the *Fingal* to sea. He also engaged a crew with several well-qualified engineers and mates. All were kept in the dark as to their true destination; only the ports of Bermuda and Nassau were mentioned. By 8 October 1861, the *Fingal* stood ready to make for sea. The "Charleston gentlemen" went aboard at Greenock and instructed the captain to weigh anchor as soon as possible. His orders were to sail 200 miles south and call at Holyhead, Wales, where Bulloch, Anderson, and Dr. Henry Holland would join them. Bulloch knew that their appearance anywhere near the vessel would spark the interest of Union spies and consular officials who could alert the British authorities. Again, Bulloch's suspicions were correct, for Union intelligence agents reported that he left Liverpool on the 8th. He returned without their knowledge the next day to deal with a last-minute problem: Lt. James North.[42]

Sec. Mallory had shot-gunned a multitude of "independent agents" into Britain with the hope of getting an ironclad built or purchased on the quick. Lt. James H. North, the most senior of these agents, asked Bulloch to transfer all of his papers, contracts, finances, and other dealings to him. Lt. North arrived in Great Britain with Major Anderson on the former racing yacht *America* (of "America's Cup" fame, renamed *Camilla* and later the *Memphis*). Anderson was less than impressed with the indolent officer who, though "only" a lieutenant, had been on active Navy service for 32 years and was very much an "old school" Navy officer. Bulloch had already discussed his responsibilities with North who was now attempting to force the issue in a more formal manner. Bulloch cursorily refused all of North's requests and reminded him that his position was sacrosanct.[43] After he slammed shut his letter-book, Bulloch made his last preparations before his 110-mile journey west to Holyhead on 11 October 1861.

Back in New York City, Bulloch's stepmother, Martha, also longed to go home to Georgia. Her motivation was to care for her ailing son Stuart Elliott (a.k.a. Daniel). Martha's effort to "go South" required the assistance of her son-in-law, Theodore Roosevelt, Sr., as well as additional funds. She hoped to raise enough money by using the bonds from Bulloch and cross into the Confederacy where she planned to remain for the duration of the war.[44]

On 10 October 1861, the *Fingal* set sail from Greenock. The "secret" endeavor was underway. It was hardly a secret, however, since Union consuls Adams and Sanford had independently contracted the same British detective, Ignatius Pollaky, to report the identical information that included a copy of the *Fingal's* custom house manifests.[45] That same day, Bulloch penned a letter that he left in the hands of Fraser, Trenholm and Company's manager, Prioleau. Bulloch stipulated that if the *Florida* was completed before his return, Prioleau was empowered to contact the senior Confederate Navy officer and place the vessel in his control, or if not, in the hands of Captain Huse.[46]

The next morning, Bulloch picked up his bag and headed for the train station to catch the express to Holyhead. Dr. Holland joined him, though they may have sat separately to complicate Union surveillance. After eluding a Union detective, Maj. Anderson arrived at Holyhead a day later.[47] Upon checking in at the Royal Hotel in Holyhead, they found a telegram confirming that the *Fingal* was at sea. However, that night a tremendous gale came on and for the next few days heavy clouds, rain and wind plagued the progress of the stout former Highland steamer. On the third day (14 October), the weather finally cleared. Bulloch hoped the ship made it to safe anchorage, knowing that Union warships could not find her in the extreme weather.

In the very early morning hours of 15 October 1861, Bulloch awakened to find the storm-drenched figure of John Low standing before him, excitedly telling him that there had been a collision. Bulloch, after realizing that this ghostly apparition was not a nightmare, woke fully, and envisioned the *Fingal* lying at the bottom of Holyhead harbor, all their equipment lost. Low quickly calmed his fears and explained that as the *Fingal* entered the harbor, she rounded the outer breakwater and encountered a brig at anchor with no lights to mark her position. In an instant, the bow of the iron-hulled *Fingal* carved out a large piece of the brig's starboard quarter. Full of coal, the brig, named the *Siccardi*, settled to the bottom upright, her masts and upper spars standing straight above the waters. Bulloch realized that the greatest threat to his enterprise was now the British customs officers who were sure to investigate. If they found the war material or Union spies discovered their location, the *Fingal* would most likely be detained or seized. They had to get moving, now![48]

Rousing Anderson and Holland from their slumbers, Bulloch and Low headed for the *Fingal*'s boat. They rowed as quickly as they could while surveying the sunken vessel by the light of the misty dawn. Clambering aboard the *Fingal*, Bulloch wrote a quick dispatch to Fraser, Trenholm and Co., explaining the event and asking them to compensate the owners of the *Siccardi*. After passing the letter back to a following boat that brought out their luggage, the crew of the *Fingal* weighed anchor and made for the mouth of the Holyhead Harbor and the Irish Sea.[49] Captain James Dunwoody Bulloch was at sea again.

The weather over the next few days favored the overloaded steamer, although she was riding too low in the water for Bulloch's tastes. Her running speed was now only nine knots, far too slow to escape Union ships. The blockade itself was not limited to the coastline of the South. It extended outward into the Atlantic along all shipping routes into the Confederacy and included the approaches to popular transshipment ports, particularly Nassau and Bermuda. Union warships were already stopping, searching, and seizing suspicious vessels that were headed toward the South. Bulloch and his fellow blockade runners soon found themselves with more immediate problems, both related to water.[50]

On October 19th, the *Fingal* was struck by another severe gale, with lashing rain and wind that forced the captain to virtually halt his engines and rely upon his sails for stabilization. In the midst of the storm, Bulloch learned that the onboard fresh water supply was perilously low. Fortunately, the *Fingal* was near the island of Terceira, the largest of the Azores, and made for Praya, a port village on the northeast quadrant of the isle. There they could reprovision, and most importantly, refill the water tanks.[51]

Typically circumspect with his criticisms, Bulloch did not name the inept captain of the *Fingal* in his memoirs, but wryly noted that he "probably acted according to his lights, which were dull." Major Anderson had no such qualms, identifying the inattentive captain as John Anderson (no relation), who upon arrival in Savannah indulged in a "regular Scotch bender."[52] Upon reflection, Bulloch noted a happy consequence of the captain's incompetence. His forced diversion to the Azores figured largely in future planning for the operations of the Confederate commerce cruisers and blockade runners.

Replenished with victuals, water, and fuel, the *Fingal* sailed out of Praya Bay and pointed her bow to the west by southwest. On 2 November 1861, the plucky steamer dropped anchor in Bermuda. Their arrival marked a historic occasion insofar as the Confederate Navy was concerned, for in port was the CSS *Nashville*, under the command of Lieutenant Commanding Robert B. Pegram. Underpowered and undergunned, the *Nashville* was more of an exercise in "showing-the-flag" than power-projection. She had run the blockade from Beaufort, South Carolina, and was on her way to England. Her escape caused Seward to fulminate with Welles about the ineffectiveness of the Union Navy's blockade.[53] For the crew and passengers of the *Fingal*, it was a chance to get the latest news from inside the Confederacy and, fortuitously, Pegram carried a letter from Mallory addressed to Bulloch.[54]

He must have breathed a partial sigh of relief as he read the letter. Mallory acknowledged receipt of Bulloch's messages concerning the *Bermuda*, as well as the contracts for the *Florida*, *Alabama*, and other naval material. His full relief came when he read that Mallory fully approved his idea for purchasing and supplying the *Fingal*, and personally running the blockade to visit the secretary in the new Confederate capital of Richmond.[55] More good news followed; the *Nashville* had several coastal pilots aboard who were to guide blockade runners from Bermuda into the Confederacy. Pegram had standing orders from Mallory to detach any of the pilots for just such duty. The pilot Bulloch chose was Capt. John Makin, whose homeport was the same as Bulloch's, Savannah.

The choice of Savannah was not the best from a purely military perspective. However, it was optimum from the commercial and personal perspectives of the principal parties to the decisions surrounding the *Fingal*. The primary planners of this adventure were Andrew Low, Charles Green, and Major Anderson, who all had business and family connections with Savannah. While their motivations may have been altruistic, the gains would be tangible. Low and Green particularly stood to gain from the transshipment of goods through Savannah. As the pilot Makin and a load of coal from the *Nashville* were packed aboard the *Fingal*, Bulloch made his plans while keeping a keen eye on Union attempts to buy up all the coal in Bermuda and bribe the crew.[56]

The Union efforts were unsuccessful, for on the afternoon of 7 November 1861 the *Fingal* cast off her lines and cleared the narrow mouth of St. Georges harbor for the final lap of her dangerous race into the Confederacy. To throw off any curious eyes ashore and aboard nearby ships, Bulloch initially set their course for Nassau. On the 8th of November, Bulloch ordered a change for their run through the blockade and into Savannah. He had a good crew that had performed well thus far, with the exception of the captain, though none had been told they would be running the Union blockade. It was time to reveal their true destination.[57]

Bulloch was plainspoken; he knew the crew suspected he would try a blockade run, but he could not confirm their suspicions for security purposes. But the time had come to confirm their thoughts and offer a proposition. Would they stay with him and his fellow Confederates to carry the *Fingal* through the blockade? If not, he would send them ashore and find new crewmen to do the deed. Noticing that some crewmen were whispering over his proposal, he pushed his plan. He had a receipt for the sale of the vessel that made him the official owner and transformed the *Fingal* into a Confederate naval vessel. They were all safe from any legal restrictions under the British Neutrality Act. In short order, the entire crew volunteered.

Two 4.5-inch guns were hauled from their crates in the cargo hold and mounted on the gangway-ports forward, while two additional guns were mounted on the quarterdeck. Bulloch reasoned that many of the Union blockaders were merely converted merchant ships like the *Fingal*. Small-arms and rifles were made ready with ammunition, but in reality, his primary purpose in arming the vessel was to buck up confidence. Bulloch and Major Anderson knew that if a legitimate Union warship confronted them, they would be blown out of the water. Bulloch's real weapons were speed, stealth, and audacity.[58]

By noon on the 11th, the *Fingal*'s course ran parallel to Wassaw Sound. The Savannah pilot, Makin, claimed that he could take the ship through the maze of inland waterways behind the outer islands and into the Savannah River, thus eluding Union ships. Just prior to this perilous journey, Maj. Anderson found the pilot passed out on the deck, "under the influence of liquor." After sobering up, Makin revealed the reason he had tried to steady his nerves with whiskey: he had lied about his knowledge of the Wassaw channel into Savannah.[59] Harkening back to his days with the Coast Survey, Bulloch knew these waters well and remained confident that he could pilot the ship himself if needed.

In the midnight darkness of November 12th, Bulloch took soundings just inside the Gulf Stream, but the night was uncomfortably clear. The discredited Makin tried to ease his concern by pointing out that the dark-line to the west was the on-coming marsh-fog. The dependable reversal of wind between land and sea would soon carry the marsh-fog out to sea, covering their approach. This time, Makin was correct. In less than an hour, a fog as thick as a cotton bale engulfed the *Fingal*. All lights were down except the binnacle, a case that contained a small lamp that illuminated the face of a gimbaled compass. The only sound was the rumbling steam engines and the waves rushing past the hull.[60]

With the crew taking constant soundings, the engines were brought back to dead slow when the depth reached six fathoms. The course was now set straight for land. At three and one-quarter fathoms, the engines were set to "all stop" and the *Fingal*'s bow turned into the gentle east wind. Everything was set for a sunrise sprint into the Savannah River. With nerves on edge and every ear tuned for any sound of a Union warship, the entire ship was stunned to hear an unearthly shriek. The source of the chilling sound was soon discovered to be a crowing rooster, preternaturally observing sunrise. Momentarily terrified with fear at such a loud and unexpected noise, the cock crowed again and then again, reverberating "far and near, alow and aloft." This time, a mad scramble took place as crewmen searched in the pea-soup fog for the unsuspecting rooster's coop. After several unsuccessful attempts, an able-bodied seamen named Freemantle managed to seize the offending creature, ringing the bird's neck with a quick twist. The crew of the *Fingal* all hoped the rooster would be their only casualty; they all were at risk of having their proverbial gooses cooked.[61]

The rooster's alarm had been correct, for by the time Freemantle finished his "combat," the sun had begun to rise. Makin told Bulloch that the sea fog would now drift eastward and into the eyes of any lookouts aboard Union ships, leaving the mainland clear. Bulloch climbed into the *Fingal*'s crow's nest and saw that Makin was right; thirty minutes later, the pine trees came into view and shortly afterwards, the sandy shoreline of Georgia's coast. The fog was still so thick at sea level that Makin still could not see. He asked Bulloch to come below and confer as to their next course. Reaching deck, Bulloch told Makin he was sure they were at the entrance to Wassaw Inlet. Makin agreed with this assessment, but pointed out that the buoys were all gone, removed by both Confederate and Union forces to restrict easy navigation. Makin believed that since the fog would take some time to clear to seaward, they should take advantage of the effect and make a dash for the main entrance of the Savannah River, some 17 miles north of their position. Makin believed they could get in there, buoys or no buoys. Bulloch and his precious cargo would go in through the front door.[62]

With orders to make all speed, Engineer McNair had the *Fingal* cracking along at 11 knots, hugging the shoreline at the shallowest points possible. Shortly, the sand, scrub and trees fell away as the shoreline turned dramatically westward. Soon, the lookout made out the walls of Fort Pulaski, still in the hands of the Confederates and commanding the outer approaches of the Savannah River. Before they got within range of the brick fort's long-range cannon, Bulloch unfurled the Confederate flag and fired a signal gun to herald their approach as a friendly vessel. The walls of the fort were soon lined with soldiers, who began to cheer and wave their caps as the hardy little ship came near. Although they were close to their goal, and safely through the blockade, navigating the Savannah River was still a tricky proposition.[63]

At the outset of the war, Georgia forces sank two wooden hulks into the main channel adjacent to Fort Pulaski, leaving room on either side for smaller coastal vessels. Makin knew of them and believed they could creep past. Unfortunately, Mother Nature hindered his best efforts, for the *Fingal*, after enduring gales and eluding federal spies and ships, went aground on an oyster bank. They would need help from Savannah. Fortunately, Major Anderson was the former mayor of Savannah and struck out for shore to telegraph the news of their arrival into the city. Meanwhile, Colonel Olmstead CSA, commander of Fort Pulaski, sent out a boat to the stricken ship. The news delivered to Bulloch wasn't good. Only a few days earlier, a fleet under Union Admiral Du Pont had landed troops and taken nearby Port Royal, South Carolina. Olmstead was worried that Union forces might send small boats and troops through the inland waterways to capture the *Fingal*. The Confederate Army officer assured Bulloch that his troops were keeping a good watch and had reinforcements on stand-by at Fort Pulaski's pier, ready to mount a defense if necessary. In the end, they only saw a few Union ships that cautiously approached the outer bar of the Savannah's mouth, curious as to the identity of this newfound blockade runner.[64]

Union naval forces had been well aware of the pending approach of the *Fingal*. Alerted by Seward's network of spies and consulates in Scotland, England, Bermuda, and Halifax, Union Navy Secretary Gideon Welles issued alerts to the three Atlantic blockading squadron flag officers, Goldsborough, Du Pont, and McKean. These detailed and essentially accurate alerts included a sketch and description of the *Fingal*, its cargo manifest, destination, expected arrival date, and specifically mentioned "Captain J.D. Bulloch." Welles made it clear to his flag officers that another failure to intercept a high-value ship would not be well received.[65]

Finally, just after noon on November 12th, naval forces under the command of Josiah Tattnall came to the rescue of the *Fingal*. With a hawser passed over from the converted river-steamboat, the *Fingal* was towed to freedom. By 4:00 P.M., the *Fingal* was alongside the Savannah River docks, the bluffs above crowded with both curious and cheering Savannahians. Bulloch wasted no time, hurrying ashore to the nearest telegraph office to send word to Sec. Mallory. Afterwards, Bulloch spared a few moments to accept the thanks of Savannahians. He was the hometown Georgia boy who was a triumphant hero, even if only for a few days.[66] In contrast, the reaction of the flag officer Du Pont and the rest of the Union was incredulous disbelief, "it is hardly possible she may have run the blockade."[67]

On the day after his arrival, Bulloch received a reply from Sec. Mallory: as soon as he discharged cargo, he was to make haste to Richmond. The following day (14 November) another officer assumed the responsibility of unloading the *Fingal* to free Bulloch and Anderson for travel.[68] On the way to Richmond, they surveyed a scene of economic and cultural chaos within a region transformed by war. Bulloch observed that the rail lines were struggling to keep up with the increased traffic, as civilians, soldiers, and war supplies competed for the limited rolling stock. The pair noted the good morale of the Southern troops, despite their poor equipment and indifferent "uniforms." A stop in Goldsborough, North Carolina, produced entertainment in the form of a freshly recruited regiment headed for Wilmington. As they rolled away on their open flat cars, exposed to the cold November air on benches nailed to the flat beds, they sang "Dixie," its refrain echoing as their train puffed out of sight.[69]

While Bulloch traveled to Richmond, his relatives in New York learned of his departure from Liverpool via a letter from Harriott. She offered to forward her in-law's letters to their Confederate kinsman, Irvine, and through the blockade to Stuart.[70] Ironically, although Bulloch was now physically closer to his extended American family, his ability to reliably communicate with them would be impossible until he returned to Liverpool.

Bulloch met with Mallory on the morning of 19 November 1861 to discuss his plan of action for the *Fingal*. The travel-weary mariner proposed loading the *Fingal* with cotton and naval stores, running her through the blockade again, crossing back to Liverpool, and attempting to repeat the feat. He suggested that profits from the sale of the cotton from the *Fingal*'s return voyage could fund the purchase of additional war supplies.

Bulloch urgently wanted the *Florida* out of Fawcett and Preston's shipyard, equipped, and into combat. There were two primary options for getting the *Florida* into the war. If Britain recognized the Confederacy, she could easily be launched and armed in Liverpool with a mission to cruise from New York to Maine, destroying commerce as the winter weather allowed. If Britain remained neutral, he would have to sail her out as a civilian ship and send a *separate* ship out with the armaments and related supplies. The support vessel would then meet the *Florida* in a neutral port where it could transfer all her material and finish her fitting out. *Florida*'s mission in that event would be to cruise off Africa, pick off a few Union merchant ships and fill out her crew. He then suggested that the *Florida* should sail via the Indian Ocean into the Pacific Ocean where she would cruise off China! Mallory must have been encouraged at the audacity of his agent who not only knew how to acquire warships, but also knew what to do with them.[71]

Drawing from his personal knowledge, Bulloch pointed out that certain New York import houses that dealt exclusively with the China trade were rolling profits in the door as fast as they could unload the goods. He felt that this class of Yankees needed to feel some economic pain (these trading houses would have included Roosevelt and Sons). Obviously desperate for a Confederate Navy command and hoping the vision of his proposition would be so grand that Mallory would believe only he could carry it off, he again requested an officer's commission. To fill out his officer's mess, Bulloch asked for Acting Midshipmen Anderson, his brother Irvine, as well as Acting Lieutenant William C. Whittle, who had crossed on the *Fingal*. As a kicker, he pressed for his friend John Low to be promoted to the rank of master. Bulloch wanted Low for his staff as well.[72]

Sec. Mallory agreed with his mission proposal, and by 23 November 1861 Bulloch was back in Savannah. There, Bulloch found that the *Fingal* had been fully unloaded and was ready to receive cotton, naval stores, and other materials that might be sold in Europe. Needing a load of coal from Columbus, Georgia, he was impatient to be away. Union troops had landed at Tybee Island and now controlled the lighthouse and could place artillery at the outer mouth of the Savannah River. These developments left the *Fingal* with only one escape route through the Wassaw inlet, the very place they had avoided on their inbound journey. But there would be no need to run the blockade if there was no useful cargo to carry.[73]

Bulloch and his wardroom of junior officers became exasperated as cargo arrived in dribs and drabs. To make matters worse, there was no word from Mallory. Finally, on 4 December, he learned that the secretary agreed with his proposal to command the *Florida* (then referred to as the *Manassas*). Mallory also granted his request for officers, as well as those that might be available from the *Nashville*. Bulloch had full discretion on where he should operate based on the capabilities of his ship (imagine a modern naval officer with such responsibility and carte blanche for operations!). He could turn over the *Fingal* to Lt. George T. Sinclair after he reached England.

On financial matters, the Navy Department placed $100,000 with Fraser, Trenholm and Co., and requested another $75,000 credit for his account. With a final, pro-forma warning to adhere strictly to the neutrality laws, Bulloch had the orders of his dreams ... if only he could get out of Savannah.[74]

He hoped to get the *Fingal* away in the next few days, but it was not until 20 December 1861 that the *Fingal* was filled with cotton for the outward voyage. The *Fingal* anchored in a bay off Wilmington Island, waiting for an opportunity to run through the blockade. However, the commander of a nearby Confederate coastal artillery battery passed word to Bulloch that three Union ships had appeared off the bar, with one pressing forward to drive off a Confederate picket boat. All night long he attempted to find a way past the Union blockaders, hoping to take advantage of squalls and fog. But his reconnaissance boats could find no channel that was not blocked by a Union ship. Bulloch suspected treasonous behavior by someone in Savannah, suggesting that the Union ships knew the *Fingal* was coming. All he could do was watch, wait, and hope.[75]

After long delays, Major Anderson reported that Lt. George Sinclair was placed in command of the *Fingal*. His estimate of Sinclair's abilities was not favorable as "he has neither brains or dash enough to get her safely clear ... yet I feel sure that either Bulloch or I could carry her out."[76] In his own account, Bulloch admits that he gave up his attempt to escape on December 24th. He took the *Fingal* back to her berth in Savannah after consulting with Flag Officer Tattnall. He reported that two crewmen who were on loan from another Confederate ship had deserted and were suspected of joining the Union blockade ships. These two men and a deserter from Fort Pulaski had, in fact, alerted Flag Officer Du Pont on the USS *Wabash*. Du Pont promptly added two steamers, armed with eight guns to the three Union ships that were blockading Savannah.[77] The city's door to the sea had been slammed shut and would remain sealed until the end of the Civil War. By 26 December 1861, Bulloch finally ran out of patience and requested that Mallory allow him to find his way back to England by some other means. It was an ill-spent Christmas. Across the Atlantic, his wife and family were experiencing their first "Boxing Day" in England, wondering when or if Bulloch might return.[78]

The remainder of 1861 dwindled away with Bulloch stranded in his native state of Georgia in his father's home city, with no close family about him and no clear prospects on how he would proceed. Despite this delay, it was still a good start to the birth of the Confederate Navy. Two major blue-water ships were under construction, supplies were flowing through the blockade, Bulloch's financial coffers were replenished to buy more weapons, supplies and ships, and more officers were on the way to Europe. For Bulloch, 1862 looked to be a promising year, if only he could get back to Great Britain.

6

Anglo-Rebel Pirates and Confederate Navy Cruisers—1862

As the residents of Savannah roused from their beds on New Year's Day of 1862, the temporary joys of holiday celebrations began to recede into the realities of their shared circumstances as members of the quasi-nation called the Confederate States of America. Business had temporarily picked up during the Christmas holiday, but during the first week of January, it slackened considerably. The lack of trade was largely due to the lack of hard currency, i.e., gold. The Union blockade had begun to bite, and bite hard. Local newspapers reported fantastic rumors of Confederate raids on Northern cities and attacks on Lincoln; such was the desperation for favorable news.[1]

The Confederacy experienced increased pressure as Union troops began to push cautiously southward into Tennessee and Kentucky. The capture of Port Royal, South Carolina, on 7 November 1861, had rattled the residents of Savannah, as well as the rest of the Confederacy. However, all was not going the Union way, for it was still trying to smooth the ruffled feathers of Great Britain when Capt. Charles Wilkes of the USS *San Jacinto* illegally seized Confederate commissioners James Mason and John Slidell on 8 November 1861 from the British mail packet *Trent*. The intensity of the British outrage over the capture was only matched by the American public's rapture. Belatedly, Seward and Lincoln realized the disastrous practicalities of going to war with the world's greatest empire (and naval power) and fighting a three-front war with the Confederates to the south, Canada to the north, and the Royal Navy to the east. Prince Albert, husband of Queen Victoria, intervened from his deathbed and softened Lord Russell's official diplomatic demand to release the commissioners.[2] Pragmatism sunk in on both sides and as Lincoln aptly quipped, the Union could only fight "one war at a time."

The European powers continued to act as geo-political gods, as they always had, with the unpleasantness in America still viewed as a minor internal problem within the always-fractious American states. It was a problem that could be contained and might be used to their strategic advantage. The *Trent* affair notwithstanding, Great Britain had to deal with its own rebellion. This one was in New Zealand as the northern provinces wanted to separate from the southern ones due to familiar problems of taxation and revenue-sharing issues, and a recalcitrant native Maori population.[3] Another consequence of the American

6. Anglo-Rebel Pirates and Confederate Navy Cruisers

Confederate blockade runner in Bermuda (U.S. Naval Historical Center).

Civil War soon manifested itself in the British economy. The Lancashire cotton mill industry collapsed, due at least in part to reduced expectations as a result of the Union blockade. Production had virtually ceased in the region by October 1861 and by January 1862 mass unemployment and soup kitchens appeared throughout northwest England.[4] All entities involved in the business of cotton, from importers to manufacturers, were soon pounding on the doors of the British government to do something about the American Civil War.

On the European continent, France's Emperor Louis-Napoléon Bonaparte (Napoleon III) warily eyed the continued political turmoil in Prussia, Austria, and Saxony concerning the creation of a unified and powerful German Confederation. Wilhelm I had assumed the crown as king of Prussia on 2 January 1862 and contended with internecine political wars and squabbling over military funding that led to the appointment of Otto von Bismarck as his prime minister.[5]

Queen Victoria, empress of the British Empire, was in deepest mourning over the death of her beloved Albert. As a result, Prime Minister Palmerston and Foreign Minister Russell had to contend with Germany and France under a head of state in absentia. And those upstart Americans — why couldn't they just sort out their peculiar internal differences amicably and quickly?

James Dunwoody Bulloch was still stuck in the wrong part of the world. His 1862 New Year had begun with the Union blockade continuing its stranglehold on shipping traffic into and out of Savannah, Georgia. Most importantly for him, a return voyage aboard the *Fingal* across the Atlantic to Liverpool was proving to be an impossibility. Three "stone ships" (old hulks sunk in the main harbor channel) combined with Union-occupied shore positions only added to the problems caused by the increased number of Union warships.

Four officers, who would have significant impact on Bulloch and the Confederate Navy, officially joined him in Savannah: "Master" John Low, Midshipmen Edward Maffitt Anderson and Eugene Anderson Maffitt, and Assistant Paymaster Clarence Randolph Yonge. Three of these men were well known to Bulloch and well connected with the Southern aristocracy. Anderson was the son of Major Edward Anderson, the former and future Mayor of Savannah. Maffitt was the son of Bulloch's former commanding officer, John Newland Maffitt. The other man, Clarence R. Yonge, was a distant cousin, whom Bulloch picked to fill his critical need for a clerk back in Liverpool. Formerly assigned to the Confederate gunboat *Lady Davis*, a converted iron tug, Yonge seemed to be an ideal choice.[6]

Queen Victoria and Prince Albert, circa 1861 (authors' collection).

Ten more days progressed while Union warships circled off the mouth of the Savannah River. Across the Atlantic in Liverpool, the *Florida* was almost ready to put to sea. Union agents and U.S. Consul Thomas Haines Dudley were constantly acquiring or inventing information about the vessel and her Confederate connections. They promptly passed this information to British authorities and the U.S. Navy. On 9 January 1862, Charles K. Prioleau, of Fraser, Trenholm, urged Lt. James North to take decisive action. While Lt. North dithered, Prioleau could only hope that Bulloch would soon return.[7]

By January 12th, Bulloch considered the port of Savannah to be closed and was likely to remain that way unless a European power intervened.[8] He asked Mallory to let him and his small detachment return to Liverpool by the fastest method possible. Time was of the essence and the lack of transoceanic telegraph precluded him from knowing the precise fate of his ships in Liverpool. For Bulloch, the most important personal issue was his expectation of commanding a warship, either the *Florida* or, preferably, the *Alabama*.[9] Four days later, Bulloch officially turned the *Fingal* over to Lt. George Sinclair, having just received the requested orders from Sec. Mallory allowing him return to England.[10] He could not know that the *Fingal* would be the only Confederate ship he would ever command. He would be involved in the construction, manning, crewing, and supplying of myriad commerce raiders, blockade runners, and ironclads, but he would never again come as close to combat action as he had with the *Fingal*.

Ironically, before Bulloch and the small detachment under his command departed Savannah, "his" former ship appeared before his very eyes. While scouting the Union ship dispositions at the mouth of the Savannah River, he saw off shore what he thought was his old command, the *Bienville*. Though he did not know it in 1862, or even when he wrote his memoirs in the early 1880s, he was right. The gunboat USS *Bienville* had taken part in the capture of Port Royal, South Carolina, and was now part of the Atlantic blockading squadron.[11] The ship that he had brought into commission and refused to turn over to the Confederacy was now one of the federal warships that had him trapped!

Before leaving Savannah, Bulloch quickly acknowledged what should have been very good news from Mallory.

> I had the honor to receive your letter of the 17th instant, enclosing me a commission as commander in the Navy ... while I am deeply sensible of the honor and am grateful to yourself personally for this evidence of trust and confidence; I can not but declare that it is beyond my expectations and in excess of my deserts. The Commission you now send places me above many officers who would be my seniors if the Navy list were arranged according to relative rank in the old United States service. You are sufficiently aware of the feelings of naval officers on the subject of promotion and will readily conceive that the assignment to me of this advanced rank will create much criticism and a feeling of discontent in many quarters which will vent itself on me as its cause.[12]

Bulloch's assessment of this "good news" and the result of his advancement ahead of his peers would prove to be all too accurate. But those concerns were for later; Bulloch was practical and pragmatic as ever. He had a coveted commission, he had orders, and he had a small detachment of junior naval officers to get across the Atlantic. He had worked out a contingency plan with Prioleau in Liverpool in case of transportation troubles. He contacted the firm's office in Charleston, SC. Fraser and Company had two ships scheduled to make a run for the Atlantic, one in Charleston and one in Wilmington, NC. The Charleston ship was smaller, with a shorter cruising range. This ship was headed to Nassau, which would require an intermediate stop in Havana, before taking a British ship to England.[13]

The Wilmington ship was much larger and headed directly for Liverpool, with only a fuelling stop in the Azores. One other quality of the Wilmington vessel caught Bulloch's experienced eye as well. She was built for the coast trade in New York, but had been making coastal runs from Wilmington, NC, to Boston, MA before the war and he reckoned she could manage a transatlantic voyage. Thus, the *Annie Childs*, formerly named the *North Carolina*, was his best and only choice.[14]

Bulloch with Master John Low, Midshipmen Anderson and Maffitt, and Paymaster Yonge, arrived in Wilmington, NC, on 24 January 1862. The *Annie Childs* was loading a cargo of cotton and other typical Southern commodities such as pine resin and tobacco while simultaneously taking on coal. By 1 February 1862, the ship moved south to Orton Point, some twelve miles from the river's mouth, and prepared to make its run.[15]

Leaving nothing to chance, Bulloch contacted the commander of the local Confederate Army forces, Gen. J.R. Anderson, who procured a small tugboat for the fast-moving naval agent. Captain Hammer, commander of the *Annie Childs,* and Bulloch then daringly sailed the little tug down the river every day to scout out the locations of the blockaders and potential points of egress over the river's bar.[16] Unfortunately, the main channel was the only route out for the heavily laden blockade runner. Hiding the hull against the shoreline or behind obscuring islets was not an option; they would have to rely on stealth, weather, speed, and cunning. Helpful coast watchers revealed that the Union ships did not move at night. Fate still plagued his escape efforts though, for the nights were clear and cool — perfect weather for the blockaders, providing good visibility and increased sound detection. Despite the moonless night on January 30th, they would have to wait for a change in the weather.[17]

On February 5th, the weather and their luck changed. By noon, wind and clouds began to spool over the North Carolina coast from the northeast. Bulloch and Capt. Hammer saw that the change was consistent and made ready for getting under weigh. At 10 P.M., the sleek blockade runner made for the mouth of the river. They timed their sail down the river so that the full tide and the setting of the sliver of the crescent moon occurred at the same time. At 12:15 A.M., the *Annie Childs* slipped over the outer bar on a teacup calm sea, in sea-hugging fog. All held their breath now, for the skies cleared and they heard the purr of a ship's engine to one quarter. Quiet orders to the engine room shut down the one-cylinder engine in a moment and for the next half-hour the crew maintained silent-running. Once more, nature intervened on Bulloch's side, as rain began to fall. As the sound of the nearby ship faded, the engine of the *Annie Childs* restarted. Shrouded by a thick drizzle, the gray shadow of a ship melted into the Atlantic Ocean, bound for the Azores and Liverpool.[18]

Despite her fine sailing qualities, the *Annie Childs'* single engine was not designed for transoceanic travel. She made a slow passage, with the attendant problems of poor steerage in an underpowered vessel. Her hull design compensated somewhat, for Bulloch noted that she handled well in heavy seas, even when plowing through a strong winter gale in the tumultuous North Atlantic Ocean. Reaching Fayal in the Azores, the Confederates were confronted by a U.S. consul who hoped to add to his family's diplomatic and nautical fame. Charles Dabney made it nearly impossible to purchase coal. Dabney was the son of the previous U.S. consul to the Azores. As a young man, he carried his father's urgent warning to a U.S. Navy ship that resulted in a successful engagement against the British during the War of 1812. Whether by luck or design, Bulloch's panache won the day again, for the Lloyds' shipping agent in the port managed to procure a small amount of coal that would have to be managed carefully if they expected to reach the British Isles.[19]

As the last embers of coal turned to ash, the *Annie Childs* made fast to the quay at Queenstown, Ireland. Bulloch went ashore for a token amount of rest. Early on the following morning, he caught the ferry-train for Liverpool, passing through Dublin and Holyhead before reaching his English home on the afternoon of 10 March 1862.[20]

The next morning, Bulloch awoke at his home in Waterloo, a small village just north of Liverpool, and made his way into the offices of Fraser, Trenholm and Co. He was in for a great shock. The *Florida* was completed, but had not sailed! The designated captain of the ship, Lt. James North, had been recalcitrant in taking action despite Union agents snapping at their tails like bloodhounds. The U.S. consul in Liverpool, Thomas Haines Dudley, was zealous in his attentions and kept a constant flow of information to Minister Adams and British officials. What had been going on while Bulloch was in America?

The person who exacerbated this dramatic tension was Lt. James North, who received his Confederate Navy appointment on 26 March 1861 at the same rank he had in the "Old Navy." North had been senior to Bulloch by nine years, but unlike Bulloch, he did not have an eight-year break in service. Bulloch's commission as a full commander would be the can of peas under the sea-mattress of all future problems with Lt. North.[21] North was the source of ongoing murmurs, "made by several very ancient, although not very profound salts," about the need to supplant Bulloch.[22]

The James North–inspired problems began less than a week after Mallory and Bulloch's May 1861 "Meeting in Montgomery." Despite North's failure in his first assignment of buying ships and arms in Baltimore and New York, Mallory ordered him to Europe on 17 May 1861. North's mission was to acquire ironclad warships that could sweep the Union blockading vessels away from Southern ports. Mallory specifically noted that France would be the best place to start and hope of hopes, they might even sell their famous ocean-going ironclad *Gloire* to the Confederacy. Mallory promised that the Confederate Congress would appropriate $2,000,000 toward this project. As proof, he attached a complete copy of this legislation for Lt. North to give to the Confederate commissioners in Europe, along with additional instructions for Bulloch.[23]

By 21 May 1861, North was in Savannah and boarded the former racing yacht *America* with his wife and children. Along with Maj. Edward C. Anderson, he made a wild, rollicking dash across the Atlantic as a passenger. It was during this voyage that Major Anderson developed his disdain for North as a slovenly excuse for a naval officer.[24] Upon reaching Liverpool on 25 June 1861, North and Anderson made their way to Fraser, Trenholm and Co., where they found Bulloch and Huse unaware of their pending arrival.

Given the subtlety of Bulloch's public characterizations of his fellow naval officers, it's easy to assess where Lt. North actually stood in Bulloch's estimation. He saw North as a jealous competitor who was "pulling rank" to undermine his larger mission, challenge his authority, and create messes that he had to clean up. North saw Bulloch as a politically appointed and unresponsive upstart who used his connections to get ahead. This overlapping assignment of responsibilities within the European theater placed these two under-financed agents in unnecessary and unfortunate competition for resources, priorities, and authority. Despite the apprehension that the civilian Bulloch must have felt at that first meeting, relations were somewhat convivial, for they all retired to the Queen's Hotel for refreshments and dinner that evening.[25]

After North delivered his messages to the Confederate commissioners in London (Yancey and Mann), he found Bulloch and Huse hard at work trying to procure war materials on a very limited budget. He also discovered that a Confederate naval agent with no money could not accomplish much. Frustrated, he settled his family into their new home at 6 Oxford Street in London and became the classic "tourist" for most of July 1861! He visited Parliament, Madame Tussauds Wax Works, and even the queen's stables, with no apparent urgency in pursuing Mallory's unfunded agenda.[26] North was not alone in his enjoyment of London's attractions. During this same period, Bulloch, along with Maj. Anderson and Capt. Huse, also had their share of off-duty entertainment. But unlike North, they wrote less about it, adding to the slightly skewed historical perspective of North's relative diligence. Taking time from his family, North accompanied Bulloch and Anderson on July 15th for their tour of Fawcett, Preston & Company's foundry where Blakely guns and other naval ordnance were cast.

During this same critical month of July 1861, Bulloch and Anderson had not hesitated to act on Mallory's new instructions and promised funding. Together, they successfully toured sensitive military areas, such as the Woolwich Royal Arsenal, and traveled to France to investigate the purchase of maritime supplies and ships.[27]

North's lack of immediate success is somewhat understandable. He had no funding, there were few willing sellers and, unlike Bulloch and Anderson, his family was with him. The one shipbuilder that North had spoken to had been pragmatic; France and England were in a naval arms race of their own and every available shipyard that could build *ocean-going* ironclads was working to fill the orders of those two nations. All the cotton and gold in the world could not force its way through that competition.[28]

Despite his own lack of success and the limited prospects of buying an ironclad, North was not above asking for command of a warship — hinting to Mallory that he should be given command of one of Bulloch's new ships. Meanwhile Anderson and Huse acquired a ship (the *Bermuda*) to run the blockade loaded with munitions and other supplies. Was North interested in serving as the Confederate naval officer? Anderson posed the question since he knew that North was "gear adrift" in the Confederate endeavors in Europe and believed the South Carolinian lacked initiative. North rebuffed the offer and stated that he intended to continue on his empty mission.[29] Since early August, North had been living aboard the *Camilla* with his family and sailed away with Captain Decie for more yacht racing and touring of Britain before finally landing in Cherbourg, France, on 16 August 1861.[30]

Arriving in Paris after a cursory visit to a French ironclad, North again established residence for his family, visited the sights, and slowly began to act on his orders from the Navy Department. By the end of September 1861, he had toured the French army artillery school at Vincennes and met the Confederate commissioner Pierre Rost (former U.S. minister to Denmark) and a Brazilian navy captain by the name of Portugal. No contracts had been entered into and no war material had been purchased. Yet, extraordinarily, he told Mallory that if funds were available, he could achieve almost anything in France.[31]

However, only a week later as October 1861 began, North was astounded to learn that while he had been leisurely touring his way around France, Bulloch, Anderson, and Huse had placed the *Fingal* mission into motion. North dropped everything and rushed back to Liverpool, where he confronted Bulloch on October 8th demanding that he be given control of Confederate naval funds, and by extension, the shipbuilding contracts involving the *Florida* and *Alabama*. With his scheme rejected by Bulloch, North could only fume. After documenting this rebuff in a letter to Sec. Mallory, Bulloch formally notified North of his decision. He pointed out that as a *civilian*, his chain-of-command led directly to Sec. Mallory, and the financial responsibilities of his contracts lay with him personally. Due to North's meanderings through Britain and France, he could not even *find* him, much less inform him of his operations (not that Bulloch would have confided in him anyway). Bulloch placed Prioleau in charge of monetary matters while he was away. North could only return to Paris and await further orders.[32]

So it was that from October 1861 until James Dunwoody Bulloch's return to his Liverpool office on 11 March 1862, Lt. James North effectively sulked, awaited further orders from Secretary Mallory, and counted the ways he hated civilian naval "officials." North bided his time in Paris until new orders finally did reach him, whereupon he moved back to Liverpool, performed occasional inspections of the *Florida*, wandered through shipyards

6. Anglo-Rebel Pirates and Confederate Navy Cruisers

throughout Britain, and penned missives to the Navy Department about his need for money.[33] North didn't realize that much of his fate had already been decided in Richmond during the meetings between Bulloch and Mallory.[34]

Bulloch recalled the situation on the morning of 11 March 1862 in his memoirs in a calm, sanguine manner, but several pages later his anger at the unnecessary threat to his well-laid plans boiled through his narrative. Sec. Mallory had ordered Lt. Robert B. Pegram and the crew of the CSS *Nashville* to Liverpool where they were to transfer to the *Florida* and sail her away for combat operations.[35] Unfortunately, Pegram and the *Nashville* had already left England for the Confederacy. They ran into Beaufort, SC, on 28 March 1862, after capturing and burning the schooner *Robert Gilfillan* on 26 February 1862. Pegram had reached the wrong side of the Atlantic Ocean at virtually the same time that Bulloch had returned to the right side![36] Bulloch had a ship ready to sail, but had no crew and no captain.

North, in response to an early January 1862 request from Commander Raphael Semmes aboard the CSS *Sumter* at Gibraltar, had been trying to acquire clothing for the crew on credit. The Confederate government had purchased the *Sumter* at New Orleans in April 1861. Semmes converted her into a commerce raider and escaped the Mississippi River blockade into the Gulf of Mexico. From there the *Sumter* seized 18 Union commerce vessels before reaching Gibraltar. The *Sumter* needed repairs, money, new crewmen, and cooperation from the British government, none of which was forthcoming.[37] Instantly grasping the nettle, and maybe even deferring to the needs of a former higher-ranking "old-Navy" officer, North swung into action. Despite the lack of cash, he could acquire clothing on credit, but little else.

On 27 January 1862, North piquantly repeated his complaint to Sec. Mallory that if he had money, anything could be done, writing, "It is cruel in such times as these to keep me in such a state of suspense. I have a reputation at stake.... If you have nothing for me to do here, or it is not convenient to send me money, why not recall me?"[38] The *Florida* was nearly complete and Commander Semmes reported that the *Sumter* needed considerable repairs. In fact, North sent letters to Semmes on the 23rd and 25th of January offering to bring the *Florida* out and come to Semmes' rescue! Fortunately, the wiser and more experienced Semmes quickly replied to North via telegram and letter. A better plan would be for Semmes to come and get the *Florida*, but only if he could get the *Sumter* seaworthy, obtain sufficient coal from the British, elude the Union blockaders, and sail to Liverpool.[39]

Prioleau, perhaps unaware of North's communications with Semmes, had his own plan in motion for getting the *Florida* to sea. In a 3 February 1862 letter, Prioleau informed North that he had discussed the situation with Confederate commissioner Mann in London, who agreed that the ship needed to get to sea quickly. Prioleau was willing to underwrite the costs if North would take command (with the understanding that a British captain would have to take her out of Liverpool to circumvent the British Neutrality Act).[40]

In contrast to the bravado he showed Semmes, North said he would not accept an incomplete ship that had no armament. The exasperated Prioleau responded a day later, insisting that his company was going to deliver the ship to North, whether he wanted it or not, just as Bulloch had instructed before he left for Savannah. As a riposte to North's questions about Prioleau's capacity to outfit a vessel, he pointed out that "my firm have been ship owners for many years; that we now own five steamers and nine or ten sailing vessels ... we have never sent one of them to sea improperly fitted out."[41]

Prioleau followed through on his threat to relinquish interest in the *Florida* by sending yet another letter the same day, this time as "Fraser, Trenholm and Company," whereby he quoted Bulloch's instructions of 10 October 1861 that the vessel should be handed over to a Confederate naval officer. North had little choice but to accept responsibility for the vessel. North replied from London on 6 February 1862 that he accepted the vessel and Prioleau's offer of financial support. Could Prioleau furnish a crew and supplies capable of getting her to Nassau? And could she then be sailed to London to pick up a cargo? North added that, based on advice from Confederate commissioner Mann in London, he should *not* be seen on board her to avoid Union surveillance. North certainly took that advice, remaining at his new London residence at 37 Russell Square throughout the tension-filled days when the Confederacy's first purpose-built cruiser was on the verge of being seized.

With Semmes still in Gibraltar, no news of Bulloch's whereabouts, and Prioleau fairly frothing in frustration at North's inertia, North penned a message to Sec. Mallory on February 8th saying that "he was at a loss at what to do with her, as the English Government will not allow arms aboard her." Obviously North had no inkling of the precise legal chicanery that Bulloch had set in motion, or how she would be transformed into a commerce raider. North was trying, but he was out of his depth.[42]

As more days ticked off the calendar, Prioleau tried once again (February 20th) to spur North into action, stating that "the builders of the steamer, are unwilling that she should remain any longer in her present position, and at their risk." Fawcett, Preston and Co. (as well as W.C. Miller and Sons) knew that agents of the U.S. consul were banging on the doors of British Customs and every other official who might stop the flight of the *Florida*— she had to sail. Prioleau closed with the expectant demand that he was "awaiting an immediate reply." Finally, Caleb Huse, the Confederate Army agent in Liverpool, sent North a terse telegram that said he had received the following message: "immediate action necessary. I am acting. Ship will sail Tuesday morning. Nothing can stop her but your *positive* (authors' inflection) orders to the contrary."[43]

It appears that Prioleau finally decided to act unilaterally, telling Huse he had set Bulloch's plan in motion. Inaction was no longer possible; North would have to cancel the movement of the *Florida* rather than order it. North was clearly concerned that word of his failure to act would get back to Richmond. He informed Mallory that the *Florida* was departing for Havana on 25 February 1862 and it "may be necessary for you to order someone there to take charge of her." He tried to excuse his lack of initiative by noting that "the gentleman who had charge of her building objected so much that I had to give way."[44] This gentleman was obviously Prioleau, but North made it sound like it was James Dunwoody Bulloch who had raised the objection. North couldn't know, but on February 22nd Bulloch was still enroute back to Liverpool on the blockade runner *Annie Childs*. North started with good intentions, but he had waffled and been less than truthful when action, and not words, counted most.

North, finally understanding that he could not, and indeed must not, put arms aboard the ship while in port, stood down the attempt to sail the *Florida*. U.S. Consul Dudley was demanding the full attention of the Liverpool Customs House officials. On February 26th, Raphael Semmes who was aboard the *Sumter* in Gibraltar, clearly stated the problem: "Under

6. Anglo-Rebel Pirates and Confederate Navy Cruisers   71

the strict neutrality rules recently adapted by Lord Russell, and in the face of the rigid vigilance ... exercised by the British Government, will it be possible to get the ship out of Liverpool with an armament and a crew?"[45] British Customs and Bulloch would soon answer that question.

By the time Bulloch learned about the near-fiasco of the *Florida* on 11 March 1862, British Customs had thoroughly examined her fittings and her papers. British customs officials pertly replied to Union protestations: "war-like" appearances were one thing, actualities were another. They could find nothing that directly identified her as a warship intended to violate the British Neutrality Law. Dudley and Adams were apoplectic.

Bulloch sprang into action with an élan and calmness of purpose that would have made John Paul Jones proud. Knowing that his whole mission hung in the balance unless he could avoid any further interest from both British officials and the ubiquitous Union agents, he first tackled the issue of command. He contacted North in London and reminded him of his instructions to command either the *Florida* or the *Alabama*, as Bulloch had to attend his present projects first. Bulloch further noted that if North did not accept command of the *Florida*, he would offer the ship to Semmes in Gibraltar. North needed to decide quickly. Bulloch then noted that Sec. Mallory had ordered them *both* to get into action on acquiring an ironclad of some 2000 tons. He didn't wait to confer on this issue; he merely stated he would contact the Lairds about taking the contract. Finally, in an attempt to mollify past misunderstandings, Bulloch asked after North's wife and prematurely added North's new rank of "commander" at the bottom of the letter.[46] He set all this in motion on his first day back in the office after an absence of some five months!

Bulloch's decisiveness hit the mark. North responded on the 12th of March with disingenuous congratulations on *Bulloch's* promotion. Mallory would wisely raise them both to the same rank, hoping it would assuage ruffled feathers, but North's date of rank would leave him almost four months junior to Bulloch. North soon poured out his real feelings in another ill-advised letter to Secretary Mallory, writing: "Rank to a military man is everything and that rank has been taken from me ... and now that the commission I so much coveted and so ardently hoped for has been given to another, and that other a civilian, who, when in the service, was many years my junior ... I must beg to record my most solemn protest against the foregoing act."[47]

Bulloch was very aware that his promotion to the rank of commander would upset many in the Confederate Navy.[48] Mallory ignored these admonitions and Bulloch was forced to endure enmity of line officers who had waited years for nonexistent promotions while in the U.S. Navy. When Mallory was chair of the U.S. Senate Committee on Naval Affairs, he was the key instigator of a controversial attempt to remove unproductive and physically or mentally infirm officers from the service. Mallory believed in promotion for performance, not for time in service.

North's letter to Mallory went on to complain, in no apparent order, that he had received one set of orders promising him the command of the first ship launched (*Florida*) on 25 November 1861, then another set on 11 January 1862 that promised Bulloch the first vessel, and North the second (*No. 290/Alabama*). To top off the confusion, North had received yet *another* set of orders on 20 January 1862 that appeared to assign the *No. 290* (*Alabama*) to Bulloch, since the *Florida* had already sailed. By this time, North's fury at what he perceived to be multiple slights to his honor burst loose. Yes, Bulloch had done an outstanding job, but he had the full financial support of Fraser, Trenholm and Co., plus other funds, some even carried by North himself, for his contracts. Furthermore, North pointed out that since the Confederate Navy Department had not seen fit to send him any funds, he could do nothing. If he had money, he finished in a right lather, he could purchase *two* armored gunboats that very instant, but he had *no* money.

In the meantime, Commander Bulloch, now North's senior officer, tried to make the best of the situation. He knew their relationship would be doubly troubled unless he could get Lieutenant North into action in some meaningful way. On March 14th, he acknowledged North's offer of congratulations and added several helpful and friendly comments. The *Florida* was as fine a vessel as he'd ever seen in her class, surpassing the Union Navy's equivalent. He noted that during sea-trials she had made 11 knots. Moving on to the subject of the ironclad that Mallory so desired, Bulloch prompted North to be proactive, assuring him of his complete assistance at all times. Finally, on a domestic note, he sent his regards to Mrs. North again and noted that while he had been gone, Mrs. Bulloch had taken a new house at No. 2 Marine Terrace in the Liverpool suburb of Waterloo; it was a subtle invitation to visit.[49] Over the next few days, the two officers in the Confederate Navy appeared to be getting on well, though we lack North's replies to some letters from Bulloch. Bulloch advised North about a new postal system whereby letters from the Confederacy could reach Nassau by a fast steamer commanded by John Newland Maffitt. At the British colonial port, letters and packets were then transferred to British ships for safe and assured delivery to Liverpool and London.[50] North would have known that Maffitt was Bulloch's old friend and commander from his days with the U.S. Coast Survey. Maffitt knew the Southern coastline as well as any man alive; he would be a good choice to take over a ship designed to raid Union commerce vessels. Bulloch may have gone out of his way to mention Maffitt, who detested Secretary Mallory, in a subtle attempt to assure Lt. North that Bulloch was willing and able to act independently.

Bulloch's fine ability in assessing the capabilities of people for key trust relationships in business, social, and military affairs came to the forefront now in his effort to get the *Florida* safely away from Liverpool and into combat. The appointment of John Low as a ship's master was also a masterstroke.[51] Even though John Low was only 25 years of age at the outbreak of the Civil War, he had significant practical experience at sea, knowledge of the export-shipping business, and a long-standing acquaintance with Bulloch.[52] Additionally, Low's invaluable assistance in getting the *Fingal* into Savannah had not gone unnoticed. Thus, when Bulloch had Low accompany him back to Liverpool on special duty, he was anticipating the need for personnel who were capable of realizing Mallory's vision of a truly global commerce raiding naval campaign.

It was Low's hour to excel. Bulloch entrusted him to get the *Florida* across the Atlantic to the Bahamas. He was to make contact with John Newland Maffitt, either directly, or by contacting the manager of Adderley and Co. who represented Fraser, Trenholm and Co. in the Bahamas. Bulloch had a good idea of Maffitt's schedule and the seascape of the area surrounding Nassau, so he could brief Low well on the "probables" of the mission. Next, Bulloch needed a British captain who could keep his mouth shut and his eyes wide open, in order to sign off on the loading and customs papers, and recruit a competent crew. There was also the little matter of how he would get the *Florida* armed. But, first things first; who would sail her out cloaked in British colors?

6. Anglo-Rebel Pirates and Confederate Navy Cruisers 73

Bulloch engaged the services of Capt. James A. Duguid, a fully certified British master mariner. With Duguid's assistance and contacts, he was then able to gather an engine room black gang (so named due to the coal dust and soot that covered every exposed surface of their bodies) and crew for deck duties. The "legend," or cover story for the *Florida*'s destination, was that she was bound for Palermo, Italy, and the articles of shipping that Duguid signed indicated that she might sail to other ports in the Mediterranean, or perhaps to the West Indies. The shipping articles innocently stated that the voyage would not last longer than six months and would terminate in Britain. In fact, the *Florida* would never return to her native port.[53]

To solve the problem of getting the *Florida* armed, Bulloch had the advice of the only other Confederate officer, or agent, who was nearly his equal, not only in skill and knowledge, but simple derring-do: Captain Caleb Huse of the Confederate Army. Just like Bulloch, he used ingenuity and creativity as the situation warranted.[54]

Arriving in England before Bulloch, Huse met with the Confederate officials there, and promptly acquired weapons and other war material from European sources. His greatest success to date had been the purchase of 100,000 rifles and ten artillery batteries of six guns each, complete with harnesses for horses. To transport this massive cargo of armaments to the Confederacy, even the mighty Fraser, Trenholm and Company was forced to expand its shipping fleet. Joining the *Bermuda* and another existing ship, *Melita,* were the "new builds," *Bahama* and *Economist*. The strategy of Huse and Fraser, Trenholm and Co. called for some of this veritable fleet of weapons carriers to strike for Nassau, where their cargos would be discharged into faster, shallower draft vessels capable of running the Union blockade. Others, such as the *Melita*, would pause in Bermuda to re-coal, and then attempt to run the blockade directly. There were so many weapons and supplies to be put aboard the *Bahama*, Huse told his boss, Col. Gorgas the head of the Confederate Ordnance Department, that he had problems stowing the artillery pieces. Huse also had problems with Union agents watching his every move in Germany and England.[55]

Learning of the massive weapons shipment planned by Huse and Fraser, Trenholm and Co., Bulloch knew he had a way to transport his naval guns across the Atlantic.[56] He would simply piggyback his comparatively small naval battery on the *Bahama*, where she would trans-ship the guns and other material onto a smaller vessel that would meet the *Florida* near Nassau. Huse was happy to oblige since he now had excess capacity and he would garner Bulloch's expert advice in the management of these essential maritime affairs. The *Bahama* herself would be commanded by Capt. Eugene L. Tessier, a man who had already made his mark by commanding the *Bermuda* when she made her thrilling run through the blockade into Savannah in October 1861.[57]

By 21 March 1862, James Dunwoody Bulloch had all the pieces in place to give the appearance that the *Florida* was a typical new-build, fast cargo ship on her maiden voyage. This was certainly nothing new for the shipbuilding industry of Liverpool, but it was a new venture for the Confederacy. This vessel would be the first purpose-built commerce raider warship for the Confederate Navy. Bulloch shared his thoughts and hopes for his cruisers in a letter to Maffitt:

> Day after to-morrow I despatch for Nassau a gun-vessel, built in England under contract with me for the Confederate Navy. In all sailing and steaming equipment she is very complete, but I have been forced to dispense with all outfit suited to her true character ... I hope it may fall to

your lot to command her, for I know of no officer whose tact and management could so well overcome the difficulties of equipping her, or who could make better use of her when in cruising order.... Another ship will be ready in about two months, and I will take the sea in her myself by some means or other, although I perceive many difficulties looming in the future.... Two small ships can do but little in the way of materially turning the tide of war, but we can do something to illustrate the spirit and energy of our people, and if we can arrange to meet, may yet repay upon the enemy some of the injuries his vastly superior force alone has enabled him to inflict upon the States of the Confederacy.[58]

On 22 March 1862, the *Florida* (though still officially named the *Oreto*) set sail under the nominal command of Capt. James A. Duguid, her papers all in order.[59] As she steamed down the Mersey River, her 52-man crew had more than a few suspicions, but as yet, no idea of exactly what was to come. Although U.S. Consul Dudley *knew* that the *Florida* would become a Confederate warship, he could not prove it because Bulloch had taken every precaution to ensure that he couldn't. Worse yet, the bills of lading and customs papers listed a perfectly legal but fictitious destination (Palermo). This subterfuge left British and Union officials with no idea of where she was really headed. They had no useful intelligence to help the U.S. Navy intercept the ship.[60] Confusion was part of Bulloch's plan, for he knew the enemy's defenses could not cover every chokepoint. The commerce raider was poised to fall upon Union merchant ships like a wolf among sheep and write a new page in the history of maritime warfare.

Bulloch knew that attacks by the miniscule Confederate Navy would have little effect on the overall economy of the Union. But commerce raiding did offer the Confederacy the ability to inflict punitive action against the Union, comparable to Sheridan's razing of the Shenandoah Valley or Sherman's future "March through Georgia." More to the point, the commerce raiding strategy would terrorize the coastal population of the North and infuriate the wealthy maritime industry that supported the Lincoln administration. The Great Powers noted the impotence of the U.S. Navy as U.S.-flagged ships were sunk all over the globe, even within sight of the U.S. mainland. Germany's submarine and surface interdiction campaigns in the two twentieth-century world wars borrowed this concept with equal tactical success and, like the Confederacy, in a losing cause.

Evidence of the success of Confederate raider strategy began even before the *Florida* sailed. On 26 February 1862, Capt. Thomas Craven, commander of the USS *Tuscarora*, received a letter from the U.S. *Chargé d'Affaires* in Spain (Horatio J. Perry) warning him to be on the alert for the *Florida* and the *Bermuda*. Based on information from Minister Adams, he believed they were headed for Palermo, where *both* would be converted into warships.[61] When Commander Pickering on the USS *Kearsarge*, received that same report from U.S. Consul Sprague in Gibraltar, he promptly ordered the USS *Ino* to Palermo. Bulloch was delighted that the U.S. Navy had taken the bait; they were chasing the feints of real and imagined Confederate raiders![62]

Meanwhile, the *Florida* waited until it was beyond sight of land and the prying eyes of British coastal shipping traffic and then eased its helm to the southwest and headed for Nassau and the Bahamas. There was nothing more Bulloch could do now. He had set all the pieces in motion. The game would have to run its course and, with luck, Low would find Maffitt and the *Florida's* armaments and supplies waiting for him in Nassau.

Bulloch turned his attention to the ship known as *No. 290* (*Alabama*). This new and even more powerful ship had to get to sea before the Union surveillance and propaganda hellhounds could derail the game plan for this first-rate raider. He discovered that while W.C. Miller and Fawcett & Preston had surpassed themselves in getting the *Florida* completed on time, the larger *Alabama* was proving to be more difficult for the Lairds. This was largely due to his requirement that commerce raiders be of highest quality *wood* construction, a divergence from the shift to iron hulls. The requirement for a wooden hull was purely practical. Since the commerce raiders would be sailing throughout the world, they might need to be repaired anywhere. Liverpool-quality maintenance and repair for iron hulls only existed in a few places, and not necessarily at locations convenient to the needs of the Confederate Navy.[63]

Bulloch soon discovered that Union agents were once again watching his every movement and attempting to buy or manufacture information from shipyard workers. A few days after the departure of the *Florida*, he met with the other Confederates in London, including North. The meeting on 26 March 1862 must have been an extraordinary affair, judging by the letter of complaint that North lofted off to Sec. Mallory three days later.[64] One can imagine Commander Bulloch's discomfort while standing in the same room with his former senior officer. Bulloch, better than anyone, knew how it felt to not be promoted in the naval service. While North had not exactly been a Horatio Hornblower in his initiative, he had been working against long odds in trying to get ship contracts with no money. As badly as he may have felt over the situation, this was war and Bulloch would not be deterred from accomplishing his mission. He probably hoped that this perceived slight might serve as a motivator for North to take action and prove Mallory wrong.

Bulloch completed his meetings in London and went back to Liverpool with Union informants dogging his heels every step of the way. On 11 April 1862, he summarized the overall situation for Sec. Mallory since the departure of the *Florida*. The Union was engaging in black propaganda by accusing the "Anglo-rebel pirate" ship *Florida* of having attacked an American ship named *Yorktown*. Bulloch knew that that the *Florida* was still crossing the Atlantic and did not even have its armament. This false report had caused such concern within the international shipping community that Lloyds of London was forced to deny the story. Lloyds purchased large advertisements in major newspapers that proclaimed the truth of the *Yorktown's* safe arrival in New York. Lloyds, and Bulloch, hoped the truth would discredit the Union representatives in Britain and restore calm to shippers. Unfortunately for Bulloch, Union diplomats were beyond embarrassment when it came to advocating their cause.[65]

Bulloch was exasperated at the level of scrutiny being applied to *No. 290 (Alabama)*, which he laid squarely at the feet of unscrupulous Yankees and Britain's overzealous determination to maintain strict neutrality. If the rigorous inspections continued, *No. 290 (Alabama)* would leave port "un-completed" as a warship just as the *Florida* had been. The Lairds' managers went so far as to suggest that Bulloch leave out potentially suspicious deck bolts that were designed to mount the main gun batteries. Ever the optimist, he believed he could circumvent this problem by having the work completed in a private shipyard, away from the prying eyes of both British customs and the Union agents.[66]

Bulloch was pleased when *No. 290 (Alabama)* finally moved to the more private graving yard (dry dock) where her engines and boilers were installed. The Union intelligence effort was getting bolder every day as Dudley in Liverpool and Adams in London strove to prevent the ship from sailing and hoped to provoke the British into seizing her. Additional good news for Bulloch was the April 12th departure of the Trenholm ship *Melita* from London with a large supply of gunpowder and other munitions. Perhaps more importantly, the passengers on board the *Melita* included Commander Rafael Semmes and Lt. John McIntosh Kell, who left the irreparable *Sumter* in Gibraltar. Their departure confused Union officials who believed that Semmes and his crew would take charge of at least one of Bulloch's ships. However, Semmes and his officers were headed home to the Confederacy via Nassau, probably believing that their raiding days were over.[67]

By 3 May 1862, Bulloch set about obtaining a crew for his ship when he appealed to Commissioner Mason in London for assistance. He wanted the names of warrant officers that Semmes had recommended for further service and asked that they remain in Britain to serve on his new raider. He dared not meet them himself, due to Union surveillance.[68]

On 15 May 1862, the Confederate Navy's second covertly built commerce raider was launched; the name listed on the slipway was "*Enrica*."[69] Bulloch selected this name as the Spanish equivalent of a lady acquaintance (Henrietta or Harriet). The same lady performed the christening duty of smashing a bottle upon her bow, and was probably Harriet Low, a daughter of Andrew Low, who lived in Leamington Spa with her sister Amy. He heartily disavowed subsequent Union reports that the ship's "legend" was that she was built for Spanish owners, but later facts provided by one of the Laird brothers add credibility to this claim. The detective Maguire reported that Bulloch and his wife Harriott attended the *Enrica*'s launching. Richard Broderick, a shipwright, dutifully retrieved Mrs. Bulloch's bonnet when it dropped from one of the office windows. Bulloch not only recognized Maguire, he knew the persistent and inventive detective by name![70]

On the Sunday after the launch of the *Enrica*, Bulloch was astounded by a request for assistance from James North for his ironclad! North was building a ship that the Confederacy did not need, using money he did not have. On top of trying to get the Confederacy's second commerce raider to sea, Bulloch had to deal with a potentially disastrous project created by his fellow Commander. Where, he prayed, would the money come from to pay for this ship?

While Bulloch and North struggled to maintain a civil relationship despite their latest differences, the Union intelligence effort, stung by its failure to stop the CSS *Florida* was now in overdrive. Consul Dudley in Liverpool informed the U.S. State Department on 4 April 1862 that he believed *No. 290* (*Alabama*) was a duplicate of the *Florida*. This error shows that while the Union intelligence was spot-on in identifying her purpose, it didn't have the precise details of her build, for the *Alabama* was a very different design.[71] By May 23rd, Dudley asked Adams to confirm with the Spanish embassy in London whether or not the vessel was intended for Spanish owners. A British Army officer said he heard it *directly* from one of the Laird brother's own lips that she was intended for the Spanish government. The Spanish embassy said "no," inferring they were perfectly capable of building their own ships.[72] With that information in hand, Dudley directed his agent network to mount a full-time surveillance effort.

As Union agents continued to search for new informants and ways to discern his intentions, Bulloch soon found that Sec. Mallory had turned all his best-laid plans upside down. As he readied the *Alabama* for sea-trials, on 11 June 1862 he received a massive packet from Mallory. His instructions were staggering. First, Mallory said that *North* should be given

6. Anglo-Rebel Pirates and Confederate Navy Cruisers

command of the first ship built in Liverpool; which was impossible since the *Florida* had already sailed and Bulloch had sent orders via John Low for Maffitt to assume command. How could that be fixed? Second, Semmes and his crew were to man the *Alabama*. Bulloch's dreams of commanding his fine, new warship had not only been dashed, they were crushed. He was to remain in Britain to supervise the construction of two vessels that were suitable for operations on the Confederate coastline. Letters from North and Bulloch encouraged Secretary Mallory to believe that Bulloch was on the verge of achieving his top priority: ocean-going ironclads. Since Mallory assumed that North either had left, or would soon be leaving, in the *Florida*, only Bulloch was left to see these ships through to completion.

Bulloch masked his devastating disappointment by urging North to hasten to Liverpool as quickly as possible. Although he had lost his command, Bulloch still planned to be aboard the *Alabama* on the following day to put her through her paces in sea-trials. He also noted that Mallory had enclosed a copy of North's 15 March 1862 letter to the Confederate Navy Department head, for some unknown reason. Bulloch hinted that North should stop sniveling. If Bulloch could follow orders that he did not like, why couldn't North?[73]

In fact, the *Alabama's* sea-trials did not occur until 15 June 1862, giving North time to respond to Bulloch's letter rather than travel to Liverpool as requested. Two days after the sea-trials, Bulloch confessed to North his full frustration with Mallory's constant changes of orders, the bickering over ship designs, and constant financing problems. He also noted, in the politest form possible, North's arrogance in having "already contracted for one [vessel] in accordance with your views," which were completely at odds with Bulloch's.

What had North said in his letter that fully lit Bulloch's flares?[74] North had smugly recounted to Bulloch that Mallory placed a $150,000 credit on North's account with Fraser, Trenholm and Co. He then misinterpreted Mallory's direction "to take command of the vessel built by Captain Bulloch" to mean the *Alabama*. The Secretary still intended North to command the *Florida*, and Semmes the *Alabama*. North erroneously thought he was supposed to outfit and command the *Alabama*! He closed in a superior tone saying that he was ready to either take command of the *Alabama* or continue to work on "his" ironclad, which, by the way, had been in work for a month already! And one other thing; he enclosed a copy of the plans for his ironclad for Bulloch's perusal, which was the first that Bulloch had seen of the sea-going behemoth. Bulloch wasn't just frustrated on 17 June 1862 when he read Commander James North's letter, he was rubbish-bin-kicking, throwing-the-inkpot-at-the-cat, mad.[75]

Not since the *Black Warrior* affair in Havana did Bulloch have so strongly to master his emotions and find a way to take prudent action. He set aside all ego and immediately provided a terse description of the actions that North must take. It was beyond doubt that North was expected to take command "afloat" and that according to Mallory's orders he should come to Liverpool immediately. Bulloch expected the *Alabama* to be ready to sail on or about July 4th. If he was going to take command, North needed hurry to Liverpool. Bulloch would need a *detailed* set of plans for the ironclad to have a better picture of the mess that had landed in his lap.[76] While the two Confederate commanders and naval agents struggled with the snafu created by Sec. Mallory, the Union counterintelligence noose continued to tighten around the *Alabama*. Federal agents and informants observed her sea-trials, and by the time of Bulloch's projected sailing date, even knew the name and address of the man contracted to build her furniture![77]

Bulloch, meanwhile, had to find a British captain to get the *Enrica*, as she was now known since her launch and christening, away from Liverpool. The steady drip, drip, drip of Union information leaking to the British government was beginning to have its effect at the highest level. On the other hand, Bulloch had his own informants who were knowledgeable of the prime minister's developing interest in the ship that was possibly in violation of the spirit of the British neutrality law. In his memoirs, Bulloch notes that he "consulted" a friend, who recommended Mathew J. Butcher. Captain Butcher was serving as a first officer on a Cunard steamship (the *Karnak* or *Karnac*), but he had the necessary master's certificate that allowed him to command at sea and sign all necessary papers. He was also willing to listen to a better offer.[78] Bulloch casually notes that he had met Butcher several years before the war in Havana; so again, he was doing "business" with people he knew well (and who performed equally well). After a quick conversation and an introduction to the Lairds' management, it was fixed that Butcher would handle all further preparations for the *Alabama*'s voyage, *via* instructions from Bulloch.[79] While Butcher nominally supervised the provisioning of the *Alabama*, Dudley's agents were literally their shadows and even the consulate staff followed the Confederates.[80]

At the same time, Bulloch made arrangements to depart in the *Alabama* himself. He learned that the Thomsons in Scotland were being recalcitrant regarding the contract for North's Clyde-build ironclad. They informed North that "transfer of our contract to another party will not be in accordance with either the spirit or the letter of our agreement with you." The Thomsons had North's feet to the fire and obviously they were not as amiable as the Lairds were with Bulloch.[81] Assuming responsibility for this problem would not be easy.

Assiduously following Mallory's presumed orders for North to take command of the *Alabama*, Bulloch officially transferred her to North on 2 May 1862. He also worked on contracts for two ironclads with Lairds. His disquiet and lack of confidence in North seeped through in a letter to Sec. Mallory on 4 July 1862. He knew that something wasn't quite right.[82]

The very next day, North sent a coded message to Mallory (using Cobb's Miniature Lexicon cipher) that once again demonstrated his total misunderstanding of British law and Mallory's intentions. He proposed taking out the *Alabama* as soon as the armaments and munitions were aboard.[83] North was unable to comprehend that the *Alabama must* sail unarmed, as had the *Florida*, and be met by another support vessel beyond British territorial waters before taking on armament. Bulloch had already fine-tuned his procedures after the missteps of the *Florida's* departure.

In May, Bulloch had enlisted the aid of a shipping agent to contract for a sailing vessel out of London that could carry heavy cargo; one that was not too fast, or flashy. It would have been difficult to avoid unwanted attention in Liverpool. Even with the shift to London, he knew that Union agents would learn of his plans, but he hoped at least to delay their ability to assemble all the pieces of evidence and discern his intentions. The vessel was the *Agrippina* and her captain was Alexander McQueen. Loaded with coal at the docks in London (some 350 tons) and all the *Alabama's* armaments and provisions, she appeared totally disconnected from any activities in Liverpool.[84] While this portion of the mission had been in operation for some time, the situation in mid–July was becoming more fluid and perilous by the hour. The confusing orders and interpretations of Sec. Mallory's intent were not helping matters one bit.

6. Anglo-Rebel Pirates and Confederate Navy Cruisers

On July 8th, Bulloch told North that he had received *another* set of instructions from Mallory. These orders confirmed his previous understanding of the situation. Raphael Semmes would be the commander of the *Alabama* and not James North. Bulloch promptly revoked the transfer of "nominal" command of the *Alabama* (dated 28 June 1862) since "now appearing by later advices that you are not the officer detailed for the command of this ship." These "later advices" included several letters that were hand-delivered by Lt. George T. Sinclair, the same officer who had relieved Bulloch on the *Fingal* in Savannah back in January. He arrived from Nassau where he had delivered Mallory's orders to Semmes regarding his new command, the *Alabama*.[85] Sinclair also delivered Semmes' letter to Bulloch affirming his plans to return to Liverpool and then meet the *Alabama* in some remote place that Bulloch had selected. In the meantime, Bulloch would continue to ship cargo via the *Agrippina* and get the *Alabama* ready to sail. The 4 July 1862 launch date had come and gone and the assignment of a commander had turned several circles, from North, to Bulloch, back to North, and finally to Semmes. The complications of having to get a warship under weigh and provisioned with the captain and officers hundreds of miles away, created additional challenges.[86]

U.S. protestations reached a fever pitch again, and between the 10th and 11th of July the solicitor for the Liverpool Customs House, Felix Hamel, revisited Dudley's evidence that the *Alabama* violated the neutrality law and should be seized. Hamel slammed the door shut on U.S. hopes again, frankly stating there was no direct evidence that the vessel was intended to be a warship. Dudley and Adams were fit to be tied.[87] Bulloch quickly got wind of this latest rejection through his own agents in Liverpool. U.S. Minister Adams, however, would not give up, for he now believed it was time to go directly to Lord Russell at the British Foreign Office.

If Bulloch thought matters could get no worse, he failed to account for the petulant James North who was predictably upset about losing command of the *Alabama*. Previously, Bulloch had always maintained his decorum, but North's antagonistic letter was too much. He ran out his literary cannons on 10 July 1862 and fired a pointed rebuttal telling North that he had nothing to do with Mallory's change in orders. In fact, since the *Alabama* was not yet commissioned under the Confederate flag, North had only commanded an "idea." If North had any orders in his possession that superseded the ones he had received, Bulloch would be more than glad to hand over full control of the *Alabama*. Based on documents at hand, Mallory had given command of the *Alabama* to Raphael Semmes, which was his due, given his combat performance aboard the *Sumter* and promotion to captain. North should be happy that at least he *might* have a chance to command a warship sometime in the future.

Finding his wind again, Bulloch then ripped into the behavior of fellow Confederate naval officers who pettily resented his promotion to commander and regarded him "as one to be left alone." He closed on a paternal note, hoping that they would not "avoid each other's glance again" as North had done that morning when he pointedly ignored him. He reminded North that they both were old enough and experienced enough to be above such behavior.[88]

Bulloch had to get the *Alabama* away and the only way to ensure success was for him to be on it. He welcomed this chance to escape from the circling flock of political, financial, and personal albatrosses. On the other side of the Atlantic, Mallory continued to generate orders; on 12 July 1862 he reiterated his orders for Semmes to command the *Alabama* and that Bulloch should render all help available — and get more ironclad contracts. The indefatigable commander was already doing just that, with no idea of Mallory's intentions or orders on hand.[89] As a post-script and without explanation, Mallory told him that if North asked for funds to "return to the Confederacy," Bulloch was to "please supply them." Bulloch would have understood Mallory's meaning; North was being cashiered.

Mallory clearly expected North to take command of the *Florida*. He had instructed Maffitt to take command *only* if North did not arrive via the *Bahama* with the ship's armaments. Mallory had to be peeled off the overhead when he heard that North had "refused" command.[90] Not surprisingly, Mallory had taken North to task for his "failure to follow" and take command of the *Florida*. Mallory felt that North's expressions of "surprise and astonishment" at his assignments and his whining about Bulloch's promotion were "out of place." North was to turn over his accounts to Lt. Sinclair and return to the Confederate States.[91] On 29 July 1862, when Mallory better understood the confusion he had created and sensed that North was making progress in his Scottish ironclad acquisition, he quietly, but without apology, revoked North's recall.

Mallory didn't need to worry, for out of all the confusion, the best possible assignments had been made. Maffitt had the *Florida*, Semmes would command the *Alabama*, and Bulloch would make it all happen. Bulloch had turned-to and was desperately working to get the *Alabama* away from Liverpool. He needed to be, for U.S. Minister Adams was racing to compile his case to present to the British Foreign Office with equal speed.

U.S. Consul Dudley found himself the target of Adams' impatient anger when he failed promptly to supply affidavits from his agents. Adams did not realize or care that revealing their identities might place the informants in danger. Although the Liverpool Customs House would again refuse to seize the *Alabama*, Adams raised the political stakes by giving Dudley's report to Robert Collier, a member of Parliament. Collier had been the queen's counsel and judge advocate of the admiralty. His opinion on the evidence would be damning to the British government and the Confederates if he agreed with the Union's arguments.[92]

It didn't take the experienced Collier long to ascertain that the U.S. minister had the goods on Bulloch and the Confederate Navy. On July 16th, Collier opined that the *Alabama* was clearly intended to be a privateer for use by the Confederate government. As a British-built ship, he believed it violated the Foreign Enlistment Act. He reckoned that Adams had more than enough justification to request the British government to seize the ship immediately. Adams, overjoyed with Collier's opinion, wasted no time in hiring a solicitor, Andrew T. Squarey, to assist Dudley in acquiring the necessary affidavits and documents. Though Dudley was still concerned about "burning" his agents, he and Squarey soon had six massive affidavits in work.[93]

Two of the affidavits established Bulloch's links with both the Confederacy and the *Alabama*. The third affidavit established his connections to the *Florida* and the rest documented the hiring of crew by Capt. Butcher and the details of the *Alabama* and Confederates activities in Liverpool. While Squarey and Dudley feverishly organized the mass of evidence into a coherent package, the duo added another three affidavits by the time they delivered the compilation to Minister Adams in London.[94]

Bulloch was aware of Dudley's efforts with the Liverpool Customs House and had been driving completion of the *Alabama* in a race to get her to sea. Bulloch had his own inside sources who reported Adams' efforts, for in a 21 July 1862 letter to Sec. Mallory, he closed by noting "the U.S. Minister is besieging the (British) Foreign Office with demands to stop her."[95] The labyrinth that was British law assisted Bulloch's efforts. Adams's package of affidavits, accompanied by a letter that was more of a demand than a request, bounced among the various branches of the British government including Customs, the Foreign Office, and the Treasury. Despite inefficiencies within the British governmental system, Adams' protestations finally reached Lord Russell who promptly instructed the chief law officer, Sir John Harding, to investigate.[96]

Back in Liverpool, Dudley kept raising the counter-intelligence ante against Bulloch. He hired a photographer to capture images of the *Alabama*, while he quietly negotiated a contract with a sailor he hoped would spy for the Union while aboard the ship! Dudley was covering his bases in the event the vessel was able to get away. Robert Collier, at Adams' request, had once more reviewed the enhanced package of affidavits placed before Lord Russell and Sir John Harding. He wrote Adams on 23 July 1862 that there could hardly be a stronger case for proving a violation of the Foreign Enlistment Act. In fact, if the Act was "not enforced on this occasion [it] is little better than a dead letter."[97] The Union diplomatic corps in Britain anticipated a near-certain victory against the Confederacy. Lord Russell put the matter into motion with a legal opinion by Robert Collier that Sir John Harding could not ignore. Barring an act of Mother Nature, the Union had both the ship and the man. The British were sure to seize the *Alabama* along with Bulloch and his allies at Lairds. But natural forces did intercede—on the side of James Dunwoody Bulloch and the Confederate Navy.

Just as the Union legal package and documents from Lord Russell finally arrived at the offices of Sir Harding, the chief law officer promptly suffered a mental breakdown and resigned from office, without informing the rest of the British government![98] Secreted 40 miles west of London in Reading with family friends, Harding's condition worsened. Only when the British Foreign Office's legal advisors finally inquired as to when he would render a legal finding did they discover that not only would Harding not be rendering an opinion, he had been declared insane and placed into an asylum. To exacerbate this calamitous state of affairs, Harding had all the Union's affidavits with him — and refused to give them up! It was 28 July 1862 when the Foreign Office discovered the situation. But, they were already too late.[99]

Two days before, on 26 July 1862, Bulloch received word from a "most reliable source" that the *Alabama* would have to leave within 48 hours or be seized. He had a source with access to relevant information from inside the British Foreign Office at the very highest level. Not waiting for a legal finding from the Crown's senior counsel, Lord Russell had decided on his own to seize the *Alabama*.[100]

Placing full confidence in the accuracy of his information, Bulloch went into action. He arranged for the Lairds to put the *Alabama* through an "all-day" sea-trial on the 28th of July — the very same day that the Foreign Office discovered the damning Union affidavits were in the hands of a certified madman! Bulloch sent notice to Captain Butcher's residence to gather more crewmen, have the ship coaled, and made ready to sail. In his confidential message, he directed Butcher to take on more coal and all the stores possible. The *Alabama* would not be returning to Liverpool.[101] Knowing that the enterprise was now balanced on the point of a marlinspike, he made sure to tip the odds in his favor. Master John Low, CSN, would go out with Butcher, just as he had with Captain Duguid and the *Florida*. Leaving nothing to chance, Bulloch arranged for "entertainment" for the vessel's grand send-off. The entertainment would be the curtain that hid the true intentions of the vessel from Union agents — he hoped.[102]

As the sun and tide rose on 28 July 1862, the *Alabama* made for an anchorage at Seacombe on the west side of the Mersey River near the ferry terminal. The feverish preparations for her extended sea-trials went on throughout the day and into the night. Meanwhile, the two other members of the Crown's legal counsel, Atherton and Palmer, had seen and heard sufficient evidence to compose a legal opinion even without the Union's legal packet in Harding's possession. It was now a race that pitted pen and shoe leather against time. Bulloch's pen was equally busy, ordering Acting Assistant Paymaster Clarence R. Yonge to join Captain Butcher aboard the *Alabama* and provide all possible assistance. Yonge was to take full account of all the vessel's stores and equipment and then serve under Raphael Semmes' command. Yonge was instructed to quietly entice the "temporary" crew to sign on with Semmes in the Bahamas. He was not to admit that he himself was a part of the Confederate Navy until Semmes read his commission and assumed command.[103]

Bulloch promptly sent a message to McQueen on the *Agrippina* in London: set sail at once for the Bay of Praya in the Azores.[104] Early on the morning of 29 July 1862, a group of local dignitaries and guests boarded the *Alabama*, which was gaily bedecked with flags and pennants. Bulloch had laid on plenty of liquor and food to keep the party entertained, along with extra riggers and engineers. To all appearances, it was just another ship trial on the Mersey River by one of Liverpool's most prestigious firms, the Lairds. At 9:00 A.M., she weighed anchor and headed down the Mersey and toward the sea. Following behind was the steam-tug *Hercules*, acting as a tender to the "new-build." For the next six hours, the shipboard guests and crew enjoyed a fine summer's day of sailing with light winds and calm seas. Ashore, the Queen's counsel rendered its opinion: seize the *Alabama* immediately![105]

The British again acted too late. At 3:00 P.M. on 29 July 1862, while the British counsel's legal decree shuffled from the Foreign Office to Treasury and Customs, Bulloch signaled the steam-tug *Hercules* to come alongside. He informed the guest-party that the *Alabama* would remain at sea overnight for additional trials and that they would board the *Hercules* to return to Liverpool. Turning to the Liverpool pilot aboard the *Alabama*, George Bond, he enquired if he knew Moelfra Bay off the Welsh coast. When the pilot nodded his assent, Bulloch instructed Captain Butcher to take the vessel there, where, hopefully, he would join him on the morrow. Going down the ladder onto the deck of the *Hercules*, Bulloch knew the game was well and truly afoot, for all the pieces and players were in motion, including the Union Navy's.[106]

As Bulloch watched the *Alabama* sail into the receding summer sun, he knew there was more to the Union game than mere diplomatic gesticulations. There was direct military threat to his plans. The USS *Tuscarora,* under the command of Capt. Thomas Craven, had repositioned from Gibraltar, where it had been watching the CSS *Sumter*, to a cruising station offshore from Southampton, England. Bulloch knew that the eager Craven would have intelligence from U.S. Minister Adams on the situation. If the U.S. captain found the unarmed *Alabama* or the *Agrippina* in international waters, they would be blown out of the water outright or seized and towed into a British port to embarrass the government into action. Ever prudent, Bulloch set his own counter-intelligence operation into action and had a "spotter" in Southampton to alert him if the *Tuscarora* departed.[107] He told the captain of the *Hercules* that he required her services early the next morning.

At 7:00 A.M. on 30 July 1862, Bulloch arrived at Woodside landing to find the *Hercules* standing by, steam up, with all the additional equipment for the *Alabama* already stowed on board. The shipping master was there with forty-plus crewmen for the *Alabama* along with their wives and girlfriends. However, when Bulloch and the shipping master ordered the men aboard, they refused. The sailors and their ladies demanded at least one month's advanced pay. For once, even the wily Bulloch was briefly out-foxed. There was no time for negotiation, so without debate, he agreed and ordered all aboard — quickly! Casting off all lines, the steam-tug made smartly for the Mersey's main channel. Upon reaching the New Brighton area, Bulloch ordered a diversion through Rock Channel, a short cut to Moelfra Bay on the coast of Wales. They had to get aboard and get under weigh before the USS *Tuscarora* discerned their movements.[108]

Bulloch was right to be concerned, for during the night of the 29th and the early morning hours of the 30th of July, one of Dudley's agents had observed the movement of supplies aboard the *Hercules* and, more importantly, knew the *Alabama* was anchored off the Welsh coast. Dudley telegrammed the news to Adams in London and thundered at the Liverpool Customs officer-in-charge (Samuel Price Edwards) to investigate. While the customs officer went through his motions once again, Bulloch and the *Hercules* completed the second part of the "great getaway."[109]

At 4:00 P.M. on 30 July 1862, the *Hercules* came alongside the *Alabama*. The weather had deteriorated with occasional rain squalls, leaving dull, cloudy conditions. The two ships had some cover from prying eyes as the sailors, their womenfolk, and supplies were transshipped. Bulloch had two things on his mind as loading operations were underway. First, he had to alert Captain Butcher about the USS *Tuscarora* and the safest route to avoid detection. Second, he had to get the additional sailors signed on, with their pay safely deposited into their women's hands, so they could be deposited ashore. But, to avoid the first problem, he would have to deal with the last, the crewmen and their consorts.[110]

Knowing the sailors and women brought out on the *Hercules* were hungry (for the harbor tug was not equipped with a galley), Bulloch had the *Alabama*'s steward lay on a large supper for everyone, with plenty of grog as well. He knew full well that a full belly and well-lubricated mind would make everyone more amenable to "negotiation." After the supper and the passing of the smoking pipes, Bulloch called them all aft and explained that since the ship had passed her overnight sea-trials, the owners didn't want to waste time and expense in returning to Liverpool. Would they like to sign on for a voyage to Havana with possible stops on the way? If the vessel didn't return, they had his guarantee that they would be sent back home, all expenses paid, and they would get one month's advance pay there and then. All but two or three men agreed and signed the articles of sailing with the money paid by Bulloch disappearing into female purses. As usual, Bulloch was ready for such an event, for the "articles ... had been prepared" in advance, and they would be used again in the near future.[111]

As he resolved the problem of the signing up a crew, the weather degenerated. Bulloch needed to get the women off the *Alabama*, and more importantly, get the Confederacy's second cruiser away from the British Isles. While the new sailors hove to with the existing crew to get supplies from the *Hercules* transferred to the *Alabama*, he pondered the intelligence on the USS *Tuscarora*. With concurrence of Capt. Butcher and pilot George Bond, he decided to sail up the Irish Sea and circumnavigate Ireland to reach the open waters of the Atlantic. Ironically, Bulloch would sail the same waters as Captain John Paul Jones during his raids along the British coast during the American Revolution.[112]

At midnight, the *Hercules* cast off and an hour later, the *Alabama* turned her bow north. The weather continued to worsen and riding a sou'wester through the wild Irish Sea was not a cruise to be taken lightly, even with a seasoned crew and ship. Bulloch was sailing a patchwork crew on a brand new ship through a boiling cauldron. If they survived, the *Alabama* would have a real shakedown cruise.[113]

As the darkness of the early morning hours receded into daylight, the *Alabama* flew by the Calf of Man, a rocky island in the center of the Irish Sea. Throwing up all her sails, she was soon making 13½ knots in a steady breeze and at 1:00 P.M. passed South Rock and approached the Irish coast. As the sou'wester moved on, in Britain, a diplomatic storm had risen in its place. The Liverpool Customs House finally received the Foreign Office order to seize the *Alabama*. But the *Alabama* was Scot-free, or at that moment, Irish-free, making for the Azores. Dudley, in a diplomatic frenzy, sent details of her escape to the U.S. ministers in thirty-five countries and to every U.S. consul in each of the cities of the Great Powers of Europe. He made sure that everyone knew the Union would be unrelenting in tracking down the vessel and woe to any country that helped the Confederates.[114]

At 7:00 P.M. on 31 July 1862, the *Alabama* passed between Rathlin Island and Fair Head and an hour later, stopped her engines in the lea of the ancient volcanic landmark known as Giant's Causeway on the northeast coast of Northern Ireland. After hailing a nearby fishing boat, Pilot George Bond and Bulloch arranged to sail into port. Shaking hands with Captain Butcher in a driving rain, Bulloch made his way over the side, knowing the vessel was as in as good a set of hands as any, bar his own. He left Butcher with a detailed set of orders that left little to doubt.[115]

As Bulloch and Bond recovered from their drenching in a Portballintrae hotel with dinner and drinks, the *Alabama* weighed anchor and continued her progress around Ireland and into the Atlantic Ocean. Butcher was on his was to Praya Bay in the Azores where he would meet McQueen and the *Agrippina*. Butcher and Yonge would then take charge of McQueen and the arrangements to transfer supplies, armaments, and munitions. Butcher was instructed to take as much coal as possible from the *Agrippina*, keeping ready to sail "at a moment's notice." After Raphael Semmes arrived, Butcher was to consider his duties duly discharged. Should any problems arise, he was to send a letter via the British consul in the Azores.[116]

The following day (1 August 1862), a fine sunny Friday dawned with a mild westerly wind. In a juxtaposition that must have been ironically humorous to the usually dignified Bulloch, he borrowed a boat and with George Bond, rowed along the Irish coast to Portrush, where they caught a train to Belfast. Traveling by steamship and train through Fleetwood to Liverpool, he found news awaiting him at his office about the USS *Tuscarora*. He had been none too soon in sailing the *Alabama*. Craven and the *Tuscarora* arrived at Moelfra Bay on 1 August 1862, just one day too late![117]

While Bulloch settled behind his desk at 10 Rumford Place, the recriminations between and among the Union diplomats, Union Navy officers, and British officials were flying fast

6. Anglo-Rebel Pirates and Confederate Navy Cruisers   85

and thick. Benjamin Moran, secretary to U.S. Minister Adams in London, accused the British officials of ineptitude and the Liverpool customs officer-in-charge, Edwards, as being an outright liar. Adams thought Capt. Craven and the crew of the *Tuscarora* incompetent and was furious with the U.S. Navy in general. When Sec. Seward found out about the affair, he was so incensed that he wanted to reinstate privateering against the British. Fortunately, Congress reined him in, or Lincoln would have had that second war he didn't want. There was very little that Secretary of the Navy Gideon Welles could do other than kick his desk and fume. Welles did make the feeble gesture of sending Capt. Charles Wilkes, the instigator of the *Trent* affair, out in a new ship, but only succeeded in further antagonizing the British and helped Mallory achieve his goal of weakening the blockade.[118]

On August 3rd, Bulloch informed Sec. Mallory of the *Alabama's* escape. He added that correspondence via Nassau was now safe since "private hands" delivered it to John Fraser and Co. in New York City, the same firm that had assisted Capt. Caleb Huse in his passage to Britain. He expected Semmes to arrive at any moment.[119]

The following day, Bulloch wrote another letter to Mallory, this time in the form of a referral for a Mr. S.G. Porter. Capt. Huse needed someone to "take charge of a valuable shipment of arms for the War Department," in other words, run the blockade. Without mentioning that Captain Seth Grosvenor Porter was the husband of Harriott's sister Annette, he noted that Porter served with him several times before as a ship's officer and even commanded a vessel. Bulloch told Mallory that he would have given Porter an appointment as an acting lieutenant on the *Alabama* if he had been given command of the ship. He fully briefed Porter on all aspects of the current situation in Liverpool, in particular the Laird rams. As long as the finances flowed, he saw no problems. Bulloch, in a poignant final sentence, implored Mallory to grant him command of one of the Laird rams when they were completed. With that sealed into an envelope, Porter dashed off.[120]

Turning to the more pressing issue of the *Alabama*, even though she was out of sight, she was not out of Bulloch's mind. He was keen to see Raphael Semmes and his officer staff in Liverpool and deliver them to the Azores to man the *Alabama*, but he also needed additional able-bodied seamen to work her decks. For that, he would have to chance recruiting in Liverpool and hope that the Union agents would not get wind of his efforts. The most urgent problem was Semmes. Where was he?[121]

To explain where Semmes was and where he had been, it is necessary to return to the Bahamas and the story of the *Florida*. She arrived in Nassau on 28 April 1862 after 37 days at sea, mostly using her sails in order to preserve her coal supplies. John Low, her master, found that the support ship *Bahama* had still not arrived.[122] After contacting the local Adderley and Co. Confederate agent, Louis Heyliger, Low reported that Maffitt had not arrived as of May 1st, so he moved the *Florida* to Cochrane's new anchorage.[123] He wanted to be away from prying eyes (namely U.S. Consul Samuel Whiting, who initially thought the *Florida* was a blockade runner).[124]

Maffitt arrived a few days later and relieved Low of his responsibilities for the *Florida*.[125] Meanwhile, on May 17th, Raphael Semmes and John McKintosh Kell, along with other officers from the *Sumter*, departed from London in one of Fraser Trenholm and Co.'s "former" arms carrier ships, the *Melita*.[126] At the time, Semmes had no orders from Mallory or any guidance from Bulloch (who was still junior in rank to Commander Semmes). Yet, in an extraordinary example of "what if," Bulloch offered to place himself under Semmes' command and relinquish the orders he had from Mallory to command the *Alabama*. If Semmes had acceded to Bulloch's offer, he would not have wasted critical time in crossing the Atlantic. As it was, Semmes' apparent lack of involvement in the *Alabama* made it more difficult for the Union to prove its case. If he had remained in Liverpool, it is likely the British government would have moved quickly due to his well-known depredations in the *Sumter*.[127]

Semmes and his party arrived in Nassau on 8 June 1862 after twenty days at sea to find that the British warship HMS *Bulldog*, commanded by Capt. H.F. McKillop, had seized the *Florida* on the 26th of May.[128] He also found a new set of orders from Sec. Mallory that not only gave him command of the *Alabama*, but a letter recommending him for promotion to captain. Semmes knew that neither Bulloch nor North had any idea about the new orders and he knew that Bulloch was racing to get the *Alabama* to sea before the Union could pressure the British into seizing her, so he needed to act quickly.[129]

Semmes wrote to James North telling him that he would take command of the *Alabama*. He also asked North to inform Bulloch *immediately* and to proceed with fitting her out as if Bulloch were commanding her himself. Here, Semmes was playing his cards two ways. If he failed to return, he knew Bulloch could ably command her, in light of North's potential for misunderstanding and misrepresenting the truth. He also wrote to Bulloch explaining the new situation. Semmes entrusted this letter to Lt. George T. Sinclair, who had the opportunity to take a fast British warship to Halifax, then to Liverpool. This, of course, was the critical "later advices" letter that Bulloch received on 8 July 1862, and the same letter that precipitated the near-complete breakdown of relations between Bulloch and North.[130] But this was unknown to Semmes, who like Bulloch before him, was on the wrong side of the Atlantic. Knowing the *Bahama* would be returning directly to Liverpool, Semmes, Kell, Marine Lt. Howell and surgeon Francis Galt, along with two midshipmen sharing the same last name (Sinclair), booked passage back to England. In the meanwhile, they were all more-than-interested bystanders to the legal war involving the *Florida*.[131]

Raphael Semmes, captain of the CSS *Alabama* (*Illustrated London News*, 6 December 1862).

The *Florida* had been released on 27 May 1862 on orders of the local governor, Charles J. Bayley, after the queen's advocate advised that the ship was legally registered and British-flagged. She had done nothing to violate the Foreign Enlistment Act. Still, the British moved the *Florida* from her remote anchorage into Nassau harbor and stationed a customs officer aboard to monitor on-loaded goods. Maffitt could see her from a distance, but could do little more than watch. The conversations Semmes and Maffitt had in the tropical luxury of Nassau's Royal Victoria Hotel amid good food and "some very pretty and musical Confederate ladies" can only be imagined, but they likely mimicked the temperature — very warm.[132]

Meanwhile, the Royal Navy warship HMS *Greyhound*, commanded by H.D. Hickley, arrived to relieve McKillop and the *Bulldog*. The *Greyhound's* lookouts believed they spotted artillery shells being brought aboard the *Florida*. Fearing they would be boarded, Duguid, the *Florida's* legally constituted captain, ordered the anchor raised for he wanted to move the vessel before she could be seized again. The crew refused, claiming their original articles of shipping had been violated, and they peacefully mutinied. Under the law of the day, Duguid had little choice but to place them ashore and have them brought before the local authorities. A bad situation had just gotten worse for Bulloch's first cruiser.

The local magistrate agreed with the mutinying sailors that their contracts had been violated, but he also agreed with Duguid that he did not have to pay the crew's passage back to Great Britain. This made the situation even worse, for yet again the ship had no crew, no coal, and no armament. But it was possible to make the situation even more intractable for the Confederates, for the unpaid sailors of the *Florida* intended to get even. They stormed the *Greyhound's* quarterdeck and told Commander Hickley their tales of Confederate duplicity and their belief they had been abandoned in contravention of their shipping articles, damned landlubber of a magistrate or not. Hickley, well-briefed by the outgoing naval station officer, McKillop, already had his suspicions and what he heard made him all the more certain. The *Florida* should be seized and sent to Halifax for judgment by the Vice-Admiralty Court under Admiral Alexander Milne. On June 15 1862, the British Royal Navy seized the *Florida* for the second time.[133] In Liverpool, Bulloch watched the *Alabama* undergoing her sea-trials, oblivious to the trials of the *Florida*.[134]

But for the deadly serious consequences, the whole affair began to assume comic proportions; once again, Gov. Bayley with the advice of the queen's advocate (Anderson) released the *Florida* on the morning of 17 June 1862. Anderson unequivocally told Commander Hickley there was, as yet, no evidence that showed an attempt to violate the Foreign Enlistment Act. Temporarily flummoxed, Hickley could only shake his head, but now U.S. Consul Whiting had heard enough from the discharged crew. The *Florida* was no blockade runner, she was a Confederate warship-in-waiting and Whiting was going to do his best to succeed where Dudley and Adams had failed. That morning, Whiting marched up to Gov. Bayley and demanded that he seize the vessel and send it to the Vice-Admiralty Court in Halifax. This typically rash demand reflected Whiting's inexperience in not coordinating his efforts with Hickley, for Gov. Bayley, knowing the evidence would not hold up in court, readily agreed to Whiting's demand, but not in Halifax. The case would be heard in Nassau's Vice-Admiralty Court. This failure by Whiting would be critical. But the fat was in the fire now; Gov. Bayley had the *Florida* seized for the *third* time.[135]

Raphael Semmes, trained as a lawyer himself, could do little but watch and offer legal advice from a distance. He commiserated with Maffitt, but had to maintain a very low profile. If Semmes appeared near any of the individuals who were charged with violating the Foreign Enlistment Act or the Queen's Proclamation of Neutrality, the jig was up for the *Florida*. The best Semmes could do was to observe the legal proceedings while learning what might be useful for his cruise aboard the *Alabama*, assuming he could get out of the Bahamas and back to Britain. And that was no certain thing at that moment.

John Low and Capt. James Duguid filed sworn depositions on 27 June 1862 and decided their best move was to get out of the Bahamas and back to Liverpool as quickly as possible. Bulloch needed intelligence on what was transpiring. Judge John Campbell Lees convened the Nassau Vice-Admiralty Court on July 1st, as both Low and Duguid boarded the *Minna*, a blockade runner captained by Otto Upton, that was headed directly to Liverpool.[136]

So, why didn't Raphael Semmes head back to Liverpool on the same ship? Semmes knew that back in England, Adams and Dudley were closely watching Bulloch's efforts. His appearance in Liverpool at the same time as the sailing of the *Alabama* would have been damning evidence insofar as the Union was concerned. No matter when Semmes arrived back in England, he certainly could not be seen sailing merrily down the Mersey aboard the *Alabama*, for he was already notoriously famous for his operations with the *Sumter*. Bulloch would ensure that the ship's senior officers would be transported to the *Alabama* separately to reduce Union suspicions. At the risk of literally missing the boat, Semmes decided to delay his travel to Liverpool and sailed a few days later with one of the best blockade-runner captains, Eugene Tessier, on the *Bahama*.[137]

John Newland Maffitt, first captain of the CSS *Florida* (U.S. Naval Historical Center).

In the intervening ten days between Low's sailing aboard the *Minna* and Semmes' departure on the *Bahama*, the *Florida* court case dragged on. In Liverpool, Bulloch frantically prepared the *Alabama*, dealt with the recalcitrant James North, and countered Union counterintelligence operations as best he could.[138]

When Semmes, Kell, Galt, and the other Confederate officers finally sailed away from Nassau on 10 July 1862, there was a great sense of both relief and expectation all around. Semmes and his staff were excited by the prospect of finally getting a proper warship under them to take the fight to the Union. U.S. Consul Whiting believed he had thwarted a great Confederate scheme (not knowing that Semmes would command the *Alabama*), while Maffitt sighed in relief. With Semmes and his fellow "pirates" gone, Maffitt noticed a sea change in the Vice-Admiralty Court and that the pace of proceedings picked up. Three weeks after Semmes' departure, the Vice-Admiralty Court judge pronounced his decision on the *Florida's* fate. She was returned to her owners due to insufficient evidence regarding violations of the Foreign Enlistment Act.[139]

Both of Bulloch's commerce cruisers had narrowly escaped the clutches of British law within the same week. The *Alabama* sailed down the Mersey on the 29th of July, just ahead of a British seizure order, while the Vice-Admiralty Court in Nassau released the *Florida* on August 2nd. Thanks to his careful attention to legal detail, he and his ships seemed to have nine lives.[140] The most immediate issue insofar as Bulloch was concerned was that Raphael Semmes was finally on his way to Liverpool; but would he arrive in time to take command of the *Alabama* before it was seized or sunk?[141]

As soon as he learned that Semmes and his officers were heading directly to Liverpool, courtesy of Semmes' letter via Lt. Sinclair, Bulloch contracted with Fraser, Trenholm and Co. to re-engage the *Bahama* for a quick turnaround voyage "to Nassau," though the real destination would be Terceira in the Azores.[142] Five days after Bulloch forwarded this information to Sec. Mallory, Raphael Semmes and his group of officers sailed into Liverpool aboard the *Bahama*. If ever there was a reason for the Union counterintelligence and diplomatic effort to be in a state of fear, now was the time. Before Semmes had even stepped off the *Bahama*, the two best combat and logistical commanders in the Confederate Navy were working in concert like a well-oiled machine.[143] If the entire Confederate Navy had acted with such purpose, the history of naval warfare in the American Civil War would have been profoundly different.

In fact, during the few days that Raphael Semmes was in the Liverpool area, he stayed with James and Harriott Bulloch at their home in Waterloo. Semmes provided a rare glimpse into the Bulloch's family life in England, "I met his excellent wife, a charming Southern woman, with whom hospitality was a part of her religious faith. He was living in a very plain, simple style, though large sums of public money were passing through his hands ... I had not only the pleasure of his society during a number of anxious days, but he had greatly assisted me, by his counsel and advice, given that modesty and reserve which always mark true ability."[144] This was high praise indeed from the man who would become one of only two Confederate Navy admirals, and the only naval officer to also hold rank as a Confederate Army general.[145]

We can only speculate on the conversations between Bulloch and Semmes about getting the *Alabama* away, for both men are silent on those discussions in their respective memoirs. But we do know that they realized the opportunity that was at hand for Semmes to achieve a great expression of Mallory and Bulloch's commerce-raiding strategy. They would attack Union civilian and military commerce, in the North and South Atlantic, Caribbean, and the China trade routes. After the *Alabama*'s cruise, only the *Shenandoah* would cover more of the globe.[146]

On 11 August 1862, Bulloch notified Mallory that the *Alabama* was safely away, as was its support vessel, the *Agrippina*; they would rendezvous to transfer armament and other stores. He noted that Semmes and his officer staff, along with other crewmen would sail on the morrow. Bulloch (obviously with Semmes' concurrence) would go out with Semmes' party to ensure a fluid transition and answer any questions Semmes and his officers might have about the vessel. Referring to Union counterintelligence efforts, he reported that Dudley was unable to prove the *Alabama* (or her constructors, the Lairds) had violated the Foreign Enlistment Act or the Queen's Proclamation of Neutrality.[147]

Bulloch's letter continued with a short discourse on the *Alabama*'s armaments and a promise to forward a packet of papers, plans and other drawings "as soon as possible." He provided a remarkable insight into the personal and professional pressures that he faced in his unique position.[148]

When in February last you did me the honor to send me a commission as commander in the Navy I felt fully aware that your act would be criticized and the traditional ideas of naval officers on the subject of relative rank would be shocked, and I therefore promptly expressed to you my reluctance to accept that particular commission.... In the letter acknowledging the receipt of my commission as commander I requested you to change it to that of lieutenant and to place me in the list where I should have been had I never resigned from the old service. It mattered not to me one iota by what title I was called....

Private advices inform me that influence has been used to prevent my being employed in the active duties of the sea, it seeming to be thought by a certain Class of naval men that I should be sufficiently rewarded by the appointment of Navy agent or constructor in Europe. These gentlemen seem willing to grant me the ability necessary to build and equip ships, but are unwilling that I should be put to the test of proving my ability to command them....

Having already built two ships for the Navy, the second of which is as fine a vessel of her class as any service can show, and which I was to have commanded myself, I am, as you have been informed, busily at work upon two armor-clad ships of entirely new design. In no event and under no circumstances of action upon your part will I relax my efforts to complete them in an efficient state, but I earnestly beg leave to urge my claim to command one of these ships in person. I desire, if you approve the designs sent you, to be allowed to complete these ships without interference on the part of others, and to select the one for my own command. Whoever you may appoint to command the other shall receive my cheerful assistance in equipping her for sea, but as I can alone be responsible for the character of the ships, I respectfully request to be untrammeled in the completion of their designs....

If I had no ambition beyond that of a private agent to do the work assigned him properly, I should be content to labor in a quiet sphere, but I aspire to purely professional distinction, and I feel that to toil here, as it were, in exile and then to turn over the result of my labors for the use of others is willingly to consign myself to oblivion. To retain the commission of commander and yet never to command a ship seems to me a mockery.[149]

In Bulloch's nautical world, there were two types of officers: either shore-duty sand crabs or *fighting* sailors who served on warships. Only one of these was worth his salt. Bulloch didn't care about promotion; he just wanted to command a warship.

The *Bahama* finally sailed with Bulloch, Semmes, and the other Confederate officers two days later than expected.[150] Their departure was not exactly covert, for on the sunny Wednesday morning of her sailing, the crew of the tug that towed her into the Mersey channel gave her three resounding cheers that the crew and passengers of the *Bahama* enthusiastically answered. Once again the Confederates were away; this time in broad daylight in front of a cheering crowd.

The *Alabama* reached Terceira in the Azores on 10 August 1862, three days before the *Bahama* left Liverpool. As the *Bahama* raced to catch-up to the *Alabama*, its interim commander, Capt. Butcher, got her ship-shape after a somewhat stormy ten-day voyage. Butcher told the local Portuguese customs and port officials that she was the *Barcelona*, bound for Havana and service with the Spanish government in its current troubles with Mexico.[151] The Portuguese officials were satisfied and assigned the vessel three days of quarantine, and then went over the side, leaving the covert Confederates to their work.

Just after the quarantine period, Assistant Paymaster Yonge went ashore with a working party from the *Alabama* to procure fresh food and water. In a portent of the trouble he would cause, the inebriated Yonge spread the word that the "*Barcelona*" was actually a Confederate warship intended to destroy Union merchant ships. It was most inopportune for Yonge to be spouting off, for in port at the same time was the Union whaler *Rising Sun*.

6. Anglo-Rebel Pirates and Confederate Navy Cruisers

Word reached her captain as well as U.S. Consul Charles Dabney. Yonge's shipmates were not pleased with his loose lips; the *Alabama* was not yet armed and a passing Union cruiser could blow them out of the water.[152]

Fortunately, on 18 August 1862, the crew of the *Alabama* spotted the *Agrippina* making her way toward their anchorage, whose progress had been slowed due to her heavy cargo of naval armaments and the Atlantic swell. Unable to anchor alongside the *Alabama* that evening due to the ocean swell, Capt. McQueen dropped anchor a safe distance away. To have immediately hauled alongside her would have added fuel to the fire that Yonge had already lit ashore.[153]

Early on the following morning, the *Agrippina* came alongside the *Alabama* and anchored. The transshipment of all the naval guns, armaments and other stores began in earnest. Operations continued until the long summer's light faded into darkness. The following day, the unloading and stowing of equipment continued without let up. At mid-morning, a shout from the lookout brought operations to a momentary halt. Another ship was steaming toward them at speed. For a few anxious moments, Butcher and McQueen considered their situation, but the mysterious steamer soon popped out a signal flag. Bulloch had arrived with the *Bahama* and the *Alabama*'s officers. Semmes and his executive officer, John McIntosh Kell, had their first look at the ship that would carry them into history.[154]

As Capt. Eugene Tessier eased the *Bahama*'s helm to take station near the *Agrippina* and *Alabama*, Semmes admired Bulloch's handiwork. Onboard the ship, still officially known as the *Enrica*, Semmes and Bulloch witnessed a scene of organized confusion as deckhands continued the non-stop process of transferring weapons and stores from the *Agrippina*. Butcher came across from the *Alabama* to the *Bahama* where he consulted with Bulloch and Tessier. Semmes (as senior officer), decided that the *Alabama* should raise anchor, while the *Bahama* towed *Agrippina* to a better and less visible anchorage.

Perhaps goaded by Consul Dabney, the Portuguese had not been ignorant of what was transpiring off their shores. Customs officials approached the *Alabama* on August 20th and ordered her to move to the nearby port of Angra, the designated port for merchant vessels in the Azores.[155] Instead, the three vessels sailed out of sight and down Terciera's southern coastline making for the peninsula of Monte Brazil. After rounding the peninsula, the Confederate flotilla anchored in the lee of the peninsula in a deep anchorage of 15 fathoms, where unloading operations recommenced and lasted until dark.[156]

On the following day, August 21st, Butcher, still ostensibly the captain of the *Alabama*, received a letter from the British consul. Portuguese officials were insistent that the three ships move to "East Angra." The British and Portuguese officials suspected that the ship was being armed. Semmes and Bulloch, one a real lawyer and the other a "smooth" operator, simply weighed anchor and moved into international waters to continue transferring weapons. Only after nightfall did the three vessels anchor at East Angra. If the "covert" Confederates hoped for a good night's sleep, they didn't get it.[157]

An excited watch officer awakened Semmes about midnight with the alarming news that, "a man-of-war schooner was firing into" the *Alabama*. Cool as ever, Semmes replied that Portuguese dared not "fire into me" but only "at me ... let them fire away, I expect he won't hurt you." To the astonishment of the officer and the amusement of Bulloch, he went back to sleep. The next morning, it was ascertained that the source of the firing was a mail steamer that had fired three signal shots to awaken the sleeping passengers ashore who were waiting for its arrival.[158]

As the sun rose, Semmes had commenced coaling operations on the morning watch. At 7:00 A.M., Portuguese customs officers and the British consul came aboard to insist the ships follow international protocols. Playing along, Butcher went ashore to the Customs House to present the proper papers and make the salutary apologies for their failure to anchor in the correct place due to their ignorance of local requirements.

After Butcher returned and reported to an anxious Semmes, the Confederate captain opened a barrel of cartridges for the big guns and distributed other weapons. Semmes knew that the British consul was suspicious of their behavior, but this visible show of force convinced the local authorities that any attempt at seizure would come at a very dear price. When the crews had completed the necessary hard labor, they "spliced the main-brace," the traditional libation of a ration of rum for all hands on deck. The *Agrippina* moved off to anchor nearby and the crews of the *Alabama* and the *Bahama* settled in for a well-deserved night's rest. Again, the Confederates' rest was disturbed, not by the Portuguese, but by the harbinger of a storm in the form of a large sea swell in the anchorage.[159] The following morning, after the storm cleared and the swell dropped, coaling began again along with the stowage of fresh fruit and vegetables. Work continued on correcting minor problems with gun carriages, while Semmes and Bulloch held their last councils of war.

Sunday, 24 August 1862, was the day they had all been waiting for, James Dunwoody Bulloch in particular. Having decided he could wait no longer to complete the slow progress of transferring coal, Semmes had Butcher take the *Alabama* into international waters once more with the *Bahama* following. In the early afternoon, the *Alabama* slowed her engines and fired a shot from the starboard bow gun as the signalman lowered the English ensign and hoisted the Confederate ensign aloft. A small ship's band bleated out a rough version of "Dixie," while the united cheers of the crews from the two ships echoed across the water. With the sailors in good spirits, Semmes ordered them all aft to the quarterdeck. Everything depended on Semmes's eloquence now, for a warship without a crew was merely a target.[160]

Semmes extolled the heroic virtues of the Confederate cause and implored the men to join him for a cruise aboard the warship that was now known as the *Alabama*. They would be well paid by the standards of the day. The men who signed on drove hard bargains, but Semmes did not complain, for he fully expected the sailors to demand a signing bonus, called a "bounty." Fortunately for his purse, they did not. Eighty men signed on; it was better than he had any right to expect, but not as good as he had hoped. Semmes wanted one hundred men. The rest of the day and the evening were spent in allocating advances and allotments for wives and other dependents in Liverpool. By 11:00 P.M., all was finished and with one last "cordial adieu" to Semmes, Bulloch stepped over the side of "his" ship, accompanied by Captain Butcher. It was the last time he would set foot on the *Alabama*.[161]

As the *Alabama* steered her course to the northeast, Semmes extinguished the fires of her engines, set his fore and main trysails, and sailed away into the howling fury of another gale. As Bulloch and the *Bahama* turned for Liverpool, all visual evidence of the *Alabama* soon vanished in the swirling rain. It was a fit beginning for the Confederate Navy's most destructive commerce cruiser.[162] When the *Bahama* reached Liverpool on 1 September 1862, Bulloch immediately notified the Confederate commissioner in London, James Mason, that the *Alabama* was "safely at sea, fully equipped, under our own national flag, and with a crew of 82 able seamen, besides a staff of 27 officers."[163] He was bursting with pride at the accomplishment.

If the Confederates in Great Britain had known of the events in America, they would have been doubly proud. In the last days of August, the Confederate Army had routed Union forces in the Second Battle of Bull Run (or Manassas) and only a desperate rearguard action kept Union Army from being destroyed at the outskirts of Washington, D.C. Things were so bad for the Union that even the Native Americans joined the insurrection. In Minnesota, the Sioux Nation was on the warpath. The Union was beleaguered on every side it seemed. At that moment in 1862, prospects were bright for the Confederate States of America on both land and sea.[164]

7

Of Incalculable Value — 1862

With the *Florida* and *Alabama* away on their missions of destruction, Bulloch's decks were now clear for the Confederate Navy's most important need. Since the Battle of Hampton Roads, involving the USS *Monitor* vs. CSS *Virginia* on 9 March 1862, Sec. Stephen Mallory's passion had become an obsession. He had to have transoceanic ships capable of smashing the Union blockade and raiding Northern coastal cities. The Union Navy had grave concerns about the havoc caused by Confederate commerce raiders, but the war-changing threats taking form in British graving docks shook the Lincoln administration to its very core.

As preoccupied as Bulloch had been with the details of outfitting his raiders and helping his Army and State Department counterparts, he had not neglected Mallory's highest priority. Back in April as he was trying to get the *Alabama* away, he subtlety suggested to Mallory that he should concentrate his resources where they could be used to best advantage. He didn't want to waste money on commerce raiders that were having a negative impact on the British "commercial classes." It was the next item in Bulloch's letter that is epochal for maritime historians. He reported that the clash between the *Monitor* and *Virginia* (*ex*-USS *Merrimack*) had upset the balance of power as far as the Great Powers of Europe were concerned. Britain, at the moment the world's greatest empire due in large part to its sea power, found itself doubting its true strength.

London's Fleet Street newspapers shouted that the entire Royal Navy had been rendered worthless, except for Her Majesty's ironclad HMS *Warrior* and its sister ship *Black Prince*. In an instant, the Royal Navy decided to convert several screw-propulsion "line of battle" ships into iron-plated warships armed with Captain Cowper Coles' revolving gun turret. Coles was charged with overseeing the construction of an additional *four* new purpose-built ironclads based on his designs. One builder, Samuda of London, believed they could have it launched by mid–1863! While the British Royal Navy had already been pursuing ironclad technologies, the battle of the American ironclads provided impetus and popular support for accelerating these programs. The British had no desire to be caught with their sea-boots off if they had to confront Louis-Napoléon of France who had the lead in this naval armament race. Now, they also had to reckon with the upstart Americans.[1]

The irony of Bulloch's words must have echoed in Mallory's memory. As chair of the U.S. Senate Committee on Naval Affairs, Mallory had tried for years to get a revolving gun battery funded and completed. He had been one of the first Americans to recognize that iron and steel were the future of naval warfare. The chance "gift" of the partially burned

7. Of Incalculable Value

hull of the USS *Merrimack* provided the Confederacy a base from which to build the first operational ironclad, renamed the CSS *Virginia*. Due to a lack of secrecy and the timely appearance of John Ericsson's *Monitor*, the Confederacy lost a key advantage in naval warfare, technology dominance. This was a recurring theme throughout the conflict. The Confederates out-innovated the Union, but lacked the means to translate their ideas into rapid action.

When the *Monitor* appeared in Hampton Roads off Norfolk and Ft. Monroe late on 8 March 1862 and stood toe-to-toe with the *Virginia* the next day, every naval power in the world knew they *had* to have ironclad ships. Without them, they would not only risk being second-rate, but also irrelevant. The Confederate Navy energized a global naval arms race, violently manifested in the Battle of Jutland in World War I and at Surigao Strait in World War II, the most significant and last confrontations of steel ships using turreted guns.

Because of this ironclad ship arms race, the Confederacy could now expect even more exhaustive counter-intelligence efforts to keep them from obtaining an ocean-going ironclad. Wooden commerce raiders were troublesome, but they could be dealt with, as could the Confederacy's homegrown coastal and riverine ironclads. The threat of a Confederate ironclad steaming into New York harbor, shelling Wall Street, and holding the city to ransom was a nightmare scenario that the Union had to prevent.

Bulloch, ever resourceful, knew how to overcome the problems of supply, demand, and available resources. He advised Mallory that the hulls for a series of ironclads could be laid down in the Confederacy's various ports, such as Savannah and Charleston, based on a standard set of plans. Meanwhile, working from the same plans in Liverpool, Bulloch would get all the iron plates, fittings, engines, rivets, and other material built in Britain and then "marked and shipped" via blockade runners into Confederate ports. These "weapons-packages" could then be unpacked and assembled into instant ironclads with the help of British experts. This is a principle so visionary that its equal was not seen until Kaiser Corporation in World War II created the modular construction of the famous Liberty cargo ships.[2]

Assembling a British-built, iron-hulled ship in a Southern port wasn't without precedent. Bulloch had good reason to be confident that this approach to acquiring ironclads would succeed. Back in 1834, a Savannah banker, ship owner, and cotton broker named Gazaway Bugg Lamar and John Laird fabricated and assembled America's first successful commercial iron-hulled steamship, the SS *John Randolph*. It had been shipped to Savannah in pieces where five Laird employees assembled the ship using machinery supplied by Fawcett, Preston, & Co. These were the same two companies that built the CSS *Florida* and *Alabama*.[3] At the time the *Randolph* was built, Bulloch was an impressionable 11-year-old boy living in Savannah. The Bullochs also had a close emotional connection with the owner of the *Randolph*. Lamar had survived the wreck of the steamship *Pulaski* when it sank in June 1838. Lamar, like Bulloch's brother-in-law Robert Hutchinson, lost his wife in the disaster.[4]

Bulloch also was aware of more recent plans to assemble an American-built steamship in a foreign port. The New York shipbuilding firm of "Roosevelt and Joyce" was in the process of fabricating a steamer for service as a Chinese river passenger ship. It was assembled in Whampoa in the spring of 1863, launched as the *Kinshan* in May, and placed into operational service between Hong Kong and Canton in October.[5]

Mallory, and especially Bulloch, *knew* that the best way for the Confederacy to build combatants required the highest quality workmanship that was only available in Europe. Bulloch proposed a fast, safe, reliable, and inexpensive strategy to integrate this workmanship into purpose-built designs. His approach was just as valid then as it was when the U.S. Navy incorporated modular weapons systems designs into its twenty-first century Littoral Combat Ship.[6]

Bulloch also updated Sec. Mallory on the latest advances in naval guns capable of penetrating iron plates. He planned to get a copy of Cowper Coles' revolving gun turret design for Confederate use. He probably obtained the plans from the Lairds, who were related to Cowper Coles and became Bulloch's life-long friends.[7]

Three days later, Commander James North was able to report to Mallory that he had found a builder on the Clyde in Glasgow who had agreed to build an ironclad warship. It was immense, displacing some 3,200 tons. North wanted to know if the Navy Department desired another of the same size, or whether they preferred several smaller ones.[8]

Lt. North, perhaps seeking to prove his relative merit as a Confederate Navy agent, ignored Mallory's directive to coordinate with Bulloch and failed to inform him of these efforts. The ironclad ship drew far too much water to be of any use in the shallow Confederate ports. Bulloch had been working in blissful ignorance of North's initiatives. Bulloch already had researched precisely the size and type of vessel best suited to the Confederacy's needs. Experienced shipbuilders (i.e., the Lairds) believed that a vessel of approximately 1,900 tons, 230 feet in length with a draft of some 15 feet, would be ideal for the South's shallow ports and coastline.[9]

On the Sunday after the launch of the *Alabama*, Bulloch received North's request for assistance for his ironclad project. This request included the vessel's impractical dimensions and tonnage that the builder, J. & G. Thomson, had proposed. It was a third-again larger than what was needed based on Bulloch's research. The only American ports that it could reasonably enter on the eastern seaboard were the Union ports of New York City or Boston! Bulloch had to at least try to make North realize the absurdity of his project.

First of all, he pointed to North's earlier request for copies of the ship drawings of the *Florida* and *Alabama*. He had thought North merely wanted them to file away; surely North wasn't trying to use them as a basis for constructing an ironclad ship? It simply wouldn't work due to the weight, balance and other basic naval design issues. He had already told Mallory that the Confederate Navy would be best served by building the hulls in the South. Bulloch continued to believe that "it would not be advisable to go into a heavy contract for a *cruising* ship of that material" (i.e., with an iron hull). Hinting strongly about the infeasibility of building such a ship at the stated price, Bulloch said the price for a vessel of 2,500 tons was about £208,000 (about $800,000 U.S.) and delivery time was 15 months. Bulloch warned that if anyone offered to build it for "less time and less money," he should demand a contract clause that stipulated monetary forfeiture "for non-fulfillment of contract."

Bulloch didn't need another rancid fish on his plate and the Confederate Navy did not need this ship. While the *Alabama* was still in Liverpool, he had invited North to come and see the ship with the hope that he would take note of her "internal arrangements" and see for himself that what he was proposing simply could not work.[10]

Bulloch wrote to Mallory on 11 August 1862, just before he sailed to meet the *Alabama* off the Azores. He mentioned that the two vessels he had contracted with Lairds to build were "getting on finely."[11] Mallory had intelligence on Union Navy efforts in the field of ironclads and Bulloch had similar information on British and French naval developments. However, the problem of delayed communications hampered their mutual understanding of the geopolitical forces at work. Mallory and Bulloch may have seen events through the prism of Confederacy versus the Union, but the vision in Washington was one of the Union versus the British Empire, or any other empire that aided their Southern enemies. Preventing the Confederacy from acquiring British or French ironclads was a matter of national survival. To understand the context of Bulloch's situation, a short overview of ship developments up to that point in time is helpful.

Lt. James North's ironclad, *No. 61*, later to be known as the *Danmark* (authors' collection).

The Crimean War (1853–1856) had aligned the joint forces of the British, French, and Ottoman Empires against the Russian Empire in yet another European war for geopolitical influence. The major field of conflict was in the Crimean Peninsula, where the declining Ottoman Empire had little power. In 1853, the Russian fleet, employing a new type of artillery shell, destroyed the Turkish Navy at Sinope on 30 November 1853. Louis-Napoléon reckoned that the Russian Fleet would anchor beneath the protective guns of their naval fortifications where any attacking ships would suffer greatly. In a moment of inspired genius, Louis-Napoléon ordered the creation of several light-draft, armor-plated, and heavily armed floating batteries.

With remarkable speed, a composite team of French and British naval, army, and civilian engineers created an armored battery prototype. This joint-building program included not only the armored batteries, but mortar boats and gunboats as well. These were all towed from France and England to the Black Sea. On the night of 14 October 1855, the Battle of Kinburn began and throughout the next day, the Russians desperately rained down shells upon the attacking armored batteries, but only inflicted minor injuries. French crews silenced the naval fort's guns and even breached its walls in several places. The news of this successful combination of technology and tactics rippled to the shores of every maritime power.[12]

In America, this success came as no surprise to Robert and Edwin Stevens, two frustrated brothers who designed and began construction on an armored battery over ten years earlier! The Stevens brothers managed to wrest a shipbuilding contract from the U.S. Congress in the wake of the 1841 Canadian border war scare between the United States and Great Britain.

The Stevens brothers proposed a design that was truly breathtaking.[13] Its features included the ability to partially submerge its hull to reduce its target signature and a high-speed steam-driven screw propulsion with all critical machinery beneath the waterline.

Ericsson's *Monitor* would incorporate many of these characteristics twenty years later. Unfortunately, the brothers struggled with numerous engineering and technical problems and the failure of Robert Stevens' health. Throughout the late 1840s and early 1850s, work progressed slowly but in 1851, the U.S. Secretary of the Navy ordered the cessation of all work; the chief of naval construction wanted her scrapped.[14]

Perhaps inspired by the Russian victory at Sinope, the brothers decided to radically redesign the ship. She would be a massive 420 feet in length and displace 4,683 tons with a mixed battery of seven rifled and smooth-bore naval guns, and forced-air ventilation for the crew. It was an audacious vision and work progressed quickly from 1854 through 1855. However, in 1856, Robert Stevens died as did all progress on the battery until 1859, by which time the U.S. Navy was losing its patience.[15] By 1861 the U.S. Navy had spent one-half million dollars on the project, and was prosecuting a war that required offensive naval operations. There was little need for a defensive floating fortress. When the war began, the ship that might have been first in so many ways, lay in her dry dock, unfinished and unloved by everyone except the lone remaining Stevens brother, Edwin.[16]

The Stevens' battery had one important influence. During the period in which she had been conceived, designed, and partially built, Stephen Mallory had been a U.S. senator and chair of the Senate Committee on Naval Affairs. Mallory supported the Stevens' concept, as did Thomas Butler King, the influential "floating diplomat" for Georgia and the Confederacy at large. King was a U.S. congressman and progressive member of the Committee on Naval Affairs during this period. Finally, Bulloch certainly knew of the Stevens project. Since he had lived in both New York City and the New Jersey areas before the Civil War, he undoubtedly knew of and had possibly seen the Stevens' battery.[17]

In answer to Louis-Napoléon's armored ship *La Gloire*, the British built the HMS *Warrior*, the world's first operational iron-hulled *and* armored vessel. In reality, the *La Gloire* was merely a cut-down wooden broadside battleship with armored plating. Although the French naval architect Dupuy de Lôme proclaimed his vessel to be capable of "oceanic cruises," he privately admitted *La Gloire* had limited sea-going capability and "was not destined to act far from European waters."[18] The *Warrior*, on the other hand, was a quantum leap forward in design and had much better sea-handling characteristics. Like her French competitor, she still employed naval guns organized in the traditional broadside manner. While she was innovative in certain aspects, the *Warrior* was certainly not what the Stevens brothers would have called a radical improvement in naval warfare design. For the careful Royal Navy, however, it was enough to calm public fears. It was an important element of the naval arms competition between Britain and France that was just beginning to hit full stride at the start of the American Civil War.[19]

While America had the Stevens brothers and France had de Lôme, Britain had Capt. Cowper Coles. Coles was present at the Battle of Kinburn during the Crimean War's first use of armored batteries. He was also the designer and builder of an innovative shallow-draft artillery raft at the Battle of Taganrog in the shallow Sea of Azov. Coles' unique contribution to armored ship development for the Royal Navy was the hemispherical gun turret. He had observed that the French and British armored artillery battery designs left the gun crews too exposed. The admiralty considered Coles' provocative concept in 1855–56, but it was not until 1859 that a private constructor built an experimental turret. Infighting among multiple levels of the British government and admiralty hindered Coles' efforts.[20]

7. Of Incalculable Value

The Confederate seizure of the Norfolk Navy yard and conversion of the former USS *Merrimack* into an ironclad spurred the Union into action. Union Secretary of the Navy Gideon Welles was desperate for an answer, others, including Secretary of War Stanton, became hysterical, fearing that the ironclad *Merrimack*/CSS *Virginia* would lay waste to Washington and the entire Union coast! Into that breach stepped Captain John Ericsson, a Swedish-American inventor, engineer, and irascible naval genius. After presenting warship designs to Louis-Napoléon in 1854, Ericsson had gone to America, where he became the man of the moment through fortuitous circumstance. When he saw Ericsson's plans, Welles was prescient enough to realize this answered the immediate problem. These plans featured a vessel with a single revolving turret, machinery placed beneath the waterline in a shallow draft, and a virtually waterline-flush deck that had forced air ventilation for warm-weather operations. Under these circumstances, the USS *Monitor* was born.[21]

When the Union *Monitor* met the Confederate "secret weapon" at Hampton Roads in March 1862, the battle between the Confederacy and the Union was a draw, but on the strategic geopolitical front, it was a victory for the Union. The success of the *Monitor* sent a salient message to Britain: If they interfered in American affairs, the U.S. Navy could send the Royal Navy's wooden ships to the bottom whenever they came within range of U.S. coastal waters. Ericsson, busy designing a giant ocean-going monitor, claimed that within a year he could have ships that could force both the British and French Empires from North America. The leadership in Washington agreed with that assessment, for they embarked on an ambitious campaign to build sea-going monitors.[22]

In the second week of September 1862 as James Dunwoody Bulloch surveyed the latest progress reports on his ironclad "Laird rams" (as they were known to the British and American press), he was confident they would be launched, hopefully as Confederate warships. On the other hand, Hampton Roads drew the attention of British newspapers and journals. Overnight, the fractious American "cousins" altered the balance of naval power. It was a situation that could not stand without challenge. The plot had now thickened beyond just the Foreign Enlistment Act and the Queen's Proclamation of Neutrality. If one of Bulloch's ocean-going armored ships was set loose, particularly one that was technically superior to the *Monitor*, Britain could find itself at war with the Union. The prospect of a U.S. Navy iron fleet deployment against the home isles would force Britain into recognizing the Confederacy for naval support; it would be a world truly "turned upside down." What had been a two-nation naval arms race was now a four-nation race, and who might join next, the German Confederation, Russia, Japan?

The late summer of 1862 was a period of relative calm for Bulloch. He had time to pen an extensive letter to Sec. Mallory on 10 September 1862 describing his adventures with the *Alabama* and his trip to the Azores with Semmes.[23] He even provided timely financial advice to Confederate commissioner James Mason on 15 September 1862 regarding the pricing of cotton in relation to a proposed "cotton bond." While the Confederate government had not yet fully exploited its most valuable export to raise money for the war effort, Bulloch hinted to Mason that it ought to do so. Confederate ironclad building was expensive and demanded serious financial capital. He thought 20 cents a pound was a fair price for "middling" cotton, having consulted "several gentlemen ... who knew the state of the cotton market in the Confederate ports." In reality, all Bulloch had to do was lean across his desk in the Fraser, Trenholm and Co. office to one of Prioleau's managers to get the latest market intelligence. Despite the recent "grand successes of our arms" (the victory of the Confederate Army at the Second Battle of Bull Run/Manassas), Bulloch darkly thought that the Northerners would still "harden their heart" against the South. An internal revolution, dictatorship, or anarchy would most likely befall the North he reckoned; all of which, to varying degrees came to pass over the next two years.[24]

The news of the South's battlefield victory fired up British politicians and moved the American sideshow to center stage. Palmerston told Lord Russell that if the Confederates took Washington and Baltimore, Britain and France should "address" the two sides and negotiate a permanent separation. If Lincoln's Union refused, Palmerston thought Britain should recognize the Confederacy as "established fact." Russell thought Britain should give the Confederacy outright recognition as an independent nation.[25] Palmerston was under fire from the press and the public on multiple fronts regarding the American Civil War. The South seemed to be winning as massive unemployment hit the Lancashire mills while the Union's new ironclads threatened the global geopolitical balance, i.e., British pre-eminence. If Palmerston could put out the North American fire, he might defuse all these situations and restore the *status quo*.

U.S. Minister Adams in London had a ringside seat to the Parliamentary debates, while Consul Dudley got a journalistic "earful" in Liverpool. They knew matters between the Union and Britain hung in the balance, as the failure to stop Bulloch's cruisers stuck in their craw like a bitter peach pit. They had to get Bulloch's armored rams seized from the Lairds' shipyard.[26] If not, there would be war between the Union and Britain, possibly with France joining in, and perhaps the Russians too, for they had close relations with the Union. The entire world might be at war.

And how were the British-built ironclads progressing? Commander James North provided insight as he competed with Bulloch for leadership in the Confederate Navy's armored shipbuilding program in Britain. In a letter to Mallory on 19 September 1862, North said his Thomson ship, *No. 61,* had "nearly all her frames up ... and all the larger pieces of machinery finished." In an intriguing comment, he liked the prow design sent by "Mr. Porter." The Confederate Navy Department was assisting with the design of North's armored ship.[27] "Mr. Porter" was John L. Porter, chief constructor of the Confederate Navy, in essence the Confederate Navy's naval architect.

After registering the obligatory complaint about the lack of funds, North described his visit to the Lairds' shipyard in Liverpool on the day before where he observed Bulloch's rams. North reported that one was "half in frame," while the other had "her keel down; they will be fine vessels when finished." He added that he would be sending reports on the British government's daily "experiments ... in gunnery" against naval armor. North was witness to the new initiatives instigated by the clash of the Union and Confederate ironclads at Hampton Roads. The British were on a crash armored-ship program and they wanted to know how thick the armor needed to be, and at what angle it should be in order to defeat the latest naval guns.[28]

The Union counterintelligence was operating at a super-heated level and was after the same information. While the intelligence collected about Bulloch's rams dealt with immediate threats, their collection effort also provided critical technical intelligence about *British* shipbuilding capabilities in the area of armored ships. The Lairds had laid down an ironclad frigate with guns arranged in broadside (without turrets) on 30 October 1861.

Originally named the HMS *Captain*, it was changed to *Agincourt*, perhaps as a message to Louis-Napoléon that Britain would respond to the French "iron" challenge on the high seas. (The Battle of Agincourt was a major English victory against a larger French army in the Hundred Years' War.) Progress was slow as the British determined how best to armor and arm their ships to meet the new threat from the Union. Technological advances were outstripping the speed of shipbuilders in the new field of armored ships and armor-piercing guns and projectiles.[29]

The Lairds and the Royal Navy both benefited from Bulloch's order for two armored rams. The ships incorporated the ideas of Cowper Coles' turrets, the latest British guns, and armor plating. Moreover, the two rams were designed to operate in the same waters as the Union monitors, but with better sea-handling capabilities. If Union interest was high, British interest was higher at least from a technology perspective. The Royal Navy could see the emergence of the next generation of naval warfare, paid for by the Confederate Navy. Thanks in part to the round robin of Confederate, British, and Union technical development and intelligence collection, Britain's ironclad designs were becoming outdated even as they were built. Bulloch's rams were an important step toward a true sea-going ironclad.

Meanwhile, the political and diplomatic playing field was dramatically altered on 22 September 1862 when Abraham Lincoln issued his first Emancipation Proclamation. Lincoln had made a game-changing move that radically improved his position throughout the international geopolitical scene. No nation could openly oppose a country fighting to outlaw human slavery.

Only two days later, Bulloch penned a lengthy response to Mallory's letter dated July 30th, oblivious to the new political situation. Bulloch updated the secretary on his contract for Le Mat revolvers (which fired grape-shot) and armored ship plans in France. He then noted that the Paris firm of Girard and Co. had approached him about payment for revolvers. Since the contract was with the Confederate Navy Department, they assumed that Bulloch was responsible. Bulloch told Girard that he could not pay for the revolvers in cash, but he negotiated a deal that guaranteed payment secured by future cotton deliveries. This uncomfortable event allowed Bulloch to get to his main concern: finances.[30]

Although he had been able to pay all installments on time, he needed a steady flow of Navy Department funding. If not, he would be slapped with late payment fees that would be "injurious to our national credit." This indicates clearly that Bulloch's shipbuilders knew perfectly well who would be using their completed vessels: the Confederate Navy. And this brought Bulloch to his next point: too many cooks were spoiling the broth.[31]

The appearance of Commander George Sinclair in Liverpool at the beginning of the summer, in the midst of the getting the *Alabama* ready for sea, had been inopportune. Sinclair arrived with orders for Bulloch to "furnish him the means of building a 'propeller-clipper' (ship) that Sinclair would command, and also to provide him $60,000 as a cruising fund." Bulloch was stunned by this request. He explained the untenable financial reality of their situation. Fortunately, Sinclair was cut from the same cloth as Bulloch and realized the need to maintain the Confederate Navy Department's meager credit and find another way to fund his project. Sinclair had connections in the British financial world and believed he could borrow the money to finance the construction of his ship. Bulloch left Sinclair to his own devices for he had enough to do, Sinclair could keep Mallory apprised of his progress.³² Now, Bulloch let his other shoe drop: the problem of nefarious "contractors."

Numerous individuals had arrived fresh off the blockade runners with contracts in hand, but with no financial credit or means to act upon them. The Navy Department had agreed to these schemes and encouraged these "contractors" to appear at Bulloch's door with the expectation that he would arrange financing. These demanding speculators caused numerous problems for both the Confederacy and Bulloch. Their shaky deals placed his personal and professional reputation at risk. If these deals went sour, disgruntled parties would make the easy stroll to the U.S. consul's office in Liverpool. On top of this, these characters were running about Britain hunting for financial loans and compromising the Confederacy's secrecy.³³

Bulloch was specifically irritated because "Mr. [George Nicholas] Sanders has left England ... and did not inform me of his intention to leave nor for what purpose." Sanders had been involved in a deal with an Edgar P. Stringer to acquire ships in exchange for cotton bonds. When Stringer demanded that Bulloch sign the bonds at a rate of only 8 cents on the pound (instead of the going rate of 20 cents per pound), he refused. Bulloch recounted his version of the story to Mallory to ensure that his points on financial matters in Europe were well understood before Stringer's inevitable complaints made their way to Richmond.³⁴ Unfortunately for Bulloch, his dealings with Sanders, even at a distance, would provide another uncomfortable link to the American Civil War's most infamous event: the assassination of Abraham Lincoln.

The first days of October began as September had finished for Bulloch, quietly. He had no idea, as yet, of the Battle of Corinth in Mississippi or the Battle of Perryville in Kentucky. The Union had won at Corinth on October 3rd, lost tactically at Perryville on October 8th, but won strategically in its overall "Confederate Heartland" campaign.³⁵ The tremendous geopolitical victory that Bulloch did hear about, which occurred in the second week of October, was a decisive Union victory. Newspapers across Britain trumpeted the news of Lincoln's Emancipation Proclamation and instantly the Confederacy was on the diplomatic defensive. The Confederacy's dependency on slavery, which literally carried the economy of the South on its back, had now been turned into the North's greatest moral weapon. And the depredations of the *Alabama* were beginning to make British ship insurers and shippers alike very nervous.³⁶ The Confederacy clearly was on the wrong side of right insofar as the British public was concerned. The British ruling class' understanding of this new reality, particularly Palmerston and Russell, would be pivotal.

As he awaited official British reaction, Bulloch could do very little except to carry on with his naval business. At the very least, he knew that Union efforts to thwart the sailing of his armored ships would increase. He was quiet about his activities in October of 1862, but Union counterintelligence filled in some of the gaps.

U.S. Consul Dudley received reports that the Laird rams would be using a new type of steel plate made by heating individual plates together to form a much thicker and stronger hull; Mersey Steel and Ironworks were rolling 1500 tons. On October 16th, Dudley reported that the first ram would be completed by mid–December. Security was watertight at the Lairds' yard and no one was being admitted unless they were known. Dudley would have to call on his "special detective" from London to glean some crumbs of intelligence that he could pass to the British government, but he was not too hopeful.³⁷

Shortly after Dudley reported to Seward, James Dunwoody Bulloch dealt with a more personal problem. One of his children, either James Jr. (4), Jessie Hart (2), or Henry Dunwody (1), was seriously ill. He and Harriott resorted to visiting a pediatric doctor in London. Fortunately, the child recovered.[38]

In America, his stepmother Martha received news of James Dunwoody and Harriott as well. Martha wrote to Susy (Susan) in Philadelphia telling her that Harriott had seen Irvine, Bulloch's half-brother, in August (before he sailed with Semmes on the *Bahama*) and that she had received a photograph of James Dunwoody Bulloch, Jr. The delight in Martha's letter at hearing that all were safe and sound is palpable.[39]

In Richmond, Secretary Mallory came to grips with the funding issues of the Confederacy's European shipbuilding program. On 27 October 1862, he sent Bulloch "a draft on Fraser, Trenholm and Co. for [$]1,000,000 of bonds" and he hoped "to send the first of a second million next week." Mallory's next letter referred to a "secret session" of the Confederate Congress. It described the cotton bond program and how the Confederate government was finally acting on Bulloch's pleas about finances.[40] Two days later, Mallory told Bulloch to name the two new rams "*North Carolina*" and "*Mississippi*." And if the rapid onset of armored ships had not been enough to terrify the world at large, Mallory closed this very short letter by asking Bulloch to investigate "experiments of firing guns underwater, the gun itself being submerged as well as the target." Effective underwater weapons were technically infeasible at the time, but Mallory envisioned the modern submarine warfare of the twentieth and twenty-first centuries.[41]

Back in Liverpool, Bulloch dealt with operational issues such as inquiries from James North about Whitworth guns for his ironclad and the progress of his rams. Bulloch reckoned that Whitworth's guns were the equals of Armstrong's weapons (another British naval gun builder), but the British government favored Armstrong. Concerning his own rams, he described one as being "one-third plated, not armoured, and the beams will soon be across" while the other was "half in frame" (a more realistic assessment than the alarmist reports from Dudley's agents).[42]

The subject of what type of naval guns to use on both North's ironclad and Bulloch's rams came up again on 6 November 1862. Bulloch resolved the problem by process of elimination, the "armament of turret ships being limited, of necessity, to a very few guns." He decided to mount the largest caliber guns possible. This is exactly the same advice Ericsson provided to Union Secretary of the Navy Welles: use the biggest gun possible to smash the opposing the vessel, whether it was armored or not. Bulloch also needed a formal acknowledgement from North of his changed orders so that he could "re-transfer" responsibility for the *No. 61* contract back to North.[43]

There was no small amount of competition. North implored the Thomson brothers not to let Bulloch "get ahead of us.... They (in Liverpool) will be working under sheds during the winter, so that we must look out." While North said he wanted to complete his build at the same time as Bulloch, he desperately wished to redeem his reputation by finishing his *No. 61* first.[44]

While James North struggled to sustain the construction of his ironclad, Bulloch was fully in his one-man (naval) band mode. He discovered that Le Mat revolvers had "serious defects" that forced him to decline any more unless they were "subject to inspection." He then noted that the manufacturing costs for revolvers in England ranged from 63 shillings for an "ordinary revolver" to five pounds each for a Girard "grape-shot" revolver made by the "London Armory Co.," inferring that the Navy Department had paid too much for too little quality.[45]

As North had observed, the Lairds constructed eight sheds for the armored rams and equipped them with gas (for lighting) "to insure additional hours for work during the short, foggy days of this climate." Bulloch decided how he would arrange the escape of the first ram after she was ready for sea in early April 1863. Citing the need for secrecy, he dared not reveal his plan to Mallory in a letter, but he hoped that the secretary trusted him to deliver the ship without violating the British neutrality laws. In a premonition of a shift in British policy, he added, "I am sanguine of success, unless the conduct of the British government to both belligerents is entirely changed." The British government was feeling the heat from the general public after Lincoln's Emancipation Proclamation, the steady news of the ships sent to the bottom by the *Alabama* and the constant pounding on the door by U.S. Minister Adams caused the British lion to growl.[46]

As a result, Bulloch knew that he would have to crew the rams differently. He proposed that the Navy Department select a core group of good naval and marine officers, along with some non-commissioned officers, who had proven Southern "citizenship." This first detachment should sail to the Island of Madeira, notify Bulloch of their arrival by both British and Portuguese mail, and be ready to sortie from the island in an instant should local authorities get inquisitive as they did with the *Alabama*. In that event, the senior officer should entrust a letter with the British consul addressed for Capt. W. Arkwright of the British steamer *Carnatic* saying he had "gone out for a few days." If the situation remained unsafe, the Confederate steamer could sail to Ponta Delgada after leaving notice, again with the British consul, for Capt. Arkwright. Finally, if the British consul were suspect in his sympathy, "one officer in plain clothes and warned to be discreet" could be left behind with a description of the *Carnatic* and then personally deliver the Confederate commander's message. Bulloch was leaving nothing to chance.[47]

Moving on, Bulloch noted that he reckoned the second ram would be ready by the first of June 1863. Referring back to his 12 July 1862 letter, he reaffirmed his desire to get them afloat, but "I feel bound to submit with becoming grace to any assignment of duty you may think the interests of the public service require." He then turned to the possibility of building *more* armored ships.[48]

There was additional capacity in Liverpool, but Bulloch didn't have enough money to pay off the ships currently under construction. The resourceful agent still thought that he might be able to get new builds under way even without funds. He was in discussion with a willing builder of an "ironclad ship of about 2,300 tons, drawing 14 feet" and with "certain parties who are willing or are professing their willingness to build without any cash advances." This willingness was contingent upon Fraser, Trenholm and Co.'s promise to guarantee payments. Bulloch coyly noted that the potential financial backers of this ironclad were "persons of capital and influence" and their promise to build, supply and arm the proposed vessel, including delivering it offshore, was almost too good to pass up. Was he being played by financial sharps or were they legitimate? Without names it is hard to pass judgment, so we can only rely on his demonstrated ability to differentiate among the charlatans, schemers, frauds, and other self-interested parties that beat a regular path to his door with similar promises.[49]

Amazingly, Bulloch also turned his mind to naval matters *within* the Confederacy, mentioning that he had read reports in Northern newspapers that "you are building quite a number of rams in the home ports." He suggested that engines could be contracted for and built in Liverpool and then shipped to the Confederacy. Bulloch then repeated his admonition that the Confederate Navy Department must issue the contracts, and *not* private individuals who invariably caused financial problems for all concerned.[50]

Returning to his own front in the naval war, Bulloch retained Lt. Hamilton as an attaché to help him oversee the construction of a new gunboat by Fawcett and Preston, the prime contractors for the *Florida*. Hamilton would have been Bulloch's first officer on the *Alabama* under Mallory's original orders. But Semmes had enough officers, so he left Hamilton with Bulloch. However, Fraser, Trenholm and Co. decided to build their own gunboat and wanted Hamilton to manage the effort, and Bulloch acceded to their request. He kindly requested that Mallory consider Hamilton for command of the vessel when completed due to "his disappointment in not going out as first-lieutenant on the *Alabama* ... [and] the intelligence and interest he has shown in superintending the ship." Along with the fact that he was already *in situ* made him an obvious choice. More importantly, Bulloch had confidence in him.[51]

Closing with comments on recent events, he recounted an extraordinary report from Captain Julius of the *Tonawanda*, one of the *Alabama*'s seizures. Julius said that "she is the fastest ship under canvas" he had ever seen. Bulloch thought that if the war kept on until the next summer "the Confederate Navy will be upon the sea in no contemptible force." He only wished he was afloat in one of those ships, particularly the *Alabama*, writing, "I confess to feeling a disappointment with at having been obliged to part with her."[52]

Across the Atlantic, Martha Bulloch tried to sustain the familial bonds by collecting and dispersing family news as best she could. Martha orchestrated the shipment of important domestic supplies to Lucy (Lucinda) Ireland Sorrel Elliott, the widow of Martha's son Daniel Stewart from her first marriage to Senator John Elliott. Daniel (commonly called "Stewart" or "Stuart" after 1853) led a life filled with mishap and tragedy. He joined the Confederate Army at the outbreak of war and died of tuberculosis in August 1862. He was buried in the Roswell Presbyterian Church Cemetery. Martha's packages traveled from New York to Charleston via Nassau-based blockade runners and included cloth for Lucy's mourning dress. Mittie would help ship the packages while her husband was out of town. This subterfuge inspired the game of "Running the Blockade" that her children played in Central Park. Anna played the role of a runner and tried to get past her younger brother Theodore, who assumed the role of the blockading Union Navy.

On 10 November 1862, the adults introduced a new version of the game. Martha wrote her daughter Susan in Philadelphia, "If you send a letter to Mr. Caskie, direct the inner envelope to Lucy and the outer to Gen. Dix Commandant of Fortress Monroe." This seemingly offhand comment provided a tantalizing glimpse into the intensely personal and complicated nature of North-South communications during the American Civil War.[53]

Major General John Adams Dix was a political general from New York, a former governor, secretary of the treasury, and senator. He was well known to Theodore Roosevelt, Sr., who met with Dix during the war at his headquarters in Fort Monroe, Virginia. Perhaps more importantly, the widow of General Dix's brother, Lt. Col. Roger Sherman Dix, had just married Harriott Bulloch's father! Mary Dix married Bulloch's father-in-law Colonel Osborne Cross of the U.S. Army Quartermaster Corps on 8 Jul 1862. This was less than six months after the death of his first wife, Louise, the mother of Harriott Cross Bulloch.[54] When Theodore Roosevelt met with Bulloch's new uncle, General Dix, at Fort Monroe in October 1862, they must have discussed their mutual rebel in-law.[55]

The reference to "Mr. Caskie" in Martha's letter of November 10th is to James K. Caskie, the brother of Bulloch's first wife (Lizzie), and a wealthy Richmond tobacconist and merchant. Bulloch and the rest of his extended family maintained close relationships with his former Caskie in-laws prior to the war. Despite the outbreak of hostilities, the Caskies continued to receive packages from Martha as well as from Bulloch's wife, Harriott, via the blockade runner *Giraffe*. James Caskie also played a role in forwarding official letters to and from Bulloch and the Confederate Navy Department. In a January 1863 letter to Mallory, Bulloch says, "Send your letters to Mr. James K. Caskie, who has already forwarded you one from me."[56] It is unknown whether Bulloch used the double-envelope communication system via Dix for any official communications. General Dix wisely made no mention of Bulloch or the Roosevelts in his memoirs.[57]

Five days later, Martha Bulloch wrote to Susan again, saying, "We have not written to Harriott yet because we have heard that the House to which we direct is in bad repute here, consequently, our letters would not leave N York."[58] Union postmasters had their eye on suspected Confederate mailboxes after President Lincoln's proclamation of 16 July 1861 made all communications between the North and South unlawful.

Back in Great Britain, on 21 November 1862, James North asked Bulloch whether he had seen the Whitworth gun in action and judged its performance. Bulloch replied that he "believed it [the Whitworth] to be the strongest now made." Whitworth's guns were the "most perfect and thorough" he had ever seen — high praise from a perfectionist himself. Bulloch also allayed North's financial concerns over *No. 61*; her next payments would appear in Thomson hands on the appropriate date.[59]

Bulloch had other pressing matters. A decision had to be made about the fate of the *Sumter*, Semmes' blockaded cruiser that still languished in Gibraltar harbor. Commissioner Mason finally decided she should be sold, with all equipment, to the highest bidder. If no bidders could be found, Fraser, Trenholm and Co. would buy her for the "appraised price." Three days later, Bulloch received and forwarded Mallory's letter to Prioleau acknowledging his company's "munificent gift" of a gunboat for the Confederate Navy. This gunboat was the ill-fated (as far as the Confederacy was concerned) *Alexandra*. It was named for the Princess of Wales who entered London on the same day that the ship was launched (7 March 1863).[60]

In the midst of all this, Bulloch met with Commander Matthew F. Maury, CSN, after he landed in Liverpool on 23 November 1862. Fresh off the *Arabia*, the "Father of Oceanography" and "Pathfinder of the Seas" was so well-known that it is remarkable that he and Bulloch met at the offices of Fraser, Trenholm and Co. Union counterintelligence must have been near apoplectic. The internationally famous Maury was on "special service" and his area of research was "the manufacture and use of gun-cotton, torpedoes, magnetic exploders and electric wire." Guncotton was an explosive used in early mines and torpedoes, created by soaking cotton in nitric and sulphuric acids that were then rinsed and dried. He was the prime research scientist for the "Torpedo Service," a covert "special service" that operated under great secrecy, similar to the Confederate Secret Service and Signal Corps.[61]

Maury carried a letter from Mallory (dated 20 September 1862) that informed Bulloch of his financial responsibilities in supporting Maury vis-à-vis pay and other expenses. Other than that, Maury was operating independently. As both men were well versed in operational security and compartmentalization (as it is now known), they both knew that the less they were seen together or knew about each other's projects, the better. The compartmentalization of their overlapping missions regarding the acquisition of commerce raiders, however, would prove to be another Mallory-inspired mess that Bulloch had to clean up. Like Maffitt, the brilliant, but physically infirm, Maury was no admirer of Mallory. The secretary was happy to have Maury out of his thinning hair and out of the country.

Maury's international prominence would hold no charm for U.S. Consul Dudley and his agents, either. U.S. Minister Adams would get less sleep now. Tailing Bulloch was bad enough, but Maury could operate "above the waterline" and in the public eye. His propaganda value to the Confederacy alone was incalculable as he rendered the quasi-nation a patina of scientific respect, which in science-obsessed Victorian Britain was nearly a religion.[62]

Matthew Fontaine Maury, Confederate Navy commander, European agent, and mine warfare expert (U.S. Naval Historical Center).

As Maury caught a train to London, Bulloch returned to the matter of the *Sumter*. On 25 November 1862, he ordered James A. K. Wilson, an agent for Fraser, Trenholm and Co., to sell the *Sumter*. Wilson was to proceed to Gibraltar with all speed, obtain an inventory of the ship from Lt. Chapman concerning its equipment and stores, and then to auction her. Wilson had power of attorney along with Bulloch's admonishment that he was to act in "due regards to ... interests" of the Confederacy, i.e., get the best price possible.[63] He hoped to be rid of the *Sumter* within the next two weeks and expected a net return of £6,000 from the sale (about $24,000 U.S. in 1862).[64]

As December began, Bulloch struggled with unreliable communications with Richmond, trying to fathom which letters Mallory had and had not received and how they might have influenced his instructions. In the meantime, Maury needed Bulloch in London, where he arrived on December 3rd, to discuss a project. James Spence, a wealthy Liverpool merchant and cotton broker was in London trying to raise money using cotton bonds from Mallory. Bulloch did not hesitate to criticize the tardiness of the Confederate government in addressing finances, particularly with the news that a French firm, Erlanger and Co. of Paris, proposed an immense loan to the Confederacy. Future events would darken the silvery financial cloud promised by Erlanger and Co., but Bulloch's point was valid. For now, he had money enough for the next few months to pay for the rams, but he would need more money soon. He noted that the increased Union counterintelligence effort was giving his efforts "great publicity."[65]

In America, or rather in the Union, Martha Bulloch still attempted to ship items across the Atlantic to Harriott and James. On the 5th of December, Martha reported that she went "to 36th St. [New York] where a lady gave her another address to Harriott," and she sent another "bundle by Miss Tiernan."[66] Even though Martha Bulloch was in the North and James and Harriott Bulloch were in an ostensibly "friendly" country, they knew that their mail was being watched and obviously opened. The eyes of Seward, Stanton, and Welles were upon them.

The heartening news of the tremendous success of the Confederacy's land forces at Fredericksburg, Virginia, was several weeks away for Bulloch as he considered the 8- and 9-inch naval guns intended for North's ironclad, *No. 61*. Having received technical information from Col. William Clay, the managing director of the Mersey Steel & Iron Co. of Liverpool that manufactured breech-loading field guns, Bulloch stated that since Clay had never made any guns of this size, he could only give a very conservative estimate of the price that James North would be charged. At £500 for the 9-inch and £400 for the 8-inch guns, North had a case of severe sticker-shock when he received Bulloch's letter, as this was a lot of money in 1862.[67] The following day, Bulloch received an early Christmas present. Four letters from Sec. Mallory arrived dating from 23 July to 4 November 1862. One of them included a check for $1,000,000 to be "paid out of the proceeds of the (cotton) bonds now in the hands of Mr. Spence." Interspersed within these letters were issues and orders, large and small, including a request to have Confederate Navy commission forms engraved and printed. Bulloch responded on the same day, patiently acknowledging each of Mallory's letters and even explaining the reason he had not acted on Mallory's previous request for the commission forms (he had not received the desired designs from Richmond).[68] The rest of Bulloch's 18 December 1862 letter is revealing, for Mallory had received and approved his plans for the armored rams:

> I am gratified to learn that you approve of my designs for the two armor-clad ships.... As their life must necessarily begin with a sea voyage of over 3,000 miles, it was absolutely necessary to secure fair seagoing qualities and good speed, which, I think, could not have been accomplished on less draft and dimensions. I designed these ships for something more than harbor or even coast defense, and I confidently believe if ready for sea now, they could sweep away the entire blockading fleet of the enemy. Some of the Federal ironclads are undoubtedly formidable, and our two could not probably cope with them in smooth water. But then ours could shun the heavy, unwieldy tubs the enemy have thus far built and would drown them out at sea.[69]

Bulloch clearly believed that his rams would be able to do what none of the British, Union, or French ironclads had managed to achieve: transoceanic cruising for combat operations. To demonstrate how well Bulloch was on top of technical activity in relation to armor and arms tested, he ventured to offer Mallory some advice:

> The results of experiments here and on the Continent have led to the belief that nothing is gained by inclining the sides of armored ships, especially if intended for sea service. At Shoeburyness and in Holland plates have been penetrated at whatever angle placed, even as acute as 65°, hence all iron ships building in Europe have vertical sides to get more room.[70]

7. Of Incalculable Value

His following comments illustrate how closely Bulloch was co-operating with British technical experts on the art of armored ship construction:

> Upon the conclusion of the treaty for authority to use the revolving turret [for his Laird rams], I found that our dimensions were almost precisely those adopted by Captain Coles for the Royal Sovereign, and the size and weight of guns, as well as the method of mounting them, are so nearly identical that one would suppose there had been previous consultation, which was not the case. Captain Coles suggested one important improvement, viz, to make the turntable and turret itself eccentric, so that when the guns were run out the weight would be balanced and the training more easily effected.[71]

Regarding the other large ironclad mentioned in his previous letter, Bulloch had decided to reject the "mysterious" investors' offer. It cost too much, relied on risky new technology, and his conversations with Matthew Maury led him to believe that the ironclads currently being built by the Confederacy were fully capable of their intended missions. Consequently, he was happy to continue building wooden ships of the commerce-raiding type, though of course, money would have to be forthcoming. Great Britain was still a cash up-front shipbuilding environment and the British builders didn't want to be left holding the bag if the Confederacy suddenly collapsed. Bulloch closed his report saying that he was looking forward to the arrival of another $100,000 that Mallory had promised. That amount would keep things going for another six weeks. After that, he and the other Confederate agents, with the assistance of Fraser, Trenholm and Co. and James Spence, would have to fend for themselves and trust to their luck.[72]

Had Dudley or Adams gotten hold of Bulloch's letter of December 18th, war might have ensued between Great Britain and the Union. Intelligence that one of the acknowledged technical experts on armored ship design was cooperating with the Confederate Navy would have been explosive. Bulloch's comments about British naval officers' admiration of Confederate and Union accomplishments in the field of ironclads in such a short time, also illustrate their concern that the British were falling behind.

However, there would be no sea-going Confederate ironclads to admire if Bulloch and North could not obtain financing and equitable treatment by the British government. The money situation for James North seemed to improve just a few days before Christmas 1862. Bulloch was very surprised to learn that North was on the verge of closing a lucrative cotton deal. He had managed to get a promise to buy cotton (from the Confederate government) at 8 to 10 cents per pound. Bulloch was amazed at the price and told North that was "in favour of your closing [the deal] at once." He then followed with sage advice that was not only good for James North, but also would have been even better if the Confederate government had heeded: "Men will rarely part with money for paper, unless the collateral security is ample and tangible." Bulloch remonstrated that he should close the deal quickly.[73]

On the Sunday after his first Christmas in England, Bulloch was attending to some letters at home when he came across another one from James North (sent on the 26th and delivered late on the 27th). North was still trying to nail down designs and financing for the guns on *No. 61* in Glasgow. Bulloch's response provided a revealing disclosure of the state of the Confederate Navy's funding. While there had been recent deposits of funds from the Navy Department to Fraser, Trenholm and Co., the company had such a large outlay of advance payments to other departments that even the deep pockets of the "Bankers of the Confederacy" were temporarily empty. Bulloch had promised to make no more draws

The Laird ram "El Tousson" in Liverpool (*Harper's Weekly*, 19 December 1863).

upon their resources and told the Thomsons in Glasgow that no funds would be heading there for *No. 61* until January.

As Bulloch bluntly explained, "All further operations are for the present at a deadlock." If North could forward him a statement of what he needed for a cash deposit, he would see if Fraser, Trenholm and Co. could at least meet that need. In the meantime, Bulloch recommended that North pursue his cotton sale with all possible speed, noting that cash is best, for "the character of the person is nothing, if he purchases for cash." He added a warning about a "gentleman" involved in North's potential cotton sales: "Mr. E.P.S. [Edgar P. Stringer] is something more than sharp, and I advise you to be cautious."[74]

Bulloch finally closed his letter-book on an extraordinary year, not only for himself, but also for the Confederate Navy and the history of naval warfare. He had successfully returned from a run through the blockade, having taken the *Fingal* into Savannah with an enormous load of war material. He had gotten the *Florida* and *Alabama* safely out of Liverpool and had another "gift" gunboat under construction, even with a strong Union counterintelligence effort trying to pressure the British government into subverting his operations. Now, he had two ocean-going armored rams under construction as well as numerous "lesser" efforts that included purchasing weapons, funding and managing personnel, and covertly evaluating new weapons. James Dunwoody Bulloch was a one-man Navy Department. But would 1863 improve upon these successes? Not even Bulloch's seemingly clear crystal ball could see what was coming. It would be a pivotal year. He would have to conjure even greater feats of naval magic to overcome the forces that were aligning against the Confederacy.

8

Grim Aspect and Formidable Equipment — 1863

As the New Year's Day 1863 festivities in Liverpool faded into memory, James Dunwoody Bulloch looked forward to launching the world's first transoceanic armored warships. He had two of these formidable ironclads under construction in the Lairds' shipyard in Liverpool, while his erstwhile counterpart, Commander James North, had an armored ship on the way at the Thomsons' shipyard in Glasgow. Then, there were the commerce raiders of Lt. John Hamilton (the *Alexandra*) and Lt. George T. Sinclair (the *Canton/Pampero*) rapidly nearing completion at the Lairds' and Thomsons' shipyards, respectively. The Confederates were building these ships as fast as their finances and the available ship building ways would allow. Little did Bulloch and his fellow officers know that the Confederacy's grand strategic dreams were about to collide with broader, geopolitical realities.

Back in the Union, Lincoln's Emancipation Proclamation took effect on January 1, 1863. Even though the Proclamation only applied to those states that were in rebellion and not to the slaves in the North, it was very well received in Europe. In the Confederacy, "cottonclads" under the command of Confederate Major General John B. Magruder achieved a remarkable victory over Union forces at the Battle of Galveston Bay. Union naval forces had seized this primary port in Texas in the fall of 1862. In response, Magruder's Marine Department created their own "armored" vessels using compressed bales of cotton. With desperate bravery, they captured the famous Union gunboat *Harriet Lane*, and forced the ignominious withdrawal of the remaining Union naval forces and the abandonment of the army forces ashore.[1]

In Europe, Bismarck, the minister-president of Prussia, orchestrated a dramatic budget increase for his military forces. Bismarck, who became known as the "Iron Chancellor," aligned himself with Russia, not only in the partitioning of Poland, but also in controlling its restless citizens when they attempted to force concessions from the czar. The foundation for a series of devastating conflicts was laid in 1863 that would engulf the entire world after the turn of the century.

But it was a series of events on the far side of the world that would more directly determine the fate of James Dunwoody Bulloch's blue-water Confederate Navy. It is possible that events in China had as much to do with the demise of the Confederate States of America as did the Battle of Gettysburg. China was the country that Thomas Butler King dreamed would be the economic panacea for the Confederacy. For if Confederate forces could reach

California, her ports and her gold, coupled with a transcontinental Confederate railroad (built with French assistance), the South would become a truly continental power with unimpeded access to China. The Great Powers would need the Confederate States of America for ready access to Chinese markets, or so the Confederate strategists believed.

European powers, particularly the British Empire, already had a political, economic, and military presence in China and wanted to ensure that they retained control of its development. However, a massive civil war had been raging in China for over a decade prior to the American Civil War. Commonly referred to as the Taiping Revolt, it began in 1850 when a Christian religious charismatic named Hong Xiuchuan convinced a few hundred thousand countrymen that he was the conquering brother of Jesus. By 1851, the Taiping ("Heavenly Kingdom") grew into a near million-man army. As the American Union began to disintegrate, the Taipings had captured most of south and central China. Most importantly, they controlled the fertile Yangtze River region.[2] The collapse of a stable nexus of power at the center of the Chinese state worried Great Britain, but the Foreign Enlistment Act of 1819 stipulated neutrality and complicated Britain's ability to actively influence events. The same legal sanction that James Bulloch had, so far, been successfully evading, also prevented the British government from overtly intervening in China, or so it seemed.

By 1861, China's lack of a strong central government threatened to unravel the diplomatic fabric that Britain had so carefully woven into its economic and military control of the Far East. It was the British Empire at its best, expending the least amount of the exchequer's pound for maximum profit. There was more than a bit of British cultural paternalism in its assumed duty and ability to orchestrate proper control of China. Any Chinese or Taiping resentment that British interference may have engendered was easily dismissed as indigenous myopia.[3]

Increased piracy and armed robbery of British and other Europeans, coupled with a declining capacity for *any* form of Chinese government security on her coasts or waterways, meant a greater demand on Royal Navy assets. More importantly, at least to Palmerston and Russell, if the Taipings or any other Chinese factions could not be properly "restructured" (read: "controlled"), British interests were at risk. The British certainly understood the Chinese proclivity for playing the various maritime trading nations against one another; they learned that from experience in India. Something had to be done, and quickly. Fortunately, several of the British Empire's more aspiring and adept civil servants had been considering their options. Robert Hart, a British interpreter attached to the Chinese Imperial Maritime Customs service had a solution.[4] He promoted the idea of deploying a British-built flotilla of modern steam warships that could navigate and police China's inland waterways.

By mid-summer of 1861, both Prince Kung, the Chinese emperor's brother and diplomat for European affairs, and British Ambassador Sir Frederick Bruce reached a tacit agreement on Hart's proposal. Thoroughly aware of Queen Victoria's recent Proclamation of Neutrality as it applied to the Confederate warships, Sir Frederick carefully avoided public scrutiny of the Chinese deal. In turn, the British Foreign Office, like Bulloch, considered its options for adhering to the letter of an inconvenient law while building and delivering a fleet of gunboats to a favored belligerent.[5]

While the Chinese emperor scraped together the funds to pay for an entire flotilla, Hart's superior, the optimistically named Horatio Nelson Lay, became more involved in the project. As the inspector-general of the Imperial Maritime Customs Service, Lay would later loudly proclaim that *he* had originated the idea for the flotilla that would bear his name. The 30-year-old Lay had been employed in China for 15 years and was fully aware of the geopolitical climate after the U.S. and Great Britain had stepped back from the precipice of war over the *Trent* affair (Mason and Slidell were headlining London newspapers at the time). He quietly pushed the China flotilla scheme through Lord Russell's Foreign Office and directly to Prime Minister Palmerston.

Lay tested the waters of public opinion by asking the editor of the *Times* of London, John T. Delane, what possible positive editorial support he might expect should his China escapade be made public. He also contacted Capt. Sherard Osborn, who had commanded HMS *Furious* off China (1857–1859) about his interest in commanding the still-to-be-built flotilla of ships.[6] While the ambitious inspector-general did not intend to command this flotilla at sea, like Bulloch, he orchestrated its creation, organization, and operations.

By the time Lay returned to China, Prince Kung seemed to have fulfilled Lay's naval dreams when he named him as inspector-general of the flotilla. Nothing was specified about overall command, however. On 14 March 1862, Lay received the first Chinese funds and alerted Sherard Osborn that he should seek release from his naval command, as the project was moving forward. On 29 May 1862, Osborn reached Lay in London, having been released by the Royal Navy. They organized the Chinese Government Agency, complete with a list of objectives, operational procedures, as well as a list of legal and organizational questions surrounding the building and manning of the ships that required legal counsel opinions. Favorable answers to these questions were key to both their naval aspirations and, unknowingly, to those of James Dunwoody Bulloch and the Confederate Navy. All of these parallel developments were occurring virtually at the same time as the launch and escape of the *Alabama* from Liverpool.[7]

Before Lay could properly submit his explanatory memorandum to Lord Russell on 16 June 1862, the China project was already common knowledge. The First Lord of the Admiralty, the Duke of Somerset, posted a note to Russell the day *before* (15 June 1862) excitedly supporting the idea. Not surprisingly, some of the phrasing within Somerset's letter was the same as Lay's "official" submission, but the key issue was neutrality. For British subjects (military or otherwise) to serve upon British-built warships that had been outfitted for a foreign civil war by British subjects, the Neutrality Ordinance of 1854 would have to be repealed. Like Bulloch, Lay was not hesitant to imply that he would take his business elsewhere if his maritime shipbuilding and supply needs could not be met in England.[8]

The quiet display of *realpolitik* by the British Foreign Office would have made the rising Bismarck of Prussia proud. Just as the Confederate diplomat Thomas Butler King had surmised, Lord Russell commented in late June 1862, "Our trade with China is now of vast importance—all the more as the U.S. by their quarrel have deprived us of so much of our valuable importations."[9]

Horatio Nelson Lay believed he now had a clear field of action and filed for a Queen's License. This request would allow Lay and Osborn to perform naval and military service for the Chinese emperor's government, build and outfit ships for service in China, and most importantly, *enlist* British subjects for naval and military action in China. If Bulloch's activities raised diplomatic eyebrows and Palmerston's blood pressure, this was a whole new kettle of cuttlefish. One could hear the collective sucking in of breath between clenched teeth at the British Foreign Office when they read Lay's application. While the stalwart civil servants within the Foreign Office recognized the contradictory policy implications, Russell merely looked away and passed Lay's request to the Home Office for determination.[10]

Convoluted cabinet-level discussions aided by judicious legal advocates resulted in a Queen's License for everything that Lay and Osborn wanted: with the exception of the part about enlisting British sailors in Britain. However, a letter from Lord Russell to Sir Frederick Bruce in late July 1862 reassured Lay and Osborn that they could still obtain good men for the gunboats. The clear implication was that as long as British sailors were recruited offshore, just as Bulloch had done, Lay would be in strict compliance with the letter of the law. The Royal Navy and the Foreign Office would not allow the Home Office's mincing sensibilities to get in their way. They worked directly with Lay and Osborn to facilitate the necessary contracting and logistic purchasing arrangements for ships and war material to launch their China flotilla!

While Lord Russell ruminated on Union protestations over the *Alabama*, Bulloch ran about Liverpool recruiting offshore sailors and buying up naval stores right, left, and amidships. The Royal Navy did the same thing, but for its own "covert" China flotilla.[11] The Royal Navy effort was good for the economy and advanced British geopolitical goals. Although Bulloch's efforts were an even greater economic boon, the political implications were less clear.

The Home Office remained at odds with Russell's Foreign Office and the Royal Navy's efforts to support the Lay-Osborn project. More legal machinations and opinions were demanded and issued over the problems of enlisting British subjects and authorizing a license to build or buy ships for a foreign civil war. Lay, like Bulloch, feared his ships would be seized for violating the neutrality laws. As a result, Russell was keen to help Lay, but was equally willing to let Bulloch and the Confederacy hang. Lay and Osborn were already considering "hiring" a crew in Hong Kong or, following Bulloch's model, afloat.[12]

Seeing an opportunity to decisively deal with the China problem, Lord Russell was determined to provide Lay with the ships and everything else he needed. After considerable legal and political jousting between the Foreign and Home Offices, the official Order in Council was issued on 30 August 1862: Lay and Osborn were in business. The order was issued just in time, for two days earlier, Lay had precipitously purchased five ships, lock, stock, and cannon-barrel. During this time, the *Alabama* escaped to sea and enlisted a British crew in the Azores. When Bulloch returned to the Liverpool piers on the *Bahama* on 31 August 1862, he heard the news that "someone" had just bought five gunboats for use in China's civil war. This extraordinary development, sanctioned with a Queen's License to boot, would have encouraged him to believe that the coast was clear for the Confederate Navy's armored ship program, despite Adams' and Dudley's best representations. The British exploited or created a loophole in their own legal system to pursue imperial interests in China.[13]

Flush with anticipated success, Lay and Osborn confidently expanded the flotilla to seven steam warships and one support vessel that were ready to depart in the first week of January 1863.[14] As Bulloch scanned the Mersey waterfront on the way from his home in Waterloo to his office at 10 Rumford Place in Liverpool, he wondered long and hard about British intentions toward the Confederacy. Lay was steaming an entire squadron through a

8. Grim Aspect and Formidable Equipment

legal loophole the size of Portsmouth Harbor. While Bulloch struggled to launch his own flotilla, he must have shared some of Lay's optimism. At the moment, though, Bulloch had to solve more immediate problems and they all revolved around money.

By 5 January 1863, Bulloch's accounts were almost exhausted. He needed to place contracts for the guns and ordnance to outfit his rams. He also needed additional financing to pay off the entire build. He hopefully looked to Commissioner James Mason in London for news on the much-touted Erlanger bond sales. When would he and the other Confederate agents and representatives in Europe receive any of the proceeds promised by the French financier? How long should he wait upon this promised financing miracle before once again making his own financial arrangements?[15]

Bulloch was happy to bring Mason up to date on his success with the *Alabama* and the *Bahama*. He also hoped that Lt. Chapman had been successful in selling the *Sumter* in Gibraltar. Chapman, the officer who had been left in charge of the ship, reported his status to Bulloch who passed it along to London. Even though it was now British property, Bulloch speculated that the USS *Chippewa* might venture to stop the *Sumter* on her voyage back to Britain. A British buyer bought her and he reckoned the Union Jack flying at the mast might give the Union captain pause. The *Sumter* was British property now and the *Trent* affair was still a black cloud on the periphery of everyone's memory.[16]

A few days later on 7 January 1863 Bulloch wrote an encrypted letter to Sec. Mallory describing the legal maneuvering and Union attempts to stop the *Alabama* from sailing and having her seized. Bulloch told Mallory that he learned (though he does not say how) that:

> [In] one of [the] foreign secretary's letters to [the] Federal minister ... the unexpected illness of the Queen's Advocate [Harding] had caused delay in getting a legal opinion, and when a substitute for that officer was consulted he advised that the ship should be detained. I learned that something of the kind was going on and hurried off the ship ... am greatly concerned lest the complaints of the Federal minister may induce the British authorities to act more promptly in any case of the kind; that our ironclads may be permanently shut up if not seized; evident from conduct of [the] British Government that foreign enlistment act will be very strictly construed when applied to our acts. Dread of offending [the] United States seems to be British rule.... Incautious step might involve forfeiture of ships. Shall go [on] as if sure of success.... Not able to raise money yet on bonds or cotton.[17]

In the hindsight of history and what is now known about the Lay-Osborn flotilla, this coded missive documents the Confederacy's perspective regarding the evidence of British duplicity in their subjective and inequitable application of their own Neutrality and Foreign Enlistment Acts. It seems clear that if the situation might benefit the British Empire, the British government would apply a flexible interpretation of the neutrality laws. If the situation might harm imperial interests, severe restrictions were in order. While Bulloch understandably complained about Union pressure on the Foreign Office, what neither Bulloch nor U.S. Minister Adams fully understood was the policy implications of the Lay-Osborn China project.[18] Britain masked its true intentions toward more strategic interests, focused on China at that moment, behind the appearance of being concerned with overlapping Union and Confederate neutrality issues in North America.

As the Chinese Year of the Dog turned into the Year of the Pig (1863), Bulloch had to deal with James North. This time, he complained about his inability to sell cotton to finance further construction on his *No. 61* ironclad. Bulloch empathized with North's problem, but had to remind him that although the unwieldy ironclad was still officially in Bulloch's name, his plate was full in dealing with *his* own projects. He did not have time to supervise a build he knew very little about. He left the matter in North's hands. Either North could resume control of the build or he would let the matter collapse under its own weight. Bulloch sent the Thomsons £22,000, but there was no more money. He was not optimistic for additional funding even with the hopeful advices of Commissioner Mason and agent Spence. Bulloch advised North to talk to William S. Lindsay and Co. They might get him through his financial bind for at least one payment. W.S. Lindsay would become important in Confederate naval affairs in the future, but for now Bulloch was off to Ireland.[19]

He returned to Liverpool about 16 January 1863 to find matters still in the same state of inertia: no money. Keeping busy for a few more days by attending to the Laird rams, Bulloch confided his anxiety to Commissioner Mason. He admitted that he saw no clear way to raise the funds needed to complete the rams. He did not want to interfere with the grander financial schemes or skew the hoped for success of the Erlanger bonds, which promised a cornucopia of money for the Confederacy. He updated Mason on the status of the *Sumter* noting that she had sailed for Britain, shadowed by the USS *Tuscarora*. Wryly, Bulloch noted that the British were happy to pocket the commission for the sale of the Confederacy's first truly successful commerce raider, but refused to escort her back to Britain to avoid confronting the Union Navy. A Royal Navy man-of-war departed Gibraltar for England at the same time as the *Sumter* that was now British property.[20] All the while, the Lay-Osborn flotilla was completing its outfitting and its loading of stores.

In the meantime, Bulloch finally rid himself of the responsibility for James North's *No. 61*. The morning of 26 January 1863 he notified the Thomsons that "for reasons which no longer exist ... said contract ... is hereby, retransferred to James H. North, Esq." Bulloch's hands were finally clean of the Scottish beast.[21]

On the home front, news from James and Harriott Bulloch's family was still reaching America. In New York, Martha Bulloch wrote to her daughter Susy Elliott West that James Caskie had received a package from Harriott in England. Caskie was in Richmond and the package had been run through the blockade aboard the Clyde-build, Confederate Navy steamer *Giraffe*. Three points could be made about this delivery. First, the Bullochs (and the South at large) were still able to penetrate the Union blockade, and second, a "Secret Route" mail service between the Confederacy and Union was still functional as evidenced by Caskie's ability to contact Martha Bulloch from his home in Richmond. The third, and most important point, as far as the Bullochs and Roosevelts were concerned, was that James Dunwoody, Harriott, and all their children were well.[22]

Despite the positive family news from the Bulloch household, on the professional front the Confederate agent was still frustrated by the lack of financial support from the Department of the Navy. He didn't hesitate to write to Mallory about it either. In early February 1863, Bulloch enciphered a message about the situation. It was a veritable litany of problems. Lack of money had delayed contracts for ordnance stores even though Fraser, Trenholm and Co. promised to meet all payments. Most worrisome were the "insurmountable difficulties" in getting the rams completed rapidly. In fact, he morosely observed: "No armoured ships for Admiralty have ever been completed in time specified ... great labour and unexpected time required to bend armour-plates ... the riveting, is far more tedious than anticipated." His next comment was the most telling, for he thought, "British government will prevent iron ships leaving, and am much perplexed; object of armoured ships too evident for disguise."[23] In closing, Bulloch believed it might be time to have ships built in France.[24]

Bulloch was spot-on in his analysis of the problems of building what was then leading-edge naval warfare technology. The metallurgical science behind armored ships was not well understood. What the exasperated Bulloch could not explain was the "unforeseen causes" behind the delays in other areas, or the British government's increasing recalcitrance surrounding attempts to circumvent the Neutrality Act. He had an inkling that something was up, for the Lairds built two of the eight ships belonging to the Lay-Osborn flotilla. The widespread knowledge within the maritime community that the ways had been "greased" for the rapid creation of the flotilla spoke volumes of quiet government support. In a little more than a week, Bulloch and the rest of Britain would find out what was transpiring.[25]

The 4th of February saw a potential brightening in a sky clouded by financial worries. Commissioner James Mason wanted to know how much money Bulloch needed to meet immediate payments on the rams. The commander, ever careful with his pennies and pence, quoted the full amount required to finish off both rams, some £80,000, but he only asked for £20,000. The fact that the Confederate Navy Department had sent drafts for $2,000,000, which were earmarked for the construction of more ships like the *Alabama* and advanced steam engines, did not help, for these funds were still in fiscal limbo.[26]

The financial strain began to wear on the recently patched-up professional relationship between North and Bulloch. North was upset that Bulloch provided a copy of a previous dispatch to Fraser, Trenholm and Co., whom North saw as a competitor for scarce funding. Despite Bulloch's promise of funding priority, he needed money *now*; at least enough to make a down payment on the armaments for *No. 61*. Completing all three armored vessels at the same time, as Mallory wished, would be impossible without funds. North suspected that Bulloch would give funding priority to the Laird rams and he was very reluctant to share information with Charles Prioleau after their recent and unpleasant exchanges related to the *Florida* and *Alabama*.[27]

Bulloch responded promptly, admitting that he had not even looked at the document that North had enclosed, presuming that he wanted it forwarded to Fraser, Trenholm and Co. as a requisition order. He had seen their address on the outside of the document and merely passed it on. Trying to calm North, he retrieved the letter and returned it. Bulloch assured him that as soon as Erlanger funds or Mallory's drafts became available, North's requests would be met. He even post-scripted that North could have the monies from the sale of the *Sumter*.

During this timeframe, the warships for the "other" civil war prepared to get under weigh. Bulloch had assumed that the success of the Lay-Osborn flotilla placed his Laird ironclads and the *Alexandra* on solid footing. If warships for the Chinese civil war could be built, outfitted, equipped, and manned in Liverpool, so could these Confederate warships. In a nation governed by laws, he expected equal treatment under the law. This proved to be a naïve assumption. In April and May, the Lay-Osborn flotilla, departed from Britain for China.[28] However, with the safe departure of the China flotilla, there was no longer any legal or political imperative for Lord Russell to grant the Confederacy the same privileges. By February, Bulloch was already well aware that there had been a shift in British policy that would treat his ships for the American Civil War quite differently. Twenty years later, the passage of time had only slightly tempered Bulloch's wartime sensitivity about the duplicitous behavior on the part of Lord Russell and the Foreign Office: "I do not now affirm that Earl Russell carried out the neutral policy of the (British) government with a deliberate purpose to favour one belligerent; all that I say is, that the course pursued by him was not in accordance with the principles laid down by himself and his colleagues, and by the judgement of the Lord Chief Baron of the Exchequer."[29]

Although this passage seemed to refer to the fairness of British policy that favored the North over the South in America, it also applied to the uneven application of the Neutrality and Foreign Enlistment Acts to the advantage of the Lay-Osborn flotilla. Needless to say, the Confederate Navy's leading foreign agent had used more colorful language in February 1863. Before this change in policy became general knowledge, Bulloch redoubled his efforts to get a transoceanic-capable ironclad into the Confederacy's hands, which meant he had to shift his focus to France.

Back in Richmond, Mallory affirmed Bulloch's acquisition of ironclads with open-ocean-cruising capability. Mallory observed that the *Monitor* had sunk in "comparatively" smooth water and that the *Galena* and *New Ironsides* were "neither invulnerable nor seaworthy."[30] Carrying on with his hopes for the successful launch of more vessels like the *Alabama* and *Florida*, Mallory encouraged Bulloch to meet with the Confederate commissioner to France, John Slidell, concerning the "practicability of fitting out your ships ... in French ports." Mallory clearly understood, as did Bulloch, that the high-water mark of Confederate Navy operations in Britain had passed. It was time to look elsewhere for a more conducive environment for the Confederacy's shipbuilding program.[31]

Communication delays, contradictory directives, and possibly stolen telegrams now plagued the Confederate effort at a critical moment. On 9 March 1863, Bulloch sent an enciphered message to Richmond via Baltimore (i.e., the "Secret Route"). Writing in a short cryptic manner due to the nature of the cipher code, he said, "Completion of armoured ships having been delayed, change of plan can be made. You can send officers to France as soon as possible. Will go to consult with our commissioner in France (Mr. Slidell) in a few days."[32]

Fortunately, Sec. Mallory received Bulloch's message of 23 January 1863 and had presciently decided to go ahead and send crews for the armored ship. Among the party of officers and sailors were Commander Thomas Jefferson Page and Lieutenants James I. Waddell, Robert R. Carter, William C. Whittle Jr., and Walter R. Butt. Mallory instructed that "all these men can be sent to the Continent ... or to any place they can join their ship." The Confederate Secretary of the Navy ended his message by noting that he approved of Bulloch's thoughts about building ships in France.[33]

As Bulloch went to meet with Slidell and his contacts in Paris, Dudley and Adams compiled yet another massive dossier. This time, their target was the *Alexandra*, the wooden hulled "gift" from Fraser, Trenholm and Co. Their concerns were obvious since the same consortium that had constructed the *Florida*, namely Fawcett & Preston along with W.C. Miller and Sons, was building the *Alexandra*. One of Dudley's best Liverpool informers reported that William Miller himself said that the new ship would be even faster than the *Florida*. With news about the successes of the *Alabama* and *Florida*'s commerce raiding already flowing into Britain, Dudley wasn't just alarmed; he was terrified at the prospects for Union shipping.[34]

8. Grim Aspect and Formidable Equipment

Alexandra, the "gift" Confederate raider (*Illustrated London News*).

While the wooden cruiser *Alexandra* was the most immediate threat to the Union, Bulloch's rams were not far behind; they received the full attention of Union counterintelligence. Dudley's informers had already told him that each ram had six watertight compartments, with engines capable of supplying a fast cruising speed. Even more revolutionary and perhaps with a nod to the innovation proposed by the still-born Stevens' ironclad, they had a compartment that allowed water to be pumped in and out, thus reducing the vessel's target signature above the waterline.[35]

While Dudley's agents focused on the shipyards on the Mersey and Clyde Rivers, Bulloch slipped out of Liverpool. More than ever sensing the dwindling prospects for Confederate aspirations in Britain, Bulloch surfaced in mid–March 1863 at the shipyard of Lucien Arman in Bordeaux, France. Once again, *a priori* intelligence had launched him into action. Confederate commissioner Slidell had taken the step of sending a business agent to alert Bulloch that Louis-Napoléon's government was amenable to a quiet shipbuilding program for the Confederacy. He leapt onto the first train and ferry to the Continent, eluding an exasperated Union agent.[36]

The beginning of the Confederate warship program in France represented the pinnacle of Bulloch's efforts for the Confederate Navy. The spring of 1863 was a season of hope in France and the Confederacy.

Arman's yards impressed Bulloch greatly, particularly their ability to build smaller ships in a modular fashion. More importantly, Arman was building two armored naval batteries at that moment, which spoke volumes about the technical proficiency of the French shipyard artisans.³⁷ Other than finance, his chief concern was the same as in Britain: a neutrality law. Hopefully, Arman could accomplish in France what Lay-Osborn had been able to accomplish in Britain: the sailing of armed warships to fight in a civil war. Arman told Bulloch not to worry; he need only fill out the proper applications to obtain "authorization to complete, arm, and despatch the ships for a specified purpose, which was in itself lawful." The government would not ask for any more information. In fact, Arman had conveniently spoken directly with Emperor Louis-Napoléon about building clipper ships to carry out trade between San Francisco, China, and Japan. They would of course have to be armed due to the instability in China. The Taiping Revolt, for which the Lay-Osborn flotilla was sailing at that very moment, gave Arman a convenient cover for himself and deniability for Louis-Napoléon. Any ships that Arman built could be sold to either the Chinese or the Japanese governments.³⁸

Bulloch had no way of verifying Arman's statements, but they were consistent with Slidell's information. Arman's subterfuge dovetailed with the Confederacy's grand geostrategic dream concerning China. Commissioner Slidell's former legal associate, Judah P. Benjamin, now Confederate secretary of state, had pushed for a railroad from New Orleans to the Pacific Ocean before the war (across the Central American Isthmus of Tehuantepec). As a congressman, Thomas Butler King envisioned and promoted a transcontinental railroad and canal across Panama to improve trade and communications with China as early as 1848. Slidell, with Benjamin's support and with Thomas Butler King still in Paris as an at-large emissary, floated the idea of a Confederacy stretching from sea-to-shining-sea (with a shiny set of rails connecting the two oceans) past Louis-Napoléon and his advisors. The Confederacy would be more than happy to support a puppet government in Mexico of Louis-Napoléon's design if he would support the Confederacy.³⁹

In November 1861, Thomas Butler King concluded a commercial agreement with France that would establish a trade route from Bordeaux and Le Havre to New Orleans and Savannah (if the Union blockade was ever broken).⁴⁰ Benjamin, Slidell, and Bulloch all hoped that Louis-Napoléon would recognize the Confederacy and take a firm hand in Mexico, with the Confederates rendering assistance in any way possible. The Confederacy's recent unsuccessful attempt by General Sibley to reach California via Texas was an expression of that goal. With French assistance, the Confederacy could still achieve continental conquest. Slidell's conversations stirred Louis-Napoléon's interest and imagination.⁴¹

On a practical level, Bulloch liked what he saw and heard from Arman. He told the French shipbuilder that he wished to contract for four clipper corvettes of 1,500 tons each, with 400hp steam engines, and batteries of between 12 and 14 rifled guns capable of firing 6-inch shells. He told Arman he would return to Liverpool to arrange the necessary finances for the project.⁴² As he made his way to a ferry bound for Great Britain, the Union hatched a plan in New York City to apply even more pressure to the Confederate naval building program in Britain.

On 15 March 1863, Union Secretary of the Treasury Salmon P. Chase convened a meeting with Navy Secretary Gideon Welles, John Murray Forbes (a Bostonian businessman), and William Aspinwall (a wealthy New York businessman and shipbuilder). Chase, who may have felt guilty about letting Bulloch walk out of his office less than two years ago, was ready to support the U.S. Navy's solution to problems the Confederate agent had created. On one hand, the Union wanted Britain to seize Confederate ships while they were still being built. On the other hand, internal political pressure had forced Abraham Lincoln to authorize Union privateer operations on 3 March 1863. Minister Adams warned that this pointedly anti–British measure would surely lead to war.[43] The U.S. Navy's solution to the first problem was a simple application of Yankee ingenuity: the Unites States would just buy the Confederate ships. They would offer more money than Bulloch or his bankers could possibly afford and the infusion of U.S. capital into British shipbuilding might assuage concerns about precipitous activities by American privateers.

Dubbed the Forbes-Aspinwall Mission, the two men would take a bankroll of $10 million in U.S. government bonds to London and get a loan of £1 million from the Baring Brothers bank. They would then buy any Confederate ship they could identify. U.S. Minister Adams was

Lord Henry John Palmerston, the British prime minister during the American Civil War (authors' collection).

kept totally in the dark, with only U.S. Consuls Dudley and Morse in Britain to know of their secret mission.[44] Bulloch had no idea of this new threat, though Confederate counterintelligence may have heard rumors of the Union Navy's idea since the concept had been considered earlier in 1863.[45]

Bulloch returned to Liverpool by 17 March 1863 and had to tell the frustrated North that the Confederate Navy coffers remained bare. There was not enough money to pay one-third of North's requirements for his ironclad, and more ominously, he had less than one-half of the amount needed for a currently overdue payment for one of his rams. Enigmatically, Bulloch alluded to a funding stream that Mathew Fontaine Maury had developed and Mallory hoped could provide funds for everyone. Bulloch told North that the lack of funds was not his fault and to not take it personally. They all suffered from financial starvation. At least he had some small happy news; the *Agrippina* would be off on its resupply mission for the *Alabama* on March 21st.[46]

For the next few days, he dealt with the contract involving the purchase of two marine engines and calculated specifications for the vessels that Arman would construct in France. While he did this, the political heat in Britain began to rise on the issue of the Neutrality Act and the "unpleasantness" occurring in North America.[47]

As Dudley and his faithful legal sidekick, A.T. Squarey, finished the compilation of the massive dossier on the *Alexandra*'s violations of the Neutrality Act, the British Parliament debated the Foreign Enlistment Act on 27 March 1863. Pro-Union members of Parliament (MPs) focused on the Palmerston government's failure to stop the *Alabama* and chastised him for not doing everything possible to take a fully neutral position in the war. When MPs Richard Cobden, John Bright, and William Forster sat down from delivering their accusatory condemnation of British actions and inactions, Palmerston stood up and glared back before speaking. "Pam," as the British public knew him, barked at the pro-Union MPs, calling them, "mouthpieces of the North." He would not change the Foreign Enlistment Act for the yapping of a mere puppy of a nation, the great British bulldog growled back at the Union. Despite the bravado, Palmerston and Russell knew that if the innermost details of the Lay-Osborn flotilla decision leaked into the body politic, they were in trouble. To preserve cover for that operation, they had to do something — fast.[48]

In fact, they had already known that the political winds were shifting, for on 21 March 1863, Russell and U.S. Minister Adams met in London. Russell admitted to Adams that he "knew" there were two ships being built in Britain for the Confederate Navy. Five days later, on the eve of the Parliamentary debate, they had held a long conference on matters involving the Foreign Enlistment Act. Russell prepared for pre-emptive action. He was keen to use the furor over the Confederate shipbuilding to mask his actions concerning the Lay-Osborn program, hoping that Parliament would not discover its innermost details. The chances of blowback were rising every day.[49]

The British Parliament continued to debate the Foreign Enlistment Act on 28 March 1863, when Dudley dropped his dossier and complaint against the *Alexandra* onto the desk of the Liverpool collector of customs. The following day, John Murray Forbes arrived in Liverpool as a Union agent of Secretary Chase on his mission to buy Confederate Navy ships in England. He went immediately to Dudley's offices; another match was about to be lit in Bulloch's shoe. The next day, Adams handed the complaint package to Lord Russell and the Foreign Office. In the white-hot heat of public scrutiny and the British press, Russell knew this latest U.S. tirade had to be handled precisely. Bulloch knew that his efforts were being publicly debated and that Liverpool generally supported Southerners and their cause. He also knew that much of the British public disapproved of his commerce raiders and the slave economy that they supported. Yet strangely, in a short note to Mallory on 30 March 1863, all Bulloch had to say was, "Ironclads nearly ready. Still doubtful if they can be got out." Although Russell had not declared his change in policy, Bulloch's sources within the Foreign Office remained active and alerted him to a shift in policy that would prevent the South from overtly obtaining English-built warships.[50]

The next day, Bulloch left for Paris to meet with John Slidell and begin the French-based Confederate shipbuilding program.[51] In the early spring of 1863, every major initiative was balanced precariously for the Confederate Navy in Europe. In the Confederacy, a combined Union operation using land and riverine naval forces had been prevented from gaining a northern approach on Vicksburg. The ironclads that Mallory desperately wanted could have turned this temporary Confederate success into a resounding victory.[52]

While Bulloch was in transit to Paris, everything began to happen at once. John Murray Forbes, after meeting with U.S. Consul Dudley in Liverpool, realized that the Union counterintelligence effort in Britain was sadly underappreciated and underfunded. He immediately advanced Dudley money to buy the services of more agents and wrote to Gideon Welles about the need for increased funding and better use of the intelligence collected in Britain. Forbes also assured Dudley that William Aspinwall would provide financial assistance. Forbes, hoping to maintain operational security, decided not to tell U.S. Minister Adams of his and Aspinwall's primary mission in Britain. Their cover story feigned that they were searching for men to emigrate to the U.S. (where they would enlist in the Northern armies, an action that also violated the Neutrality Act). Unfortunately for the Union cause, Forbes should have been more forthcoming with Adams.[53]

In America, Martha Bulloch wrote to her daughter Susy in Philadelphia that an Englishman had brought letters from James and Harriott as well as from Irvine, who was aboard the CSS *Alabama*. Martha was delighted by the news that James Dunwoody and Harriott had a new little baby boy, Stuart Elliot Bulloch, named after Bulloch's recently deceased stepbrother, Stuart Elliott. She complained that she had been continuously writing to James and Harriott, but they had received none of her letters. This news confirmed Martha's suspicions that Union authorities in New York were intercepting her letters.[54]

While Martha Bulloch complained of stolen mail, the Confederate Navy in Europe was about to lose its first warship to a form of legal theft. Since receiving Dudley's complaint about the *Alexandra* on 30 March 1863, Lord Russell's Foreign Office had been actively investigating the claim. Four days later, Russell wrote to U.S. Minister Adams that one ship, the *Phantom*, mentioned in Dudley's complaint was clearly not a warship, but the *Alexandra* was a different matter. She would be thoroughly investigated to see if she was in violation of the Foreign Enlistment Act, and Adams could count on that. What Russell did not tell Adams was that he wrote to Prime Minister Palmerston (on the same day) that he had decided to seize the *Alexandra* and the attorney general had agreed with the decision.[55] Matters moved quickly now. In the next twenty-four hours, the Law Office advised the Foreign Office to detain the *Alexandra* for violating the Neutrality Act. Their reasoning was based on the ship's apparent design and structure — as well as intent.[56] The following day, the British government seized the *Alexandra*.

News of the seizure of the *Alexandra* spread like wildfire among Southern sympathizers in Liverpool and the press spread the word throughout the rest of Britain.[57] During this time, Bulloch was traveling between Paris and Nantes. When Major Hurr of the Confederate Army hand-delivered a letter from James North in Tours, France, on April 6th, he probably passed along the news of the *Alexandra* affair. Bulloch was not surprised, for his very presence in France demonstrated that he had no illusions about shipbuilding in Great Britain. It was "France or bust" for the Confederate Navy.[58]

Confederate agents, sympathizers, and commissioners continued their best efforts to retrieve the *Alexandra* from the British government. While in France, Bulloch was learning the subtleties of doing business in the Gallic world. Confederate Commissioner John Slidell, who spoke fluent French, exploited his personal relationship with Louis-Napoléon to lay the foundation for Bulloch's endeavors and leverage the current political situation between France and Great Britain. The two nations, consistent with their historic suspicions, were currently on bad terms.

Several events in Europe assisted Slidell in his representations to Louis-Napoléon and the French government. France had annoyed Britain by annexing Savoy and Nice. Britain was also concerned about the rising German confederation of Wilhelm I and Bismarck. The most immediate German threat collided with Scandinavian interests in the Schleswig-Holstein region adjacent to Denmark in the northernmost portion of Germany.

In addition to the activity on the European Continent, Louis-Napoléon increased his meddling in Mexico, which gave the British Empire an even greater headache in the New World. Britain didn't want the French in an area where it still hoped to exercise primary economic and political influence. The Union government wasn't happy either as it knew that Louis-Napoléon was consorting with the Confederates. The United States had agreed to a treaty with Britain during its filibustering days for joint control over a Nicaraguan route to the Pacific. Both British and American (Union) government interests were closely aligned on this issue. Neither wanted French interference in the Americas. All of these events from late 1862 and early 1863 came into play as James Dunwoody Bulloch established himself in France.[59]

Louis-Napoleon III, the French ruler, sympathized with the South in the American Civil War (authors' collection).

In Paris on 13 April 1863, Bulloch caught up on correspondence that had been forwarded from Liverpool. Predictably, one troublesome letter was from James North, who was desperately seeking funding for his *No. 61* project. Once again Bulloch had to inform him that there were *still* no funds available from the Erlanger bond sales. In a more than irritated tone, Bulloch said, "I am exceedingly mortified and worried at the idea of having large obligations to meet, urgent appeals to enter into new contracts, and being absolutely without means." He hoped that the arrival of Gen. Colin J. McRae, whom Richmond had tasked to oversee all the Confederacy's overseas financial matters, would alleviate the problem.[60]

Bulloch sorted out the final details and contracts with Arman on 15 April 1863 and departed Paris for Liverpool. There was much to ponder while riding the train through the early spring French countryside to the Channel ferry. The French firms were just as keen to have money up front to begin their contracts as the English had been. On top of that, Arman's shipyard was unable to build two of Bulloch's desired ships; they were too busy. Arman subcontracted two of the ships to Jean Voruz, a shipbuilder based in Nantes. This increased exposure doubled the opportunities for Union counterintelligence to uncover the French ship construction efforts. To add to this litany of concerns, his expe-

8. Grim Aspect and Formidable Equipment

rience with Slidell in Paris told him that the politics of Britain were simplistic compared to the Byzantine bureaucracy of France.[61] If the Confederate Navy managed to pull this off, it would be a miracle.

Upon arriving in London, Bulloch found a scene of consternation, chaos, and confusion. Fraser, Trenholm and Company's affairs were in the full glare of public exposure as the British government slowly moved to bring the *Alexandra* case to court. Dudley's enhanced counterintelligence efforts, thanks to the assistance of Forbes-Aspinwall, were taking their toll as well. Then, there was the financial side of matters; something had to be done.

On 16 or 17 April 1863, all of the principal Confederate agents in Europe organized a council of war in London. The attending Confederate agents were: James Spence and Charles Prioleau representing "civilian" financial concerns, Mathew Fontaine Maury, James Heyward North, and James Dunwoody Bulloch for the Confederate Navy (all commanders in rank), along with Maj. Caleb Huse and Maj. J.B. Ferguson, agent of the Confederate Army quartermaster general (Ferguson took the meeting's notes).

The first subject was the state of financial affairs for the Confederacy in Europe with each of the agents providing an assessment of their respective needs. Realizing that their total needs far exceeded any possible credit that even Fraser, Trenholm and Co. could provide, the inter-service council decided to withdraw *all* of their securities from the British financial market and wait to see what resulted from the "Erlanger proposition." At the end of the meeting, Maj. Huse demanded that Ferguson turn over his remaining funds for his arms contracts. Ferguson refused and the rest of his letter, written on 18 April 1863, carefully described what he believed was financial malfeasance on the part of Maj. Huse. The financial strain was beginning to tear apart Confederate aspirations and any hope of coherent overseas operations.[62]

But the Union wasn't having it entirely its own way at the moment either. Despite providing good advice on the optimum course of U.S.–British relations, the Forbes-Aspinwall mission would soon explode in the face of the Union. Forbes urged the Lincoln government to avoid issuing "Letters of Marque and Reprisal" (privateering), as it would inevitably draw Britain into a war with the United States. The British merchant and upper classes were against the Union, but the ever-expanding working classes favored the North and were firm supporters of emancipation. A strong propaganda effort would generate political pressure that the British government could not ignore. As for the Navy, Washington needed to immediately remove Admiral Charles Wilkes from his post in the West Indies. His "Trent Affair" had nearly instigated a war between Britain and America and his continued heavy-handed campaign throughout the Caribbean incensed Whitehall and the Admiralty.

Yet, despite their elaborate and well-intended partisan efforts, everything came to naught on the 7th of April when the London *Times* exposed the primary Forbes-Aspinwall mission. Union agents were attempting to purchase the very same warships that Adams had caustically claimed were subject to seizure under the Neutrality Act. The Yanks had set a new standard of diplomatic hypocrisy. Instantly, Uncle Sam had burnt fingers and a singed beard. The two pseudo-agents went running for cover while they explained their activities to the unamused Charles Adams. Using their ability to inspire British wrath as an emblem of their zealous loyalty, Forbes and Aspinwall continued to assist Dudley behind the scenes in strengthening his counterintelligence and propaganda efforts.[63]

Meanwhile, Bulloch was back in Liverpool, maintaining an even-lower profile due to Dudley's enhanced counterintelligence resources, while trying to attend to his normal business. It was impractical for him to even visit the Lairds' shipyards to examine the progress on his rams. He had to rely on reports, which was not a good way to supervise a very complex shipbuilding project. With the firm of Fraser, Trenholm and Co. getting serious attention from British authorities, he spent more time at his home office in the Liverpool suburb of Waterloo.

Bulloch lingered in London for a few days in late April between his regular treks to and from Paris, Calais, Nantes, and Bordeaux. On May 1st, he met with Lt. Bob Carter in London after he was detained in France "for political reasons" before returning to Liverpool. He was back in London by mid–May where he informed Mallory that there were no changes to the inimical problems that plagued the Confederate Navy's shipbuilding program in Britain (lack of money, Union counterintelligence, and shifting application of the neutrality laws). He only opaquely referred to his overriding project.[64] This latest project had eminated from a message that Sec. Mallory sent on 19 March 1863.[65]

In Mallory's message, he instructed Bulloch to "arrange ... for the transfer of the vessels to (the) French owner ... in a French port." Bulloch followed Mallory's advice meticulously and quietly. In fact, in his letter to Mallory of 16 May 1863, he said that the "matter must be arranged with the greatest prudence and caution ... I shall ... mention the subject to none but Mr. Mason and Mr. Slidell."[66] In what was Bulloch's singularly most audacious play to date, he was going to "sell" the Laird rams out from under the noses of the British government and the ever-prying eyes of Union agents. The buyer was to be a willing French agent — who would then sell the rams back to Bulloch! This hyper-convoluted scheme involved the British, the French, the Union, the Russians, and even the Pasha of Egypt!

In typical Bulloch fashion, his game plan for outwitting the British and Union was based on the trustworthiness of the principal players, with political perfidy being the wild card. He concluded an agreement with the Frenchman Adrien Bravay that called for his firm to buy the rams from the Lairds (as Bulloch's surrogate) at a guaranteed price. Bravay would then sell the rams to another foreign buyer that was beyond British jurisdiction. Monsieur Bravay would receive a profitable commission for his efforts, of course.[67] The Confederate Navy would be reimbursed for all the funds it had spent and move on; simple as that. At least that's what Bulloch wanted the British and Union governments to believe. But James Dunwoody Bulloch and the Confederate Navy desperately needed those armored ships, so he added another layer to his scheme. Bravay would sell the ships all right, but the buyer would then sell the ships *back* to Bulloch and the Confederacy. This was derring-do of the highest order.[68]

Bulloch concluded the initial part of his operation during his visit to Arman and Slidell in Paris during the first of March. He had to establish a clear "legend" for the Laird rams. To protect his friends and partners, the Lairds, Bulloch once again turned to his legal advisors. They were given the task of finding a way through the legal maze.[69]

Thus, when he closed his May 16th report to Mallory saying he was "in great haste to leave for Paris by the next train" (from London), he had reason to hurry. Everything was hanging in the balance in Liverpool at the Lairds' shipyards insofar as his rams were concerned. He needed to get to Paris and ensure that Bravay was worthy of the trust he had placed in him. He also had to keep advised of the Lairds' actions. The elder Laird was a staunch pro-Southerner, but his sons might wilt under pressure and sell the rams just to be rid of the whole problem.[70]

While Bulloch was en route to Paris, events on the American battlefields helped shift momentum toward the Confederacy. General Robert E. Lee inflicted serious damage to the Union Army with his victory at Chancellorsville in April. From that time, Lee had been preparing for his surge north into the Union proper; Lincoln's government knew it, and all the Great Powers knew it — including France. The Confederacy could not win the war by just waiting for the next Union attack. The hour and the day of decision for whether or not one government or two would survive on the main body of the North American continent was coming. For Louis-Napoléon's imperial dreams in the Americas, a weak Union and a sympathetic Confederacy was an ideal outcome.[71]

When Bulloch arrived in Paris in mid–May, he flung himself immediately into securing the funds to pay for his new French ships. He also had to snatch the Laird rams from the clutches of John Bull while cultivating *new* contractors to build *more* armored ships in France. Up to that point in time, the French shipbuilding effort had been operating in fits and starts. The lack of finances delayed the start of construction until April 15th, a month after he signed the original contract with Arman. Even when the builds began, Arman was not happy with the payment arrangements, and would not be until weeks later. Why? Because Arman did not like the idea of unsecured Confederate payments that were only backed by the Erlanger bond. Bulloch's arrival in late May placed him at the center of an ongoing financial feud between all parties concerning payment: how much, to whom, when, how, and with what security? Answers to all of these questions were unknown, including who was in charge of disbursing the funds.[72]

For the next several weeks, Bulloch and Voruz worked to resolve Arman's financial concerns. Bulloch dashed back and forth to Nantes to check on his ships, and to Paris for meetings with Slidell. Arman and Voruz, wary of Erlanger's reputation for financial sharpness, took the lead in negotiating a deal that would satisfy their worries and get the Confederates their ships. On 9 June 1863, Bulloch and Voruz were at the Grand Hotel in Paris when Voruz received a message from Emile Erlanger: would Voruz kindly have Bulloch "certify the copy of the contract"?[73]

While Bulloch got the financing for the French contracts in order, the legal process surrounding the *Alexandra* in Liverpool had slowly, but inexorably, made its way through the British system. Since the seizure on 5 April 1863, government lawyers had been researching the case (while Dudley's agents dogged Lt. Hamilton's every step) and decided a change in venue was in order. The trial was moved from decidedly pro-Southern Liverpool to the Court of Exchequer in London. Bulloch had picked a very good time to visit France, for he was literally out of sight, but not out of the mind of Union officials.[74]

Though not in Liverpool, he was well apprised of events there. He knew that Lairds would be concerned about the level of government inquiries about the rams. Work had nearly ground to a halt on the armored ships; the situation was just too volatile at the moment. Once again, Bulloch had a knack for anticipation and action at just the right time. His operational dexterity was comparable to a man crossing a partially frozen and rapidly moving river, leaping from one piece of ice to another.

Solicitors in Liverpool told him that "the mere building of a ship in England for whatever purpose was not contrary to the provisions of the foreign enlistment act; that the seizure of the *Alexandra* ... [was] illegal ... but that the ironclads were liable to the same proceedings ... if they should be seized we could not expect to release them from the Court of Exchequer during the war, if at all."[75] Bulloch's legal counsel reiterated that it wasn't just a case of selling the rams in a sham sale; it would literally have to be an ironclad deal with sufficient *bona fides* to satisfy the British government in full. By the opening of the *Alexandra* trial on 22 June 1863, Bulloch had preemptively instructed the Lairds to sell his rams. If he did not sell them, he asserted, the British government was likely to seize them and he would lose not only the ships, but also all the money the Confederacy had invested. The Lairds were to sell the rams for a "reasonable profit" and to "release [Bulloch] of all further obligations under the contract."[76]

In his memoirs, as echoed by the official letter copy in the ORN, Bulloch specifies that he wrote Laird a "formal" letter, inferring that another letter or discussions had taken place. They surely had conferred, for the Russian government (which supported the Union) soon approached Laird about buying the rams. Was it a play by the Union counterintelligence at calling his bluff, or was it truly a legitimate Russian offer? It's likely that he smelled a water rat, but either way, he was going to do everything in his power to control the destiny of his rams. He rushed to the Paris offices of Bravay to "regulate the correspondence on the part of the French purchasers, to suit the advice of my English solicitor."[77] And one last impetus spurred Bulloch's improvisation: Clarence Yonge, Bulloch's fellow Georgian and distant cousin, had washed upon the shores of England as a traitorous and dangerous bit of jetsam who threatened to sink his ship-acquisition efforts.

Capt. Raphael Semmes had cashiered Yonge from the *Alabama* while in Jamaica after another episode of drunkenness (using ship's money) and bragging about the *Alabama*'s mission. Yonge, who had served as Bulloch's clerk at 10 Rumford Place, returned to Liverpool as an informant. Aided by a healthy financial Union stipend, he filled the ears of U.S. Consul Dudley with everything that had transpired aboard the *Alabama*, and asserted that the Laird rams were for the Confederacy.[78]

Bulloch learned of Yonge's presence via the direct telegraphic connection between London and Paris, but he also understood the information that Yonge could provide. Adams and Dudley were absolutely ebullient with expectation over the effect of Yonge's explosive evidence. Bulloch was outraged at Yonge's personal and professional betrayal.

The trial at the Court of Exchequer quickly descended into farce. Sir Hugh Cairns, the lead defense counsel, systematically destroyed the government's case. Not only did he use portions of the legal advice given by Solicitor General Palmer during a Parliamentary debate (about the *Alabama* affair), but demanded equal enforcement of the Foreign Enlistment Act. This was a direct poke at the Union and an allusion to both the Forbes-Aspinwall fiasco and the Lay-Osborn flotilla. He also appealed to the financial benefits of supporting the shipbuilding industry (always a crowd pleaser in Great Britain), and there was Mr. Yonge himself.[79] Sir Hugh, and supporting counsel, so destroyed Yonge's credibility that his reputation was permanently defined as an untrustworthy drunkard. Even Lord Russell despised Yonge for abandoning his wife and then marrying a quadroon in Jamaica! Evidence from such a man was beneath even the remotest consideration; at least that is what Dudley wrote about Lord Russell's opinion. But was that accurate?[80]

The geostrategic situation facing Palmerston and Russell encouraged Russell to protest just enough to keep his legal options open for a favorable interpretation of the Foreign Enlistment Act that met imperial needs. Britain could not appear to be kowtowing to the Union, but it could not give in fully to the Confederacy and risk a war with Lincoln's Union. Britain had other strategic concerns: the French were aggressively belligerent both in Europe and in Mexico, Wilhelm and Bismarck were stirring the Baltic, and the Poles were in revolt against the Russians.

The *Alexandra* verdict that came back from Sir Jonathan Frederick Pollock on 26 June 1863 was as fine as the edge of a British cavalryman's saber: the ship had been built as specified by the contract and the buyer could use it however they saw fit. The judge of the Court of Exchequer had spoken; the Foreign Enlistment Act had not been broken. The Union was stunned silent, and it was now the Confederates' turn to be ebullient.[81]

However, it was a Pyrrhic victory for the Confederacy. Palmerston knew it, Russell knew it, and Bulloch had known it since February. The verdict affirming the legality of the building and sale of the *Alexandra* was exactly what Lord Russell needed to promote the policies that best served Britain's strategic interests and validated the legality of the Lay-Osborn flotilla. Now, the British government could overtly use *policy* as a means to hinder the Confederates activities. A policy decision would keep the irritating, but dangerous Union happy. It would also reduce the Confederate chances for victory and prevent the South from assisting Louis-Napoléon's imperial designs in the Caribbean and Central America. There was one other factor: the blockade of the South prevented cotton from reaching France, which might encourage Louis-Napoléon to focus on domestic issues. As far as Bulloch was concerned, divining British government intentions from now own belonged to the province of seers. Britain's course of action was no longer guided by laws, but by adverse geopolitical winds.

The *Alexandra* decision had been a bitter birthday present for Bulloch who had turned 40 just the previous day, 25 June 1863. He pondered his situation in a letter to Mallory describing efforts to sell the rams, continuing disappointment at a lack of command (due to the forced sale of the rams), Clarence Yonge and the *Alexandra* trial, and the desultory financial results obtained from the Erlanger bond sales.[82] The best news was that Bravay was now the "owner" of the Laird rams! As Bulloch turned his focus to France, armies of Union and Confederate soldiers confronted each other around the bluffs of Vicksburg on the Mississippi River and outside the obscure village of Gettysburg in Pennsylvania; July 1863 would be the pivotal month of the American Civil War.[83]

With the legal question of the *Alexandra* having been settled (though the issue of whether Fraser, Trenholm and Co. would gain actual ownership was still pending) and the Laird rams now ostensibly owned by Bravay and Co. as representatives of the Pasha of Egypt, Bulloch was emboldened to act even more decisively. On 2 July 1863, he was spotted at the Lairds' shipyard. Bulloch must have thought that his presence would not excite undue attention since the rams no longer belonged to him, but he was wrong.[84] Dudley and his enhanced counterintelligence network had been diligently canvassing the shipbuilding effort surrounding the two vessels that the Lairds had designated as *No. 294* and *295*.[85]

Dudley's men had observed the keels being laid and soon learned that the British-registered steamer *Gibraltar* would transport their guns; even worse, the first of the rams was to be launched on the 4th of July. To avoid a very unhappy birthday, Dudley went into his well-practiced mode of compiling an extensive dossier and formal complaint for the Liverpool Customs House officers. Still smarting from the perceived slap in the face from the British Court of the Exchequer over the *Alexandra*, Dudley was extremely motivated. Commerce raiders were one thing; ironclads that could *directly* attack Union cities were another.

As the Union began to rattle the chains of the British government yet again, Bulloch was back at his desk at 10 Rumford Place. He was trying to deflect any new problems with Commander James North in Scotland. A "private and confidential" courier was leaving for the Confederacy in the next week or so. He advised North that if he had any messages for Sec. Mallory, he should send them "attention of Lt. Whittle," since Bulloch would be absent (Lt. William C. Whittle distinguished himself aboard the CSS *Nashville* and was intended to be part of the crews that would man *No. 294* and *No. 295*). After asking North how he was getting on, he briskly added that he was leaving for Paris the following day. If North needed any further assistance, he could contact Commissioner Slidell.

Bulloch's last business before leaving for Paris was about money. He straightened his back and penned a letter to James Spence, the financial agent of the Confederate Navy. Was *any* portion of Mallory's $2 million in bonds available for future use, "say in five or six months?" He was already looking forward to his French armored ships. He wanted Spence to be as "categorical in your statements as circumstances will, in your judgment, admit. I am obliged to leave for Paris in the morning" and could he please send his response to the, "Hon. John Slidell, 19 Rue de Marignan." Bulloch wanted to be sure of his finances before he put his signature to any contract with the French shipbuilders; he was trusting, but pragmatic.[86]

After locking up his Liverpool writing desk, he paid his compliments to the Fraser, Trenholm and Co. office workers and headed for home in Waterloo to Harriott and his children for evening supper. The following day, the Fourth of July, he resisted the urge to witness the launch of *No. 294*, a ship he knew that he could never command, and left for Paris.[87]

The Fourth of July 1863 could have been memorialized as the date of Bulloch's greatest achievement. The Confederate Navy's first foreign-built armored ship was now in the water.[88] Instead, it was just another case of lost opportunity and a valiant, but ultimately futile, effort. Its *raison d'être* was extinguished that same day on the Mississippi River when Confederate forces surrendered Vicksburg after 40 days and nights of Union onslaught. Also that same day, Gen. Robert E. Lee's army was defeated at Gettysburg after three days of epic struggle. The news of these terrible losses would bring double tears for the Confederates in Europe.[89]

Bulloch arrived in Paris on July 6th and found a parcel from Arman waiting for him; it was a preliminary set of plans for a new armored ship. Bulloch was already creating more armored ships. Like a good poker player, he was covering his position, and improving his odds.[90]

It was good that Bulloch did, for the next day, on 7 July 1863, the Union struck back. Dudley stormed into the Liverpool Customs House and dropped his request for seizure of the Laird rams onto the desk of the officer-in-charge. Dudley then caught the train to London to meet with Adams. Dudley carried complete copies of his dossier and witness affidavits, including those obtained from Clarence Yonge and George Chapman who had worked on the rams. Especially damning were the statements from Master Mariner William Russell and Master Shipwright Ellis, both of whom, as experts in ship operation and ship

8. Grim Aspect and Formidable Equipment 131

Paris Grand Hotel (right) was the meeting place for Bulloch and other Confederate agents and officials (authors' collection).

construction, respectively, claimed that the only purpose of the vessel was for war.[91] If the *Alexandra* affair caused consternation to the Confederates, there would be outright chaos in Liverpool if the Union could prove its case, except in the mind of the pragmatic Bulloch. He had anticipated the Union and British moves to protest and seize the rams. Although he was steeled for the worst, he hoped his dramatic maneuverings would change the end game, which was the purpose of his trip to Paris.

July 8th was a warm summer morning in Paris when Bulloch reported to Sec. Mallory that he personally inspected *No. 294* only a few days before her launch. He observed that the ironclad was as perfect as could be under the circumstances. He even noted that her masts had been mounted on the same day he had arrived in France (6 July). Bulloch and the Confederates in Paris had not yet received word that *No. 294,* and her sister ship, *No. 295,* were now under the threat of seizure due to Dudley's most recent complaint. For the moment, he enjoyed the bliss of ignorance as he wrote with considerable pride to Sec. Mallory of the characteristics and specifications of his ironclad rams.

As if giving a guided tour, Bulloch talked Mallory through a set of plans that accompanied his letter. Sheet "A" showed the semi-water tight compartments, the crew accommodation in the forecastle and poop, and of course, the turrets that made the vessels so lethal. Sheet "B" contained detailed "upper and lower deck plans," while Sheet "C" displayed the "mid-ship section ... the side water tight compartments, the depth of the bottom compartment, which can be filled to increase the immersion of the armor plating when desired." These features must have delighted and fascinated Mallory. It was the Stevens' ironclad brought to life, and actually afloat. The final plan, Sheet "D," was the sail plan and was "sufficiently explanatory."[92] It was the next paragraph that was pure dynamite.

Commenting that he had included a "detailed and very elaborate" drawing of the rams' turret design, Bulloch went on to say that it "was not exactly Captain Coles' turret ... but he [Coles] approves all the deviations from the minute details of his system." If U.S. Minister Adams and Consul Dudley had known of this technical collaboration, British blandishments that there was no violation of the Foreign Enlistment Act would not have curbed Union outrage.[93]

Bulloch compared the design characteristics of his turret with Coles,' the different formation and installation of the armor; and the iron forged with as few bends as possible to make it stronger. This was an early implementation of metallurgical stress in warship design. As delighted as a child on Christmas Day, he described *No. 294*'s essential numbers, her draft and her total weight. Bulloch figured she drew 9.6 feet mean and displacement was 1,361 tons. He knew, as would Mallory, that the rams' draft would be too deep for their original intended purpose of sailing up the Mississippi River to recapture New Orleans and control the river.[94] However, he had given much thought to what mission they *could* be used for and would send his ideas in a "special despatch."

The *tour de force* letter concluded with a remark that would have sent Seward and Welles, into cardiopulmonary seizures.[95] Bulloch quipped that he would "soon be prepared to make you a detailed report upon the various systems of plating employed as followed in the British and French *government yards*" [authors' emphasis]. His access to this information would have astounded the Union, but it revealed his adroitness in using social connections and his own counterintelligence network (which, unlike the Union's effort, remains clouded in secrecy).[96]

While Adams and Dudley fretted about British dithering over the Laird rams, Bulloch was executing his plan to get the rams to sea sometime in October.[97] He recorded his thoughts and actions in a July 9th letter to Secretary Mallory and more importantly, his vision of how the Confederate Navy should use these ships to their best advantage.[98]

His "special courier," Lt. Whittle, memorized and was told to report all of the nuanced details. Whittle was slated to serve aboard one of the rams and Bulloch needed him back as quickly as possible. Bulloch hoped that the rams would soon be "released from the trammels of British interference." He still believed that the Bravay/Pasha of Egypt legend would hold up under British and Union investigation. But the issue of the crews was the first problem that played upon his mind.[99]

The fact that the rams were obviously intended for "other purposes," due to their "grim aspect and formidable equipment" meant that reliable seamen could not be obtained from the "floating population of European seaports." No, this time the Confederacy needed its own blood and sinew — "veterans who are now sweeping irresistibly through Maryland and southern Pennsylvania under the leadership of our great General Lee" and could they be mostly artillerists? Unlike the predictability of the Union diplomatic protests, Bulloch had no premonition that Lee and the South had suffered dreadful losses at Gettysburg and Vicksburg. He optimistically commented that engineers and firemen as well as typical seamen could be found in Europe to man the rams' other needs.[100]

Now, he got to the central point of his letter: how the rams should be employed. They should be immediately sent to disrupt the blockade off Wilmington, North Carolina, Lee's strategic logistic lifeline to the outside world. There, one ram would fall upon the Union ships at New Inlet and the other upon the blockaders at the mouth of the Cape Fear River. "By steaming quietly in at early daylight, they might entirely destroy the blockading vessels; not one should be left to steal away and to make known the fact of the ironclads being on the coast." This was a bone-chilling tactic. No quarter was to be shown in the first instance, but then he carried on: "Crews might be ready at Smithville or Fort Caswell, to be put on board the ships as soon as they had destroyed the blockaders ... the two vessels would be ready to strike a decisive blow in any direction, north or south."[101] He was desperately anxious to have the ships manned by patriotic Confederates for the rams were too valuable to be entrusted to profiteering adventurers.

While pausing to admit that he might be a bit "presumptuous," Bulloch had a few suggestions for Mallory. He worried that the rams' sea-handling capabilities would restrict them upon the Mississippi River, largely due to their "length and breadth." With the aid of smaller ironclads and tugs to assist them in turning through the river's tight bends, they might be successful in breaking the Union fleet before Vicksburg. Still, he reckoned the rams would be like a boxer fighting with one hand tied behind his back in the tight quarters of the Mississippi River. All this would be bitter reading for Mallory in Richmond and a grievous plague upon Bulloch's mind when the news of the city's fall reached him in Europe. It was a disaster that could have been prevented if the Confederacy had only taken prompt action on his practical suggestions.[102]

The Atlantic coast was where the rams could shine, Bulloch reckoned. They could fall upon every blockader between the "Capes of Virginia to Sabine Pass (Texas)" and by "cruising up and down the coast could prevent ... interruption of our foreign trade for the future." If the Union government persisted in refusing the South its liberty, well, the rams could ascend the Potomac and attack Washington, D.C., creating "a powerful diversion in favor of any operations General Lee might have on foot." At that moment, however, Gen. Lee was in full retreat, attempting to save his army.[103]

Bulloch recommended that the rams could sail into the Portsmouth, New Hampshire, harbor and hold the city and its valuable shipyard under its guns, in retaliation for the Union Navy's destruction of Jacksonville, Florida. To avoid a similar fate, the city would have to pay $10,000,000 dollars in gold — or $50,000,000 in greenbacks within four hours. Considering Bulloch's reserved and understated personality, his proposal seems harshly mercenary, a cruel attempt to exact retribution upon the Union. This is a prime example of the American Civil War's effect upon its participants, whether willing or not. Bulloch thought operations such as his proposed Portsmouth expedition would have a "striking effect in Europe." If executed in full, the effect would certainly have been war between Britain and the United States.[104] Bulloch closed his letter by noting that Lt. Whittle would proceed to Halifax and Bermuda where he planned to take a blockade runner into the Confederacy. The following day, 10 July 1863, found Bulloch unexpectedly back to solving issues surrounding the *Alabama*. He received a letter from Capt. Alexander McQueen of the *Agrippina* post-marked in June from Bahia (Brazil).

McQueen had sailed from Liverpool with fresh munitions and other supplies for Semmes and the *Alabama*, but when he arrived in Bahia, the *Alabama* was gone. Semmes had left instructions for McQueen with the British consul. Unfortunately, the British consul had been transferred and took the letters with him. So, when McQueen enquired at the new consul's offices, he had no instructions. This, coupled with scuttlebutt that McQueen heard on the streets that the *Agrippina* was connected with the *Alabama*, led him to believe that his letters had been compromised. McQueen then told Bulloch that three men had deserted the *Alabama* in Bahia and reported what they knew to the U.S. consul. To make matters worse, the game was up when McQueen showed his clearance papers to the Brazilian customs officers and gunpowder was listed as part of his cargo. The president of Brazil, informed of what was transpiring, wrote to the British consul, who hauled McQueen to his office for an explanation. The consul instructed McQueen, in no uncertain terms, that he was to sell his load of cargo and gunpowder, find a load of commercial freight, and sail directly back to Britain.[105]

McQueen closed his letter with some intelligence and some complaints. On the intelligence side, he said the USS *Mohican* was shadowing the movements of *Agrippina* and the bark *Castor*, a Liverpool-based tender for Maury's commerce raider, CSS *Georgia*. After the U.S. consul complained on 16 May 1863, Brazilian authorities forced the *Castor's* captain (Attard) to stop coaling operations on behalf of the *Georgia*. With the benefit of hindsight, McQueen complained that if he had been "cleared for Rio" none of this would have happened. After making some minor repairs to the *Agrippina*, McQueen sailed for England without contacting the *Alabama*.[106]

The *Agrippina* had performed admirable service for the *Alabama* in the Azores and during two subsequent voyages, but she had now outlived her usefulness. Bulloch reckoned that Semmes had more than enough funds on hand to buy whatever stores he needed (or could not obtain from his captured prizes); Bulloch decided to sell the *Agrippina* when she returned. If Semmes needed another supply vessel, he would simply buy one. With the *Agrippina* out of the way, he would have one less problem to manage and the U.S. Navy would have one less source of information as they tried to divine his movements. Bulloch hastily jotted down this update to Mallory and placed it in the hands of Lt. William C. Whittle, who was leaving Paris that day to begin his successful run through the blockade and on to Richmond.[107]

On 13 July 1863, Bulloch headed to Bordeaux, France, where he hoped to begin construction of at least two more ironclads. Gen. McRae had the wheels of Confederate finance squeaking along again and promised him $300,000 from his long-held treasury draft. Only the lack of finances would deter his project now. He confidently urged Mallory that he should be left "untrammelled by the operations or functions of any other agent of your department; Purely business matters must be managed in a systematic way."[108]

9

Harassing Perplexity — 1863

At the midpoint of 1863, Bulloch looked toward France to continue the success he had first enjoyed in Great Britain. Even with its potential for added disappointment, he hoped for smoother sailing. On 13 July 1863, he left Paris for Bordeaux, accompanied by Arman's business agent, Henri A. de Rivière, and the French financier Emile Erlanger. The shipbuilder Jean Voruz feared that "they will be obliged to come to terms with Arman for the armoured ships." The business negotiations among Bulloch, Arman, and Erlanger, for the proposed armored ships would be complex and tense.

The next day in Arman's shipyard, Bulloch inspected his wooden corvettes, a three-masted vessel with square rigging that was similar to, but smaller than a frigate or ship-of-the-line. He was delighted with their progress, finding that, "nearly two-thirds were in frame ... and the finishing ... is quite equal to that in the best British dockyards or in the Navy yards of the United States under the former government." He believed that Arman was "imbued with the same liberal ideas as Messr. Laird ... whose desire to give satisfaction in the character of his work is greater than the inclination to screw an extra profit out of it." Bulloch had the capacity to separate his appreciation of quality work from the profit-making capitalists who would take full advantage of the Confederate government's desperate situation, but he was a bit naive about the altruistic nature of Arman. However, there was much to do; so much, in fact, that it was necessary to send a subordinate to Nantes to inspect the work on the other two corvettes under construction there. He would visit later to personally check on the quality of workmanship and progress.[1]

On 16 July 1863, Bulloch signed a contract with Arman to build two additional armored ships; Emile Erlanger was the financial intermediary who guaranteed the payments. Bulloch grumbled to Mallory a few days later that he knew Erlanger and Arman had come to some kind of backroom "arrangement." He had agreed to the banker's commission of five per cent but allowed, "I am quite sure that somehow or other the commission has been included in the estimate of prices.... If I openly declare my knowledge of the fact ... the builders will decline to go on ... and we shall have no ships at all." He was quickly shedding his naiveté regarding the motivations of his newfound French friends, quality workmanship, or not.[2]

Still, Bulloch was happy. With the $2,000,000 appropriation from the Confederate Congress on 6 May 1863, he could "build, arm, and equip 20 of such" armored ships as those in Bordeaux.[3] Incredibly, on the same day in Richmond, the Confederate Treasury delivered devastating news: the proceeds from the sale of the Erlanger bonds were only 40%

Port of Nantes, France, where two of Bulloch's ships were built (authors' collection).

of what was expected. In Mallory's own words, it was "a grievous disappointment." The new realities of the funding situation would take weeks to reach Bulloch.[4]

Bulloch's current accounts were in good shape after Gen. McRae delivered a £300,000 Treasury draft from the "instalments [sic] of the loan." At least he had a bit of relief in his dealings with the contractors. Little did Bulloch realize that there was essentially no other money forthcoming for the Confederate Navy. He still hoped to have the Laird rams at sea in October. If British authorities refused Bravay's application to arm them in Liverpool, he would move them to France and add the armament there. This optimism did not extend to the *Alexandra*; Bulloch reckoned that the cruiser was "permanently lost to us for all practical purposes."[5]

For the next week, Bulloch traveled around France assessing progress and instilling a sense of urgency in all of his projects. On Tuesday, July 28, while in Paris, he wrote to James North in Glasgow inquiring about the sale of his ironclad. Bulloch, despite not knowing the true state of the Confederate Navy's finances, wisely implored North to sell *No. 61*. The money realized would buy *two* armored ships in France without the interference they suffered in Britain.[6]

Subtly comparing North's unwieldy ship with his own, Bulloch told Commander North that his two armored ships were "formidable" and were "well suited in size and draft of water for service in our shoal rivers and harbors. Their particular feature is the mode of finishing the after-body, ... to accommodate two screws. This will enable them to turn and maneuver very quickly and easily." They only cost £80,000 each (about one-third the amount of North's).[7]

In closing, Bulloch said that he would leave Paris by next Thursday and would be back in Liverpool on Saturday. Again trying to motivate North to act on the *No. 61*, he commented that "the chances of getting her out are still slim. The *Alexandra* is still in the hands of the customs authorities and is not likely to be given up until the bill of exceptions is argued." The slowness of the British legal system would wrap itself around the *Alexandra* like inescapable tendrils of seaweed, holding her tight in port. In Glasgow, James North wrote another check to a naval gun manufacturer for £1,000. He was totally insensitive to the financial and political reality confronting the Confederate Navy and was still pouring money into his ironclad.[8]

By late July, news of the catastrophic Confederate losses at Gettysburg and Vicksburg began to filter into Europe.[9] While Bulloch was traveling back to Liverpool, James North told one of his sympathetic Glasgow suppliers that the "news from Dixie is very black. I see not just now one bright spot. I hope God may still be with us."[10] God, as the French were all too keenly aware, once again appeared to be favoring the side with the largest army.

On the 4th of August as he settled behind his desk at Fraser, Trenholm and Co., Bulloch once again turned his attention to his "in" box. One of the first priorities was to convince James North to stop wasting money on his ironclad and to sell it. Once more, the lack of funds, tardy communications and no clear command structure were fouling the progress of all their endeavors.[11] Bulloch told North,

> [Since] the sale of your ship had been determined upon, I ceased to consider her completion as a future charge upon the Navy Department's funds and contracted for two ironclads in France upon the expectation of promised remittances from the Treasury Department at Richmond. I felt safe in doing this, as should the promised money fail to arrive I thought the proceeds of your sale would amply suffice to complete them, and that you would be glad to take them off my hands. I still think the chances of getting so large and formidable a ship out are hopeless, and that you will sooner get to sea by putting the money in another ship elsewhere, yet if under Mr. Mason's advice you think proper to go on with your present undertaking I will assist you in any way within my power. As soon as the Treasury warrants arrive I will make arrangements to meet your wants, if it is possible to do so ... you should inform me what gross amount you will require.... You are aware that the loan ... is paid by instalments [sic] and that we cannot get a very large sum at once.[12]

It was "a hasty letter," but Bulloch tried to make it clear that the *Alexandra* case was the death knell for overt Confederate warship construction in Great Britain. It was time for North to stop wasting the meager resources of the Confederacy on the lost cause of an impractical ironclad. He appealed to North's fundamental professional goal (just as Bulloch desperately desired): command at sea. Could he not see that he would be much more likely to get afloat in one of Bulloch's armored rams?

Back in Richmond, Mallory was desperate for news about the ironclads. He wrote Bulloch the day before, 3 August 1863, saying that his last report of any kind was via Lt. William Murdaugh in mid–May and his last information about the ironclads was dated the 12th of *March*, nearly five months ago! Mallory implored that the "country is looking anxiously to the completion of your vessels and to learn of their safely leaving for our coast." The double jolt of Gettysburg and Vicksburg had plunged even the highest levels of the Confederate government into deep shock. The lack of news was evidence of Union tightening of the blockade as well. The Confederate government had trouble merely communicating beyond its borders, much less shipping materials out of, or into its ports.[13]

Bulloch had no way of knowing that Mallory had not received any of his recent messages. But as he read through his pile of newspapers and messages and conversed with Prioleau and others, he knew that the defeats at Gettysburg and Vicksburg had significantly reduced the Confederacy's chances of survival. Only extraordinary means could bring the country back from a slide into oblivion. The armored ships under construction in France might constitute those extraordinary means, if only they could be finished and delivered in time.

It was a mountain of correspondence, actions, orders, and directives that Bulloch dealt with that first week of August. Having answered North on Monday, it was not until Thursday (August 7th) that he managed to address the numerous issues that Sec. Mallory had raised from the capital in Richmond. Orderly as always, Bulloch addressed each letter and each question in his response.

First, Bulloch hoped that Lt. Whittle had arrived safely and briefed Mallory fully about the situation in Europe. Moving to the subject of North's ironclad, he described the sequence of events, including the improbability of getting any warships away from Great Britain. The altered British policy stance led to a decision to sell *No. 61* and use the proceeds to purchase "armoured ships on the Continent." Completion of North's unwieldy ironclad would consume "the entire $5,200,000 ... [that] has been appropriated from the loan for naval contracts in Europe." He made it clear that full responsibility for this on-going fiasco of financial blundering and interference lay outside his control and mandate. Richmond had created this mess and that unless specifically instructed by Secretary Mallory, he wasn't going to scuttle any of his own efforts to clean it up.[14]

Moving on to his activities in France, Bulloch foresaw no problems with completing the wooden corvettes on schedule. But the armored ships were going to be another story. He pulled no punches here, saying, "I am not at all sure that we shall have less difficulty with the ironclads in France than we have had elsewhere. Vessels of that description cannot possibly be disguised, nor can it be pretended they are built for any other uses than those required for offensive warfare. Unless ... the French Government were prepared for an open rupture with the United States, such vessels would not be allowed to equip in a French port, or to leave without enquiry and explanation. At any rate, no hint or intimation has yet been obtained to the contrary, although some very direct enquiries have been made." He promised to cooperate with Commissioner Slidell's attempts to change French neutrality policies so that the vessels could be fitted out and sailed without difficulties. Bulloch closed this portion of his letter with the comment that he had made discrete inquiries about buying existing ironclads from "one of the European navies," but that most of these were too large, too small, or had too much draft to suit "our especial purposes."[15]

In what would become one of his most successful acquisition efforts, Bulloch updated Mallory on his efforts to purchase a "swift-paddle steamer" for service as a blockade runner. Although he "had no funds that were not wholly pledged" for other projects, he was in negotiation that very day for a fast double-screw ship that had a cargo capacity of 1,000 cotton bales.[16]

Turning next to the Confederate Treasury's inability to supply the "funds contemplated in the 'Secret Act of Congress,'" Bulloch acknowledged that this development "does not take me by surprise, because I did not see how it would be possible to place £2,000,000 in Europe except by a new loan." He had anticipated this development and exercised caution by only contracting for the four wooden corvettes and two armored ships.[17]

The rest of his letter sounded a more cheerful note as he reported the expected performance capabilities of the French vessels. The corvettes will "have great speed — 14 knots

... the ironclads will draw 14 feet 6 inches extreme ... [with] a speed of 12 knots. They will have two screws and will be handled with great ease." Bulloch pointed out that there would be additional design changes, but the critical issue remained money. He had not yet received a draft for £64,492 (plus change), but when it arrived, he would sign it over to Spence, the Confederate finance agent. His missive completed, and with a contemplative sigh, he turned to other affairs.[18]

Not mentioned in Bulloch's letter was the fact that the Confederacy had lost control of the Mississippi River. The Laird rams, intended to wrest control of the Mississippi from the Union, were on the verge of being lost as well. He made no mention of any of these depressing issues, much less Gettysburg, yet both men knew time and tide had changed for the Confederacy, perhaps irrevocably.[19]

In the middle of the following week, Bulloch responded to Voruz's questions about his French ships and shared his thoughts about using Blakely's naval guns. Bulloch retained his penchant for covert operations and catered to the Frenchman's long-term financial interests, saying, "It is my intention to confide my affairs to as few hands as possible ... so that our relations may be extended even in case of peace." Moving to equally practical affairs before closing, he hopefully opined that his government would have to "apply for the construction of its [marine] engines." The good relationship he had with Voruz might "lead in the future to still more considerable orders." He promised to "write a week before my arrival in Nantes."[20]

Even as North fretted over his *No. 61*, the *Alexandra* lay ensnared in the British bureaucracy. Arman and Voruz were building corvettes and armored ships in France and the fate of the Laird rams remained in limbo. Throughout the rest of August, Lairds' shipyard rushed to complete *No. 294*, which had already been launched. Her turrets needed to be installed prior to outfitting the naval guns (if and when they might be put in place was another matter); the launch of *No. 295* was still pending.

U.S. Consul Dudley, flush with funds courtesy of William Aspinwall, had his counterintelligence effort in high gear. He had current information on North's *No. 61* (even to the point of knowing that she would be named the *Virginia* and she still had significant work to be completed) and he closely followed the progress of the Laird rams. So far, Bulloch's smokescreen had satisfied British authorities, who merely relayed Adams and Dudley's accusations to Bravay for answers. Bravay maintained his story that he was the representative of the Pasha of Egypt and that the vessels were under French ownership, *merci beaucoup*. Having no verifiable contrary evidence, the Foreign Office told Adams that there was nothing to be done. But several issues were about to come together that would dramatically alter Lord Russell and the British government's stance concerning the rams and alter the rest of Bulloch's operations in Britain for the remainder of the American Civil War.[21]

When Bulloch sent Lt. Whittle across the Atlantic in early July 1863 to brief Sec. Mallory in Richmond, he also directed the young officer to ascertain who would command the Laird rams if they could be gotten away from Liverpool. He was ever hopeful of command and envisioned Semmes at the helm of the other ram. Mallory had been considering the issue of who would command the rams since Bulloch's March dispatches, if not before. Ever since Commissioner John Slidell convinced Mallory that French support for the Confederate cause was assured, he became obsessed with routing all future naval efforts through

France. At this critical point in the war, Mallory ignored the on-site advice from Bulloch about the situation in both Britain and France. In late 1862, Bulloch had recommended a crew-transfer *a la Alabama* with the officers and crewmen sailing directly the ships from the Confederacy (with seasoned, patriotic "artillerists"). Instead, Mallory decided to send officer staffs to France via England for both ships. From both an operational and security standpoint, this was a mistake. Large numbers of idle Confederate naval officers would certainly come to the attention of both Adams' and Dudley's counterintelligence network. Worse, Mallory was overriding Bulloch's sage advice.[22]

In the meanwhile, the turrets of *No. 294* were put in place on 28 August 1863. The following day, *No. 295* slid down the shipyard's ways into the waters of the Mersey. The Confederate Navy now had the world's two most advanced armored ships afloat and very nearly completed. On the following day in Richmond, Mallory sent formal orders to Commodore Samuel Barron to run the blockade out of Wilmington, NC, and take command of the two rams that Bulloch would deliver to him at sea, probably sometime in October. Mallory hoped the rams would be "an instrument for the relief of your noble and suffering country."[23] At that moment in Britain, however, the rams seemed to be instruments of diplomatic destruction for the relations between Washington and London.[24]

Throughout August, U.S. Minister Adams sent diplomatic demands to Lord Russell about the Laird rams, messages that contained increasing evidence and vitriol. On the 1st of September, Lord Russell replied to Adams that the evidence was flimsy and there was no proof that the Confederates owned the rams.[25]

In Richmond, Mallory was understandably anxious over the affairs of the naval department in Europe, which provided about the only hope of rescuing the fortunes of the Confederacy. Bulloch noted with exasperation that "a series of dispatches from the various heads of departments at Richmond, addressed to your commissioners and officers in Europe ... were intercepted by the enemy, who at once gave their contents to the public. These dispatches were published throughout Europe ... thereby giving great publicity to our affairs and so directed attention to the various agents of the Government, especially in England, that the difficulty of executing any work which might be considered as in violation of the 'foreign enlistment act' or in opposition to the neutrality this country has imposed upon itself, was greatly increased." As a result, Bulloch had been even more cautious in his reports, sending "brief but frequent statements in cipher."[26]

Despite his best efforts at keeping his operations secret, the lackadaisical attitude of his fellow Confederates compromised many of his efforts. Lord Russell tried to ignore U.S. Minister Adams' diplomatic bluster, but the British public could read for themselves what the Confederates were up to in Great Britain in their own words. Lord Russell could not explain that away, which of course raised the political heat in the House of Commons for Prime Minister Palmerston and his cabinet. All of which helped Adams in the court of public opinion.[27]

Bulloch offered another respectful admonishment to Mallory for placing too much faith in the Erlanger bond scheme, saying, "I have all along feared that you were overestimating the amount of money to be realized from the loan." He met "several gentlemen connected with the operation," and he smelled a financial rat. He had Lt. Whittle relay his opinions to Mallory on the subject: Richmond was being taken for a financial ride.[28]

After dispensing with the issue of the acquisition of a fast steamer to carry a marine engine through the blockade (a mission headed by Lieutenant Bob Carter) and a brief report on the Laird rams, he updated Mallory on the overall environment in Britain, and the "favourable" decision about the *Alexandra*,

> [It has not] made our operations in Europe less difficult. Federal spies have ... increased ... and I am convinced that nothing more should be attempted in England ... every possible description of warlike implements for the North is freely allowed ... armour plates are being rolled in this country for United States ships and recruiting is ... going on in Ireland for the Federal Army ... a vessel cannot clear for an island, even though it be a British island contiguous to the Confederate States, without enquiry, interruption, and delay. And a shipbuilding anywhere in private yards with the external appearance of a man-of-war is not only watched by Yankee spies but by British officials, and is made the subject of newspaper discussion, letters ... protests from lawyers ... and even petitions from the Emancipation Society.

To close this point, Bulloch rendered a stout opinion on the state of Britain's use of the neutrality laws saying, "Britain discriminates too palpably in favour of the North to deceive anyone but an Englishman as to the fears if not the sympathies of the present ministry." For their part, British officials were invariably perplexed, and often annoyed, that each side of the American Civil War viewed them as biased in favor of the other.[29]

Finally, Bulloch returned to the pragmatic and ever-present problem: a slim budget. He copied into this letter an extract from one he had sent to Gen. McRae concerning the funding needs of the Confederate naval department in Europe. There was no money for any new projects. At least he had time, "several months — say six or eight," before he needed the full amount specified in the letter (£1,018,250) to complete his existing commitments.[30] As Bulloch placed this letter into the "normal" mail, he had no that idea that within 96 hours his own words would be quoted by U.S. Minister Adams to Lord Russell—and fuel the next issue that fouled the props of the rams' escape.

Adams returned to his London office after his summer vacation on September 3rd to find an unwelcome letter from Lord Russell. The foreign minister had refused to seize the Laird rams. Adams replied immediately that if either of the rams attacked U.S. people or property, a "grave" situation would then exist between Britain and the Union. As Adams' messenger dashed to the Foreign Office with his letter, in Liverpool, Bulloch dealt with his own unexpected problem that further damaged his effort to get the Laird rams away. An officer from the CSS *Florida* stood in Bulloch's office at 10 Rumford Place with a letter in hand from his captain, John Newland Maffitt. Bulloch had heard nothing from Maffitt since the *Florida* escaped from Mobile on 16 January 1863.[31]

Maffitt's letter to Bulloch was a tale of mechanical woe: the *Florida* had landed at Brest, whereupon the Confederate commander paid his compliments to Vice-Admiral Count de Gueyton and advised him of his needs for repairs and refueling, all of which were in compliance with French neutrality laws. Bulloch immediately realized the *Florida* needed a full refit and contacted both Fawcett, Preston and Co. as well as W.C. Miller to get a ship's surveyor to Brest and "report her condition." The *Florida* was one issue, but it was her crew that muddied the waters further. Maffitt paid his enlisted crewmen only enough to travel to Liverpool, telling them they would not receive their full pay until they returned to the Confederacy, unless Bulloch instructed otherwise.[32]

The dream of well-qualified crewmen to man the rams was within his grasp, but Bulloch realized that the *Florida's* arrival in Brest, coupled with the release of a large number of disgruntled, unpaid Confederate sailors to journey across France and into England was manna from heaven for the Union counterintelligence efforts. Even if a Union agent had not detected Maffitt's officer in Liverpool, the telegraphs between Brest, Paris, London, and Liverpool were clacking the news. To further complicate matters, the *Florida* would eventually need sailors to replace the ones Maffitt had dismissed. Any increase in manning required an application to the French government and attracted unwanted attention to Confederate efforts in France, just as Bulloch was getting his shipbuilding program going there. The release of idle sailors was a common practice in peacetime, but it created a wartime nightmare for Bulloch.[33]

The following day, U.S. Minister Adams received a jolt when he opened the latest message from Dudley. The sea-trials of *No. 294* were complete and she was ready to sail. Adams sent off a message to Lord Russell and when he had no response by the next day, a Saturday, he fired off a diplomatic broadside to Russell. This note stated plainly, "It would be superfluous in me to point out to your lordship that this is war." If Britain allowed the rams to sail, the Union would view them as a threat to the national security of the United States of America. Britain was aiding and abetting the Confederate cause in its "illegal" rebellion. Adams's "superfluous" comment would become famous, but it was his near direct quotation of Bulloch's vision of using the rams against the cities of New York, Boston, and Portland (along with breaking the blockade) that demonstrated the effectiveness of the Union intelligence effort against the Confederacy. Adams believed he had a lit match held above a cannon pointed at the British lion's head. Dudley caught the train to London; he wanted to be in the capital when war broke out between the Union and Britain.[34]

While Adams and Dudley fretted about the British response and whether they would be expelled as agents of a belligerent nation, Lord Russell already had decided his course of action some two days before (3 September 1863). He would seize the rams. It was the same day that news of the *Florida*'s predicament in France and of her displaced crewmen reached England. What had caused Russell's position over the seizure of the rams to change since his last message to U.S. Minister Adams?[35]

While some historians endorse the supposition that the threat of war by the Union caused Britain to back down, Lord Russell was following the precept he had formulated in the wake of the *Alexandra* decision. The Neutrality Act would be enforced as a matter of government policy, irrespective of the law and any legal findings that might support Confederate claims. Contemporary written evidence supports this argument. Prime Minister Palmerston was on a visit to Wales when Lord Russell made his decision, and upon his return to London, he informed Palmerston. He told the prime minister that he had the solicitor general's endorsement for his action "as one of policy, though not of strict law." The loss of the rams to the Confederate Navy was the result of an amalgamation of factors. Each one added weight until the scales of justice tipped the balance from the rule of law to the expediency of politics: Secretary Mallory failed to follow Bulloch's advice about personnel as large numbers of talkative Confederate Navy officers and enlisted men moved throughout France and Britain; Bulloch lacked adequate and speedy funding; Union counterintelligence fed inflammatory information to the British press; and Union diplomats issued formal complaints at every possible opportunity. All these factors contributed to the Confederate loss, but there were broader policy issues in play for the British.[36]

Lord Russell applied his flexible policy on the Neutrality Act to cover his actions authorizing the Lay-Osborn flotilla. He also kept a weather eye on the situation with Louis-Napoléon and France, along with the rising tensions between Prussia and Denmark, not to mention Poland and Russia. If the Royal Navy needed an "instant" addition to its fleet, the Laird rams were game-changers. Although the younger Lairds were business confidants and the elder Laird sympathized with the Southern cause, their choices were clear if its ancient enemy (France) or new rivals (Germany or Russia) threatened Her Britannic Majesty's Empire.[37]

Although Lord Russell had decided his course of action, he had to bolster not only public opinion but also legal support for his policy on how to apply the Neutrality Act.[38] In the meantime, work on the two rams in Liverpool was proceeding at an even more furious pace.[39] On the 8th of September, Russell informed Adams and Dudley that the rams would be detained. Both Union diplomats knew that detention was not enough; they had to be seized. The American diplomats had heard, believed, and promoted rumors that the Confederates were planning to board the rams and sail them away. Their angst was unnecessary; Russell ordered his assistant, Austin H. Laynard, to stop the rams if they made any move down the Mersey toward the sea.[40]

And where was Bulloch? There is total silence in his memoirs and in the official correspondence from the 3rd when he was in Liverpool through the 16th of September 1863 when he was in Nantes, France. He was most likely making the rounds necessary to maintain business, financial, and political viability of his French shipbuilding efforts in Bordeaux, Paris, and Nantes. Using a surrogate, he relayed instructions concerning the rams to Bravay in Paris, who passed them on to Lairds. Bulloch knew that France was a good place to be, for the rams were getting maximum attention in Liverpool and maximum action in London. The future of his Laird rams was being decided in the halls of the British Foreign Office, the Home Office, and by the highest legal counsels.[41]

British politicians at the cabinet level, including Prime Minister Palmerston, agreed with Russell's actions. But Palmerston pointed out to Russell that it would be difficult to obtain clear proof that a) the Confederates were the actual owners of the rams and that b) they intended to attack the Union. That standard of proof would be required to give his action legal standing. Russell had already broached the first point in a terse diplomatic response to U.S. Minister Adams on the 11th of September, implying that while the Union might rule without legal precedent, Great Britain did not. That point was brought home the next day when the Law Office rendered its opinion.[42]

The Crown's legal officers told Lord Russell, and the entire cabinet, that the government had overstepped its authority. There was no legal justification for halting the "exportation of ships of war or ships which Her Majesty shall judge capable of being converted into war." In a remarkable turn of events, both the British Law Office *and* U.S. Minister Adams were assisting the Confederates in keeping the rams! Adams' persistent and insolent protestations were beginning to annoy the usually unflappable Lord Russell. As for Prime Minister Palmerston, he didn't give a damn what the "Yankees" thought. Pam wasn't going to allow the British Lion to be forced into submission by Yankee whelps. Without ironclad evidence, Adams was only adding to the Union's problems, as the British Law Office confirmed Britain's legal right to do nothing.[43]

Bulloch had no knowledge of these particulars as he concluded a contract with Voruz in Nantes on September 17th that called for the purchase of fifty-six naval guns. The guns were to be manufactured to French naval standards, with the payments handled by "the banking house of Messrs. Erlanger." The French financial octopus was steadily reaching its tentacles into every Confederate pocket.[44]

The tenacious Union counterintelligence effort shifted its energies to closely monitor Bulloch's efforts in France. Beckles Willson provides an extraordinary description of Bulloch as a classic "secret agent," who wore shabby clothing and shaved off his trademark mutton-chop sideburns and moustache to elude Union agents. On September 18th, one of the Union agents sighted Bulloch in Brest, and quickly relayed the information to Paris and to Dudley in Liverpool. Dudley, in conjunction with Henry Sanford, had become the *de facto* head of the Union counterintelligence effort.[45]

Bulloch's presence at Brest was coincident with the CSS *Florida*'s change of command from the ailing Lt. Maffitt to Lt. Joseph N. Barney, who would temporarily oversee the ship's refit. While in Brest, Bulloch personally surveyed the ship and arranged to pay the shipyard before he left.[46] Two days later, he was back in Paris where he managed his French business and caught up on correspondence. As usual, there was a letter from James North in Glasgow about his iron albatross, *No. 61*. North's letter, dated 15 September 1863 had, in Bulloch's own words, "followed me to Bordeaux and back to Paris."[47]

While he may have been out of the ironclad-building business in Great Britain, Bulloch had high hopes for the high-speed blockade runner he had bought there (the *Coquette*). She was to make a run into the Confederacy to obtain cotton on behalf of the Navy Department and then run the cotton through the blockade all the way to Europe. The Confederate Navy finally was acting on Bulloch's recommendation to enter the cotton market and directly finance its requirements.[48]

Even though he remained doubtful about the whole *No. 61* project, Bulloch sent North £15,000 drawn on his Fraser, Trenholm and Co. account. To avoid default, he asked North to request funds in small, manageable amounts. The unexpected arrival of the *Florida* had seriously skewed financial planning. Bulloch closed on a somber note, "I do not think we will get any more [war] ships out of England, and it is a great pity to have so much locked up there." Bulloch's ability to collect and analyze information remained spot on, for he clearly was prepared for bad news.[49]

The next day (September 21st), the British Foreign Office refined the final text of the news that Bulloch and Mallory feared most. Hammond, undersecretary of the Foreign Office, had re-examined Lord Russell's actions and determined that Bravay's ownership was a cover. The shape and structure of the vessels indicated they were clearly warships and the Pasha of Egypt denied that he had anything to do with the rams. With no legitimate owner willing to step forward, Hammond reckoned the rams should be detained.[50]

Lord Russell carefully covered all of his diplomatic bases by sending inquiries to the Russians, Danes, and Turks. The Russians had approached the Lairds about the rams (which did not amuse Palmerston, Russell, or the Royal Navy), while Denmark warily eyed the power plays of Wilhelm I and Bismarck along the Baltic. The Turks? Who knew if they were merely one of Bulloch's "blinds" intended to throw them off the scent? What if they were actually interested in the rams? Then there was Louis-Napoléon. Palmerston had already floated the idea of an outright purchase of the Laird rams (on September 13th). As he pointed out to Lord Russell, the Royal Navy was falling behind France in ironclads.[51] U.S. politicians were not helping matters, for on 26 September 1863 Lord Russell responded to an incendiary speech by U.S. Senator Charles Sumner by saying that Britain did not bow to threats from anyone.[52]

While the British government chastised politicians and chased the Laird ram issue to ground, the French government became more than suspicious about Confederate dealings there. Confederate Commissioner John Slidell summoned Bulloch to Paris with unsettling news. Voruz's confidential clerk had disappeared several weeks before and the U.S. Minister William Dayton had sent copies of Voruz' correspondence to the French foreign minister. These documents allegedly proved that the Confederates were not just building warships in Great Britain, they were also building them in France!

Bulloch was astounded that these facts would be considered news and asked "but surely the government itself authorised [their] building?" How could this be? Slidell answered that although the minister of the marine had authorized the deal by direction of Louis-Napoléon, the foreign minister could still intercede if the activity became public knowledge. Slidell had no concrete intelligence about what French Foreign Minister Lhuys, or U.S. Minister Dayton actually knew. Louis-Napoléon had the classic option of "plausible deniability"; whether he would use it, remained to be seen.[53]

Bulloch returned to Liverpool from France on 27 September 1863 to oversee the dispatch of Lt. Bob Carter and the new high-speed blockade runner *Coquette*. Carter's immediate mission was to get one of Mallory's long desired marine engines into the South for installation aboard a Confederate-built hull. Seventy-two hours after Bulloch's return, the *Coquette* had completed its sea-trials and he hoped to "get her off by the 16th."[54]

Still uncertain about the exact intentions of the British Foreign Office toward his Laird rams, Bulloch told Mallory of his fears, "I would strongly advise that you should direct all work to be suspended in England and material to be sold." Hoping to unload North's ironclad, he hinted that, "other property here might be condemned and confiscated." Complaining of the need for frequent travel and his ever-increasing load of correspondence, Bulloch asked for a trustworthy "young officer" to assist him. Bulloch closed by saying that he would return to France as soon as the *Coquette* got away.

In early October, Bulloch and Lt. Bob Carter journeyed north to Glasgow. Ostensibly, they were there to complete the purchase of the *Coquette* and arrange for her journey south to Liverpool. Perhaps not coincidentally, they noticed another fast vessel at Glasgow that had great potential as a Confederate commerce raider, but was committed to a voyage to Australia. Named the *Sea King*, she was the newest marvel created by the great Scottish naval architect, William Rennie. For the moment, Bulloch's attentions were focused on getting the *Coquette* under weigh. And well that they were, for the axe finally fell on Confederate dreams of British-built armored ships.[55]

On 8 October 1863, Lord Russell instructed Foreign Office Undersecretary Hammond to have the Treasury Office seize the Laird rams. A rumor that one of the rams was preparing to sail reached the Foreign Office and prompted Russell to act on his commitment to seize them.[56] For the present time, work was allowed to continue on the ships to avoid unemployment among the Laird shipyard workers. Bulloch was forced to continue making payments on ships he could not obtain.

Bulloch returned to Liverpool on October 11th, but due to bureaucratic inertia, the British had not yet physically seized the rams. He returned to his home in Waterloo only to puzzle over another James North-induced problem. Bulloch had to relay the "unfortunate" news that Gen. McRae denied North's request for funds to continue work on *No. 61*. The Confederate Treasury had instructed McRae to hold all funds in France. Bulloch observed that all his correspondence seemed to be about "pecuniary" matters, thus he was obliged to tell everyone he had no money. The Confederate naval effort in Great Britain was dying from adverse political winds and a lack of money. There seemed to be little that Bulloch could do about it.[57]

On Thursday night, October 15th, James Dunwoody Bulloch's greatest technical achievement, and the Confederacy's dream of war-winning destroyers of the Union blockade came to an official end. The British customs officers finally took physical possession of the first Laird ram and they both were soon secured from any potential Confederate effort to sail them away.[58]

On 20 October 1863, Bulloch reported to Sec. Mallory that his earlier suspicions were now confirmed: the British government would not allow the Confederacy to have the rams. Like all good Navy officers, he conducted a candid self-examination of all the particulars surrounding his role in the failure of the ram project, trying to discover and avoid repeating any mistakes.[59]

He had sold the rams to Bravay, believing that if they were in French hands, the British would not interfere with their sailing. He was wrong in that belief. In fact, the British had thoroughly tested the whole charade. Before the seizure of the rams on 22 September 1863, Captain E.G. Hoare, the Royal Navy attaché in Paris, met Bravay at his home with "the intent of the purchase ... of such formidable ships."[60] Bravay managed to convince the officer of his story, or so he thought, but Hoare outbluffed him when he offered to buy the rams outright. Bravay tried to extricate himself by claiming he had to complete the rams according to "their designs" and deliver them to a French port before he could sell. The British captain went away with a knowing smile as Bravay dabbed the perspiration from his brow. Bulloch knew the British were onto their scheme.[61]

Bulloch next proposed that Louis-Napoléon might intercede on behalf of Bravay. To that end, he had sent a carefully worded letter to Slidell in Paris about Hoare's visit. What could the French government do to help the situation? He traveled to London the following day and met Commodore Barron, who had arrived in Britain (along with the indefatigable Lt. William C. Whittle) to find that his armored squadron was under lock and key. They proceeded to Paris and conferred with Slidell about their options. Bulloch believed that the British would not release the rams unless Louis-Napoléon gave the British government a guaranteed absolution of responsibility for any actions the Union might take. For this ploy to work, Monsieur Napoleon would have to be willing to let John Bull step aside if Uncle Sam decided to pick a fight over the issue.[62]

Bulloch completed his soul-searching letter by wondering if he had placed too much trust in Slidell and Mason's assurances that France fully and officially supported their efforts. He suspected that Bravay should have openly declared his ownership of the rams and asked the British for permission to move them to France for completion rather than suggest that they were for Egypt. At least the Confederate Navy could have saved money, time, and effort. As it was, the "gray navy" lost the ships, time, effort, and was on the verge of losing its money as well. Bulloch was running out of ideas for salvaging anything at all, lamenting that "my hands are tied."[63] Knowledgeable Northerners recognized the significance of this victory: "Undoubtedly to us this is a second Vicksburg."[64]

For the British, it appeared that they had achieved a blessed equilibrium. The Union was ecstatic; Lincoln's government believed it had tamed the British Lion, forcing it to behave like a more friendly neutral. The British were able to take the rams out of the equation for upsetting affairs in Europe, and most importantly, out of the hands of the French. Lord Russell believed that his flexible application of neutrality policy also preserved the legality of the Lay-Osborn flotilla. Yet, in China, the Lay-Osborn project began to unravel.

As the Laird rams issue reached its superfluous apogee, the Lay-Osborn flotilla arrived in China. The nebulous legality of the flotilla's "neutrality" was obvious to not only Chinese, but also to British observers. A letter in the English language *North China Herald* in Shanghai pointed out the reality of Lord Russell's untenable problem. The decidedly unclear "loyalty" of Lay and Osborn, created the question, "Do we recognise these two gentlemen and their subordinates as British subjects and as such entitled to British protection, or are we to leave them to the tender mercies of the local authorities" if they should fall afoul of Chinese law? Coming to the crux of the issue, the anonymous correspondent presciently stated, "The day is not far distant when we shall find a British gunboat interfering for the protection of British property against the rapacious demand of a Chinese cruiser, commanded and manned by men still owing allegiance to Her Majesty. That this calamity may be avoided is the earnest wish."[65] But calamity was coming very soon for Lay, Osborn, and Lord Russell's flexible neutrality policy. Bulloch and the Confederate Navy would have another opportunity to make up for the loss of the rams.

In the meantime, Bulloch was in Liverpool, attending to the practical means that could provide the Confederate Navy the funds it needed to buy any number of ships, should they become available. He was loading the *Coquette* with a marine engine and spare parts. Her performance was exemplary, making over 13½ knots on her sea-trials.[66]

If Lieutenant Carter was successful in running the *Coquette* through the blockade, Mallory could "carry out ... the design of sending out cotton to meet the engagements of the Navy Department in Europe." Bulloch mused that if Mallory wished to establish a regular service, he could purchase "two or three light-draft paddle steamers of high speed" to work in concert with the *Coquette*. The *Coquette* could haul cargo to the British islands nearest the Confederacy, where the light-draft paddle steamers would dash into the Confederacy. It was a typically practical suggestion and like most of Bulloch's theories, it was successful in practice.[67]

According to Prioleau, at least 200,000 bales of cotton had been run through the blockade and there were plans to *expand* the scope and scale of this profitable business. At the present prices, Bulloch reckoned 200,000 bales of cotton would cover all the Navy Department's needs. The Confederate government needed to take control of this trade, even though it would ruffle the feathers of Confederate businessmen, such as Prioleau. Bulloch had already brokered some minor cotton shipments on the Navy's account using Fraser, Trenholm and Co. and their agent in Bermuda, Louis Heyliger. Whenever Bulloch knew that a cargo of Confederate Navy cotton was bound for Liverpool, he could draw credit for it against its sale price and stabilize his financial situation.[68]

Bulloch told Mallory explicitly that if such a payment system could be established on a regular basis, there would be enough money available for other naval agents. Drawing on his experiences with North and Maury, he needed to have total knowledge of their projects to forecast their financial needs and "make the necessary financial arrangements." He was hoping to avoid the constant juggling of finances for competing projects.[69]

As he dreamed of financial deliverance, Bulloch had to endure the unexpected drain on his funds through North's continuing work on *No. 61* and Maffitt's ill-timed arrival. Bulloch paid off the *Florida's* crew and covered her refit costs. Coupled with the expenses of the *Coquette* mission, Bulloch said frankly, "I shall be without a farthing in England." In fact, when he made the final payment on Mallory's marine engines, his account with Fraser, Trenholm and Co. was overdrawn. Bulloch needed decisive action if he and the Confederate Navy's European initiatives were to have any chance of success.[70]

His immediate concern was to get the *Coquette* under weigh for the Confederacy via Bermuda, and then return to Paris as quickly as possible. He needed to check on the progress of his new French builds and review his remaining options for the Laird rams with Slidell and Bravay. As October slipped away into November, he saluted Lt. Carter and wished the *Coquette* fair winds. Bulloch could only hope that his projects in France would prove as successful.

It was fortunate for his peace of mind that Bulloch was unaware of the events that were transpiring in France during his last transit between Liverpool and Nantes. The clerk that had disappeared from Voruz's office resurfaced on 10 September 1863 in the offices of the U.S. consul to France, John Bigelow. Initially, Bigelow believed the Alsatian clerk was just another of the countless adventurers, or outright lunatics, who frequented the Union's diplomatic offices with tales of Confederate duplicity. However, in this instance, the middle-aged man at the door was "sober and deliberate of speech, as if he had been trained to measure his words." In Bigelow's first-person account of this meeting, he only referred to the man as "Mr. X," but court records later confirmed his identity as "Petermann."[71]

Petermann claimed that there were several ships under construction for the Confederacy in both Nantes and Bordeaux. Although Bigelow had heard rumors, nothing had been confirmed. Petermann said that some of the ships under construction were armored rams that had propulsion systems ready for installation; "artillery and shells" had been ordered for their guns. Bigelow at first thought these claims were preposterous; the French government would not allow any ship of war to be built without the proper authorization. The unruffled Alsatian countered that "official authorization for the construction, equipment, and arming of these vessels had already been issued from the Department of the Marine," and he was prepared to prove it.[72]

Bigelow recognized the enormity of Petermann's claims if they could be substantiated but "none at all without proofs which cannot be disputed or explained away." Petermann implacably replied that he could supply "original documents and what is more, ... with my proofs in hand you can effectually secure the arrest of the ships." Petermann then delivered the *coup de grace*, producing the authorization from the Department of the Marine that "appeared on its face to have been procured through false representations." Petermann said that Bigelow could examine the documents at his leisure to confirm their authenticity. Bigelow, knowing that the clerk was not motivated by altruism, told him he could expect 20,000 francs upon the defeat of "Confederate naval operations in France." With that, Bigelow and Petermann arranged another meeting for September 12th when he would provide more evidence.[73]

U.S. Consul Dudley had tried to use Charles Yonge against Bulloch and the Confederates, but his weak character was exposed and exploited under legal examination. By contrast, Consul Bigelow now had the ultimate inside man, for Petermann was a confidential secretary at Voruz's firm and he had the actual documents. The clerk's character, however questionable, didn't matter in this case.[74] The documents would do all the talking and the authorities would not question the legality of their acquisition. Petermann returned to Bigelow's office as promised with a veritable dossier of material, including a letter between Arman and Voruz that identified a ship they were building for Bulloch (for the sum of 720,000 francs) *and* confirmed Erlanger's involvement. Bigelow fairly swooned with joy. As he wrote later, the "note from M. Arman ... to M. Voruz ... would alone have answered our purpose." But there was more, much more, including letters directly from Bulloch to Voruz.[75]

John Bigelow, the U.S. consul in Paris, exposed Bulloch's acquisition of French-built flotilla of armored rams and wooden cruisers (Library of Congress).

After settling the financial side of Petermann's industrial espionage for the Union, Bigelow absorbed all the material. What he saw convinced him and Minister Dayton that the scope and scale of the support for the Confederate operation ran all the way to the top — Emperor Louis-Napoléon.[76]

Dayton took almost a week before submitting copies of the Petermann dossier to the French minister of Foreign Affairs, Drouyn de Lhuys, on 22 September 1863. Three days later, de Lhuys began an investigation, but the Department of the Marine moved with the same initial lack of haste as had the British. The ships in question were not far along in construction, so there was no apparent need to hurry. Bulloch had just been in Paris on the 20th, and was not aware of the extent of the clerk's treachery.[77]

The French government finally acted on October 22nd when the Department of the Marine revoked Arman's authorization for arming the wooden corvettes. This complication would have overwhelmed a lesser man. For it was the same day that Bulloch finalized details of the *Coquette's* mission, settled the accounts of the *Florida's* discharged crew, and lamented the lack of funds for North's ironclad. When he arrived in Paris about three days after the *Coquette* cleared for Bermuda on 25 October 1863, Bulloch was still hopeful that Confederate Commissioner John Slidell could intercede and salvage the Laird rams as well as the French corvettes. November looked to be as bleak as October.[78] He would take little comfort in the knowledge that November was not going to be a good month for Lord Russell either.

In China, Russell's effort to take sides in the other civil war began to unravel. Several weeks of negotiations among the emperor of China, Prince Kung, Horatio Lay, and Captain Sherard Osborn had ended in stalemate. The Prince would not agree to the British command relationships for the "China flotilla." Prince Kung demanded that he and the lesser mandarins had to have operational control, while Osborn resolutely argued that all orders would emanate from Her Majesty's government. He would be in total charge of all ships, at all times. The affair descended into dramatic farce on November 9th when Osborn ordered the flotilla to be disbanded, effective immediately.[79]

The Lay-Osborn Flotilla caused Lord Russell and the British government immense embarrassment over its "flexible" neutrality policy and gave the Confederate Navy one last glimmer of hope of acquiring a war-winning, blockade-busting fleet. It would take time for news of the China flotilla to wend its way around the globe, but it would spread like wildfire when it reached the first tendrils of the telegraphic branches of the British Empire.

It wasn't until 26 November 1863, that Bulloch mentioned any details about his French initiatives. In a letter to Mallory written from Liverpool, he noted that when he "last saw them about ten days ago" the armored ships were "nearly three-fifths finished." Thus, sometime around November 16th Bulloch was in Bordeaux where the ironclads were being built. But where had he been in the preceding two weeks?[80]

The answer is simple: everywhere. He went to Le Havre to inspect the works of Mazeline, one of France's greatest marine engine builders; he had been to Rive-de-Giere in Loire at the works of Petin, Godot and Co. who was making the armor plates for the Bordeaux rams. Then there was a visit to a "private" French naval gun foundry. He withheld the name from his correspondence because he believed that he had not been followed, but the French and British were opening his mail. He checked on the progress of refitting the *Florida* in Brest and traveled through Paris. Even with France's modern (by nineteenth century standards) network of rail and telegraphic connections, Bulloch had raced through an itinerary that would have exhausted a modern-day business-class traveler.[81]

Consequently, when Bulloch returned to Liverpool toward the end of November 1863, he had a lot to tell Secretary Mallory. He had received $2,000,000 in cotton certificates via the Confederate Treasury and Gen. McRae. He had another warrant for £437,500 (over $3,000,000 U.S. in 1863) from the Erlanger loans. Suddenly, the possibility of actually having funds burst through Bulloch's financial clouds like a summer's rainstorm, pouring funds into his parched coffers. He profusely apologized for his earlier letters to Mallory, who had belatedly recognized the wisdom of Bulloch's advice for obtaining funds for his European naval projects.[82]

Bulloch confirmed that cotton certificates could buy both "second-hand ships" and supplies. Cotton was as good as money in hand. The assignment of Gen. McRae as the sole financial agent for cotton certificates and securities meant that a "fixed market value can ... be soon established for them." He would patiently wait to see if McRae's efforts could meet the $2,000,000 warrant. In the meanwhile, he exhorted Mallory to allow him to buy light-draft, high-speed steamers. They would be capable of making rapid transits from Bermuda, the Bahamas, and Cuba into the Confederacy. A fleet of such ships would guarantee a steady delivery of cotton for conversion into cash. The vessels could easily be sold if peace were to break out, or after the war they could be armed with a single pivoting naval gun for "the police of the coast." The prospect of steady funding had positively transformed Bulloch's outlook.[83]

On another cheerful note, the *Alabama* and the *Florida* and other commerce raiders had been so successful that the "American flag is fast disappearing from the ocean." Most American ships had been reflagged under foreign ownership. With only a few ships left to attack, Bulloch did not see the point in pursuing additional commerce raiders. Instead, he advocated building ships for "offensive warfare." In case Mallory had already been thinking along those same lines, Bulloch had already procured some "estimates and plans" and would coordinate financial arrangements to build these ships with Gen. McRae, pending Mallory's approval to proceed.[84]

He closed the letter to Mallory with a detailed accounting of all expenditures, including those of Sinclair's ship, Maury's "special project," the *Florida's* refit, and of course, North's *No. 61*. Candidly, Bulloch said, "I hope that officer will decide to sell her before it is too late." In a not-so-subtle hint, he begged Mallory's pardon for "the untidy appearance of this dispatch. I am much pressed for time in bringing my correspondence" for he had "no clerk to assist" him.[85]

The next day, he addressed Mallory's request for more information about his armored ships in Bordeaux. Each ram would have "one 300-pounder of 12 tons, mounted in the forward turret and pointing in the line of the keel, with no side ports or lateral training." The rear turrets would have "two 70-pounders ... arranged to fire over the stern or forward at an angle of about 25° with the keel." While the armored turrets and the huge firepower may have captivated Mallory's attentions, Bulloch was most proud of the rams' handling capabilities. The design called for two sternposts, with two screws powered by separate engines so that "by reversing the motion of the screws, the vessels may be turned as on a pivot." These ships could turn within their own length and quickly bring their guns to bear. Mallory would get the full details when John Maffitt returned to the Confederacy to convalesce. Bulloch next turned to more worrisome matters.[86]

American newspapers reported that the French government knew that ships were being built in France for the Confederate Navy. Mallory had read the stories himself; and Bulloch, through clenched teeth, had to acknowledge that they had been compromised.[87]

Parisian newspapers claimed that the French government would not allow any of the ships to be completed, but Bulloch asserted that this was not true. Just like the British, the French would not seize them until they were "ready for sea." Although French Foreign Minister de Lhuys had reportedly told U.S. Minister Dayton that "none of the ships [would] be allowed to leave France," he did not fully believe the report. However, he did admit that news of his frequent visits to the various shipyards and suppliers had elicited widespread "suspicion" that helped to substantiate the compromised information provided by Voruz's confidential clerk.[88]

Bulloch learned that Petermann had disappeared with "some letters and papers relating to the business. Mr. Voruz has not yet discovered the full extent to which he has been robbed ... [and] how far he can prove complicity on the part of the United States officials. We know that the stolen papers contain absolute evidence that the ships are for us," for Minister de Lhuys had stated so to "one of the builders." Bulloch angrily stated that he had the certificate of authorization signed by the minister of the Department of the Marine, Chasseloup-Laubat. Neither the French, nor the Union, could ever truthfully say that the Confederate States of America had violated French neutrality laws. Upon that, he was sure. But he was also sure that France would soon have to declare its policy relating to "American affairs positively."[89]

Bulloch began to sense *déjà vu* about the situation in France. Minister de Lhuys accepted Dayton's dossier of stolen documents without even questioning whether they were stolen. Bulloch argued that any other government official in a lawful country would have thrown out the illegally obtained documents and tossed Dayton out on his ear. Instead, the French minister confronted Arman and Voruz and made them confess their dealings with the Confederacy. The builders believed they could still finish the ships, as Bulloch had predicted, but his ability to get them out of France would "depend upon the position of affairs in America at the time of their completion." If the Union continued to have the upper hand in the war, French neutrality law would be enforced to the Confederacy's detriment. The French were positioning themselves to place their bet only after it was clear which side would win. Bulloch would proceed with hopes of success, but his every course of action was driven by wildly variable and unpredictable political winds.[90]

The Confederates certainly had good intelligence as to what the French government knew about their operations. But neither Bulloch, nor Confederate commissioner John Slidell, knew the internal machinations that were at work within the French government.

Foreign Minister de Lhuys was no great supporter of Louis-Napoléon's imperial vision. The "cotton famine" that had struck the British economy had an even more devastating effect on the French economy and on the country's purse. He was unhappy that Louis-Napoléon had used him as a pawn in a deadly game that risked war with America, not only over the Confederacy, but Mexico as well. Then there were the British; they were tightening their policy on neutrality and were supposed to be adhering to a cooperative policy over the conflict in America. If this wasn't enough, Denmark and Prussia were beginning to look like they might square off. A war on the very doorstep of France could easily draw them in there. This was not a time for imperial dithering; for de Lhuys, France was immortal, but Louis-Napoléon was not. He would do what was best for France. The Confederates simply did not know and could not see *la grande image*.[91]

Bulloch was operating in an increasingly hostile environment, and his luck with the British and the *Alexandra* was no better:

> The animus of the British government is sufficiently apparent. The difference between the speech of the present attorney general in Parliament, when it was his cue to defend the government for the escape ... of the *Alabama*, and that which he has lately made in support of the plea for a new trial in the case of the *Alexandra* is most striking. Lord Russell furnishes Mr. Adams with lawyers to plead for him in court and with spies and detectives to pick up testimony.[92]

On December 3rd, Mallory wrote from Richmond that he had not heard from Bulloch for some time. He presumed that his reports had been captured aboard inbound blockade runners. The anxious Secretary said, "You will readily appreciate the earnest interest with which the grave affairs in your hands are followed." Mallory, the Confederate Navy, and the Confederate nation were desperate for Bulloch's ironclads.[93]

Writing from Paris on 6 December 1863, Bulloch completely understood Mallory's anxiety and told him that due to lost dispatches, and possible tampering with his mail, he would be using a special messenger to send sensitive messages to Richmond. Too much information had leaked into the press. He then brought Mallory up to speed that the Laird rams had been "exchequered" and there would be a trial in January 1864:

> Builders and French owners have employed the very best counsel, who are of [the] opinion that the case will go against the British Government and that French owner's title will be fully estab-

lished.... If case is decided in favor of French owners, they will resist any attempt to appeal the case; will formally claim the ships as their property and throw themselves upon their own government for protection. Then will be determined how far we can expect the aid of French government in all our undertakings.[94]

Bulloch was correct in his assessment. Their success would depend on French (i.e., Napoleon's) intentions, but he had little idea of the greater political realities that influenced French actions. Foreign Minister de Lhuys was intent on keeping France on the side of the Union, out of Mexico, out of further debt, and with plenty of dry powder, ships, and credit in case the Danish-Prussian-Polish-Russian situation went hot. The Confederates were simply babes in the business of international affairs and unable to fathom the *realpolitik* of the Victorian Age.[95]

However, Bulloch understood finances and phonies in the cotton trade. He told Mallory that he had received "no proposition from Stringer or Sanders." Sanders, in fact, "has nothing in progress under [his] original contract and has shown much shuffling. The [Navy] department will save largely by doing its own business."[96]

Of all his various and frustrating dealings with builders, sailors, contractors, lawyers, politicians, and assorted middlemen, Bulloch found people like Stringer and Sanders the most exasperating. In his memoir, Bulloch confessed, "Nothing gave me so much harassing perplexity, or tried my patience and forbearance to so great a degree, as the supervision of private contracts." These men had considerable political influence in the South and great ideas in Europe, but they had no money or other means of raising money other than looking for a handout from Bulloch. Their lack of discretion was only matched by their eagerness to complain to Richmond about Bulloch's lack of cooperation.[97]

Despite the revelations in France, Bulloch's work on the French corvettes was proceeding well and that there was "no intimation of interference yet."[98] After posting his letter, Bulloch dashed away to gather up important papers into his valise and catch the train to London, and onto the Channel ferry to France. During his journey, the fate of North's ironclad was decided. On December 14th, North wrote Mallory from Paris, after "a meeting and consultation of the commissioners, senior naval officer [Barron], and financial agent [McRae]," it was decided unanimously to sell *No. 61* without loss of time. The seizure of Lt. George Sinclair's *Pampero* in Glasgow had finally convinced North and the rest to act.[99]

On December 21st, Lt. John Hamilton, the star-crossed officer who had been omitted from the crew of the *Alabama* and who lost command of the *Alexandra* when the British seized it, joined Bulloch in Paris to help keep his French building projects alive. As Lt. John M. Brooke observed, "The amount of work and bother that he [Bulloch] has to get through within twenty-four hours would kill most any other man."[100]

On 26 December 1863, Bulloch found himself back in Liverpool. He had been fortunate to spend Christmas and Boxing Day with Harriott and his children after getting away from Paris. His letter on that date did not reflect a holiday mood, however; money problems were proliferating. He had to report that Gen. McRae was unable to cover Mallory's Confederate Treasury draft of £437,500. Even worse, there were insufficient funds to meet Bulloch's forthcoming payments. He needed more cotton sales — and soon. He was going to test the financial waters using cotton certificates shortly and he hoped for help from an unidentified gentleman who was "well known to you [Mallory] by reputation and who has already communicated with the department."[101]

The Lay-Osborn flotilla (National Maritime Museum London, A7541).

Closing his Boxing Day letter to Mallory, Bulloch said he was just back from the Continent to post letters on the mail ship to Bermuda. All work was proceeding satisfactorily, though "not so fast as I could wish." He ruefully wished that "all our people in Europe could only be kept perfectly quiet for a short time, so that public attention might be distracted or led away from our designs." For this Christmas wish, U.S. Consuls Dudley and Bigelow would share the role of unreconstructed Scrooges to all things Confederate.[102]

In New York, Bulloch's stepmother Martha and sister Anna received a worrisome Christmas present in the form of a letter from Harriott in Liverpool. Harriott reported that James was not in Liverpool and that their son Dunwody was "encased in steel." Young "Dunnie" was receiving a treatment to straighten his arms and legs as a result of having contracted rickets, a disease that bows the arms and legs of children. Harriott also mentioned that she had recently seen Mrs. Raphael Semmes, but added a sad note that brought home the enormity of the personal losses that the Confederacy and Union had endured in 1863. Her younger brother Edwin, a Union Army soldier, had been killed in battle during the summer. It was the 31st of December and provided a fitting, somber ending to 1863.[103]

But on the far side of the world on the same day, well before James and Harriott Bulloch celebrated the promise of the New Year in Liverpool, or Martha Bulloch and the Roosevelts had even awakened, a telegraph clattered to life in Suez, Egypt. It was a dramatic telegram from the *Times* of London correspondent:

> Prince Kung having refused to ratify the agreement made by Mr. Lay with Captain Osborn, Captain Osborn proceeded to disband his force. The European Ministers protested against Prince Kung having the ships on his own terms, and Prince Kung then requested Mr. Bruce to sell the ships for him. Mr. Bruce having requested Captain Osborn to undertake their disposal, a part of the squadron were to sail for England, and Captain Osborn, with the *Keangsoo, Quantung*, and *Amoy*, had sailed for Bombay. Captain Osborn may be shortly expected in England.[104]

10

Act Upon Your Own Judgment — 1864

On first day of 1864, Mary Boykin Chesnut provided a succinct commentary on the plight of the Confederacy in her insightful diary; "One more year of 'Stonewall' would have saved us. Chickamauga is the only battle we have gained since 'Stonewall' died, and no results follow as usual.... If General Lee had had Grant's resources, he would have bagged the last Yankee or have had them all safe back in Massachusetts." The acerbic wit of Mary Chesnut defined the Confederacy's problems: lack of dynamic leadership in the field, other than Robert E. Lee, and lack of resources. She did not even mention the Confederate Navy. The successes of Raphael Semmes and the Alabama made good newspaper copy, but success across the oceans did not resonate with Southerners who were facing a growing threat of Union armies that ravaged their farmlands.[1]

The ongoing conflict between the Confederacy and the Union was a mere sideshow for Great Britain and France in the first weeks of 1864. The embers of the Schleswig-Holstein situation were threatening to turn white-hot and bring Wilhelm I of Prussia into direct conflict with Christian IX of Denmark over control of the two duchies. They both had largely German populations and since the twelfth century, they had complex relationships with their more powerful Danish and German neighbors. Their "true" allegiance was not clear and competition over who "owned" them was fierce.[2]

During the First Schleswig War (1848 to 1851), Great Britain stepped in and helped confirm the integrity of Denmark as a European nation. The resulting protocol, signed by Austria, France, Prussia, Britain, Russia, Sweden, and Denmark, also required the two duchies to remain neutral. Great Britain included Sweden and Denmark in the agreement since the two Baltic naval powers could help check Prussian naval aspirations. Wilhelm I and Bismarck wanted Kiel, for if they controlled this Baltic seaport, the German Confederation could and would build a navy to challenge Great Britain.[3]

The latest crisis between Denmark and Prussia started when Christian IX signed a new Danish constitution on 18 November 1863. It mandated rule over the entire Danish monarchy. The future of European peace balanced upon the word "entire." Bismarck did not hesitate. The Germans produced a resolution calling for the occupation of Holstein by "Confederate" forces — in this case, the German Confederation. Christian IX withdrew his troops from Holstein, hoping to placate Wilhelm I and Bismarck, while shortening his lines of defense in the event of open war. On Christmas Eve 1863, Saxon and Hanoverian

A contemporary illustration of the last Confederate raider, CSS *Shenandoah* (U.S. Naval Historical Center).

troops marched into Holstein and took control. For the next 80-odd years, Europe would tremble at the sound of German boots marching across its landscape, each time more destructive than the last. But at that moment in 1863, Lord Russell and the British Foreign Office knew that a short fuse had been lit in Europe that could explode into a continental war. Even worse, the Germans and the Danes were frenetically buying supplies and munitions for war.[4]

If Lord Russell's civil servants had not been working long hours at the Foreign Office throughout the holidays due to marching Germans, the sudden availability of the Lay-Osborn flotilla meant that their night lamps were on now. At least two sets of Confederates would be after Osborn's ships: the American and German. Who else? The French, Russians, Swedes, South Americans, and Japanese could all use a few extra warships.

On January 6th, the *London Nonconformist* carried a front-page article about the failed Lay-Osborn project, reporting, "The force is disbanded. The squadron is dispersed for sale and Captain Osborn is on his way home." The first weeks of January offered new opportunities and additional competitors in the naval weapons market. This information would not have escaped Bulloch's notice; it certainly hadn't escaped the attention of Palmerston and Russell's enemies in the British Parliament. There would be baying from the backbenches of Parliament for answers soon. The Cabinet was in full damage control mode for this foreign policy catastrophe, while it tried to avert an impending disaster between Denmark and Prussia.[5]

Bulloch coveted at least some of the eight ships of the China flotilla. Not only were they built and acquired right under his nose in Liverpool, they were designed for the shallow waters of China's inland rivers. They were well armed with the latest British weapons and two of them were commanded by former blockade-running Royal Navy officers, Hugh Burgoyne (*Pekin*), and Charles Forbes (*Keangsoo*). Bulloch was very aware of the diplomatic game that Her Majesty's government had played with the Foreign Enlistment Act. These

British-built-and-manned warships were intended for one of the belligerents in a civil war. If the Chinese could have them, why couldn't the Confederacy?

Bulloch was in Liverpool for much of January 1864, still trying to get the two Laird rams into the hands of Bravay and out of the clutches of the British legal system. He also attended to his ever-present bills by applying proceeds from recent cotton sales through Fraser, Trenholm and Co. He had not yet used the cotton certificates provided by the Secret Act of the Confederate Congress to finance the ironclads. He feared using them in any open business deal, for they might reveal the Confederate Congress' involvement. He also wanted to avoid locking up large amounts of money for projects that might not come to fruition. The British were interpreting the neutrality laws without regard to legality, so he knew that no more overt warship projects could be started there; France remained uncertain, but Louis-Napoléon still seemed sympathetic.[6]

Bulloch's assessment of the tenuousness of France's neutrality position was well warranted. On 26 January 1864, Foreign Minister de Lhuys appeared at a cabinet council meeting to discuss French neutrality, or lack thereof. Lhuys believed that Louis-Napoléon's reckless activity in Mexico weakened France both financially and militarily at a time when it could least afford it.[7] German nationalism was growing while France's power on the Continent appeared to be waning. France needed the support of the United States and Britain, which would require a policy of strict neutrality enforcement. It was an opportune moment for the foreign minister, since Louis-Napoléon was away from Paris. In a charged cabinet meeting chaired by Empress Eugénie, de Lhuys' arguments carried the day. The wily French foreign minister gained total jurisdiction over all Confederate shipbuilding operations in French ports. It remained to be seen what the emperor would say, or do, when he discovered de Lhuys' political maneuvering at the expense of the Confederacy.[8]

By the time Bulloch arrived in Paris the following day, the European continent was again holding its breath in anticipation of hostilities between Denmark and the German Confederation.[9] Four days later, a joint Prussian-Austrian force assaulted the Danish fortifications at Dannevirke. The French and British resolutely focused their diplomatic efforts to contain the crisis. Bulloch's attempts to get any of the Confederate ships would now compete for attention with the *realpolitik* of the Great Powers. Louis-Napoléon simply had bigger potatoes to fry.

Bulloch arrived in France with the intention of getting Bravay to appeal to the French emperor directly regarding the Laird rams. Louis-Napoléon continued to express his personal sympathy for the South, but he would not ask the British government to release the Laird rams to Bravay. The events in Denmark meant that neither France nor Britain wanted armored ships on the open market unless they were sold to "allies" like Denmark. They certainly could not afford to risk a war with the United States that would jeopardize French interests in Mexico or interfere with British maritime trade.[10]

Bulloch immediately met with Confederate commissioners Slidell and Mason, along with Commodore Samuel Barron, to assess the situation. Slidell, Mason, and Barron quickly agreed that the rams could not be taken out of England. They instructed him to sell the rams immediately and recover as much of the Confederate investment as possible, hoping to invest the money in future projects in France.[11]

On February 7th, Bulloch was forced to annul the contract with Bravay for the Laird rams. It was an act "that caused me greater pain and regret than I ever conceived it possible to feel." This time, the sale had to be legitimate, but they were not to be sold to the Union under any circumstances. He believed the "completed" value of the rams was £210,000 and the uncompleted value was £182,000. Bravay and Bulloch would split any profits over these amounts. Bravay acknowledged this proposal formally on February 10th by merely signing the bottom of the letter.[12]

Despite this setback, the events in Schleswig-Holstein would soon profit the Confederacy. On February 18th, Commander James North, who had left Glasgow to take up residence in Paris, announced that the Danish government would buy his unfinished ironclad, No. 61, for £240,000.[13]

News of French Foreign Minister de Lhuys' strict neutrality policy reached Bulloch in Liverpool on the same day. Louis-Napoléon's covert attempt to advance the Confederate cause (and his Mexican dreams) through the Department of the Marine without informing the Foreign Ministry had failed disastrously. Union Minister Dayton, Consul Bigelow, the French press, and a very irate de Lhuys had neutered the emperor's imperial aspirations. The French shipbuilders were instructed that the Confederate "ironclads cannot be permitted to sail, and that the corvettes must not be armed in France, but must be nominally sold to some foreign merchant and dispatched as ordinary trading vessels." That was that.[14]

Bulloch, who had already lost his cherished Laird rams, was not going down without a fight for the French ironclads. This time, the Danish situation worked to his advantage. He concocted a plan with Arman to sell one of the ironclads to a Danish banker. The banker would then assume the role of an official representative of the Danish government when, in actuality, the deal would only be a private agreement among Arman, Bulloch, and the banker. The French ironclad would ostensibly set off for Denmark and rendezvous with a ship loaded with a Confederate crew and munitions. The Confederates could then take control of the ironclad, supply her, and sail for North America. Bulloch's letter of February 18th reveals that he had long suspected de Lhuys would announce this dramatic change in French neutrality policy. He wrote Mallory on February 9th outlining his covert plan. Just as in Liverpool, Bulloch was a half step ahead of politically manipulated lawyers.[15]

Although he had expected the worst of the French, he didn't have to like it. Bulloch fulminated that they had proffered hope and an open hand of support, but then slapped the Confederacy fully in the face. He could only muse upon what might have been a glorious composite naval squadron comprised of the two ironclads building at Bordeaux and the four corvettes at Nantes. They would have "enabled [their] commander to strike severe and telling blows upon the northern seaboard." All he could do now was to offer opinions and options to Sec. Mallory. The success of the *Alabama* and her satellite commerce cruiser, the *Tuscaloosa* (one of the *Alabama*'s prizes that Semmes converted into a raider under the command of John Low), had driven Union commerce ships either into port or under foreign flags. There was nothing left to capture; there was also no money. In fact, Bulloch had to continue making payments on the detained ships that were under construction until they were actually sold—a bitter and expensive pill to swallow.

Bulloch still had creative ideas: could not light draft, high-speed paddle wheel steamers be bought? Such ships could be equipped with external coalbunkers and a single naval gun, and sent on blockade-busting raids from Bermuda, Cuba, and the Bahamas. The naval guns could be installed offshore to maintain neutrality; the ships could then be sold if they made it through the blockade. The fear of such raids would disturb Union transports and blockaders alike. It was a desperate strategy, but like most of his ideas, it could have succeeded if only the Confederacy had acted more promptly.[16]

Details of what had transpired in China were slow in reaching Lord Russell's offices at the British Foreign Ministry. When they did arrive in the mid-to-latter weeks of January 1864, there was immediate concern that the vessels could wind up in the hands of governments or individuals unfriendly to Her Majesty's "interests." This fear was well founded.

Back in August 1863 when Semmes and the CSS *Alabama* steamed into Simon's Town, South Africa, they found the *Kwang-Tung* of the Lay-Osborn flotilla already there. The *Kwang-Tung* had been laid down as hull #297 in Lairds' shipyard and was under the command of the adventurous and convivial Allen Young of the Royal Navy. Commander Young wasted no time inviting Captain Semmes and his officers onboard the *Kwang-Tung* for dinner on August 10th and 11th. He warned them of the presence and location of the USS *Mohican*, a federal gunboat searching for the *Alabama*.[17]

If this meeting aggravated Secretary Welles' and Consul Adams' ulcers, they would have been doubly concerned when the *Alabama* entered Singapore on 22 December 1863. Who should be there but Commander Young and the now-for-sale *Kwang-Tung*? Just in case there was any doubt about their encounter, Young sketched the *Alabama*'s destruction of the *Texan Star* (aka *Martaban*) in the Malacca Strait shortly after both ships departed port. This engraved illustration was dated on Christmas Eve and prominently pictured the *Kwang-Tung* in the background.[18]

In China, Sir Frederick Bruce agreed with Capt. Osborn that the ships of the China flotilla should be kept from falling under the control of Chinese warlords. But his reason for sending them back to Britain and India was to keep them from the Confederate States. As he later explained, "There is no doubt that agents of the confederates were on the look out to purchase the more powerful vessels of the squadron from the Chinese had they been left in their hands, and it is equally certain that the Chinese would have sold those vessels as being unsuited to them."[19]

Lord Russell approved of Sir Frederick's actions and sent word to every port where the China flotilla might call. All of the vessels were to be placed in protective custody when they arrived. He intended to prevent their sale "to agents for the Confederate States of America." The depredations of Semmes and the *Alabama* in the South China seas had been too successful and Bulloch's covert activities too wide-reaching. Semmes may have factored the opportunity of acquiring the *Kwang-Tung* or other ships of the China flotilla into his decision when he sailed into the East China Sea and contemplated visiting Shanghai. The *Alabama*'s appearance off the southwestern coast of India in mid–January 1864, just prior to the *Kwang-Tung*'s arrival in Bombay, reinforced the concerns of both the British and Union diplomats. The British government feared Bulloch's reach, even into China and India.[20]

In the full and final bitter irony of the total collapse of the Confederate foreign warship acquisition strategy, Bulloch lost the opportunity to buy an entire squadron of British-built ships. The opportunity vanished before it was fully formed for the same reasons that Bulloch had lost the squadron of ships that he had bought and paid for in France. The Great Powers of Europe could not allow the Confederate States to pursue a maritime-based war against the Union on a scale that would endanger their own national or imperial interests. The British needed to protect its colonies in the Western Hemisphere. France needed to prevent the Union from "liberating" Mexico, and both nations needed to have their hands free and resources available to fight the Germans, who crossed into Denmark on February 18th.[21] The blue-water Confederate Navy died because of Franco-British political and foreign policy expediency, more than any other factor.

As February 1864 drew to a close, affairs for the Confederate Army were no better. The only good news was a tactical victory by Maj. Gen. Nathan Bedford Forrest at Oklona, Mississippi, on the 22nd. Only his lack of logistic support kept Forrest from destroying the Union forces under the command of Gen. William Sooy Smith.[22] The Confederacy was like a punch-drunk prizefighter, able to hit back, but lacking sufficient energy to deliver the finishing blow.

From late February through March of 1864, Bulloch was in constant transit between Liverpool, London, and Paris in full "damage control" mode. He was attempting to bring shipbuilding projects in Britain to a close and dealing with related political issues in London and Paris. He had to get the CSS *Florida* away from Brest and meet with Bravay, Voruz, and Arman to salvage his projects at their shipyards.

His traveling companion for some of these journeys was none other than the famous Confederate spy Rose O'Neal Greenhow. Affectionately known as the "Rebel Rose," she had run the blockade and arrived in England in September 1863 with her daughter Rosie. Over the next eleven months, she shuttled between London and Paris promoting the Confederate cause. Greenhow regularly met with socially and politically prominent Europeans and Confederates, including Commissioners Mason and Slidell, and even U.S. Minister Charles Adams, Lord Derby, and Louis-Napoléon.

She was with Bulloch in Paris in early February. On the first Saturday of that month, he escorted Rose to the train station and ensured that she was comfortably situated in the "Ladies Only" salon on the train to the English Channel. Seven weeks later, he was back in England and this time accompanied her on the train and ferry ride from London to Paris. Before he returned to London five days later, he waited for Rose to return to her apartment and put her young daughter to bed. He was leaving early the next morning and wanted to bid her goodbye.

Greenhow's assessment of Bulloch indicates that she knew him well: "He is one of the most active [and] intelligent of our agents. God speed him in his work. Altho I have seen but little of him in Paris, I am very sorry he is going, for it is a pleasant thing to feel that a true friend is near and such he is to me."[23] This diary entry also suggests that they worked together in England. The only other hint of their cooperation is found in a letter from John L. O'Sullivan to Jefferson Davis written on 19 February 1864 in Liverpool. O'Sullivan, the former U.S. minister to Portugal and a Confederate sympathizer, discussed his business meeting with Bulloch that day and added that the beautiful and talented Rose was "quite a lioness in society, influential men are constantly seeking her, & she them."[24] One of the topics that Bulloch probably pressed on Greenhow was how to shape the political debate regarding "covert" Confederate shipbuilding. He became incensed enough to send Mallory copies of the British Parliamentary debate and implored him to respond. Sir Roundell Palmer had made accusations that were based on a forged letter, probably written by Union propagandists.[25]

While Bulloch railed about British politics, Abraham Lincoln took direct action on the same day to convince Louis-Napoléon that the Union would not tolerate any French interference via Mexico. The French had landed 25,000 troops in Mexico and Lincoln was concerned they might link with Confederate forces and threaten the Union's western flank. On March 12th, the Union launched its Red River Campaign in an attempt to invade Texas via Louisiana. The bitterly fought, but unsuccessful campaign lasted until May 1864.[26]

A few days later, the *Florida* managed to return to sea. With exquisite timing, Bulloch obtained new naval gun carriages and fuses from Nantes and placed them aboard the *Florida* via another steamer in neutral waters. The old tactics still worked. The financial strain these operations placed on Bulloch's purse were lessening due to the cotton for the Confederate Navy Department's account that was on the way from Halifax. Unfortunately, there was no reduction of political and governmental tensions in France.[27]

The Schleswig-Holstein War between Denmark and Wilhelm I's German Confederation nudged its way into the American Confederacy's affairs a few days later. Bulloch explained to Mallory that when the Confederate principals (Slidell, Barron, et al.) had met in Paris and decided to sell the rams, the consensus had been to slow down the pace of construction. He added that "because of the critical state of Europe, which might any day be involved in a general war" the Confederacy's chances at obtaining the rams might improve. Bulloch and Slidell imagined a topsy-turvy future with France and the German Confederation at war allowing the Confederacy to come to the aid of France with her advanced ships. In return, the French would grant recognition and intervene against the Union via Mexico. He imagined a "world at war," but he was some 50 years too soon.[28]

Bulloch also concocted a more tactical plan to gain control of his French corvettes in neutral waters and supply them with crews naval armaments and munitions. Meanwhile, he was annoyed at being officially "noticed" by the British government. The Court of the Exchequer had filed a brief against Lairds, Bravay, and Bulloch about the Liverpool rams. Yet, he angrily added, the British government was quietly trying to buy the rams at the same time! The Confederacy was a victim of political Darwinism.[29]

Meanwhile, he continued to acquire war supplies and blockade runners, an otherwise demanding activity that had become so routine that it almost disappears from his correspondence from late 1863 through the first months of 1864. He was assisting Lt. William F. Carter in getting a blockade runner completed and fitted out for General McRae. The steamer would carry critical materials (cast steel, tin and zinc) for the Confederate gun manufacturing works. He hoped to get the vessel off between the 1st and 5th of April.[30]

While Bulloch was getting Lt. Carter's blockade runner completed and away, a new opportunity presented itself. A former native of New Orleans, Robert McDowell, appeared in the offices of Fraser, Trenholm and Co. with John Palliser, a marine engine manufacturer. The Confederate Navy Department had contracted with Palliser to build three pairs of marine engines. Unfortunately, they were taking longer than expected. Palliser had come to ask for a contract extension, but at the same time he and his partner McDowell developed a proposal for Bulloch and the Confederate Navy. They wanted to form a small joint stock company and build a fast steamer under Bulloch's direction, according to his specifications, and sell the ship to the Confederate government.[31]

Bulloch, delighted with the proposal, urged Mallory to accept it, saying that he would send a copy of his plans for the ship design with Lt. W.F. Carter. He would contact Gen. McRae in Paris to arrange his support and financing. In the meantime, Palliser and McDowell had already been sent to one of the "most eminent ship builders in this Kingdom."[32]

While Bulloch pursued practical naval matters, "the critical state of Europe" became even more critical. On March 17th, a Danish naval squadron blockading Schleswig-Holstein repulsed a Prussian naval attack. The fears of both Great Britain and France had been realized: the rise of a Baltic navy that might challenge, and in turn, destabilize Europe. Both Denmark and Germany reinforced their naval forces and coveted the Confederate ships, both wooden and ironclad.[33]

By early April, Bulloch was in motion again on the Continent. Cdr. Matthew F. Maury had covertly purchased a mechanical nightmare named the CSS *Rappahannock*. It was a former Royal Navy steam sloop-of-war; but needed an immediate refit in Calais. Maury's other ship, the CSS *Georgia* (languishing at anchor five kilometers from Bordeaux), had to be sold outright. The *Georgia* was another example how the great Maury, known internationally as the "Path-finder of the Seas," was no Bulloch when it came to the practical matters of acquiring useful ships. The *Georgia* had a difficult-to-maintain iron hull and poor sailing qualities. As Bulloch had known from the beginning, Confederate cruisers had to be wooden-hulled with copper-clad bottoms.[34] More importantly, he desperately reworked his options to save his ironclads that were upriver from the *Georgia*. The slipways of Bordeaux held the Confederate Navy's last great hope.[35]

On 12 April 1864, while he was en route to Calais to see the *Rappahannock* and its captain, Charles Fauntleroy, a Confederate victory in the West helped ensure a brutal, no-holds-barred end to the American Civil War. At Fort Pillow, forty miles above Memphis on the Mississippi River, 2,500 Confederate cavalrymen under the command of Maj. Gen. Nathan Bedford Forrest attacked roughly 600 Union troops composed of an equal number of white and black troops. After a bitter contest where Confederate artillery and sharpshooters took a horrific toll on the Union defenders, Forrest demanded unconditional surrender. After twenty minutes, the Union garrison gave their answer: full refusal. Forrest, who would become the first grand wizard of the Klu Klux Klan, resumed the battle and drove the remaining Union troops out of the fort and down onto the Mississippi River's bluff in a hellish cross-fire. Only sixty-two of the "colored" Union troops survived. As one naval officer viewing the aftermath said, "Here there were unmistakable evidences of a massacre carried on long after any resistance could have been offered, with a cold-blooded barbarity and perseverance."[36] Although Confederate records and other accounts of the event indicate the Union reports of atrocities were exaggerated, the battle became known at the "Massacre of Fort Pillow." Fort Pillow became a rallying cry for the Union to finish the Civil War, no matter the cost.

The prospects for the "other" confederacy of states that were trying to unite as a great nation would be more positive on the 18th of April. On that day, 10,000 Prussian troops stormed the Danish garrison at Dybbøl killing some 1,700 Danish troops in the process.[37] The grim reports of the Ft. Pillow massacre and equal measures of Union revenge reached Europe several weeks later. Both Lord Russell and Minister de Lhuys knew that they were dealing with two hawkish powers, driven by two unrelenting leaders, Wilhelm I and Abraham Lincoln. The thought of dealing with Seward and Bismarck would churn stomachs in London and France. The German Confederation was rising, while the Confederacy in North America was teetering.

In Liverpool, Bulloch anticipated the arrival of the *Georgia* before the end of the month. Commodore Barron had dumped another mess into his lap that the resourceful Bulloch would have to clean up.[38] In the early morning hours of 2 May 1864, the CSS *Georgia* arrived in the waters of the Mersey River and nudged into Birkenhead dock on the next tide to have her armaments removed and complete her conversion to a merchant ship. In compliance with Barron's request to pay off the crew and sell the cruiser, Bulloch was "anxious to get the ship docked as quickly as possible so as to render it more difficult to eject her."[39]

The *Georgia* had been under Union surveillance in France and when she arrived in Liverpool, Adams filed a complaint (with yet another impressive dossier) with Lord Russell and the Foreign Office. Adams, rightfully concerned about Bulloch's ability to maneuver within the limits of British law and the dockyards of Liverpool, threatened a diplomatic break if the *Georgia* returned to a career as a raider on the high seas.[40]

After tending to the many issues related to disposing of the *Georgia* and his other ship and supply projects in Great Britain, Bulloch prepared to meet with Commodore Barron and Captain Fauntleroy about the *Rappahannock*. With the CSS *Georgia* generating a diplomatic and surveillance firestorm for Bulloch in Liverpool, it was obvious that the *Rappahannock* would have to remain in Calais. Bulloch was doubtful that the *Rappahannock* would ever get away, but he was prepared to assist if needed. To make matters worse, local French authorities initiated legal actions against the *Rappahannock* to hold her in Calais. He would go to Calais and deal with Maury's mess himself and then meet with Arman in Nantes about how he might get his armored rams out of France.[41]

In Calais on May 10th, he dined aboard the *Rappahannock* with Lt. Commanding Fauntleroy and recommended selling the ship. The ironclads were critical. He didn't need another poor-performing raider to chase ships that didn't exist mudding the political waters. But the internecine warfare among the French departments and Louis-Napoléon rendered a single, rational course of action regarding the *Rappahannock* nearly impossible.[42]

After assessing the situation onboard the *Rappahannock*, he traveled to Nantes via Paris for meetings with Arman about the armored rams. In the first meeting, Bulloch took along George Eustis, the personal secretary of Commissioner Slidell. Arman laid out his plan to get one of the Bordeaux rams into the hands of the Confederacy. He would sell one to a Swedish representative, who was actually holding it for Denmark, for use in its war with Prussia. He "predicted" that the French Foreign Ministry would investigate, discover it was a truthful sale, and then allow the vessel to sail with a French crew to Gothenburg, Sweden. Arman then believed the Union and French ministers would be mollified and lower their guard regarding the *second* ram.[43]

At the second meeting between Arman and Bulloch, Capt. Eugene Tessier (Bulloch's *de facto* agent in France) attended. This time they discussed how to transport the armaments for the second ram using a qualified and discrete captain as well as necessary deckhands. Were there enough in the ports of Brittany to supply the special needs of an armored steamship? More importantly, Bulloch inquired earnestly of Arman, would the French government allow the second ram to sail? Arman assured him that the emperor had confided in him personally that it would be allowed. These operational plans were so secret that Bulloch did not risk putting them on paper.[44]

Before departing for Nantes he reviewed all these matters with Slidell and Barron as well as other sensitive intelligence issues, including the impending arrival of Semmes and the *Alabama* in a European port. The ship, captain, and crew needed rest and overhaul.[45]

He also had to respond to a well intended, but untimely order from Mallory. In a letter dated March 29th, Mallory ordered Bulloch *not* to sell the Laird rams unless a presidential directive from Jefferson Davis himself approved the sale. These were impossible orders. The Confederacy no longer had any control over the fate of the Laird rams.[46]

Bulloch still had hopes for his French rams. He agreed to sell them after the Paris meeting with Mason, Slidell, and Barron. The consensus decision was to finish the corvettes and maximize their value before attempting to sell them. However, he agreed to let Arman attempt to convince French Minister of Marine Lhuys that he had finished all his dealings with Bulloch. Perhaps then Bulloch could spirit the corvettes out of port *a la Alabama*. They had "an express agreement" that the sale of the corvettes would be "purely fictitious."[47]

Shortly thereafter, they amended the plan due to the hostilities between Denmark and the German Confederation. A Swedish representative would take "nominal" ownership of the vessels and a Swedish naval officer in Bordeaux would supervise their completion. He planned to sail one of them to Gothenberg, Sweden, using a French crew under a French flag to reduce suspicion. Thus, Arman told Bulloch, when the second ram sailed from Bordeaux, it could be arranged to stop anywhere that Bulloch preferred. The French crew could be taken off and a Confederate crew placed aboard, along with all her necessary war material.[48]

However, just as one of the straws that Bulloch was grasping seemed to gather substance, his secret plan to gain control of the rams went badly awry. As he scouted French shipyards for usable steam warships, Arman met with Louis-Napoléon about the rams, expecting Napoleon to quietly give his assent. Instead the French emperor "rated him severely" and threatened Arman with immediate imprisonment if he did not sell *all* the ships immediately and with full *bona fides*.

The emperor's complicity had been exposed due to the combined diligence of U.S. Minister Dayton and Consul Bigelow's French solicitor, the dogged determination of Foreign Minister de Lhuys, and the increasingly unamused French press. Coupled with the apparent military successes of the Union in America, its rumblings over Mexico, and the war between Denmark and Prussia on his very borders, Louis-Napoléon was in a corner. Arman and the Confederacy caught the back blast of the emperor's failing dreams.

A shaken Arman retreated to his offices and found the first buyers he could, who were chosen for their deep pockets, sheer speed of purchase, and, perhaps to spite Louis-Napoléon, the Prussians were first in line. Arman also sold one ram to the Danish government. The Danes also considered the other ram, but it ended up with the Prussians.[49] This was absolute diplomatic dynamite; the worst fears of the British Royal Navy were now unfolding. Denmark bought North's ironclad and one of Bulloch's turreted rams and the Prussians were getting the other one. There was now a Confederate-enabled naval arms race in Europe.[50] On 25 May 1864, Arman sold the first ram and two of the wooden corvettes to Prussia. The modern German Navy (*Kriegsmarine*) had begun. Meanwhile, Bulloch operated in blissful ignorance of these events. Arman's silence might be explained by his fear of Napoleon's prison.

Bulloch didn't learn of the emperor's edict until the afternoon of June 9th when Eugene Tessier burst into his office with a letter from Lucien Arman. After he heard Tessier's verbal report and ripped open the envelope, he was stunned. Arman had sold "both the rams and both the corvettes to Governments of the north of Europe in obedience to the imperative orders of his Government." Bulloch provided Mallory full details of the French fiasco saying, "It is now my painful duty to report upon the most remarkable and astounding circumstance that has yet occurred in reference to our operations in Europe."[51]

Tessier told Bulloch that one of the shipbuilders at Nantes had given him a copy of a letter from the minister of the marine (Louis-Napoléon's "fall-guy" in the episode). The marine minister told the shipbuilders that he knew they were building a ship of war and demanded that they sell it immediately. The minister expected complete *bona fide* paperwork verifying that it was a "true sale" to the satisfaction of the Foreign Office. Anything less and the shipbuilders would be joining Arman in prison.

When Bulloch heard this last part of the story, he exploded, telling Mallory that he "thought this kind of crooked diplomacy had died out since the last century." He had the original certified copy of the permit to build the vessels signed by French Minister of Marine Lhuys. Bulloch instructed Tessier to return immediately to Nantes and represent his outrage to the shipbuilders there and communicate his "protest at the proceedings."[52] Chicanery was not limited to the French, for he also had to fend off bogus attempts to sell him ex–Royal Navy warships. The dishonest shipbroker picked a bad time to defraud the short-tempered naval agent and soon disappeared like a Mersey fog in a freshening wind.

Undaunted, Bulloch concluded contracts for six blockade runners in Liverpool, including two designed for the shallow waters of Florida. On the positive side of the ledger, he sold the *Georgia* to Edward Bates of Liverpool on June 1st, and counted himself lucky. Not only had he netted almost £15,000 into his account, the *Georgia* was now somebody else's problem. The British buyer was well aware that the Union Navy was targeting the former commerce raider for capture, but Bates was willing to trust the matter to fate and his insurer.

Minister Adams refused to believe the legitimacy of the *Georgia's* sale and ordered the Union Navy to capture the ship. Commander Craven in the USS *Niagara* caught up to the *Georgia* off the coast of Portugal on 15 August 1864 and sent her to Boston as a prize. Russell retaliated by declaring that *no* belligerent warship could enter British ports, Union or Confederate. This time, Adams' paranoia created problems for Gideon Welles, whose ships needed coal and food supplies even more than Mallory's.[53]

On June 13th as Union armies assaulted the political and agriculture heart of the Confederacy and the Prussians shelled the Danish town of Als, Bulloch left Liverpool for the 60-mile trip east to Sheffield to visit the Cyclops Steel and Iron Works. He was recruiting Bessemer steel mechanics for service in the Confederacy's developing steel industry. He intended to leave for Paris immediately afterwards and attend to the complicated business and vexing political issues in France. However, by the time he arrived in Sheffield, all of Europe was alive with the news of the arrival of Captain Semmes and the CSS *Alabama* at Cherbourg, France (a short four-hour ferry ride from Southampton, England).

When Bulloch set out for Paris, he no doubt anticipated that his involvement with the *Alabama* would be similar to the logistical support he provided to the *Florida* when it was in Brest the previous August. He would make shipyard arrangements, care for and pay the crew, assist with a likely change of command, and navigate the always-turgid political waters. The *Alabama* arrived off Cherbourg harbor on 11 June 1864 and anchored the next day with an exhausted Rafael Semmes still in command. The *Alabama* was as tired as Semmes, who like Maffitt of the *Florida*, was ready to step down as captain. The beleaguered *Alabama* was in port for only three days when on June 14th the USS *Kearsarge* sailed into the French harbor.[54] The stage was set for one of the most dramatic encounters in naval history.

As these events unfolded just 185 miles to the west of Paris, the *Alabama's* creator was also in France. Bulloch kept track of the pending dual between the *Alabama* and *Kearsarge*, while he went forward with his plans to meet with Minister Slidell and Arman in Paris. Accompanied once again by Slidell's secretary, George Eustis, Bulloch then met Arman where they poured over the letter from the French minister of the Marine Department. This review validated the actions of Arman and further convinced Bulloch that official French "treachery" forced the pre-emptive sale.[55]

In Cherbourg, Semmes was tired, but his fighting spirit was not. He sent a message to the *Kearsarge*'s commander, Capt. John A. Winslow: "If you will give me time to re-coal, I will come out and give you battle." It was a romantic gesture in a war that had turned so horrible. Unfortunately for Semmes and the *Alabama*, he needed fresh gunpowder that he could not acquire in a neutral port. Bulloch was probably among the throng of onlookers who traveled from Paris to observe the event. Although the *Kearsarge* sank the *Alabama* on 19 June 1864, Semmes and most of his crew survived. It was a fitting end to the *Alabama*, but a signal victory for the U.S. Navy and a huge propaganda boost for the Union. It gave the European governments more reason to doubt the viability of the Confederacy. For Bulloch and the Confederate government officials in France, they now had to care for, pay, and transport home surviving crewmen.

Fortunately for Semmes, Kell, Bulloch's brother Irvine, and 10 other officers and 27 crewmen of the *Alabama*, the British yacht *Deerhound* saved them from drowning and capture. The *Deerhound* deposited the drenched Confederates on the friendly soil of Great Britain at Southampton that evening. After the battle, Bulloch had crossed the Channel back to England. The next day, he traveled from London to Kelway's Hotel in Southampton with Commissioner Mason and Rev. Francis Tremlett to get a firsthand report from Semmes and check on the status of his brother, along with the other officers and men from the *Alabama*.[56]

For the next two weeks, Bulloch was fully engaged with the details of tending to the *Alabama's* crew, traveling to and from Paris, London, and Liverpool, considering his options for getting warships to sea, and pressing ahead with the Confederate blockade runner program. When he finally reappeared in the official records on July 8th, he was back in Liverpool, explaining in a brief note to Secretary Mallory that the "unusual press of business" kept him fully occupied. In the almost telepathic language that he and Mallory had come to share, Bulloch tidied up affairs in France, and looked for ways to retrieve the situation. Oddly, his letter made no mention of the loss of the *Alabama*. Perhaps he preferred to let Commodore Barron break the news of her loss to Sec. Mallory.[57]

Bulloch's "press of business" included an agreement with skilled Sheffield mechanics to manufacture engines and armor in the Confederacy. Perhaps they could improve upon the Confederate Navy Department's technical drawings that were not precise enough for British manufacturers. Bulloch had to advise Mallory that precision was critical if this early type of modular construction was to succeed.[58]

The last two items of business were even more hopeful. First, a telegram from Commodore Barron that day (8 July 1864) reported the French intention to release the *Rappahannock*. Accordingly, Bulloch planned to immediately "get her armaments and stores out of England." Then, he described the progress on the blockade runners he was constructing under a new system he had devised with General McRae. McRae organized the finances and Bulloch supervised construction, ship trials, and their "dispatching ... to sea." Simple and practical — the way the Confederate Navy Department should have been operating all along. Unfortunately, time was trickling away faster than Bulloch and his European cohorts could adapt.[59] News of General Grant's relentless siege against Petersburg, Virginia, had reached Europe; if successful, it would mean the collapse of the Confederacy.

A week later, on 15 July 1864, Bulloch sent a quick letter to Mallory, along with copies of earlier messages, via Alan Hanckel, who was leaving for the Confederacy. There was not much to say about the situation in France. Although the British government had still not paid for the Laird rams, all the necessary contracts and other paperwork were complete and he expected payment any day. He could say with pride that the blockade runner fleet was fast growing. In addition to the six already under construction, he had purchased five more, and he was about to "lay down four more, two of which will be large twin-screw ships." He had the shipbuilding bit between his teeth now. Encouragingly, some of the engineers and mechanics that Thomas Ludlam had organized were ready to depart as well. In closing, he provided a letter of introduction for Alan Hanckel, who had "assisted me in matters wherein I could not have trusted anyone but a countryman."[60]

Sec. Mallory bemoaned the loss of the *Alabama* and the poor performance of the high-speed blockade runner *Coquette*. The *Coquette*, whose initial performance was a marvel, had now become an engineering nightmare. Her boiler pipes repeatedly fouled, reducing her speed, and as a result, she was in constant danger of capture. But Mallory's most important message for Bulloch was this: no matter what the practical expediency of the Confederate Navy's needs, and regardless of the strategic effectiveness of commerce raiding, he had to replace the *Alabama*, and quickly. The Confederacy had to have another blue-water commerce raider. Mallory's orders, which would not reach him for several more weeks, set into motion one of the greatest naval missions of the American Civil War. Neither man would know it at the time, nor would they live to see its full influence on naval strategy, but that mission would demonstrate the truly global reach of naval power. It was a concept that James Dunwoody Bulloch's nephew, Theodore Roosevelt, would understand and use in the twentieth century.[61]

While Bulloch managed the construction of numerous blockade runners and situated the crews from the *Georgia* and *Alabama*, he continued his desperate efforts to salvage the two rams in Bordeaux and the four corvettes in Nantes. Bulloch is equally comic, extraordinary, and befuddling, in his portrayal of the complex situation. First, he met with Arman three times in late June and early July and agreed that for the short term, it was best to lie back and "reflect upon what was best to be done." Meanwhile, he instructed Capt. Eugene Tessier, his trusted agent in France, to monitor the progress and condition of the rams in Bordeaux. Tessier was to avoid interfering, but needed to preserve Bulloch's investment "rights under the original contracts."

Officials representing several governments had visited Nantes and were interested in purchasing the corvettes. In Bordeaux, Tessier also observed that the armor was improperly mounted in order to complete the rams rapidly and get them away. He knew that Bulloch would not accept such shoddy workmanship. Bulloch was not happy. Arman had his money and the rams, while all he had was a valid contract. He alerted Commissioner Slidell to the situation on the 12th and 22nd of July hoping for additional diplomatic pressure or legal support.[62]

Slidell's assessment of the situation on 24 July 1864 is either an example of his blind credulity toward Louis-Napoléon or incredibly duplicitous behavior on the part of the imperial regime. Slidell told Bulloch that the French government would "connive at the completion of the ships for us provided Mr. Dayton [the U.S. minister] can be kept in ignorance of the circumstance." To that end, the minister of the marine suggested that Bulloch only visit the Bordeaux shipyard as "a stranger." He didn't accept the veracity of the French offer, much less the conditions. The French builders were rightfully concerned with the actions of its government and were not in a position to help him

To avoid future disappointment and betrayal, Bulloch decided to sell all of the ships and informed Slidell that he would acquire a good solicitor. He would then meet with Arman and Voruz, and draw up an agreement that would at least recover the Confederate Navy Department's expenses. In fact, the German Confederation had already offered one million francs for one of the corvettes (the *Yeddo*). Although Bulloch continued to believe that Arman remained ethical in his financial finagles, he couldn't resist sending the exasperated Mallory a polite "I told you so" about the behavior of the French government.[63]

Three days later, on 30 July 1864, one of his new blockade runners departed for Bermuda. Named the *Owl*, the ship carried state-of-the-art detonators and wire for mines, the martial fruits of Commander Mathew Maury's labor. The Ludlam engineers and mechanics would depart the next week (August 6th) aboard the normal Bermuda packet to avoid problems with the Foreign Enlistment Act. Next, Bulloch arranged a contract between the mechanics and a South Carolina businessman (G.B. Tennant) to maintain the appearance that it was strictly a commercial enterprise. When the men arrived in the Confederacy, Tennant transferred his contract to the Confederate Navy Department's chief clerk, Edward Tidball. After placing Mallory's official stationery and officer commissions aboard the *Owl*, Bulloch planned to travel to France the following day to "settle all our operations in France."[64]

He arrived in Calais as planned and immediately met with Commodore Barron and Lt. Fauntleroy of the *Rappahannock*. Barron explained that the French government, for some unknown reason, had decided that the *Rappahannock* could only sail with 35 crewmen and not the 100 crewmen and officers that were aboard when she arrived. They all agreed that it would be madness to sail her undermanned, particularly with Union ships like the *Kearsarge* lurking about. With no change in the French government's stance, the *Rappahannock* would have to be sold.[65] The Confederate naval effort in France, like Britain, was systematically unraveling and in less than heroic circumstances.

Bulloch dashed back to Britain to finalize departure arrangements for Mallory's mechanics and the 150-pounder Armstrong guns and carriages originally intended for North's ironclad. By August 5th, he was in London on his way back to Paris to meet with General McRae, Commodore Barron, and Commissioner Slidell. Secretary Mallory had reaffirmed his urgent desire to get another cruiser to sea as a replacement for the *Alabama*. Bulloch needed to coordinate the "sale of certain ships" to raise funds to finance additional raiders. Equipping a raider at sea would be far easier with an existing ship. It would "simply" require him to identify and purchase the right ship and recruit talented ship carpenters who could improvise at sea. Bulloch was now on the prowl for likely vessels.[66]

10. Act Upon Your Own Judgment

Bulloch intuitively understood the critical state of affairs in the Confederacy. The newspapers recounted the march of Union armies into Tupelo, Mississippi (July 14th) and the battle for Atlanta in his home state of Georgia (July 22nd). And Bulloch? He was on the way to Paris hoping to get at least one of the rams away to the Confederacy. It would require an eleventh-hour miracle, for as he crossed the English Channel and traveled south to Paris, the Confederate Navy and Army were fighting and losing the Battle of Mobile Bay.

On August 6th, he went immediately to Commissioner Slidell's office in Paris for an update on status of his French ships. Still hopeful that he would be able get them out of France, Slidell dashed his dreams within a few moments. The French government "would not permit any of the ships to sail except as the property of a non-belligerent power ... the builders declared they could not perform their contracts." Bulloch had harbored visions of an enduring Confederate nation, for he mused to Mallory that "I was desirous of completing the ships leisurely, so that we might obtain possession of them at the end of the war." As he wrote those wistful words to Mallory, back in Richmond, the secretary could hear the echoes of cannon fire at Petersburg.[67]

Commissioner John Slidell summed up his activities in France the next day in a letter to Confederate Secretary of State Judah P. Benjamin: "Bulloch is now here for the purpose of closing the sale and delivery of the ships built at Bordeaux and Nantes. This is a most lame and impotent conclusion of all our efforts to create a Navy; but he thinks, and I agree with him, that this is the better course to pursue under all the circumstances." Perhaps no better statement encapsulates the bitter disappointment of the Confederate Navy's fruitless efforts in France, but at least they were getting their money back, with some to spare.[68]

A few days later, while he was closing down affairs with Arman and Slidell, Bulloch received a letter from James North concerning some of the last vestiges of the *No. 61* ironclad. North, who was in Versailles, had some £105,000 in bonds from the sale of his ironclad. Bulloch realized that the Navy Department stood to lose a considerable amount of money if he converted the bonds to cash immediately. Since he didn't need the funds at that moment, he advised North to let Gen. McRae retain control of the bonds.[69]

For the next several weeks, Bulloch ironed out the details surrounding the sale of the French ships with particular attention to the possibility of being cheated. Despite these precautions, it appears that both Bulloch and the Confederate Navy came away from the French affair as victims of profiteering chicanery, as there were plenty of commissioned culprits in every transaction. Back in Liverpool on 25 August 1864, Bulloch provided his insightful analysis of the situation:

> SIR: ... our two English "rams" 294 and 295 have finally and formally passed into the possession of the British Admiralty.... The Messrs. Bravay having failed to perform the service agreed upon consented to waive all claim for remuneration.... Wishing to conceal the connection between Messrs. Bravay and myself and to destroy any trace of the money from them to me, I arranged with Monsieur A. Bravay that he should pay the entire amount as he received it from the Government to "third parties," with whom I had come to a previous understanding on the subject.
>
> Thus on the 8th instant Mr. Bravay handed "those parties" £191,000 out of which £3,000 was returned to him for unsettled expenses and £188,000 was passed over to me for the credit of the Navy Department....
>
> Mr. Arman having ... sold two of the corvettes and the two rams to Prussia and Denmark,

did not hesitate to express the opinion that I could not recover them ... I hope and indeed expect, to recover the money expended, with perhaps a moderate interest. Mr. Arman has already paid me 1,250,000 francs on account of the Yeddo. He is to send me from time to time as he receives payments from Prussia and Denmark ... the corvettes were sold for ... a profit of 200,000 francs on the corvettes and 300,000 francs on the rams.... There was never any pretence of concealing them from the Emperors Government, because they were undertaken at its instigation, and they have failed solely because the policy or intentions of the Emperor have been changed.[70]

In the end, he could see that the wily French Foreign Minister de Lhuys had curtailed Louis-Napoléon's imperial ambitions. The milk had already been spilt and he would salvage what he could. He had other pressing matters: more wire for mines, detonators, the sailing of the *Owl*, and cotton bonds. All in a typical day's work.[71]

August ended with Bulloch's financial circumstances in surprisingly good order. Though, as he ruefully admitted, it was due to the forced sale of desperately needed French ships, the Laird rams and North's *No. 61*. There was a hopeful flurry when the U.S. Navy seized the *Georgia* upon her departure from Liverpool. The desperate Confederate community anxiously watched to see if this latest Yankee effrontery would stir the British Lion, but so far, there was only bluster. There were trips to Sir William Armstrong's gun foundry where he inspected a new prototype, but it was too heavy for the small, fast, single-gun vessels that Bulloch needed.

Still, it was chin up and onward, for he wrote Mallory that he could now fulfill his outstanding order to "get such vessels to sea as may be available against the remnant of American commerce and the whaling fleet of New England." He even hoped "to obtain a ship capable of harassing the enemy upon his own coast." Bulloch may have considered the idea of attacking the Union whaling fleet and discussed it with Lt. Bob Carter before his blockade run into the Confederacy on *Coquette*. However, the idea had been fully developed in Richmond several weeks before.[72]

As contrasted with the many audacious but relatively trivial guerrilla raids sponsored by the Navy Department, on 19 August 1864 Secretary Mallory proposed a daring mission that demonstrated the Confederate Navy's grasp of strategic naval warfare. Mallory conferred with Commander John Brooke and Lt. Bob Carter about destroying the Union's whaling fleet in the North Pacific, quite literally at the farthest end of the world. Carter and Bulloch had seen the perfect vessel for this mission while they were in Glasgow nearly a year earlier. Designed by the eminent naval architect William Rennie, the *Sea King* was widely admired for her speed and performance.[73] Mallory urged Bulloch to acquire the *Sea King* if at all possible. Assuming success, he forwarded a succinct mission assessment and advisory from Commander Brooke.

On August 29th, Bulloch he wrote a sterling endorsement of his loyal and efficient clerk, Moses P. Robertson. Until the arrival of Robertson from the Confederacy in May 1864, he had been inundated handling all the details for getting naval plans, designs, supplies, and all other such activity in motion, as well as accounting for large amounts of money. Robertson had rapidly organized the Confederate Navy Department's administrative affairs in Europe and compiled detailed financial statements for each ship. He now had cost-performance analyses of all the projects, from the *Florida* to the new blockade runners. He wanted Robertson to have a firm annual salary of £500, the going rate for a professional quality bookkeeper in Britain, as a trusted Southerner charged with protecting volumes of confidential information.[74]

In the Confederacy, the final desperate battle for Atlanta was underway near Jonesborough on 1 September 1864. Bulloch Hall and the town of Roswell had been in Union hands since 5 July 1864. On the 7th of July, Sherman destroyed the town's cotton mills as fitting retribution for the "traitors." Though Bulloch never lived in Roswell, the industry that Roswell King created and his father helped develop was eradicated. Fortunately, his family home, Bulloch Hall, survived. The news of Atlanta's burning, surrender, and occupation would not reach Europe for several more weeks.

Meanwhile, Bulloch alerted his shipbroker contacts to be on the lookout for vessels that might be converted to commerce cruisers and available for purchase. He hoped "to get one or two fast sailing vessels to send against the whaling fleet and one which can hang about the North Atlantic and make occasional dashes against the coastal trade." He was already seriously considering an anti-whaling fleet mission, long before he received word from Mallory about Brooke and Carter's similar scheme.[75]

Bulloch hinted in his September 1st letter to Mallory that "I am satisfied that there is not for sale in England a single warship with a lifting screw, but nevertheless I feel sufficiently confident to venture the assurance that before long you shall hear of another cruiser under our flag ... I am sure you will approve my caution in not reporting the means by which this is to be affected in advance." This letter was Bulloch's subtle way of saying that he knew exactly which ship he would transform into the "next *Alabama*." Just because there was no *warship* available with a lifting screw didn't mean that there wasn't a *commercial* ship with those characteristics. He was well aware of the *Sea King*'s construction and availability. In fact, Bulloch had already asked Commodore Barron to select and send officers to lead the mission. He wanted the proposed ship's commander in Liverpool at once.[76]

In considering the available inventory of ships that could be used as gunboats, he dismissed Mallory's idea of purchasing laid-up warships from the Royal Navy. His solution was to obtain two very large double-screw ships that could mimic the operations of the highly maneuverable CSS *Tallahassee*.[77] The new raiders would depart by December 1864 and January 1865, respectively. Whether there would be a Confederate flag to sail under by then was anybody's guess.[78]

He was also contracting for six small torpedo boats like the one that had seriously damaged the Union's massive ironclad, the USS *New Ironsides*, the previous October off Charleston. A draftsman had Mallory's rough drawings in hand and construction could soon begin, for he was flush with money. In addition to funds from the sale of the French and British ships, profits from cotton sold on behalf of the Confederate Navy were now arriving on a regular basis.

Bulloch had begun the search for contractors to build two shallow-draft, fast steamers to help protect Wilmington. All the shipbuilders in Britain were at maximum capacity at the moment and it was literally a case of take a ticket and wait your turn in line. At least he had acquired four small marine engines that he could send aboard the *Emma Henry*. This delivery would be delayed since the engines required a direct, nonstop shipment to the Confederacy, which meant a longer wait for suitable blockade runners.[79]

No matter. Like the United States would do some 80 years later in World War II in its campaign against German U-boats, Bulloch intended to "out-build" the Union block-

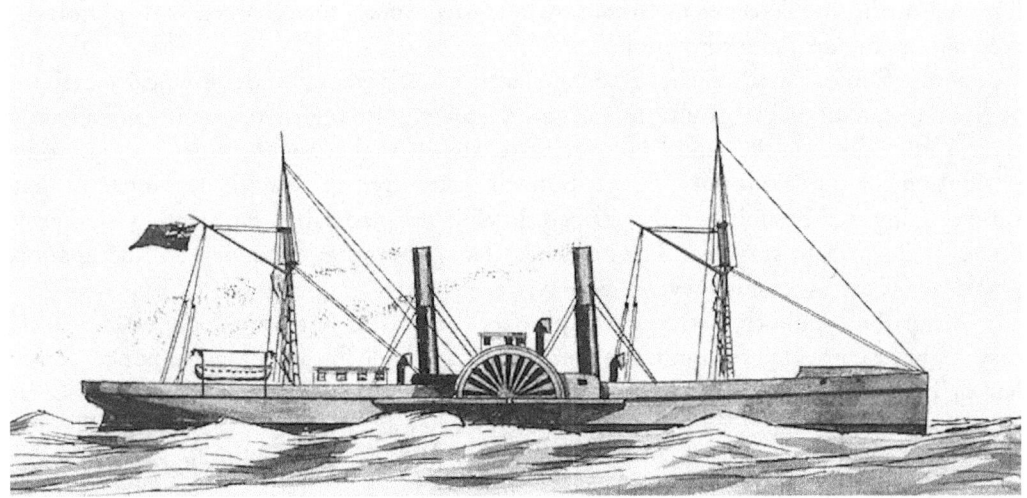

The SS *Bat*, one of Bulloch's contract blockade runners (U.S. Naval Historical Center).

ade. The Union might catch some blockade runners, but like pesky Georgia mosquitoes, they couldn't catch them all. Bulloch intended to swarm the Union Navy with numerous fast, shallow-draft ships. Two weeks later, Bulloch sent the details of these fast, elusive ships to Mallory.

The first four of these remarkable vessels were the *Owl*, *Bat*, *Stag*, and *Deer*. Their draft was shallow enough to run into waters the Union blockaders could not. Most importantly, they could carry about 800 bales of cotton and enough coal to reach the Confederacy in one trip from either Bermuda or Halifax. Bulloch had been confident enough in their performance that the *Owl* had already been dispatched — he reckoned she might already be in Wilmington. The *Bat* was on her way to Halifax, where she would reprovision for her dash down to Wilmington. The *Stag* and *Deer* would follow by the first week of October.[80]

Bulloch's energetic effectiveness astonished even the implacable Mallory and was a testimony to his agent's optimism, organizational skills, and the capacity of British shipyards. It was an extraordinary achievement and Bulloch had another ten steamers under construction. The first two of these were steel-hulled paddle steamers of 260 feet in length, 33 feet by the beam and drawing only 9 feet; they displaced 1400 tons and had 300hp engines. Bulloch proudly said they had been "designed and modelled with care." He reckoned they could easily make 14 knots with a three-day load of coal and 1,500 bales of cotton. It was an impressive level of performance.[81]

The next two, slightly smaller paddle steamers were designed with the shallow waters of Texas and Florida in mind; they would draw only 5 feet with a load of 750 bales of cotton, coal, and other supplies.[82] Another two paddle steamers were on the ways with powerful engines and steel bottoms plated with iron. These ships could carry 1000 bales of cotton below the main deck in sealed compartments, three days of coal, with space for another 150 tons of cargo; they would draw between 9 and 10 feet.[83]

The two other paddle wheelers would have steel frames and hulls that could carry 800 of the largest cotton bales. Bulloch's years of experience in hauling cotton cargo aboard the *Black Warrior* and the *Cahawba* were proving invaluable for the Confederate effort now.

Six feet was the predicted draft for these vessels under weigh. The build for this class of ship would soon expand to four, all of which were named for near-shore aquatic birds (*Curlew*, *Plover*, *Snipe*, and *Widgeon*). All of these ships were constructed by Jones, Quiggin & Co., of Liverpool, under contract to John K. Gilliat & Co., a London banking firm with longstanding ties to the Southern states.[84]

The last two ships in Bulloch's veritable squadron of blockade runners and raiders were twin-screw steamers that would be fast and able to turn about quickly. Bulloch described them as having "disconnected engines, which will be fully able to repeat the operations of the *Tallahassee*. I am having them rigged in such a way that they can carry a good amount of square canvas with which to eke out their fuel, but the spars are so arranged that they can quickly and easily be reduced to the ordinary schooner rig, for running the blockade." These were to be the "dash and destroy" gunboats that Mallory desired so desperately. Indicative of Bulloch's political sophistication, the ships (*Mary Augusta* and *Luisa Ann Fanny*) were named after the wives of his financial benefactors, John and Algernon Gilliat, of J.K. Gilliat & Co.[85]

In addition to the *Owl*, *Bat*, *Stag*, and *Deer* that had either sailed or would depart in the next few days, Bulloch optimistically planned to dispatch the remainder of his "flotilla" of blockade runners. One would sail in November, *four* in December, three in January, and "two in April 1865." This impressive list of fourteen ships did not even include four others that were under construction for the Confederate Navy in Scotland, one of which would sail for the Confederacy before the end of the war. Despite the efforts of Adams and the British politicians, Bulloch's shipbuilding efforts were in high gear and accelerating.[86]

Unless he heard otherwise from Mallory, Bulloch planned to place Confederate naval officers in command of these vessels. For contracting and legal purposes, the ships would be owned and operated under British masters at least until the Confederacy could pay for them in cotton, and perhaps longer. Lord Russell had warned that any Confederate government-owned ships trading between Britain and the Confederacy "would be forbidden to enter English ports ... except under the restrictions imposed upon all men-of-war of belligerent powers." They would only take on minimal supplies and discharge no cargo and be forced to sail onwards. To avoid this restriction, Bulloch strongly urged the Navy Department to hire qualified pilots under nominal foreign ownership and establish a regular supply service.[87] The Confederacy was in a race with the ever-increasing onslaught of the Union armies and the steadily tightening noose of the blockade that was choking off the South's few remaining open ports.

On September 16th Bulloch had exciting news: he had a replacement for the *Alabama*, named the *Sea King*. Richard Wright (the father-in-law of Charles K. Prioleau) served as Bulloch's broker to maintain the appearance that the purchase was purely commercial.[88] She had just completed her first voyage and Bulloch admiringly described her thusly: "She is full rigged as ship, with rolling topsails ... has a lifting screw ... and she has made 330 miles in 24 hours by observation. You will be gratified to learn this good fortune in finding a ship so admirably suited to our purpose." William Rennie had wrought perfection in teak and iron as far as Bulloch was concerned. Lloyds of London had just inspected he *Sea King* and found her hull, lifting screw shaft, and all else completely ship-shape. Bulloch was taking every precaution to prepare the *Sea King* for her epic mission to the North Pacific and back.[89]

To get the *Sea King* away, manned, and armed, Bulloch would have to exercise even greater caution and subterfuge than he had with the *Florida* and *Alabama*. The British and French governments were seizing any vessel that even appeared as if it might function as a Confederate warship. Bulloch had no illusions concerning the difficulties he faced:

> Every ship when purchased must change owners in a manner prescribed by law, and she cannot sail without a prescribed form of clearance at the custom-house. There must be an ostensible owner to make the necessary declarations for taking out the register, and he must be a British subject.... Such is the fear of offending against the foreign enlistment act inspired by the Government, that it is very difficult to get anyone, fit for the trust, to come forward as the owner of a vessel under such circumstances, and it is only within a day or two I have been able to find a gentleman to act this part for me, and now only upon the assurance that the ship shall not fire a gun until the register has been sent back to England to be cancelled.[90]

There would be difficulty in getting crewmen as well, but he was not going to send the *Sea King*, now referred to as the *Shenandoah*, on her mission without sufficient armament. Like the *Alabama*, the *Shenandoah* would initially have a civilian crew that would rendezvous with a supply ship to transfer aboard her war material and other supplies. She would have "four 55-hundred-weight 8-inch shell guns" with "two 32-pounder Whitworth rifled guns." He intended to "put as much coal on board as can be carried, leaving only space for provisions, thus enabling her to keep the sea for a long time."[91]

With his *Shenandoah* project fully in motion, Bulloch also had six torpedo boats under construction. They were built according to the plans of the Confederate Navy's constructor, William A. Graves. Bulloch enhanced this design with a stronger stem (to better withstand the force of the torpedo spar striking another vessel) and an improved stern to account for the iron plates in place of wooden hulls.[92]

Bulloch was able to report progress on the *Louisa Ann Fanny* and *Mary Augusta*, the twin-screw steamers that were intended to protect blockade runners running into and out of Wilmington and conduct night attacks on the blockading squadron. A Scottish shipyard, William Denny & Company of Dumbarton, had finally taken on the contracts. Their reluctance to accept the work wasn't due to fear of the British customs or the neutrality laws; they were simply too busy with other work! Although the two ships would be fast (12 knots minimum) and have strengthened decks and spaces suitable for gun batteries, the canny Scottish shipbuilders on the Clyde knew how to avoid suspicion while hiding their technical improvements like a Swiss watchmaker.[93]

By September 23rd, Bulloch reported to Mallory that the "steamers now building for Government service are rapidly approaching completion." He would soon start sending "all goods not contraband of war in our own bottoms." This initiative would avoid expensive freight and reshipment costs and delays through Bermuda and the Bahamas (as well as Cuba). As Bulloch ruefully noted, no war material could be shipped from Britain to the islands. They were all British, with the exception of Cuba, and were subject to the British neutrality laws.[94]

In late September 1864, Lt. Bob Carter arrived back in Liverpool with several dispatches for Bulloch from Richmond, but the most critical information was in Carter's head. He brought a complete verbal report of his discussions with Commander Brooke and Sec. Mallory about the *Shenandoah's* mission. Carter's return was fortuitously timed. Bulloch had already acquired "from Captain Maury a set of the whale charts published in connection with his Physical Geography of the Sea." Mallory's memorandum dated 19 August 1864 was also invaluable. Even by Bulloch's normally busy pace, his speed in getting the *Shenandoah*, her officers, crew, supplies and munitions together had been extraordinary.[95]

Commodore Barron chose Lt. James Iredell Waddell as the *Shenandoah's* commanding officer, or "lieutenant commanding" as the Confederate Navy designated a lieutenant who commanded a ship. By the 5th of September, Barron had a confidential conference with Waddell in Paris about the mission and ordered him to meet Bulloch in Liverpool. Although Waddell did not reach Liverpool until the 12th, he arrived well enough in advance to assist in organizing the mission.[96] Most importantly, he was in Liverpool when Lt. Carter arrived with the crucial new mission information. Carter, having already been to the "end of the world," would give Waddell advice about the far North Pacific. One important talent that Waddell brought to the mission was his incredible skill in navigation; he had been an assistant professor of navigation at the U.S. Naval Academy before the war. If any Confederate officer could carry off the mission, it was Waddell.[97]

Yet, Waddell had not been Bulloch's first choice to command the mission. He had wanted Lt. William Murdaugh, but Barron said that he was unavailable, having been assigned "special duty" with the Bureau of Ordnance. Bulloch knew that Murdaugh was a hard-charger in the mold of Maffitt and Semmes, but future events would prove that Barron's selection of Waddell was providential. Bulloch's choice of Lt. William C. Whittle for executive officer was more successful. Whittle had been in Paris with Barron and frequently carried messages between the Commodore and Bulloch. He, like Waddell, had intended to serve aboard one of the British- or French-built rams. To avoid a similar fate, the raiding mission that Bulloch, Waddell, and Whittle were trying to get under weigh would have to be launched quickly. They would need to exercise quiet precision to stay one step ahead of Dudley's ever-watchful network of spies.[98]

As Waddell and Whittle executed Bulloch's instructions to organize the *Shenandoah's* other officers and a few enlisted crewman (for most had been sent back home to the Confederacy), he hired a support vessel and a trustworthy master to carry out gun batteries and other supplies. All this occurred while Bulloch supervised the completion of two steamers intended for raiding duty out of Wilmington, NC. Understanding that even he couldn't manage all of this at once, he informed Mallory in his September 29th letter that he was retaining Lt. Bob Carter to assist in supervising construction of two high-speed blockade runners. Carter had practical knowledge and Bulloch planned to give him command of the first small twin-screw steamer when it was launched in January 1865. Both "Wilmington Raiders" were progressing nicely and would be equipped with two 7-inch, 110 pound Armstrong guns.[99]

By September 29th, another talented officer and Bulloch's old shipmate Commander Hunter Davidson, reached Liverpool. He and Bulloch had already had several substantive conversations about mine warfare, which was then known as "submarine defences."[100] Based on Davidson's advice, Bulloch acquired quantities of copper, zinc, acid, and small chains to create submarine mines and their detonating devices. The Confederacy had successfully used mines already on the Mississippi River and along the Atlantic coast, but research by Davidson and his fellows in the Torpedo Service had pushed the boundaries of innovation. In a desperate attempt to keep Wilmington and Galveston open, they had developed weapons that were even more effective.

In contrast to his early years in Liverpool, when he was alone, ship-rich, and cash-poor, Bulloch now found himself surrounded by Confederate naval officers of every rank and persuasion, with enough money to purchase numerous ships from the Mersey to the Clyde. It was a do-or-die effort by the Confederate Navy and for the Confederacy itself. By the time Bulloch returned home for supper on the 29th of September, Grant's army at Petersburg, Virginia, had begun to continuously hammer at the defenses around Richmond until like a nutshell, it cracked.[101] The Confederacy needed a miracle.

To that end, junior officers detailed for the *Shenandoah* mission drifted into Liverpool from across France and Britain. Bulloch dispersed them to confuse Union intelligence and more pragmatically, reduce their living costs. On October 3rd, two of the midshipmen (Browne and Mason) wandered into his office at 10 Rumford Place. They needed uniforms, supplies, and of course, money.[102] He was astounded by their lack of regard for operational security and shooed them out the back door with the admonition to "live quietly as possible" and most importantly to NOT return to his office for any reason.[103]

Bulloch signed a contract for the *Shenandoah*'s support vessel, the *Laurel*, and ordered his brother Irvine to the *Shenandoah* as acting master. Irvine had survived the sinking of the *Alabama*, now he was being sent on a mission that would make the *Alabama*'s cruise seem like a mere Sunday boating trip. Irvine's considerable experience would be of great assistance to Waddell.[104]

Bulloch laid his plans well for the getaway of the *Sea King* (*Shenandoah*). Since her purchase, the nominal owner, Richard Wright, chartered the vessel for a series of seemingly innocuous freight runs along the British coast. Brazenly, she sailed up the Thames River into the heart of London, literally under the noses of U.S. Minister Adams and Consul Morse. Meanwhile in Liverpool, the *Laurel* loaded naval guns, ammunition, and other supplies that would transform the merchant *Sea King* into the warship *Shenandoah*. U.S. Consul Dudley was watching. He knew that Fraser, Trenholm and Co. had issued orders to the *Laurel*'s officers and that she would also transfer her cargo to the *Sea King*. Dudley also knew that Henry Lafone, a well-known Confederate sympathizer and agent, had gotten the *Laurel* cleared for Matamoros, Mexico, via Havana, Cuba. The earnest Dudley was right about everything except the destination of the *Laurel*.[105] He had bought Bulloch's "legend" hook, line, and sinker, for Bulloch had instructed Lafone to casually leak the story about her destination. All the consular office could do was notify Union Minister Adams in London and the nearest Union ships, and that would take time. Bulloch just had to have his timing right and both the *Sea King* and the *Laurel* would be a half step ahead of the Union Navy and away to sea.[106]

As tight as security measures had been about the mission, Union Secretary of the Navy Gideon Welles had heard rumors of a strike against the Union's whaling fleet. In April 1864, Napoleon Collins, captain of the USS *Wachusett*, reported to Welles about its mission while he was cruising in the South Pacific. A whaling ship captain had reported that the *Sea King*, while she was on her "maiden" sea cruise, would be converted into a raider to seek out and destroy Union whalers (the *Sea King* was of such superior design that she would have had a ready military customer, no matter what the circumstance, since it was well known that her design was suited to military uses). In the intervening months, Welles communicated his concern with Adams and Dudley over the possibility of more Confederate cruisers. Welles would ensure there was surveillance of British ports (from international waters, of course). He wanted no repeat of the *Florida* and *Alabama* escapes.[107] As promised, the USS *Niagara* was cruising off the mouth of the Thames River looking for the *Sea King* to emerge and searching for a Spanish ship (the *Cicerone*) that was thought to be carrying armor and a turret for a Confederate ironclad. The USS *Sacramento* patrolled the English Channel looking for the *Sea King* or the *Laurel*, should either appear.

On October 5th, while Dudley's agents swarmed and Union cruisers stared menacingly at every suspect vessel sailing from British waters, Bulloch issued a comprehensive letter of instruction to Lt. Commanding Waddell. Effectively an operations order, Waddell was to destroy Union whalers in their known fishing grounds; "Considering the extent of ocean to be sailed over, the necessarily incomplete equipment of your ship at the beginning of the cruise, and your approaching isolation from the aid and comfort of your countrymen, a letter of specific instructions would be wholly superfluous." Waddell was tasked with leading a mission around the world's oceans into its most hostile and violent waters, North Pacific and the Arctic Sea. This was audacious and near suicidal for all but the finest of ships and seamen. Waddell had plenty of officers, but he lacked experienced crewmen. To obtain seamen, he would have to depend on his ability to induce the men that sailed on the *Laurel* to sign onto the cruise when he was beyond British waters. It was a desperate hope for a dangerous mission for seamen who were already suspicious of Confederate promises.[108]

As Waddell perused the contents of Bulloch's operations order, he learned the details of the plan to outwit the Union Navy. The *Sea King* would sail from London on October 8th with Lt. Whittle aboard, *incognito*. Whittle would ascertain the ship's capabilities and how she could best be rapidly converted into a raider. Her civilian commander during the escape would be Captain Peter S. Corbett, who had been fully briefed. The destination of the *Sea King/Shenandoah* would be Funchal in the Madeira Islands. Waddell and the *Laurel*, meanwhile, would sail from Liverpool on the same day with the other Confederate officers and as many other potential seamen as Bulloch and Henry Lafone could find.[109]

On October 6th, Bulloch sent Lt. Whittle to London where he clandestinely met Richard Wright, the shipping agent who had purchased the *Sea King*. His instructions to Whittle were from the pages of a Victorian Era adventure magazine. He was to meet Wright in London on the next day at Wood's Hotel in High Holborn. He was to use the name of "Mr. Brown" and be seated in the hotel's dining room at 11 A.M. with a napkin stuck in the buttonhole of his coat. Wright would approach him and ask if he was "Mr. Brown." Whittle would respond in the affirmative, and withdraw to a secure place where they could exchange official identification papers. From there they would meet with Captain Corbett. The *Sea King* had to leave by the 8th; the *Laurel* would sail from Liverpool after Bulloch received Wright's telegram confirming their departure from London. Timing and secrecy was everything.[110]

Anticipating success, Bulloch issued orders for Waddell on Friday, October 7th, to proceed to the island of Madeira aboard the *Laurel*. Bulloch's nose was twitching about Union surveillance once more and he decided to preempt his own operations order by sending his raider out to sea early. The commander of the *Laurel* was Lt. John F. Ramsay, Confederate Navy, who was also a Royal Navy reserve officer.[111]

Ironically, that same day in the Western Hemisphere, the Union ship that had gotten the first intelligence about the *Sea King/Shenandoah* mission, captured Bulloch's first commerce raider, the CSS *Florida*. In a gross violation of international law, Captain Collins and the USS *Wachusett* attacked and captured the *Florida* in the dead of night while she lay at anchor in the harbor of Bahia, Brazil. The *Wachusett* towed the *Florida* out of the harbor as the feeble Brazilian naval forces and shore installations attempted to stop the illegal seizure. The Brazilian government was apoplectic with rage and the Union press was exultant when the news reached them. The stakes had been raised for Bulloch and the necessity of another Confederate raider.[112]

At 5 A.M. on Friday morning, the *Sea King* sailed down the Thames River and into the English Channel. She slipped by the USS *Niagara* and was soon beyond the ken or grasp of the USS *Sacramento*. Bulloch's plan was working, thus far.[113]

On the morning of October 8th, Bulloch received Wright's telegram: the *Sea King* had sailed. Bulloch promptly ordered Lt. Ramsay and the *Laurel* to proceed to Funchal, Madeira. The *Sea King* had been instructed to arrive no earlier than the 17th of October to allow the *Laurel* time to arrive first and take on coal for transshipment without raising suspicion. Ramsay and Waddell were to rendezvous outside Funchal where both ships would then proceed to a secluded anchorage to transfer weapons, munitions, and supplies. After satisfying the needs of Lt. Commanding Waddell and his ship, Ramsay and the *Laurel* were to then sail across the Atlantic to the Bahamas. There, he would meet with Louis Heyliger of Fraser, Trenholm and Co. and get the latest intelligence about the feasibility of running the blockade into the Confederacy.[114]

The *Laurel* did not sail until the morning of October 9th, possibly because of problems in gathering Waddell, his dispersed officers and the extra crewmen aboard. In the Confederacy, on the same day that the *Laurel* left Liverpool, Sherman consolidated his positions around Atlanta. It would be weeks before Bulloch heard of Atlanta's fate and Waddell would know nothing of these events for months.[115] With the raider and her consort away, all Bulloch could do now was hope for the best. He had myriad projects that needed his attention, like the blockade runner *Stag*. He readied the vessel for departure in two weeks with a load of wire for underwater mines, and other assorted "torpedoes" material, along with three more British mechanics. Bulloch ruefully noted that the *Agnes E. Fry* had returned to Bermuda after unsuccessfully attempting to run the blockade, with his seventeen mechanics embarked. He expected those men to try again.[116]

He had the marine engines that Mallory wanted and shipped four pair of small engines the week before from Glasgow aboard the steamer *Emma Henry*. He would send another six by the *Susan Beirne*, and another two by the *Tartar* (formerly the *Wren*). He would run these through the blockade directly from Glasgow without the risk of refueling or transshipping their cargo in Bermuda or the Bahamas.

As Mallory had requested back in August, Bulloch transferred $31,507.97 to Captain Patrick C. Martin's account in payment for a cargo of provisions, clothing, and ordnance.[117] Martin was a blockade runner and Confederate agent living in Montreal who previously assisted Confederate schemes to release prisoners on Lake Erie. Bulloch's payment supported Martin's involvement with John Wilkes Booth, who was planning to abduct President Lincoln. After receiving payment from Bulloch, Martin perished in a storm in December 1864 as he sailed his schooner *Marie Victoria* from Montreal to Maryland via Halifax. He had claimed to be transporting Booth's "theatrical wardrobe," but swords and pistols were discovered among Booth's belongings when Martin's schooner was salvaged.

The written record provides no indication that Bulloch had any inkling of Martin's true mission or how the provisions and ordnance would be employed.[118]

While Bulloch tended to business, Lt. Commanding James I. Waddell commissioned the *Sea King* as the CSS *Shenandoah* as planned on October 19th, near Madeira.[119] Bulloch soon regaled Mallory with the story of yet another Confederate fox that had slipped out of the chicken coop while the Union farmer looked in the wrong direction. But the unequal treatment granted to the Union "belligerents" still stuck in his craw: "The British Government will scarcely give our public ships common shelter, and we cannot send an unarmed vessel in the direction of North America without embarrassing and annoying enquiries from the customs and board of trade officials. Yet United States ships of war are permitted to lie in English ports and watch British ships, as in the case of the *Georgia*, previously reported, and are allowed to cruise and make captures of neutral ships off the largest port of the kingdom and in waters which were once considered exclusively British."[120]

Bulloch sent a verbal update to the Mallory via Commander Hunter Davidson, who returned to the Confederacy via Bermuda before the end of the month. Ten of the small engines had already been shipped and the remaining two would be enroute in about a week. He expected to complete and ship the six torpedo boats to Wilmington by December. He had overcome the problem of fitting the engines designed by the department's chief engineer (William P. Williamson) into the ship designs of the naval constructor (Graves). Williamson's original engine drawings were imprecise and did not correspond to the technical descriptions from Graves. As he wryly commented, distance and communications were an issue in such matters; he left the obvious suggestion for better coordination back in Richmond unspoken.[121]

Drawings of two large screw steamers and two small steamers designed for "special service" at Wilmington were going out with Davidson for Mallory's perusal as well. The small steamers had the appearance of mere towboats (or tugs); but in reality, they could easily be converted into small gunboats armed with large fore and aft naval guns. He reckoned that any action in the confined, shallow waters outside Wilmington would be a slugfest; he needed to make sure the small steamers had a fighting chance. More specific plans for the two large steamers could wait until next summer since it was unlikely that the Confederate Navy could strike a severe naval blow until the coming June of 1865.[122]

Bulloch warned Mallory that an unscrupulous Frenchman was headed to Richmond with a scheme to get one of the Bordeaux rams for the Confederates, for a fee. Bulloch sniffed that he had gotten the *Sea King* away, which was the third time he'd accomplished such a feat. If it was possible to repossess of one of French rams, he could manage it "without the aid of speculative adventurers."[123]

On the subject of getting naval guns for the two gunboats, Bulloch was as good as his word. On 27 October 1864, Bulloch reported to Mallory on the results of his visit to Sir William Armstrong's cannon foundry at Newcastle-upon-Tyne. He found that the 150-pound shunt gun was ready for shipment. He hoped it would arrive before "the Federal attack upon Wilmington, which the Northern papers assert is near at hand." Bulloch was gleaning the latest intelligence from Union newspapers arriving off the fast transatlantic steamers. As Bulloch knew and the leadership of the Confederacy and Union would soon learn, it was Wilmington that was crucial to the survival of the Confederacy, and not Charleston, or even Richmond. If Wilmington fell, the death warrant of the Confederate

States of America was sealed.[124] On October 27th, Bulloch noted that Lt. Bob Carter was returning to the Confederacy shortly, and that he would provide a plan for outfitting and operating the two large double-screw steamers. Never lacking in attention to detail, Bulloch considered mounting the guns on a new, compact iron traversing carriage that he had seen at Armstrong's foundry; they cost the same as their wooden equivalents.[125]

The following day, Bulloch updated Mallory on shipments headed toward the Confederacy. The *Susan Beirne* sailed from Glasgow with guncotton, items originally intended for James North's ironclad and the six pairs of marine engines. Norman S. Walker, the Bermuda Confederate agent, would handle transshipment of the cargo to a blockade runner.[126]

On a personal note, Bulloch's stepmother, Martha, passed away, on October 30th. She had been ill since July and died at Tower House, in Madison, New Jersey. Her son Irvine was steaming southward in the Atlantic Ocean toward the tip of Africa aboard the *Shenandoah* after making its first successful capture on October 28th. Martha never had the chance to acknowledge the poignant letter that her son posted just before he left England. Irvine would not find about Martha's death until the next year. Bulloch probably heard the sad news from his sister Mittie.[127]

The first week of November saw Bulloch shuttling about Liverpool investigating the progress of his various shipbuilding projects, while waiting for more definitive intelligence on the *Shenandoah*. Bulloch had not heard from Capt. Corbett. The reason for the captain's silence was simple. He was in jail. On the same day that the *Shenandoah* captured her first victim (the *Alina*), the British consul arrested Corbett for violating the Foreign Enlistment Act in Tenerife, capital of the Portuguese Canary Islands, lying 440 miles off the Atlantic coast of Morocco.[128] It would be November 11th before Bulloch knew that the *Shenandoah* was "fairly at sea under the Confederate Flag." After his arrest, Corbett was sent to Liverpool for trial. There, he delivered Lt. Ramsay's written report from the *Laurel* and briefed Bulloch in person.[129]

The *Sea King*, now commissioned as the CSS *Shenandoah*, and the *Laurel* had met "without accident and at the appointed time." However, the *Laurel* had arrived early and lay at anchor in Funchal Roads for several days, exciting the attention of the Union and British consuls. The U.S. consul tried, without success, to have the Portuguese seize the *Laurel*. In the meantime, the *Sea King* arrived on October 18th. The *Laurel* promptly weighed anchor and joined the *Sea King* off Las Desertas (literally a deserted island), located near Madeira. The weapons and other stores had been transferred by the early morning of the next day. As the *Shenandoah* steamed over the horizon, the *Laurel* sailed for the Canary Islands. At Tenerife, Captain Corbett and the *Sea King's* crewmen who had refused to sign onto the *Shenandoah* cruise disembarked. This group of disgruntled sailors promptly knocked on the door of the British consulate.[130]

When Captain Corbett returned to Liverpool, "a greater portion" of the *Sea King's* crew accompanied him. Bulloch was concerned enough about the impact of the statements from the disgruntled seaman that he wrote Henry Hotze, editor of the Confederacy's propaganda newsletter, the *Index*, even before he reported to Secretary Mallory. Bulloch speculated that either Corbett or Ramsay's sales pitch had lacked tact or "from some freak of the men, by far the greater portion declined to enter the service." He speculated that "the indifference evinced in the settlement of the *Alabama's* affairs, and the unfavourable impressions made upon many of her men, has spread among seamen generally, and will render it very difficult for us to man ships in future." Bulloch wanted Hotze to get out in front of the story of the *Shenandoah* (without reference to its former identity as the *Sea King*) since "some of the local papers may be tempted to publish garbled accounts of returned seamen."[131]

Not surprisingly, both Ramsay and Corbett reported that the *Shenandoah's* main problem was lack of crewmen. Waddell had offered bounties of a £15 per man, but he enticed only a few. The ship was so short-handed that the entire officer staff worked as deck hands to accomplish even the most basic functions. The Rennie-designed ship required far fewer men than similar vessels, but still needed a minimum crew. Even with this shortfall, the news that the Confederacy had responded to the seizure of the *Florida* rattled the confidence of Union merchants and government. The Confederate Navy had a "*New Alabama*" that would pursue the Achilles Heel of the Union economy to the ends of the world. The destruction of the New England whaling fleet would affect industrial production as well as home lighting and send insurance rates and whale oil prices into orbit. Even more important to some Southerners, the *Shenandoah* would strike at the core economic interests of the Connecticut Yankees who symbolized the radical North, just as Charleston represented the radical South.[132]

After updating Mallory on the status of the *Shenandoah* and confidently anticipating her accomplishments, Bulloch returned to the pragmatic present. He needed to throw the Union Navy off the scent for a few more days to allow the *Shenandoah* to reach Australia unmolested. Whatever shortcomings Captain Corbett may have had as a recruiter, he made up for them as a secret agent and a source of plausible misinformation. On November 22nd, Bulloch playfully wrote this short but triumphant note to Henry Hotze: "Thanks for the 'Slip' Mr. Mabbs was kind enough to send. The report was a blind thrown out by Capt Corbett and seems to have been taken up as true by Lloyds. The Liverpool papers of today all announce the 'loss of the *New Alabama*' but the *Shenandoah* is all right."[133]

The temporary captain of the *Sea King* had planted a false story of the Shenandoah's loss that Lloyds accepted as true without attribution to Confederate sources. "Mr. Mabbs," a *nom de guerre* for Bulloch, had composed a "slip" of paper with the false story that helped the *Shenandoah* give them all the "slip" as the raider made good its escape. This *double entendre* pun must have brought a knowing smile to his face as he penned this uncharacteristically humorous note. The note also provided a rare glimpse into Bulloch's truly secret operations that he does not mention in his memoirs and omitted from the official records.

On a more sobering note, Bulloch realized that another vessel such as the *Shenandoah* was not likely to be available. He continued to believe that if the war continued into the summer of 1865, he could deliver a serious naval strike against the Union. Bulloch hoped to deploy one of his new screw steamers that would be manned by a crew coming out from the Confederacy. He had contracted for a large steamer with the external appearance of a passenger ship and could be rapidly converted to a warship "as formidable as the late steamship *Alabama*." Bulloch still spoke of the *Alabama* as a dearly departed loved one.[134]

The grim turn of events in the Confederacy would alter his assessment about future operations. On November 16th, General Sherman began his epic "March to the Sea" through Georgia. He would not stop until he reached Savannah, or was destroyed by Confederate forces, which seemed highly unlikely. The bitterest stage of the Civil War had begun.[135]

With the *Shenandoah* away on her cruise, Bulloch turned his eyes to the logistics of his flotilla of blockade runners that included the *Runber, Whisper, Susan Beirne, Deer,* and *Crocodile*. Some of the items shipped, like blankets, were typical; however, much of the cargo included mine warfare supplies and equipment for cannons and guns. He affirmed that his double-screw steamers, both large and small, were progressing nicely.[136]

On November 23rd, Bulloch was finally able to settle some of the very last business involving James North. That same day in Paris, Commodore Barron wrote to Mallory that since there was no prospect of a command for North, he proposed "ordering him to return to the Confederacy."[137] Evidently, Bulloch did not celebrate Thanksgiving in 1864, for his plate was full with Confederate business. The first course dealt with financing the operations of the *Tallahassee* and *Chickamauga* and payments to the Crenshaw firm that "had on several occasions rendered ... valuable services ... to our cruisers in the ports of Brazil." A Richmond merchant sent to London to form a blockade running company, William Crenshaw was also producing the engine for an unspecified "armoured ram," possibly one being built in the Confederacy. The second course was his attempt to sell tobacco on the Liverpool market. Charles Prioleau told Bulloch frankly that it was hardly worth it, since the price was too low. Bulloch gave Mallory a careful explanation of how he was balancing his books. There were a lot of beans being shuffled about and the prospects for pudding were slight, but for the moment Bulloch was operating in the black.[138]

December opened with Bulloch still occupied with blockade runner shipments to the Confederacy. But, in this instance, they related to goods shipped for Commander James North, who would soon be headed back to the Confederacy himself. In response to a request from the ever-annoying North, Bulloch's clerk, Moses P. Robertson, tacked on the reassuring comment that North's goods had been shipped and were "all insured."[139] But, there was another reason why it was Robertson and not Bulloch who had replied. Bulloch was yet again in motion on a mission that would constitute his greatest feat of maritime legerdemain during the American Civil War.

Bulloch saw opportunity in the October 1864 post-war chaos of the Second Schleswig-Holstein War between Denmark and the German Confederation.[140] During the war, both the Danish and Prussians had purchased several of Bulloch's French ships in the aftermath of the Arman/Louis-Napoléon fiasco. However, due to inertia or a subtle work slowdown at the instigation of Arman, one of the Danish rams was not completed by 30 October 1864 when the Treaty of Vienna was signed. This left Arman with a "useless" state-of-the-art armored ram on his hands. Or so it seemed.

In early autumn, Bulloch received a proposal from Arman who offered to "deliver to me at sea one of our French ironclads." He declined this offer; no longer trusting Arman and realizing that U.S. Minister Dayton was still vigilant for Confederate activity in France.[141] However, the Danish Government was reeling from financial and territorial losses of the conflict and subsequently approached Arman about the *Sphinx*. The Danish minister of marine wanted to annul their contract. The ship had not been finished in time, and a peacetime Danish Navy did not need it. More than likely, the Danes could not afford it.[142]

When the *Sphinx* moved to Copenhagen in November, Arman again sent his agent, Henri de Rivière, to see if it might be possible to "arrange for a re-delivery of the ram to the Confederate States." The game was afoot and Bulloch was ready to try again. In fact, Bulloch wrote:

10. Act Upon Your Own Judgment 183

The circumstances had wholly changed. The vessel was clear of French interference. She was in Copenhagen, or at least she was en route for that port, and the purchasers were desirous to annul their bargain. Mrs. Arman proposed to instruct his agent to manage the negotiations at Copenhagen so as to give me time to collect a staff of officers, prepare the necessary supply of stores and a tender, and to select a suitable rendezvous. He [Arman] said that when I was ready his agent would get leave to engage a Danish crew to navigate the ship back to Bordeaux, but instead of returning to that port he would take her to the appointed rendezvous, and deliver her to the Confederate officer appointed to command her.[143]

While Bulloch was away for the first 16 days of December 1864, Moses P. Robertson had been answering the mail in Liverpool. Bulloch was arranging to get "his" armored ship back from the French and across the Atlantic to strike at the Union. A transoceanic, turreted and armored ram would far exceed anything that the Union Navy might bring to bear. There was no force afloat that could check the depredations of the *Sphinx*, soon to be commissioned as the CSS *Stonewall*. If Bulloch could get the *Stonewall* across the Atlantic and break the blockade before Wilmington, it would create panic in Northern port cities. The marauding Confederate vessel could dash into any port not defended by a monitor and destroy it with impunity. The Union had monitors, but not *that* many and they virtually no capability in the open ocean.[144]

Bulloch's plan to get the CSS *Stonewall* into the hands of the Confederate Navy was more complicated than those for the *Florida, Alabama,* or *Shenandoah*. But certain tried and tested methods were still effective. He would need to arrange an at-sea rendezvous to transfer a complete crew, supplies, and other war material. This time, he'd have to do it in European waters, within range of enemy cruisers, and before the very eyes of Union spies and the uncooperative governments of Britain and France.

On the plus side of the planning ledger, the *Stonewall* already had her main gun batteries in place; a mighty 300-pounder and two 70-pounders, courtesy of Sir William Armstrong's state-of-the-art gun foundry. The ship was sold to Denmark through Sweden and had first sailed to Sweden. It was under the ostensible ownership of a Danish banker, Mr. Rudolph Puggard. Union authorities did not suspect that the ship could wind up in Confederate hands while it was in Denmark, under the Swedish flag.[145] That was a plus as well.

The next part of the plan was trickier and relied heavily on de Rivière's acting ability, plus some subtle naval engineering subterfuge. M. de Rivière had to negotiate a deal that benefited the Danes and compensated Mr. Puggard. The rationale for annulling the sale would have to seem plausible.[146]

After all parties had agreed to the contract annulment, M. de Rivière would submit the paperwork to the French consul in Denmark, with copies to the Danish minister of the marine. M. de Rivière was confident in his success. Bulloch, while not as confident, given his well-earned distrust of the French, was willing to try desperate means, for the South was being torn apart. Sherman's "March to the Sea" was nearing its end on the Georgia coast. Soon Savannah, scene of Bulloch's epic blockade run aboard the *Fingal* in 1861, would be in Union hands.[147]

Assuming the Danes and French approved the contract annulment, and he was able to hire a temporary Danish crew, the next hurdle was to clear Danish customs, and ostensibly sail the *Stonewall* toward Bordeaux. Henri de Rivière would try to entice as many Danish crewmen as possible to join the anticipated cruise of the *Stonewall* without exciting the attention of the Danes, French, or Union officials. The Frenchman would seek out the chief engineer who had been with the *Stonewall* during her construction. These precautions would all be expensive, but cost was no obstacle for Bulloch now.[148]

To preserve operational security, Bulloch's agreement with Henri de Rivière merely stated that the *Stonewall* would be delivered to a place of his choosing where the ship, armaments, equipment and "other stores" would be handed over to Bulloch's chosen officer or agent. He closed this extraordinary agreement by saying that he would proceed to England with all haste to "make necessary arrangements there." For his part, Henri de Rivière would leave for Copenhagen immediately to put the plan into action. Captain Thomas Jefferson Page would join him a few days later to arrange provisioning the ship and begin a quick study of his new command. Page was a quiet and taciturn man, but one who had already had an amazing military career.[149]

In the U.S. Navy, he had served off the coast of China and Japan, battled pirates, sailed a steamer up the Paraguay and Bermejo Rivers in Argentina, performed coastal surveys of the New York coastline, and served under his fellow Confederate officer Mathew Fontaine Maury. He joined the Confederate Army as an artillery officer defending Richmond before being commissioned in 1863 as a captain in the Confederate Navy.[150]

Bulloch cautioned Page to resist loading too many supplies aboard the *Stonewall* in order to reduce the chances of garnering undue attention. With that, Bulloch and de Rivière sprang into action. Bulloch and de Rivière also concocted a series of coded phrases to report the status of the *Stonewall*. The key term Bulloch wanted to hear via telegram was, "Coffee is bought."—this meant the *Stonewall* would sail the next morning. Commodore Barron went into action as well, writing out official orders to Capt. Page that he was "to put himself in contact with Commander J.D. Bulloch C.S. Navy ... you will receive and commission ... a Confederate States man-of-war."[151] As good as his word, Bulloch appeared in London two days later and urgently requested William Crenshaw to provide the services of a steamer for a brief but "secret mission." He knew that there just happened to be such a steamer ready to sail for the Caribbean. If Crenshaw could help out, it would be of immeasurable service to the Navy Department. If he could reply immediately by telegram to this urgent request with a simple "yes," Bulloch would describe the proposition more fully.[152]

Crenshaw had no idea of the particulars for the "secret mission," but he did know that the "plan and arrangements of the ship would have to be altered to meet your wants." Crenshaw surmised that Bulloch would need the blockade runner rather longer than the initial letter had inferred. He needed to know if the mission was worth the possible loss of another month in getting the railway equipment into the Confederacy. Crenshaw's ship, the *City of Richmond*, was under the command of Bulloch's old shipmate Hunter Davidson and had already been insured for a trip to Bermuda and the Bahamas. Those were the facts, and if Gen. McRae concurred with Bulloch's needs, the ship was his to use.[153]

Crenshaw must have had second thoughts on the security of sending his message by mail, for the next day he personally visited Bulloch at his temporary headquarters at 5 James Street, London. They had a frank discussion about the urgent need for the *City of Richmond* that was convincing enough to intrigue him into full cooperation. Bulloch probably shared the full story of the "secret mission" with Crenshaw who was also a Confederate Army officer and he agreed to release his ship as soon as possible. Bulloch promised to personally inform Secretary Mallory of his gracious assistance.[154]

A few hours later, across the Atlantic Ocean, Sherman's marauding army reached the outskirts of Savannah. Rather than fight, Gen. Hardee's Confederates constructed a pontoon bridge and escaped into South Carolina. The following day, 21 December 1864, the mayor of Savannah, R.D. Arnold, surrendered the city.

Three days before Christmas, Bulloch asked Commodore Barron to send his son Lt. Sam Barron, Jr., to London where he could assist with the transportation arrangements for the *Stonewall's* Confederate crewmen. Bulloch planned to use sailors from the *Florida* who had made their own way back to Britain after being released from detention in the Union. Still angry over the illegal seizure of their ship, they were highly motivated to get the *Stonewall* into action. Bulloch had just learned that the *Shenandoah* had destroyed "three Yankee ships off the South American coast." This news cheered the crew of his new masterpiece, and lifted his spirits as well.[155]

Back in Liverpool in time for the holidays with Harriott and his children, Bulloch worked right up to Christmas Day. He dashed off another quick note to Commodore Barron in Paris. Yes, he had received orders relating to Dr. Green and Acting Paymaster Curtis (for the *Stonewall*), but he was still looking for orders on Barron's son who should be part of the crew as well.[156]

Bulloch updated Mallory about the goods he had shipped aboard the *Babthorp* for a "special project" involving Commander Maury, as well as another cargo sent by the sailing ship *Amy* for Nassau. The *Runber*, which had the large shipment of submarine mine equipment aboard, had wrecked in Angra Bay on the Island of Terceira in the Azores. Fortunately, most of the cargo was saved and transferred to the *Ruby*, a small steamer. He now had all these items heading for the Confederacy. Bulloch cheerfully reckoned that the first of the small steamers would be ready to go by 10 January 1865. They were delayed because "Christmas holidays suspend work for at least a week in England." Still, the torpedo boats were in an advanced state and they should be ready to transport by 20 January 1865.[157] He closed his last significant message of 1864 to Sec. Mallory saying, "I have been absent from Liverpool for three weeks, and have been engaged in arranging for an expedition far more formidable than anything yet attempted from this side. If we are blessed with success the fact will probably be known to you before this letter reaches Richmond, and it would therefore seem superfluous to report details when everything may fail." [158] He added newspaper clippings about the *Shenandoah's* successes that showed her movement toward her ultimate goal to cheer Mallory. But both men knew that time was rapidly running out; the desperate hope of the *Stonewall* remained problematic.

Working from London again on 28 December 1864, he met with Commodore Barron and wrote his final operations memorandum of 1864, which he outlined the sequence of events:

> First. Captain Page leaves London for Copenhagen tonight. Second, The ironclad, being prepared for sea, is to leave Copenhagen as if for a trial trip, and instead of returning to Copenhagen will proceed to the rendezvous in the manner agreed upon and now in possession of Lieutenant Carter, dated December 22, 1864, with this deviation, that she is not to stop at Nieuwe-Diep, but is to proceed direct to a position in plain sight of Ushant and thence to Quiberon Bay, in Belle Isle, and afterwards to Angra, etc.... As the movements of the supply ship are subordinate to and must be governed by those of the ironclad, the following arrangements of telegrams are adopted to secure concert of action: When Captain Page reaches Copenhagen and can determine the practical issue of the undertaking, he will telegraph through R.

Puggard and to A. Mabbs [Bulloch's *nom de guerre*], 17 Saville row [the address of Henry Hotze, Confederate propagandist], in accordance with previously arranged telegrams, ... although, if possible, the telegrams now adopted will alone be used.[159]

Bulloch then provided the following list of code phrases for various contingencies and his expectation that the ironclad would not sail until it received an answer to its telegram:

Meaning	*Code Phrase*
de Riviere or Page to Captain Bulloch	R. Puggard to A. Mabbs
The affair is in a favorable condition	Can now fill your order for teak
We can sail at any time	Will you buy at price quoted?
Will sail to-morrow.	Will close at price quoted.
Will require ___ days to reach a position opposite mouth of Thames	Will hold to offer ____ days.
Cannot carry out programme as arranged. Leave at once for London.	Can not buy on your limit.
Expedition must be totally abandoned.	Negotiation closed.
Niagara is not at Antwerp.	No other bidder in the market.
We have arrived here.	Will try to buy here.
Can leave here in (cipher) days.	Can inform you in (cipher) days.
Have been finally stopped here.	Can not operate here.
Ship is off.	Ready for offer.
Ship has been gone one day and have heard of no interruption.	Can keep offer one day only.
Ship stopped.	Offer withdrawn.
I am progressing favorably also.	You may do so.
Sail as soon as you can.	You may buy at price quoted.
Do not sail until further advice.	Hold for another advance.
Our ship has been stopped.	Must decline the offer.
Can not get another ship for (cipher) days	Will receive another offer in ____days.

Bulloch then concluded the plan with: "If the ironclad is compelled to put into any harbor, and the telegrams to announce that fact as herein arranged are sent by Henri to A. Mabbs, and the number of days of delay are also telegraphed as per arranged telegrams, then, the ironclad [being] ready to sail, a telegram will be sent to announce her sailing as if from Copenhagen, and she will await reply."[160]

There it was. On a single sheet of Victorian sized writing paper, the single most complex Confederate naval operation that James Dunwoody Bulloch would direct in the American Civil War was laid out. Its success depended on multiple people, movements, and events, along with impeccable timing, to converge at a given spot on the Atlantic coast of France. If the *Stonewall* made it out of Copenhagen and met Davidson and the *City of Richmond*, could it make it across the Atlantic Ocean in winter? And if she survived the crossing, could the *Stonewall* make any difference in the outcome of the war? Only the coming months of 1865 could answer those questions.

11

I Know Not What Your Circumstances May Be — 1865

The 6 January 1865 edition of the *British Standard* relayed staggering statistics detailing Sherman's destruction to Bulloch's home state of Georgia: $40 million worth of cotton burned, 1,000 slaves freed, 4,000 prisoners and 30 artillery pieces captured. The newspaper did not tell the tale of the total devastation of civilian homes, farms, plantations, and industry.[1]

In this same week, on January 4th, Bulloch sent a coded telegram to de Rivière and Page in Copenhagen: "You may buy at the price quoted." Understanding its meaning to be "sail as soon as you can," the *Stonewall* set sail on the 7th and headed for France. Their coded response to Bulloch was "ready for offer" that provided the welcome news that the "ship is off." Bulloch and de Rivière's secret plan was in motion and Captain Thomas Jefferson Page was aboard.[2]

With the possible exception of James Dunwoody Bulloch, the news of the America Civil War certainly had shaken the confidence of even the most ardent Confederates in Liverpool and all across Britain. To Bulloch, all seemed calm and orderly even when he learned that a fierce snowstorm forced the *Stonewall* into the port of Elsinore (Helsingør) Denmark on 8 January 1865.[3] Yet, doubt and tension can be detected in the small turns of phrase in his orders to his fellow Georgian and blockade-running companion, Lt. John Low, who was now captain of the *Ajax*. The *Ajax* was one of the two small steamers intended to protect the Cape Fear region and Wilmington, NC. Bulloch was entrusting the mission of getting the small ship away, across the North Atlantic in the winter, and through the blockade to his most experienced and loyal officer.[4]

Low's orders were to depart Glasgow by January 12th in the role of a "supercargo." As an *incognito* civilian cargo master, he would confer with the "ostensible owner" about whether or not to stop in the Madeira Islands on the way to Nassau for coal. After the *Ajax* reached Nassau, Low was to pay off the British crew and captain and then provide them passage back to Glasgow. They were instructed to bring back the ship's register to answer any questions from British customs. In Nassau, he would contact the ever-helpful agent Louis Heyliger about current affairs in the Confederacy. If possible, Low was to run into Wilmington; if not, then make for Charleston. If that proved impossible as well, he would try for Galveston and bring out a load of cotton. After that, Bulloch could "only wish you God Speed."[5] Clearly, Bulloch knew that events in the Confederacy were coming to a climax.

Still operating from London where he could coordinate the rapidly evolving situation concerning the *Stonewall*, Bulloch wrote to Lt. George S. Shryock on Sunday, January 8th, that Lt. Samuel Barron would meet him in the early morning hours aboard the *Rappahannock* at Calais. Shryock was to assign all the former crewmen of the *Florida* to Barron for service aboard the *Stonewall*. In addition, Lt. Borchert, who was in charge of the remaining *Rappahannock* crewmen, was to join Lt. Barron and his men aboard the night steamer to London. Shryock and Lt. Read were to arrive on the same night ferry and travel immediately to London where they would meet with Bulloch for last minute briefings and papers. There must be no deviation from this plan and Bulloch did not need to "point out to you how important this is."[6]

The final logistic pieces were now in play. On January 10th, there was a flurry of activity: Lt. Shryock went to Greenhithe, England, where he found the *City of Richmond*. He and the men of the *Florida* and *Rappahannock* reported to Commander Hunter Davidson for "a passage to join the C.S. ship *Stonewall*." Shryock received additional men according to a list supplied by Acting Paymaster Curtis. These men would form the crew of the *Stonewall*, though for purposes of naval etiquette, Commander Davidson would be the senior officer in charge until they met Page on the *Stonewall*. When they did meet, Shryock was to transfer his men to Captain Thomas Jefferson Page, who would take command and issue all further orders.[7]

Finally, Bulloch gave Lt. Shryock a stack of important papers for Commander Davidson to deliver to Mallory, Secretary of the Treasury George A. Trenholm, and the Confederate agent in Bermuda, Norman S. Walker. He also gave Shryock a parcel of "much importance for Captain Page" that he was to deliver personally. The *City of Richmond* awaited Shryock's arrival and he was to get aboard her "at the earliest possible moment on the morning of the 11th of January."

Bulloch told Commander Davidson that the officers and the sailors from France were on their way to meet him. He warned, however, that in the event British authorities prevented them from debarking the ferry, he should have an alternate plan. The timing of the mission required the *City of Richmond* to sail no later than the 11th to keep its rendezvous with the *Stonewall*. Unfortunately, Bulloch had no further word of the ironclad's location since the telegraph of the 8th when she diverted to Elsinore.[8]

Davidson had to estimate the *Stonewall*'s progress on the chart and plot his course for a rendezvous at Quiberon Bay off Belle Isle, France. If the ironclad was not there, Davidson needed to remain as long as possible. If she still did not appear, Davidson was to sail for Bermuda; Bulloch would have letters and advice waiting for him there. The best advice that he could give Davidson at the moment was to be watchful for the USS *Niagara* which was cruising the North Sea and English Channel, hoping to capture the *City of Richmond* and her double load of Confederate Navy sailors and officers. In closing, he invoked a higher power as he lifted a prayer for Davidson, "may God give you success."[9]

In the pre-dawn hours of Wednesday, January 11th, Lt. Shryock met Bulloch in London to collect last minute letters, packages, and instructions.[10] By the time Shryock boarded the train to Greenhithe, the headline that every Southerner and Confederate sympathizer in Britain feared to read burned their eyes to tears: "THE CAPTURE OF SAVANNAH."[11]

That same morning, Commander Davidson and the *City of Richmond* arrived at Gravesend, less than five miles downstream from London on the Thames. Davidson sent

Lt. W.F. Carter ashore to meet the officers and men from the *Florida* and *Rappahannock*. After embarking the sailors, the weather steadily deteriorated as the anxious Davidson waited for Carter to reappear with Shryock and Read. Finally, the two Confederate lieutenants appeared through the blustery Wednesday afternoon squalls. The *City of Richmond's* crew strained at the capstan until the anchor was clear and the ship was under weigh.[12]

It was a wild crossing; Davidson was forced to take shelter under the lea of the great breakwater at Cherbourg harbor. The *City of Richmond* was too small and underpowered to challenge the effects of the gale that swept the Bay of Biscay. The weight of the cargo, mostly railroad stock, was an even more important consideration. The reduced freeboard ensured a cold and wet ride and made her less responsive to the helm in the heavy seas. Davidson could not turn back, for as he telegraphed Bulloch from Cherbourg on the 13 January 1865, "It was indeed most lucky that I determined to come down the [English] Channel, for the steamer would have suffered on the English side from heavy seas, besides which, I might have been forced into one of the harbors on that side." That would have been a disaster, for British customs or one of the lurking Union cruisers might have seized Davidson and his ship.[13] Once again, Bulloch's fabulous luck held, for the foul weather kept the Union cruisers at bay and masked ship movements from prying eyes. Unfortunately, the weather also forestalled Confederate actions. The *Stonewall* made her way to Niewe Diep (a Dutch port adjacent the French border) through the heavy seas where it met Lt. Bob Carter and took on her main load of coal. Bulloch knew that the weather was delaying his operations for this large storm front also raged off the east and west coasts of England. The storm wrecked the blockade runner *Lelia* on its maiden voyage out of Liverpool within sight of the Mersey. Tragically, 47 of the *Lelia's* 59 crew and passengers drowned, including Commander Arthur Sinclair and gunner Thomas Cuddy (formerly of the CSS *Alabama*).[14]

The next Monday, Bulloch updated Captain Page via Bob Carter on the new timing and location of the rendezvous between the *Stonewall* and the *City of Richmond*. Reflecting on the fullness of the *Lelia* tragedy, he opened his telegram to Page by saying that no one could forecast the severe gale, "even though it may have been foreseen." Bulloch realized that his plan had been overly optimistic. He should have factored additional time into the plan to account for the North Atlantic winter.[15]

Bulloch believed that Captain Page would meet the supply ship at Quiberon Bay, by January 28th, but if it did not appear, he should wait a few more days before deciding whether or not to sail directly to the Bay of Angra (Azores). Page could meet the *City of Richmond* in the Azores or sail directly into a French or British port. Bulloch recommended a French port where he could leverage any assistance that Arman might be able to provide and avoid interference from Adams.[16]

The *City of Richmond* finally sailed from the shelter of Cherbourg on January 18th and headed south toward Quiberon Bay. Captain Davidson later remarked that the ex–*Florida* and *Rappahannock* men were "all very manageable, and we get on very well."[17] Page and the *Stonewall* did not leave Niewe Diep until January 20th, but made good progress through the Channel. After dropping off the Dutch pilot on a fishing boat near Dungeness, England, at 10:00 A.M. on the 21st, she finally proceeded down the English Channel with "a light wind and smooth sea." In the meantime, the *City of Richmond* anchored at Quiberon Bay on January 20th, the same day as the *Stonewall* departed Niewe Diep. There she lay quietly at anchor, Davidson did not allow any communication with the shore.[18]

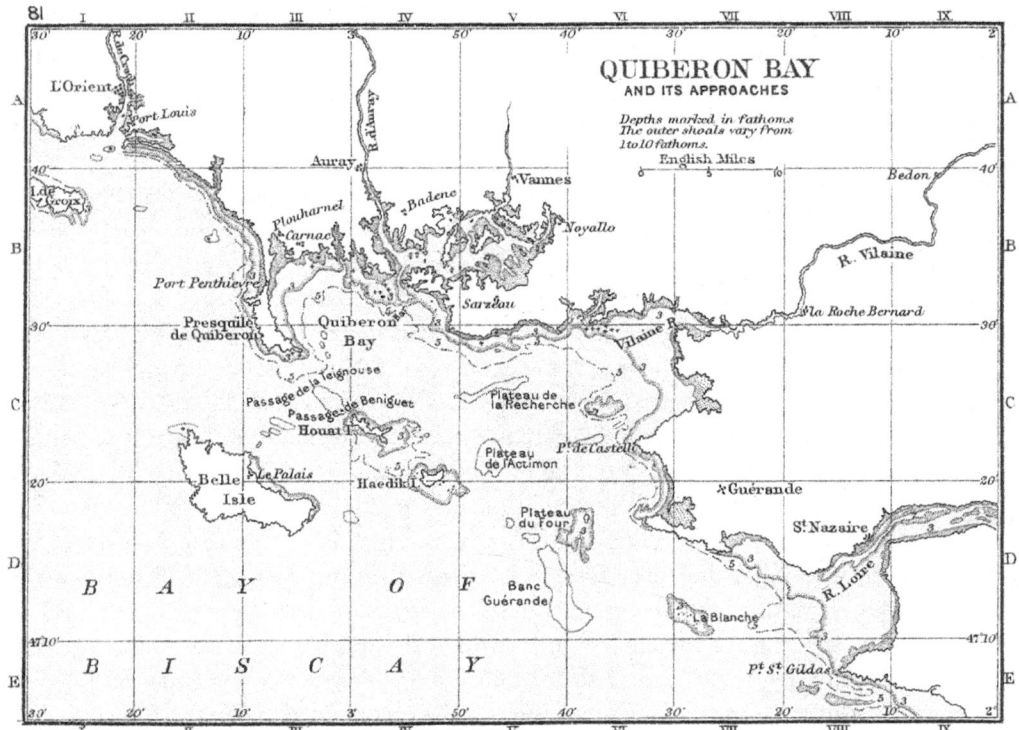

Quiberon Bay, where the CSS *Stonewall* and *City of Richmond* met (authors' collection).

On the morning of 24 January 1865, Page and the *Stonewall* steamed into Quiberon Bay to the enormous relief of Commander Davidson who had been anchored there for the past four days. The ironclad was a sight, Davidson reported: "She was in a filthy condition, and required more labour to clean her than to get the stores on board and stowed afterwards. The weather was very bad and wet, too, and prevented us from lying alongside."[19]

They struggled to get the *Stonewall* ship-shape for her Atlantic crossing while Bulloch was in Liverpool anxiously awaiting word from Page and attending to routine affairs. One of the Navy Department's chief engineers, Michael Quinn, had arrived in Liverpool with a shopping list of needed items. Quinn's experienced eye discovered numerous errors in Richmond's plans for 12 pairs of marine engines. As before, Bulloch informed Mallory that any future requests for engines should be exact and contain cross-sectional drawings of the vessels they were intended to fit. As a coda to that point, he told Mallory that the six steel-hulled torpedo boats he had ordered were almost finished.[20]

On January 26th, Bulloch also took time to assess the current state of the Confederate Navy Department's financial affairs in Europe. The large amount of money committed toward the *Stonewall* expedition, combined with his loan to the Confederate Treasury in Europe left him short of cash once again. He certainly intended to follow Mallory's orders and support General McRae, but he suggested that the secretary approve a more expedient and reliable system of bond payments to cover his expenses.[21]

Two days later, the *Stonewall* and the *City of Richmond* left their anchorage and headed southwest across the Bay of Biscay toward a coaling station at San Miguel, the largest island in the Azores. Making nine to ten knots, both vessels again ran into gale-force winds and seas. Davidson, who had a good perspective to observe the performance of the *Stonewall*, wrote that " the *Stonewall* would often ship as heavy a sea as I have ever seen ... seeming at times to cover her from the knight-heads to taffrail [from bow to stern] but yet she never seemed to be injuriously affected by them, but would keep her course very steadily." [22] Continuously pounded by heavy weather, Davidson forged ahead of Page by some five miles on the morning of January 30th, as the little ironclad struggled in the fierce seas.

At midday, the weather broke enough for Davidson to turn his ship and check on the *Stonewall*. "How do you do?" Davidson signaled. Page answered back, "All right." Davidson then queried, "Shall I go?" Page replied, "Am very short of coals, and must make a port, Ferrol." Davidson signaled, "Shall I follow you?" Page answered: "Suit your convenience about following." Thinking about his own mission and the fact that *City of Richmond* had "lost the moon" for its run through the blockade, Davidson decided to press on across the Atlantic.[23]

About 1:00 P.M., Davidson signaled "Adieu," which was met by "Many thanks" from Page. At 1:30 P.M., the two Confederate vessels broke off and two hours later, the *City of Richmond* faded out of sight. Page's course was north by west, keeping out to sea while the gale blew itself out before turning down to Spain and the port of Ferrol.[24]

As the South's final hope lumbered through the roiling Atlantic, the war in North America entered its final stages. By 15 January 1865, Fort Fisher had fallen and the South lost the gateway to its last port with rail connections to the Army of Northern Virginia. Only the port of Galveston was available to large blockade-running steamers, and it was too remote to affect the war in the East. Hunter Davidson and the *City of Richmond* would never sail into Wilmington with their cargo of railroad equipment.

Ignorant of the fall of Fort Fisher and Sherman's march into Virginia, Capt. Page and the crew of the *Stonewall* were more concerned with their own survival. Soon after the *City of Richmond* departed, Page discovered a serious leak. Water flowed into the captain's cabin and after an inspection, they discovered that heavy seas had worked the two rudder heads loose. A temporary repair held the rudders in place, but they now required an immediate port call for critical repairs. At any moment, a large wave could dislodge the rudder and create "apertures well calculated to endanger the safety of the vessel."[25]

On February 2nd, the *Stonewall* reached La Coruña, Spain. It had been a hellish five days for a warship originally designed to operate in the relatively benign waters of the Mississippi River. After paying his compliments to the ranking Spanish naval officer (an admiral) who pronounced the *Stonewall* a legal belligerent, Page inquired if he could carry out repairs. Spanish authorities agreed, though the admiral alerted Madrid of a possible confrontation with the U.S. Navy. The *Stonewall* limped to an anchorage at Ferrol where the Spanish navy had a large marine and engineering repair facility.[26]

While the crew attempted to regain their composure after their narrow escape from the wild wintry seas of the Bay of Biscay, the tendrils of Union counterintelligence tried to accomplish what Davy Jones could not. By the time Capt. Page began the tedious process of unloading the ship's stores and other heavy material, the Union Navy was in motion, more akin to flailing, while they sorted out the intelligence. Bulloch, with the assistance of de Rivière, Tessier, and Davidson, had surpassed himself in sleight of hand.

The rattled Union diplomats believed that both the CSS *Shenandoah and* the CSS *Stonewall* were in the western approaches to Europe! In fact, as Capt. Walke of the USS *Sacramento* departed Cadiz on February 4th, he received information that the *Shenandoah* was at Vigo, Spain (just north of Portugal). Walke steamed the *Sacramento* so hard she blew her aft engine, forcing her into Lisbon for repairs, whereupon he learned that the *Stonewall* was at Ferrol. The frustrated Walke reported that the *Shenandoah* was not at Vigo; after repairing his engine, he proceeded north to Ferrol. The fear of the Confederate ironclad alone was enough to damage a Union warship.[27]

Bulloch received Page's update on the 5th or 6th of February, for his letter to Commodore Barron about the situation arrived in Paris on Tuesday, February 7th. Bulloch had also gotten an erroneous report that the *Stonewall* was in Lisbon. As the facts became known, Bulloch realized he would be in more of a political race than a military one. The Union would attempt to muscle the Spanish government into holding the *Stonewall* as they had done with the *Sumter*.

This time, there was a key difference. Bulloch's ironclad could fight its way out of port if necessary. Its weapon systems and armor were something the *Sumter* did not have. The Spanish knew it, the Union knew it, and so did Bulloch and the Confederate sailors. But could they hold off the Union political attack long enough to get the *Stonewall* repaired and on its way?[28]

Page was having problems effecting repairs due to the interference of Union ministers in Spain. On the same morning that Bulloch received his update about the ironclad, the Union *chargé de affaires* to Spain, Horatio Perry, called on the Spanish minister of state, Sr. Benavides, in Madrid. Perry wanted the *Stonewall* seized, not just blockaded in port. He cited the British example of the Laird rams' seizure and the *Rappahannock*'s detention. Benavides asked for copies of all this information in writing and he would see what could be done.[29]

While Perry was in his office detailing his complaint to Spain, Bigelow advised Perry to seek out Mercier, the French ambassador to Spain. He wanted French support for detention based on the ship's origin in Bordeaux. It was a tall order, particularly for a country that had little reason or inclination to deal with the Union government. The years of American and Spanish rancor over Cuba, among other issues, were not easily forgiven or forgotten.[30]

On February 6th, as Bulloch's message containing the erroneous location of the *Stonewall* was on its way to Commodore Barron in Paris, Perry implored the French Ambassador to Spain, Mercier, to help him seize the Confederate ship. Mercier replied that he needed specific directions from French Foreign Minister de Lhuys. He did not "feel at liberty to take any steps in the matter." Perry hurried back to the Spanish Ministry of State to press his complaint alone. After carefully rewording the overly harsh language, the Spanish finally agreed to the Union protest and issued an order to suspend work on the *Stonewall* that went into effect by February 7th. Round one had gone to the Union, but it wasn't over yet.[31]

Perry then reiterated his demand to hold the *Stonewall* in port. To this, the Spanish sub-secretary of state, Sr. Banuelos, rolled his eyes, threw up his hands, and asked, "With what!?" Ferrol had only outdated artillery batteries and ancient forts. Perry mumbled that he had no indication that the Confederates would try to fight their way out of Ferrol, and he wanted the Spanish government to at least make a token effort. The Spanish, like the Union Navy, were under the spell of the supposed invincibility of the mighty *Stonewall*. They were reacting exactly as Bulloch had predicted months before. The mere fear of powerful ocean-going ironclads could force coastal cities and governments into appeasement.[32]

Round two in the diplomatic battle over the *Stonewall* opened in Paris on February 8th when Captain Page's urgent telegram finally reached Confederate commissioner John Slidell. It requested the commissioner to remind the Spanish embassy in Paris that the *Stonewall* was a "duly authorised vessel of war belonging to the Navy of the Confederate States" and she was in need of supplies. Slidell exploded and chased up Barron. Why hadn't he heard about this already? Apparently Page had been in Ferrol for at least five days! Barron, apparently relying on Bulloch for his information, admitted that this letter had reached him the day before (Tuesday), but it said the *Stonewall* was in Lisbon! Slidell, still fuming, marched off to the Spanish embassy in Paris to extricate the *Stonewall* and Capt. Page from the clutches of the Spanish and Union authorities.[33]

While Slidell pleaded with the Spanish government, Bulloch learned of Page's plight. He quickly developed plans to send technical support into the Spanish port since the commanding Spanish naval officer said the "case was under consideration ... and that he thought all would be all right in a few days."[34] Not to be outdone, Commodore Thomas Craven got his command in gear while the Union diplomats engaged in polite verbal combat. The Union Navy was on the way as well.[35]

On Friday, February 10th, the USS *Niagara* appeared off the Spanish coastline, steamed into La Coruña, and took a position some nine miles distant from the *Stonewall*. The Spanish government had learned that Union representations about the *Stonewall* were false on all key points, and they were not amused by the strong-arm tactics of the Union warship at the anchorage. Page and the Confederates aboard the *Stonewall* could only glare at the Union lookouts across the wide bay who were staring back at them through their telescopes. The *Niagara* dared not make a move to "cut-out" the *Stonewall* as with the *Florida* in Brazil. The armored ram could blow it out of the water at close range. On the other hand, the Confederates could not move. It was a stalemate.[36]

Having obtained enough clear information by Saturday, Bulloch was "greatly pained to inform" Mallory of the *Stonewall*'s uncertain situation. He also felt that the Confederacy had been "cheated and deceived by some of the parties ... which clearly justifies my original distrust of them." His rancor over the entire French fiasco was not to be politely hidden. His message closed with an acknowledgement that Fort Fisher had fallen which "seriously disarranges our plans for sending in supplies, but all of us who are charged with such duties will speedily consult and make new and suitable arrangements." It was a chin-up message, but Bulloch knew as well as the beleaguered Confederate Secretary of the Navy Mallory what the loss of Ft. Fisher meant. With the *Stonewall* stuck on the wrong side of the Atlantic in disrepair, there would be no last hope of smashing the Union blockade.[37]

Back in Liverpool, Bulloch awaited additional "particulars of" the problems facing Page. Fortunately, based on his first message, Bulloch had already diverted Lt. W.F. Carter and the blockade runner *Louisa Ann Fanny* to go to the aid of the *Stonewall*. He sent the former chief engineer of the CSS *Georgia* (Mr. Pearson) to assist Page's engineer (Mr. Brooks).[38]

Bulloch then chased down Arman via telegram, since he wanted "one of his foremen to accompany Capt. Tessier to Ferrol." Bulloch sent his most trusted man on the Continent, Tessier, to Ferrol, but he wasn't finished. He established a line of credit with a local finance house (Sr. Perez and Co.) to underwrite Page's expenses. He knew that the *Stonewall* was not designed for rough seas and the condition and quality of the work performed in Copenhagen was an unknown. Sensing Page's lagging morale, he passed along an encouraging report about a Richmond ironclad that had launched a successful raid on Union transports. He also reported the news of a new ironclad in Charleston that was expected to attack the Union blockaders any day now. All this occurred on February 14th, the same day that the *Louisa Ann Fanny* arrived in Ferrol. It was an inspired example of using nineteenth century technology to its limits to coordinate command and control and financial arrangements via telegraph and deliver personnel and supplies via a fast steamer. The only distraction in the frantic wartime business of Valentine's Day was the birth of Bulloch's daughter Martha Louise. Harriott gave birth to their fifth child and second daughter at the Bulloch home on 3 Wellington Street, Waterloo.[39]

Aboard the *Stonewall,* Page faced another problem, but this time it was his own crew. The young officers had not been happy with the ship's performance in the wild weather of the Bay of Biscay. What if they encountered a similar problem in the middle of the Atlantic when they were far from any port? The repairs carried out by the Spanish workers did not inspire confidence either. The officer staff, with the exception of Lt. Bob Carter, Page's first officer, authored a joint letter to Commodore Barron in Paris, who relayed his concern to Bulloch.[40]

As a mere commander who was not on the scene, Bulloch was hesitant to intervene in the apparent morale problem on board the *Stonewall*, but he told Barron: "There is a marked difference between Capt Page's letter to me and that of the 'Watch Officers' to you. He says he does not endorse their views and you will observe that the latter is not signed by Lieut. R.R. Carter. Capt Page more over expresses his willingness and determination to repair defects and proceed upon his voyage." Bulloch promised Barron that he would go to Ferrol himself, but *only* if Page or Barron thought his presence was crucial. He was "frequently called by duty to various parts of Great Britain," so he needed to remain there if possible.[41]

His duties in Great Britain included cleaning up the long-running fiasco surrounding the *Rappahannock*. With Barron's concurrence, he intended to "lay her up ... provided she cannot be disposed of in any other way" as Mallory had suggested. He also had to untangle a contract with Tipping and Lawden of Birmingham for 1000 "Girard Pistols." Bulloch was not happy about sending them "so large a sum of money upon an expired contract."[42]

Perhaps his most pressing problem involved the pending arrival of additional officers and crew from the CSS *Florida*. They had been in Union prisons since their illegal capture in Brazil during the previous October. After the U.S. was forced to admit to violating Brazilian sovereignty, the Navy reprimanded Commander Napoleon Collins, released the CSS *Florida* (which sank under suspicious circumstances on 28 November 1864), and deported the crew without any assistance. The Confederate crewmen would be in Liverpool the next morning, 16 February 1865. Bulloch told Barron that "a steamer sails from Southampton for St. Thomas [Virgin Islands] on the 17th and 2d of each month," thus implying that he intended for the crew to join the *Stonewall* in the Caribbean.[43]

The next day, while he was attending to the *Florida's* crew, Bulloch became exasperated with Captain Page's indecisiveness. Page had requested a conference in Paris, with Bulloch in attendance. In response, he told Barron:

> If a consultation is considered necessary ... I will of course make arrangements to join the conclave. The letters and telegrams you get must be of different significance from those I am receiving. I have been under the impression that the temporary interference of the Spanish authorities was all that delayed the repairs of the ship. If Page is to go to Paris I will comply with a telegraphic summons to join you, but I do not see how he can leave Ferrol before seeing the persons I have sent to join him there and who being experts and well acquainted with the construction of the ship will be able to give him efficient aid & advice. I really do not see how any survey can be held upon the ship in Paris. Nothing but a personal examination & trial could justify a judgement.[44]

Page was certainly coming to Paris; even the Union Navy knew it. Commodore Craven aboard the USS *Niagara* at Ferrol said that Page departed aboard a Spanish government vessel on February 17th to La Coruña. From there he traveled by train to Madrid and Paris. Craven even knew that repairs on the vessel were completed and that she was ready for sea. Bulloch would have had an apoplectic fit if he had known of this gross breach of operational security. Barron soon affirmed that Bulloch needed to come to Paris. Page had doubts about the *Stonewall's* seaworthiness and he had even greater concerns about her mission.[45]

Illustrative of the many reasons, Bulloch needed to remain in Britain was the pressing matter of the CSS *Tuscaloosa*, an offspring of the commerce raider *Alabama*. The *Tuscaloosa* was a prize vessel that Semmes converted into a commerce raider. After a relatively quiet career, Lt. John Low, the captain of the *Tuscaloosa*, called at Cape Town, South Africa, hoping to meet up with Semmes again. However, Union complaints and the change in the enforcement of neutrality laws induced the British government officials in January 1864 to seize the ship and remove all armaments. Bulloch wanted to recover the *Tuscaloosa* and had to affirm her status as legal Confederate belligerent. He also had to pay several large bills, with 9% interest, that Semmes had incurred in Brazil.[46]

As Bulloch headed toward Paris, Union pressure was mounting on the *Stonewall* in Spain. On February 21st, the USS *Sacramento* anchored near the USS *Niagara* at Ferrol. Aboard the ironclad, Lt. Bob Carter was acting commanding officer in Capt. Page's absence. As soon as Carter saw the Union ships approaching, he fired up the boilers. He would not be caught unaware like the *Florida*. The admiral of the port was obviously concerned about a repeat of the Bahia incident and would not tolerate a naval battle in "his" port. He promptly sent a senior staff officer to tell Carter that the admiral wanted him to lower his boiler fires and "warns you against any attempt to break the peace." To make matters clear to both of the belligerents, the admiral placed two guard boats near the *Stonewall*. Carter lowered her fires slightly, but unshackled her chains so he could rapidly turn the formidable ram toward any Union attack.[47] Carter need not have worried. Aboard the *Niagara* a shaken Craven had surveyed the impressive ram that was

> completely cased in 5-inch plates of iron ... her casemated 300-pounder Armstrong rifle ... can be fired directly ahead or on either beam. Abaft her mainmast, in a fixed turret, are two other rifled guns, 120-pounders ... which can be fired directly astern and one on each beam. She has two smaller guns in broadside ... four engines, two screws, and two rudders, and is provided with a long projecting spar for butting.... In smooth water and open sea she would be more than a match for three such vessels as the Niagara. In rough weather, however, we might be able to annoy if not to destroy her.[48]

Craven complained to Secretary Welles that all he could do was watch, for he feared attacking the *Stonewall* without substantial reinforcements.

The next morning, Bulloch met with Commodore Barron, Capt. Page, and probably Commissioner Slidell. Back in Ferrol, the *Niagara* and the *Sacramento* weighed anchor and returned to La Coruña where Craven reckoned they would not be subject to the 24-hour rule in case the *Stonewall* decide to sail. The generally accepted practice required an opposing belligerent ship to wait 24 hours before sailing in pursuit of an enemy ship that had previously departed the same port. Craven could argue that La Coruña and Ferrol were two separate ports within the giant natural anchorage.[49]

Despite the bad news about the military situation around Richmond and Page's obvious misgivings, the Confederates in Paris decided that "no possible effort that could be made from Europe should be abandoned." The Confederate Navy Department in Europe would go down with its flag flying. Page was to sail for Bermuda, procure more ammunition, gather a few more picked crewmen from the crew of the *Florida*, and then launch an attack on Port Royal, thought to be the logistical base for General Sherman.[50] With that, Page finally caught a train back to Spain. It would be the last significant Confederate Navy conference of the American Civil War.

Bulloch remained in Paris for several more days, preparing a detailed operations plan to document and amplify the guidance outlined in the previous meeting. With that task taken care of, he concluded his visit to Paris. As he made his way back to Britain, the myth of the *Stonewall* grew exponentially. On February 27th, Union Secretary of State Seward had intelligence that Maffitt was in charge of a "contemplated attack on New York City by four ironclad rams and five blockade running steamers." Seward was dismissive of the report, but thought enough of it to pass it along to Secretary of the Navy Welles. If Bulloch had gotten possession of the ships that he had built and paid for (the two Laird rams and his six French ships), that is exactly what he would have done. He certainly would have placed a commander with spit-and-fire in his belly to carry it out — just like Maffitt, or himself.[51]

In late February 1865, the situation within the collapsing Confederacy became more desperate by the day. Commodore Barron and his staff were ordered to return to the Confederacy. There was no need for them to remain in Europe. Bulloch assumed responsibility for remaining business under Barron's name, including the *Rappahannock*. He could retain any officer he needed to assist with these duties. Barron officially relinquished command of European operations on February 28th.[52]

While waiting for Barron's list of unfinished business, he detailed Lt. Murdaugh to survey the *Rappahannock's* condition on March 2nd. As expected, he found her completely unsuitable as a cruiser. Bulloch ordered Lt. Fauntleroy to "pay off and discharge the crew, detach the officers, and strip and lay up the ship." The *Rappahannock*'s career as a Confederate combatant was stillborn and now she was simply unnecessary.[53]

For the *Stonewall*, however, the game was still afoot. On March 11th, Commodore Barron noted, "Dick Taylor came over from Liverpool, bringing what [Capt.] Page has been waiting for more than a fortnight. He is to leave tomorrow." Although it is unclear what Bulloch was sending from Liverpool, Paymaster Taylor was most likely carrying essential bank drafts to help the ship get away.[54]

Even though the Confederacy was in precipitous decline, Bulloch continued to manage his affairs in the hope of some miraculous reversal. One of those desperate hopes was a last-ditch project by Mathew Maury. Having failed in his efforts to get effective commerce raiders to sea, Maury had been secretly conducting advanced mine warfare research.[55]

Maury believed that the only way the Confederacy could survive was to ensure that Galveston, or some other inlet in Texas, could be kept open. He intended to personally install a mine defense system, if Bulloch could ship the required wire, detonators, and other apparatus for him. Bulloch agreed that Havana would be the best port to receive the politically and kinetically explosive cargo for covert transshipment to a blockade runner. He began organizing this project with Maury that continued through the end of the war, and a bit beyond.[56]

In Spain, another winter gale howled down and across the Bay of Biscay, so Page and the *Stonewall* still lay at anchor. The Spanish expected the *Stonewall* to leave under cover of darkness, but as Page commented, "It would simply be prolonging an event which must inevitably come." Page expected and would not decline combat against the *Niagara* and *Sacramento*. Bulloch believed that the Union cruisers could eventually destroy the ironclad as long as they used their speed to avoid its ram. He had sent Capt. Tessier to report the Stonewall's departure and the result of the anticipated engagement with the Union Navy. Craven, however, was not so optimistic in the assessment of his chances.[57]

Over the next several days, the *Stonewall* attempted to depart Ferrol. Each time, the weather outside drove them back into anchorage and each time, the Union cruisers made no move to follow. To improve seaworthiness, Page unloaded about 40 tons of coal and then made ready to sail again. Informing the Spanish again of his intent, the polite old admiral told him that this time, he *must* leave. The Yankees were kicking up a political fuss, while keeping their anchors on the bottom. On 24 March 1865, the *Stonewall* finally sallied forth from the protected waters of Ferrol harbor into the Bay of Biscay, and still the USS *Niagara* and USS *Sacramento* lay at anchor. When it became apparent that Craven would not answer his unspoken challenge to combat, Page sent a message via a Spanish fishing boat for the local Confederate agent to sell his 40 tons of coal and two small boats. He left the boats behind since he expected them to be shattered by shellfire that never materialized.[58]

At sea on March 25th, Capt. Page wrote Bulloch about all that had occurred. Due to his forced departure with a light load of fuel, he had to re-coal in Lisbon. By now, he was aware of Sherman's shattering campaign through the Carolinas. By the time the *Stonewall* got there, if it got there, the entire Atlantic coast would be under Union control. What would he attack? Page understandably questioned the wisdom of his mission.[59]

Bulloch quickly received news of the *Stonewall*'s departure via telegram and Page's letter of the 27th described a wild ride down the Iberian Peninsula before reaching shelter within Lisbon harbor. The Portuguese had been cordial, but they only gave Page twenty-four hours to re-coal. Page protested that the USS *Sacramento* had been there as long as she liked. He demanded equal belligerent rights, but the Portuguese official departed without reply.[60]

Page alerted Bulloch that he would head for Nassau via the Azores rather than Bermuda to take advantage of trade winds for safety and fuel economy. Bulloch had to transfer the stores sent to Bermuda to Nassau. After affecting an interest in completing the mission, Page again expressed his doubts. He wondered whether any damage the *Stonewall* might inflict would be worth the inevitable loss of the ship and its crew? He believed that his mission was suicidal. As he finished his missive, the *Stonewall*'s lookouts spotted the *Niagara* and *Sacramento* off the bar of Lisbon Harbor. It was 6:00 P.M. and too late to depart. There was a north wind outside the harbor that favored the Union cruisers, but the Portuguese were adamant that Page had to take the *Stonewall* out on the following morning. The letter ended abruptly; Bulloch would be left hanging about what happened next.[61]

At 11:00 A.M. the next day, the *Stonewall* sailed down the Tagus River and out to sea, making a course northward, before being lost to the sight of coastal watch towers. Ironically, neither Page nor Craven wanted combat, though for differing reasons. Page believed it was futile as the Confederacy was dying. Craven believed the *Stonewall* would smash his cruisers, resulting in a massive loss of life, and perhaps he too knew the war would end soon. He certainly hoped so; the boasts of the *Stonewall's* crew would haunt him if it did not.

Back in Liverpool, Bulloch could only continue assisting Commander Maury with his mine warfare project and reassess where he might deploy his blockade runners. Texas looked to be the only viable destination, but it offered faint assistance to the rest of the Confederacy. There were no rail or river connections from Texas to the armies in the West or the remnants of the Confederate forces in the East. And there was the matter of repatriating the sailors still in Europe. All travel to the Confederacy flowed through Liverpool.

On Saturday, April 1st, Lt. Douglas French Forrest, the *Rappahannock's* former paymaster, called on Bulloch in Liverpool to settle his accounts and make his way back home via Cuba and Texas. Forrest's journal provided an essential window into the lives of Confederate naval personnel in Europe. He also provided a glimpse of the typically frenetic activity that Bulloch managed even on a weekend. Forrest observed that "Captn. Bulloch" was "engrossingly occupied" with the details of assuming Barron's responsibilities as the commodore prepared to leave Europe. When Bulloch finally made his appearance at Rumford Place, "he was besieged by wives & sweethearts of our tars" for their pay allotments and other administrative needs that were typical of family members left ashore while their sailors were at sea. Unable to elbow his way through the crowd to meet with the commander, Forrest went to Bulloch's home in Waterloo. There, he met Harriott Bulloch and her sister who played the role of gracious hostess until her husband finally returned that night around 10:00 P.M. and made arrangements to settle his accounts. Bulloch had been attending to the widow of the Confederate shipping agent Charlie L. Hobson who had been lost on the *Lelia*. Bulloch had completely forgotten about Forrest and his anxieties.[62]

Five days later, Lt. Read dashed into Bulloch's office after a long journey from the Iberian Peninsula carrying a last letter from Capt. Page. It was dated March 27th, the day before the *Stonewall* sailed from Lisbon, and just now reached Bulloch. Apparently not trusting the telegraph, Page must have believed that there was no urgency since there was little Bulloch could do after he headed west into the Atlantic.[63]

Bulloch acknowledged that the *Stonewall's* "first effort would probably be her last." He remained hopeful that a hit-and-run attack on Port Royal could inflict irreparable damage to the Union forces in the Carolinas. However, all would depend on the intelligence Page received when he met Louis Heyliger in Nassau. If it proved impossible or imprudent to attack Port Royal, he suggested heading for the Gulf Coast to operate out of Cuba. If that option was impossible, then it would be best to lay the ship up in some foreign port as Page saw fit. Bulloch agreed that Craven's behavior at Ferrol and Lisbon had done his reputation no good and did not reflect well on the "service to which he holds a commission." The spirit of John Paul Jones and Raphael Semmes meant that Confederate sailors expected to joust upon the waters like knights of old. Bulloch sent Page his best wishes and enclosed a letter from Mrs. Page.[64]

In the 39 days between the *Stonewall's* departure from Lisbon on March 28th and its arrival in Nassau on May 6th, the Confederacy had begun its final implosion. In what has been termed the "Waterloo of the South," Gen. Robert E. Lee was forced to abandon his defenses around Petersburg and President Jefferson Davis evacuated the Confederate government from Richmond. As General Grant launched a final assault on April 2nd, numerous governmental departments burned their papers, including Mallory and the Confederate Navy. The next day, the Confederate capital fell into Union hands. As Richmond burned, Confederate forces began to disintegrate.

Back in Liverpool on 9 April 1865, evidence of the Confederacy's demise steamed directly into Bulloch's lap. The Confederate blockade runner *Chameleon*, under the command of John Wilkinson, had left Nassau and Bermuda after the Union capture of Fort Fisher. When Prioleau refused responsibility for the ship, Wilkinson turned the ship and the public funds over to Bulloch who "acted with his usual tact and discretion." Bulloch took care of the ship, the crew, and "pettifogging" lawyers who tried to extort additional money for the crew.[65]

The Confederacy's larger problems, however, were beyond Bulloch's control. After Lee had retreated from Richmond, on April 6th nearly one-fourth of his army was captured at the battle of Sayler's Creek. Lee continued toward Lynchburg via his last remaining avenue of retreat, one that took him northwest across the Appomattox River. One last time, Union forces stopped Lee's line of advance. On the same day that Bulloch greeted Wilkinson and the *Chameleon*, General Lee met General Grant at William McLean's house in Appomattox to discuss terms of surrender and peace. The most violent war in American history was ending in the most polite manner.[66]

On Wednesday, Bulloch wrote a letter to Mallory that would never reach him, for there was no Confederate Navy Department left in Richmond. What remained of the Confederate government was on the run through southwest Virginia. Bulloch and the "representatives of the Treasury department" as well as the "commissioners of the Confederate States" had agreed to suspend all naval contracts and preserve funds for the general good. Bulloch immediately informed Fraser, Trenholm and Co. he was winding up business. Any future cotton that arrived would be sold and the proceeds added to the general fund.[67] This was the last documented letter sent to the Honorable Secretary of the Confederate Navy Department Stephen Mallory.[68]

A week later, British newspapers thundered the stunning news of Lee's surrender. The descriptions of Lee's courtly manner and Grant's courteous behavior at Appomattox moved British readers, who admired the gallant General Lee, even if they didn't support his cause.[69] While Commissioner Mason and other Confederate supporters believed the struggle might be carried on in the western Confederacy, Bulloch knew better. The Great Powers of Europe would rapidly withdraw the belligerent status afforded Confederate ships as soon as they were completely satisfied that the Union government was well and truly in control of all its rebellious states. As he continued to pay allotments for members of its crew, Bulloch knew that the *Shenandoah* was still at sea, on the way to her mission in the North Pacific whaling grounds, if all had gone as planned. However, after her status as a belligerent lapsed, the *Shenandoah* would be a stateless warship and Waddell and his crew would be treated as pirates. But first, Bulloch had to solve more immediate problems: getting the remaining Confederate naval personnel home, settling debts, and winding up the business of the Confederate Navy — much of which involved Fraser, Trenholm and Co.[70]

As the remaining forces surrendered throughout the Confederacy, John Wilkes Booth shot President Abraham Lincoln on the evening of April 14th at Ford's Theater in Washington. The Union government immediately suspected the involvement of the Confederate government and arrested former officials wherever they were, including former Secretary of the Navy Mallory. The Union dragnet managed to kill Booth and capture all the persons involved except for John H. Surratt, Jr. The fugitive Surratt escaped to Canada and was headed to Liverpool.[71] Moreover, the check that Bulloch had written to Patrick Martin (who had plotted with Booth to kidnap Lincoln) meant that he was now linked to this infamous event.

Lincoln assassination conspirator John Surratt, Jr., in Papal Zouave uniform (Library of Congress).

In his memoirs, Bulloch was generous in his assessment of Lincoln, saying that the assassination was "the most lamentable event which could have happened for the South, and indeed for the whole country ... President Lincoln ... was naturally of a kindly disposition, and had on many occasions openly and frankly declared that all he wanted was to 'restore the Union.'" It is likely that the Union accusations of Confederate government complicity in Lincoln's death worried Bulloch, as he no doubt recalled his financial support to Booth's associate in Canada, Captain P.C. Martin.[72]

The assassination horrified the British public, and Union government suspicions of official Confederate government involvement in the plot alarmed and infuriated the Southerners remaining in Europe. James Mason in London was incensed at the blanket accusation of the Union government and sent a letter via Mathew Maury to Confederate Secretary of State Judah P. Benjamin. It never reached Benjamin for he too was on the run from Union pursuers. Maury was on his way to Havana with his mines, still hoping to reach Texas.[73]

In May 1865, as the scattered Confederate land forces continued to surrender throughout the South, Bulloch still had two warships under weigh. The *Stonewall* had stopped in the Canary Islands to refuel and then proceeded to the Bahamas. There, Capt. Page met with the Confederate commercial agent in Nassau, Louis Heyliger, to discuss the latest intelligence.[74] Page and his crew learned of Lee's surrender from Heyliger or perhaps earlier, when they overhauled and released an American clipper ship before reaching Nassau on May 6th. Page's departure for Havana suggests that Bulloch's final letter of April 8th was waiting from him in Nassau.[75]

Maury and his mine warfare equipment for Galveston were also headed to Havana. Bulloch, Maury, and Page may have contemplated an impromptu "joint-operation." The *Stonewall* could have attacked the blockading Union ships off Galveston, allowing Maury to deploy his defensive mines. The *Stonewall* and perhaps the CSS *Ajax*, under the command of John Low, might have been able to keep the port open. All this became a moot point by the time Page arrived in Havana, short of fuel and money, and with no war to fight.[76]

Page, in a last letter to Bulloch, said that upon stepping ashore in Havana he learned that Jefferson Davis had been captured in Georgia and Maj. Helm, the Confederate agent, could not supply any financial support. News from Texas was equally bad. The people of Texas had heard and read of Sherman's hellish treatment of Georgia and the Carolinas. They were laying down their arms.[77]

The Spanish captain-general informed Page that he expected the Spanish ambassador in Washington to confirm his government's revocation of all belligerent rights afforded to the Confederate States. He would be a pirate if he and the *Stonewall* continued operations. Unable to imagine a world not at war, Page thought France and the United States would soon declare war over Mexico and that Spain would join the fray on the side of Louis-Napoléon. The French or Spanish would love to have a formidable armored ram in the Gulf of Mexico, ready to go. He was not going to surrender her to the Union Navy without a fight. He planned to sell his ship to the Spanish or scuttle her in adjacent Castle Morro in Havana harbor.[78]

After some haggling by the Spanish business representative, who was trying to get Captain Page and Lt. Bob Carter to ask for more money, the *Stonewall* became property of the Spanish government for $16,000. The *Stonewall* was now under her fourth flag (French, Danish, Confederate, and Spanish). By the end of her career, her masts would also fly the U.S. and Japanese flags.[79]

After the Spanish Navy rendered full naval courtesies to Capt. Page, Lt. Carter, and the rest of the crew, the Confederates were paid their wages and left to make their way back to the reunited United States as best they could. Page's letter to Bulloch was dated 19 May 1865 and it probably reached Liverpool by the end of the month. The irony would not have been lost on Bulloch. The last time he left a ship in Havana, he had to pay a $6,000 ransom to set the *Black Warrior* free, but there would be no recovery from this setback. By the time Bulloch learned of the *Stonewall's* fate, there was only one Confederate naval combatant in operation, Lt. Commanding James Iredell Waddell and the *Shenandoah*. But where were they?[80]

On the day following Page's sale of the *Stonewall*, the CSS *Shenandoah* sighted the snow-lashed peaks of the Kuril Islands north of Japan, and headed toward the Kamchatka Peninsula of Siberian Russia. She was only just now reaching the edge of her ultimate intended operational area. Waddell's last official documented communication with Bulloch had been a short letter posted in Melbourne on 25 January 1865 that did not reach Liverpool until late May. Before departing Australia, Waddell probably sent additional, undocumented letters to Liverpool in mid–February via a Fraser, Trenholm and Co. owned ship, the *John Fraser*.[81]

Bulloch learned of the arrest of President Jefferson Davis soon after receiving word about the *Shenandoah's* visit to Melbourne. Davis was captured on 10 May 1865 and the announcement appeared in British newspapers on May 31st.[82] Bulloch knew it was over. He had to make every effort to get news to Waddell, as all the Great Powers began to withdraw belligerent rights from the "so-called" Confederate States of America. Most affected by this decree was the *Shenandoah*. The ship and its sailors were now precisely what Seward and Adams had declared them to be all along, pirates!

To protect Waddell, his crew, and possibly himself from the hangman's noose, Bulloch wisely advised Commissioner Mason that they needed to send a formal communication to the *Shenandoah*. The Confederate commissioner, now with no government to represent and no authority, had to find a way to officially and publicly order Waddell to cease combat operations, strike his colors and guns, and sail into the nearest port. Bulloch realized that it was far more likely that Waddell would learn of the situation prior to any communication from Mason. But he knew that a vengeful Union government would be particularly enraged by any "depredations" committed after hostilities had officially ended. The *Shenandoah* and its crew were already subject to detention as stateless pirates.[83]

Mason and Bulloch discussed notification options during the first two weeks of June 1865.[84] After initially resisting the idea, Mason finally agreed: "I think the time has come when it should be attempted, ... let me hear by note the several points to which the orders should be sent, and send me the form of the order, which after examining, I will return to you ... the order must of course be sent to Lord Russell." Bulloch must have grimaced at the thought of dealing with Russell, but it was the only way to disseminate an order to the farthest reaches of the world. More importantly, it would place the official British imprimatur on the inevitable delay in notifying Waddell and protect him from recrimination for any acts of "piracy" committed after the cessation of hostilities.

On 19 June 1865, the same day that Seward learned of British withdrawal of belligerent rights, Bulloch sent Mason his proposed letter for the British Foreign Office. It was brief and purposeful. Bulloch wanted Lord Russell to send copies to British stations at Nagasaki, Japan, Shanghai, and the Sandwich Islands (Hawaii) where the local consular officers could get a copy into the hands of Lt. Waddell, if he happened to stop in any of those ports.[85]

> Sir: ... President Davis, vice-President Stephens, and several members of the Confederate Cabinet have been arrested and are now held as close prisoners by the U.S. Government ... the principal European powers have withdrawn the recognition of belligerent rights accorded by them to the Confederate States in 1861, and have forbidden the entry of vessels bearing the Confederate States flag into their ports for any purpose of repair or supply ... I hereby direct you to desist from any further destruction of United States property upon the high seas and from all offensive operations against the citizens of that country.... The orders issued by the maritime powers with regard to the treatment of Confederate States ships hereafter indicate that you would be allowed to enter any port for the bona fide purpose of disarming and dismantling the *Shenandoah*.... If you have not money enough to pay off in full, and cannot negotiate a bill on England, pay to the extent of your funds and give each man an order on yourself, payable at Liverpool, for the balance due him, and come here to settle your accounts. The terms of a proclamation lately issued by the President of the United States are such as to exclude most of the officers of your command from the privilege of returning at once to their original homes, and I would advise all of you to come to Europe, or to await elsewhere the further development of events in the United States before venturing to go to any part of that country or the Confederate States ... I shall remain in Liverpool for an indefinite time, and you can communicate with me at my usual address.[86]

11. I Know Not What Your Circumstances May Be

Bulloch's letter reveals his complete understanding of the political situation. He mentions that Davis and much of the former Confederate cabinet had been arrested, a testament to the total collapse of the Confederacy. He took particular notice of President Andrew Johnson's proclamation that the war was over; it included a general amnesty, except for officers such as Waddell. Johnson's pardon initially excluded any Confederate civilian or military officer who served outside the Confederacy. These individuals were considered to be the most treasonous. There were several other categories of exclusionary or exempted persons, but none as harsh as this. Bulloch wisely advised Waddell to come to Europe and await events in America before attempting to go home. Bulloch's own comment that he would be in Liverpool for an "indefinite time" showed that he was in limbo himself, but at least he was safely ashore and was prepared to pay the Confederate Navy's sailors as a matter of honor. He could only hope that Waddell surrendered the *Shenandoah* before the U.S. Navy could sink the ship or capture and hang him.[87]

Bulloch's orders, with a cover letter from Mason, went to Lord Russell on June 20th; on the 22nd Russell's assistant, Hammond, agreed to forward it to the suggested consulates. Mason acknowledged Hammond's letter on June 26th, though carefully couching a reply that the *Shenandoah* "must be submitted to the laws of the country where she may arrive." Mason also requested that Bulloch's order to Waddell be sealed before being sent. Hammond responded on June 29th, relaying Lord Russell's concurrence. On 12 July 1865, the Foreign Office forwarded sealed copies of Bulloch's order to all British colonial authorities. As his orders to Waddell wound its way through the British Foreign Office, Bulloch struggled to cover the remaining debts of the Confederate Navy Department, close open contracts, and plan for a future that included his wife Harriott and their children.[88] They were essentially stateless refugees, subject to arrest in their native land, and likely targets of the victorious and even more powerful federal government of the United States. The destruction of its maritime industry by Confederate raiders had been bad enough in a financial sense, but the assassination of Lincoln had put the Yankees into a blood lust for revenge.

For the rest of the summer of 1865, Bulloch carried on with the great unwinding of the Confederate Naval Department's affairs. He also had to find his own way. With his knowledge of the cotton trade and his collocation with Fraser, Trenholm and Co., he could have bought and sold cotton on his personal account. He also had access to discounted refunds for cancelled contracts. Foremost among his unsettled liabilities was the whereabouts of the *Shenandoah*.

When Bulloch's orders reached Lord Russell at the end of June, Waddell and the *Shenandoah* were off the coast of Russia in the Sea of Okhotsk. The *Shenandoah* was just beginning her rampage against Union whalers on June 22nd when the British Foreign Office acknowledged Mason's letter (with Bulloch's orders attached). Waddell's boarding officers, including Acting Master Irvine Bulloch, recovered recent newspapers from the condemned Union whalers telling of Lee's surrender. But they also carried news of Confederate President Jefferson Davis' proclamation to fight on to the bitter end. Waddell did not trust the newspaper accounts fully since all were in Northern papers. Waddell fought and sailed on. Between the 26th and 28th of June, as Mason wrote to the British Foreign Office, the *Shenandoah* began her most intensive combat operations when she destroyed nine ships and bonded two more. The last two survived only because Waddell needed them to carry Union prisoners to San Francisco. The plan conceived in Richmond, organized in Liverpool, and carried out in the North Pacific Ocean had been executed brilliantly with 32 Yankee ships destroyed and 6 bonded — but too late.[89]

As July opened, the *Shenandoah* headed south from the Arctic Circle to avoid the increasingly dangerous ice flows. Waddell and his ship were the only Union or Confederate combatants to operate north of the Arctic Circle — a superb feat of seamanship. Now headed toward warmer waters, Waddell's mind turned to what he might achieve next. Waddell reckoned he could launch a raid on San Francisco and ransom it for gold as Bulloch had suggested months earlier.[90]

As the *Shenandoah* approached the California coast on 2 August 1865, Waddell spotted a small English barque running fast; it was the *Barracouta*. A boarding party led by Bulloch's brother Irvine soon learned the shattering news that the war was over. General Lee had surrendered, President Lincoln was assassinated, and President Davis was arrested. Recognizing the implications, Waddell immediately ordered the *Shenandoah* decommissioned as a warship and stored the heavy guns in the hold. Waddell and his fellow ex–Confederates were alone on a ship that belonged to no nation. He did not need Bulloch's warning to know that they would be hung as pirates unless, perhaps, they could reach a safe port.[91]

For the remainder of August, the *Shenandoah* stormed south across the Pacific, reaching a point where she began to shape a course for Cape Horn on 1 September 1865. Though he did not know it, hot on his heels were the American warships USS *Saranac, Iroquois, Wateree*, and *Saint Marys*. If Waddell and the *Shenandoah* managed to survive the monstrous wind and waves off Patagonia and the southernmost Pacific, they still had to slip through a tightening net of Union ships. On 17 September 1865, the British government issued a blanket proclamation to all its colonies and territories directing them to seize the *Shenandoah* if she should stop in any of Her Majesty's ports or territories.[92]

Bulloch could only watch, wait, and worry about the *Shenandoah*. He knew that Waddell would try to get the ship back to Liverpool. It offered the best hope of finance and succor for the crew of former Confederates. Whether Waddell could make it that far was another question. Toward the end of September, a vestige of the American Civil War's horrific end appeared in Liverpool. Whether Bulloch knew of the individual's arrival in the city is not known, but an accused Lincoln assassination conspirator had used Canadian connections to reach Britain. His name was John H. Surratt, Jr., the only accused assassin to escape arrest and trial. Surratt arrived in Liverpool on 27 September 1865 having disembarked from his ship, the *Peruvian*, in Ireland to avoid Union notice.[93]

Surratt hid at the Oblates of Mary Immaculate, only one kilometer away and a quick stretch of the legs up Chapel Street from Bulloch's Rumford Place offices. There is no documentation that Bulloch was even aware of his presence at the time or that he had any prior knowledge of Surratt's arrival. Still, Surratt likely knew about Bulloch's recent financial support to John Wilkes Booth via Capt. P.C. Martin and may have hoped for similar assistance. Surratt had admitted to the ship's doctor of the *Peruvian*, Lewis McMillan, that he was wanted by federal authorities before he left the ship in Moville, Ireland. Union authorities throughout the breadth of Britain were alerted and launched an immediate manhunt. Surratt's presence would have alarmed all the Confederates in Liverpool, who did not want any implied association with a notorious assassin.

On September 28th, Bulloch contacted Mason wondering about the fate of the *Shenandoah*. The British seizure order was alarming, but not unexpected in light of the intense pressure by the new U.S. government. President Johnson had intended to be less provocative in his responses to both internal and international problems, but the aftermath of Lincoln's assassination inflamed passions for revenge.[94]

The first autumnal days of October 1865 came and went as Bulloch still hoped for news of the *Shenandoah*. The weather-beaten ship had rounded South America and was racing northward, her prow slicing through the first pummeling gales of the Atlantic. The British government produced another announcement about the *Shenandoah* on October 6th: if the Royal Navy found her with weapons intact, she was to be handed over to the U.S. Navy. There would be no chance of leniency from the British legal system.[95] Unaware of her new threatened status, the *Shenandoah* crossed the Equator on October 11th. It was now clear to all aboard that they were making for Britain.[96]

In Liverpool, Surratt finally left the city on October 18th, crossing into France, possibly from the English ferry port of Newhaven.[97] The Union agents were still doggedly on his trail. Two days later, Bulloch considered his own legal, financial, and personal vulnerability in a letter to Mason. It had been four months since Bulloch's surrender orders had reached the British Foreign Office for dissemination via the British consulates. He wanted Mason to spread the word that Waddell may not have heard of the war's end until September and suggested that he should release portions of Bulloch's letter to the press. He fully realized that he "might be compromised by the publication" of the order to Waddell since it bore his signature. It would be Mason's judgment at to what should be released.[98]

The answer to the question of the *Shenandoah's* location would be answered shortly. Waddell briefly interrupted his journey in the mid–Atlantic. On October 27th and again on the 31st, he paused for burial-at-sea ceremonies for two crewmen who had died due to illness. By 1 November 1865, he was only 900 miles from Liverpool. The last great drama of the American Civil War was about to unfold, right in Bulloch's front yard.[99]

Two days later, Waddell set a northerly course one last time as *Shenandoah* neared the southeast coast of Ireland. Approaching Cape Clear on the Irish coast, the *Shenandoah* wore away to a new course that took her into St. George's Channel and up the Mersey into Liverpool. Waddell was going to dash through one of the busiest shipping areas in the world, hoping to slip past any U.S. or Royal Navy warships.[100]

On the same day, James Dunwoody Bulloch arrived in Liverpool as a passenger on the ship *City of London* from Queenstown, Ireland. The timing of his trip was either a case of irony that placed Bulloch in Ireland on unrelated business, or a sign that he had received news via the *Barracouta* and anticipated Waddell's arrival in Liverpool. In either instance, Waddell's return to Liverpool was prudent given the strength of British laws and the hope that Bulloch would still have money to pay the crew.[101]

Just before midnight on November 5th, the *Shenandoah* neared the entrance to Liverpool and launched rockets to gain the attention of the harbor pilots. After several volleys, a boat came out and met the ship. Waddell initially told the pilot that the name of his ship was the *America* and had come from Calcutta. Waddell quickly revealed the true identity of the ship to the astonished pilot who confirmed that the American Civil War had been over for so long that it was no longer news. The U.S. Navy was looking everywhere for them; it was amazing they had not been discovered by British or Union ships on the way up the Channel.[102]

After circumnavigating the globe, a feat achieved by no other combatant ship in the

CSS *Shenandoah* in Liverpool at the end of the war (*Illustrated London News*, 18 November 1865).

American Civil War, and not grounding a single time, the Liverpool pilot managed to hang the *Shenandoah* on the bar outside the entrance up the Mersey. At 7 o'clock on the morning of November 6th the tide came on, lifted the ship, and she steamed up the Mersey with the "Stainless Banner" flying one last time. Waddell directed the pilot to bring her near the *Donegal*, a Royal Navy warship. A young lieutenant from the *Donegal* clambered up the side to discover the identity of the unknown vessel, painted in black. He was as astonished as the Liverpool pilot had been the night before. At 10:00 A.M., Lt. Commanding James Iredell Waddell, captain of the CSS *Shenandoah*, ordered the quartermaster to strike the Confederate colors. The American Civil War was now over, and it ended in Liverpool, England. The *Shenandoah* was anchored off Rock Ferry, where Bulloch, and a great portion of the Confederate sympathizers and former officers and officials, could witness the proceedings through their telescopes. It was a docile ending to a brutal war.[103]

Waddell asked the lieutenant of the *Donegal* to deliver a letter to Lord Russell that officially surrendered the *Shenandoah* to Great Britain. Shortly afterward, the Liverpool customs officers announced that the men could debark, but all their belongings would have to stay aboard. No one departed the ship by instructions from Waddell, or perhaps the Royal Navy. It was well they did, for after receiving Waddell's letter, Capt. Paynter of the *Donegal* sent word that the men were to stay aboard the ship until he received instructions from Lord Russell's office.[104] Paynter sent a detail of Royal marines to board and guard the *Shenandoah* and ordered the gunboat *Goshawk* to move near the raider. Tension among the crew of the former Confederate vessel began to rise with these ominous developments. Dudley and Adams predictably demanded the immediate seizure of the vessel and crew in the name of the U.S. government.[105]

Faced with such a diplomatically radioactive situation, Lord Russell did what high British government officials always did best; he handed the whole matter over to the Crown's legal counsel. Fortunately for Waddell and his crew, there could not have been a more knowledgeable group of legal minds to pass judgment on the *Shenandoah*. The counsel included Sir Roundell Palmer, Sir R.P. Collier, and most importantly, Sir Robert Phillimore, the most famous legal mind in the world on maritime law. They were beyond wise; they were the law. Waddell was a fanatical reader of Phillimore's legal treatises, and like Semmes, even had copies aboard the ship. Waddell had assiduously followed maritime precedence in his seizures. His attention to legal detail and ignorance of the war's end (along with Bulloch's notice via Lord Russell) saved his crew's necks from being stretched by Union rope. Palmer, Collier, and Phillimore reviewed Waddell's simple legal argument, considered Adams and Dudley's complaint for seizure, and made their pronouncement: the *Shenandoah*'s crew was to be released and only those proven to be British subjects would be prosecuted. The ship itself could then be handed over to the U.S. government.[106]

On November 8th, Capt. Paynter delivered the news to Waddell and his last, lost Confederate command: the American crewmen were free to go, but any British crewmen would be detained. Waddell ordered the crew to assemble on the main deck and Lt. Whittle called the ship's muster roll by rating and name. Each man was called to attention before Captain Paynter to declare their nationality, and in a range of accents from English, to Irish, to Scottish, all declared themselves to be Confederates. Whether through sympathy or inability to challenge the nationality of these Rip Van Winkles of the sea, Paynter pronounced them all "Confederates" and set them free. With whoops of joy, the men reassembled one last time. Waddell thanked everyone for their service and dismissed them with the sounds of their cheers ringing in his ears. It was a last joyous occasion for the Confederacy and it was carried out right before Bulloch's eyes on the Mersey. As the freed crewmen of the *Shenandoah* scrambled into a ferry (the *Bee*) that took them ashore at Great George landing, Bulloch's organizational skills and foresight would be tested one last time.[107] These lost Confederates needed to be paid.[108] Waddell set up temporary residence at George's Hotel on Dale Street in Liverpool. He soon made contact with Bulloch and was relieved that he had set aside funds to support former Confederate crewmen in Europe.[109]

The Southern officers of the *Shenandoah* learned that any attempt to return to America would place them at considerable risk due to President Johnson's amnesty exemption for those who had been "academy-trained" and serving overseas. Waddell, for one, was certainly not going home any time soon. He was America's Public Enemy Number One, the chief pirate of the most egregious Anglo-American pirate cruiser. He had escaped justice due to British complicity, or so it would seem when newspapers in America reported the story.

The day after the crew was released, Dudley visited the *Shenandoah* and spoke with Capt. Paynter of the *Donegal*. Paynter said he would hand the ship over to any person that Dudley "might appoint to take charge." As this information originated from Bulloch's memoirs, it is apparent that Bulloch knew exactly what was going on with this last commerce raider. The next day, Capt. Freeman, a commercial captain hired by Dudley, came aboard to take charge of the last Confederate warship. Dudley wanted Freeman to sail the *Shenandoah* to New York and hoped to exhibit her as a war prize to the victorious and still vengeful Northern states, even though it was a "United" States of America once more.[110]

During this time, Bulloch was busy with more important matters, at least for the officers of the *Shenandoah*, as he arranged for James Baines, a Liverpool merchant, to disburse back pay for the crew.[111] By Saturday, the crewmen were paid off at the Liverpool Sailor's Home. While some men would later claim that they did not receive the full amount due to them, both Bulloch's and Lt. Whittle's memoirs and letters assert that the crewmen were properly compensated. Even Cornelius Hunt, a junior officer aboard the ship, who detested Waddell and accused him of "short-pay," expressed his admiration for Bulloch's diligence and honesty. Bulloch, Hunt said, stood "pre-eminent [a]mong the many excellent and high-minded gentlemen who ... acted as Confederate Agents in England ... during the hour of her trial."[112]

A week later, Bulloch dealt with another kind of emergency, a medical emergency. James Waddell had suffered hemorrhaging in his lungs and appeared to be at the point of death.[113] Bulloch organized medical treatment and had him moved to the Royal Marine Hotel, only a short distance from the Bulloch residence. Waddell would be there for the next several months under Bulloch's watchful care.[114]

Bulloch continued to sort out the finances of the now defunct Confederate Navy Department, and quietly assisted former-Confederate officers and sailors stranded in Europe. He also kept a keen eye on relations between Britain and America. The unwelcome return of the *Shenandoah* to England had created a predictable political firestorm in the United States. Throughout the remainder of November and December 1865, a fierce war of words raged between U.S. Minister Adams and Lord Clarendon, the new British foreign secretary, with British newspapers avidly reporting each verbal volley.[115]

The British papers highlighted the vitriolic reactions of Americans. The *New York Times* had already adopted a position advocating reprisal as an appropriate response to British-inspired depredations of the *Shenandoah* and her sister ships, *Alabama* and *Florida*: "The responsibility of dealing with Waddell devolves wholly on the British Government. If he was in command of a privateer, duly exercising belligerent rights, England cannot surrender him, nor shall we ask her to do so. If, on the contrary, he pursued his career of devastation after those rights had ceased to protect him, he became simply a pirate, and violated the laws of Great Britain quite as truly as those of the United States. And it devolves upon the English authorities to hold him responsible."[116]

It was manifestly clear that Bulloch was going to have to keep his head down and hope his own meticulous accounting practices would cover his financial tracks as well. Although Fraser, Trenholm and Co. and chief financial agent General Colin McRae would be most directly in the U.S. government's firing line, Bulloch knew that he could be unfairly targeted at any moment. The ongoing investigation in the Lincoln assassination was also an unknown. Would the paper trail to Bulloch be discovered?

At least Bulloch was relieved of the problem of transferring the *Shenandoah* to the United States. Dudley had to respect Waddell's skill in sailing the ship around the world. Dudley could barely get it out of the Irish Sea. On 21 November 1865, the *Shenandoah*, under the command of Thomas F. Freeman, sailed down the Mersey River headed toward America. With a crew of only 55 men, a few more than the 46 Waddell had originally embarked with, Freeman was chancing a winter crossing. Perhaps it was the winter weather, or as some former Confederates sardonically muttered, it was the American flag at the mast, but on 6 December 1865 the *Shenandoah* limped back into Liverpool. Her terrified crew stumbled ashore, glad to be alive, and refused to sail again. Freeman reported that the *Shenandoah* required repairs, new sails, 100 tons of coal, a new crew and a new captain; he was returning to his own company. The last Confederate warship refused to yield to the Yankee yoke.[117]

Perhaps already sensing where the roots of his future would be planted, on 9 December 1865 James and Harriott Bulloch had their children, Jessie Hart, Henry Dunwoody, Stuart Elliott and Martha Louise, baptized into the Church of England at the Parish of St. John Church in Waterloo. Bulloch's oldest son, the 11-year-old James, Jr., had already been baptized (christened) in America. If the Bullochs planned to become British subjects, this was a helpful addition to any future naturalization petition.[118]

As Christmas approached in the bitter winter of 1865, the former Confederates in and around Liverpool experienced their first festive season without war as a backdrop. Bulloch and his family had survived the most destructive war in American history, but their list of blessings was short. Like most Southerners, their only assets were determination, hope, and each other. For Bulloch, it was a time to assess an ambiguous future. There was little prospect of making a livelihood in the United States. He would have been arrested the moment he set foot on American soil. If they were to survive, the Bullochs would have to redefine their understanding of "home."

12

Under a New Flag

Until the winter of 1865–1866, James Dunwoody Bulloch's life had been one of dangerous sureties, whether as a U.S. Navy officer, a commercial shipping captain, or as a Confederate naval officer and secret agent. That was all gone, replaced by numbing uncertainty. The cataclysmic excitement of the American Civil War ended with an empty silence. The shooting war was over, but Bulloch knew that the reunited United States of America, like the ancient Roman Empire, would not be satisfied with victory. It would want the spoils of war as well.

The *Shenandoah* was symbolic of the fate of former Confederate property. After failing in the attempt to sail the ship to the United States in late autumn of 1865, and accepting the stark assessment of her unseaworthy condition, Dudley ordered her to be sold at auction. The process of inventorying and stripping her of saleable items began; *Shenandoah* would be auctioned like an unwanted piece of discount furniture.

All of the Confederate Navy Department's European agents and suppliers were nervously following the U.S. government's aggressive actions against them. Former Confederates living in foreign countries, such as Bulloch, had their U.S. passports, but they were worthless. In the U.S., they would be arrested due to President Johnson's general amnesty exclusions (the first of several). Like the Israelites out of Egypt, they could only move onward, not homeward. For Bulloch, his brother Irvine (who had returned on the *Shenandoah*), and his faithful clerk Moses P. Robertson, England was now "home."

Most of the Confederate government officials who had been in Europe when the war ended remained in place. Slidell was still in Paris and Mason moved between London and Leamington. Judah P. Benjamin, the former Confederate secretary of war and later secretary of state, arrived in Britain in late August 1865. He had survived a spectacular escape from the Union cavalry and a voyage in a small boat from Florida to the Bahamas. Benjamin was a high priority target. He ran the covert Confederate intelligence operations and "raids" behind Union lines during the war. He was also Jewish, making it all the more imperative to get out of America. His chances for a fair trial in the United States would have been nil. Since his arrival in Britain, Benjamin had been writing for a London newspaper, *The Daily Telegraph*, and training to become a British barrister. He was born in the Virgin Islands as a British citizen and had been one of America's most renowned lawyers prior to the American Civil War.[1]

One former Confederate who had been in the direct line of legal fire from the U.S. government since July 1865 was Charles K. Prioleau, the principal manager of Fraser, Trenholm and Co. in Liverpool.² Prioleau possessed the fiery disposition of the South Carolinians who began the Civil War. He wasn't going to back down from Seward or the Johnson administration. On 28 February 1866, he filed a countersuit against both the United States government and President Andrew Johnson.

Another one of Bulloch's former "associates" was in some difficulty, not with the U.S. government, but with the British bankruptcy courts. George Sanders, "a notorious Confederate agent, who came to this country to fit out a fleet of Confederate warships, and has succeeded in getting pretty deeply into debt" owed over £10,000. One of his creditors was W.S. Lindsay and Co. This was the same Lindsay who had tried to convince Louis-Napoléon to support the Confederacy. Sanders operated as deep and as quiet as any Confederate agent in the war. If the British knew of Sanders' covert, but ineffective activities, how was Bulloch going to escape a full outing in the press?³

Judah P. Benjamin, Confederate attorney general, secretary of war and state, head of covert intelligence operations, and post-war British barrister (authors' collection).

The U.S. government investigators were combing Europe to capture the financial residue of the Confederacy and support U.S. legal actions and diplomatic complaints. Yet Bulloch continued to escape direct prosecution, as he set up a new Liverpool office adjacent his old office at 10 Rumford Place. James, Harriott, and the children still lived at No. 3 Wellington Place in Waterloo, just outside of Liverpool. Bulloch and his faithful clerk Robertson began work as cotton traders with the assistance of Fraser, Trenholm and Co.⁴ Cotton continued to pay the bills while Bulloch and Robertson quietly attended to personnel issues associated with the former Confederate Navy.⁵

In 1866, Liverpool, Glasgow, and Southampton were the great arterial valves that fed the economic lifeblood from the global British Empire, taking in the raw materials and shipping out finished products.⁶ James Dunwoody and Irvine Bulloch, along with Robertson, were in the right place with the right skills for success. To take full advantage of this commercial opportunity, they would need to become British citizens. For the Bulloch brothers, the prospect of citizenship was problematic, depending on legal pressure from the U.S. government. For Robertson, a figure in the background, it was less of a worry.⁷

Sir Frederick Bruce, the minister who received the direct brunt of Washington's anger over the Confederate commerce raiders, was the same British diplomat who had been in China during the Lay-Osborn affair. Bruce had arrived in Washington on 1 March 1865 and had to weather diplomatic blasts from Seward and deliver the British responses. Sir Frederick was in an unenviable position, but he was up to the task as he was an ardent supporter of America.[8]

Sir Bruce's American counterpart in Britain remained Charles Francis Adams. The belated return of the *Shenandoah* provided the U.S. minister yet another opportunity to rekindle his smoldering lamentations against British assistance to the Confederacy. Adams had compiled a litany of complaints against the British government including the exaggerated accusation that during the war, "there has been no appearance of the insurgents as a belligerent on the ocean, excepting in the shape of British vessels, constructed, equipped, supplied, manned, and armed in British Ports."[9]

In his memoirs, Bulloch commented that only three months after Lee's surrender at Appomattox, the U.S. government brought the first of a series of cases to British courts claiming ownership of Confederate properties that were being hidden from the U.S. government. The initial case targeted Fraser, Trenholm and Co. and Gen. McRae, the former Confederate Treasury officer in Europe.[10] The British judge, Lord Hatherley, ruled that "whenever a government *de facto* has obtained possession of a property ... the government which displaces it succeeds to all the rights of the former government and to the property so acquired." The Union would have to acknowledge that the Confederate government had been a *de facto* government if it hoped to recover any of the imagined Confederate loot in Britain. The ruling also affirmed the right of British subjects to conduct business with the Confederate government while it existed. The Union would also have to pay any outstanding liens against the seized assets.[11]

Bulloch opined that "all of the official representatives of the of the late Confederate Government would have accepted it ... and would have ... assisted any authorized agent of the U.S. Government in winding up affairs so as to secure to that government their just affairs." However, Lord Hatherley's legal pronouncement only infuriated Seward. He didn't just want control of Confederate property; he wanted to prosecute anyone (British or otherwise) that had carried out business with the illicit "so-called" Confederate government. Beginning in mid–1865, the U.S. government even introduced a "bounty policy" in Europe. As a result, U.S. Minister Adams ordered Consuls Dudley and Morse to hire special agents (i.e., more private detectives) to search out any and all suspected Confederate properties and to discover who had carried out business deals. The agents received a percentage of any monies collected. In Liverpool, a cauldron of pro–Southern and anti–Union feeling, this approach was not productive.[12]

In the spring of 1866, the U.S. strategy of litigation, property seizures, and insinuations of British complicity was operating at full throttle. On March 22nd, Nathaniel I. Wilson purchased the CSS *Shenandoah* at auction for £15,582 (and 15 shillings), less than half of Bulloch's original cost.[13] On April 26th, the former CSS *Tallahassee* was turned over to Dudley for sale at auction as well.[14] Dudley and his cohorts auctioned off all Confederate ships or property they found to the highest bidder, a mocking reminder of the slave auctions once held in the South. Fortunately for the individual Confederate expatriates, British barristers and sympathetic judges were still fending off the American legal assault against them.

In mid–April, news of the U.S. Reconstruction Committee hearings reached the daily papers of Britain. The great hero of the South, Gen. Robert E. Lee, testified that "he did not know of any person in Virginia who now contemplated resistance against the United States Government." Lee's key statement dashed all romantic dreams of European intervention in the collapsed South. No Southerner would contemplate "availing themselves of any opportunity for obtaining independence which might be offered in the event of a war between the United States and any foreign power, such as France and England."[15] This was a warning to Confederates in Europe as well as to Louis-Napoléon that Mexico was an unacceptable excuse for intervention in American affairs. The United States of America, though war-fatigued, was prepared to fight again to defend the borders it had fought so hard to preserve.[16]

Despite the successful connection of the transatlantic cable in July 1866, Europe was becoming less interested in American affairs. An intermittent exception was in Britain where the "late unpleasantness" provided a convenient British political axe to grind, particularly against the Confederate commerce raiders. The brewing conflict between Louis-Napoléon and the Prussian Empire, ostensibly led by Wilhelm I but in reality by Bismarck, was occupying the thoughts of European leaders. Unlike Europe's relative disinterest in American affairs, U.S. animosity toward Britain over the Confederate Navy's operations out of England continued to fester and grow.[17]

At least Bulloch's family news from America was happy. His sister Anna married James King Gracie, a New York banker. The news in Europe was decidedly different.[18] The success of the German Confederation in snatching Schleswig province from Denmark had emboldened Bismarck even more. His real aim was the unification of all German-speaking peoples into one nation, a development that would destabilize the core of Europe. Bismarck's desire for territory under German control would find its most horrific exposition some seventy-odd years later in World War II.[19] Even with the gloomy news from Europe, there were reminders of the old Confederacy washing up in Liverpool every few weeks. One such reminder was Gen. Beauregard, "of the late Confederate service, [who] arrived by the *Scotia*, and took apartments at the Adelphi Hotel ... where his appearance attracted some interest and curiosity." Beauregard, an employee of the Southern Railway, toured the Liverpool Exchange and may have met with Bulloch.[20]

British newspapers in July 1866 noted the feeling of self-satisfaction the U.S. authorities had in reaction to the Fenian (Irish) uprising in Canada. The question over reparations for the destruction caused by the Confederate Navy's commerce raiders still hung over British and American relations. Americans believed that Britain was getting what it deserved in Canada. As British newspapers accurately observed, "The popularity of the Confederate cause in the more numerous sections of English society has been aggravated by practical questions arising out of the fitting out of the Confederate cruisers, which have been dropped rather than settled by diplomatists."[21]

Sympathetic newspapers in Britain such as the *Anglo-American Times* recognized the need for a diplomatic solution (or arbitration) over the permanent damage Confederate commerce raiders had inflicted on the U.S. carrying trade: "It is clearly for the interest of England ... to urge a settlement of the United States claims, and at the same time, ... to revise and lay down distinctly the Maritime Law on captures at sea." This was a pragmatic assessment of the problem that clouded diplomatic relations between the U.S. and Great Britain. It was time to make up with the cousins over the sea, for there were German wolves on the prowl in Europe.[22]

Bulloch kept a low profile and went on with his cotton business. He was fully aware of the pressure the U.S. government placed on Prioleau and his company through incessant investigation and litigation. At least the cotton prices were good throughout the summer.[23] Another uncertainty was the change in British government. In July 1866, Lord Russell and the Liberal party were replaced by a Tory government under Prime Minister Derby, with his son Lord Stanley as foreign secretary. Russell, who had firmly refused to negotiate with the U.S. government over the Confederate commerce raiders, was gone.[24] The new Tory government might be more receptive to U.S. complaints, especially in light of the Prussian threat. The arrival of the dual-turreted USS *Miantonomoh* in Britain early in July, on its way to visit Russia, had alarmed the British public. The U.S. was demonstrating its value as an ally or as an enemy that could deploy its powerful new Navy to the doorstep of any coastal nation.[25]

While the Lancashire summer of 1866 was much cooler that anything Bulloch had experienced as a Georgia youth, the legal and diplomatic heat between Britain and America continued to rise. On 27 August 1866, Seward compiled a summary of the U.S. claims against the British government for the damages caused by the Confederate commerce raiders. The most destructive ships on Seward's list had been obtained under Bulloch's direction.[26] Seward sent this political hot potato to Adams who dropped it into the hands of British Foreign Minister Lord Stanley.[27]

The possibility that Britain and America would enter into negotiations over the Confederate commerce raiders meant that Bulloch would be drawn into the affair that became known as the "*Alabama* Claims." Yet, the litigation that immediately threatened to ensnare Bulloch was not related to the *Florida*, *Alabama* or *Shenandoah*. It involved Bulloch's blockade runners *cum* gunboats.

On October 2nd, a British admiralty court convened to consider the fate of the blockade runners *Ariel*, *Badger*, *Fox*, *Lark*, *Owl*, *Penguin* and *Wasp*. As the *Watchman and Wesleyan Advertiser* remarked in its October 3rd edition, these were "alleged Confederate ships ... and are the property of a merchant named Prioleau." The ships had been seized in late August and early September and Prioleau wanted the presiding judge to release them. The judge decided that he first needed a "written order or authorisation from Mr. Adams." U.S. Minister Adams or U.S. Consul Dudley had to appear in person. It was an opportunity that Thomas Dudley relished. The U.S. legal representative, Vernon Lushington, managed to prove that three of the vessels, the *Penguin*, *Owl* and *Lark*, were purchased with Confederate funds and that damages might be applied for, but the presiding judge decided that the remaining four ships had to be released. Prioleau's legal team had included a "Mr. Benjamin" who was none other than the former U.S. lawyer and senator and Confederate Secretary of War and Secretary of State Judah P. Benjamin. The resilient Benjamin had become a qualified British barrister.[28]

Adams and Dudley had their way, by and large, with the British Foreign Office and Treasury (Customs) Departments since the Laird rams seizure in 1863. Although the British courts had denied most U.S. government claims against Confederate properties and finances thus far, the continuous legal pressure cost the former Confederates time and money they could not spare. Judah P. Benjamin, due to his extensive legal experience and British citizenship, had become a member of the Inns of Court without the usual three-year legal apprenticeship, and his circuit included Liverpool. Now, the U.S. government faced one of the pre-eminent legal minds of the age whenever they attempted legal action against former Confederates in the Liverpool area. Bulloch must have breathed a little easier, while Adams and Dudley fumed.²⁹

For the rest of the fall and early winter of 1866–67, Charles K. Prioleau and his firm remained under intense financial and legal pressure. The American press avidly followed the U.S. government cases filed against him and his blockade runners. However, the constant publicity negatively affected his company's ability to obtain credit in New York. Judah P. Benjamin could defend Prioleau in a British court, but he could not rebut the judgment of American business markets.³⁰ In November 1866, Prioleau filed an affidavit for a U.S. court action. He asserted that as a partner in Fraser, Trenholm and Co., the defunct Confederate government owed him £272,000 pounds. Prioleau provided a full accounting of goods and public monies handled by his firm and now that the U.S. government had seized all of these resources, it was their responsibility to pay the bill.³¹

Lord Stanley, British foreign minister, weathered U.S. postwar fury over Confederate commerce raiders (Library of Congress).

The 17 November 1866 edition of the *London Times* assessed the U.S. government's harassment of ex-Confederates, British businesses, and government this way: "America has refused compensation in cases somewhat analogous to that of the *Alabama*; but unless it can also be shown that her refusal was justified by the higher code of international morality which rests upon the common interest of all civilized nations, little will have been gained by the demonstration."³² The American Civil War would not just fade away because the Johnson administration, driven by the passion of Secretary of State Seward, would not let it go.

The British government wasn't amused by the American administration's constant badgering either. Lord Stanley refused to submit to arbitration. On 30 November 1866, he explained to Sir Frederick Bruce that there was "no precedent for any Government consenting to submit to the judgment of a foreign power or of an international commission the question whether its policy has or has not been suitable to the circumstances in which it was placed." Lord Stanley was not inclined to have the British Empire bow to external pressures.³³

Both the U.S. and British governments slowly and cautiously felt their way into unexplored legal territory. An unforeseen consequence of the American Civil War would be a permanent shift in the understanding and application of international law. Bulloch, through his dexterous manipulation of Anglo-American and Continental jurisprudence, had forced the Great Powers to rethink their legal equities. Attention to the subtlety of the law had helped fuel Bulloch's success as a brilliant naval intelligence operative and agent. Because he had played the legal game so cleverly, the rules had to be changed.

In the second week of December, Bulloch presented his copy of Peake's *Rudimentary Treatise of Shipbuilding* to his friend Arthur French. The book had been his shipbuilding bible throughout his time in Liverpool and Paris.[34] Perhaps this gift was Bulloch's way of severing his connections with the past and looking toward a future that did not include shipbuilding.

Bulloch's dedication to cotton importing and trading, as well as his tentative advances into business in partnership with Moses P. Robertson, became apparent in late 1866. The *Galveston Daily News* carried a recurring advertisement placed by James Sorley that ran for the entirety of 1867. It proclaimed: "Liberal advances on cotton or wool, consigned to my friends ... Fraser, Trenholm and Co., Bulloch and Robertson," among others. Bulloch had become concerned enough about the mounting legal problems of Fraser, Trenholm and Co. that he set up a business partnership with Robertson that would insulate him from any direct legal action by the U.S. government.[35]

Further evidence of Bulloch's whole-hearted plunge as an international trade broker is documented by the British Commissioners of Patents. On 3 October 1866 and 4 February 1867, Robertson and Bulloch applied for British patents on behalf of an American client. The patents were for "an improved tie to be used in fastening bales of cotton" and "an improved self-fastening buckle or tie to be used in fastening hoops or bands of metal round bales of cotton, wool, and other merchandize capable of being packed in bales." Robertson and Bulloch submitted these patents on behalf of Charles William Wailey, a former Confederate soldier and inventor who lived in New Orleans. As Wailey's representatives, they were successful in their applications and were each granted patents for the inventions in 1866 (#2535) and 1867 (#311).[36] While Bulloch and Robertson were making their way in the cotton business, the U.S. government prepared to have another go at Fraser, Trenholm and Co. via Charles K. Prioleau.

While the American lawyers and British solicitors prepared their case against Prioleau, Lord Stanley searched for a way to accommodate the U.S. while preserving Her Majesty's international dignity. On 9 March 1867, he wrote to his minister in the U.S., Sir Frederick Bruce, that the real question was "the liability of the British Government to make good the losses occasioned to American commerce by the operations of Confederate ships-of-war" that were owned and operated by British citizens and admitted to British ports.[37]

After carrying out a campaign of intimidation and barely legal threats from mid–1865 until the Fraser, Tuenholm and Co. case in mid–1867 (and beyond), the U.S. government had only collected $144,157.15 in Confederate assets. Much of this amount went to pay commissions to the special agents hired by Dudley and Morse. As Bulloch accurately observed, Seward's plan of "getting possession of Confederate property through such means did not result in much pecuniary profit."[38] More rational Union advocates such as Counsel Freeman Morse recognized that Seward's harassment campaign against penniless ex–Confederates and their bankrupt, or nearly so, British business partners was counter-productive. He understood that the undiplomatic attempt to bully Britain was a failure as well. Almost a year had passed since Lord Stanley had refused arbitration.

Morse decided to offer some honey to the angry Confederate bee's nest in Liverpool. He began negotiations with Charles Prioleau that would allow him full access to all its accounts and allow him to determine the true financial status of Confederate operations in Europe. Morse and Prioleau concluded an agreement that Fraser, Trenholm and Co. would a) submit all financial documents for inspection, b) list all property in their possession that belonged to the Confederate government, and c) sell all such property "to the best advantage" for the U.S. government. The proceeds of such sales would be first applied against the Confederate debts owed to the company, up to a limit of $150,000 (which Prioleau grumbled was too low). The rest would go to the U.S. Treasury. Morse had letters that purportedly proved the support of Secretary of State Seward and the U.S. Treasury for his proposals. The pragmatic Prioleau, thinking it the best way forward, discussed the plan with Bulloch and the other former Confederate officials and agents in Britain before giving his approval.[39]

Bulloch, upon seeing of the details of Morse's offer to Prioleau, believed it to be "a fair, open, and perfectly trustworthy settlement of affairs." Yet, before any of Morse's carefully negotiated plans could be put into operation, Seward threw the proverbial baby out with the bathwater in a fit of pique. Hearing from a variety of other consuls and agents from across Europe (Bigelow in Paris, for example) that there was some sort of backroom deal between Morse and Prioleau, the secretary ordered Adams to totally "disavow and reject" the settlement offer. What dumbfounded Bulloch about the whole bumbling affair was that Morse had met with him personally in London. Morse told Bulloch that his only interest was to rapidly wrap up an "equitable arrangement that would secure the rights of his [U.S.] government without detriment to just private claims [e.g., Prioleau's], and without the irritation and expense ... caused by litigation." Bulloch believed that Morse was "both sincere and disinterested in his efforts."[40]

Internecine jealousy among the U.S. government's representatives in Europe had successfully fed disinformation to the Confederate-hating Seward. Instead of an equitable settlement, the result would be prolonged diplomatic and legal conflict between the U.S. and Britain. Predictably, the legal lions of the U.S. government were in court again on 29 May 1867 filing suit against the partners of Fraser, Trenholm and Company. Seward would persist in his pursuit of vengeance.

Bulloch's comments on this era of Confederate-baiting and hunting by U.S. lawyers, agents, and detectives were both instructive and mysterious. "No United States official ever gave me the least personal trouble or annoyance after the war, except for my voluntary offer to assist in bringing the 'Morse arrangement' to an equitable settlement, I should have never come in contact with any one of them at any time." This is a remarkable statement with innumerable questions attached. James Dunwoody Bulloch was well publicized by Union, Confederate, and European press during and after the war as being *the* Confederate agent responsible for building the Confederate Navy's most effective warships. How could he escape any form of investigation or prosecution by the U.S. government? Was Bulloch receiving official or unofficial legal advice from his British business partners or Judah P. Benjamin about how to avoid legal "interest"? Did influential friends in the U.S. or Britain provide protection?[41]

Bulloch took full advantages of F.S. Hull's legal advice throughout the war and Hull could assist him as a private citizen as well. There were no residual issues surrounding the

Laird rams, so the U.S. government had no case there. He would have to rely on his own fastidious bookkeeping, professional reputation, and influential contacts to maintain separation from the legal hurricane circling Fraser, Trenholm and Company. Although not documented, it is likely that Judah P. Benjamin and Bulloch also exchanged information and advice.

Bulloch continued to enjoy a close relationship with Fraser, Trenholm and Co. through 1868, which would have included financial and legal support. When Bulloch and his partner Robertson moved out of the Fraser, Trenholm and Co. offices to set up their new business at 13 Rumford Street, they were only a one-minute stroll removed from 10 Rumford Place. The early joint advertisements strongly suggest coordinated business efforts. For example, Bulloch had authority to draw funds from the post-war "estate" of Fraser, Trenholm and Company that was set up to pay dividends to Confederate officers.

The recipients of these estate distributions included Robert Randolph Carter, who had assisted Bulloch during the war and sailed to Havana as first lieutenant on the CSS *Stonewall*. Carter was one of the many Confederates who lived in Brazil after the war, but he returned to Virginia in 1866 to manage his Shirley Plantation inheritance. Carter received at least five small installments that totaled just over £15, plus another £11 that had remained in his account at the Bank of Liverpool. Bulloch received and forwarded all these payments every six months through December 1868, using Fraser, Trenholm's embossed stationary.[42]

One other business enterprise occupied Bulloch and Robertson in 1867 that promised financial gain and political support. The partners were supporting the Virginia legislature's effort to induce British subjects to immigrate to Virginia! The Virginia Immigration Society placed the following advertisement in London, Liverpool, Manchester, and Birmingham newspapers:

Emigration to the United States

The Virginia Immigration Society has established agencies in Europe with a view of furnishing reliable information to intending emigrants. No part of America now offers such inducements to settlers as this State, whether capitalists, agriculturists, mechanics or labourers. This Society does not pay passages, but will make arrangements with steamship owners, advantageous to Emigrants. The agents in the United Kingdom are — Messrs. Bullock [sic] and Robertson, Rumford Court, Liverpool; Messrs. Cary and Macfarland, 150, Leadenhall Street, London. A.F. Robertson, Comr.[43]

This was a short-lived venture, for the announcement only ran through the third week of July 1867.

While Bulloch and Robertson, along with the rest of the expatriate Confederates in Liverpool, tried to get on with their new lives, the U.S. government continued to find ways to antagonize Britain about the *Alabama* Claims. In February 1867, Seward offered to drop all related claims against the British government — if Britain would sell the Bahamas islands to America. Manifest Destiny had returned. It was back to business as usual for America, and the business of America, so Seward believed, was to expand. The British government, very un-amused, refused this offer.[44]

Seward, less than amused himself, fretted about ways to get John Bull's attention. The answer appeared in the form of Russian diplomat Eduard de Stoeckel. Shortly before the American Civil War began, Russia offered to sell the Alaska territory to America, believing that Britain, which had fought against Russia in the Crimean War (1853–1856), might seize Alaska for itself. After the Civil War, Czar Alexander II and Russia still needed the money and sold Alaska to the United States on 30 March 1867. Initially known as "Seward's Folly" for its $7.2 million price tag, Seward saw Alaska as leverage in his dream of annexing the neighboring Crown colony of British Columbia.[45]

Seward telegraphed his scheme to swap British Columbia for the *Alabama* Claims to U.S. Minister Adams. Charles Adams shook his head at Seward's delusions and told him frankly that he believed the British would refuse it. And they did. One moment Secretary Seward was threatening Britain, the next he was trying buy them off![46]

So went the remainder of 1867 with Seward vainly attempting to get Britain to the negotiating table, always using the *Alabama* Claims as the key bargaining chip. Adams was tired of it all and submitted his resignation. He had been in London for seven years and believed the *Alabama* Claims were a dream that would never be realized.[47]

Bulloch would have been overjoyed at the thought of an arch-nemesis leaving Britain. Unfortunately, his main antagonist remained in Liverpool. Thomas Dudley was still collating information about Confederate activities in Britain and the rest of Europe.

The naturalization issue that Seward tried to attach to the *Alabama* Claims ended up muddying the diplomatic waters. Seward wanted to neatly package all of the U.S./British diplomatic complaints. However, the British Foreign Office wanted to deal with each issue separately, hoping to wear down Seward's pursuit of the *Alabama* Claims. Lord Stanley continued to rebuff Seward's persistent overtures via Sir Edward Thornton, Jr., the new British envoy to Washington, right up until Adams' last day as U.S. minister on 1 April 1868.[48]

As the new U.S. minister to Great Britain, Reverdy Johnson, settled into his offices in London during the spring of 1868, the British Foreign Office monitored more threatening events. The situation in Europe was very fluid after the short Austro-Prussian War. Bismarck constantly angled to weaken the countries adjoining the German Confederation by coercing them into giving up any territory that included German-speaking peoples (or land that interested the Prussians). Astute British military strategists knew that the Prussians wanted to isolate and then overwhelm Louis-Napoléon and France. Bismarck only needed a reasonable pretence to attack France.[49]

In May 1868 the U.S. was in the countdown for the first presidential election since the end of the American Civil War. The Republicans went for a sure winner: "Unconditional Surrender" Ulysses S. Grant. Meanwhile, the Democrats hopefully nominated the aptly named Horatio Seymour. It was universally agreed, even among the Democrats, that Seymour had no chance of defeating the unequalled hero of the American Civil War. While America descended into a political carnival for the forthcoming elections, the ultimate symbol of the "lost cause" headed to Liverpool, the former president of the Confederate States, his ex-excellency Jefferson Davis.

Davis and his family sailed from Quebec on 25 July 1868 aboard the *Austrian* and landed in Liverpool ten days later. The *Anglo-American Times* remarked that Bulloch's associates Charles K. Prioleau and James Spence greeted Davis, who after acknowledging the cheers of a small crowd, disappeared into a carriage that took the Davis family to the Adelphi Hotel.[50] James and Harriott Bulloch would have welcomed the Davis's as well, either at the hotel, or later on at the Norman Walker residence.[51]

In Spain, Admiral Juan Bautiste Topete and his forces mutinied against the Spanish

Crown, Isabella II, who fled into France under the protection of Louis-Napoléon. While the revolutionaries in Spain argued over whether or not Spain should become a republic, Bismarck plotted. In Britain, the government and the Royal Navy realized what it would mean if Spain chose a German member of the Hohenzollern royal family as its king. Louis-Napoléon would know that France was now surrounded by Germans and would declare war on Bismarck and his Confederation, just as Bismarck hoped. Lord Stanley and Queen Victoria tried to keep a lid on the explosive situation by trying to calm Louis-Napoléon and assuaging Wilhelm I and Bismarck. The lid on the pot was dancing as Europe simmered over the Spanish succession issue, as America blithely neared its presidential elections.

Bulloch would have seen the irony of this situation. If Bismarck's German Confederation went to war with Louis-Napoléon's France, all Europe could be drawn into the conflict. The German Confederation had naval aspirations and one of its most powerful ships was a Bulloch creation. The sister ship to the CSS *Stonewall* was now known as the *Prinz Adalbert*. Britain would soon need the support of its recalcitrant cousins across the Atlantic and perhaps it was time to start talking again, no matter how distasteful.

Lord Stanley had refused Seward's previous attempt to address the *Alabama* Claims as part of a "catch-all" conference. Since that time, U.S. Minister Reverdy Johnson agreed with the British and began to address each issue separately. On October 9th, Lord Stanley finally signed a protocol settling the naturalization issue. Next on Johnson's agenda was the Northwest border dispute (San Juan Island) and then "the claims question."[52]

Lord Stanley liked Johnson's manner, especially when compared to the prickly nature of the former U.S. minister. On October 17th, he signed off on Johnson's proposal to deal with the Northwest border problems.[53] This was extraordinary progress compared with the glacial pace of diplomacy between Lord Russell and Mr. Adams.

Johnson, sensing that the diplomatic wind was at his back, met with Lord Stanley on October 20th and got straight to the point. Since the naturalization and boundary disputes between the U.S. and Great Britain seemed to be a thing of the past, might they not now address the long-endured pea under the queen's mattress, the *Alabama* Claims? Johnson proposed forming a commission with equal numbers of British and American citizens who would sit, listen, and decide each claim, If they reached an impasse, they would "call in an umpire, and whose decision, with such assistance shall be final."[54]

Lord Stanley liked the concept, but pointed out the political reality. British citizens could not be expected to "pronounce judgment on the authorities of his own government." Stanley counter-proposed that arbitrators should be "the sovereign or president of a friendly state" such as "the President of the Swiss Republic and the King of Prussia." The last suggestion was extraordinary in light of the situation in the German Confederation. Lord Stanley may have suggested inviting King Wilhelm I to the diplomatic table with the hope that he would learn the ways of peaceful negotiation. The way was now clear to address the *Alabama* claims "by mutual consent, either tacit or express."[55]

During all this time, Bulloch had been going about his business as a cotton importer, trader, and merchant. He had seen the U.S. government's relentless legal attacks against Fraser, Trenholm and Co. and former Confederate agents such as Gen. McRae and Norman Walker. But he had escaped attention — so far. The departure of U.S. Minister Adams must have given Bulloch hope that he might outlast Seward's consuming anger.

The news that U.S. Minister Reverdy Johnson was getting along famously with Lord Stanley meant that an *Alabama* Claims commission might not be far behind. The *Times* of London covered a banquet in honor of Johnson on the evening of October 22nd, noting, "The ministers on both sides seemed anxious to settle the pending questions. Mr. Seward because he held office when the difficulties arose and may not desire to leave them to a successor to treat in a manner which he might reject, and Lord Stanley because he has so far been successful in his policy."[56] Perhaps the most extraordinary aspect of the *Times* correspondent's commentary on the apparent rapprochement was the location of the event: Liverpool. Even the elder Laird shook Johnson's hand and exchanged greetings. The diplomatic cuddling between the two countries was obvious and alarming to the men responsible for crippling the Union merchant marine carrying trade. Their honor and economic survival were at stake, beginning with that of James Dunwoody Bulloch.[57]

By late October 1868, the diplomatic discussions between Lord Stanley and U.S. Minister Johnson seemed to have borne fruit. On November 3rd, Johnson and Lord Stanley completed a draft set of articles to govern an *Alabama* Claims convention. Her Majesty's Attorney General Sir John Burgess Karslake also attended and helped shape the document. Johnson had no legal expert on international law at his side, much less one experienced in the British legal system. For the moment, he was basking in his apparent success. Lord Stanley and the wily Sir Karslake were holding their breath to see if Washington would agree to the articles that Stanley and Johnson signed on the 10th of November.[58]

Bulloch was fully aware of these negotiations and through his social connections probably had direct contact with Lord Stanley or Earl Derby himself. During Liverpool's Grand Southern Bazaar in October 1864, Lord and Lady Wharncliffe had attended as "guests of the Earl of Derby." As long as the Derby family held the reins of political power in Britain, Bulloch seemed safe from retribution by the U.S. government. First, he had done nothing "wrong." He had scrupulously followed British law as it existed and was interpreted at the time, and had been vindicated in every judicial proceeding. Plus, he had earned a well-deserved reputation for honesty from his peers and had even won the grudging admiration of his Union antagonists. He had little to fear, practically, from any British politician. Too many of them had been politically and financially involved with the advancement of Bulloch's cause. Bulloch knew all the secrets and he was a man who knew how to keep his own counsel. But there was a problem, actually two problems, and they both occurred within a week of each other following the election of U.S. Grant as American president in November 1868.

First, on 27 November 1868, Lord Stanley received a telegram from Sir Edward Thornton in Washington. The Stanley-Johnson articles of convention created an uproar in the U.S. Senate and stood absolutely no chance of being passed in their present form. The cabinet of outgoing President Johnson wanted the *Alabama* Claims to be settled on their watch. After all, their administration had fought and won the American Civil War. They wanted Sir Edward to return to Britain immediately and explain in person the problems the U.S. government had with the proposed articles for the claims convention. Lord Stanley, taken aback at the stern rebuff, told Sir Edward to stay put. He wanted to see all the points that the U.S. government objected to in the proposed articles.[59] Secretary Seward, and the angry whalers of Massachusetts, as represented by Senator Charles Sumner, were still on the warpath for compensation.

Bulloch's second problem came on December 3rd when the Tory government fell from power. There was no more protection from the Derby family or any of their political cronies.[60] William Gladstone and the Liberal Party were in power now, and they were reformers. Bulloch now faced multiple threats. He had no particular access to power within the new British government, "Unconditional Surrender" Grant now led the American government, and Sen. Charles Sumner was on the bully pulpit baying for British blood, or better yet, gold.

Despite the blanket "Christmas Amnesty" that President Andrew Johnson granted to all Confederates on Christmas Day 1868, Bulloch decided that his only sure route to escape U.S. government persecution was to become a British citizen. He consulted with the sagacious solicitors and barristers in Britain and decided to place himself fully under the protection of the British legal system.

While Bulloch arranged his papers and found sponsors for his application for naturalization, Lord Stanley dealt with the diplomatic skirmish over the *Alabama* Claims articles of convention. On December 8th, his last full day in office as the foreign secretary, he telegrammed Sir Edward Thornton in Washington expressing his dismay that Reverdy Johnson had apparently negotiated without proper authority.

Sir Edward read Lord Stanley's extensive reply and called on Seward a few days later. A careful grilling of Secretary of State Seward revealed that Minister Johnson had not acted according to his instructions. Seward excused his duplicitous dealing by blaming miscommunication with Johnson. The net result was that the articles had no hope of passing the U.S. Senate without extensive changes. Still, Seward felt that they had come too far, after so long, to fail at the last moment. Furthermore, he intimated to Sir Edward that he'd still like to see the convention articles approved before the Johnson administration passed into history on 3 March 1869. On that day, U.S. Grant was to be sworn in and any diplomatic successes would be attributed to the new administration.[61] Seward and Lord Stanley agreed to set in motion new language, and this time Reverdy Johnson would be operating under tighter control.

On Christmas Eve 1868, Johnson sent new convention articles to Lord Clarendon, who was now the British foreign secretary. Clarendon was the very person that Washington did not want to be dealing with on the *Alabama* Claims. Not only was Clarendon highly experienced in foreign affairs, he was an expert on maritime law. Clarendon dealt with Russia during the Crimean War and the important post-war convention that produced the Declaration of the Maritime Powers at Paris in 1856.[62]

Better known as the Treaty of Paris, the declaration abolished privateering, defined the rights to blockade, and put strict limits on the right to capture property in enemy ships. This was the very same treaty that the United Stated had refused to sign in 1856 that caused so many problems for the Union at the outset of the Civil War. When Lincoln announced the blockade of the South in 1861, it was Clarendon's Treaty of Paris that clarified the status of the Confederacy as a legal belligerent. Seward belatedly recognized this diplomatic *faux pas* and asked to sign the treaty in 1861, but Britain refused permission. U.S. Minister Johnson and Secretary Seward were now dealing not only with a professional, but the literal author of all their worrisome claims.

Lord Clarendon replied to Johnson's proposed convention draft saying that Secretary Seward should telegraph his permission for Johnson to sign it, if he agreed.[63] After that, "it might be laid before the [U.S.] Senate by the middle of January, and pronounced upon by that body before the rising of Congress on the 4th of March."[64]

As governments shut down in London and Washington, D.C., for the December holidays, the Bullochs celebrated Boxing Day in Liverpool. Children crawled and ran about. Martha Louise, Bulloch's youngest daughter, was only a toddler, and Stuart Elliott, not much older. It was controlled chaos, even with a nanny about. With James, Jr., Jessie, and Henry added into the mix, it's easy to see the Bulloch household was a merry place, for Harriott was a vivacious hostess. In the quieter moments of that Christmas season, though, Harriott may have noticed a certain pensiveness in the face of her husband. Soon he would make a change that would be memorialized on his tombstone, forever severing his links with the United States as a citizen. He and his household would become British citizens. The year 1869 would be another one of change.

The newspapers on New Year's Day 1869 reported a strong market for cotton in Britain, which boded well for the partnership of Bulloch and Robertson. The *Commercial Daily List*, a British business journal, noted that 25,000 bales of cotton had been shipped from New York to Britain since Christmas Day.[65] News of President Johnson's unlimited amnesty to all former Confederates had crossed the Atlantic as well, but Bulloch had already made up his mind. On 14 January 1869, Bulloch assembled his naturalization papers and his sponsors at the offices of Fred Hill, a commissioner authorized to administer oaths in chancery in England.

Hill took depositions and signatures certifying the merit and veracity of James Dunwoody Bulloch's desire to become a British citizen. His sponsors were John Richard Armstrong, Eugene Henry Perrin, James Spence, and John Alexander Sellar. These men were all prominent citizens from Liverpool or Birkenhead. Armstrong was a partner in Fraser, Trenholm and Co. after George Trenholm retired in January 1866. Perrin was a broker involved in both cotton and shipping. Spence had been a propagandist and agent *provocateur* for Judah P. Benjamin and the Confederacy.[66] Sellar was a "merchant and broker" entrepreneur who purchased American-flagged ships during the war and sailed them under British colors.[67]

As for Bulloch's own statement as to his reasons for being in Britain and wanting to remain, he coyly stated in his memorial to the secretary of the Home Office that he had come to Liverpool to work as a merchant. He had lived in Britain for the last six years, except for "short temporary absences" and he was a householder with an American-born wife and five children. Two of the children, Bulloch took pains to point out, had been born in Britain and were British citizens from birth. Bulloch then simply stated that he had become fond of Britain and wished to carry on in his business as a merchant due to his "business connections here." Simply put, he had put down roots and had "become attached."[68]

Bulloch's request for citizenship was surely one of the most rapidly processed naturalization requests in the history of the British Home Office, requiring only a few days between application and approval. The other significant event that occurred on 14 January 1869 was the signing of the articles of convention to settle the *Alabama* Claims.[69] The timing of this gathering of sponsors in Liverpool to vouch for his naturalization papers was no coincidence. It was a good time for Bulloch to become a British citizen.

President Johnson's unlimited amnesty for all ex-Confederates had not been enough to tempt Bulloch to return to the United States. The amnesty would not shield him from backlash over the Johnson-Clarendon articles, as they were now called, or spiteful attempts to hold him personally liable for the depredations of his raiders and Confederate financial accounts. His best chance for a stable business, social, and family life was in Liverpool. His wife and children were with him, his parents were long deceased, Harriott's mother had died, and only her absentee and remarried father, General Osborne Cross, still lived. Although the Bullochs remained close to their extended family, particularly the Roosevelts, who could and would visit them in Liverpool, their closest family members were Harriott's sister Annette who was in Liverpool and his brother Irvine. Irvine also decided to start a new life in Liverpool.

On 21 January 1869, the British Home Office granted James Dunwoody Bulloch's request for British citizenship. Bulloch would now be sailing under different colors, his third flag in eight years.

13

Once More

Safe in the protective bosom of the British Empire, with no form of extradition treaty between the United States of America and Great Britain, James Dunwoody Bulloch and his family could breathe easily in 1869 for the first time in eight long years. The American government could threaten and cajole the British government all they wanted, but his adopted country would not give up a subject of Her Britannic Majesty to a foreign power. It was a most interesting time and place in the Empire's history for Bulloch to become a British subject.

Bulloch lived in one of the most important cities of the British Empire, Liverpool. With the transatlantic telegraph cable in reliable working order and the appearance of high-performance transoceanic steamers, America was closer than ever to Britain. Near instantaneous telegraphic connection and sea-crossings of fewer than two weeks were commonplace. Personal and business communication had never been better. The import and export merchants of Liverpool were well positioned to transmit goods to and from the rest of the empire. American businesses needed British markets, but the niggling problem of the *Alabama* Claims needed to be resolved, particularly for the still-angry New England whalers and the shipping interests of New York and San Francisco.

As Bulloch was awaiting approval of his naturalization, Sir Edward Thornton, the senior British diplomat in Washington, presented a copy of the signed Johnson-Clarendon articles to President Johnson. The President quickly forwarded the articles to the U.S. Senate. In a telegram to the Earl of Clarendon in London, Sir Edward complained, "No action has yet been taken upon them by that body."[1]

A week later, Sir Edward gave Clarendon his first intelligence of the U.S. Senate and public reaction to the Johnson-Clarendon articles: the news wasn't good. Sen. Corbett of Oregon had received a blistering protest petition from over a dozen officials, agents, and surveyors, representing the Oregon and Washington Territories. They were adamant that the British border claims were in direct contradiction to the Treaty of 1846.[2] They had no intention of relinquishing San Juan Island and the Haro Archipelago. Ironically, this was the same Oregon Territory where Bulloch and the ill-fated USS *Shark* were operating in September 1846.

The New Englanders waded in next with an even harsher, though shorter, petition. On 29 January 1869, Sen. Charles Sumner of Massachusetts, the great anti-slavery orator, delivered a petition from New England businessman George Upton, who had suffered from the depredations of the Confederate commerce raiders. Its central statement was so inflam-

Liverpool docks in the late nineteenth century (authors' collection).

matory that Sir Edward telegraphed that portion before he had even received a full copy: "the so called treaty proposes to put upon the same footing claims by British subjects ... upon the British Government for piracies committed by British-built, British manned, and British-armed vessels; by vessels and armaments which left British ports under the protection of a British flag, and burned American ships, and your memorialist's among the number, upon the high seas, ... and without any action being taken on the part of the British government, when these atrocities were laid before it, to prevent the same."

Mr. Upton used the word "British" eight times in one short paragraph. There was no doubt about the rage towards Her Majesty's Empire. When the Earl of Clarendon received this message on 15 February 1869, he knew the Johnson-Clarendon agreement was in serious trouble. By the end of February, Senator Sumner's Committee on Foreign Relations unanimously (with the exception of one absent member) forwarded its recommendation to reject the Johnson-Clarendon agreement to the full Senate.[3]

With this pronouncement, and the forthcoming change of administration during the first week of March 1869, Secretary Seward, Minister Johnson, Sir Edward, and Clarendon went into damage control mode. But time ran out on Secretary Seward's dream of solving the *Alabama* Claims on 4 March 1869. General U.S. Grant was now President Grant and Commander-in-Chief of the United States of America. Seward was out and any agreement with Britain would have no chance of approval. Bulloch, now a British subject, had outlasted yet another foe.

On 13 April 1869, Charles Sumner regaled the Senate with a litany of British wrongs against the U.S. that had prolonged the American Civil War by at least two years. He then conjured up a figure of *two billion dollars* that should be included in any *Alabama* Claims settlement. That same day, fifty-four of fifty-five U.S. senators voted against the ratification of the Johnson-Clarendon articles of convention. It was dead. "Preposterous," "calculated to excite derision," "an insult," and "a humiliation" were among the terms Charles Francis Adams' son used to describe Sumner's position.[4] To replace Seward, President Grant soon appointed a new secretary of state, Hamilton Fish. The Secretary was a friend of Sen. Charles Sumner, but he was his own man.

While U.S. Minister Reverdy Johnson remained at his post in London throughout the spring of 1869, attempting to salvage the pieces of the claims agreement, the Bulloch family prepared for visitors. The Theodore Roosevelt family and their servants were headed to Europe and they were coming to stay in Liverpool! It would be a hectic time for the Bullochs. They were preparing to move to a newly built and more spacious home in the Liverpool suburb of Waterloo, but not before the Roosevelts arrived.[5]

On 12 May 1869, the Roosevelts departed New York City aboard the steamship *Scotia*, bound for Liverpool.[6] When the Roosevelt party arrived in Liverpool on May 21st, Mittie Bulloch Roosevelt wrote that they were delayed by the low tide at the Mersey River. After enduring a separation of eight years, Brother Jimmie and Irvine could wait no longer, so they caught a tender and boarded the *Scotia* late that evening at the anchorage. Theodore, Jr., and the rest of the children were on "tip toe of fidgety expectation" to see their Uncle Jimmie and were "wild with delight" when he and the children finally rushed in. The Bullochs quickly collected the entire Roosevelt entourage from the vessel, and after a twenty-minute tugboat ride, they finally arrived in Liverpool and settled into their rooms at the Adelphi Hotel.[7]

After a good night's rest, Bulloch and Harriott played host to the Roosevelts. Mittie's description of the house that had seen the Bullochs through the Civil War was a remarkable picture of an upper middle-class household at the height of Victorian Era: "Hattie and the children except Jimmie met us at the door, the same kind of little low house the front shaped in a half circle, brick, no outside blinds on any house but inside a little snuggery ... they are just on the eve of moving to a large house just built and bought by Brother Jimmie." Later when James and Harriott took the Roosevelts to visit the future Bulloch abode, Mittie wrote admiringly about

> the new house which is all complete and ready to move in next week. It is so very comfortable, 3 story brick, rough stone front, bay windows, handsome plate glass, on a perfectly flat piece of ground, having larger back yard than front, divided by the house on one side and a beautiful rockery (artificial of course) all planted, wall flowers on top ferns and everything springing up, in a few years the whole brick wall which surrounds the place will be covered with ivy, which is now planted. Following the brick wall all around a bed planted with all sorts of lovely flowers in the middle the lawn only just sodded. This whole place is about one and a half larger than that of Sisters house in Philadelphia was; the house had drawing room, Library, and large Dining room, besides Kitchen, Pantry, and on first floor upstairs nice closet room, bath rooms, etc. Brother Jimmie is going to call it Clifton.

Though he nostalgically named the new home after his boyhood roots in Georgia, Bulloch clearly was prospering in England. His financial well being stemmed from his business, social and family contacts in Liverpool and New York, and the remnants of any inheritance he may have received from his late uncle Robert Hutchison. He also may have had a stipend associated with the care of his orphaned young cousin Nannie Caskie Hutchison who came to live with the Bulloch's in Liverpool around 1869.[8]

From May 21st until May 31st, the Roosevelt family visited with James and Harriott Bulloch along with Irvine Bulloch and his fiancée Ella. The Bulloch boys and girls played games with the Roosevelt children, including Theodore Roosevelt, then known as "Teedie," and made the most of the late spring weather in Liverpool. The American cousins watched the Bulloch boys play cricket one evening, while on another occasion Mittie and Harriott Bulloch went shopping together in Liverpool's High Street area. Bulloch wrote to an old friend from his days in the U.S. Navy, Admiral Hornby of the Royal Navy, to request cards of admission to "Knowsley," the great house and estate of the Derby family. The admiral was the cousin and brother-in-law of Edward Smith-Stanley, the 13th Earl of Derby. That the wealthy family of the former British prime minister and foreign secretary were on social terms with Bulloch speaks volumes about his hearty welcome into British society.[9]

The success of Bulloch's efforts on behalf of the Roosevelts may have exceeded his own expectations, for Theodore Roosevelt, Sr., and his valet (Noel Paovitch) attended Derby Day with Irvine's future father-in-law, Henry B. Sears. Now known as "Royal Ascot," Derby Day was then, as it is now, one of the premier social events of the year. While much has been written about the rise of Theodore Roosevelt, to become president of the United States, his father, Theodore Roosevelt, Sr., also entertained thoughts of running for president in 1860. His aspirations were dashed by a bout of tuberculosis. Theodore's cultivation of social contacts like the Derbys was a natural outgrowth of his political and business instincts. Roosevelt Sr.'s success as a New York businessman, with contacts in the Far East and interests in England with the Lenox Plate Glass Company, also made him attractive to British politicians, businessmen, and socialites. They were also helpful to Bulloch's business prospects, a natural outgrowth of the mutual admiration between Bulloch and Theodore Roosevelt, Sr. While Theodore and Mr. Sears were off at Ascot, back in Liverpool Irvine's wife entertained the family with a fine mezzo soprano rendition of "The Wild Birds" and Brother Jimmie proved to be particularly adept at dancing.[10]

During the Roosevelt family reunion with the Bullochs, the new U.S. minister to Britain, John Lothrop Motley, worked to improve British and American relations. Motley was a welcome breath of fresh air in Britain after the acidic Adams and bumbling Johnson. Motley was a respected historian, spoke German, and held William II as one of his great heroes. His *History of The United Netherlands*, a four-volume work completed in 1867, was already hailed as a masterpiece; President Grant had apparently made a wise choice. Motley visited the Earl of Clarendon personally, though unofficially, on May 31st, the day before the Roosevelt family departed Liverpool.[11] With a polite handshake, the new era of British-American relations began. It would not be easy, but Clarendon liked Motley for he said of him, "His tone was friendly and we met as old acquaintances."[12]

While the new U.S. minister settled into his London offices, the Roosevelts were off on a grand tour of Britain and Western Europe. They first visited the Duke of Devonshire's estate at Chatsworth and then went to Scotland with an obligatory visit to Edinburgh.[13] Young Theodore Roosevelt kept a copious diary and remarked on the old castles and antiquities he saw, all the while trying to ward off the effects of asthma.[14]

The Bulloch family settled into their new home, named "Clifton," while the Roosevelts visited in the French Alps. In the newspapers, the affairs of Austria, France, Prussia, and

Spain occupied readers and the British government. Bismarck's speeches about unifying all Germans were playing well to the Austro-German minority in Bohemia. Vienna, however, decided that alignment with Louis-Napoléon of France was the way forward. British Royal Navy admirals nervously eyed Prussia's construction of a massive canal that would unite the North Sea with the Baltic to provide better access to the open ocean.[15]

In Spain, the bitter question of the succession to Queen Isabella II still affected the central government. The weak Spanish government discussed the sale of Cuba to Washington as they fought a growing insurrection there. In Mystic, Connecticut, perhaps as a message to the British, the U.S. seized thirty gunboats at the behest of the Peruvian government. The builders claimed they were for Spain, but the Peruvian minister said they were intended for Peruvian rebels who had hired ex–Confederate mercenaries.[16]

Admiral Geoffrey Hornby of the Royal Navy was Bulloch's long-time friend and the cousin of the Earl of Derby (authors' collection).

Throughout the rest of the waning summer of 1869 and into the first days of fall, Bulloch continued his cotton and commodity brokerage business, while Harriott managed necessary domestic affairs that transformed the new house into a home. The Roosevelts moved from Austria to Germany via the Alps, doing the asthmatic lungs of young Theodore Roosevelt no good. He suffered from relentless attacks. In the British port of Southampton, Jefferson Davis embarked for America having secured no permanent employment, but he was still feted by British society as a tragic and heroic figure.[17]

U.S. Minister John Motley came to the Earl of Clarendon's office on October 15th to relay a lengthy dispatch from Secretary of State Fish dated 25 September 1869. For security purposes, Secretary Fish wanted Motley to read the entire document to the Earl of Clarendon, which he did in one long sitting. President Grant was attempting to reopen the issue of the *Alabama* Claims. The clear stamp of his authority was in the second paragraph: "The President is inclined to believe that sufficient time may have now elapsed to ... place in your hands, for appropriate use, a dispassionate exposition of the just causes of complaint of the Government of the United States against Great Britain." Secretary of State Fish may have written the words, but this was clearly the voice of the plain-spoken Grant. Clarendon asked for a copy of Fish's exposition after Motley's departure. He simply couldn't remember all the points of contention.[18]

Before Clarendon had a chance to respond, Motley sent another message on 23 October 1869 that acknowledged inconsistencies in U.S. policies on belligerence and commerce raiding. However, the position presented in the diplomatic complaint of September 25th was *the* position of the U.S. government. The U.S. intended to prove that Britain had exceeded its rights under the Treaty of Paris. As the British author of the Treaty of Paris, Clarendon arched an eyebrow at Motley's presumptive message.[19] Clarendon let Motley stew for a while before replying.

Four days later, on October 27th, young Theodore Roosevelt celebrated his 12th birthday in the German Confederation, or plain "Germany" as he referred to it in his diary. If the Prussians seemed quiet in Europe, it was only because Bismarck's hand was at play on the periphery of the Continent. Crown Prince of Prussia Louis of Hesse was on his way to the ceremonial opening of the Suez Canal in November. He first paid a state visit to the Ottoman sultan and grand vizier of Turkey aboard the sultan's yacht. The item that caught the attention of the Royal Navy was the Prince's escort, the Prussian Navy corvette *Hertha*. The *Kaiserliche Marine* was demonstrating its capability to operate far from the cold and sheltered waters of the Baltic Sea.[20]

On November 5th, Clarendon finally acknowledged Minister Motley's request to address the U.S. complaints. He apologized for the delay and promised to address Secretary Fish's concerns shortly.[21] The next day, Clarendon sent the promised response to Sir Edward Thornton in Washington. Clarendon instructed Sir Edward to take it directly to Secretary Fish and read it to him, just as Motley had done with Clarendon. He was adept at diplomatic gamesmanship.[22]

Clarendon agreed that it would be in the best interests of both countries to settle the *Alabama* Claims. Clarendon concluded, "Her Majesty's Government will be ready to cooperate with the Government of the United States for so salutary a result, which would redound to the mutual honour of both countries, and, if accepted by other maritime nations, have an important influence toward maintaining the peace of the world." The sagacious Clarendon could see that the Treaty of Paris was no longer adequate as a standard for international law and martial maritime affairs. But first, they had to sit down at the negotiating table under suitable terms not dictated by the volatile U.S. Senate and the equally sanctimonious "Greater Britain" John Bulls of the British Parliament.[23] With the opening of the Suez Canal on 16 November 1869, the world's maritime powers now had new considerations and worries.[24]

On 22 November 1869, as the Americans and British pondered their diplomatic options, Theodore Roosevelt, Sr., returned to Liverpool. He had to attend to his plate glass importing and manufacturing business and left his family to continue their touring in Italy. He dined with Irvine, "Captain" Bulloch, and Bulloch's partner Robertson, which suggests they may have mixed business with pleasure. Roosevelt delivered family letters to Harriott the following day before heading off on more business affairs and returning to Italy.[25]

Christmas 1869 and New Year's Day 1870 came and went with a reasonable hope for "peace on earth." There was little mention of the *Alabama* Claims.[26] Then, on 12 January 1870, Motley visited the Earl of Clarendon to confess that he had not included the Earl's important 6 November 1869 message in the *Alabama* Claims papers given to the U.S. Senate. According to Clarendon, Motley defended this omission by saying that "he did not consider it official, as the memorandum was not signed or dated, as in my [Clarendon's] other dispatch of the same date." Motley also released some of these sensitive diplomatic exchanges to the U.S. Senate, resulting in automatic release to the press. Clarendon was now obliged to do the same in Britain, "as the British public had a right to expect that important information should be furnished them by their own government, and not be derived from the newspapers of another country." Motley had also insisted that these partisan negotiations would be conducted at Washington. Once again the *Alabama* Claims descended into public farce on both sides of the Atlantic.[27]

During the winter and spring of 1869–1870, the Roosevelts followed the seasonal change in Europe, moving northward though Europe like migrating birds. After a chance meeting with the pope in Rome, they traveled to Paris.[28] While the Roosevelts enjoyed the City of Light, the French government, like the British, kept a wary watch on Bismarck, who had Wilhelm I and the rest of Prussia under his spell. Theodore Roosevelt, Sr., decided it was time for his family to make its way back to America, via Britain and another visit with the Bullochs, leaving their eldest daughter Anna, known as "Bamie" (short for "bambina"), behind in Paris to attend school.

Arriving back in Liverpool around 1 May 1870, it was another joyous reunion and a chance for the telling of tales by the Roosevelt children to the wide-eyed Bulloch children. The impressionable young Theodore Roosevelt was also able to soak up some more "seastories" from his Uncle Jimmie and Uncle Irvine. On May 14th, with many well wishes and a few tears, the Roosevelts departed Liverpool on the Cunard line's first transatlantic screw steamer, the SS *Russia*. Their waves to the Bullochs were obscured by a gentle May shower and Teedie's inevitable seasickness.[29]

The Roosevelts returned to an America that was still steaming over the *Alabama* Claims. In Britain, the Earl of Clarendon marveled over the inability of the U.S. government to hold to a logically consistent line of negotiation. The Americans continued to roll out the same contentious and absurd points, including Britain's "premature" recognition of the Confederacy as a belligerent. Motley had not helped matters either, for he refused to adhere to President Grant's policy position, leading to his recall to the United States. The exasperated Clarendon told Secretary Fish, "Her Majesty's Government believe that for the settlement and disposition of the question at issue it is neither useful nor expedient to continue a controversial correspondence in which there is little hope for one of these governments being able to convince the other." This was a diplomatic way of agreeing to disagree while trying to move on to other matters of substance.[30]

The principal characters in the drama that had set all these contretemps into motion, Bulloch and his former assistant and current business partner Robertson, could watch and read about the whole affair with detached and profitable bemusement. Mittie Roosevelt expressed her personal happiness for the apparent success of brother Bulloch's business affairs in a letter to her daughter "Bamie" on May 18th.[31] In another week, the Roosevelts would all be back in New York, discussing their great adventure across Europe and, of course, how the Bullochs were doing in Liverpool.[32]

The summer of 1870 was fast approaching and the rising temperatures across Europe mirrored the growing heat in both the internal and external politics of France and Prussia. Louis-Napoléon's France was convulsed by daily rumors of a *coup d'état*. Years of imprudent finances, both legal and illegal, coupled with internecine bickering had weakened the Grand Republic. It seemed that the only thing that united the arguing French politicians, people, and Louis-Napoléon was dislike of Prussia. Like Louis-Napoléon, Bismarck believed that a war could solve his country's problems. A common enemy would unite all the quasi-independent German states into a united and much stronger Germany.[33]

Wilhelm I's announcement that he intended to proclaim himself *Kaiser* sent the French into apoplectic fits. Germany intended to raise itself up to an empire and dominate Europe! Louis-Napoléon warned Bismarck that he was prepared to strike if Germany continued its provocations. Bismarck countered by insinuating that the German Confederation was working to form a better alliance with Switzerland when no such alliance existed. The French legislature quickly demanded action.[34] At this critical moment in European affairs, Britain lost its most able hand, the Earl of Clarendon, who literally died at his desk on 27 June 1870.[35]

In July, the lid was rattling over the simmering pot of Franco-Prussian relations. As senior diplomats prepared to depart on their summer holidays, a series of testy exchanges between French Ambassador Count Benedetti and Wilhelm I, who was vacationing in Ems, brought the situation to a boil, with just a little help from Bismarck. Carefully editing the transcript of the Benedetti-Wilhelm I conversation in a way that was sure to offend both the French and Germans, Bismarck released it to the press in the form of an "authentic telegram."[36]

When the "Ems telegram" hit the streets, all Germans were enraged and most shouted for war; in France it was the same. The truth didn't matter; nothing could hold back the anger of the French people; there would be war! On 15 July 1870, the *Corps Législatif* of the French government declared war on Prussia. Europe was at war again and all the Great Powers would have to take sides. Although the British Empire was the world's mightiest, there was little she could do on the Continent other than search for a diplomatic solution and have the Royal Navy monitor the situation. Britain was content to let France meet her own fate, but Britain's failure to support France against Prussia would have long lasting effects.[37]

The mobilization of the French army was more than a news article to James and Harriott Bulloch. They had a relative in a potential war zone, for James' teenage niece Bamie Roosevelt was still attending school in Paris! Captain Bulloch took charge of the situation, arranged for Bamie's move to Liverpool, and kept everyone informed by telegram. Bamie Roosevelt was safely in Liverpool by 15 August 1870 and stayed with Uncle Jimmie and Aunt Hattie, far from the coming hostilities in France.[38] Once again, Bulloch's seemingly never-ending ability to extract himself, and others, from the most difficult circumstances came to the fore.

While Bulloch dealt with the relocation of Bamie, he and Harriott were also keeping an eye on the children of Jefferson Davis. The Davis children entered a school in Waterloo and remained there while their father returned to America to manage his business and legal affairs. The Bulloch and Davis children were regular playmates, as the school the Davis children attended was near the home of the Bullochs. Young Teedie Roosevelt had commented in his journal on 27 May 1869 that while playing with his Bulloch cousins in Liverpool he "met Jeff Davis' son and some sharp words ensued." The image of the children of former President of the Confederacy Jeff Davis playing and quarrelling with future President of the United States Teddy Roosevelt on a Liverpool playground is a remarkable irony. At the same time that James and Harriott Bulloch were getting Bamie Roosevelt situated among the Bulloch brood, Jefferson Davis was on his way back to Liverpool from New York City on a popular steamship, the SS *Russia*.[39]

Davis arrived on 19 August 1870 and remained for several days visiting his children, his sister-in-law Margaret Howell Stoess, the Bullochs, and other friends and associates.

On about August 23rd, Davis took the train to London to be reunited with his wife Varina, who had been a butterfly on the London social scene while he was in America. Although the former Confederate president was a social, political, and economic pariah north of the American Mason-Dixon Line, he was still welcomed in some British quarters. Residual respect and veneration was practically worthless in the South, where the economy was destroyed and many blamed him for losing the war. Davis hoped that Europe would offer him a better chance at success.[40]

Through the end of August, Bulloch sent Theodore Roosevelt, Sr., (and Mittie) updates about their teenage daughter Bamie and how she managed in the bustle of the Bulloch household. Back on the Continent, the Prussians had assembled over 300,000 men, but remained on their side of the border. The French generals, sensing the inevitable, had launched a preemptive attack on August 2nd. Despite their initiative, the French army was pushed back at every turn and by August 18th, the Prussian/German army had stormed across France; Louis-Napoléon was on the verge of defeat.[41]

In America, there was considerable admiration for the German army's performance, flavored with a degree of smug satisfaction, particularly in New England. The U.S. enjoyed the discomfiture of Britain due to the rise of a competing empire in Europe. The continuing refusal of Britain to negotiate over the *Alabama* Claims still rankled. As the Prussian military machine crushed France, Great Britain began to regret its failure to render support. The *Anglo-American Times* said, "England blustered, and threatened war ... she was disregarded [by Bismarck] ... making a Teutonic Empire strong enough to overawe Europe." Her Majesty's British Empire now realized that she needed strong allies.[42] The time was ripe to engage Washington again, but British diplomats would need to be very accommodating. The American public, as far west as Oregon, applauded the Germans who "have realized the nature of their position and are yearning for a change that shall emancipate them forever" from the Great Powers of Europe.[43]

To break the diplomatic logjam, both sides of the Atlantic would have to take dramatic action, which neither nation was quite ready to risk. From the American view, U.S. Minister Motley was too European and regarded "English gentlemen as that most perfect of human beings." Motley did not enjoy the confidence of the people, or the earthy U.S. politicians, including President Grant. He was an effective representative, but not the man to move the *Alabama* Claims forward.[44]

On the British side, the idea of conceding that the upstart Americans could dictate terms to Her Majesty's government and have them judged by representatives of other countries, still stuck in the craws and cravats of all levels of British society.[45] There was a cultural, diplomatic and political impasse on both sides of the Atlantic. It would take an historic event to get the attention of both America and Britain, which was not long in coming.

On 2 September 1870, 104,000 French troops including Louis-Napoléon himself surrendered to the Prussian-German army. Near panic reigned in France and in the halls of power throughout Europe, as the Prussians continued their advance toward Paris. Patriotic Frenchmen, outraged by Louis-Napoléon's cowardly behavior, staged a *coup d'état* on September 4th. The new government proclaimed itself the "Third Republic," redeclared war against the Prussian-German state, and asked for every able-bodied Frenchman to come to the aid of liberty.[46]

Louis-Napoléon's surrender shocked the British government. They did not like the French emperor, but the possibility of having Bismarck in control of most or all of Continental Europe was too much. America's first ally in its War of Independence shouted the French version of "liberty or death!" This attitude appealed to American patriots who began to question German motives that somehow seemed to threaten their own pursuit of life, liberty, and happiness.[47]

In September, during the turmoil on the Continent, Jefferson Davis and Bulloch visited Ireland and Glasgow.[48] After acting as an informal *aide de camp* to Davis, Bulloch returned to his work, while the luckless former Confederate president prepared to leave for the U.S. on October 8th.[49] The travels of Davis had once been front-page news, but the alarming events in Europe relegated him to the back pages.

The German military machine used the latest telegraph and rail technologies to inform, maneuver, and resupply their forces at a speed never before seen in warfare. The French military and government simply could not compete. The British, particularly the Royal Navy, would no longer be able to passively observe new technical developments and then supersede and out-build its adversaries. This new model of warfare required "great powers" to sustain an ongoing arms race. Those nations not prepared to defend, or attack at an instant, were doomed to extinction.[50]

It was now clear to the Roosevelts and Bullochs that the European continent would not be safe for a long time; Bamie needed to come home. Accordingly, on October 5th Theodore Roosevelt, Sr., left New York on the SS *Russia*. He stayed with the Bullochs in Liverpool and attended to business matters for several days before returning to the U.S. on November 9th with Bamie in tow. Interestingly, Bulloch decided to tag along as well. Although his reasons for accompanying his brother-in-law and niece back to the U.S. are not recorded, he probably combined his business with pleasure. He remained in the U.S. for several months, staying in Baltimore (where he could visit James Waddell), and visiting Mittie and his other Bulloch and Roosevelt relatives in New York.[51]

The inseparable nature of business and family would consume Bulloch during this visit. He leveraged the services and advice of his brother-in-law James King Gracie while tending to his cotton brokerage business. He also engaged brother-in-law Roosevelt to assist with a more delicate matter. Captain Donald M. Fairfax, the executive officer of the Portsmouth, NH, Naval Station owed him $400. Due to the war and resultant global economic downturn, Bulloch's business losses of 1870 had placed him in a precarious financial situation. He needed the money and, fortunately, his brother-in-law Theodore Roosevelt, Sr., was willing to help.[52]

Back in Europe, the French and German armies fought throughout November and December 1870. For every victory obtained by the stumbling forces of France (at Coulmiers on November 9th), the Prusso-German troops inflicted another severe defeat (Lemans on December 4th). The Franco-Prussian War began to affect global British and American interests as far away as the South Pacific. Fiji was a critically important coaling station for ships headed from California to either Australia or New Zealand where potentially significant gold deposits had been discovered in the surrounding island chain. Knowing that German commercial interests had been active in nearby Samoa since the 1850s, the settlers on Fiji requested U.S. protection from German imperialism.[53]

By January 18th, the German Confederation united into a full-fledged German Empire under Kaiser Wilhelm. Bismarck and Wilhelm would not be satisfied with just muzzling France; the new German Empire wanted new lands and naval bases. This ambition threatened the British Empire. It was time to settle the *Alabama* Claims and get the America cousins back to the family dinner table to discuss common issues and potential enemies.

British Foreign Secretary Granville and U.S. Secretary Fish energized the whole process to move as rapidly as it had proceeded slowly in the past. Bulloch never believed that Britain would accede to arbitration or external adjudication, but now the impossible was happening, thanks to Bismarck and Kaiser Wilhelm. On January 26th, only eight days after the announcement of a German Empire, the British ambassador to the U.S., Sir Edward Thornton, wrote to Secretary Fish: "I am directed by Lord Granville to propose to the Government of the United States the appointment of a joint high commission, which ... shall hold its sessions in Washington, and shall ... discuss the different questions which have arisen out of the fisheries *as well as all those which affect the relations of the United States towards Her Majesty's possessions in North America* [italics added for emphasis]."[54] It was as close as Granville could bring himself to broaching the near-unmentionable subject of the *Alabama* Claims, but Secretary Fish was sagacious enough to understand Granville's meaning.

Secretary Fish laid the British proposition before President Grant, and in his usual straightforward manner, he got to the bone of contention. If the British truly wanted a long-lasting friendship, they would have to address the *Alabama* Claims. Great Britain's approval of Grant's proposal would yield a guarantee that the U.S. government would "spare no efforts to secure, at the earliest practicable moment, a just and amicable arrangement of all the questions which ... unfortunately, stand in the way of an ... abiding friendship between the two nations."[55]

On February 1st, Sir Edward responded that "I am now authorised by his Lordship [the Earl of Granville] to state that it would give Her Majesty's Government great satisfaction if the claims commonly known by the name of *Alabama* Claims were submitted to the consideration of the same high commission." Sir Edward added that "all other claims, both of British subjects and citizens of the United States, arising out of acts committed during the recent civil war in this country [America], are similarly referred to the same question." Secretary Fish answered on February 3rd that President Grant was delighted with the British proposal and he wanted to move things along quickly.[56]

On 28 January 1871, French President Jules Favre signed a peace treaty with the German Empire. On that same day, Paris fell after twenty-two days of heavy artillery shelling.[57] France had been forced to her knees, and the German Empire now sat astride the heart of Europe. On February 17th, the victorious German army brazenly strutted through the streets of Paris in a victory parade.[58] The office lights of concerned British politicians and diplomats were on all night. The lights at the Bulloch household were on late through the night as well, for they faced a different kind of tragedy.

Nine-year-old Henry Dunwody Bulloch, known to the family as "Dunnie," contracted scarlet fever while his father was in the United States. The virtually untreatable disease was not well understood in the Victorian Era and it had ravaged his already weak body that had been afflicted with rickets. On February 21st, young Henry succumbed to the fever. Bulloch had lost his first wife, Lizzie Caskie, to tuberculosis. Now, one of his sons had died of another widespread malady. At the time of Dunnie's death, Bulloch was in the United States visiting family and tending to business. He finally bid farewell to the Roosevelts and headed back to Liverpool on March 2nd, the day after he belatedly learned the sad news.[59]

The grief in the Bulloch household was palpable, for Harriott managed a lively and loving household. To those who knew Bulloch socially such as his brother-in-law, Theodore Roosevelt, Sr., he was held to be a *bon vivant*. Bulloch's step would have been a bit slower and his demeanor more subdued as he and Harriott endured the grief of losing a precious child.[60]

Two days later, while he grieved for his young son, the threat to Bulloch's professional life took another step forward. Granville dispatched two British members to serve on the high commission. Lord de Grey and Mr. Montague Bernard (an Oxford professor of international law) departed Britain on February 11th, bound for New York, while Sir Stafford Northcote, MP, left seven days later. The British government had gone from "all stop" to "full-speed ahead" on the *Alabama* Claims.[61]

On February 27th, the commissioners produced the "Protocols of Conferences between the High Commissioners on the Part of Great Britain and the High Commissioners on the Part of the United States of America." Grant had given full negotiation rights and privileges to Secretary Fish and the commissioners.[62]

The British commissioners included Sir John MacDonald, a member of the Privy Council of Canada, and the queen's cousin Viscount Goderich, also known as Frederick John Robinson, Marquess of Ripon. The British had assembled an all-star, all-influential team. With the protocol signed and exchanged, both sides agreed to adjourn until the 4th of March.[63]

Throughout March and into April, the joint commissioners worked over the issues. Not surprisingly, the U.S. commissioners, in Articles I-XI, held that the main issue was the *Alabama* Claims, for America had "sustained a great wrong." The remaining articles covered everything from fisheries, navigation along the St. Lawrence, and the Northwest Territory dispute around San Juan Island. All these took a back seat in importance to the *Alabama* Claims.[64]

On 2 April 1871, a British census official visited the Bulloch family in Waterloo. For the first time, James Dunwoody Bulloch was recognized on the British census as a naturalized subject. The census report tells a story of a moderately successful Victorian Era gentleman merchant. In addition to his wife Harriott and eight-year-old Stuart Elliot, there was Martha, his youngest daughter, now six. Jessie and James, Jr., were away at school; the poignant absence of Henry Dunwody's name was due to his passing away in February. Harriott had a live-in cook, a Welsh lady named Jane Howland, a waitress *cum* servant, Ellen Tetley (who hailed from Shropshire), and Agnes McCormick, a 20-year-old housemaid from Scotland. Despite his economic woes, Bulloch was able to afford three full-time, in-house domestic staff. Similarly, Bulloch's partner Moses P. Robertson and his wife Annie kept house with six children and four domestic servants. In the spring of 1871, Bulloch and Robertson appeared to be prospering. Sustaining that success would be quite another issue.[65]

By April 1871, the British press applauded the speedy progress of the *Alabama* Claims commissioners. The *Times* of London hailed "the promise of a settlement of the *Alabama* dispute with genuine satisfaction." It was, however, "by no means disposed, even for the sake of permanent goodwill to go a step beyond what we believe to be the proper measure of international obligations." The British-American commissioners eventually decided to place the matter into the hands of a five-person international commission. President Grant and Queen Victoria would each choose a commissioner who would be joined by three commissioners selected by the emperor of Brazil, the president of the Swiss Confederation, and the king of Italy. France and Germany were ignored for obvious reasons. Still, British newspapers saw incredible irony in having the actions of the British government judged by foreigners.[66]

The Washington Treaty, as it became known, was signed on May 8th and ratified on 17 June 1871. It set the parameters for *Alabama* Claims tribunal including the location where the high commission would sit in judgment. The selection of Geneva, Switzerland, cemented the Swiss reputation as a neutral state devoid of favoritism. With the completion of the treaty, President Grant managed to keep a lid on the always-emotive internal politics regarding the *Alabama* Claims.[67]

Through the summer and into the fall of 1871, both sides raced to compile their cases before the December deadline when the *Alabama* Claims tribunal would first convene. Grant reluctantly named Charles Frances Adams, the combative former U.S. minister to Britain, as the U.S. arbitrator for the Geneva conference (Thomas Dudley was also included).[68] In a related move, Grant appointed Robert Schenck as the new U.S. minister to Britain. Schenck was a former Union general and was the brother of the man whose life Midshipman Bulloch had saved back when he was sailing master of the USS *Shark*.

As the Great Powers jockeyed for position, Bulloch and his former comrades continued to rebuild their lives. In late October, Bulloch wrote a letter of introduction for Mr. Harold Bower, of Liverpool. Bower was traveling to America and was eager to meet Jefferson Davis. Bower was an intimate friend of a gentleman who had accompanied Bulloch and Davis on their Irish trip in September 1870. While the introduction might have helped Davis, this favor for an influential young cotton broker was also helpful to the business of Bulloch and Robertson and of brother Irvine.[69]

In the last days of November 1871, Bulloch departed Liverpool for New York City on the SS *Russia* and on December 6th arrived in New York Harbor. Other than a visit with his Bulloch and Roosevelt relatives, his trip to America was most likely related to business interests. The other names on the passenger list of the SS *Russia* were most revealing, including "Mr. Trenholm" (William Lee Trenholm) and "Mr. Hull" (F.S. Hull, Bulloch's long-time solicitor). Most names on the passenger list included a first name or initial in front of the surname. Such was not the case for Bulloch (misspelled as "Bullock"), Trenholm, and Hull. This subtle attempt at anonymity was probably related to the excitement over the *Alabama* Claims tribunal that was due to meet in Geneva in just nine days.[70]

Why had Bulloch risked coming to New York at such a critical time? If newspapermen had discovered that the arch-creator of the disasters inflicted on U.S. merchant shipping had brazenly landed in America, Bulloch's safety would be imperiled. The answer probably lies in the affairs of George A. Trenholm and his Fraser, Trenholm and Co. subsidiary. All of Trenholm's partners and principals had been under continuous legal assault since the end of the war. In 1868, the Circuit Court of South Carolina assumed jurisdiction over all the property of partners and co-owners of Fraser, Trenholm and Co. as security until every last Confederate penny and parcel became property of the United States government. If not, "the Government ... [would] take judgement against the parties or their property in the United States."[71] As part of his "secret service," Bulloch was likely on the

Fraser, Trenholm and Co. books as an employee (even Bulloch needed a plausible cover). Based in part on his financial interests in the postwar "estate" of Fraser, Trenholm, and Company, it seems that he had other financial connections with the firm.

Though the Roosevelt correspondence during this period of time is mute on his activities, Bulloch opaquely refers to his "visit in the winter of 1871" in his memoirs. Bulloch noted that he visited the "house of a gentleman — a New Yorker, of high social position." Bulloch and the "gentleman" discussed application of the British Neutrality Act during the Civil War. The New York gentleman argued that the British favored the South. Bulloch took the opposite view, citing Union recruitment of European men to join the Union Army in contravention of the Neutrality Act. An example was the *Great Western*, a transport ship for German immigrants recruited into the Union Army. At the mention of this ship, the gentleman smiled, disappeared into his study, and to Bulloch's astonishment reappeared with a folder full of "documents and vouchers relating to that voyage." The Union and the Confederacy had both stretched the British laws, but it was only the losing side that was being taken to task.[72]

The Union's maneuverings around the British Neutrality Act were among the many issues that the British team would raise when the *Alabama* Claims began on 15 December 1871 in Geneva. President Grant had been right to worry about the British reaction to the appointment of Charles Francis Adams as the U.S. arbitrator. They bitterly, but reasonably, complained that Adams was a direct participant in events during the Civil War in Britain and could not possibly have the unbiased viewpoint expected of an arbitrator. Despite his initial "repugnance" about the thought of Adams' appointment, Grant stubbornly refused to yield. The British answered with a redoubtable character of their own: Sir Alexander Cockburn, the British lord chief justice.[73] Cockburn detested being contradicted and had a firecracker temper.

The other arbitrators at the Hotel de Ville in Geneva on that mid–December day in Geneva were the Baron d'Itajuba of Brazil, Count Frederic de Sclopis of Italy, and Jacob Stämpfli of the Swiss Confederation. Stämpfli was the former president of Switzerland, while Baron d'Itajuba was minister to France.[74] Count Sclopis was an Italian minister of state.[75]

While the tribunal had its arbitrators, the two principle parties, Great Britain and America, had legal teams as well. William M. Evarts was among the three U.S. representatives, while Lord Tenterden led Britain's legal team. By prior agreement, each side would receive the other's bound legal cases and then adjourn the following day to study the other's argument. The rest of the December 15th session was spent in administrative matters, such as determining the tribunal chairman (Count Sclopis). Then there was the discussion about seating arrangements. Sclopis would be in the middle, but should his chair be higher than the others, or not (it should). A more important matter was language.[76]

Sclopis concluded that the official language of the tribunal would be French as the Italian and Brazilian members were not fluent in English. Sir Alexander Cockburn, his mouth agape, fulminated until the end of that day's session when he approached Adams. Cockburn wanted Adams to support his demand that English be used or the other arbitrators should resign. Precise legal terms would have different meanings in French. Adams knew that the American team had already produced copies of their case in both English and French and that his counterparts had not. He told Cockburn that they could not ask other members to resign; it would be an insult to each. Cockburn walked away shaking his head.[77]

The following day, the *Alabama* Claims tribunal adjourned with the agreement to reconvene in June of 1872. This would give each side six months to study the respective legal cases. With that, each side extended the other best wishes of the Christmas season and disappeared into the half-light of the Swiss winter's day.[78]

A few hours later, the *New York Times* blasted out a long article entitled "The Geneva Tribunal.... A Powerful Indictment Against Great Britain." Although Bulloch departed New York in the SS *Russia* just before the article appeared, he would soon see this editorial rant upon his arrival in Liverpool. The American Civil War, or at least the part of it where he was a central character, was about to be fought all over again.[79]

The British Foreign Office was already shutting down for the Christmas and Boxing Day holidays when U.S. Minister Robert Schenck dropped off extra copies of the U.S. case against Britain. The British team would not open the American *Alabama* Claims until after Christmas. When the Foreign Office staff finally returned from their holiday and opened the packages — they were shocked. The U.S. case included language nearly as harsh as Senator Charles Sumner's infamous rant before the U.S. Senate.

The British Foreign Office was forced to delay its return volley of diplomatic counterarguments, for the U.S. government would not return to its offices until 2 January 1872. While the British Foreign Office crafted a forceful response to these "indirect claims," newspapers on both sides of the Atlantic waded into the issue with relish.[80]

In 1872, Bulloch's name resurfaced as an almost daily subject of conversation in legal, political, and business circles. He was mentioned countless times in the U.S. case and complaint against Britain and in the associated newspaper stories on both sides of the Atlantic. It was a good time for Bulloch to stay out of the public eye, as emotions were running high.

Charles Francis Adams remained in Europe for several weeks, not returning to the U.S. until 24 February 1872. Despite his wartime advocacy, Adams sternly reminded reporters that he could only speak on the case "as an arbiter, not an advocate" and stressed his neutral stance. He recognized the absurdity of the "indirect" claims and suggested that both sides would finally grow weary of it all and come to a settlement.[81]

When the arbitrators reconvened in Geneva on 15 June 1872, the British legal team immediately requested an eight-month recess! Everyone, especially Charles Francis Adams, understood that if the British were granted the recess, the negotiations would never reopen. Tired of the years of bickering, he came up with a brilliant solution. The five arbitrators could disallow the U.S. demand for recompense for "indirect claims" by ruling that these grievances were not within the jurisdiction of the tribunal. Both Adams and Cockburn could argue that they were only going along with the majority. Newspapers in America marveled that the decision was "acceptable to both governments [Britain and America]."[82] On 15 July 1872, the Geneva tribunal finally met to address the key *Alabama* Claims issues. It had been seven years since the end of the American Civil War.[83]

One of the first legal positions that needed to be established was "due diligence." The British argued that *due diligence* only meant following the provisions of the Neutrality Act. With respect to the belligerents, it was only obliged to carry out its legal and business affairs in a normal fashion. The American legal team argued just the opposite. In judging culpability for the depredations of the Confederate commerce raiders, the burden of *due diligence* fell upon Great Britain. The British should have pursued every possible avenue of investigation to answer each complaint. The arbitrators decided that the U.S. definition of *due diligence* was the more correct. Britain became a victim of Bulloch's success and their own strict adherence to existing laws. The tribunal ruled that the British government could have prevented, but did not prevent the deployment of ships that the United States had correctly identified as likely commerce raiders.

The gavel fell and Cockburn exploded. This broad interpretation meant that Great Britain would be liable for most of the direct damages caused by the British-built or British-supported commerce raiders. After the British "victory" of having the indirect claims dropped, the score was now U.S. 1 and Britain 1. It would get worse for the British side, but at least nothing had leaked to the newspapers. Count Sclopis had laid down ironclad rules of secrecy.[84]

The arbiters next reviewed the activities of ships the U.S. presented as commerce raiders. Deciding that many of them had caused no harm (the *Rappahannock*, for example) or had little connection with Britain, they winnowed the list down to the principal, and most well-known, Confederate cruisers, primarily Bulloch's CSS *Florida*, CSS *Alabama* and CSS *Shenandoah*. Their tenders, such as the *Laurel* and *Agrippina*, were included in the adjudications as well. If Bulloch would not be fully exposed now, he never would be. He was the driving force behind all of these ships.[85]

In the cases of the *Florida* and *Alabama*, the tribunal voted that Britain was liable for compensations. The *Shenandoah* was another matter. She had not been built as a covert warship and was commissioned at sea and converted into a cruiser by her Confederate crew. The tribunal decided that there was no way that the British government could be liable for her departure from Great Britain. However, since the British colony of Australia allowed the *Shenandoah* to refit, recoal, and add stowaway crewmen, the British Empire was liable for *all* damage inflicted after the ship left Melbourne. That damage included the destruction of the U.S. North Pacific whaling fleet.[86]

Now it came down to a question of money. The British legal team roared that they owed nothing! Once again, the British position was voted down.[87] On 9 September 1872, newspapers in America and Europe headlined the news from Geneva. Britain owed America over £3 million, or about $15 million-in *gold*— to be paid within a year of the closure of the tribunal. The final score was U.S. £3 million and Britain 0.

The indirect claims had been a red herring. It was an utter diplomatic humiliation on the international stage. The final meeting of the tribunal was held the following Saturday, September 14th, and would be, for the first time, open to the public.[88]

Bulloch had cost the British Empire £3 million in gold, had his name brought before a panel of lawyers and arbitrators, and yet, he remained inviolate. There was no knock at the door of his Liverpool home from British authorities of any kind. Life proceeded on as ever, while the British newspapers pondered what it all meant and searched for scapegoats.[89]

Bulloch's thoughts about the *Alabama* Claims judgment against Britain exactly mirror the *Week's News* opinions on the Gladstone government: "The simple fact is that Her Majesty's Government gave way to the United States, and agreed to the ... rules hastily, and without fully appreciating the extent to which ... [rules such as *due diligence*] would afterwards be [used] ... in determining the liability of Great Britain." Bulloch was a bitter critic of Gladstone for the rest of his life.[90] The Geneva damage awards indirectly impugned the honor of Bulloch and his associates. The findings implied that he had acted improperly.

On the contrary, he had strictly adhered to British law as it had been interpreted at the time, but the tribunal decided that was not enough.

For Bulloch, and other Confederate Navy expatriates still in Britain, the American Civil War was now well and truly over. For nearly eleven full years, Bulloch had been involved with matters of the Confederate Navy in one form or another. Now, it was all consigned to history and Bulloch had escaped with no damage except his wounded pride. With Minister Schenck in London, there may have been an inclination to give the heroic former Confederate secret agent the benefit of any doubts.

As October 1872 neared, James and Harriott Bulloch prepared for another Roosevelt invasion. Sailing from New York City on October 16th, the Roosevelts were once again on the SS *Russia* and bound for Liverpool, where a dock strike was resolved just before their arrival.[91] The Roosevelt family arrived in Liverpool on 26 October 1872 and was greeted once again by both James Dunwoody and Irvine Bulloch. His uncles delighted young Theodore, Jr., who had already taken an immense "shine" to his seafaring relatives. Over the years, his mother Mittie had plied young Theodore, Jr., with tales of their adventures. During their last trip, Uncle Jimmie had taken an interest in the awkward young man who was now 14, the same age as his cousin James Dunwoody Bulloch, Jr.[92]

Theodore Roosevelt, Sr., had come to Europe for two reasons. First, President Grant had appointed him as a commissioner to represent the U.S. at the Vienna International Exposition in the spring of 1873. This dovetailed perfectly with his second reason for coming to Europe: to enjoy a warm winter by moving south to the Mediterranean and Egypt. The warmer and drier air was also therapy for the still-asthmatic "Teedie," though Theodore, Sr., would never admit to coddling his young son.[93]

Much of the two-week visit in Britain was spent in Liverpool, before the Roosevelts pushed on to continental Europe and the Mediterranean Sea via London and Dover. While in Liverpool, local boys teased young Theodore. He took it in stride, assuming it was because of his accent, which marked him as a "Yankee." More likely, it was his glasses and gangly body. Fortunately, Teedie lacked that kind of self-awareness. The exciting sea stories emanating from Uncles Jimmie and Irvine made up for minor adolescent inconveniences, such as the smothering kisses of his aunts.[94]

The Roosevelts departed Liverpool with ample hugs, tears, and more unwelcome kisses, and continued their latest grand tour. The Bullochs returned to their normal routine. "Jimmie" Junior was in school, as were his brother Stuart (9) and little sisters Jessie (12) and Martha (7). Harriott still looked over the whole flock with her three domestic helpers. On the business front, the Liverpool market reported firm cotton prices as November 1872 began, with an "inclination on the part of [cotton] holders to sell."[95]

Already the *Alabama* Claims process was positively influencing international relations. When Portugal and Britain squabbled over territory on the east coast of Africa, the problem was submitted to arbitration with a member of the French government as chief arbiter. The *Guardian* newspaper commented that "Englishmen have reason to be glad that their own government is still disposed to employ a method for deciding disputes which commends itself to reason even when it fails to work quite as we could have wished." It was a grudging, backhanded reference to the *Alabama* Claims and an acknowledgment that as a future prime minister would say "to jaw-jaw is always better than to war-war!"[96] As Christmas 1872 approached, Sen. Sumner's resolution to require the "blotting out of the battles of the rebellion ... and peeling them from regimental banners" led to his censure in the Massachusetts House of Representatives. America was no longer picking at the scab; it was time for healing.[97]

The Bullochs spent their Christmas in Britain while the adventurous Roosevelts were on the Nile River portion of their 1200-mile journey.[98] By the spring of 1873, the business of Bulloch and Robertson and particularly the cotton brokers Irvine Bulloch and his partner William Barcroft faced a slow market. The world's economies were experiencing a dramatic shift in markets. The resulting global depression known as the Panic of 1873 lasted until 1879, and even longer in some countries.[99]

Theodore Roosevelt and his family sailed up the Danube River after visiting Greece and Turkey. The markets did not affect Roosevelt. He had inherited over $1 million from his father Cornelius and his business benefited from the sound financial management of his brother and partner, James.[100] Theodore Roosevelt, Sr., returned to Liverpool in the spring, where he met with Brother Jimmie. Roosevelt was in a position to offer useful advice regarding future business options, perhaps backed up with financial support.

The rest of the Roosevelt family remained in Europe, with the children scattered to various cities under private tutelage, while Mittie took "the cures" at a spa in Carlsbad, Bohemia. Roosevelt wrote to Mittie of his *bon voyage* party when he departed Liverpool on 7 June 1873 aboard the *Russia*. Bulloch, Jimmie Jr., Irvine, Moses Robertson, and Irvine's father-in-law, Henry Sears, all came down to the pier to see him off.[101]

Roosevelt had completed his appointment as commissioner at the Vienna Exhibition and engaged the U.S. consul in Dresden to find suitable homes for his children while he was back in America. Teedie was able to witness the developing nationalism of unified Germany and its culture under Bismarck's hand. For insurance, Roosevelt briefed Bulloch on his scattered flock of children. Mittie was an independent women and a force to be dealt with, but for emergencies, Brother Jimmie and Irvine were the family firemen.

August and September 1873 saw Mittie Roosevelt and her brood back in Britain. In New York, Roosevelt was busily tending to accounts and a new home, as he prepared to rejoin the family in Europe. Between August 17th and 20th, he sent just under £10 to Robertson in payment for some spirits he had just received and he deposited another £200 in Brother Jimmie's account (with £125 of that amount for Harriott). Roosevelt also penned a request to J. Hubley Ashton, the former assistant attorney general of the United States, on behalf of "Capt Jas. D. Bulloch." He gently inquired about Bulloch's unpaid shares in the SS *Bienville*. Roosevelt had already broached the subject with Ashton's former boss and member of the *Alabama* Claims commission, William Maxwell Evarts. While none of these activities were "charity," Roosevelt was generous with his time and money to ensure that Bulloch's family and partner received all the monies that were due.[102]

By early October, Mittie Roosevelt was with Harriott and Irvine Bulloch in Liverpool, but Brother Jimmie was absent on business.[103] A week later, Theodore Roosevelt, Sr., was in Liverpool again, having crossed the Atlantic to rejoin his clan before they all returned to New York. Writing from Irvine Bulloch's home at 77 Canning Street on October 18th, Theodore Sr. told Bamie that her "Uncle Jimmie" was still in Pernambuco (Brazil), but was expected to return shortly. He planned to see Harriott the following day.[104]

Bulloch's trip to Brazil most likely related to a new business venture with the most successful Brazilian magnate of the age, Baron de Mauá. Bulloch and Robertson found it tough going in the commission merchant market. Bulloch alluded to this Brazilian enterprise in his memoirs, but offered few details.[105]

Although it is unclear exactly how Bulloch met the baron and what business they had together, there are several possibilities. On the personal and political level, General Robert Schenck, the brother of Bulloch's former shipmate, had been the U.S. minister to Brazil and was now the U.S. minister to England. Additionally, Brazil was one of the most active participants in the Vienna Exposition where Theodore Roosevelt, Sr., met representatives of Baron de Mauá. The baron also had considerable business ties with Britain. His Amazon Steam Navigation Company merged with its two rivals in 1872 and was based in London. By the spring of 1873, the baron was in a legal tussle with his former São Paolo Railway Company that was now "held" in Britain. The only cloud over the baron's dealings were the shareholders of this company; they owed the baron money and threatened the financial stability of his holdings.[106] Another avenue of contact was through Liverpool. The baron's telegraphic cable project leveraged British expertise and ships.[107] Bulloch was working with one of the great entrepreneurial industrialists of the age.

Just four days before the Roosevelt brood rejoined him in New York, Theodore Sr. once again used his considerable influence to advance Brother Jimmie's claim for his shares of the *Bienville*. He had already laid the legal and political groundwork with Ashton and Evarts. Now, he went to the top. Roosevelt's brief note to Secretary of State Hamilton Fish says little, but reveals much. He reminded the secretary of their visit the previous summer and the secretary's offer to "look into" and assist Captain Bulloch's well-justified claim. Roosevelt enclosed a statement from Bulloch and pressed Secretary Fish for payment as a personal favor. Bulloch, the prime instigator of Confederate Navy depredations, was receiving personal assistance from the chief instigator of the Union's successful *Alabama* Claims.[108]

In Liverpool, Harriott managed the Bulloch household while her husband spent long periods of time overseas, with multiple trips to Brazil. Jefferson Davis, on yet another visit to Liverpool in mid–February 1874, commented that "Capt. Bulloch is in some employment in South America, but is expected here daily for a visit." During this period, Bulloch used the services of Roosevelt and James K. Gracie, his other brother-in-law, to help manage his Brazilian and U.S. financial accounts.[109] This combination of hopeful confidence in South American business, poor prospects in Liverpool, and his partner's desire to return to the U.S. led Bulloch to dissolve his partnership with Moses Robertson. On 1 May 1874 after nearly 10 years together, "Bulloch and Robertson" disbanded, with Bulloch assuming all residual debts.

Shortly thereafter, Bulloch departed once again for Brazil and Baron de Mauá's steamship company.[110] Bulloch's venture into the commission merchant trade had suffered under the Liberal government's reforming zeal. There had been a "corn crisis" and then a depression in 1873 (giving him yet another reason to dislike the Liberal Party).[111]

While Bulloch toiled in South America, Theodore Roosevelt, Sr., continued his campaign to help collect his claim against the U.S. government. On 23 June 1874, Roosevelt wrote to the secretary of the navy applying for $8,958.83 that the United States Navy owed Bulloch for the purchase of the *Bienville* (and *DeSoto*) back in 1861. This was Bulloch's portion of the sale represented in his 10 shares of New York & New Orleans Steamship Company stock. By 21 August 1874, Roosevelt filed a formal claim on behalf of his Confederate brother-in-law. During this time, Roosevelt also helped Irvine Bulloch explore employment opportunities in the U.S. as a cotton broker (the timing was poor and Irvine decided to remain in Liverpool).[112]

On 6 October 1874, Roosevelt again turned his attentions to Bulloch's claim for payment from the U.S. Navy. On that day, Roosevelt and his lawyer, Gilbert S. King, presented a formal demand for payment to the Department of the Navy.[113] Roosevelt used all his professional skills and connections to help Bulloch.

In Brazil, the business empire of Baron de Mauá held enormous debts that it could not collect and soon collapsed into bankruptcy. Bulloch's financial fate was too closely linked with his Brazilian enterprises. Even Harriott was uncharacteristically worried. In mid–November 1874, she confided her financial concerns to Theodore Roosevelt, Sr., who was back in Europe on business while Bulloch was away.

Roosevelt's son Elliott ("Ellie") accompanied him on this trip, and while tending to business in France, he left Ellie with Irvine and his wife Ella. He was in Paris when an alarming telegram arrived saying that Ellie was not well. Roosevelt hurried back to Liverpool and found his son prostrate with an asthma attack. Ellie had been playing with "Harriott's children" and was on the losing end of a pillow fight.[114]

Roosevelt spent the remainder of the month tending to Elliott at Irvine and Ella's home. He wrote Mittie that Brother Jimmie returned home on November 14th and he planned to see him the following day. Roosevelt was also in communication with his attorney back in New York, who was working with Secretary of the Navy George Robeson on Bulloch's claim.[115] Roosevelt's assistance and Bulloch's persistence paid off, but it would take another 21 years before the U.S. Congress and court system finally confirmed the correctness of the payment. Bulloch finally received $8,510.62 for his 10 shares of stock.[116]

On November 27th, Theodore Sr. reported to Mittie that Brother Jimmie was more like "his old natural self" than he had been for many years. The good news about his claim raised his spirits even more. It was a joyous and uniquely American Thanksgiving celebration with turkey and champagne all around. Roosevelt, and Bulloch celebrated after the feast with a bit of shopping, purchasing extra goodies for Irvine and his family for their generosity in caring for Elliott. Theodore and Elliott Roosevelt departed for New York on December 5th, once again boarding the luxury liner SS *Russia*.[117]

In 1875, Bulloch's name is unusually absent from public view and private letters. At 51 years of age, he was too young and healthy to retire, but too old to enter a radically new career. The only hint of his business pursuits came in the form of a June 1875 letter from Theodore Roosevelt, Sr., to James King Gracie, endorsing a business proposal from Bulloch. Roosevelt did not indicate what Bulloch was pursuing, but he closed with the positive note, "I am glad he seems hopeful and has so good a thing."[118]

James King Gracie had married Bulloch's sister Anna nine years previously. He was a successful banker and broker who came from a prominent family of politicians and bankers with connections in both New York and Liverpool. Gracie obviously had strong feelings for his Liverpool relatives; he generously remembered Bulloch's spinster daughter Martha and Irvine's wife (Ella) in his will.[119]

Bulloch's nephew Teedie was cramming for Harvard College and pursuing a frenetic exercise program. The thin, wiry little Roosevelt had discovered girls, actually one girl: Edith Carow. By the time Teedie entered Harvard in the fall of 1876, he was madly in love. Having just settled into his college accommodations, a letter with a British postmark dropped through the mail slot in his door. Uncle Jimmie had written his favorite nephew; Teedie was so pleased that he promptly wrote his father with the news. It was 22 October 1876.[120]

As Theodore Roosevelt settled into his first term at Harvard, he remained implacably faithful to Edith Carow and sported a fashionable look that was unmistakably inspired by his Uncle Jimmie. By the end of the spring term 1877, his classmates began to refer to "Teedie" as "Teddy." Even better, his Uncle James Dunwoody Bulloch was coming to America for a visit![121]

On June 28th, Bulloch departed Liverpool on the steamship *Adriatic* for his third documented return to America since the American Civil War. After a brief stop in Queenstown, Ireland, Bulloch was in New York City on Saturday, July 7th, at 9:30 P.M. Theodore Roosevelt, Sr., wrote R.J. Cortis, the agent for the steamship line that owned the *Adriatic*, to be on the outlook for Bulloch and to render him all possible assistance. Roosevelt enclosed another letter for Bulloch's eyes only. The Roosevelt clan had decamped to "Tranquility," their home at Oyster Bay, Long Island. Roosevelt invited Bulloch to come out to Oyster Bay with all possible speed the following day (Sunday). It would be a grand reunion, for his stepsister Annie Gracie and her husband James King Gracie were already there. Bulloch could conduct business with Roosevelt and Gracie while he enjoyed a family visit.[122]

Teddy Roosevelt had traveled to the Adirondacks at the end of Harvard's spring semester on 21 June 1877, and by mid–July joined the other Roosevelts and Uncle Jimmie at Oyster Bay. The atmosphere of the Roosevelt family, interspersed with Bullochs, Gracies, and other various relations and friends was a summer idyll of sailing, carriage rides, parties, and picking flowers. The opportunities for conversation between the still-impressionable Theodore and Uncle Jimmie were frequent, and it can be imagined that Bulloch asked "Thee Jr." (as he signed his letters to his father during this period) about Harvard and his future plans.[123]

Bulloch remained at Oyster Bay in an extended holiday mode until August 10th, when he traveled to Elizabethtown, New Jersey, to visit sister Susy and Hilborne West. By August 14th, Bulloch returned to New York and the Roosevelts. Four days later, Bulloch left for home aboard the *Adriatic*, arriving on August 31st. It had been a relaxing and fruitful visit for Bulloch, who continued his regular correspondence with sister Mittie.[124]

Teddy Roosevelt was back at Harvard beginning his second year when President Rutherford B. Hayes nominated his father to be collector of customs for New York. Roosevelt was interested in the post out of a sense of public duty, but he was a pawn in a battle over reform in the federal civil service system. As he fought to maintain his reputation and offer himself for public service, his mental and physical health suffered under the strain of American politics.[125]

On December 18th, Theodore, Sr., collapsed and his doctor's diagnosis was acute peritonitis. Just in time for Christmas, the elder Roosevelt strengthened. However, on 9 February 1878 a telegram from New York arrived at Harvard summoning Teddy Roosevelt home. His father was mortally ill. By the time he arrived in New York City, his father had died, in agonizing pain. His death was caused by a tumor of the bowel that had wrapped itself around the intestines like the strangling roots of a willow tree. The family was devastated. The great Roosevelt of his era was gone before he had reached his 47th birthday.[126]

There is no record of how, or when, James and Harriott Bulloch learned of the death of their beloved Theodore Roosevelt, Sr. In fact, there is little knowledge of Bulloch's activities at this time. Liverpool records only reveal that in 1878 the family moved to 63 Irbey Terrace, a house on Upper Parliament St. in Toxteth, Liverpool. Roosevelt was one of Bulloch's oldest and dearest friends. The respect and friendship they shared had bound the two families together before, during, and after the American Civil War.

For the next two years, Teddy Roosevelt would finish his degree at Harvard, while Bulloch carried on as an independent businessman. Their mutual loss would bind them together in a way that would benefit each other, American foreign policy, naval strategy, and international trade. Bulloch would become Teddy's oracle, and Teddy would become Bulloch's pride and joy, almost another son.

14

A President's Oracle

In February 1880, James Dunwoody Bulloch was nearing his 57th birthday and the peak of his post-war career as a Liverpool businessmen, broker, and sometime maritime consultant. His brother Irvine was equally successful. He had dissolved his partnership with Barcroft in 1875 and carried on as I.S. Bulloch and Co. But it was the elder Bulloch who was venerated in Liverpool. He was a gentleman's gentleman, with the manners the South had made famous, wholly immersed in Waterloo, his hometown, and Liverpool, his business town. Bulloch was well regarded on the local maritime scene for his contributions to training apprentice seamen, donations to the local Seaman's Home, and church and society functions.[1]

At the same time, Bulloch's favorite nephew, Theodore "Teddy" Roosevelt, was struggling at Harvard University on two fronts. First, Teddy's infatuation with Edith Carow had been displaced; he was lovesick over Alice Lee. The first problem caused the second. Teddy's grades began to suffer. Teddy was so obsessed with Alice that he suffered bouts of insomnia. He tried reading himself to sleep and when that didn't' work, he decided to write a book. It would cover naval history. Thanks to his uncles' sea stories, it was the topic that interested him most, other than Alice. Late in 1879, Roosevelt began *The Naval War of 1812*, a detailed look at the U.S. and British Royal Navy operations that still affected the U.S. Navy's understanding of its strategic role.[2]

Happily, on 25 January 1880, Alice yielded to Teddy's persistence and accepted his proposal of marriage. He could now get some sleep, improve his grades (he graduated *magna cum laude*), and pursue research for his book![3] The spring of 1880 brought clarity of mind regarding his future. Teddy still missed his father terribly, but if the elder Roosevelt had been alive, he undoubtedly would have approved of his son's decision to study law. His decision to enter the unseemly public world of elective politics was another matter, at least to those family members who aspired to a higher caste of society, as his more stodgy relatives were horrified by his career choice. On June 25th, his beloved Uncle Jimmie turned 57; five days later, Theodore Roosevelt graduated from Harvard University. His work on *The Naval War of 1812* languished as it competed with a post-graduation hunting trip to the American West and the expectation of marriage. With the onset of autumn on October 27th, Theodore Roosevelt and Alice Lee married and took up residence in New York City at 6 West 57th Street, two blocks south of Central Park.[4]

After settling into their home, Roosevelt picked up his writing pen with much more seriousness. In the first days of 1881, he dusted off the first two chapters on *The Naval War of 1812* that he had completed while at Harvard. Next, he had to compile and analyze a tremendous amount of information despite his lack of practical experience and formal education about the topic.[5] However, the famous Bulloch propensity for appearing at the right place, at the right time, provided a boost to his motivation.

On 15 March 1881, Bulloch left Liverpool on the White Star line steamer *RMS Republic* for New York City, arriving on March 25th. It is likely that he saw Teddy soon after arrival, having barely put down his bag. His nephew peppered him with a hundred and one naval questions. If there was ever any doubt about whether Roosevelt could tackle his subject, now, a living, breathing naval hero, and family at that, was in his own house. Fortunately, this would be a long visit, for Bulloch did not depart the United States until May.[6]

Fired with motivation, Teddy had ready access to the conveniently located and well-stocked Astor Library in New York City. His research regimen was so strict that he marched off in the morning to the Astor, pored over the relevant materials, and when the clock struck 3 o'clock, he bounded back home to collect Alice for an afternoon stroll or carriage ride.[7]

Having decided to take a belated European honeymoon, on 12 May 1881 Teddy and Alice Roosevelt ambled up the gangway of the *RMS Celtic*, another White Star liner bound for Europe. Bulloch did not depart New York on the SS *Britannic* until May 21st, but Teddy had carefully timed his itinerary to ensure that he and Alice would be in Liverpool upon Uncle Jimmie's return. Teddy spent 10 days touring Ireland with Alice before meeting up with his two uncles and his kissing cousins in Liverpool. Uncle Jimmie had answers to the nautical questions that popped into Teddy's mind during his nauseous cruise across the Atlantic. He certainly encouraged Teddy's efforts on *The Naval War of 1812*. Teddy also wrote his mother that he really liked his cousin "Jimmie" Jr., but he continued his disdain for the slobbering kisses of the younger Bulloch cousins.[8]

The census of April 1881 recorded James Dunwoody Bulloch, Jr., as a member of the Bulloch household at 63 Upper Parliament St. The same census also recorded James D. Bulloch as a "retired" cotton merchant. Also living with the Bullochs were two female domestic servants. Gone was the previous "waitress" of the 1871 census, but Agnes McCormick of Scotland faithfully remained, having been promoted from housemaid to cook. As a 57-year-old retiree with a large family and live-in household staff, Bulloch had been extraordinarily successful in a very short period of time. His status as a gentleman of independent means was due to his own industrious efforts, initially wise investments, and family bequests or stipends courtesy of Bamie and Theodore Roosevelt, James and Anna Gracie, and Nannie Hutchison.[9]

Though Teddy Roosevelt lugged his rough manuscript of *The Naval War of 1812* around Europe, there was little time to meet with either of his Bulloch uncles. Teddy and Alice still had a lot of Europe to cover. Five days after his arrival in Liverpool, Irvine's wife Ella, her mother (Mrs. Harriet Sears), sister (also named Harriet), and Teddy's sister Corinne were all headed to America on the SS *Britannic*! Roosevelt's timing had been well planned for they enjoyed a grand mini-reunion on the British side of the Atlantic.[10] After spending two days in Liverpool and another eleven days sightseeing in London, the rambling Roosevelts, Teddy and Alice, toured France, Italy (including the Italian Alps and Lake Como), Austria, and Bavaria.[11]

While portions of the Roosevelt and Bulloch families scattered to the four winds that summer of 1881, shocking news arrived from America. President James A. Garfield had been shot on the 2nd of July. The assassin, Charles Guiteau, was a deranged patronage-seeking "stalwart" (an ardent group of supporters of Vice President Chester Arthur). The American public was repulsed and there was a bizarre twist that connected Theodore Roosevelt, Sr., with Teddy's political future.[12]

Earlier in 1881, President Garfield had nominated another reformer as collector of customs for the port of New York. Back in 1877, President Hayes had nominated Theodore Roosevelt, Sr., for this same position (to replace Chester Arthur). Senator Roscoe "Boss" Conkling could not believe that a second president had given him the political slap. This time Conkling resigned, creating a bitter political face-off that culminated with the assassination of Garfield. Conkling was instantly implicated as co-conspirator in a plot to kill President Garfield. In another ironic twist, when Garfield succumbed to the bullet lodged near his spine, Chester Arthur, the former New York customs officer, was now president of the United States. The assassination ended Conkling's political career and cleared the way for legislation to reform the U.S. government's civil service.[13]

While Roosevelt mused over the news from America, he and Alice made their way to the Netherlands. There, he exhumed his manuscript from the bottom of the trunk and began work again. As he reviewed the text and considered the task ahead, he was becoming less sure of his ability to come to grips with his subject.[14] Fortunately, Teddy and Alice were headed back to Britain. On September 10th, the Roosevelts reached Liverpool for a two-week stay with the Bullochs. He just missed the opportunity to join his uncle and see the Prince of Wales officially open the North Docks. No matter, it was fodder for conversation after a hearty welcome and a segue for discussing Teddy's *1812* manuscript.[15]

Roosevelt admitted that by September 14th he was spending almost all his time with Uncle Jimmie, talking naval history. When he saw the files that Bulloch had accumulated pertaining to Confederate operations in Europe, Teddy was impressed. He urged his uncle to publish a work covering his significant role in those efforts. In between helping him arrange his papers, Roosevelt suggested that he include the exciting blockade-running adventure aboard the *Fingal* in addition to the story of the *Alabama* and other commerce raiders. Roosevelt could tell that Uncle Jimmie was pleased with his interest in the old sea captain's Civil War accomplishments, even if he had served on the "wrong" side. His nephew contended that he would have been on the Union side if he had been old enough to fight, but that didn't stop him from admiring Bulloch's knowledge and commitment to do what he thought was right. In this same letter, Roosevelt joyfully wrote that he both respected and loved his Uncle Jimmie, thinking him the most modest and kindly old-soul he'd ever known. Bulloch would reciprocate that love and respect throughout his life.[16]

This letter also marked the impetus for Bulloch's memoir of the Civil War, *The Secret Service of the Confederate States in Europe*. Roosevelt took credit for persuading Uncle Jimmie to write his memoirs. He accurately observed that only his uncle had the necessary information and papers to describe the successes and failures of this fascinating international aspect of the American Civil War. Teddy's claim coincided with Bulloch's own comments in Volume I of his memoirs, where he wrote, "The Introduction and Chapter I were written in the autumn of 1881." Bulloch would note in the forward of his work that there were persons who "thought that the future historian should be furnished with the facts relating to the foreign-built navy of the Confederate States." It is a remarkable commentary on the synergy between uncle and nephew that both would be writing naval histories at the same time. Roosevelt wrote about a war that had occurred before he had even been born, and Bulloch wrote about a war that he had experienced and directed first-hand.[17]

At this time in history, the world was ready for a new vision of the strategic role of naval forces. In Germany, the growing *Kaiserliche Marine* of Kaiser Wilhelm I and Chancellor Bismarck was still largely a coastal defense force. Germany had a small squadron of ironclads based at Wilhelmshaven during the Franco-Prussian War of 1870, but they had not been used. In fact, the performance of the German navy and its leadership was so poor that German army generals had led the admiralty since the end of the war. In 1881, Bismarck decided to construct sea-going ironclads, but the build up would be spread over a ten-year period.[18]

British naval developments had been moving in step with the empire's needs. British sea power had allowed the empire to flourish in splendid isolation since Trafalgar in 1805.[19] Seventy-six years later, other imperial aspirants emerged as competitors. In September 1881, the scramble to divide Africa into European spheres of influence had begun in Tunisia and would spread throughout the continent.[20] After the Franco-Prussian War, the French strengthened their naval forces with the addition of the world's first steel-hulled warship, the *Redoutable*. The ties between France and Japan also disturbed forward-thinking American naval strategists. American naval power had opened Japan to trade, and Britain carefully watched French activities from China to the South Pacific.[21] Although China remained a politically fractured nation, Japan was coalescing. The new minister of the Japanese navy, Enomoto Takeaki, was an aficionado of the French naval doctrine that envisioned smaller, higher performance warships, such as cruisers and torpedo boats. Japan realized that it needed to reduce its dependence on Britain and develop closer relations with France.[22]

Kaiser Wilhelm I united Germany and challenged the British Empire and its navy during the late nineteenth century (authors' collection).

The United States Navy declined precipitously after the Civil War, even with the rise of Ericsson's innovations. In September 1881, the U.S. Navy was suffering from fifteen years of inadequate funding, corrupt shipbuilders, and lack of political support. The nation had turned inward, trying to fill up Teddy Roosevelt's beloved West. This was the situation for the principal naval powers on 14 September 1881 when Theodore Roosevelt and Bulloch had their wide-ranging conversation on all things pertaining to naval warfare.

Late in September 1881, Teddy and Alice Roosevelt boarded the SS *Britannic*, bound for New York, leaving James Dunwoody and Harriott Bulloch once more to their quiet lives.[23] For Bulloch, his retirement now had real purpose. He would doggedly arrange and write *his* answer to the unjust U.S. government aspersions contained within the *Alabama* Claims. Bulloch's memoirs would tell the real story of the Confederate Navy in Europe, written by the man who had been there and done it all.

It must have seemed like old times for Bulloch, back behind a desk, writing and shuffling vast amounts of familiar documents, but this time around there were no rushed orders to captains who dared confront Union warships. His only shipmates were the gray ghosts of a navy that no longer existed. Yet his actions had dramatically affected world history and changed naval warfare, even he could sense that.

Irvine Bulloch left Liverpool just before Christmas to join his wife, Ella, in the U.S. and accompany her back to Liverpool, where they arrived on 30 January 1882.[24] Irvine brought family news from America updating his brother about sisters Mittie and Anna and Teddy and Alice Roosevelt. Teddy was studying law at Columbia, and had been elected as assemblyman for the 21st district of New York. While Teddy attended to the duties of his new office, he also spent long hours on *The Naval War of 1812*. He delivered his manuscript to the publishing offices of Putnam on 3 December 1881. The exhausted Roosevelt was able to relax for the Christmas holidays. He had won the race to meet the publisher's deadline, while his uncle's writing project plodded onward. Perhaps it was the critical success of *The Naval War of 1812* that did it, or some undiscovered prompting from Teddy, but when Roosevelt's book was published in April 1882 Bulloch rededicated himself to his two-volume tome that same month.[25]

Theodore Roosevelt went on to write thirty-seven more books, but it was *The Naval War of 1812* that established his credentials as a first-rate naval historian. In Britain, France, and Germany critics proclaimed total admiration for Roosevelt's exacting and scholarly work. By 1886, the U.S. Navy placed a copy in every ship's library. It had multiple printings and was required reading at every serious school of naval history and warfare. Bulloch was bursting with pride at Teddy's success, and though his nephew deserved the accolades, it is undeniable that Bulloch's assistance was essential. Roosevelt had superb research and analytical skills, a benefit of his Harvard education. But when it came to practical naval experience and vocabulary, it was the hard-won achievements and insight of Bulloch that gave his work depth and context. While Irvine Bulloch may have helped, it was Uncle Jimmie who Roosevelt recognized in his preface: "In conclusion I desire to express my sincerest thanks to Captain James D. Bulloch, formerly of the United States Navy ... without whose advice and sympathy this work would probably never have been written or even begun."[26]

While Roosevelt's book provoked considerable comment from American and European reviewers, the Great Powers were slow to embrace modern naval strategies and technologies. In Germany, a young naval officer named Alfred Tirpitz was testing the employment of torpedoes and torpedo boats. The British and French conducted similar experiments, but were primarily interested in protecting the near-shore, littoral areas of their homelands. They seemed oblivious to the concept of projecting power abroad as the British Empire had done during its glorious rise during the nineteenth century.[27]

In June 1883, Bulloch's memoirs appeared in Britain. Titled *The Secret Service of the Confederate States in Europe or, How the Confederate Cruisers were Equipped*, Bulloch's two-volume book was not an academically edited or referenced work like Teddy's. It had no index, bibliography, illustrations, photos, or maps. On the other hand, as Roosevelt pointed out, it was a book that *only* Bulloch could write. In the preface, Bulloch acknowledged that his style was unavoidably chaotic, largely due to multiple events occurring at the same time. He made no apologies as to his purpose "to furnish a truthful record of the efforts made by the Confederate Government to organize a naval force during the Civil War." Bulloch succeeds in this goal as his character shines throughout the book. Even his most severe critics never questioned the personal and professional honesty that is reflected in his only published work.[28]

Alfred Thayer Mahan, American geostrategist and naval officer, had a close and mutually supportive relationship with Theodore Roosevelt (U.S. Naval Historical Center).

Bulloch appears to have funded the publication of his book in Britain, but several hundred sets of sheets were shipped to America and published by none other than Teddy Roosevelt's publisher and partner, G.P. Putnam and Sons. In 1884, coincident with Putnam's first U.S. edition of Bulloch's book, Teddy invested $20,000 in his good friend's company (George Haven Putnam). This contract guaranteed Teddy a share of Putnam's profits and a voice in what would be published. Although there is no evidence of Roosevelt's direct involvement, it is clear that G.P. Putnam had no difficulty in recognizing the value of the book that Teddy's uncle had written. Despite its limited numbers, Bulloch's book quickly became a must-have for students of naval and international affairs.[29]

As Bulloch said in a letter to an acquaintance only a month before the publication of his book in Britain, "It has been written as a duty, and as a contribution to the materials for which a future historian may draw his facts for an impartial account of the great Civil War."[30] This observation was particularly true since the U.S. government had not yet published any of the 30 volumes in its "Official Records of the Union and Confederate Navies in the War of the Rebellion."

Within a little over fourteen months, two members of the same extended family, the Roosevelts and Bullochs, published two great works on America's most significant naval campaigns in two critically decisive wars. They were sustaining a nautical family tradition that extended back to the very beginnings of the republic via James Stephens Bulloch, who invested in the early steamships and Nicholas J. Roosevelt, a partner of Robert Fulton.[31]

Using technology developed some thirty years after the American Civil War, the Kaiser's navy applied lessons learned from Bulloch in its U-boat and Q-ship campaigns of World War I and II. Roosevelt took away lessons from Bulloch's work as well. They would reappear as strategies and policies in his public service career. It would be a middle-aged U.S. Navy officer who would synthesize Bulloch's and Roosevelt's ideas into the naval treatise that set in motion the great awakening of the world's naval powers: Captain Alfred Thayer Mahan.[32] Mahan understood and articulated the subtleties of Bulloch's frustrations as the weaker naval power whose innovative, war-winning naval strategies were beyond the reach or recognition of the Confederacy's leadership.

As Bulloch's book rocked the naval and diplomatic world in May-June 1883, Teddy Roosevelt's political career was in its second year. Invited to a speaking engagement on May 28th at the Free Trade Club, Roosevelt assailed politically motivated tariffs. Afterwards, over cigars and drinks, Roosevelt met Commander Henry H. Gorringe. The commander had recently resigned from the U.S. Navy after a highly publicized clash with Secretary of the Navy William Chandler about the need for a larger fleet. Roosevelt discovered a kindred spirit in Gorringe. He had fought for the Union in the Civil War, published a book on his explorations of the Rio de la Plata in South America, and recently brought the obelisk known as Cleopatra's Needle from Alexandria, Egypt, to Central Park in New York City. Gorringe was an ardent and vocal supporter of Roosevelt's dreams for a stronger U.S. Navy as enunciated in *The Naval War of 1812*.

Commander Gorringe had also acquired a hunting ranch in the American West. With Elliott Roosevelt's fabulous big-game hunting stories fresh on his mind, Teddy mused aloud to Gorringe that he'd like to try something like that. Naturally, the retired naval commander invited him to come west with him in the fall of 1883. Roosevelt accepted Gorringe's invitation, but he had to delay his departure. Alice was pregnant. While Roosevelt busied himself with plans for a new and larger home, he came down with cholera. In July 1883, he and Alice retreated to a resort in the Catskill Mountains where he could recuperate. Fortunately, Teddy was sufficiently recovered by August to return to Oyster Bay, Long Island.[33]

With his own health restored, Teddy didn't let Alice's pregnancy keep him from traveling to the American West in the first week of September 1883. For the next few months, Roosevelt experienced a way of life that he had only read about in books or heard in stories about Uncles Jimmie and Irvine. The trip would change his perspective about life and America's place in the world. Across the Atlantic, Uncle Jimmie's book frequently appeared in newspaper ads and received positive reviews.[34]

It was a November *New York Times* review of *The Secret Service of the Confederate States in Europe* that helped fix the reputation of Bulloch's effort in literary and historical circles. "In these volumes we have the most important Southern contribution that has yet been made to the history of those naval operations of the Confederacy that were conducted from the Old World as a base."[35] Of all the great ironies of Bulloch's life, few could rival this. A leading newspaper of a city that he had hoped to destroy was now acclaiming him as a noteworthy author. Unlike several other veterans, from both the North and South, Bulloch never published another book, article, commentary, or even a letter to the editor. Apart from an excerpt from his memoirs that the Southern Historical Society Papers reprinted in 1886, Bulloch's name only appears once in any bibliography of the Civil War.[36]

In February 1884, the more prolific author, Theodore Roosevelt, returned from his Dakota idyll. Teddy was so thoroughly entranced with the Dakota wilderness that he invested a sizable portion of his inheritance in a cattle ranch.[37] Other responsibilities were looming now, for his wife, Alice, was about to give birth. On February 12th while waiting in New York for her labor to begin, Assemblyman Roosevelt was called away to the state capital in Albany. When he left, Alice was in bed pregnant under the same roof as his mother, Mittie, who was in bed with a cold. His sisters Corinne and Bamie were there to care for them and Alice's parents were staying in a nearby hotel. Thinking that both of his ladies were in good hands, Teddy expected to return quickly from Albany, well in time for the delivery.[38] On the 13th of February, Roosevelt was basking in the congratulations of his fellow New York politicians over the birth of his first child, a healthy girl. Just before noon the same day, a second telegram brought ominous news. His mother and his wife had taken a turn for the worse; they both were near death. Roosevelt raced for the train station. By the time he arrived at his home in New York City, Alice was only barely alive and Mittie was drifting in and out of consciousness. Mittie Bulloch Roosevelt died of typhoid fever at three o'clock in the early morning hours of 14 February 1884. At two o'clock in the afternoon of the same day, Alice Lee Roosevelt died of Bright's disease (kidney failure). Teddy Roosevelt's depth of anguish was profound. *The New York Times* said simply in its February 15th edition: "Theodore Roosevelt met with a severe affliction yesterday in the death of his young wife and mother. Mrs. Roosevelt Sr., was a Savannah lady, her maiden name being Bullock [sic] ... Roosevelt's wife was a Miss Lee of Boston ... she leaves an infant child."[39]

The news of the double Valentine's Day tragedy rocketed across the Atlantic Ocean that same day. It was probably Teddy's older sister Bamie who telegraphed Bulloch and his brother Irvine with the first awful news of Mittie's death and Alice's critical condition. Bulloch responded with a brief telegram and a lengthy letter that same day. He wrote "Dearest Bamie" saying that never had any telegram delivered such sad news, as had the one that had borne the brief message about Alice and Martha Roosevelt. Bulloch was overwhelmed by grief and commiseration at the same time, for although the 49-year-old Martha Bulloch Roosevelt was only his half-sister, she had always been his closest family.

Bulloch fully empathized with his young nephew's loss, for it reminded him of the tragic loss of his own young mother, Hettie (32), when he was only seven. His first wife Lizzie Caskie was born on February 15th and died just before her 23rd birthday after less than three years of marriage. These experiences were all too familiar and all of these special women had been taken far too young. In Alice's case, the tragedy was compounded, for she left behind an infant girl. It was all too much to bear and a telegram offered far too little room to expound his feelings. Bulloch closed his letter to Bamie by saying that both he and Irvine would be writing letters when they knew more fully what had happened. It would be several generations before either the Roosevelts or Bullochs could truly celebrate Valentine's Day.[40]

The double funeral of Alice Lee and Martha Bulloch Roosevelt on 16 February 1884 sent Theodore Roosevelt into an extended state of grief, denial, and shock. Bamie cared for Teddy's infant daughter, Alice Lee, while Roosevelt threw himself into politics. He also sold his New York house, for the memories there were now too painful. With the end of the New York Assembly's session in June 1884, Roosevelt headed west to his ranch where could leave his troubles behind.

Shortly after the demise of Alice and Mittie Roosevelt, news of Judah P. Benjamin's death on May 6th in Paris reached British papers. While Bulloch suffered the vagaries of the cyclical British economy, Benjamin had prospered within the British legal system. Yet, their similarities were substantial. They never accepted a U.S. pardon, opting for British citizenship instead. The secrecy of Benjamin, to an even greater degree than Bulloch, would torment future historians. The *New York Times* described Benjamin simply as "the distinguished jurist, formerly Secretary of State of the Southern Confederacy."[41]

As figures like Benjamin passed from the stage of history, new players such as Bismarck and Kaiser Wilhelm emerged. They were racing the French for control of the heart of Africa. In 1883 when territorial issues began to develop pertaining to Niger, British affairs were in the able hands of Lord Derby as head of the Colonial Office.[42] As the European powers divided up the world, Teddy Roosevelt pursued his dream of being a rancher in the Dakota Territory during the tooth-chattering winter of 1884–85. In Liverpool, Bulloch's career ambitions took a bizarre turn.

On 25 November 1884, Bulloch wrote Jefferson Davis to request a favor. He hoped that the recent U.S. election of the Democrat Grover Cleveland might offer a chance for former Confederates. Until now, the Party of Lincoln was unable to "act with conciliatory fairness to all sections for the country or to shape out a national policy which should affect the States, and arouse support or opposition, without reference to geographical divisions or the special questions which caused their separation in 1861." With the Democrats now in power, Bulloch believed that there was no "valid reason why representative men from the South, that is to say men who took part with their State during the war, should not be freely admitted to Federal offices of trust, or why they should be restrained from seeking these by all honourable means." This last comment set the stage for Bulloch's extraordinary request: "I wish to obtain, if possible, the office of United States Consul at Liverpool, and I write to ask what you think should be my proper course of procedure and whether, in your opinion a man who has no party record, and can claim nothing in the score of party services, would stand any chance of being listened to?"[43] It was a jaw-dropping bombshell of a request. The ostensibly retired Bulloch, then went on to set out his case:

> My education, past services and experiences, have been such as should fit a man for a consular office, and my long residence in Liverpool has given me very special familiarity with the Maritime Laws of Great Britain and the local usages of this particular port. Besides this, I have passed a large part of my life in close association with seafaring men, and others who have to do with ships and commerce, and I understand their habits and modes of thought.[44]

Finally, Bulloch suggested that Davis contact Senator Lucius Lamar of Mississippi on his behalf, as Lamar "had once professed a warm friendship for me." Bulloch had written Lamar several times over the past years, but received no reply. Either through naiveté, or a total failure to appreciate how politically "hot" he still was, Bulloch briefly considered that Lamar's political position required the politician to be "indifferent to me ... [Lamar's] public duties are too engrossing to admit of his indulging in private correspondence."[45]

Now that the Democrats were in power, Bulloch believed that the country could set aside the old bitterness. Perhaps he believed that the publication of *The Secret Service of the Confederate States in Europe* exonerated his activities fully, and that enough time had passed to set aside any lingering resentment over the *Alabama* Claims. If Lucius Lamar, a former Confederate colonel and agent in Russian, France, and England could become Cleveland's secretary of the interior, why couldn't he achieve a lowly consular post? He knew that Davis still had the respect and ear of some congressmen, but he failed to appreciate that any publicly exposed endorsement from Davis would have assured its failure.

Bulloch was unable to consult with Teddy Roosevelt who was in Dakota until a few days before Christmas 1884. During the Republican nominating convention in Chicago he had worked against the unsuccessful Republican candidate James G. Blaine's nomination. However, as a loyal Republican, he was obligated to support Blaine despite his reputation of being anti–Southern.[46]

Whether through discussion with wiser heads in Britain, or sober political advice from America, Bulloch decided to withdraw his request for Davis' support. In a letter dated 9 January 1885, he told Davis that he had reconsidered his request for appointment to the U.S. consular office in Liverpool. Bulloch realized that his role as the Confederate Navy's agent in Europe made him politically unacceptable, even under a Democratic administration. The Boston and New York shipping magnates would never trust someone who had caused them so much harm. He had come to the sad but accurate conclusion that he "would stand no chance of getting the appointment."[47]

After this, Bulloch receded into reluctant retirement, while his nephew Teddy Roosevelt returned to his Dakota ranch. As both Roosevelt and Bulloch entered into a period of reflection, the Germans set off a new round of imperialistic expansionism in Southern Africa. In 1883 a Bremen-based merchant instigated the encroachment by establishing a trading post 150 miles north of the British Empire's Cape Colony. Bismarck's Germany gained British acquiescence in their African and other colonization efforts by 1885. Bismarck acted quickly since he knew that Kaiser Wilhelm I had a short time to live and Frederick, Wilhelm's son, was an admirer of Britain (Queen Victoria was his grandmother). Bismarck wanted to promote German nationalism and create an anti–British climate in Germany that would isolate the future kaiser from British influence. Bismarck released the uncontrollable forces of German nationalism that, under Kaiser Wilhelm II, led to the world's greatest naval arms race. This quest for military supremacy to support nationalist aims fuelled the engine of world history inexorably toward World War I and its even more destructive coda, World War II.[48]

The progeny of Bulloch's shipbuilding program provided a glimpse into the future of transoceanic armored vessels and the need for forward operating bases. The *Stonewall's* sister ship *Cheops* wound up in Germany as the *Prinz Adalbert*. The Royal Navy assimilated his Laird rams as the HMS *Wivern* and *Scorpion*. The Japanese Imperial Navy bought the *Stonewall* from the United States in 1871, and by 1885 it was *still* in active service. Bulloch and Roosevelt also developed personal relationships that influenced the decisions of key military and political leaders including the Derby family and Lord Salisbury. James Dunwoody Bulloch had an outsized affect on world history in the American Civil War, and his influence reached into the future in ways no one could have imagined.

Out in the American West, Roosevelt enjoyed the rigors of ranching in Dakota, though he did return east for summer holidays, including a September side-trip to the New York State Republican Convention. The biggest development, though a very personal one, was his rekindled romance with childhood sweetheart Edith Carow. By mid–November 1885, they were secretly engaged.[49]

In March 1886, Roosevelt headed west for another cattle roundup. He also chased and arrested men responsible for stealing a boat and started a new book. It was a lively and opinionated biography of Thomas Hart Benton, the redoubtable U.S. senator from Missouri who had championed westward expansion called "Manifest Destiny." Roosevelt used *Benton* to promulgate his view of America's rightful expansion.[50] The great dreams of the pre–Civil War Southern Democrats were alive and well. Jefferson Davis, John Slidell, and Judah P. Benjamin all envisioned an America that ruled the Caribbean, portions of Canada (British Columbia), and islands in the Pacific. Linked with Roosevelt's passion for the U.S. Navy and his well-remembered conversations with Uncle Jimmie on the use of naval power, the foundations were laid for the rise of the American Empire.

Senator Lucius Lamar, former Confederate agent, whom Bulloch contacted regarding the U.S. consul position in Liverpool (U.S. Senate).

While Roosevelt roped cattle and recorded the life of Thomas Hart Benton and American expansion, Bulloch met with an old sea-faring friend from his days in the Coast Survey. Capt. Silas Bent had arrived in Liverpool with his family aboard the steamship *Germanic*. Bulloch told Silas that he had learned of the death of his old shipmate John Newland Maffitt on 15 May 1886 and passed on the details.[51] Both men remembered the audacious and remarkable Maffitt with the admiration born of comradeship. With the loss of Maffitt, none of the great Confederate cruiser captains still lived. Rafael Semmes of the *Alabama* died in August 1877 and James Iredell Waddell of the *Shenandoah* passed into the light of heaven in March 1886.[52] The long, harsh cruises had taken their toll, but their fame was everlasting. Now, only their maestro remained alive: James Dunwoody Bulloch.

On the world stage, the defeat and death of "Chinese" Gordon at the hands of Sudanese rebels in Khartoum reverberated throughout 1885 and contributed to Bismarck's brazen leap into colonialism. German freebooters had coerced East African tribal leaders into signing treaties that offered German protection over an area covering 100,000 square kilometers.[53] The sultan of Zanzibar was outraged when he learned of this land grab. In March 1885, he telegraphed London: Had he not been loyal to Queen Victoria? The Germans were claiming lands that had belonged to his ancestors for generations. The sultan dispatched General Lloyd Mathews to lead a Zanzibar force ashore to the region of Kilimanjaro to stop any further German incursions. British efforts to cultivate the sultan as an ally had included the sale of Bulloch's former commerce raider the CSS *Shenandoah* in 1866 and it became his personal yacht. Renamed the *El Majidi*, she ended her career off the Somali coast during a great storm in 1879.[54]

Lord Salisbury decided that the best way forward was to divide East Africa into spheres of influence, but his Conservative Party was soon ousted from power. This change annulled the agreement as Gladstone once again ascended to office.[55] The Germans were not going to let the Sultan of Zanzibar stand in their way. Consequently, during August and September of 1885, the German ships *Stosch, Gneiseau,* and *Prinz Adalbert* arrived off the sultan of Zanzibar's main headquarters and coerced him into ceding a portion of his realm to German "protection."

In the Dakotas, Roosevelt finished his book after an epic spate of writing in June 1886, saying, "Benton, greatly to the credit of his foresight, and largely in consequence of his strong nationalist feeling, thoroughly appreciated the importance of our geographical extensions ... [Benton] had engrained in his very marrow and fibre the knowledge that inevitably, and beyond all doubt, the coming years were to be hers [America's] ... while other nations held the past, and shared with his own the present, yet that to her belonged the still formless and unshaped future." Roosevelt had laid down the first plank in his view of the United States' leading role on the world stage.[56]

Arriving back in New York in the fall of 1886, Roosevelt found himself dragged into the New York City election as the Republican candidate for mayor. Roosevelt was an enthusiastic but sacrificial lamb to the New York Republican machine. It was all over by the first days of November: Roosevelt finished a respectable third. With politics out of the way, he was free to escape to Europe with sister Bamie to meet up with his "secret" fiancée, Edith Carow.[57]

Sneaking aboard the *Etruria* on 6 November 1886, Theodore and Bamie identified themselves as "Mr. And Mrs. Merrifield." They gave up the ruse after they were under weigh, having mailed Teddy and Edith's engagement and wedding announcements just before boarding the ship. In the days before radiotelegraph, they were safely at sea and beyond the reach of nattering New York society columnists.[58]

Nine days later on November 15th, Theodore Roosevelt and Bamie landed in Liverpool, duly identified as "Miss Roosevelt" and "T. Roosevelt." While crossing the Atlantic, the Roosevelts met a young British diplomat, Cecil Arthur Spring-Rice. He made such a positive impression that by the time they arrived in Liverpool, Roosevelt had asked "Springy" to be best man at his wedding in London.[59]

By sending out wedding announcements before their departure, Roosevelt's friends and family knew they were being married in London. It is likely that Bamie or one of the other family members telegraphed the Bullochs in Liverpool about their impending arrival as well. It is also possible that Roosevelt telegraphed his venerable old uncle to let him in on the secret. Teddy was extraordinarily sensitive about the fact the he was remarrying. If any man could empathize with his situation and keep a secret, it was his Uncle Jimmie.

On 2 December 1886, Teddy Roosevelt and Edith Carow married at St. George's Church in Hanover Square, London. Following the ceremony, the couple emerged from the church into a thick wintry English fog, whereupon they took a carriage and disappeared on their honeymoon. For the next fifteen weeks, the Roosevelts toured England, France, and the sunny climes of Italy. Roosevelt, ever the politician, mixed with intellectuals and members of society, including the Marquess of Salisbury, who also just happened to be the British prime minister.

Their discussions probably included Africa, for on December 4th, the sultan of Zanzibar learned of the Tripartite Commission's unfavorable decision about his lands that Germany had subverted. Whether the sultan liked it or not, he was being dictated to by Europe, as all of Africa would experience by the time the "scramble for Africa" ended.[60]

The newlyweds returned to America on 27 March 1887, again departing from Liverpool aboard the *Etruria*. This time they were clearly identified as Mr. and Mrs. Theodore Roosevelt, "Ranchman." Britain had gotten its first good look at the future president of the United States.[61]

Records of Bulloch and Roosevelt contacts during this period are mute and there are two likely factors. First, Roosevelt's complicated feelings about his second marriage to Edith led to actions that were equally complicated and secretive. Although Bamie stayed with the Bullochs in November, Teddy rushed straight to London to meet up with Edith. There is no evidence that any of the Bullochs were present on December 2nd at their wedding in London. At the conclusion of Roosevelt's European honeymoon, there was no surviving record of their meeting prior to departing from Liverpool. Of the dozens of letters exchanged between the Bulloch's and the Roosevelt's extended families, very few have surfaced.[62]

For the rest of 1887, Edith was consumed with setting up house and addressing the care of "Baby Lee," Roosevelt's daughter by Alice Lee. There was some tension between Bamie and Edith on that subject, since Bamie had been the child's de facto mother. For his part, Teddy focused on reentering the political scene, starting another book (*Gouverneur Morris*), and managing his Dakota ranch. By the end of the year, he considered writing an epic, multi-volume work, to be entitled *The Winning of the West*. Roosevelt wanted to synthesize his views on Manifest Destiny from *Benton* with his experiences in Dakota, and merge them with his European experiences and understanding of U.S. naval matters. He had grand visions of America's strategic future. It would be breathtaking.[63]

Europe took a deep breath of its own in the first days of March 1888. Kaiser Wilhelm I died on March 9th and Crown Prince Frederick took power as Frederick III. Unfortunately, Frederick was afflicted with a misdiagnosed case of throat cancer. His unbearable son, Crown Prince William, could hardly wait for his father to die. Prince William was militant, vain, and enamored with the idea of empire.[64]

While Roosevelt pursued his writing in early 1888, the Bullochs prepared for a wedding of their own. On April 4th, their daughter Jessie Hart married Maxwell (Max) Hyslop Maxwell at St. Agnes Church, Toxteth, Liverpool. Maxwell was a successful merchant in Liverpool with prosperous career and political aspirations. It was a delight for James Dunwoody and Harriott Bulloch to see one of their children safely away from the family nest.[65] James Dunwoody Bulloch, Jr., now 30 years old, was having some success in the insurance business and continued the family's military tradition as a member of a local Liverpool militia troop.[66]

Max and Jessie decided to honeymoon in the U.S. with an itinerary that included visits with Jessie Bulloch's American relatives later that month. Jimmie Bulloch, Jr., accompanied the newlyweds on the SS *Germanic* that arrived on April 21st in New York. Their stops included a visit with Teddy Roosevelt in mid–May and again in late June at Oyster Bay, Long Island. Teddy acknowledged how well suited Jessie and Max were for each other. He scoffed at Jessie's silliness when she panicked at getting lost while walking from the boathouse to her Aunt Anna Bulloch Gracie's home. Unimpressed with Max, he compared his conceit and commonness with Jimmie Junior's more pleasant and manly demeanor. Jimmie left their company to attend to insurance business in Lynchburg, Virginia.[67]

By May 1st, Teddy Roosevelt was head down at his desk at Sagamore Hill, plowing forward on his historical epic, *The Winning of the West*. On 15 June 1888, when Roosevelt returned from his afternoon stroll, he learned that Frederick III had died. World history was now about to charge off into a new and violent direction, for Crown Prince William, titled as Kaiser Wilhelm II, was bent on increasing the German Empire at any cost.[68] Most Americans were focused inwardly. They were filling-in the great empty areas of the West that they had so recently won. News from "over there" was of much less interest and concern. Even Roosevelt, despite his European family and personal connections, attended to domestic issues.[69]

Despite being knocked senseless playing polo in late July and the more personal trauma of his wife Edith's miscarriage ten days later, Teddy Roosevelt headed off to Idaho in August. Soon, even more tragic news flew from America to the Bulloch household in Liverpool. On the 24th of August, their eldest son was violently ill and seven days later, James Dunwoody Bulloch, Jr., aged 30, was dead in Lynchburg, Virginia. The heart-rending news was telegraphed across the ocean to his parents, presumably by his sister Jessie or his Aunt Anna Bulloch Gracie. Due to his remote location, it is unknown when Teddy Roosevelt heard the news. The two young men had been born the same year (1858), in the same city (New York City), played together as boys on the Mersey River bank, and had just reunited in New York. Bulloch had now lost his eldest son, his young mother and father, his first wife, and another young son, Henry. Even in an age without vaccinations and antibiotics when death due to virulent disease was common, it was emotional agony. Teddy Roosevelt and his Uncle Jimmie had an indescribable shared connection. There are, however, no records of the event in the Roosevelt family letters, a testament to careful or perhaps careless preservation of family history.[70]

Roosevelt returned to New York in early October to continue work on *The Winning of the West*; it was due to the publisher by Christmas of 1888. In November, Teddy made a curious reference to an $1800 payment that his sister Bamie had sent to "Uncle Jimmie Bulloch." When Edith told him about Bamie's generosity, he volunteered to pay Bamie half the amount at $100 per year. Although Bulloch had been retired since the early 1880s, he and Harriet had a modest, but comfortable life-style that included two household servants through the early 1890s. Although Bamie's payment might have been related to Jimmie Junior's death in Virginia, it more likely was to help Bulloch cover debts from his failed investments and lack of employment. Bulloch's fanciful notion of becoming the U.S. consul to Liverpool back in 1884 was motivated by a desire to be active as well as his need for money. Bulloch was in the uncomfortable position of having to accept financial support from his American family including his Roosevelt niece and nephew.[71]

In the spring of 1889, Benjamin Harrison assumed the presidency. To Roosevelt's delight, the president, with some ambitious lobbying by Roosevelt's friend Henry Cabot Lodge, offered him a low-paying appointment as a civil service commissioner. Lodge had assumed the low pay would insult Roosevelt, but the ambitious Roosevelt saw it as career opportunity and a chance to undermine politicians like Boss Conkling who had wronged his father.[72]

Out in the Pacific Ocean, German activity in the Samoan archipelago intruded into U.S. celebrations of the presidential inauguration. This time, German imperialism resulted in a naval confrontation between the *Kaiserliche Marine* and the United States Navy. The

Germans, ever keen to establish new naval bases, sent three warships into the area (the *Adler, Olga* and *Eber*) in December 1888. The German squadron opened fire on the village of Apia in the same month, hoping to force Samoan acquiescence to a German naval base. The U.S. countered with three warships of its own, the USS *Trenton, Vandalia* and *Nipsic*. The British sent HMS *Calliope* to monitor the tense standoff and guard British interests. War seemed imminent.[73]

Before the warships confronted each other, Mother Nature intervened with a brutal hand. On 15–16 March 1889, a tremendous typhoon wrecked all of the American and German warships at Apia's harbor with the loss of fifty American and ninety German sailors and marines. Only the HMS *Calliope* escaped disaster. To avoid further loss, all parties decided the negotiating table was the better method to resolve the Samoan question, thus avoiding a premature conflict between Germany, America, and Britain.[74]

By the summer of 1889, Roosevelt was busily investigating U.S. Post Office corruption. It was exciting stuff for a new government officer like Roosevelt, but nothing that would launch him up the ladder of power. In Liverpool, on July 29th, Bulloch wrote to Jefferson Davis to help deflect some unwarranted criticism that Davis had received from General P.T. Beauregard. This criticism would persist into the twentieth century. Beauregard had publicly questioned Davis' failure to accept an opportunity to buy several East India Company ships in early 1861. Bulloch had not been aware of the offer, but he knew the ships very well. His unequivocal assessment was that they were not suitable. Even if the Confederacy had the money to buy them and the crews to man them in 1861 (which they did not), the ships would have been useless as either cruisers or blockade runners.[75]

Only a few days later, British newspapers reported that Kaiser Wilhelm II reviewed German sailors on the "lawn in front of Osborne House" in honor of Queen Victoria and the Prince of Wales. Queen Victoria catered to the young Kaiser's vanity by making him an honorary admiral in the British Navy.[76]

Theodore Roosevelt's tome *The Winning of the West* had become a best-seller in America, and in the fall of 1889, it was released in Britain to critical praise. Roosevelt refined and translated the old dreams of Manifest Destiny for a new age. He wrote of future American imperialism, while in Germany, Kaiser Wilhelm II prepared for the immediate expansion of his empire — the *Reich*.[77]

In December 1889, an era that had lingered on in the nation's consciousness truly began to pass when Jefferson Davis, the Confederate States of America's only president, died. The British press reported the news with pages bordered in black. On December 7th, Bulloch pulled out his best writing paper to express his sympathy to his wife, Varina Davis:

> The first thought that arises in the mind and hearts of the small colony of Southerners in this land of refuge, is one of sympathy with you and the children of him who was the chief figure in the Great War of Secession, and the Chief victim of its failure.... The fact that he was deprived of the political rights restored to every other Southern man who took part in the war, and that he was made to feel in a very literal sense that he had no citizenship in the land of his birth will be a record in the history of this United States.... At some future day an impartial historian will tell the story of those troubling years, 1861 to 65, and Mr. Davis' name will then be found grouped with those who have made great sacrifices for conscience sake, and have devoted every faculty earnestly, faithfully, unselfishly, to their country's service.[78]

Bulloch's empathetic letter was telling on many levels. It revealed that Bulloch, as well as the other Confederates who never returned to America, regarded themselves as exiles in a country of convenience. They might have sworn the queen's oath as loyal subjects, but the lost Confederates recognized the reality of their situation. They would always be the exiled jetsam of a failed country. Like other refugees that had washed upon the shores of British benevolence, they would be taken in, sheltered, and protected. They would work for the empire's good, but they would never be truly British. The other telling comment by Bulloch pertains to U.S. citizenship.

His letter to Varina Davis points out that the U.S. government refused to restore Jefferson Davis's full civil rights. Bulloch knew that *he* could return to the United States as an American citizen if he had chosen to do so. His simple statement highlights a common misperception that Bulloch was never pardoned and could not return to America. When he wrote this letter, Bulloch had made at least four trips to the U.S. after the Civil War. He openly traveled under his own name as a British citizen; he did not need a pardon. President Johnson's final general "Christmas Amnesty" of 1868 made it all a moot point; all, except for Jefferson Davis. Even in 1869, Bulloch feared that President Johnson's pardon might not be enough to protect him from Seward's ruinous legal and financial retribution. The fact that he might be linked to the Lincoln kidnap plot was in his mind as well. Like Davis, Bulloch believed that he had acted honorably and had done nothing wrong. Unlike Davis, who was bound to maintain residence in the United States out of a sense of personal loyalty, Bulloch had no such ties or responsibilities.

By the winter of 1889–1890, Americans were capable of a more charitable view of Jefferson Davis' life. It had been a quarter century since the war's bloody end. Northerners and Southerners both mythologized the horrific contest by. Grand old Yankees thought they had fought the "Noble War" to preserve the Union and free the slaves. Confederate veterans remembered defending their homes against invasion and for an equally noble "Lost Cause" of states' rights. Across America, great veterans' societies met regularly, and oft-times held joint celebrations and reunions to commemorate their great sacrifices. The death of Davis was the passing of the ultimate Southern Spartan; denied honor in life, but granted a small measure of commemoration and sympathy after his death.[79]

As the country looked forward, New Year's Day 1890 was portentous for American history and Teddy Roosevelt. He attended a White House reception and basked in the glow of the power emanating from President Harrison's office. This was the first recorded instance of Roosevelt entering the White House, but it wouldn't be the last. The most significant milestone for America that year, however, was the addition of four new states, North Dakota, South Dakota, Montana, and Washington. Roosevelt's beloved Dakota Territory was now part of the Union, and with the bolting-on of Washington the dreams of earlier Manifest Destiny prophets were being realized.

In Germany, Otto von Bismarck resigned as chancellor in March, leaving Queen Victoria's grandson Kaiser Wilhelm II at the helm of a united German Empire. His primary international goal was to challenge the British Empire at every turn and become her equal.[80]

Between 1890 and 1891, only fleeting references to the Bullochs survive, but it is clear that the Bullochs and Roosevelts remained in frequent contact. In January 1890, Teddy asked sister Bamie to post a letter to Uncle Jimmie Bulloch, since he had misplaced his address. In April of that same year, Bulloch's son-in-law Max Maxwell returned to the U.S. and dined with Teddy and Edith. For Teddy, the experience was reminiscent of Max's previous visit, once again boring Teddy "to extinction."[81]

The Bullochs continued to live in their unpretentious but comfortable home at 30 Sydenham Avenue in the Liverpool suburb of Waterloo. Their 26-year-old daughter Martha Louise was a spinster music teacher, living with her parents. The music lessons must have taken Bulloch back to his days in Connecticut when as a ten-year-old youth he nurtured his own musical talents. The faithful cook Agnes McCormick continued her long years of service to the family. There were fewer mouths to feed and the steady flow of visitors had begun to ebb. Completing the household was a teenage housemaid to assist Harriott, as Bulloch, the "Retired Naval Officer," continued to employ two full-time servants.[82]

During this time, Teddy Roosevelt pursued with all his vigor his role on the Federal Civil Service Commission, while maintaining an acute interest in naval affairs. On 10 and 11 May 1890, he sat down to read a provocative new treatise entitled *The Influence of Sea Power upon History*, by Alfred Thayer Mahan. Captain Mahan was a history professor at the Naval War College in Newport, Rhode Island, who had independently collated Roosevelt's and Bulloch's perspectives. The result was an epiphany, engendering a whole new understanding about the strategic role of sea power. As a specialist on naval history and strategy and a consistent proponent for upgrading the U.S. Navy, Roosevelt was well qualified to grasp the implications of Mahan's thesis.

Mahan argued that sea power was the key element of a great power. The U.S. needed to build many powerful and fast warships and deploy them to the corners of the world's oceans. If the United States concentrated these warships at key choke points, such as the Strait of Gibraltar or Suez Canal, *America* could control the flow of commerce and military forces anywhere in the world. Mahan's exposition used cogent historical examples on the interdependence of America's maritime development and power projection with its political will, economy, geography, and industrial base.[83]

By the time the sun rose on 12 May 1890, Roosevelt was fired with the vision that America must become the world's leading naval power. Bulloch had been his inspiration and Mahan had articulated the vision. Now, all Roosevelt needed to do was attain the right position to be able to act. Roosevelt was not alone in his reading. The admirals of the British Royal Navy, the Japanese Imperial Navy, and Kaiser Wilhelm II's *Kaiserliche Marine* all read Mahan and embraced the imperative to control the world's oceans.[84] The ultimate irony was that each of these fleets had bought one or more of Bulloch's "lost" armored rams several decades earlier, to help launch them into the "modern" warship age. The British had acquired the two Laird rams, the Japanese the CSS *Stonewall* (first named *Kotetsu* and then *Azuma*), and the Germans the *Prinz Adalbert*, one of the French rams.[85]

Before Roosevelt could channel his newfound passion for expanding the U.S. Navy, a family crisis diverted his energies. His brother Elliott had become a serious alcoholic following an accident that left him dependent on painkillers. Elliott fled to Europe with his wife and children and landed in Vienna. From there, his wife, Anna Hall, pleaded with Teddy for help. Teddy immediately made arrangements with sister Bamie for a rescue mission, but before she could travel abroad there was more bad news. One of Elliott's servant girls accused him of infidelity and she was pregnant. Teddy was furious. Bamie would have to confront Elliott about his alcoholism, philandering, and sort out Anna who was also pregnant, and her children, Anna Eleanor and Elliott Junior. Bamie Roosevelt left for Europe in early February 1891, and by the end of the month was in Vienna with Elliott and Anna. Elliott had already surrendered himself into a treatment center in Austria. There is no record of how Teddy or Bamie contacted the Bullochs during this initial crisis response, but Bulloch was well aware of the situation and was prepared to respond when needed.[86]

By June 1891, Bamie found herself up to her ears with Elliott's fiasco. Elliott denied that the servant girl's child was his, but Teddy knew that Elliott was lying. Elliott's doctors and Bamie agreed to let him move to Paris, where Anna delivered their third child, Gracie Hall. Unfortunately, it wasn't long before Elliott again hit the bottle and resumed his physically abusive behavior.

Teddy took it upon himself to resolve the Elliott problem. In August 1891, after Bamie returned to the U.S. with Anna and the children, he applied for a writ of lunacy to take over Elliott's affairs. The nation's press went wild over the story. The rest of the Roosevelt clan was not amused by Teddy's heavy-handed approach or his predictable escape to the American West.[87]

Meanwhile, Britain and Germany were behaving with astonishing quietude considering Kaiser Wilhelm II's previous belligerence. Circumstances had changed so much that in July 1891, Wilhelm II sailed to Britain for a state visit. He even had his portrait painted in his "honorary" Royal Navy admiral's uniform![88]

After returning to the East Coast, Roosevelt rode out the rest of 1891 dealing with Civil Service Commission business and in late December came down with severe bronchitis. By New Year's Day 1892, Teddy was back in fighting form and decided he had to go to Europe and convince Elliott to return home. Eight days later, Teddy Roosevelt sailed for Europe. Upon reaching Paris, he convinced Elliott to sign over control of his finances and property and commit himself to yet another alcoholic asylum in the United States. Teddy remained in the French capital for another seven days with Elliott. He then traveled to Southampton where he boarded the SS *Lahn* on January 27th and arrived in New York City after ten days at sea.[89]

As several Roosevelt biographers have noted, Elliott sailed to New York separately a few days after Teddy's departure. Registered as "E. Roosevelt," Elliott sailed from Liverpool on February 3rd with his eight pieces of luggage aboard the White Star line's SS *Teutonic*. Elliott's departure was fully one week after his brother sailed for New York.

Teddy Roosevelt had just crossed the Atlantic with the intent of rescuing his brother from alcoholism and myriad other physical and mental afflictions. Elliott's scandalous behavior endangered the family's good name and Teddy's own political aspirations. Why would Teddy spend all this time, trouble, and money only to abandon the unreliable Elliott in England and then trust him to cross the ocean alone? The answer is simple, he didn't. Traveling with the troubled Elliott on the SS *Teutonic* was none other than the 68-year-old James Dunwoody Bulloch, registered as "J.D. Bullock." Uncle Jimmie had come to the rescue once again. It was only after Teddy deposited Elliott in Liverpool and entrusted him to the care of Uncle Jimmie that he made his way back to New York. After getting Elliott safely enrolled at the asylum, Bulloch returned to Liverpool by the SS *Britannic* about a month later.[90]

For Roosevelt, the rest of 1892 was filled with Civil Service Commission business and the painful realization that the Republican Party was slowly, but inexorably, losing control of the country. With a presidential election looming in November, this trend did not bode well for his future aspirations. All he could do was turn to his writing and watch fate take its hand, as it did on November 8th when Grover Cleveland was again elected president after one term out of office.

Fate was also at work in Germany on December 1st. That day, Alfred von Tirpitz presented a set of battle plans and strategies to Kaiser Wilhelm II. Tirpitz had routinely clashed with the Secretary of the *Kaiserliche Marine* Admiral von Hollman over their competing visions of the German navy that were evident to the kaiser. Tirpitz wanted battleships and accompanying strategies that were consistent with Mahan's theories of naval power projection. It was a view that revolutionized the German war machine and challenged British naval supremacy.[91]

The year 1892 ended on an even more somber note for the Roosevelts and Bullochs. Elliott Roosevelt's wife, the 29-year-old Anna Hall, died of diphtheria on December 7th. Anna, "one of the most beautiful and popular women in New York society," was also the mother of future first lady Anna Eleanor Roosevelt.[92]

Records of the contacts between the Bullochs and Roosevelts are once again sparse during this period. James Gracie briefly acknowledged a spate of seven condolence letters from the Bulloch clan in late June. His wife (Bulloch's sister), Anna Bulloch Gracie, had died on June 9th.[93] In August 1893, Bulloch also wrote to his niece (Teddy's sister), Corinne Roosevelt Robinson. In one of his few surviving personal letters to a Roosevelt, Bulloch thanked Corinne for remembering to place flowers upon sister Mittie's grave on his behalf. He also updated her about general doings with his own family. Jessie Bulloch Maxwell and her husband, Max, had gone off to a wedding up in Scotland, and Bulloch had shared Corinne's previous letter (of 20 July 1893) with both Irvine and Ella Bulloch. James and Harriott Bulloch were enjoying an Indian summer in their lives.[94]

Bulloch's family connections and influence continued to play a larger than life role in national and international politics. Earlier in 1893, a distant Roosevelt cousin, James "Rosey" Roosevelt, was appointed first secretary to the U.S. embassy in London. Unfortunately, Rosey's wife, Helen Astor, the daughter of one of America's wealthiest men, died on November 12th after a brief illness. Rosey needed someone to act as hostess in London and look after his children, aged 12 and 14. Bamie had been one of Helen's bridesmaids and instantly cabled cousin Rosey to offer her assistance. Bamie soon found herself on the SS *Lucania* sailing for England via Liverpool, and arrived on December 16th.[95] It would be in London that the physically handicapped but vivacious spinster would meet and marry the American embassy's dashing naval attaché, William Sheffield Cowles. The familial connection between the Bullochs, Roosevelts, and Bamie's rising naval officer suitor were too strong for anything but frequent and friendly contact.

In another political surprise, the Democratic regime of President Cleveland retained the staunch Republican Roosevelt in his Civil Service Commission position. Seeing no particular political threat from the bombastic New Yorker, Teddy was allowed to continue beavering away non-stop at his position throughout early 1893. Happy to have a steady job, Roosevelt concentrated on developing his vision of Americanism. Applying the influence of Uncle Jimmie and the writings of Mahan, he began to advocate his own version of Manifest Destiny. With President Cleveland's recognition of the Republic of Hawaii in the summer of 1894, Roosevelt saw an urgent need for America to build a naval base there. It also needed to build a first class U.S. Navy.

Another critical need was a U.S.-owned canal across Central America that could control the transit of merchant and naval warships to and from the Atlantic and Pacific Oceans. It was a dream that Thomas Butler King, John Slidell, Judah P. Benjamin, and James Dunwoody Bulloch had actively championed. Most internationalists and naval experts trumpeted the obvious need, or better yet, the right, for American expansion. Roosevelt was carrying the banner for Manifest Destiny now bolstered by an ambitious vision of the U.S. Navy as the nation's principal means of power projection.

Just as Uncle Jimmie remained relevant for the future of the U.S. Navy, he would make a vital contribution to the documented history of the American Civil War. Obviously impressed with the extensive correspondence contained within his memoirs, the U.S. Navy History Department's editorial staff announced in the *New York Times* that they had contacted Bulloch about his archives. They wanted to include any papers Bulloch would care to share in the *Official Records of the Union and Confederate Navies in the War of the Rebellion*, as the 30-volume work would be called. The initiator of the project was Professor James R. Soley, a former U.S. Naval Academy lecturer, librarian of the U.S. Navy, and Harvard contemporary of Teddy Roosevelt. Since most of the Confederate Navy Department letters were destroyed, Bulloch's status in the firmament of naval history had risen even higher. His letters would comprise most of one volume and significant parts of several others.[96]

Naval matters in the present tense, however, were of more immediate concern in Britain and Germany, largely due to Africa (again). The discovery of vast gold deposits a few miles south of Johannesburg in 1886 unleashed economic and demographic chaos on the quasi-independent Boer Republic. The conduct of the invading foreign miners outraged the pious Boers who attempted to control the situation by increasing the residency requirement for citizenship. This imposition inflamed the mostly British, American, and German *uitlanders* (outsiders).[97]

German businesses and subtle official German exchanges with Kruger's Boer government added to the unease. In response, the British government deployed additional Royal Navy assets to South Africa to counter possible incursions of the *Kaiserliche Marine* that were flying the sinister "black eagle" ensign. The British Empire, primarily through Cecil Rhodes (who founded the diamond company De Beers and named the country of Rhodesia after himself), was keen to gain control of the Boer gold, even if it meant the destruction of the Boer Republic. The amount of gold pouring out of the "Rand" could more than pay for the expense of a war and was worth protecting.[98]

In the same month that the Republic of Hawaii was welcomed into the warm embrace of Uncle Sam, the Greek tragedy that never seemed to end for the Roosevelt family struck again. Elliott Roosevelt was suffering from effects of a drunken-binge-induced carriage wreck and his own internal demons. On August 14th, he tried to commit suicide by leaping from a window and died in a convulsive seizure. Teddy Roosevelt knew of his brother's severe depression and erratic behavior, but did not visit him in New York because he knew that Elliott would rebuff him. Guilt-ridden, Teddy raced north from his Washington office. The sight of Elliott, serenely looking like his old self in death, haunted Roosevelt. After seeing to his funeral, Roosevelt predictably headed west, but this time the escape did not have its normal calming effect and he soon returned to Oyster Bay.[99]

Soon after Elliott's death, Bulloch wrote to his sister Corinne that Bamie Roosevelt had been in Liverpool. She stayed with her cousin Jessie Bulloch Maxwell for several days before departing on September 5th aboard the *Teutonic*. Bamie took the news of her brother's death especially hard. Her absence at his funeral was doubly difficult. Trying to comfort Corinne, Bulloch noted that Mittie had often remarked what a wonderful little boy Elliott had been. Bulloch had missed seeing him during his short trip to New York almost 13 years ago, as Elliott was in India on a hunting trip. After seeing him as a pathetic drunk just two years previously, he preferred to remember his nephew as a little boy.[100]

By the end of 1894, Teddy Roosevelt again considered running for mayor of New York City. Largely due to his wife Edith's objection to the thought of leaving Washington, he regretfully declined the opportunity. Misreading his motivations, the new mayor offered him a better paying job as city street cleaning commissioner. Roosevelt had no interest or inclination to accept the job. He decided to spend one more year on the Federal Civil Service Commission and then consider his next move.[101]

In February 1895, Cuba was in the news again. The Cubans had risen up against their Spanish masters and were fighting for freedom. Arguments raged in Washington about what America should do: invade or support the Cuban revolutionaries? Roosevelt, not wanting to be left out of any shooting match, sent a desperate request to the governor of New York for an officer's commission in any regiment that might fight in a war with Spain. Teddy did not want to sit on the sidelines as his father had done in the American Civil War.[102]

By May 1895, the opportunity that Teddy Roosevelt had been awaiting presented itself. He resigned his position with Federal Civil Service Commission to take on the rambunctious position of New York police commissioner. There he would remain, cleaning up the politically corrupt police department throughout 1895 and into 1896. British newspapers filed favorable reports on the American political dynamo at work in New York City. American newspapers pondered whether Roosevelt should run for president.[103]

Roosevelt, however, wasn't ready for a presidential run — yet. He needed to work his way through the New York Republican Party system first. That would be a problem; his party suffered a resounding defeat in the November 1895 elections. The results so infuriated Roosevelt that he penned a letter to a long-time friend General James Harrison Wilson, a former Civil War hero, and vented his anger. Teddy laid out his vision for America if he were president. He'd throw the Spanish out of Cuba, go to war with Britain, and seize Canada. For good measure, he would take control of the Orinoco River in Venezuela before British tentacles could embrace more of South America.

The spirits of Jefferson Davis, Judah P. Benjamin, and Thomas Butler King must have been shaking their heads, wondering why there had been a Civil War at all. Here was a Republican hell-bent on American dominance. One of the men who had been involved in American attempts at expansion into Central and South America was still alive and well: Roosevelt's uncle, James Dunwoody Bulloch. Bulloch had made a filibustering run into Nicaragua, was at the center of in the *Black Warrior* affair in Havana, and had naval and commercial experience in South America with the benighted Brazilian, Baron de Mauá. Roosevelt had access to specific intelligence from the man who had literally been there.[104]

The world's leaders would learn many sobering lessons about empire-building like the one taught in South Africa. Cecil Rhodes' mercenary leader Dr. Leander Jameson attacked the Boer Republic and managed to get within 14 miles of Johannesburg by 2 January 1896. The mercenaries were quickly surrounded by an ever-increasing mass of Boer irregulars. Jameson surrendered and was sent to England for trial. Kaiser Wilhelm II, sensing an opportunity, prepared to declare war if the British government pronounced their support for Jameson's action.

Despite British assurances and apologies, the Kaiser would not let the matter go away quietly. On 4 January 1896, he telegraphed the Boer president, Peter Krueger, to congratulate the feisty Boers and offer full support to the Transvaal Republic. British outrage over the "Kruger Telegram" was such that the Royal Navy ordered a "flying squadron" to South Africa. It was only after Queen Victoria dampened British rhetoric and admonished her grandson that the kaiser explained that he was merely standing up for the principles of law and order. With that, German and British diplomacy returned to its tentative, but peaceful *status quo*.[105]

Predictably, Roosevelt spent much of 1896 struggling with his own New York Republican Party. For a city police commissioner, his letters and speeches had a decidedly international outlook. He complained about President Grover Cleveland's spineless approach to the Cuban rebellion and the British Guyana boundary dispute with Venezuela. He argued that America should just kick Spain out of Cuba and do the same with the British in South America.

In addition to Venezuela, the British Empire remained embroiled with the French and Germans in Africa. Naval power was a key element for all of the great powers in these remote locations. Having a colony was not the same as keeping it. For that, they needed a naval force able to defend, or attack, whenever required.[106] The contretemps in South Africa had convinced Britain that the Germans, under Kaiser Wilhelm II, had replaced France as their most sinister threat. The Germans believed that they had a right to expand anywhere they wished, but to exercise this right, the Germans needed a powerful navy.

The now elderly Bulloch retained a front row seat to these naval maneuvers as more than an interested bystander. His niece Bamie Roosevelt had married William Cowles in November 1895, and they brought the commander into their family circle. In early May 1896, Teddy wrote Bamie in London, telling her about dining with Mahan and discussing the navy's battleships and the "Transvael fiasco." He also humorously related how surprised Uncle Jimmie had been during his recent visit with Bamie and Commander Cowles in London. Bulloch was amazed at the "intelligent interest" Bamie took in her naval attaché husband's pursuits. These "pursuits" would have included both the problems in South Africa as well as Bulloch's informed insight about British-American equities in South America.[107]

Roosevelt's political situation would change on 3 November 1896 when William McKinley, a Republican, became President. Roosevelt's party was back in power. He had campaigned vigorously for McKinley and hoped for an appointment in his administration. What he dearly wished for was to be the assistant secretary of the navy. Teddy had been preparing for this appointment since the summer of 1896. While on vacation at Oyster Bay, he consumed a veritable library on current naval affairs.[108] Then in early 1897, Roosevelt worked on a revised edition of *The Naval War of 1812*. Sir William Laird Clowes of the London *Times* and editor of the Royal Navy's official history had requested the update. Teddy was a guest speaker at the U.S. Naval Academy and he had frequent conversations with Alfred Thayer Mahan who was now a regular dinner guest at Roosevelt's home at Sagamore Hill. The New York City police commissioner was well prepared to become the assistant secretary of the navy.[109]

Roosevelt's able friend Senator Henry Cabot Lodge campaigned relentlessly for Roosevelt's appointment. However, Roosevelt's outspoken views on what America "should do" about foreign policy made McKinley nervous. The man actually advocated war to deal with Cuba and Spain. Two factors worked in Roosevelt's favor for this coveted position. The New York Republican Party believed he would be less of a nuisance if he were in Washington and Roosevelt assured Secretary of the Navy John D. Long that he would adhere to any and all of President McKinley policies. Finally, on 6 April 1897, Theodore Roosevelt was sworn in as Assistant Secretary of the Navy Roosevelt.[110]

When Roosevelt first sat down at his Navy Department desk on April 19th, he was like a child at Christmas whose every wish had been fulfilled. Teddy spoke frequently of James Dunwoody Bulloch, his very favorite uncle, promoting him to "admiral" in his stories. He touted Bulloch's exploits in the Confederate Navy, from building the *Alabama* to running the blockade in the *Fingal*. Roosevelt did not forget his mother Mittie's role in his love of the navy either. She regaled him with story after story about blockade runners, warships, and his heroic uncles. All this had helped motivate him to write *The Naval War of 1812* and become America's greatest proponent of naval power.

To his office he added "props" that would visibly demonstrate to visitors that he understood where the U.S. Navy had come from and where it was going. He dragged the old desk of Gustavus Fox, his predecessor under Gideon Welles during the Civil War, from storage and moved it into his new office. Roosevelt was delighted that the desk had ironclad monitors carved into its sides. The beginning of the modern United Stated Navy was instigated, at least in part, by an unreconstructed Confederate secret agent named James Dunwoody Bulloch and his sister's motherly urgings to an impressionable, energetic, and determined young man.[111]

The delightful news of Roosevelt's appointment as the assistant secretary of the navy must have made Bulloch's shirt buttons pop off. *His* nephew was the number two man in the U.S. Navy Department. To be recognized as one of his greatest influences was a gratifying honor. Poignantly, Harriott Bulloch, Roosevelt's vivacious old aunt in the mold of his mother Mittie, would learn of Teddy's success just two months before she succumbed to a stomach ailment.

On 3 July 1897, Harriott Cross Bulloch, the blonde Southern belle who had mended James Dunwoody Bulloch's heart and woven a life with him under all conditions, died at No. 30 Sydenham Avenue, Liverpool.[112] The 68-year-old Harriott and James had lived in their home in the Toxteth District since 1886. Bulloch sailed on alone now. At least his daughter Jessie Bulloch Maxwell remained in Liverpool with her husband Max. Martha Louise remained unmarried and lived with the family in Liverpool. Stuart Elliott Bulloch, his sole remaining son, also lived in Liverpool. Teddy Roosevelt wrote Bamie shortly afterwards agreeing with her arrangements in support of "dear old Uncle Jimmie." Bamie then returned to the U.S. and convinced her brother to arrange the transfer of her husband, Commander Will Cowles, from an antiquated gunboat to a more capable cruiser, the USS *Topeka*.[113]

Roosevelt meekly kept his promise not to rock Secretary of the Navy Long's boat, at least in public. Off the record and off hours, Roosevelt was busy meeting and eating at the Metropolitan Club with a universe of politicians, naval officers, intellectuals, businessmen, and all their hangers-on. Roosevelt was in the center of a bubbling cauldron of American imperialism. All of the personalities at the Metropolitan Club believed that Manifest Destiny's time had come: America should take Hawaii outright, seize Cuba, and ensure that America ruled supreme over the Western Hemisphere. The synergy of American business, technology, and politics that Mahan had postulated was firing Roosevelt's imagination.[114]

In a June 1897 speech at the U.S. Naval War College in Rhode Island, Roosevelt raised the roof when he called for a dramatic boost in shipbuilding. He cited the need for newer and bigger Navy warships. He pointed to the Japanese, British, Germans, and Spanish who were in an all-out naval arms race. By comparison, America's Navy was far behind. The U.S. could not rely on another 90-day industrial miracle like the one wrought by Ericsson during the Civil War. Modern warfare and weapon systems required advance preparation. The alternative was destruction or irrelevance. Roosevelt's speech recognized the lessons he had learned from Bulloch and the Confederate Navy. The Confederate Navy had projected naval power around the world, but lacked overseas ports and repair facilities to support continuous operations. The modern U.S. Navy needed to apply these lessons using Mahan's strategies to build fast, powerful warships augmented by overseas naval bases capable of projecting and supporting this new naval power. Roosevelt's speech was reprinted all across America and Great Britain. Bulloch read with his own eyes what his precocious nephew advocated within the U.S. Navy.[115]

Roosevelt was doing more than just talk. Shortly after his arrival at the Navy Department, Roosevelt asked Captain Caspar Goodrich for a new set of war plans to address Japanese threats against Hawaii and destroy any Spanish fleet that might interfere with an American invasion of Cuba. Before June was out, President McKinley annexed Hawaii, under strong pressure from pro-Manifest Destiny politicians such as Roosevelt's friend and patron Senator Henry Cabot Lodge.[116]

When rebellion broke out in Cuba on 11 January 1898, Roosevelt was delighted, thinking it would immediately lead to war. He telegrammed the adjutant general of New York's National Guard reminding him of his previous application for an officer's commission. At the same time, Roosevelt remonstrated that the U.S. Navy was headed for war — unprepared! Commodore George Dewey, who commanded the U.S. Asiatic Fleet through Roosevelt's personal intervention, had sufficient forces to deal with the Spanish, but the U.S. naval forces in the Atlantic were scattered. Roosevelt wanted the fleet concentrated and ready to speed across the Atlantic and attack Spain directly.[117]

Roosevelt's agitation stirred the McKinley administration, for Roosevelt's boss, Secretary of the Navy Long, sent the North Atlantic Squadron to Key West to refuel and standby for orders. Long also sent the USS *Maine* to Havana where it could provide sanctuary for any American citizens trying to escape the disorder spreading across Cuba.

The *Maine* arrived in Havana Harbor on 25 January 1898, and on 15 February 1898 at about 9:40 P.M., the ship exploded. News of the catastrophe reached Washington that night. Captain Sigsbee, commander of the *Maine*, reported massive loss of life and shocked survivors. By the next day, the headlines screamed "THE MAINE BLOWN UP" followed by "SPANISH TREACHERY" and similar staples of yellow journalism that were guaranteed to inflame patriotic passions. At least 254 U.S. sailors and marines were killed outright and another eight would die of their wounds. William Hearst, the newspaper publisher, knew what had happened; the Spanish had used an explosive device to destroy the ship. Hearst also uttered his famous quote that was more than an observation. It was a demand: "This means war."[118]

The U.S. Navy convened a board to investigate the explosion, but Roosevelt was also convinced of Spanish perfidy. When Secretary of the Navy Long went home early on February 25th, feeling ill, Roosevelt was left as acting Secretary of the Navy. And act he did. He ordered Commodore Dewey to sail the Asiatic Squadron to Hong Kong and block any movement by the Spanish Pacific Fleet. And one more thing: prepare to attack the Philippines. When Secretary Long returned the next day, he found that Roosevelt had sent the U.S. Navy, and the United States of America after it, to war. There was little or nothing he could do. Bulloch's nephew was acting on his long ago musings about what a well-coordinated, fast moving naval force might achieve. Roosevelt blended those ideas with Mahan's theory of naval warfare to create the new American geo-political strategy. All that remained was to give it a try.

Theodore Roosevelt dramatically increased the strength of the U.S. Navy as president, to project the nation's global power (U.S. National Archives).

Roosevelt knew that Spain was preparing for war and buying up available ships. In a direct and unabashed adaptation of Bulloch's tactics thirty-five years earlier, Roosevelt began to buy merchant ships for conversion into commerce raiding cruisers. He specified that the ships were to be delivered to a precise location within an agreed time. It was the *Florida*, *Alabama*, and *Shenandoah* all over again. Bulloch had been the master of this kind of off-the-shelf naval warfare and had taught his nephew well.

Throughout March, the nation awaited the outcome of the *Maine* investigation. The verdict came on 28 March 1898. An underwater mine sank the *Maine*. On 19 April 1898, the U.S. Congress voted to deliver Cuba from Spain and with that, America went to war. Two days earlier, the German *Reichstag* approved Admiral Tirpitz's "Navy Bill" which funded a modern armada of over 16 battleships and laid the groundwork for a future, global war.[119]

On the same day that Congress voted to support Cuban independence, Roosevelt resigned his position with the Navy and joined the Army. Secretary of War Russell Alger needed three regiments of experienced frontiersmen, such as cowboys and trappers who knew how to shoot and ride horses. Roosevelt, rancher and polo pony cowboy, seemed ideally qualified and Secretary Alger offered Roosevelt command of one of these regiments four days after he joined the volunteers. Roosevelt wisely declined command, but eagerly accepted the position of second in command of the First United States Volunteer Calvary, better known as the Rough Riders.[120]

A few days later, on May 1st, the results of Roosevelt and Mahan's new naval strategy

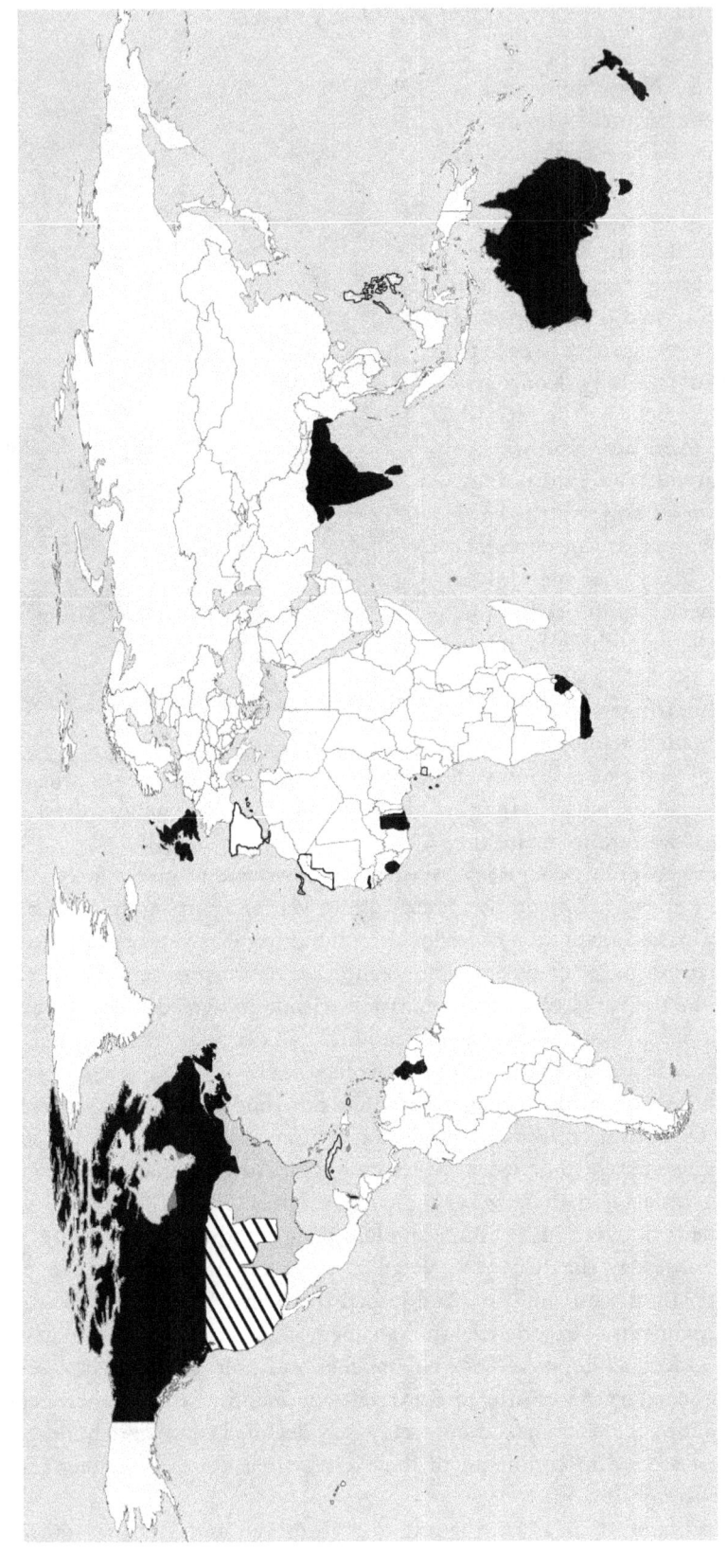

for America were in: Commodore Dewey and the U.S. Asiatic Fleet not only defeated, but virtually annihilated the Spanish Asiatic Squadron at Manila Bay.[121] European naval powers were astonished, none more so than the Spanish obviously, but also the British Royal Navy. There was a new imperial power, the United States of America.[122]

By mid-May, Lieutenant Colonel Roosevelt was on his way to San Antonio, Texas, where he and his Rough Riders would be transformed into a military fighting force. The unit remained in San Antonio until May 29th when they shipped out to Tampa, Florida, by train. The journey through the old Confederacy was reminiscent of Bulloch's train ride from Montgomery in 1861. Roosevelt was finally going to war. He had heard his mother's and Uncle Jimmie's stories, but now he would test his own mettle under fire. By June 23rd, the Rough Riders woke up to their first morning roll call on foreign soil.[123]

By the end of June 1898, Roosevelt and his men had experienced combat and learned to deal with the heat and the even more deadly mosquitoes. On July 1st, he fought the single battle that gave Roosevelt his lasting military fame. The Battle of San Juan Hill began with an attack against Kettle Hill, a smaller elevation on the heights leading to the 125-foot San Juan Hill. Roosevelt and his men crawled through brush and heavy suppressing fire to capture their first objective. From his vantage point, Roosevelt could see that the American unit attacking San Juan Hill was struggling to advance up the steep slopes. Ordering his men to fire onto San Juan Hill, Roosevelt's men then rushed down from Kettle Hill and up San Juan Hill where they routed the Spanish. The Americans were now looking down on Santiago, Cuba. The Rough Riders soon joined other American forces to lay siege around Santiago and Teddy was promoted to colonel of the regiment. The Rough Riders remained at Santiago until July 18th, when they were withdrawn due to rampant yellow fever.

Four days earlier, Roosevelt's other heroic uncle, Irvine Stephens Bulloch, died of Bright's disease and a cerebral hemorrhage in Selby Town, Wales. He had been a splendid officer with near-legendary navigational skills. With his brother's support, Irvine served aboard Semmes' *Alabama* and Waddell's *Shenandoah*. No American sailor surpassed his service afloat during the American Civil War. In life, Irvine had always followed in Brother Jimmie's personal and professional footsteps. In death, he painfully reduced Bulloch's circle of nearby family and friends from his antebellum days of peace and prosperity. John Low, his stalwart companion since Savannah, was among the few who remained.[124]

The welcome news of Roosevelt's safety and daring exploits were in the European newspapers. Though it would require over 100 years before Teddy was posthumously awarded the Medal of Honor, his men adored him as a true leader and the American public was enamored as well.[125]

On 15 August 1898, the exhausted and yellow-fever-ravaged Rough Riders returned to New York. Roosevelt had encouraged this redeployment through a critical letter that leaked to the press. The return of Roosevelt as a war hero made him the Republican Party's overwhelming choice as their candidate for governor of New York. Whether the party liked or agreed with him or not; the people wanted it and he easily won the Albany State House in November.[126]

Opposite page: The 19th Century Empires in Flux: The rise of the British (black), decline of the Spanish (bold black outline), and the American Republic ascending (gray, and white with black stripes) (G.L. McKay).

By the middle of 1899, Teddy was so popular that Henry Cabot Lodge suggested that he might be a vice presidential candidate. While Roosevelt pondered the issue for several months, international issues intruded upon American headlines. On 11 October 1899, war broke out between the British Cape Colony and the Boer republics of Transvaal along with the Orange Free State. The influx of *uitlanders* into the Boer Republics, the failed negotiations between London and Pretoria, coupled with continuing German interference, had finally combusted into war.[127]

For the elderly James Dunwoody Bulloch, the Boer War took on particular interest. His sole remaining son, Stuart Elliot Bulloch, was a member of the 2nd Life Guards of the British Army. Renowned as the senior regiment of the entire British Army, membership was a prestigious accolade.[128] As Germany, America, and Britain were dividing up Samoa, the Boers and the British fought a ruthlessly brutal war in South Africa. For Roosevelt, time and destiny had finally arrived. On June 19th, Teddy Roosevelt was nominated as the Republican candidate for vice president of the United States of America, with incumbent President William McKinley as his running mate. On November 6th, McKinley and Roosevelt won a landslide victory over the Democratic Party ticket, headed by William Jennings Bryan.[129]

British newspapers marveled and fretted at Roosevelt's meteoric rise. Here was a fighting president who knew what he wanted and how to get it. Clearly, the British Empire would have to pursue a policy of engagement. Its "splendid isolation" was being destroyed by the rise of "new imperialism": Germany in Europe, America in the Western Hemisphere, and Japan in the Far East. All wanted control of important spheres of influence without interference; it was a changed world. As for James Dunwoody Bulloch, he was delighted with the achievements of his favorite nephew. Bulloch had been one of the people that Teddy had credited with influencing him most. Yet, Bulloch would never see Roosevelt sworn in as vice president or become president just six months later on 14 September 1901 after McKinley was assassinated.

Bulloch had been diagnosed with cancer. At the end of the first week of January 1901, James Dunwoody Bulloch suffered cardiac arrest and died at No. 76 Canning Street. He had been staying at the home of his daughter and son-in-law, Jessie and "Max" Maxwell. James Dunwoody Bulloch, "a man of amiable character and engaging manners," was 77 years old.[130] He was buried in the Toxteth Park Cemetery, Liverpool, under a tombstone that reads "American by Birth, Englishman by Choice."

15

From Splendid Isolation

The eminent historian Philip Van Doren Stern argued that only Robert E. Lee was the equal of James Dunwoody Bulloch for his contributions to the Confederacy, particularly during its final two years.[1] Every serious treatment of American Civil War foreign policy, intelligence operations, blockade running, commerce raiders, ironclads, and naval strategy has recognized Bulloch's energetic and creative contributions. Despite these accolades, many historians chide Stern for this "enthusiastic" assessment of Bulloch's importance. These authorities tend to narrowly focus on those efforts that failed to reach the Confederacy or his successes that were not sufficient to secure victory.

If ultimate victory is the standard of individual success, every Confederate action must be considered a failure. A more accurate assessment is that despite the military successes of Lee and Bulloch, they could not save a flawed and under-resourced ideal. While not perfect, Bulloch's plans and projects were all hugely successful both in concept and in execution. In less than four years, Bulloch was directly, and sometimes solely, responsible for acquiring or leasing a staggering total of 49 cruisers, blockade runners, tenders, gunboats, and ironclads. His blockade runners carried tons of vital military supplies to the Confederate Army and Navy between 1863 and 1865. Bulloch also materially assisted the Confederate Navy and his fellow overseas agents with an 71 additional logistic vessels.

COMMERCE RAIDERS

Military historians have rightfully focused their attentions on Bulloch's commerce raiders. His raiders caused immediate and irrevocable harm to the U.S. merchant marine. Each one of his three commerce-raiding cruisers, CSS *Florida*, *Alabama*, and *Shenandoah*, did more actual damage than all the other Confederate cruisers combined. These three ships were responsible for sinking 130 of the 179 Union ships that Confederate cruisers destroyed during the Civil War. Together, they struck devastating and permanent blows against Union maritime commerce and its whaling fleet. They also strengthened the international legitimacy of the Confederacy and diverted U.S. Navy resources.

Bulloch had total responsibility for every aspect of the three commerce raiders from initial financing, outfitting, manning, and deployment, to the plans for cruising and resupply. He also designed and supervised the construction of the *Florida* and *Alabama*. He achieved all of this with virtually no staff in a hostile legal, political, and military environ-

Union-agent drawing of a Laird ram (U.S. Naval Historical Center).

ment where any misstep or delay would have resulted in failure. When each of the three ships returned to European ports, it was Bulloch who was there to meet them, pay the crews, tend to the dead, wounded, and their families, and fend off legal and diplomatic attacks.

Even Bulloch's Union adversaries were awestruck at his ingenuity and capacity to outwit them at every turn. And yet, while commerce raiding garnered headlines and inflamed the passions of diplomats, politicians, and shipping moguls, Bulloch himself recognized that it was not a war-winning strategy. As World War II general Omar Bradley famously observed, "Amateurs study strategy, professionals study logistics."

LOGISTICS AND BLOCKADE RUNNING

Bulloch's development of global logistical support for his commerce-raiding cruisers is a commonly overlooked factor in their success. He leased or purchased seven different multi-function tenders that supplied his warships after they had safely made it to sea. Unable to obtain sufficient fuel or war materials in neutral ports, Bulloch overcame this shortfall through an early version of underway replenishment that modern navies perfected in the latter half of the twentieth century. An example is the *Agrippina*, the CSS *Alabama's* unsung consort, that enabled operations from the British Isles to the Western Caribbean and South China Seas, and every ocean in between.

However, it was in the field of blockade-running logistics where Bulloch achieved his greatest and most often overlooked success. Early in the war (1861) as the de facto captain of the *Fingal*, he demonstrated the effectiveness of carrying military goods through the blockade in government-owned blockade runners. In 1863, the Confederate leadership finally agreed to his urgent recommendation to take control of the profitable blockade-running business. Almost overnight, the Confederacy had ample credit and cash in its overseas accounts and more shipbuilding orders than the British shipyards could handle. During these desperate days of the Confederacy, Bulloch was directly responsible for getting 19 blockade runners to sea. Fifteen of these made a total of at least 64 successful runs though the blockade. When the war ended, he had another six ships under construction. Bulloch also directly participated with other Confederate agents in the contracting, manning, or inspection of 35 other logistics vessels that made another 75 blockade runs. He assisted with yet another 31 privately owned ships that carried government-contracted goods.[2]

These achievements are even more remarkable when his warship construction efforts are added to the mix. During the last two years of the war, he completed four additional gunboats and had five more under construction. All of these vessels were built as unarmed but strongly reinforced merchant ships intended to run the blockade and then be reconfigured into warships. Lest there be any doubt about their suitability as warships, all nine of these gunboat/blockade runners were taken into foreign navies after the war (Turkey, Greece, Brazil, and Argentina) and had average active life spans of over 25 years.[3]

IRONCLADS

Most historians view Bulloch's ironclad rams as failures since they did not participate in combat. They were, however, his finest shipbuilding innovations. Contemporary Union officials believed that his two Laird ironclads had to be stopped, even at the risk of war with Great Britain. In actuality, the more capable ironclads were under construction in France along with a flotilla of four supporting corvettes.

The French rams, known as *Cheops* and *Sphinx*, were advanced designs with innovative turreted guns. Their twin screw propellers and rudders allowed them to turn within their own lengths and they had the ability to countersink to reduce their silhouette during combat. The transformation of the *Sphinx* into CSS *Stonewall* represents Bulloch's most brilliant achievement in terms of political, financial, and legal guile, with a dash of sheer audacity. It was the first vessel of its kind to transit the open ocean, a feat that some thought impossible, and was accomplished in mid-winter. Even as the Confederate nation breathed its last, the unchallenged *Stonewall* was poised to rain death and destruction at any place of its choosing. The impact of the *Stonewall* on American history if the Civil War had not ended will be a perpetual "what if."

Although some historians have dismissed Bulloch's four ocean-going ironclads as overrated, each ship achieved varying degrees of success in peace and war. After the British government seized the much-feared Laird rams, they became the Royal Navy's *Scorpion* and *Wivern*. The *Scorpion* would outlive Bulloch, remaining active with Bermuda's harbor defense force until it was sunk, raised, and lost in 1901 and 1903. After the war, the Royal Navy dispatched the *Wivern* to Hong Kong where it outlived Teddy Roosevelt, remaining on active service until 1922! All four of Bulloch's French corvettes that were to have supported the ironclads served as effective warships after the war. They ended up in the Prussian (*Augusta* until 1885 and *Victoria* until 1891) and Peruvian Navies (*America*, lost during an 1868 tsunami, and *Union*, scuttled to avoid capture in 1871).[4]

By the time the *Stonewall* arrived in North America, it was the Confederate nation that had failed, but not Bulloch's effort or ingenuity. After the war, the ironclad became the Japanese Imperial Fleet's most powerful warship and defeated a rebel force of English and Prussian-built ships in 1869 at the Battle of Hakodate Bay. The *Stonewall's* sister ship (*Cheops/Prinz Adalbert*) served in the Prussian and German navies until 1871, when it was discovered that (as Bulloch suspected) her French timbers were rotten. The nascent German navy was able to apply lessons learned from this advanced armored vessel and began a remarkable naval development program. That program yielded similar armored cruisers that became more powerful versions of Bulloch's commerce raiders.

INTELLIGENCE OPERATIONS

As documented in this account of his life, James Dunwoody Bulloch's shipbuilding activities are broadly known. However, the intelligence aspects of his career are more opaque. As a secret agent, he used codes and ciphers, surrogate "cut outs," informers, spies, spotters, the latest technologies, code names, and disguises. He confided in very few, and then only based on their "need-to-know." Despite the prominent place that the CIA gives to Bulloch, and other accounts of his covert action in the Civil War, the full story of Bulloch's intelligence activities remains untold.

Most published accounts address his ability to stay one step ahead of the army of Union spies and informers.[5] There is ample evidence in official documents that these well-paid and unsavory adversaries collected and fabricated intelligence about his ship acquisition programs. The U.S. Navy reported that Bulloch contributed 120 of these documents to the compilation of the *Official Records of the Navy* (ORN).[6] However, there are a total of 345 letters in the ORN that he either wrote or received (193 authored letters and 152 received). They are spread over five different volumes of the ORN, but most are in the volume that focuses on his overseas operations (Series II, volume 2). Bulloch's memoirs cite 87 letters that also appeared in the ORN, but he cites another 21 that are unique to the memoirs and not contained in the official records. (Bulloch authored 4 of them and the other 17 were received from Barron [2], R.R. Carter [2], Davidson [2], Waddell [1], Maffitt [1], Mallory [1], Mason [1], McRae [1], Murdaugh [1], Page [3], and Semmes [2].)

The published letters say very little about his intelligence operations other than those activities related to shipbuilding that were exposed during the *Alabama* Claims proceedings. Unfortunately, the 21 letters cited in his memoirs and other sensitive documents that Teddy Roosevelt helped organize after the war have never been discovered and were most likely burned.[7] This sad fact leaves us with only a hint of Bulloch's other intelligence operations. With the few letters and commentaries from other available sources we know that he proactively fed false information to Union spies and British government officials. Bulloch's memoirs remain a time-tested and accurate source, but he sometimes misled the reader by omitting key facts. He told the truth, but not the whole truth.

Bulloch carefully protected his sources and did not share or mention compromising correspondence in his memoirs. The source of his information from the British Foreign Office about the *Alabama* remains a mystery and he only broached the subject because it was already in public view. Based on a careful analysis of his statements and actions, it's clear that this source remained active at least through 1864. As an example of redacted correspondence, he made no mention of his regular interactions with the Confederate propagandist and agent Henry Hotze or contacts with the famous Confederate spy Rose Greenhow in his memoirs. He also withheld all of his correspondence to, or from, these and other Confederate secret agents from the official records. It's clear that Bulloch maintained a regular correspondence with Hotze to help manipulate people and events to his benefit. He also used Hotze and his London offices as a conduit for his covert communications and avoided any mention of his meetings with Rose Greenhow. Her recently discovered diary confirms that she met with Bulloch on multiple occasions in London and Paris prior to her fatal return to the South on Bulloch's ill-fated blockade runner, the *Condor*.

Given his location in Great Britain, Bulloch was also the financier of covert Confederate naval operations within the British Empire. This aspect of his intelligence operations seems to have eluded the many analysts and historians who have

Emperor Meiji, who allied Japan with the British Empire against Russia, acquired Bulloch's CSS *Stonewall* that was victorious in the Battle of Hakodate (U.S. Naval Historical Center).

studied the Canadian elements of the conspiracy to assassinate President Lincoln. In late 1864, Secretary Mallory ordered Bulloch to write a check drawn on "secret funds" to Patrick Martin, a Confederate blockade runner operating from Canada. At the time, these funds supported the plot to kidnap Abraham Lincoln. Martin's project later morphed into the successful assassination plot. Fortunately for Bulloch, Captain Martin went down with his ship in December 1864, as he was enroute to Maryland with supplies for John Wilkes Booth. When John Surratt, the last surviving member of the Lincoln assassination conspiracy, arrived in Liverpool in 1865, Bulloch had to maintain a very low profile.

There is no evidence that the Roosevelts or anyone else ever acknowledged Bulloch's connection with the assassination. But this single transaction is more than likely the greatest single contributing factor to Bulloch's decision to remain permanently in Britain. An oft-repeated canard is that Bulloch could not return to the United States after the war because he was denied amnesty. One source of this inaccuracy was President Teddy Roosevelt himself. In his autobiography, he described his Bulloch uncles who "shortly after the close of the war ... were at that time exempted from the amnesty."[8] Roosevelt's statement was true as far as it went, for until 25 December 1868, Bulloch was in a class of "exempted" Confederates who could not accept reinstatement as citizens. However, President Andrew Johnson's 1868 Christmas Day proclamation granted amnesty to all Confederates, including Bulloch. This amnesty occurred almost a month before Bulloch obtained his British citizenship. While it is true that he never executed a loyalty oath or accepted amnesty, as a British citizen, it wasn't necessary.

There were other factors in his decision to remain in England. The roots that his family had planted in Liverpool no doubt influenced Bulloch's decision to reject amnesty and remain in England. Two of his five children were British-born and he had a strong circle of friends, family, and business associates in Liverpool. However, only British citizenship could protect him from persecution by a vindictive U.S. government. His deeds as a Confederate secret agent were tainted by a distant connection to Lincoln's assassination, a connection that, if discovered, would have ruined any hope of a life as a U.S. citizen.

This concern did not prevent him from visiting his Roosevelt relatives and business associates in the United States. One common mistake repeated in numerous sketches of Bulloch's life is that he never revisited his native land or if he did, it was under an assumed name. In fact, he made at least five documented trips to the United States after the war, and he always traveled under his real name, although it was frequently misspelled.[9] For example, when the SS *Java* arrived in New York City on 9 November 1870, the name "Jas D. Bullock" appeared on the manifest along with his brother-in-law Theodore and niece Bamie who were listed respectively as "T. Roosevelt" and "Miss Roosevelt."[10]

Abraham Lincoln, c. 1860. Bulloch was unknowingly involved in John Wilkes Booth's plot to kidnap Lincoln, which may have prompted his self-imposed exile to Great Britain (U.S. National Archives).

FOREIGN POLICY, DIPLOMACY AND INTERNATIONAL LAW

Bulloch's early life in the Navy and merchant marine provided vital schooling in this important dimension of his impact on world affairs. As a naval officer and ship captain, he traveled to South America, Europe, the Caribbean, and Pacific where he made lifelong friendships and contacts. More than a front row observer, he played an important role in most of the major international events within the North American continent during the 15 years leading up to the American Civil War.

His heroic actions in the Oregon Territory during the wreck of the USS *Shark* endeared him to his shipmates and their family members who rose to prominent military and political positions in the U.S. and Great Britain. While in the Pacific fleet, Bulloch also charted and projected American interests in the newly settled Oregon Territory, participated in the Mexican-American War, and witnessed the initial excitement of the gold rush. Later, as a popular merchant sea captain, he transported miners and gold to and from the California fields. He also transported American adventurers and mercenary "filibusters" to the battlefields of Central America and played the leading role in a dramatic diplomatic confrontation with government officials in Havana. Bulloch's *Black Warrior* affair almost precipitated a premature war with Spain in Cuba that would have robbed his Rough Rider nephew of his glorious rise to political power 34 years later. All of these events gave impetus to a Southern variant of Manifest Destiny that would reach its zenith with the presidency of Teddy Roosevelt.

During the American Civil War, he sought out and took advantage of neutrality laws and international protocols that withstood every legal challenge. He literally sailed a fleet of ships through the loopholes in the British and international legal systems from 1861 until 1863 when the repercussions from the Lay-Osborn affair took full effect. The successful construction, outfitting, manning, and deployment of the Lay-Osborn flotilla to China gave Bulloch false hope that he would be given equal treatment under the law. The British government discovered that its double standard in stretching the practical application of its Foreign Enlistment and Neutrality Acts was risky, and ultimately, harmful to the nation. The rule of law in England had to take a back seat to the overriding imperial policy imperative that could not allow Bulloch to have his ironclad rams.

Bulloch spent the years immediately after the end of the American Civil War establishing himself as a Liverpool businessman with his partner and former clerk. To his consternation, the "Bulloch" name frequently appeared in the papers and diplomatic correspondence as a result of the legal acrimony that led to the *Alabama* Claims and the Geneva tribunal. The diplomatic wrangling between Britain and America was finally settled in 1872 when the international tribunal ordered Britain to pay the United States some $15,500,000. Most of this amount was for the damage that Bulloch's cruisers had wrought. Britain's penalty hinged on a broadly defined failure to exercise "due diligence" in preventing these ships from sailing and operating under Confederate colors. The *Alabama* Claims was a landmark event in international law and led to the greatest unintended consequence of Bulloch's commerce raiders. The Geneva tribunal established a precedent of settling disputes through a system of international arbitration and was a precursor to the World Court (International Court of Justice) and the United Nations.

Many analysts have assumed that the *Alabama* Claims process embittered Bulloch's outlook. It is true that the repeated epithets of fraud, piracy, and illegal activity deeply wounded his sense of honor. In his mind, the tribunal's finding against Great Britain gave legitimacy to the Union's assaults against his character. He was certain that he had never defrauded anyone, much less conducted illegal activity. He took pains in his memoirs to document the legality of his actions and the accountability of his financial records.

In a testament to his personal and professional integrity, Bulloch was never accused of any personal or financial misconduct. He never had to endure the literal and figurative trials of his cohorts, Charles Prioleau and General Collin McRae. They were acquitted, but harassed into bankruptcy. It is remarkable that two key players in the prosecution of the U.S. *Alabama* Claims case even went out of their way to advocate Bulloch's case against the U.S. Navy. Shortly after settlement of the *Alabama* Claims, Secretary of State Hamilton Fish met with Theodore Roosevelt, Sr., and helped him collect Bulloch's long-overdue payment for pre-war shares in the SS *Bienville*. Another ally who provided advice and assistance was Senator William Evarts, the former secretary of state and senior *Alabama* Claims prosecutor.

NAVAL WARFARE STRATEGY

It was Bulloch's success in supplying the Confederate armies, even more than his ability to launch warships, that placed his wartime contributions on the same plane as Robert E. Lee. The plans and operations that formed the basis for his ability to gain unfettered access to the open ocean using powerful offensive weapon systems continue to have relevance into the twenty-first century. The wartime imperatives that enabled these efforts merit closer attention.

Bulloch effectively launched and sustained his commerce raiders, but he knew that the Confederate Navy had a greater need for ships that could break the blockade and gain access to the open ocean. The South's improvised casemate ironclads and torpedo boats achieved limited success in protecting inland waters. Unfortunately, these vessels were too few and too restricted in their sea-keeping capabilities to open any of the ports they protected.

The Confederacy simply lacked the industrial capacity and skilled workers to produce the machinery, amour, and armaments in sufficient quantities. Bulloch's answer to this problem was to manufacture these items in Great Britain and run them into Southern ports along with foreign experts who could supervise their assembly. This elegant solution also avoided problems with neutrality laws and placed smaller ships exactly where they were needed most. The many delays in the approval of this plan and lack of precision engineering design expertise in the South prevented full implementation of Bulloch's gunboat/torpedo boat program before the end of the war. The U.S. finally replicated his innovations for modular construction of ships and marine engines during World War II and beyond.

Even though the South was the disadvantaged naval power, Bulloch, like General Lee, did not think he could win the war by remaining on the defensive. He wanted to deliver serious offensive blows into the face of the Union. If the entire flotilla of British and French-built rams and corvettes had sailed under Confederate command, they could have inflicted serious destruction upon the North. Bulloch firmly believed that the South could have won the war by naval means if the requisite ships and materials had become available as planned. Unstated in this belief is his certainty of the moral superiority of his cause. Bulloch and other Confederate leaders repeatedly planned and launched attacks against the North's will to fight, knowing that it was impossible to subdue the Union's ability to make war. They hoped that when the profiteering elitists of the North realized that their mercenary army could not protect their personal and financial interests, they would sue for peace.

There's no doubt that Bulloch inspired Teddy Roosevelt's interest in the U.S. Navy and naval history. His mother, grandmother, and aunts all regaled him with stories about his uncle's heroic exploits. This inspiration transformed into mentorship over the next several years as uncle and nephew pushed each other to write about naval matters. As Bulloch helped Roosevelt analyze the lessons and history for *The Naval War of 1812*, he responded to his nephew's pleas to write about his own Confederate naval service. Bulloch wrote and published his memoirs at the same time that Alfred Thayer Mahan published *The Gulf and Inland Waters* as part of a semi-official Navy trilogy about the Civil War (1883). The others in the series were by navy history professor and Roosevelt's friend James R. Soley (*The Blockade and the Cruisers*) and Bulloch's old Coast Survey shipmate Rear Admiral Daniel Ammen (*The Atlantic Coast*). Bulloch's account would have been particularly useful to Professor Soley's effort. Perhaps not coincidentally, Soley solicited and received 120 of Bulloch's documents that he later compiled and published in the *Official Records* document.

Although he never wrote a treatise on tactics or strategy, Bulloch's ideas are clearly articulated in his official letters and memoirs. For example, he believed that the key to the Union's victory was its destruction of the South's interior lines of communication. Echoing Mahan's sentiments that were unknown to Bulloch at the time, he observed, "I have always thought that the consequences which resulted from the operation of that [Farragut's] force in the waters of the Mississippi were more fatal to the Confederacy than any of the military campaigns."[11] Combined with his emphasis on logistics and offensive operations, Bulloch and Mahan were like-minded on the importance of sea power.

Although Mahan intended his naval strategy for application within the United States, Great Britain, Japan, and Germany were among his earliest and most ardent advocates. All four nations aggressively applied Mahan's concepts with varied results. Teddy Roosevelt, shortly after becoming assistant secretary of the navy in 1898, set in motion the destruction of the Spanish Empire. Later as president, he plunged the nation headlong into the Age of American Imperialism that included the creation and control of major sea lines of communication such as the Panama Canal. Roosevelt transformed the "what ifs" of Bulloch's Confederate Navy into a reality for the United States. Bulloch inspired and enlightened these beliefs that were later bolstered by Mahan's strategic framework.

Bulloch and the rest of Roosevelt's family tutored him on how to use his unique access to the highest level of U.S. and British society, business, and government as means to an end. These relationships helped insure that Britain had a powerful ally in the great conflicts of the early and middle twentieth century. It could also be reasonably argued that the beginnings of the "special relationship" between Britain and America originated in the Bulloch's Liverpool parlor with the quiet conversations between Bulloch and his nephew Teddy.

In an interesting twist of fate, Chinese naval strategists of the twenty-first century have inherited similar problems and beliefs as their Confederate predecessors. The Chinese see themselves as blockaded by U.S.-dominated island chains that restrict their access to the open ocean. The Chinese perspective is eerily reminiscent of Bulloch's: they must confront an aggressively superior U.S. Navy that is backed by a corrupt and materialistic society.

To alter this dynamic, the Peoples' Liberation Army Navy (PLAN) of China has furiously studied Alfred Thayer Mahan's concepts. They are adapting his imperatives for unimpeded access to the sea to enable economic prosperity and justify a naval build-up. In Mahan's day, the extent of territorial seas was only three nautical miles, a distance just beyond the maximum range of nineteenth century naval artillery. Territorial limits are now generally set at 12 miles with contiguous and economic zones that extend to 200 miles and beyond. Precision-guided tactical naval weapons have ranges up to 1000 miles and strategic weapons have a global reach. The Chinese view the "first island chain" (running from Japan, to Taiwan, the Philippines, and Malaysia) they same way as the Confederacy saw its offshore barrier islands. This area contains essential internal waters that must be controlled as an integral conduit for interior communications. Access to the open ocean through the "second island chain" (from Japan, to Guam and New Guinea) is China's version of breaking the blockade.[12]

China recognizes the need for island bases to project naval power and by default, geostrategic power. Like the Confederate Navy, the Chinese cannot stand toe-to-toe against

American naval power, but must develop asymmetric weapon systems to challenge the U.S. Navy's control and access to vital sea lanes. Just as Bulloch supported any type of weapon system that could hold the Union Navy at risk, the Chinese have done the same. Their ongoing development of weapons such as anti-ship ballistic missiles and small, cheap and expendable anti-ship missile ships are designed to keep American carrier and amphibious groups far away from Chinese shores. In another worrisome parallel with Bulloch's thinking, the Chinese believe that they are confronting a morally corrupt society that, like the school bully, will turn and run as soon as its nose is bloodied.

In considering the likely actions of China and other aspiring but disadvantaged maritime nations, intelligence analysts are examining the current inventory of ships and facilities, fleet exercises and training, budget allocations, and strategic writings. An additional and instructive step would be to answer this question: "What would someone as clever as Bulloch do in a similar situation?"

Personal

James Dunwoody Bulloch was a man universally lauded for his integrity, hard work, and ingenuity. While acknowledging these attributes, many biographical sketches also depict him as a wooden figure, often cold and calculating. A completely different picture emerges from the few surviving personal letters and is echoed by those who knew him best. He was a sensitive soul who cared deeply about his family, friends, and those many sailors and their families who depended upon him. Family letters also reflect his ability to provide solace and his deep grief at the loss of a loved one. On festive occasions, he was the life of the party, who danced and sang for the entertainment of all. When he decided to remain in England after the war, he fully immersed himself into the life of the local business community and society. Bulloch was generous in his support of favored Liverpool charitable activities including the church, Boys Orphanage, School of Technology, and various maritime organizations.

The image of the gallant naval officer who played violin, spoke several languages, loved to dance, and always had a merry twinkle in his eye, captivated his sister Mittie Bulloch. Her stories transformed Bulloch into a larger than life character in the imaginations of her children. In doing so, she unintentionally helped walk Bulloch down the iconic, but anonymous cultural path paved by the nineteenth century poet Henry Howard Brownell and the popular writer Richard Henry Dana.

In 1923, a society writer for the *Atlanta Journal-Constitution*, Peggy Mitchell, interviewed the last remaining bridesmaid from Mittie Bulloch's marvelous wedding to Theodore Roosevelt, Sr., at Bulloch Hall in 1853. Enthralled by the stories, Mitchell, who was already intrigued by the idea of writing an American Civil War novel from a Southern perspective, began to intensively research local people, places, and events.

Years later, when her novel *Gone with the Wind* became a worldwide success under her given name of Margaret Mitchell, she was asked many times upon whom she based the characters of Scarlett O'Hara, Rhett Butler, and Ashley Wilkes. Mitchell asserted that none of these characters were based on real people, but many commentators have noted the resemblance of Mittie Bulloch to the personality and beauty of Scarlett. Although nobody could confuse the roguish Rhett Butler with Mittie's brother James, the same romanticized story of Bulloch's exploits that Teedie Roosevelt heard as a child were repeated to Mitchell. The composite portrayal of a dashing Georgian blockade runner who was also Roosevelt's vision of the ideal man, was reflected in the characters of both Rhett and Ashley.

Margaret Mitchell's fictional characters in *Gone with the Wind* are known to millions, but the real man faded into obscurity, just as he would have wished. James Dunwoody Bulloch was President Theodore Roosevelt's hero and the greatest naval hero America ever forgot.

Appendix 1

Bulloch's Family, Friends, and Foes

Adams, Charles Francis (1807–86), U.S. minister to Great Britain (1861–68) and U.S. arbiter for the *Alabama* Claims, son of President John Quincy Adams.
Ammen, Daniel (1820–98), JDB's shipmate on the *Gallatin*, Union officer and rear admiral, author of *The Atlantic Coast*, 1883.
Anderson, Edward C. (1838–82), Confederate Army major who investigated and then assisted Caleb Huse in Liverpool; ran the blockade into Savannah with Bulloch on the *Fingal*.
Anderson, Edward Maffitt (1843–1923), Confederate midshipman, with JDB on the *Annie Childs*, son of Major Anderson, named after Cdr. John Newland Maffitt.
Arman, Jean-Lucien (1811–73), Bordeaux shipyard owner, built JDB's ironclads *Sphinx* (CSS *Stonewall*) and *Cheops* and corvettes *Yeddo* and *Osacca* (CSS *Mississippi* and *Louisiana*).
Armstrong, John Richard, one of JDB's four sponsors for British citizenship, a partner in Fraser, Trenholm and Co. after George Trenholm retired in January 1866.
Armstrong, William G. (1810–1900), JDB visited his gun foundry at Newcastle-upon-Tyne and purchased several naval cannons.
Aspinwall, William H. (1807–75), Northern businessman and shipbuilder, sent to England with Forbes to purchase Confederate-contracted ships, financed Union surveillance efforts.
Barney, Hiram (1811–95), U.S. customs official in New York, who received J.A. Roosevelt's report of JDB's plans and activities as a Confederate secret agent.
Barney, Joseph Nicholson (1818–99), commanded the *Florida* in Brest, September 1863 to January 1864.
Barron, Samuel (1809–88), commodore intended to command JDB's ironclad flotilla, senior Navy officer in Europe, October 1863 to February 1865.
Bayley, Charles J. (1819–1873), pro–Confederate British governor of the Bahamas (1857–64).
Benjamin, Judah P. (1811–84), Confederate attorney general, JDB's first point of contact (1861), Secretary of War (1861–62), Secretary of State (1862–65), former U.S. senator (LA), postwar U.K. barrister.
Bigelow, John (1817–1911), U.S. consul to Paris (1861–65), succeeded Dayton as minister in 1865; wrote book about effort to counter JDB; traveled to Europe on the same ship as Mrs. Bulloch.
Bismarck, Otto E.L. von (1815–98), prime minister and chancellor of Prussia and German Empire (1862–90).
Bond, George A. (1825–1877), Liverpool pilot for the *Enrica/Alabama*.
Bravay, Adrien, French broker who attempted to rescue the Laird rams from seizure.
Bright, John (1811–89), pro–Union member of Parliament.
Brooke, John Mercer (1826–1906), met with JDB about ordnance; naval scientist and designer, developed plan for the *Shenandoah*.
Bruce, Frederick W. A. (Wright-Bruce) (1814–67), British minister to China during the Lay-Osborn affair (1859–65), minister to the U.S. (1865–67) during *Alabama* Claims negotiations.
Bulloch, Anne Irvine (1770–1833), JDB's grandmother, mother of Jane, Ann, John Irvine, and James Stephens.
Bulloch, Archibald (1730–77), JDB great grandfather, son of James and Jean Stobo; married Mary De Veaux 1764, president of Georgia, died in office.
Bulloch, Charles Irvine (1838–41), JDB's stepbrother, son of James Stephens and Martha.
Bulloch, Elizabeth (Lizzie) Euphemia Caskie (1831–54), JDB's first wife.
Bulloch, Harriott Cross Foster (1829–97), JDB's second wife.

Appendix 1

Bulloch, Henry (Dunnie) Dunwoody (1861–71), JDB's son, died of scarlet fever.
Bulloch, Hester Amarinthia Elliott (1797–1831), JDB's mother, wife of James Stephens Bulloch.
Bulloch, Irvine Stephens (1842–98), JDB's half-brother, served on the *Alabama* and *Shenandoah*.
Bulloch, James (1701–80), JDB's great-great grandfather, emigrated from Scotland.
Bulloch, James (1765–1807), JDB's grandfather, eldest son of Archibald, married Anne Irvine.
Bulloch, James Dunwoody, Jr. (1858–88), JDB's eldest son, died suddenly in Virginia.
Bulloch, James Stephens (1793–1849), JDB's father, died teaching Sunday school in Roswell.
Bulloch, Jean Stobo (1710–50), JDB's great-great grandmother, daughter of Rev. Archibald Stobo.
Bulloch, John Elliott (1819–21), JDB's brother, son of James Stephens and Hettie.
Bulloch, Martha Louise (1865–1947), JDB's daughter, never married.
Bulloch, Martha Stewart Elliott (1799–1864), stepmother of JDB and Corinne Elliott Hutchison, mother of Susan, Georgia, and Daniel Elliott; mother of Anna, Mittie, Charles, and Irvine Bulloch.
Bulloch, Stuart Elliott (1863–1939), JDB's youngest son.
Burgoyne, Hugh Talbot (1833–70), awarded Victoria Cross, blockade runner, with Osborn on *Pekin*, commanding officer of JDB's ironclad HMS *Wivern* (1865–67), lost at sea with the HMS *Captain*.
Butcher, Matthew James (1832–1909), British captain of the *Enrica/Alabama*.
Cairns, Hugh McCalmont (1810–85), British barrister, declared JDB's shipbuilding legal, represented Fraser, Trenholm and Co. in the *Alexandra* case, lord chancellor (1868, 1874–80).
Carter, Robert (Bob) Randolph (1825–88), commanding officer of JDB's blockade runner *Coquette*, helped plan the *Shenandoah's* mission, executive officer of the CSS *Stonewall*, JDB sent postwar payments.
Carter, William F., commanded the *Louisa Ann Fanny*, blockade runner and tender to the CSS *Stonewall*.
Caskie, James Kerr (1818–68), JDB's brother-in-law by first wife; helped deliver JDB's letters to Mallory, received packages through the blockade from New York and Liverpool.
Caskie, John (1790–1867), father-in-law, president of the Bank of Virginia.
Caskie, Mary Edmonia, see: Hutchison, Mary Edmonia Caskie.
Chapman Robert T. (1831–1905), served on the CSS *Sumter* and *Georgia*, took charge of the *Sumter* in Gibraltar, carried the Great Seal though the blockade, defended Ft. Fisher.
Chase, Salmon P. (1808–73), U.S. secretary of treasury, interviewed Bulloch about the *Bienville* and authorized the Forbes-Aspinwall mission.
Chasseloup-Laubat, Count Justin Napoléon Samuel Prosper de (1805–73), French marine minister, supported JDB's French warships.
Clarendon, George William Frederick Villiers, 4th Earl of (1800–70), British foreign secretary (1853–58, 1865–66, 1868–70) under Palmerston, Russell, and Gladstone.
Cobden, Richard (1804–65), pro–Union member of Parliament.
Cockburn, Alexander (1802–80), British *Alabama* Claims arbiter, lord chief justice.
Coles, Cowper Phipps (1819–70), Royal Navy captain, inventor of revolving gun turret; helped JDB improve the design of the Laird rams; died on his experimental ship HMS *Captain*.
Collier Robert P. (1817–86), pro–Union member of Parliament, former queen's counsel and admiralty judge advocate, argued to seize the *Alabama* and release *Shenandoah's* crew.
Collins, Napoleon (1814–75), captain of USS *Wachusett*, warned Welles about the *Sea King*, illegally attacked and captured the *Florida* in a Brazilian port; rear admiral, USN (1874).
Corbett, Peter Suther (1817–73), nominal captain of the *Sea King*, successfully planted a false story about its sinking, acquitted of violating the Foreign Enlistment Act.
Cowles, Anna "Bamie" Roosevelt (1855–1931), JDB's niece, Theodore Jr.'s sister, married the U.S. naval attaché to London in 1895, frequently met, dined, and stayed with JDB and Harriott.
Cowles, William Sheffield (1846–1923), Bamie's husband, U.S. naval attaché to Great Britain.
Craven, Thomas (1808–87), captain of USS *Tuscarora* and *Niagara*; JDB outwitted him in escape of *Florida* and *Alabama*, captured former CSS *Georgia*, avoided combat with CSS *Stonewall*.
Crenshaw, William Graves (1824–97), Confederate merchant and Army officer, formed a blockade-running company in London, loaned JDB the *City of Richmond* as a tender to the *Stonewall*.
Cross, Annette, sister of Harriott Cross Bulloch, married Seth Grosvenor Porter, the brother-in-law of Cornelius Van Schaack Roosevelt, Jr. (Theodore, Sr.'s brother)
Cross, Edwin (1833–63), JDB's brother-in-law, Union soldier, killed in the war.
Cross, Osborne (1803–76), father-in-law, brigadier general in quartermaster corp, U.S. Army.
Dabney, Charles W. (1794–1871), U.S. consul to the Azores who harassed JDB on the *Annie Childs* and *Alabama*.
Dana, Richard Henry, Jr. (1815–82), lawyer, politician, author, wrote *To Cuba and Back* (1859) with vivid description of JDB.
Davidson, Hunter (1827–1913), JDB's shipmate on the *Shark*, purchased mine warfare supplies, carried messages; commanded *City of Richmond* (*Stonewall's* tender and blockade runner).
Davis, Jefferson (1808–89), Confederate president, JDB's postwar visitor in the U.K. (1868, '69, '70, '74, '76, '81) and confidant.

Davis, Varina Banks Howell (1826–1906), wife of Jefferson Davis, frequently visited her sister in Liverpool and briefly lived in Great Britain, at Davis' death, JDB wrote sympathy letter.

Dayton, William L. (1807–64), U.S. minister to France (1861–64).

Delane, John T. (1817–79), London *Times* editor, supported the Lay-Osborn flotilla.

de Mauá, (Ireneo Evangelista de Souza) baron and viscount (1813–89), JDB business associate, Brazilian transportation and communication mogul.

De Veaux, Mary (1748–1818), JDB's great-grandmother, married to Archibald Bulloch.

Dix, John Adams (1798–1879), U.S. Union major general who assisted TR, Sr., New York governor, U.S. senator (NY) and secretary of the treasury; related by marriage to JDB (step-son-in-law).

Dudley, Thomas Haines (1819–93), U.S. consul and Bulloch's chief antagonist in Liverpool (1861–65); member of the U.S. *Alabama* Claims arbitration.

Duguid, James Alexander (1816–82), initial British captain of the *Florida*, with Low on *Minna*.

Dunwody, John (1786–1858), JDB's uncle by marriage to Jane Bulloch, law partner of JDB's father.

Elliott, Daniel Stewart "Stuart" (1826–62), JDB's stepbrother, son of Martha Bulloch from first marriage to John Elliott, joined the Confederate Army, died of tuberculosis.

Elliott, John (1773–1827), Martha Steward Bulloch's first husband, U.S. senator from Georgia.

Elliott, Lucinda (Lucy) Sorrel (1829–1903), the widow of Daniel (Stuart), received mourning dress through blockade from mother-in-law Martha Elliott Bulloch.

Erlanger, Friedrich Emile (1832–1911), German banker in France who sponsored a large loan to the Confederacy and guaranteed the payments of JDB's French ironclads.

Eustis, George, Jr. (1828–72), former U.S. congressman from Louisiana (1855–59), Slidell's secretary in Paris who went with JDB to meet with Arman.

Evarts, William M. (1818–1901), lawyer on the *Alexandra* case and the *Alabama* Claims; U.S. secretary of state, attorney general, and senator; assisted Bulloch with his *Bienville* claim.

Farragut, David G. (1801–70), first and most famous U.S. admiral, Bulloch's commanding officer on the USS *Decatur* on Brazil station.

Fauntleroy, Charles Magill (1822–89), commanding officer of the CSS *Rappahannock* and blockade runner *Economist*, executive officer of the CSS *Nashville*.

Ferguson, James Boswell III (1822–96), Confederate Army quartermaster agent, accused Huse of corruption.

Fish, Hamilton (1808–93), former governor and senator from New York, Grant's secretary of state, began *Alabama* Claims negotiations, met with Theodore Roosevelt Sr., and supported JDB's *Bienville* claims.

Forbes, Charles Stuart (1829–76), former blockade runner, Royal Navy captain of *Keangsoo*, served Maximilian in Mexico, authored books on Iceland (1860) and Garibaldi's campaign (1861).

Forbes, John M. (1813–98), Northern railroad man sent to England with Aspinwall to purchase Confederate-contracted ships; supported increased Union surveillance in Europe.

Forrest, Douglas French (1837–1902), *Rappahannock's* paymaster, met with JDB in Liverpool.

Forster, William E. (1818–86), pro–Union member of Parliament.

Frederick III, William N. C. (1831–88), married Queen Victoria's eldest daughter Princess Victoria, German emperor for 99 days, died of throat cancer, succeeded by Wilhelm II.

Gilliat, Algernon (1837–1925), partner of a pro–South British cotton and banking company; the blockade runner *Mary Augusta* was the named for his wife Mary Augusta Georgina.

Gilliat, John Saunders (1829–1912), partner of a pro–South British cotton and banking company; the blockade runner *Louisa Ann Fanny* was named for his wife, Louisa Ann Frances.

Gladstone, William E. (1809–98), Liberal British prime minister (1868–74, 1880–85); agreed to *Alabama* Claims.

Gorgas, Josiah (1818–83), Confederate Army general in charge of Ordnance Dept.

Gracie, Anna Louisa Bulloch (1833–93), JDB's half-sister, daughter of Martha and James Stephens Bulloch.

Gracie, James King (1840–1903), JDB's brother-in-law, married Anna Bulloch, New York financier assisted JDB, left $10,000 each to Irvine Bulloch's wife Ella and JDB's daughter Martha Louise.

Granville, Earl (Leveson-Gower) (1815–91), British foreign secretary initiated *Alabama* Claims negotiations.

Graves, William A. (1821–94), Confederate Navy's constructor, with poor designs for JDB's torpedo boats.

Green, Charles (1807–81), partner of Andrew Low, brother-in-law of John Low, Confederate agent who helped finance the *Fingal*.

Greenhow, Rose O'Neal (1817–64), Confederate spy "Rebel Rose" and overseas agent, met with JDB in England and France; drowned running into Cape Fear on JDB's *Condor*.

Hamlin, Hannibal (1809–91), Lincoln's first term vice president, U.S. senator (Maine), he and JDB stayed at the Astor Hotel in New York on 2 April 1861.

Hamilton, John Randolph (1828–1909), intended to be JDB's first lieutenant on the *Alabama*, designated to command the *Alexandra*.

Hanckel, Alan Stuart (1837–94), JDB courier (1864), agent for Fraser, Trenholm and Co. in Liverpool.

Harding, John D. (1809–68), chief law officer of the Crown, suffered a mental and physical breakdown the allowed the *Alabama* to escape.

Hart, Robert (1835–1911), British interpreter and 2nd inspector general of China's Imperial Maritime Customs service, originated the Lay-Osborn flotilla initiative.
Hatherley, William Page (1801–81), British judge and lord chancellor (1869), ruled in favor of Fraser, Trenholm and Co. against the U.S. (1865), co-sponsored Benjamin for the British court.
Heyliger, Louis C., Confederate shipping agent for Adderley & Co. in Nassau.
Hickley, Henry Dennis (1826–1903), captain of the HMS *Greyhound*; led second and third seizure of the *Florida* in Nassau.
Hoare, E. G., Royal Navy captain and attaché to Paris; investigated Bravay and the Laird rams.
Hornby, Geoffrey Thomas Phipps (1825–95), knighted Royal Navy admiral, cousin and brother-in-law of 13th Earl of Derby, JDB's friend, *aide-de-camp* to Queen Victoria and Wilhelm II.
Hotze, Henry (1833–87), Confederate agent and editor of the London *Index*; JDB's conduit for intelligence information.
Howison, Neil McCoul (1805–48), JDB's commander on the USS *Shark*.
Hull, Frederick Shepard. (1817–75), JDB's Liverpool solicitor, cleared the path to build raiders.
Huse, Caleb (1831–1905), Confederate Army major; JDB's counterpart for the Ordnance Dept.
Hutchison, Corinne Louisa Elliott (1813–38), JDB's stepsister, married to Robert Hutchison, drowned in the wreck of the *Pulaski*.
Hutchison, Mary Edmonia Caskie (1822–52), JDB's sister-in-law, second wife of Robert Hutchison.
Hutchison, Robert (1802–61), brother-in-law by his first marriage to stepsister Corinne and by marriage to first wife's sister Mary; early sponsor and benefactor in his will.
Isaac, Samuel (1812–86), owned blockade runners, Confederate contractor in London,
Jackson, Nancy (1813–?), domestic slave of JDB's father; freed in Connecticut court.
Johnson, Reverdy (1796–1876), U.S. minister to the U.K. (1868–69), U.S. senator (MD) and attorney general.
Kane, Elisha Kent (1820–1857), U.S. Navy doctor, arctic explorer, author, hero of the Mexican-American War, JDB carried remains to New Orleans, shipmate of Murdaugh and Bob Carter.
Kell, John McIntosh (1823–1900), Semmes' executive officer on the *Sumter* and *Alabama*, rescued in the *Deerhound* and carried to South Hampton.
King, Roswell (1765–1844), cotton mill partner of JDB's father, founder of Roswell, GA.
King, Thomas Butler (1800–64), state of Georgia and Confederate emissary to Europe, former U.S. congressman, advocate for China trade, transcontinental railroad, and Panama canal.
Kung, (Gong, Yixin, 6th Prince) Prince (1833–98), Chinese emperor's brother and diplomat for European affairs, agreed to the Lay-Osborn flotilla.
Lafone, Henry (1830–1917), Liverpool shipping agent for Bulloch (e.g., *Laurel*) and blockade runners.
Laird, John (1805–74), Scottish founder of shipbuilding firm managed by his sons William, John, and Henry in 1861 who built the *Alabama*; pro–Confederate member of Parliament (1861–74).
Lamar, Gazaway Bugg (1798–1874), Savannah banker and cotton broker, sponsored the SS *John Randolph*, fabricated and assembled in Savannah by Laird and Fawcett, Preston, & Co. (1834).
Lamar, Lucius Quintus Cincinatus, II (1825–93), U.S. senator (MS) (1877–85), secretary of interior (1885–88): former Confederate colonel; minister to Russia and special envoy to England and France.
Law, George (1816–81), rail and ship owner and politician who owned part of the Panama railroad, and the SS *Georgia*; presidential candidate lost nomination to Fillmore.
Lay, Horatio Nelson (1832–98), inspector-general of the Chinese Imperial Maritime Customs Service, promoted the failed Lay-Osborn flotilla, later fired and replaced by Robert Hart.
Lhuys (l'Huys), Edouard Drouyn de (1805–81), French foreign minister who opposed JDB's French warships.
Lindsay, William S. (1817–1877), shipbuilder, member of Parliament (1854–65), advocated Southern independence, met with Napoleon III, Confederate creditor.
Low, Andrew (1803–1894), Green's partner, John Low's uncle, on *Fingal* with JDB, daughters remained in Great Britain, father-in-law of Juliette Gordon Low, Girl Scouts founder.
Low, Harriet (1848–1891), possible namesake of the *Enrica/Alabama*, daughter of Andrew Low, lived in Leamington Spa with sister Amy, married Major George Coke Robertson,
Low, John (1836–1906), JDB's lifelong friend, served on *Fingal*, *Florida*, and *Alabama*; commanded *Tuscaloosa* and *Ajax*; attended funeral and received JDB's sureties upon his death.
Maffitt, Eugene Anderson (1844–86), Confederate midshipman, son of John N. Maffitt, with JDB on the *Annie Childs*.
Maffitt, John Newland, Jr. (1819–86), captain of the *Florida* and blockade runners including JDB's *Owl*; JDB's commander on the USCS *Morris* and *Gallatin*, son of Methodist minister.
Maguire, Matthew (1815–96), Liverpool detective who followed JDB.
Mahan, Alfred Thayer (1840–1914), influential naval strategist, authored *Gulf and Inland Waters*, *Influence of Sea Power upon History*, et al., Theodore Roosevelt, confidant and frequent guest.
Mallory, Stephen R. (1813–73), Confederate secretary of the navy, former U.S. senator (FL).
Mann, A. Dudley (1801–89), first Confederate commissioner to London (with Yancey), reassigned to Belgium; participated in Ostend Manifesto as U.S. assistant secretary of state (1853–55).

Martin, Patrick C. (?–1864), Canada-based blockade runner, drowned December 1864; conspired with John Wilkes Booth to kidnap Lincoln; JDB provided over $30,000 for supplies and ordnance.
Mason, James Murray (1798–1871), Confederate commissioner in London, captured with Slidell on the *Trent*; former U.S. senator (VA).
Maury, Matthew Fontaine (1806–73), Confederate scientist and naval agent in Europe, developed mine warfare, purchased two ineffective cruisers, CSS *Georgia* and *Rappahannock*.
Maury, William L. (1813–78), commander of the CSS *Georgia*, cousin of Matthew F. Maury.
Maxwell, Jessie Hart Bulloch (1860–1941), JDB's daughter, wed Max Maxwell, spent last years in their Liverpool home.
McCormick, Agnes (1851–?), JDB's Liverpool housemaid and cook for over 20 years.
McKillop, Henry Frederick (1822–79), captain of HMS *Bulldog*, seized the *Florida* in Nassau.
McNair, Angus, JDB's Scottish engineer on the *Fingal*.
McQueen, Alexander (1826–1906), master of the *Alabama's* tender, the *Agrippina*.
McRae, Colin (1813–77), Confederate Army general, chief European financial officer.
Miller William C. (1803–69), with his sons, Liverpool shipbuilder of the *Florida* and *Alexandra*, and blockade runners.
Milne, Alexander (1806–96), British Royal Navy admiral, commander of North America and West Indies Station (1860–64), presided over the Halifax Vice-Admiralty Court.
Mitchell, Margaret "Peggy" M. (1900–59), author of *Gone with the Wind*, who wrote a long article about Bulloch Hall, and Theodore Roosevelt's wedding to Mittie.
Montagu-Stuart-Wortley-Mackenzie, Edward M.S.G. (1827–99), 3rd Baron of Wharncliffe, participant in Liverpool's Grand Southern Bazaar, headed a pro–Southern association.
Morris, Charles M. (1820–95), commanding officer of the CSS *Florida* in 1864.
Morse, Freeman H. (1807–91), U.S. consul in London who met with JDB after the war.
Motley, John Lothrop (1814–77), Grant's minister to Great Britain (1869–70), recalled to the U.S.
Murdaugh, William H. (1826–1901), JDB's courier, Ordnance Bureau special duty, surveyed the *Rappahannock*, selected to command one of JDB's unfinished gunboats, served with Kane.
Napoleon III, Louis-Napoléon Bonaparte (1808–73), emperor of France (1852–70); exiled to England; nephew and heir to Napoleon I.
North, James Heyward (1815–93), Confederate navy agent in Europe, competed with JDB about seniority, priorities, money, and control; built large ironclad in Scotland that was sold.
Osborn, Sherard (1822–75), commander of the Lay-Osborn flotilla, an unsuccessful British effort to intervene in China's civil war; Royal Navy admiral and arctic explorer.
Palmer, Roundell (1812–95), British solicitor general (1861–63), attorney general (1863–66), lord chancellor (1872–74, 1880–88); pro–Union but acknowledged CSS *Shenandoah's* legitimacy.
Page, Thomas Jefferson (1808–99), commanding officer of the CSS *Stonewall*.
Palmerston, Lord Henry J. Temple (1784–1865), Liberal British prime minister (1859–65).
Paynter, John Aylmer (1814–76) commanding officer of the HMS *Donegal* received *Shenandoah's* surrender in Liverpool, released the "Southern" crew, later vice admiral.
Pegram, Robert B. (1811–94), Confederate Navy captain of the CSS *Nashville*; in Bermuda 1861, provided JDB instructions from Mallory and a pilot for the *Fingal*.
Perrin, Eugene Henry (1830–1919), one of JDB's four sponsors for British citizenship, Liverpool cotton and shipping broker.
Petermann (a.k.a. Petersmann, Peterman, or Trémont), clerk for French shipbuilder Voruz who sold information about JDB's French contracts.
Phillmore, Robert J. (1810–85), queen's counsel, advocate general in admiralty; author of *Commentaries upon International Law*; ruled on the *Shenandoah's* legitimacy.
Pollaky, Ignatius Paul "Paddington" (1828–1918), British detective hired by Adams and Sanford to track JDB, and others; in 1881 lampooned in Gilbert and Sullivan's *Patience*.
Porter, David Dixon (1813–91), U.S. Navy admiral, Bulloch's commander on the SS *Georgia*, (1852–53).
Porter, John L. (1813–93), chief constructor of the Confederate Navy.
Porter, Seth Grosvenor (1835–1910), blockade runner captain, married Annette Cross, and brother-in-law of JDB and Cornelius Van Schaack Roosevelt, Jr. (TR, Sr.'s brother).
Prioleau, Charles Kuhn (1827–73), principal of Fraser, Trenholm, & Co. in Liverpool, financed Confederate operations, owned blockade runners, shared office space with JDB.
Puggard, Rudolph, Danish banker, nominal owner of the *Stonewall*.
Quinn, Michael, Confederate Navy chief engineer, met with JDB about marine engine designs.
Rivière, Henri Arman de, Arman's business agent, coordinated the acquisition of the *Stonewall*.
Robertson, Moses P. (1823–1905), JDB's clerk and postwar partner.
Robertson, William H. (1788–1859), U.S. consul to Havana during the *Black Warrior* affair.
Robinson, Corinne (Conie) Roosevelt (1861–1933), JDB's niece, Theodore Roosevelt's sister, corresponded with JDB, named for Martha Bulloch's stepdaughter who drowned in a shipwreck.

Roosevelt, Alice Hathaway Lee (1861–84), TR's first wife (1880), honeymooned in Europe, visited JDB (1881), died within hours of TR's mother, Mittie; JDB sent heartfelt condolence letter.
Roosevelt, Anna "Bamie," see Cowles, Anna.
Roosevelt, Anna Eleanor (1884–1962), JDB's great-niece, daughter of Elliott Roosevelt, wife of Franklin Delano Roosevelt.
Roosevelt, Cornelius Van Schaack, Jr. (1827–87), brother of Theodore Roosevelt, Sr., brother-in-law to Harriott Bulloch's sister Annette Cross Porter.
Roosevelt, Edith Kermit Carow (1861–1948), Theodore Roosevelt's second wife.
Roosevelt, Elliott (1860–94), JDB's nephew, brother of TR and father of Eleanor Roosevelt.
Roosevelt, James Alfred (1825–98), reported JDB's activities to treasury official Barney; son and partner of Cornelius, the nephew of Judge James I. Roosevelt and Theodore Roosevelt, Sr.
Roosevelt, James (Rosey) R. (1854–1927), secretary of the U.S. embassy in London; Bamie was his hostess when his wife Helen Astor died (1893); half-brother of Franklin D. Roosevelt.
Roosevelt "Judge" James I. (1795–1875), U.S. district attorney for Southern New York in 1861
Roosevelt, Martha (Mittie) Bulloch (1834–84), JDB's half-sister, mother of Theodore Roosevelt, Anna (Bamie), Corinne (Conie), and Elliott (Ellie).
Roosevelt, Silas Weir. (1823–70), JDB's brother-in-law, brother of Theodore Roosevelt, Sr.; married Mary West, sister of JDB's brother-in-law Hilborne West.
Roosevelt, Theodore. (1858–1919), JDB's nephew, Assistant Secretary of the Navy (1897–98), governor of New York (1898–1900), president of the U.S. (1901–09).
Roosevelt, Theodore "Thee" Sr. (1831–78), JDB's brother-in-law, husband of Mittie Bulloch, father of Theodore Roosevelt, Corinne (Conie), Anna (Bamie), and Elliott (Ellie).
Rost, Pierre A. (1797–1868), first Confederate commissioner to Paris and then Spain.
Russell, John (1792–1878), Liberal British secretary of state foreign affairs (1852–53, 1866–68) prime minister (1846–52, 1865–66).
Sanders, George Nicholas (1812–73), wanted JDB to cover his debt of over £10,000, Confederate agent provocateur in Canada; former U.S. Navy agent in New York and consul to London.
Sanford, Henry S. (1823–91), U.S. minister to Belgium; organized European espionage.
Schenck, James F. (1807–82), commended JDB's heroism in saving his brother Woodall, served in the Union Navy, promoted to rear admiral.
Schenck, Robert Cumming (1809–90), U.S. minister to Brazil (1851–53) and Great Britain (1871–6), brother of Lt. Woodhull and Rear Admiral James Schenck; former Union general.
Schenck, Woodhull S. (1815–1849), JDB's shipmate that he rescued on the USS *Shark*.
Sclopis, Count Paul Frederic de Salerano (1798–1878), head of the *Alabama* Claims tribunal, an Italian minister of state.
Sears, Harriet Louisa Clitz (1832–1909), American-born mother of namesake Harriet ("Hattie") and Irvine's wife Ella, wife of Henry, traveled to the U.S. with Corinne Roosevelt.
Sears, Henry Beaufort (1824–80), father of Irvine's wife Ella, American businessman, moved to Liverpool before the war, befriended JDB and Theodore Roosevelt, Sr.
Sellar, John Alexander (1831–99), one of JDB's four sponsors for British citizenship, Liverpool merchant and broker, purchased American-flagged ships during the war.
Semmes, Raphael (1809–77), captain of the *Alabama*, stayed with Bulloch in Liverpool.
Seward, William Henry (1801–72), U.S. secretary of state (1861–9), former U.S. senator (1849–61) and governor of New York (1839–42); survived assassination attempt when Lincoln was killed.
Shryock, George S., Confederate Navy officer who assembled officers and crew for the *Stonewall*.
Sinclair, Arthur (?–1865), CSN Commander, father of George T. Sinclair, drowned in the *Lelia*, 1865
Sinclair, George T. (1816–85), relieved JDB on the *Fingal*, delivered message from Mallory about Semmes taking command of the *Alabama*, built the *Canton/Pampero* in Scotland.
Slidell, John (1793–1871), Confederate commissioner to France, captured with Mason on the *Trent*, former U.S. minister to Mexico, and senator (LA).
Smith-Stanley, Edward (1775–1851), 13th Earl of Derby, married Charlotte M. Hornby.
Smith-Stanley, Edward George G. (1799–1869), 14th Earl of Derby, U.K. prime minister (1852, 1858–59, 1866–68), agreed to *Alabama* Claims settlement, owner of Knowsley Hall near Liverpool.
Soley, James R. (1850–1911), compiled 30-volume ORN (JDB contributed 120 documents), authored *The Blockade and the Cruisers*, assistant secretary of the navy (1890–93).
Somerset (12th Duke), Edward Adolphus Seymour (St. Maur) (1804–85), The First Lord of the Admiralty (1859–66), supported the Lay-Osborn flotilla.
Soulé, Pierre (1801–70), U.S. minister to Spain during the *Black Warrior* affair, co-authored the Ostend Manifesto; U.S. senator (LA) (1847, 1849–53).
Sorley, James (1820–95), Galveston cotton merchant who advertised for JDB (1867–68), met in Liverpool postwar, former Port of Galveston customs and Confederate Army agent.

Spence, James (1816–1905), Confederate financial agent, Liverpool cotton broker, propagandist, author of *The American Union*, one of four co-sponsors of JDB's British naturalization request.

Squarey, Andrew Tucker (1821–1900), Dudley's solicitor for the *Alabama*; partner of Duncan, Squarey, & Blackmore, erroneously identified as "A.F. Squarey" in U.S. *Alabama Claims*.

Stanley, Edward H. (1826–93), Lord Stanley (1844–69), succeed father as 15th Earl of Derby, and served as his secretary of foreign affairs (1866–68).

Stevens, Edwin Augustus (1875–1868), with brother Robert, inventor of advanced ironclad warship.

Stevens, Robert Livingston (1787–1856), with brother Edwin, inventor of advanced ironclad warship.

Stobo, Jean (1710–1750), great-great-grandmother, daughter of Rev. Archibald Stobo.

Stoess, Margaret Howell Graham de Wechmar, (1842–1930), Varina Davis' sister, married the Bavarian consul to Liverpool (Charles Stoess) in 1869.

Stringer, Edgar P. (1822–94), associate of Sanders, director of Mercantile Trading Co., a shipping and insurance firm, introduced North to Thomson Co., owned blockade runners.

Sumner, Charles (1811–74), anti-slavery U.S. senator (MA) (1851–74); argued for $2 billion for "indirect" *Alabama Claims*.

Surratt, John Harrison, Jr. (1844–1916), accused Lincoln co-conspirator, escaped to Canada and Liverpool.

Tattnall, Josiah (1795–1871), Confederate Navy commodore, at Savannah took charge of the *Fingal* from JDB, later commanded the ironclad CSS *Virginia* (*Merrimack*).

Tessier, Eugene L. (1819–1901), captain of JDB's first blockade runner from Great Britain (*Bermuda*), captain of *Florida* and *Alabama* tender (*Bahama*); JDB's agent in France for the *Stonewall*.

Tirpitz, Alfred von (1849–1930), admiral of the Imperial Naval Office in 1897.

Tremlett, Francis W. (1821–1913), anglican vicar, unofficial chaplain of the Confederate Navy in England, accompanied JDB to Southampton to greet the *Alabama* survivors, 1864.

Trenholm, George A. (1807–76), Confederate secretary of treasury, principle partner of Fraser, Trenholm & Co.

Vanderbilt, Cornelius (1794–1877), U.S. railroad and shipping magnate with Central American transit interests.

Voruz, Jean Simon (1810–96), Nantes shipbuilder, constructed two of JDB's corvettes that were sold to Peru, his clerk exposed JDB's contract.

Waddell, James Iredell (1824–86), captain of the CSS *Shenandoah*.

Walker, Norman S. (1831–1913), Confederate Army major, shipping agent in Bermuda.

Walker, William (1824–60), freelance U.S. mercenary general "filibuster"; recognized as president of Nicaragua: JDB captained ship with supplies and reinforcements (1856).

Welles, Gideon (1802–78), U.S. secretary of navy (1861–69); newspaper owner.

West, Hilborne T. (1818–1907), JDB's brother-in-law, husband of Susan married at Bulloch Hall, medical doctor and businessman in Philadelphia.

West, Susan ("Susy") Ann Elliott (1820–95), JDB's stepsister, married Hilborne West at Bulloch Hall, 1849.

Wharncliffe, Lord, see Montagu.

White, Hollis (1813–1880), U.S. treasury agent and officer of Niagara Falls Bridge company, reported that JDB was headed to Liverpool as a Confederate secret agent on 5 May 1861.

Winslow, John Ancrum (1811–73), captain of the USS *Kearsarge*, engaged and sank the *Alabama*.

Whiting, Samuel (1816–1882), U.S. consul to Nassau (1861–63), tried to stop the *Florida*; as captain of the SS *Marion*, carried Union family members out of Ft. Sumter prior to bombardment.

Whittle, William C., Jr. (1840–1920), JDB's courier, crossed with JDB on the *Fingal* and *Annie Childs*, JDB recommended as executive officer of the CSS *Shenandoah*; son of a Confederate Navy commodore.

Wilding, Henry J., acting U.S. consul to Liverpool before Dudley arrived.

Wilhelm I, Frederick L. (1791–1888), king of Prussia (1861–88), first German emperor (1871–88).

Wilhelm II, William V. A. (1859–1941), king of Prussia and last German emperor and kaiser (1888–1918), grandson of Queen Victoria, advocate of Mahan and naval power.

Martha "Mittie" Bulloch Roosevelt, Bulloch's half-sister, was the mother of future U.S. president Theodore Roosevelt (U.S. National Park Service).

Wilkes, Charles (1798–1877), instigated the *Trent* affair as commanding officer of the USS *San Jacinto*, illegally seizing Mason and Slidell, conducted unsuccessful search for JDB's cruisers.

Wilkinson, John (1821–91), as captain of the blockade runner *Chameleon* turned it over to JDB.

Wilson, James A. K. (1833–70), agent for Fraser, Trenholm and Co., purchased blockade runners, and the CSS *Sumter* from JDB and renamed the *Gibraltar*.

Wright, Richard (1812–71), Scottish-born shipbuilder and owner with brother William from Canada; purchased the *Sea King* (*Shenandoah*) for JDB; Prioleau's father-in-law.

Xiuchuan, Hong (1814–64), self-proclaimed brother of Jesus, led the Taiping Rebellion (1851–64) against the Qing Dynasty, established the "Heavenly Kingdom" in southern China.

Yancey, William Lowndes (1814–63), first Confederate commissioner to Europe with Mann, resigned in 1862, elected to Confederate Senate.

Yonge, Clarence Randolph (1833–?), paymaster and clerk, with JDB on *Annie Childs* and in London, deserted from the *Alabama*, discredited in *Alexandra* trial, JDB's distant cousin.

Appendix 2

Bulloch's Fleet of Ships

Total Cruisers, Ironclads, Gunboats, Blockade Runners, and Supply Ships Purchased, Owned, Leased, or Managed: 49
3 Commerce Raiders
4 Ironclads
13 Gunboats
24 Blockade Runners (plus the tender/runner *Laurel/Confederate States*)
5 Tenders/supply ships (includes the *Laurel*)

Total Gunboats, Blockade Runners, and Supply Ships Inspected, Consulted, Sold, or Partially Manned: 71
5 Gunboats assisted with *Alexandra, Georgia, Hawk, Rappahannock,* and *Sumter*
13 Blockade runners inspected, manned, or managed
22 Supply ships contracted or manned
31 Blockade runners with Confederate contracts and possible JDB assistance.

Commerce Raiders that Bulloch Had Built or Purchased (3 total):
CSS **Alabama** (*No. 290, Enrica*): commissioned 24 August 1862, commanded by Capt. R. Semmes, 65 prizes (53 sunk, 9 bonded, 1 converted to raider, 1 sold, 1 released), sunk by USS *Kearsarge* 19 June 1864 in English Channel.
CSS **Florida**, (*Oreto, Manassas*): commissioned 17 August 1862, commanded by Cdr. J. N. Maffitt (until September 1863), Lt. J.N. Barney (September 1863–January 1864, never sailed from Brest), and Lt. C.M. Morris (January–October 1864), 58 total prizes (21 by consorts; 45 sunk, 12 bonded; 1 recaptured), illegally seized by US Navy in Brazil October 1864, scuttled 28 November 1864.
CSS **Shenandoah** (*Sea King*): commissioned 19 October 1864, commanded by Lt. J. I. Waddell, 38 prizes (32 sunk; 6 bonded), surrendered to Great Britain 6 November 1865, transferred to U.S., sold to the sultan of Zanzibar in 1866 as *El Majidi*, foundered in 1879.

Ironclads that Bulloch Built (4 total, 1 commissioned; all 4 entered foreign navies with an average life span of over 40 years):
El Tousson (*No. 294,* CSS *North Carolina*): seized, sold to Royal Navy as *Scorpion*, Bermuda harbor defense, sunk and lost 1903.
El Monassir (*No. 295,* CSS *Mississippi*): seized, sold to Royal Navy as *Wivern*, Hong Kong harbor defense until 1922.
CSS **Stonewall** (*Sphinx, Staerkodder, Olinde*): French-built, surrendered in Havana, returned to the U.S., sold to the Japanese as the *Kotetsu* (renamed *Azuma*), active service until 1888.
Cheops: French-built, sold to the Prussian navy as the *Prinz Adalbert* until 1871

Gunboats Bulloch Contracted, Owned, or Managed (13 total, 5 unfinished; all 13 saw service with foreign navies):
Adventure (*Tientsin,* CSS *Waccamaw*): sold to Argentina as gunboat *Amazona* in 1866, renamed *General Brown* and *Chacabuco*, in service until 1893.
Ajax (CSS *Olustee*): sailed for Confederacy under John Low, but returned to Great Britain 9 June 1865; sold to Argentine navy.

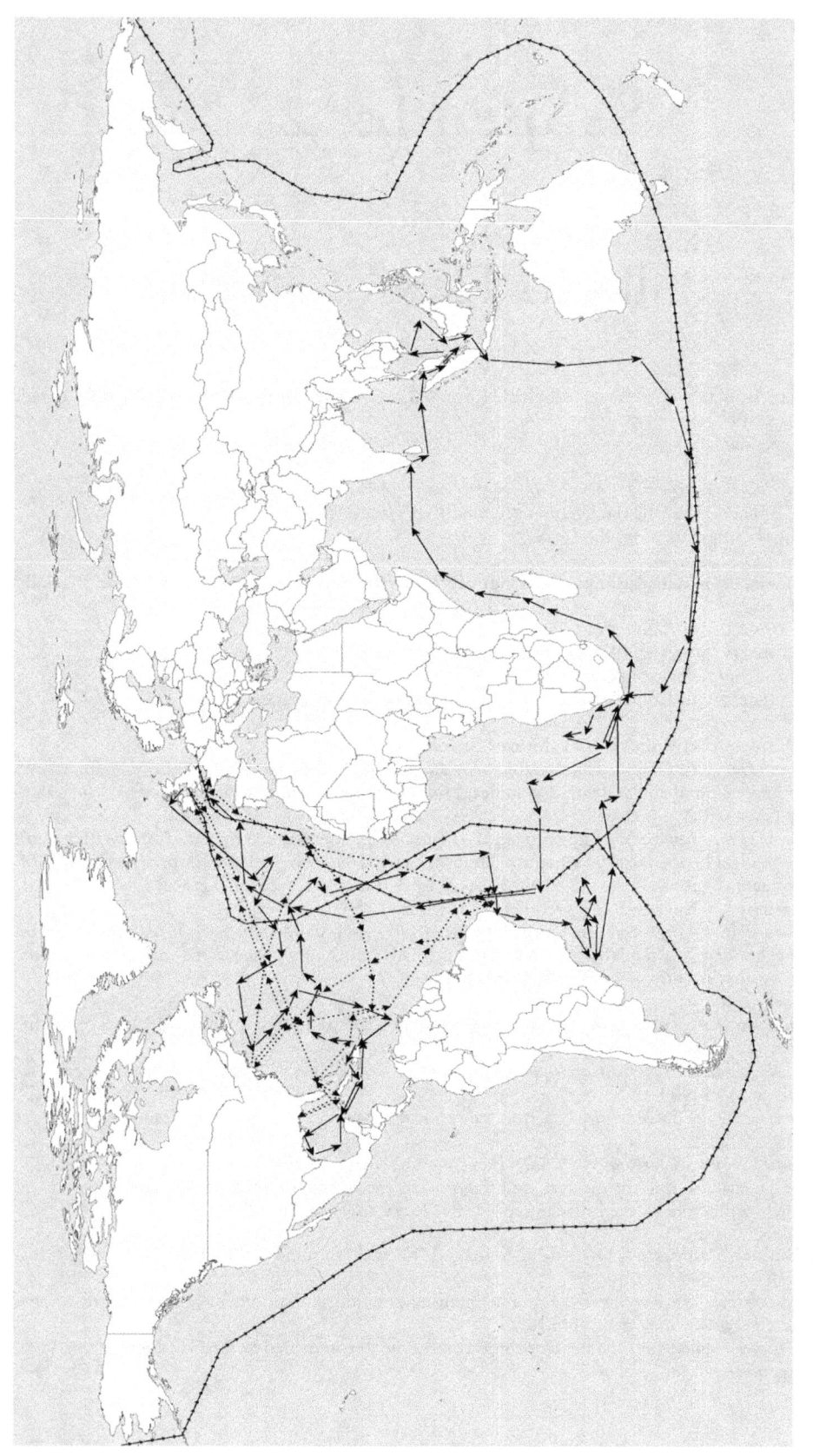

Routes of Bulloch's commerce raiders, *Alabama* (long black arrows), *Florida* (dots with arrows), and *Shenandoah* (short-segment "stitching") (G.L. McKay).

Shanghai (CSS *Texas*): Nantes-built corvette, sold to Peruvian navy as *America* (1864), lost during an 1868 tsunami.
Yeddo (CSS *Mississippi*): Bordeaux-built corvette, sold to Prussia as *Augusta* (1864), in service through 1885.
Enterprise (II) (*Yangtze*, CSS *Black Warrior*): sold to Brazil as a transport in 1866 as *Brasil*, in service until 1877.
Hercules (CSS *Vicksburg*): unfinished, sold to the Argentine navy.
Louisa Ann Fanny (CSS *Waccamaw*): never ran, survived, sold possibly to Spain or as armed transport for Venezuela or Brazil.
Mary Augusta (CSS *Black Warrior*): unfinished, sold to Brazil as *Vassimon*, converted to armed transport.
Penguin: unfinished, sold to Greece as *Amfitriti*, converted to royal yacht, hulked in 1906.
Rosina (*Rosine*): unfinished, sold to Turkish navy as *Eser-I-Nusret* and converted into a dispatch vessel until 1890.
Ruby III: unfinished, sold to Turkish navy as *Medar-I-Zafer*, converted into a dispatch vessel until 1890.
San Francisco (CSS *Georgia*): Nantes-built corvette, sold to Peruvian navy as *Union* (1864), scuttled to avoid capture in 1871.
Osacca (CSS *Louisiana*): Bordeaux-built corvette, sold to Prussia as *Victoria* (1864), active until 1891.

Blockade Runners Bulloch Purchased, Leased, or Managed (25 vessels including the former tenders *Bermuda* and *Laurel/Confederate States,* 6 were unfinished at the end of the war; 15 of them made 64 successful runs, 3 never ran, 16 survived the war, 5 entered naval service for the U.S., British, Greek, and Spanish governments):
Albatross: unfinished, sold to Royal Navy as HMS *Isabel*, active through 1876.
Bat: captured (1864), taken into U.S. Navy, sold as *Teazer*, and sold to Canada as *Miramichi*, active through 1897.
Colonel Lamb: 2 runs, survived, sold to Greek government as *Ariel* and *Bomboulina*.
Condor: ran aground off Ft. Fisher in 1864 (Rose Greenhow drowned).
Confederate States: 2 runs (see former tender *Laurel*): survived.
Coquette: 13 runs, survived; renamed *Maryland* active through 1873.
Corcovado: unfinished.
Curlew: unfinished.
Deer: captured and sold 1865 as *Palmyra*, active through 1870.
Evelyn: 4 runs, survived.
Falcon: 4 runs, survived, sold to Argentina.
Fingal: 1 run, converted into ironclad CSS *Atlanta* and captured 1863, taken into U.S. Navy as USS *Atlanta*.
Flamingo: 2 runs, survived, sold to Argentina.
Gibraltar (*Habana*, CSS *Sumter*): 1 run, Fraser, Trenholm and Co. returned to Confederates, carried Blakely guns, survived.
Hope: 2 runs, captured 1864, sold and renamed *Savannah*, sold to Spanish navy as frigate *Churruca* until 1888.
Lark: 8 runs, last steamer to run out of a Confederate port, survived until 1890.
Mary Celestia: 8 runs, wrecked at Bermuda 1864.
Matilda: ran aground leaving Great Britain under command of Lt. W.F Carter, CSN, 1864.
Owl: 5 runs, survived.
Plover: unfinished.
Ptarmigan: 2 runs, survived, sold to Argentina as *Pampa*.
Snipe: unfinished.
Stag (*Zenobia*): 2 runs, captured and sold to Argentina in 1865 as *Cenobia* (renamed *Villeta, Santa Fe, Maria Luisa*), active through 1870 (not the *Stag/Kate Gregg* built by Denny in Glasgow).
Widgeon: unfinished.
Wren (*Tartar*): 6 runs, seized by crew 1865, sold by Key West prize court, returned to owners (1868), active through 1884.

Tenders Bulloch Purchased or Leased (5 total; also 2 blockade runs):
Agrippina: tender for CSS *Alabama*, survived.
Bahama, tender to *Alabama*, supply ship, in service until 1884.
Bermuda: (*Czar*), tender to CSS *Florida*, 2 runs, captured 1862, taken into U.S. Navy as USS *Bermuda*.
City of Richmond: contract tender for CSS *Stonewall*, never ran the blockade, survived, sold to Brazil 1866.
Laurel: tender for *Shenandoah*, 2 runs (renamed *Confederate States*), survived

Gunboats Bulloch Inspected, Manned, or Sold, but Did Not Own or Lease (5 all survived and were reconfigured as merchant vessels):

Alexandra: detained (1862), converted to a merchantman as *Mary* (1864), detained in Nassau by the British customs until the end of the war.

Georgia (*Japan*): iron hull, acquired by Cdr. M.F. Maury, commissioned 1862, captured 9 prizes (3 sunk; 6 bonded), Bulloch sold in 1864, U.S. Navy seized and sold 1865, wrecked in 1875.

Hawk: intended for Virginia Volunteer Navy, resold at Liverpool January 1865

Rappahannock (HMS *Victor*, *Scylla*): acquired by Cdr. M.F. Maury, commissioned 1863, decommissioned 1865 in France, survived and sold to the U.S.

Sumter (*Habana*): sold to Fraser, Trenholm and Co. in 1862 at Gibraltar, renamed *Gibraltar*; see blockade runner *Gibraltar*.

Blockade Runners Bulloch Inspected, Manned, or Contracted, but Did Not Own or Lease (13 ships total, made 75 runs; 7 survived, 3 taken into U.S. Navy):

Agnes E. Fry: 4 runs, ran aground and destroyed, 1864.

Alliance (*Fox*): captured 1864, sold.

Cornubia (*Columbia*, *Lady Davis*, USS *Cornubia*, *New England*): 18 runs, captured 1863, entered U.S. Navy, sold 1866.

Crescent (*Nita*): 2 runs, captured and taken into U.S. Navy (1863), sold in 1865.

Dare: ran aground and destroyed on maiden voyage in 1864.

Eugenie (*Hilda*): 10 runs, survived, sold at Liverpool.

Greyhound: 1 run, with spy Belle Boyd captured inbound to Cape Fear (1864), sold.

Herald I (*Antonica*): 24 runs, driven ashore and destroyed in 1863.

Lilian: 5 runs, captured 1864, taken into U.S. Navy, sold, Spanish gunboat *Victoria de las Tunas* (1870).

Mary Ann (*Mary Anne*, *Russia*): 5 runs, captured and sold (1864), abandoned in 1865.

Phantom: 4 runs, ran aground and destroyed in 1863.

Presto: 2 runs, destroyed in 1864.

Susan O'Beirne, (*Susan Beirne*, *Susan Burne*), 1 attempt (1864), survived, sold to Buenos Aires from Glasgow.

Supply Ships Under Contract to Bulloch (22 total):

Amy: sailing brig to and from Nassau and Liverpool with cotton for Navy Dept. in 1864.

Babthorp: sailing brig with goods for Maury to Bermuda, November 1864.

Cecile: lost between Charleston and Nassau with 400 barrels of powder.

Conway: cotton for Navy Dept, to and from Nassau and Liverpool, May 1864.

Crocodile: sailing vessel from Liverpool carrying submarine defenses November 1864.

Chameleon (CSS *Tallahassee*, CSS *Olustee*, *Atalanta*, *Amelia*): turned over to Bulloch at Liverpool, survived, transferred to the U.S. in 1866, sold to Japan as the *Haya Maru*.

Diana: steamship with Navy Dept., goods from Liverpool to Bermuda, September 1864.

Driving Mist: sailing vessel with cotton and guns for Navy Dept. to and from Nassau, Bermuda, and Liverpool, June–December 1864.

Egriteria: probably sailing vessel with cotton for Navy Dept. to and from Nassau and Liverpool.

Emily II: steamer, with 2 small marine engines and Lt. Howell CSMC from Glasgow to Bermuda, never ran blockade, survived.

Emma Henry: steamer, carried marine engines, captured coming out of Cape Fear, 1864.

Enterprise: probable British sailing vessel, carried cotton for Navy Dept. from Nassau to Liverpool, 1864.

Giraffe (*Robert E. Lee*, USS *Fort Donelson*, *Isabella*): captured carrying supplies for Navy Dept., survived.

Harriet Pinckney (*Leda*): Confederate Army–owned, standby tender for *Rappahannock*, supply ship direct England to Bermuda or the Bahamas, sold August 1864, wrecked in 1896.

Julia Usher (former *Annie Childs*): steamer owned by Fraser, Trenholm and Co., carried crew of *Sumter* from Liverpool to Nassau.

Madonna: sailing vessel carried naval ordnance supplies from Glasgow to Bermuda.

Maria: probable sailing vessel, carried cotton for Navy Dept. from Nassau to Liverpool, April 1864.

Melita: steamship carried Navy Dept. ordnance supplies, Semmes and Kell to Nassau, April 1862.

Ruby II: steamer carried mine warfare supplies salvaged from the *Runber*, from Angra Azores to Bermuda, captured.

Runber (*Run Her*): steamship wrecked at the Azores with load of mine warfare supplies, 1864.

Tryom: sailing bark carried supplies and cotton to and from Nassau and Liverpool, 1864.

Whisper: supply steamer carrying mine warfare supplies, returned to Great Britain after one failed run, survived.

Blockade Runners with Confederate Contracts and Possible Bulloch Assistance (31 total):
Annie, Badger II, Banshee II, Ceres, Charlotte, City of Petersburg, Dee, Denbigh, Don, Flora I, Flora III, Florie, Hansa, Hebe, Heroine, Horne, Juno I (Helen), Little Ada, Little Hattie, Merrimac, Neptune, Night Hawk, Pearl, Savannah (Old Savannah, Everglade), Swan II, Tallahassee (Atalanta), Venus, Vesta, Wasp, Wild Rover, Will of the Wisp.

Bulloch's U.S. Navy Service Afloat (Key: ship name, type, dates assigned, operating areas, other):
USS ***United States***, frigate, 21 June 1839–31 March 1840, Western Atlantic out of Boston, acting midshipman.
USS ***Potomac***, frigate, 31 March–31 July 1842, Brazil Station, warranted midshipman.
USS ***Decatur***, sloop-of-war, August 1841–winter 1842, Brazil Station, served under David Glasgow Farragut.
USS ***Delaware***, battle ship-of-the-line, winter 1842–44 March 1844, Brazil Station and Mediterranean Squadron.
USS ***Pennsylvania***, receiving ship, 27 June–29 August 1844, in port at Norfolk.
USS ***Erie***, store ship, 14 June 1845–April 1846 and February–June 1847, transited from New York to Pacific Station, passed midshipman.
USS ***Shark***, schooner, April–September 1846, Hawaii to Oregon Territory, acting master, wrecked coming out of Columbia River.
USCS ***Warren***, sloop, June 1847–November 1848, Pacific Squadron, U.S. Coast Survey.
USS ***Lexington***, store ship, 23 November 1848–12 June 1849, transited from San Francisco to New York.
USCS ***Morris***, schooner, 29 August 1849–November 1849, New England, U.S. Coast Survey, served under John Newland Maffitt.
USCS ***Gallatin***, schooner, November 1849–May 1851, Virginia to South Carolina, U.S. Coast Survey, under Maffitt.
USS ***Washington***, brig, May–19 November 1851, New England, acting master, U.S. Coast Survey.

Bulloch's Merchant Marine Service (5 total ships):
SS ***Georgia***, side-wheel steamship, 22 March 1852–29 June 1853, New York City to Chagres (Panama) via Havana and New Orleans and return; first officer under David Dixon Porter (March 1852–May 1853), lieutenant and commanding officer (June 1853).
SS ***Black Warrior***, side-wheel steamship, 23 July 1853–3 December 1855, New York to Mobile, (later New Orleans) via Havana and return, commanding officer.
SS ***Cahawba***, side-wheel steamship, 26 December 1855–4 June 1859, New York to New Orleans via Havana and return, one "filibuster" trip to San Juan de Nicaragua (August 1856), commanding officer.
SS ***DeSoto***, side-wheel steamship, 27 August 1859–29 June 1860, New York to New Orleans via Havana and return, commanding officer.
SS ***Bienville***, side-wheel steamship, 1 August 1860–23 April 1861, New York to New Orleans via Havana and return, commanding officer, part-owner.

Chapter Notes

CoGB   *The Case of Great Britain as Laid before the Tribunal of Arbitration*
JDB   James Dunwoody Bulloch
NYT   *New York Times*
ORA   Official Records of the Army in *The War of the Rebellion: A Compilation of the Official Records of the Union and Confederate Armies*
ORN   Official Records of the Navy in *The War of the Rebellion: A Compilation of the Official Records of the Union and Confederate Armies*
TR   Theodore Roosevelt
TR, Sr.   Theodore Roosevelt, Sr.
TRC   Theodore Roosevelt Collection, Houghton Library, Harvard University, Cambridge, MA

Chapter 1

1. London *Daily Telegraph*, 9 Jan 1901.
2. *Savannah Morning News*, 12 Jan 1901.
3. *Ibid.*
4. U.S. State Department, "*Alabama* Claims," http://history.state.gov/milestones/1861-1865/Alabama.
5. U.S. Central Intelligence Agency, "Intelligence in the Civil War, Intelligence Overseas, James Bulloch," https://www.cia.gov/library/publications/additional-publications/civil-war/p31.htm.

Chapter 2

1. U.S. Congress, *Biographical Directory*, s.v. "Archibald Bulloch" http://bioguide.congress.gov/scripts/biodisplay.pl?index=B001050.
2. James Cook, *The Governors of Georgia* (Macon, GA, Mercer University 2005), 14–15.
3. *Ibid.*; U.S. Congress. *Biographical Directory*, s.v. "Archibald Bulloch."
4. New Georgia Encyclopedia, "Archibald Bulloch," http://www.georgiaencyclopedia.org/nge/Article.jsp?path=/HistoryArchaeology/ColonialEraTrusteePeriod/People-4&id=h-682.
5. James D. Bulloch, *Secret Service of the Confederate States in Europe*, vol. 1 (New York: G. P. Putnam's Sons, 1884), 41.
6. *Ibid.*, New Georgia, "Archibald Bulloch"; Kenneth Coleman in *A History of Georgia* lists Archibald Bulloch as a Whig Party member.
7. Charles C. Jones, *Biographical Sketches of the Delegates from Georgia to the Continental Congress* (Spartanburg, SC: Reprint Co., 1972); W.B. Stevens, *A History of Georgia, from Its First Discovery by Europeans to the Adoption of the Present Constitution in MDCCXCVIII*, vols. I–II. (New York: D. Appleton, 1847).
8. *Ibid.*
9. Joseph G. B. Bulloch, *A Biographical Sketch of the Hon. Archibald Bulloch, President of Georgia, 1776–77* (Privately published, 1900), 11.
10. Nicholas I. Roosevelt was a partner of Robert Fulton, the steamship inventor, and an ancestor of both Roosevelt presidents. JDB would become an uncle to TR by virtue of his half-sister's marriage to TR, Sr. See: Bulloch, *Archibald Bulloch*, 12–13.
11. U.S. Congress, *Biographical Directory*, s.v. "Elliott, John," http://bioguide.congress.gov/scripts/biodisplay.pl?index=E000124.
12. Connie Huddleston, "A Social and Economic History of the James Stephens Bulloch Family of Bulloch Hall, Roswell, Georgia," 10. John Elliott and Martha Stewart married 6 Jan 1818.

13. *Ibid.*
14. *Darien Gazette*, "Death Notice," 22 Sep 1821.
15. *Charleston Observer*, "Marriage and Death Notices," 4 Aug 1827; Brent Holcomb, "Senator John Elliott," http://www.quarterman.org/who/senelliott.html.
16. Huddleston, "A Social and Economic History of the James Stephens Bulloch Family," 11.
17. Daughters Susan and Georgia Elliott traveled from New York on the Ship *Hamilton* 16 Nov 1829. James Stephens Bulloch was executor of John Elliott's estate. See: Probate file for John Elliott, Probate Court, Liberty County Courthouse (Hinesville, GA, 1827–1834), 11.
18. *Savannah Daily Georgian*, 21 Feb 1831, cited in Huddleston, "A Social and Economic History of the James Stephens Bulloch Family," 11.
19. Charles J. Johnson, Jr., *Mary Telfair: The Life and Legacy of a Nineteenth-Century Woman* (Savannah: Frederic C. Beil Publisher, 2002), 93–94.
20. Johnson, *Mary Telfair*, 94. All of the children were baptized at Midway Church. See: Midway Church records, Midway, Liberty County, GA.
21. *Ibid.*
22. *Ibid.*
23. *Daily Commercial Bulletin* (Missouri), 16 Jul 1838. Corinne married Robert Hutchison a few months prior to the marriage of Martha and James; she and her two young daughters Corinne and Catherine died in the sinking of the steamship *Pulaski* in 1838 off the coast of North Carolina. Robert Hutchison was also on board the *Pulaski*, but survived.
24. Estate inventory of John Elliott, Will Record B, 1824–1850, 41, Probate Court, Liberty County Courthouse, Hinesville, GA.
25. Probate file of John Elliott. Daniel Stewart died in 1829.
26. Bernard C. Steiner, History of Slavery in Connecticut (Baltimore: Johns Hopkins University Press, 1893), 52, 53; James Mars, *Life of James Mars, A Slave Born and Sold in Connecticut* (Hartford: Case, Lockwood, 1868), Appendix, 33.
27. James Stephens Bulloch, letter to Robert and Corinne Hutchinson, 7 Jul 1837, Robert Hutchison papers, MS 2226, 1:1, Georgia Historical Society (Savannah, GA).
28. David Menschel, "Abolition without Deliverance: The Law of Connecticut Slavery, 1784–1848," *Yale Law Journal* 111, no. 1 (Oct 2001): 194–196.
29. James Stephens Bulloch, letter to Robert and Corinne Hutchinson, 7 Jul 1837, Robert Hutchison papers, MS 2226, 1:1, Georgia Historical Society (Savannah, GA).
30. Menschel, "Abolition without Deliverance"; Mars, *James Mars,* appendix, 33–35.
31. Roswell King ledgers, Roswell (Georgia) Historical Society and Archives.
32. Bulloch Hall history cites letters to the editor of the *Savannah Daily Georgian* from 1842; David Williams, The Georgia Gold Rush: Twenty-Niners, Cherokees, and Gold Fever (Columbia, SC: University of South Carolina, 1993); Henry Merrill, *The Autobiography of Henry Merrill Industrial Missionary to the South*, ed. James L. Skinner III (Athens: University of Georgia, 1991), 177.
33. Michael D. Hitt, *Bulloch Hall* (Roswell, GA: Self-published, 1995), 2. Willis Ball was the master builder for Bulloch Hall.
34. U.S. Navy Department. *Register of the Commissioned and Warrant Officers of the Navy of the United States, including Officers of the Marine Corps, and other for the Year 1848* (Washington: C. Alexander, 1848), 66; U.S. State Department General Records, National Archives. Record Group 59, Microfilm Publication M1372, 694 rolls, Passport Applications, 1795–1925, s.v. "A. Hutchison" and "J.S. Bulloch." Robert Hutchison applied to Secretary of State John Forsyth for a passport for both himself (#1040) and his nephew (#1041), giving a physical description of young JDB; Hutchison was planning a trip to England and France.
35. J. Thomas Scharf, *History of the Confederate States Navy* (1887; reprint, New York: Gramercy, 1996), 783–784; Wilson Lumpkin letter to James K. Paulding, 28 Mar 1840, Brock Collection, Misc reel 5071, University of Virginia Library (Charlottesville, VA).
36. JDB Service Record, 26 Jan 1934, Navy Historical Center (Washington, DC); US Navy Dept., *Dictionary of American Naval Fighting Ships*, vol. VII, ed. RADM Ernest McNeill Eller (Washington: GPO, 1981), 413–414; U.S. Naval Historical Center, Dictionary of American Naval Fighting Ships, *DANFS Online*. "Potomac," http://www.hazegray.org/danfs/frigates/potomac.htm.
37. Naval Historical Center, *DANFS Online*, http://www.hazegray.org/danfs/sloops/decatur1.htm; Scharf, *Confederate States Navy*, 783–784. The USS *Decatur* departed New York 16 Mar 1840, but did not arrive on Brazil station until Jul 1841.
38. Bulloch, *Secret Service*, I: 91–92; sources vary on the precise dates of the *Decatur* and Farragut's activities. See: Alfred T. Mahan, *Admiral Farragut* (New York: D. Appleton, 1892), 90; Jared Sparks, ed., *The American Almanac and Repository of Useful Knowledge for the Year 1842* (Boston: David H. Williams, 1843), 77; Naval Historical Center, *DANFS Online*, s.v. "Decatur" http://www.history.navy.mil/danfs/d2/decatur-i.htm.
39. Scharf, *Confederate States Navy*, 783–784.
40. Naval Historical Center, *DANFS Online*, http://www.hazegray.org/danfs/line/delaware.htm; Scharf, *Confederate States Navy*, 783–784. Other commanders were Captains Charles Morris and Henry W. Ogden.
41. U.S. Navy Order log; JDB Service Record.
42. Scharf, *Confederate States Navy*, 783–784.
43. U.S. Navy, *Register 1848*, 68.

44. Scharf, *Confederate States Navy*, 783–784; Naval Historical Center, *DANFS Online*, http://www.hazegray.org/danfs/sloops/erie.htm.

45. Gregory P. Shine, "Sympathy and Prompt Attentions: Fort Vancouver's Relief of the U.S. Schooner Shark on Sept. 13, 1856." *Campfires & Candlelight Resource Guide 2007* (Washington: National Park Service, 2007). The *Shark* was 198 tons displacement and 26 meters in length with two masts. Commodore Perry gained international fame when he and his fleet of warships convinced the Japanese to open their ports to western trade in 1854.

46. Sam W. Haynes and Christopher Morris, eds., *Manifest Destiny and Empire: American Antebellum Expansionism* (College Station: Texas A&M University, 1997).

47. U.S. Interior Department, "Find a Park," "Fort Vancouver," http://www.nps.gov/fova/historyculture/index.htm

48. U.S. Congress, House of Representatives, "Report of Lieut. Neil M. Howison, United States Navy," 30th Cong., 1st Sess., House Misc. No. 29 (Washington: 1867): 3.

49. *Ibid.*, 3–5; Shine, "Sympathy and Prompt Attentions," 11.

50. Howison, letter to James S. Bulloch, 5 Aug 1847, Mariner's Museum (Newport News, VA).

51. *Ibid.*; Gregory P. Shine, "'A Gallant Little Schooner': The U.S. Schooner Shark and the Oregon Country, 1846," Oregon Historical Quarterly 109, no. 4 (Winter 2008): 554, 559, 560. Two carronades believed to be from the *Shark* were discovered in Feb 2008, but the gold remains undiscovered.

52. Jas. Findlay Schenck, letter to J.S. Bulloch, 25 Nov 1848, Mariner's Museum (Newport News, VA).

53. U.S. Congress, "Report of Lieut. Neil M. Howison," (1848): 3, 10.

54. *Ibid.*, 5–7. Hunter Davidson "cross-decked" from the USS *Portsmouth* for temporary duty on the *Shark*. Davidson would earn his fame as a Confederate commander in charge of torpedo boats and mine warfare.

55. Howison, letter to Bulloch, 5 Aug 1848, Mariner's Museum.

56. U.S. Navy, *Register for 1848*, 68 and *1849*, 125 and 127; Schenck, letter to Bulloch, 25 Nov 1848, Mariner's Museum. The Coast Survey has evolved into the Office of Coast Survey within the National Oceanic and Atmospheric Administration (NOAA).

57. On 23 Oct 1848 while in port Monterey, CA, the *Warren, Ohio, Dale, Lexington,* and *Southampton* were all undermanned due to desertions; the USS *Ohio* reported 145 deserters. See: *Niles Weekly Register*, vol. 75, "Navy" (Philadelphia: 24 Jan 1849): 50.

58. *Ibid.*, 178; Virtual Museum of the City of San Francisco, "Gold Rush Chronology 1846–1849," http://www.sfmuseum.com/hist/chron1.html.

59. Betty B. Caroli, *The Roosevelt Women* (New York: Basic Books, 1999), 30–32. Hilborne West would later become a medical doctor.

60. Hitt, *Bulloch Hall*, 6.

61. *Niles Weekly Register*, vol. 75, "Navy" (Philadelphia: 13 Jun 1849), 370; Official Navy Order log; JDB Service Record.

62. Caroli, *Roosevelt Women*, 27–28, 31.

63. Chester G. Hearn, *Admiral David Dixon Porter* (Annapolis: Naval Institute Press, 1996), 17. Bulloch's pay went from $62.50 per month ($50 base plus $12.50 sea pay) to $92.50 (additional $30 Survey Pay). Superintendent Alexander Dallas Bache, a great-grandson of Benjamin Franklin, and Lt. Mathew Fontaine Maury (head of the U.S. Naval Observatory, "The Father of Oceanography," and a future Confederate naval officer) had a bruising political battle over control of the Coast Survey.

64. JDB Service Record.

65. U.S. Navy, *Register for 1849*, 125 and 127; Schenck, letter to Bulloch, 25 Nov 1848, Mariner's Museum.

66. Lindley Butler, *Pirates, Privateers and Rebel Raiders of the Carolina Coast* (Chapel Hill: University North Carolina, 2000), 149; Jacquelin A. Caskie, *The Caskie Family of Virginia* (Charlottesville: Conway, 1928); U.S. Congress, Senate, *Annual Report of the Superintendent of the Coast Survey for the Year Ending, Nov. 1851*. 32d Congress, 1st Session, Senate Ex. Doc. No. 3 (Washington: Robert Armstrong, 1852), 115.

67. Official Navy Order log; JDB Service Record.

68. Emma Martin Maffitt, *The Life and Services of John Newland Maffitt* (New York: Neale, 1906), 68.

69. Donald R. Hickey, *The War of 1812: A Forgotten Conflict* (Urbana: University of Illinois, 1990), 221–255.

70. George Hull Camp letter to his wife Jane Margaret Atwood dated Feb 21, 1850 in Cox and Walsh, *Selected Correspondence of George Hull Camp* (Macon, GA: Indigo Publishing Group, 2008), 152–153.

71. Senate documents, otherwise publ. as Public documents and Executive documents Senate Document 3, Appendix 3, 115: List of navy officers on Coast Survey duty, 1 Mar 1851; JDB Service Record; Maffitt, *Maffitt*, 78–79; U.S. Congress, Senate, *Annual Report of the Superintendent of the Coast Survey* . 32d Congress, 1st Session, Senate Ex. Doc. No. 3, 41–42, 118; U.S. Navy, *Register 1852*, 66–67, 116.

72. JDB Service Record.

73. Caskie, *Caskie Family*, 52–54. Lizzie was the daughter of wealthy tobacconist John Caskie of Richmond, who married Martha Jane Norvell and had several children, including Elizabeth Euphemia, better known as "Lizzie," born Feb 15, 1831.

74. JDB Service Record.

Chapter 3

1. H.W. Brands, *The Age of Gold: The California Gold Rush and the New American Dream* (2002; reprint, New York: Anchor, 2004), 405.

2. Rene De La Pedraja, *A Historical Dictionary of the U.S. Merchant Marine and Shipping Industry: Since the Introduction of Steam* (Westport, CT: Greenwood, 1994), 672.

3. JDB Service Record; *NYT*, 25 Mar 1852; Panama Railroad, "The Panama Railroad & the US Mail," http://www.panamarailroad.org/mail.html; Potash and Company, "Pacific Mail Steam Ship Collection," http://www.potashco.com/potash_2.htm; John, H. Kemble, *The Panama Route 1848–1869* (Berkley: University of California, 1943). The PMSC remained welcoming to Southern-born officers even after the American Civil War.

4. *NYT*, 29 Oct 1852.

5. Warrant signed by Secretary of the Navy John P. Kennedy and President Fillmore; JDB Service Record lists 11 Feb.

6. TR, Sr., letter to Martha (Mittie) Bulloch Roosevelt, 5 Jun 1853, TRC bMS Am 1785.2, #2; *NYT*, 7 Jun 1853.

7. *NYT*, "Later from Havana," 30 Jun 1853.

8. *NYT*, Jul 5, 1853. "Capt Bullock and lady" sailed from New York to Richmond via Norfolk on 4 Jul 1853 in the steamship *Jamestown*.

9. Virtualology, *Appletons Encyclopedia*, "Hall of North and South Americans," s.v. "George Law." http://www.famousamericans.net/georgelaw/; *Daily Alta*, 11 and 13 Oct 1853; The Ships List, "Steamships on the Panama Route," http://www.theshipslist.com/ships/descriptions/panamafleet.html; Don Ross, "Era of the Clipper Ships," http://www.eraoftheclippership.com/page62.html. Law's notoriety excited enough enthusiasm for him to be nominated as the 'Know Nothing' party's presidential candidate in 1856, but the incumbent, President Millard Fillmore, defeated him.

10. *NYT*, 25 Jul 1853. On 16 Jul 1853, the *Black Warrior* under Captain Shufeldt arrived at New York City from Mobile via Havana. See: *NYT*, 18 Jul 1853.

11. Aqua Explorers, "The Black Warrior Shipwreck," http://www.aquaexplorers.com/BlackWarrior.htm. *Black Warrior*: 225 feet (68.5 m) long, displacement of 1556 gross tons (approx. 1446 metric tons), 37-foot (11.27 m) beam. The fare for a one-way passage to either Havana or Mobile was $65, which was $20 less than the first class "Ladies Saloon State Rooms" on the *Georgia*.

12. John H. Morrison, *History of American Steam Navigation* (New York: Stephen Daye, 1958), 455–456. The ships were named after Alabama rivers, the Cahawba (or Cahaba), a tributary of the Alabama River and the Black Warrior, a tributary of the Tombigbee River.

13. TR, Sr., letter to Martha Bulloch Roosevelt, Aug 18 and Oct 3–5, 1853, TRC, Transcripts, early family correspondence.

14. *NYT*, 11 Oct 1853.

15. U.S. Congress, Senate, *Journal of the Executive Proceedings of the Senate of the United States of America from December 6, 1852 to March 3, 1855 Inclusive*, vol. IX, 32nd Cong. 2nd Sess. (Washington: GPO, 1887), 168.

16. *NYT*, 21 and 29 Dec 1853.

17. Richmond *Times-Dispatch*, 23 Oct 1905.

18. *NYT*, 10 Jan 1854.

19. *NYT*, 18 Jan 1854.

20. Robert Jones, "Photographs of headstone and burial card," email to authors, 6 Feb 2009.

21. *NYT*, 13 Feb 1854.

22. Henry Lorenzo Janes, "The Black Warrior Affair," *The American Historical Review* 12 (Jan 1907): 280–298.

23. *Charleston Daily Courier*, 28 Feb 1854 to 16 Mar 1854.

24. *NYT*, 1 May 1854.

25. Janes, "Black Warrior Affair," 282–283; *NYT*, "Obituary of William H. Robertson," 6 Jun 1859.

26. Naval Historical Center, DANFS Online, s.v. "Fulton" http://www.history.navy.mil/danfs/f5/fulton-ii.htm.

27. *NYT*, "From Havana," 21 Mar 1854. The correspondent comments that the captain-general of Havana tried to rule Cuba with an "iron-rod" and micro-managed all aspects of Cuban life.

28. U.S. Congress, House of Representatives, "Seizure of the Black Warrior," 33rd Cong., 1st Sess., House Ex. Doc. No. 76, 15 Mar 1854 (Washington: A.O.P. Wilson, 1854), 33.

29. Harry F. Guggenheim, *The United States and Cuba* (1934; reprint, New York: Arno, 1970), 17–18. *NYT*, 30 Mar 1854.

30. *NYT*, 30 Mar 1854.

31. *NYT*, 28 Mar 1854.

32. Soulé was unpopular in Spain after he wounded the French ambassador to Spain (Turgot) in a duel. See: Guggenheim, *United States and Cuba*, 18.

33. Robert May, *The Southern Dream of a Caribbean Empire* (Baton Rouge: Louisiana State University, 1973), Chapter 3, "The Cuba Movement, 1854–1855." Relations with Spain improved immeasurably with the resignation of Soulé in 1855.

34. *NYT*, 4 May 1854.

35. JDB Service Record.

36. *NYT*, 11 Sep and 4 Oct 1854.

37. JDB, letter to Secretary of the Navy J.C. Dobbin, 3 Jun 1854.

38. *NYT*, 9 Feb and 3 Aug 1855. With the change in destination from Mobile to New Orleans, the company changed its name to the New York and New Orleans Steamship Company.

39. Martha Bulloch Roosevelt, letters to and from TR, Sr., 2, 8, 9, 13, 18, and 21 May 1855, TRC, bMS Am 1785.2 (97 & 100).

40. Morrison, *American Steam Navigation*, 487; The Ships List, http://www.theshipslist.com/ships/descriptions/panamafleet.html. William Collyer also constructed the *Cahawba*.
41. *NYT*, 20 Feb, 19 Mar, 20 and 27 May, and 20 Jun 1856.
42. *NYT*, 12 Aug 1856.
43. Robert E. May, *Manifest Destiny's Underworld: Filibustering in Antebellum America* (Chapel Hill: University of North Carolina, 2002), Chapter 1.
44. See: "The Remembrances of Solon Borland," http://files.usgwarchives.org/ar/pulaski/history/borland-solon.txt for more on Nicaragua.
45. Robert L. Scheina, *Latin America's Wars: The Age of the Caudillo: 1791–1899*, vol. 1 (Washington: Brassey's, 2003), 229.
46. *Ibid.*
47. *NYT*, 12 Aug, 1 and 15 Sep 1856.
48. Scheina, *Latin America's Wars*, 225–231; Walker mounted two more filibuster expeditions in Central America. On the first, the U.S. Navy intercepted him. On the second, the British Royal Navy captured and handed him over to Honduran authorities who executed him by firing squad on 12 Sep 1860. Walker was 36 years of age.
49. J.G.B. Bulloch, *Archibald Bulloch*, 17; TR, Sr., letter to Martha (Bulloch) Roosevelt, 25 Jan 1857, TRC, bMS Am 1785.7(38), #23. Roosevelt erroneously dated his letter 1856 instead of 1857.
50. Osborne Cross, *A report, in the form of a journal, to the quartermaster-general, of the march of the regiment of mounted riflemen to Oregon,* U.S. House, Ex. Doc. 31st Cong., 2nd Sess., part II (Washington, DC), 126–240; See: J.G.B. Bulloch, *Archibald Bulloch*, 17; Raymond W. Settle, *The March of the Mounted Riflemen* (1940; reprint, Lincoln: University of Nebraska, 1989), 18. Louise was the daughter of Colonel Bartholomew Von Schaumburg, a former German count. Osborne Cross helped blaze the Oregon Trail in 1849 and kept a journal that was published by the War Department and by a private publisher.
51. Virtualology, *Appletons Encyclopedia*, "Hall of North and South Americans," s.v. "Trueman Cross," http://famousamericans.net/truemancross/; Settle, *Mounted Riflemen*, 33–35; General Cross died in New York City in the Roosevelt Hospital on 15 Jul 1866.
52. TR, Sr., letter to Martha (Bulloch) Roosevelt, TRC bMS Am 1785.7(38), #23; Naturalisation papers dated 21 Jan 1869, Bulloch, James Dunwody (sic), Certificate 6059 (Official National Archives of the U.K. Government) lists date of marriage as 1857. There was an added element of excitement after Bulloch left New Orleans. Mr. Stringer of the Bank of New Orleans absconded in the *Cahawba* with $50,000. "The telegraph line ... was ... cut, thus preventing the detention of the steamer." Mr. Stringer confessed that he hid the loot in one of the *Cahawba*'s staterooms. See: *NYT*, 27 Jan, 2, 4 and 5 Feb 1857.
53. *NYT*, 25 Feb 1857.
54. Elisha Kent Kane, *The U.S. Grinnell Expedition in Search of* Sir John Franklin*: A Personal Narrative* (New York, Harper & Brothers, 1854); Ken McGoogan, *The Race to the Polar Sea: The Heroic Adventures of Elisha Kent Kane* (Berkeley, CA: Counterpoint, 2009); Mark M. Sawin, *Raising Kane: Elisha Kent Kane and the Culture of Fame in Antebellum-America* (Philadelphia: Philosophical Society, 2008). Franklin and his party of 128 men would die of disease and exposure, 1845–1851; two future Confederate naval officers who sailed with Kane were William Murdaugh and Bob Carter; both would be crucial as JDB planned of the cruise of the CSS *Shenandoah*. Kane's procession started in New Orleans and terminated in Philadelphia.
55. Caroli, *Roosevelt Women*, 34–38; Bulloch, *Secret Service*, I: 18–50.
56. TR, Sr., letter to Martha Bulloch Roosevelt, 31 May 1857, TRC, bMS Am 1785.7(38); Martha Stewart Bulloch, letter to Susan Elliott West, 15 Oct 1858, TRC, bMS AM 1785.2 (19), #2; U.S. Interior Department, Census Office. Eighth Census, 1860, Morris Township, Morris County, NJ, series M653, roll: 703, p. 68, s.v. "Capt J. D. Bullock"; *NYT*, 5 Oct 1858; Martha Stewart Bulloch, letter to Susan (Elliott) West, 15 Oct 1858,TRC, bMS AM 1785.2 (19), #2.
57. Henry Howard Brownell, *Lyrics of a Day: or, Newspaper-Poetry* (New York: Carleton, 1864), 78–80, 83–85. "The Burial of the Dane" was written on the "Steamship Cahawba, at Sea, Jan. 20th, 1858." "At Sea" was also written aboard the *Cahawba* (3 Feb 1859) and addressed to Bulloch. Farragut would be impressed with Brownell's work and appointed him acting ensign and secretary aboard the USS *Hartford*, where, during the Battle of Mobile Bay, he wrote the poem "Bay Fight." See: Henry H. Brownell, *Lines of Battle* (Boston: Houghton Mifflin, 1912), introduction, 13, 16.
58. Edmund Morris, *The Rise of Theodore Roosevelt* (New York: Coward, McCann, & Geoghegan, 1979), 32.; Martha Stewart Bulloch, letter to Susan (Elliott) West, 28 Oct 1858, TRC, bMS AM 1785.2 (19), #4. TR was born at the Roosevelt home, No. 28, East Twentieth St., New York City.
59. Richard H. Dana, *To Cuba and Back: A Vacation Voyage* (London: Smith, Elder, 1859), 5–6.
60. *Ibid.*, 20.
61. *NYT*, 20 Oct 1859.
62. *NYT*, 19 May 1860 and 22 Aug 1860. The *Bienville* was a 1558-ton side-wheel steamer built by Lawrence and Foulks of Brooklyn, New York, with a length of 253 feet and 38 feet by the beam. She was built for first class passenger comfort with considerable cargo capacity as well.
63. U.S. Congress. *Biographical Directory*, s.v. Herschel Johnson, http://bioguide.congress.gov/scripts/biodisplay.pl?index=J000139.
64. Galbraith Schlisinger, *Of the People: The 200 Year History of the Democratic Party* (Santa Monica, CA: General, 1992); Joel H. Silbey, *A Respectable Minority: The Democratic Party in the Civil War Era, 1860–1868* (New York: Norton, 1977).
65. Constitutional Union Party, http://www.ourcampaigns.com/RaceDetail.html?RaceID=58519.

66. Allan Nevins, *Ordeal of the Union. Volume 4: The Emergence of Lincoln: Prologue to Civil War* (London: Charles Scribner, 1950).
67. U.S. Federal Election Commission, "Federal Elections: 1860" (Washington: GPO, 1982).
68. James M. McPherson, *Battle Cry of Freedom* (1988; reprint, London: Penguin, 1990), chapters "The Revolution of 1860" and "The Counter-Revolution of 1861," 202–275.
69. Bulloch, *Secret Service*, I: 29.

Chapter 4

1. *NYT,* 23 Nov 1860.
2. Steven A. Channing, *Crisis of Fear: Secession in South Carolina* (New York: W.W. Norton, 1970), 280–286.
3. *NYT,* 24 Dec 1860.
4. *NYT,* 25 Dec 1860. Commodore Josiah Tattnall, was staying at the Astor House, while Morris was at Brevoort House. Tattnall had recently returned from the Far East where he assisted a British squadron under fire from forts at the mouth of the River Pai-ho on the Yellow Sea coast of China. Charged with violating neutrality, Tattnall replied, "Blood is thicker than water," which entered American lexicon overnight. Morris later commanded JDB's commerce raider, the CSS *Florida.*
5. *NYT,* 2 Jan 1861.
6. *NYT,* 23 Feb 1861.
7. McPherson, *Battle Cry,* 240–241; David Detzer, *Allegiance: Fort Sumter, Charleston, and the Beginning of the Civil War* (San Diego: Harcourt, 2001); Jefferson Davis, *The Rise and Fall of the Confederate Government* (1881; reprint, New York: Da Capo, 1990), vol. 1, part 3, chapters 1 and 2.
8. U.S. Library of Congress, "Abraham Lincoln's Inauguration," http://www.americaslibrary.gov/cgi-bin/page.cgi/jb/civil/lincoln2_1.
9. *NYT,* 25 Mar 1861.
10. *Ibid.*
11. Bulloch, *Secret Service,* I: 27–28.
12. McPherson, *Battle Cry,* 249–250; John G. Nicolay, and John Hay, *Abraham Lincoln: A History* (New York: Century, 1890), 3: 248; Abraham Lincoln, *The Collected Works of Abraham Lincoln,* vol. IV, ed. Roy P. Basler (New Brunswick, NJ: Rutgers University, 1953), 157–159.
13. Bulloch, *Secret Service,* I: 27.
14. *Ibid.,* 27–28.
15. *Ibid.,* 28.
16. *NYT,* 2 Apr 1861. U.S. Vice President Hannibal Hamlin and his wife, Ellen, were also at the famous New York Astor Hotel.
17. See: James Phinney Baxter, III, *The Introduction of the Ironclad Warship* (1933; reprint, Annapolis: Naval Institute, 2001), 39, 46 for details on private-government mail contract vessels.
18. See: John, Niven, *Gideon Welles: Lincoln's Secretary of the Navy* (New York: Oxford University, 1973), 3.
19. Bulloch, *Secret Service,* I: 30; U.S. Interior Dept., Battle Summaries, "Fort Sumter," http://www.nps.gov/hps/abpp/battles/sc001.htm.
20. Davis, *Rise and Fall of the Confederate Government,* vol. I, part 3, chap. 1 and 2.
21. Bulloch, *Secret Service,* I: 32.
22. *Ibid.,* 33.
23. *Ibid.,* 34.
24. U.S. Treasury Dept., *Decisions of the Comptroller of the Treasury, containing decisions of Robert B. Bowler, Comptroller, and Edw. A. Bowers, Assistant Comptroller,* vol. II (Washington: GPO, 1896): 84–89.
25. *Ibid.;* also in U.S. Congress, Senate, *Reports of Committee of the Senate of the United States,* Senate Rept. 1010, 53rd Cong., 3rd Sess., vol. 2 (Washington: GPO, 1895). Appendix I contains the full decision. Although JDB was a minority shareholder, he held had more shares (10) in the vessel than any other Southern owner.
26. Bulloch, *Secret Service,* I: 34.
27. *Ibid.,* 35.
28. *Ibid.*
29. *Ibid.,* 36; *NYT,* 22 Apr 1861.
30. Bulloch, *Secret Service,* I: 36.
31. *Ibid.,* 36–37.
32. *Ibid.,* 37.
33. *Ibid.,* 38.
34. *Ibid.;* Liverpool Record Office, *Register of Baptisms in the Parish of St. John Waterloo, in the county of Lancaster* (London: Shaw & Sons, 9 Dec 1865), 1; Martha Bulloch Roosevelt, to Anna Bulloch Gracie, 26 May 1869, TRC Early Family Correspondence to Sep 1869 From Liverpool, #207.
35. U.S. War Dept., *The War of the Rebellion: A Compilation of the Official Records of the Union and Confederate Armies,* ser. 3, vol. 1 (Washington: GPO, 1899), 445–447. On 10 Jun, Seward forwarded the report to Morse, who acknowledged receipt on 19 Jul.
36. Bulloch, *Secret Service,* I: 39–41.

37. *NYT*, 5 Sep 1860; William Pool, ed., *Landmarks of Niagara County* (Syracuse,: D. Mason & Company, 1897), 99; Hollis White, letter to George D. Lamont, May 3, 1859, Thurlow Weed Papers, Rush Rhees Library, University of Rochester (New York); Robin W. Winks, *The Civil War Years: Canada and the United States*, 4th ed. (Baltimore: John Hopkins, 1998), 60.

38. *NYT,* 26 Mar 1861.

39. Bulloch, *Secret Service*, I: 23.

40. U.S. Interior Department, Census Office. Eighth Census, 1860, City of Philadelphia, Philadelphia County, PA, series M653, roll: 1157, p. 568, s.v. "Dr. H. West." Martha Bulloch and her children Anna and Irvine also resided in New Jersey and New York during this period and may have only been an occasional boarder with her daughter Susan Elliott West.

41. Bulloch, *Secret Service*, I: 40.

42. See: James I. Waddell, CSS *Shenandoah: The Memoirs of James Iredell Waddell*, ed. James D. Horan (New York: Crown Publishers, 1960) for an account of how a Southern naval officer smuggled himself into the Confederacy.

43. Bulloch, *Secret Service*, I: 40–41.

44. Tennessee Historical Society, *Tennessee Encyclopedia of History and Culture*, "George Washington Barrow," http://tennesseeencyclopedia.net/imagegallery.php?EntryID=B009.

45. Bulloch, *Secret Service*, I: 41. Tennessee seceded on 8 Jun 1861.

46. *Ibid.*

47. Most of the Confederacy's first offices were located in the Clancey Hotel, near the intersection of Bibb and Commerce Streets.

48. Bulloch, *Secret Service*, I: 41.

49. *Ibid.*, 43.

50. Bulloch, *Secret Service*, I: 46; Ernest McNeill, ed., *Dictionary of American Naval Fighting Ships*, vol. II, 569–570. The *Habana* was a bark-rigged screw steamer. As the *Sumter*, it was the Confederacy's first commerce raider.

51. Bulloch, *Secret Service*, I:46.

52. *Ibid.*

53. *Ibid.*, 47.

54. *Ibid.* Raphael Semmes, in the CSS *Sumter*, first confirmed the Confederate Navy's inability to use foreign ports for condemnation procedures.

55. James P. Baxter, "The British Government and Neutral Rights, 1861–1865," *American Historical Revie*, 34, no. 1 (Oct 1928): 11. Queen Victoria's letters give context to the security issues that Great Britain saw as foremost of concern. See: Frank Merli, *Great Britain and the Confederate Navy: 1861–1865* (Bloomington: Indiana University, 1970), for a more modern take on the naval side of this issue.

56. See: John S. Gordon, *A Thread across the Ocean: The Heroic Story of the Transatlantic Cable* (New York: Walker & Co, 2002), for the fascinating story of how the telegraph became the "internet" of the age that knitted together the British Empire and briefly dominated communications as a result.

57. Merli, *Great Britain and the Confederate Navy*, 41–42; Georg F. Martens, et al., *Nouveau Recueil Général des Traités et autres Actes relatifs aux Rapports de Droit international*, 2nd series, vol. XV (Gottingue: G. A. Kaestner, 1857), 791–792. Lincoln's government would never acknowledge the "belligerency" or legitimacy of the Confederate States, but in 1863 a U.S. Supreme Court prize case ruling held that the Confederacy was in a state of civil war.

58. Robert D. Meade, *Judah P. Benjamin: Confederate Statesman* (New York: Oxford University, 1943). This remains the best reference on Benjamin, especially for his international connections and grasp of international law.

59. The Avalon Project, Lillian Goldman Law Library, Yale Law School,"Proclamation of April 17, 1861" http://avalon.law.yale.edu/19th_century/csa_p041761.asp.

60. See: *NYT*, "The Privateers of Jefferson Davis in Court," 28 Jun 1861 for an ironic footnote on Confederate privateers and the trial of the CSS *Jefferson Davis*.

61. Eric H. Walther, *William Lowndes Yancey: The Coming of the Civil War* (Chapel Hill: University of North Carolina, 2006), 309. Mann had been the U.S. assistant secretary of state 1853–55. See: NYT, 5 Feb 1855 for Mann's resignation and involvement in the Soulé-Ostend Manifesto.

62. Ethel Trenholm S. Nepveux, G*eorge Alfred Trenholm and The Company That Went to War* (Charleston: Electric City Printing, 1994). There has yet to be a full examination of the Fraser, Trenholm and Co. documents located in Liverpool, nor an analysis of the principal partners of the firm, particularly Charles K. Prioleau.

63. Lyman Cobb, *The Reticule and Pocket Companion, or, Miniature Lexicon of the English Language* (New York: Harper & Brothers, 1861). Semmes mentions that he and Mallory used *Reid's English Dictionary* when Semmes could not find a copy of *Cobb's Miniature Lexicon* in New Orleans, and a review of the enciphered letters of Mallory, North, and Bulloch confirms the use of Cobb's cipher. See: Raphael Semmes, *Memoirs of Service Afloat, during the War Between the States* (Baltimore: Kelly Piet & Co., 1869), 104.

64. Bulloch, *Secret Service*, I: 48.

65. *Ibid.*

66. Bulloch, *Secret Service*, I: 48; Canada, Parliament, *Sessional Papers of the Parliament of the Province of Canada, Volume 20, Issue 4* (Quebec: Hunter, Rose, and Lemieux, 1862), #21.

67. William A. Tidwell, *Come Retribution* (Jackson: University of Miss., 1988), 171.

68. The St. Albans raid is perhaps the most notorious and well-known Confederate covert operation, with even a romantic Hollywood movie to add to its historical sheen. There were lesser-known "actions" such as the attempt to burn down New York City and blow-up a major rail bridge near Nashville. See: Edward A. Sowles, *History of the St. Albans*

Raid (St. Albans: Vermont Historical Society, 1876); Edward R. Ellis, *The Epic of New York City* (1966; reprint, New York: Basic Books 2004), 317; Tidwell, *Come Retribution*, 166.

69. Tidwell, *Come Retribution*, 172–173.

70. Newspaper messages became a common form of "open" transmission of secret information by the end of the war. Mittie used such devices, as did Irvine Bulloch, to alert the Bulloch-Roosevelt ladies to his location when he visited New York City *after* the Civil War. See: Caroli, *Roosevelt Women*, 46–47. JDB may have stayed at the St. Lawrence Hall Hotel in Montreal, which had many prominent guests, including the Prince of Wales in 1860 and John Wilkes Booth in 1864, after it had become known as the Confederate Headquarters in Canada.

71. Liverpool Record Office, *Register of Baptisms*, 1.

Chapter 5

1. Queen Victoria's letter to Palmerston on 30 May 1861 provides an intriguing view of the British Empire's thoughts on Canada during this time, since it was "of great importance that we should be strong in Canada, and thinks an increase in Artillery as important as the sending of two more battalions.... The Naval forces would, however, require strengthening even more. It is less likely that the remnant of the United States could send expeditions by land to the North while quarrelling with the South, than that they should commit acts of violence at sea." See: Victoria, *Letters 1854–1861*, 440.

2. There is conflicting evidence concerning the actual date of Bulloch's arrival in Liverpool. In the ORN, ser. II, 2:83, JDB's letter to Mallory dated 3 Jun 1861 declares his arrival in Liverpool, while other sources indicate arrival on Jun 4th or 5th after a passage of 14 days, 14 hours via Londonderry. See: Canada, Parliament, *Sessional Papers*, #21. JDB may have posted a letter to Mallory by the return voyage of the *North American*. If he did, the letter then had to be posted to the Confederacy through the Union lines, suggesting an early version of the "Secret Line." The route ran from England to Halifax, Nova Scotia, and then to coastal pickup points on Chesapeake Bay, where couriers received dispatches for the Confederate capital.

3. Bulloch, *Secret Service*, I: 51.

4. John D. Bennett, *The London Confederates: the Officials, Clergy, Businessmen and Journalists Who Backed the American South during the Civil War* (Jefferson, NC: McFarland, 2007), 26.

5. *Ibid.*

6. Bulloch, *Secret Service*, I: 52; the "Great Powers" were: France, United Kingdom, Prussia, Austrian Empire, and Russia.

7. *Harpers Weekly*, 29 Jun 1861, 406, 413 (image).

8. Bulloch, *Secret Service*, I: 52–53; Nepveux, G*eorge Alfred Trenholm*, 25–27.

9. Bulloch, *Secret Service*, I: 66.

10. *Ibid.*, 66–67. One of the barristers was probably Sir Hugh McCalmont Cairns, who would represent the builders in the *Alexandra* case. See: Wilbur Devereaux James, *The Confederate Rams at Birkenhead* (Tuscaloosa, AL: Confederated Publishing Co., 1961), 24, 34.

11. *Ibid.*, 68.

12. *Ibid.*, 58–59.

13. Robert Thorpe, conversations with author, 17–18 Jul 2009. In his forthcoming book on W.C. Miller, Thorpe notes that compared to the *Philomel*, the *Florida* was stretched by 50 feet amidships to accommodate additional boilers and engine. The HMS *Steady* was keeping an eye on British interests along the eastern seaboard of USA at the same time that CSS *Florida* was patrolling the area. Also, see: ORN, ser. II, 2: 83–87.

14. *NYT*, 29 Aug 1859.

15. Ocean Liner Virtual Museum, "Cammell Laird: Shipbuilders to the World (1824–1993)," http://www.oceanlinermuseum.co.uk/Cammell%20Laird%20Shipbuilders%20to%20the%20World.htm; Cammell Laird, "The History of Cammell Laird," www.cammell-laird.com. By 1839, the Lairds built their first screw-propelled steamship for the North American market and by the mid–1840s regularly constructed ships for the Admiralty. In 1857, they opened a large shipyard at Birkenhead, across the Mersey River opposite Liverpool that is still in use today. Hereafter, the *Oreto* will be referred to as the *Florida*.

16. Sanford, letter to Seward, 4 Jul 1861, Despatches, Belgium, *vol.* 5 and Dispatch 14, Morse, letter to Seward dated 19 Jul, 1861, within a covering Dispatch, 23 Aug 1861, quoted in Hariet Chappell Owsley, "Henry Shelton Sanford and Federal Surveillance Abroad, 1861–1865," *The Mississippi Valley Historical* Review 48, no. 2 (Sep 1961), 214.

17. ORA, ser. 2, vol. 2, 18. James Alfred Roosevelt, was the nephew of Judge James I. Roosevelt and TR, Sr.

18. Milton, *Lincoln's Spymaster*, 29 (Huntington Library, DU-4573, Wilding, letter to Adams, 12 Sep 1861).

19. The best reference detailing the CSS *Alabama*'s construction is Andrew Bowcock, CSS *Alabama: Anatomy of a Raider* (London: Chatham, 2002). The model is on display at the Liverpool Maritime Museum.

20. ORN, ser. II, 2: 85. JDB also received a letter via Lt. James H. North CSN, and Major Anderson CSA. This was the first remittance to the Confederate Navy account to reach Great Britain.

21. Bulloch, *Secret Service*, I: 58–65.

22. *Ibid.*, 70–71; McPherson, *Battle Cry*, 338–345.

23. *Ibid.*; This is Hartlepool, "History" http://www.thisishartlepool.co.uk/history/westhartlepool.asp. The small port had a convenient rail link with nearby coalmines.

24. ORN, ser. II, 2: 83–87. Bulloch was in London when he wrote this letter. He may have been coordinating supply efforts with Major Huse. The munitions shipped on the *Bermuda* included a million percussion caps.

25. Bulloch, *Secret Service*, I: 71; Naval Historical Center, *DANFS Online*, s.v. "Bermuda" http://www.history.navy.mil/danfs/b5/bermuda-i.htm.
26. *Ibid.*
27. Michael F. Hughes, "The Personal Observations of a Man of Intelligence: Sir James Fergusson's Visit to North America, 1861," *Civil War History* 45, no.3 (1999): 243; *Questia*, Web, 23 Dec 2010. Lord Derby's letter is dated 13 Nov 1861. The Roosevelt family in New York knew of the *Bermuda*'s arrival and JDB's involvement with the operation. See: TR, Sr., letter to Mittie Bulloch Roosevelt, 14 Feb 1862, TRC.
28. Bulloch, *Secret Service*, I: 111; Anderson, *Confederate Foreign Agent*, 82, 89–90.
29. Victoria, *Letters*, 350–451, 453.
30. Edward C. Anderson, *Confederate Foreign Agent: The European Diary of Major Edward C. Anderson*, ed. William S. Hoole (Tuscaloosa, AL: Confederate Publishing, 1976), 47, 49; Bennett, *The London Confederates*, 54, 55; JDB saw the play "My Lord & My Lady" at the Haymarket Theatre on Aug 12th with Anderson and Charles Green. He was probably with Anderson at the Olympic Theatre on Aug 24th for "Porter's Knot, & Wandering Minstrels." Charles Green was a partner of Andrew Low who the Confederate War Department sent to England in Jul 1861. "Mr. Isaacs" was the principle owner of Isaac, Campbell and Sons.
31. *NYT*, 29 Aug 1861.
32. Bulloch, *Secret Service*, I: 110; ORN, ser. II, 2: 86.
33. Eric J. Graham, *Clydebuilt: The Blockade Runners of the American Civil War* (Edinburgh: Birlinn, 2005).
34. Anderson, *Confederate Foreign Agent*, 55. Bulloch may have visited Glasgow as early as the end of Jun 1861, if the reports of Acting Consul Wilding were accurate. He noted in a message to U.S. Minister Adams on 3 Jul that "a person answering [JDB's] description was here about two weeks since and has gone to Glasgow." See: Wilding, letter to Adams, 3 Jul 1861, Thomas Dudley files at Huntingdon Library, CA, DU-4573.
35. Harriott Bulloch's arrival date is based on the advertised Cunard Line sailing schedule.
36. John Hussey, *Cruisers, Cotton, and Confederates* (Wirral, U.K.: Countryvise, 2008), 95.
37. "Cut-outs" are individuals who can claim plausible deniability and who have no knowledge that their actions might constitute illegal activities.
38. Regina Rapier, *Saga of Felix Senac. Being the Legend and Biography of a Confederate Agent in Europe* (Atlanta: Self-published, 1972), 127; Nepveux, *George Alfred Trenholm*, 35.
39. Bulloch, *Secret Service*, I: 122; ORN, ser. I, 12: 331; Anderson, *Confederate Foreign Agent*, 82, 89–90.
40. *Ibid.*, 112–113; Hussey, *Cruisers, Cotton, and Confederates*, 102. The impetus for Low's timely arrival may have come from JDB, Mallory, Andrew Low, or John Low himself. Low and his family were familiar with Glasgow and Liverpool shipping and shipbuilding trade and had considerable useful connections.
41. ORN, ser. II, 2: 96–97.
42. Bulloch, *Secret Service*, I: 113; ORN, ser. I, 6: 411–412.
43. ORN, ser. II, 2: 98–99.
44. Martha Stewart Bulloch, letter to Susan Elliott West, 20 Jul 1861, TRC, bMS Am 1875.7(4), #3.
45. Owsley, "Henry Shelton Sanford," 218; ORN, ser. I, 6: 411–412.
46. Bulloch, *Secret Service*, I: 113; ORN, ser. II, 2: 142–143.
47. Anderson, *Confederate Foreign Agent*, 79–80.
48. *Ibid.*, 114–115.
49. Bulloch, *Secret Service*, I: 117; Anderson, *Confederate Foreign Agent*, 79–80. Anderson recalls that he and Low awakened JDB, which is unlikely given Low's relationship with JDB.
50. *Ibid.*, 116.
51. *Ibid.*, 117.
52. Anderson, *Confederate Foreign Agent*, 105.
53. ORN, ser. I, 12: 222.
54. Bulloch, *Secret Service*, I: 118.
55. *Ibid.*
56. *Ibid.*; ORN, ser. I, 6: 745.
57. Bulloch, *Secret Service*, I: 120–121.
58. *Ibid.*, 121.
59. Anderson, *Confederate Foreign Agent*, 92, 93.
60. Bulloch, *Secret Service*, I: 123.
61. *Ibid.*, 124; Anderson, *Confederate Foreign Agent*, 96–97. The story of the crowing cockerel was retold a number of times in several blockade running accounts. In this case, both Anderson's contemporary diary and JDB's memoirs tell the same tale.
62. Bulloch, *Secret Service*, I: 125.
63. *Ibid.*, 126.
64. *Ibid.*, 126–127.
65. ORN, ser. I, 1: 202; ORN, ser. I, 6: 355–356, 367–370 (sketch of the *Fingal* by Ed. Brennan is on page 369), 391, 405–406, 411; ORN, ser. I, 6: 202; ORN, ser. I, 12: 226–227, 330–331.
66. Bulloch, *Secret Service*, I: 127.
67. ORN, ser. I, 12: 324.
68. *Ibid.*, 128.
69. *Ibid.*, 129–130.

70. Martha Stewart Bulloch, letter to Susan Elliott West, 16 Nov 1861, TRC, bMS Am 1875.7(4), #7.
71. ORN, ser. II, 2: 105–106.
72. *Ibid.*
73. *Ibid.*, 132.
74. Bulloch, *Secret Service*, I: 133; ORN, ser. II, 2: 114–116. JDB carefully edited the letter that appeared in his memoirs as compared to the compete version in the ORN. He was probably shielding the partners of Fraser, Trenholm and Co., who at the time of the release of his memoirs still owed the U.S. government monies.
75. Bulloch, *Secret Service*, I: 136–138.
76. Anderson, *Confederate Foreign Agent*, 104.
77. ORN, ser. I, 12: 432–433, 438.
78. Bulloch, *Secret Service*, I: 138–139.

Chapter 6

1. Richmond *Daily Dispatch*, 7 Jan 1862.
2. Victoria, *Letters*, 469–470, 473–474. Queen Victoria comments that this Dec 1st draft "was the last the beloved Prince ever wrote." Albert died on 14 Dec 1861.
3. John Holland Rose, et al., eds. *The Cambridge History of the British Empire*, vol. 7, part 1 (Chicago: University of Chicago, 1932), 103.
4. Eugene A. Brady, "A Reconsideration of the Lancashire Cotton Famine," *Agricultural History* 37 (Jul 1963): 156–157, 161; Edwin Waugh, *Home-Life of the Lancashire Factory Folk during the Cotton Famine* (1867; reprint, Charleston: Bibliobazaar, 2007).
5. David Blackbourn, *History of Germany, 1790–1918: the Long Nineteenth Century*, 2nd ed. (Oxford: Wiley-Blackwell, 2003), 183–210.
6. ORN, ser. II, 2: 123–124. JDB's letter confuses the names of the two midshipmen that are correctly identified here. See: Maffitt, *Maffitt*, 344, 377; Naval Historical Center, "Online Library" s.v. "Lieutenant E. Maffitt Anderson" http://www.history.navy.mil/photos/pers-us/uspers-a/em-ander.htm). The fathers, John Newland Maffitt and Edward C. Anderson, entered the Navy together and named their sons after each other. Christiana Bulloch, a sister of Bulloch's grandfather, Governor Archibald Bulloch, married the Hon. Henry Yonge in 1774. Henry branded Christiana a "rebel" when she gained control of his property during the American Revolution after he was banished to Florida as a British loyalist. See: Joseph G.B. Bulloch, *A History and Genealogy of the Habersham Family* (Columbia, SC: R.L. Bryan, 1901), 138.
7. ORN, ser. II, 2: 125.
8. *Ibid.*, 130. It is likely that JDB had heard in Richmond of the not-so-secret conversion of the former USS *Merrimac* into the ironclad CSS *Virginia*, and like many other naval offices, he hoped for a miraculous sweeping of Union wooden ships from the sea.
9. Bulloch, *Secret Service*, I: 140–141.
10. Sec. Mallory's new orders appear to have been sent in response to JDB's first missive, as it is dated 10 Jan 1862, thus a full week after his 3 Jan request, and three days before his second letter of 13 Jan 1862. See: ORN, ser. II, 2: 127.
11. See: Naval Historical Center, "Online Library" s.v. "Bienville," http://www.history.navy.mil/photos/sh-usn/usnsh-b/bienvill.htm, for fascinating pictorial evidence of the USS *Bienville*'s activities during this period.
12. ORN, ser. II, 2: 134.
13. Bulloch, *Secret Service*, I: 149.
14. The *Annie Childs* was a steam-powered, screw propulsion steamer of 618 tons. See: Ron Vinson, "List of Merchant Steamboats in NC (1861 to 1880)" http://www.historync.org/NCsteamboatlist1861–1880.htm; Steven R. Wise, *Lifeline of the Confederacy: Blockade Running During the American Civil War* (Columbia, SC: University of South Carolina, 1988), Appendix 6, 242.
15. Bulloch, *Secret Service*, I: 149.
16. *Ibid.* JDB was the *de facto* leader of every operation he came in touch with during the war.
17. *Ibid.*, 150.
18. *Ibid.*
19. Bulloch, *Secret Service*, I: 150–151; U.S. State Dept. "American Consulate in the Azores," http://www.usconsulateazores.pt/HistoryOfTheConsulate.htm.
20. *Ibid.*
21. Warren Spencer, *The Confederate Navy in Europe* (Tuscaloosa, AL: University of Alabama, 1983), 19–20.
22. John M. Brooke, *Ironclads and Big Guns of the Confederacy, the Journal and letters of John M. Brooke*, ed. George M. Brooke, Jr. (Columbia, SC: University of South Carolina, 2002), 162.
23. ORN, ser. II, 2: 70–72. This document reveals the hopes of the new government regarding assistance from Britain and France in the early halcyon days of the Confederacy.
24. Thomas R. Neblett, *Civil War Yacht; Chronicles of the Schooner America* (Mustang, OK: Tate, 2009); 216, 273; Anderson, *Confederate Foreign Agent*, 45; Naval Historical Center, DANFS Online, s.v. "America" http://www.history.navy.mil/danfs/a8/america-i.htm.
25. Anderson, *Confederate Foreign Agent*, 20–22.
26. Spencer, *Confederate Navy*, 21.

27. Anderson, *Confederate Foreign Agent*, 27–28; Spencer, *Confederate Navy*, 21. North took no action until Jul 22nd when he visited the British Navy's ironclad *Warrior*. North returned to the *Warrior* on Jul 28th, but merely walked around her hull. His only other constructive activity in Jul was a desultory discussion with a shipbuilder. Based on Anderson's damning diary, Mallory's often harsh criticisms, JDB's inferences, and James North's own diary, Spencer and other commentators have not dealt kindly with North's comparative lack of results. However, no biography of North has yet appeared to fully examine his role in the Confederate Navy.
28. ORN, ser. II, 2: 87. The date of 16 Aug 1861 was inserted by the ORN editors, for North was actually at sea again aboard the *Camilla* with her owner, Decie. See: Spencer, *Confederate Navy*, 221, fn15.
29. Anderson, *Confederate Foreign Agent*, 45–46.
30. Neblett, *Civil War Yacht*, 278; Spencer, *Confederate Navy*, 23.
31. Spencer, *Confederate Navy*, 23; ORN, ser. II, 2: 88.
32. ORN, ser. II, 2: 98–99; Anderson, *Confederate Foreign Agent*, 77; Spencer, *Confederate Navy*, 25.
33. Spencer, *Confederate Navy*, 39; ORN, ser. II, 2: 125.
34. ORN, ser. II, 2: 105–165. The myriad and confused orders, changes, and personnel re-assignments can only be attributed to Sec. Mallory who did not fully appreciate the havoc delayed communications would cause. Mixed with North's attitude, it was a recipe for increased friction between two key people in the Confederate Navy's overseas operations.
35. Sec. Mallory sent copies of the order to Pegram to JDB to take with him to Britain, but there no copies of the order sent to Pegram by Sec. Mallory in ORN.
36. Naval Historical Center, "Online Library" s.v. "CSS Nashville" http://www.history.navy.mil/photos/sh-us-cs/csa-sh/csash-mr/nashvill.htm.
37. *Ibid.*, s.v. "CSS Sumter" http://www.history.navy.mil/photos/sh-us-cs/csa-sh/csash-sz/sumter.htm and ORN, ser. II, 2: 136. Two letters from Semmes to North dated 23 and 24 Jan 1862 illustrate the communications problems.
38. ORN, ser. II, 2: 138.
39. *Ibid.*, 140–141.
40. *Ibid.*, 141.
41. *Ibid.*, 141–142.
42. *Ibid.*, 144–145.
43. *Ibid.*, 147.
44. *Ibid.*
45. *Ibid.*, 147–148.
46. *Ibid.*, 164–165.
47. *Ibid.*, 176–177.
48. *Ibid.*, 134–135.
49. *Ibid.*, 166.
50. *Ibid.*
51. *Ibid.*, 105–106. JDB requested Low's appointment as an acting master on 19 Nov 1861 in a letter to Mallory. JDB specifically notes that "the East Indian trade ... is pouring large profits into the hands of certain well-known merchants in New York"; clear evidence that he and Mallory understood the need for a global naval war. Low's appointment as master took effect on 20 Jan 1862.
52. Spencer, *Confederate Navy*, 45–46. A vast corpus of papers is in the Georgia Historical Society in Savannah, GA, providing a glimpse of a "cotton society" truly "gone with the wind." Files concerning the Green, Low, and Bulloch families, et al., describe the wonderfully incestuous relationship of business and marriage that marked the period.
53. Bulloch, *Secret Service*, I: 153 and ORN, ser. I, 1: 753.
54. Caleb Huse, *The Supplies for the Confederate Army* (Boston: T.R. Marvin & Son, 1904). Huse had also taken six-months leave from the Union Army, which he spent in Europe, thus he had timely knowledge and contacts there for the Confederacy.
55. James J. Barnes and Patience P. Barnes, *The American Civil War through British Eyes: Vol. 2, Apr 1862–Feb 1863* (Kent, OH: Kent State University, 2005), 2: 103–105.
56. Bulloch, *Secret Service*, I: 160. JDB had to settle for a lesser weapons battery, consisting of four 7-inch rifled guns. The *Florida's* guns were most likely from the Fawcett Preston Foundry in Liverpool that cast the 7-inch Blakely guns and converted the 32-pounder naval smooth bore guns 6.25-inch rifles. Both of these guns are at the Washington Navy Yard; one is stamped as "Blakely's Patent No. 37 Fawcett Preston & Co. Liverpool, Makers 1861." See: John C. Reilly, Jr., *The Iron Guns of Willard Park* (Washington: Naval Historical Center, 1991), 77, 85.
57. Naval Historical Center, DANFS Online, s.v. "Bermuda"; Ethel S. Nepveux, "Eugene Tessier." *Confederate Historical Association of Belgium News* 34, no. 2 (2006): 62–64 http://www.chab-belgium.com/pdf/english/Tessier.pdf.
58. Bulloch, *Secret Service*, I: 159–162. Low carried this letter to Maffitt and a copy for Mallory. JDB did not provide this letter or other correspondence for inclusion in the ORN that would have compromised family or friends such as Duguid.
59. *Ibid.*, 159–160.
60. *Liverpool Mercury*, 8 Apr 1862. Liverpool newspapers were flummoxed about the true identity and destination of the *Florida*; Dudley enclosed this edition in a message to Seward on 9 Apr 1862, illustrating the Union's desperation for useful intelligence.
61. ORN, ser. I, 1: 316.
62. The USS *Tuscarora* and *Ino* were entangled in another international imbroglio. The paymaster and a crewman

from the CSS *Sumter* had been illegally seized in Tangier, Morocco, at the instigation of the US consul. A near-riot broke out among Confederate sympathizers requiring Union forces to extract all concerned. See: ORN, ser. I, 1: 312–316.
 63. Bulloch, *Secret Service*, I: 226.
 64. ORN, ser. II, 2: 176–177.
 65. *Ibid.*, 183–185.
 66. *Ibid.*
 67. *Ibid.*, 185–186.
 68. ORN, ser. I, vol. 1, 770–771.
 69. Stephen Chapin Kinnaman, *The Most Perfect Cruiser* (Indianapolis, IN: Dog Ear Publishing, 2009), 121–122. Kinnaman presents a convincing argument that the *Enrica* was launched on the morning of the 14th at high tide based on Yard Data books and not the 15th as cited in JDB's memoirs.
 70. Bowcock, CSS *Alabama*, 41. Bowcock provides a transcript of Maguire's report that is held in the Mariner's Museum in Newport News, VA; Bulloch, *Secret Service*, I: 227–229.
 71. David H. Milton, *Lincoln's Spymaster: Thomas Haines Dudley and the Liverpool Network* (Mechanicsburg, PA: Stackpole Books, 2003), 39. Hereafter, the *290/Enrica* will be referred to as the *Alabama*.
 72. Dudley, letter to Adams, 23 May 1862, Huntington Library, DU-4573.
 73. ORN, ser. II, 2: 206.
 74. *Ibid.*, 207–208.
 75. *Ibid.*, 207.
 76. *Ibid.*, 207–208.
 77. Milton, *Lincoln's Spymaster*, 40.
 78. Frank Merli, *The Alabama, British Neutrality, and the American Civil War* (Bloomington: Indiana University, 2004), 128. Merli says George Barnett, a Cunard shipping agent, brought Butcher to JDB's office in Liverpool.
 79. Bulloch, *Secret Service*, I: 231. Butcher was a member of the Royal Naval Reserve. While Merli surmises that Butcher joined the RNR to burnish his resume in order to get command of a Cunard ship, it is equally likely that is was a stipulation of the British government's mail ship program. Cunard ships performed the trans–Atlantic mail runs for the government and those vessels, like JDB's former command, the *Bienville*, were built to be converted into auxiliary warships in times of conflict. See: Baxter, *Ironclad Warship*, 39, 46.
 80. Milton, *Lincoln's Spymaster*, 40.
 81. ORN, ser. II, 2: 208.
 82. *Ibid.*, 212. JDB notes that copies of the plans for the ironclads would go via Nassau and New York, in order to reach Mallory in Richmond.
 83. *Ibid.*, 212–213.
 84. Bulloch, *Secret Service*, I: 237.
 85. Sinclair caught a ride on a British warship from Nassau to Halifax where he then boarded the SS *Arabia* to Liverpool. Semmes, who ended up taking the *Bahama* back to Liverpool with other members of his ward room knew that Sinclair might arrive a week or so ahead of him, so he sent his letter to Bulloch via Sinclair. See: ORN, ser. II, 2: 191, Mallory letter to Bulloch dated 7 May 1862; ORN, ser. II, 2: 213–214. Mason letter to North dated 8 Jul 1862; Semmes, *Memoirs of Service Afloat*, 351–353.
 86. ORN, ser. II, 2: 213.
 87. Merli, *Great Britain and the Confederate Navy*, 91.
 88. ORN, ser. II, 2: 214–215.
 89. *Ibid.*, 215–217.
 90. Maffitt, *Maffitt*, 238–239.
 91. ORN, ser. II, 2: 215. Mallory told North to return directly to the Confederacy and that if he had not the funds, to apply to "Commander Bulloch" to "supply them." Mallory's use of "Commander" in front of JDB's name was a direct and intentional slap-down of North's arrogant attitude.
 92. Milton, *Lincoln's Spymaster*, 44.
 93. *Ibid.*
 94. *Ibid.*, 44–45.
 95. ORN, ser. II, 2: 222–226.
 96. Milton, *Lincoln's Spymaster*, 45; Merli, *Great Britain and the Confederate Navy*, 91.
 97. *Ibid.*
 98. Merli, *Alabama*, 82–83, 94, 101, 202. Harding's wife withheld the news of her husband's mental collapse.
 99. Milton, *Lincoln's Spymaster*, 46. Harding may have suffered a stroke. See: Merli, *Great Britain and the Confederate Navy*, 92. Merli and Milton's timeline of Collier's involvement in Adam's submission to Lord Russell do not agree, but Milton's version seems to more closely follow the actual events.
 100. Bulloch, *Secret Service*, I: 238.
 101. *Ibid.*
 102. *Ibid.*
 103. *Ibid.*; Merli, *Great Britain and Confederate Navy*, 92–93; ORN, ser. I, 1: 772.
 104. Bulloch, *Secret Service*, I: 245.
 105. *Ibid.*, 238–239; Merli, *Great Britain and the Confederate Navy*, 92–93.
 106. *Ibid.*
 107. Bulloch, *Secret Service*, I: 241.

108. *Ibid.*, 239–240.
109. Milton, *Lincoln's Spymaster*, 48–49.
110. Bulloch, *Secret Service*, I: 240.
111. *Ibid.*, 240–241.
112. *Ibid.*, 242; Naval Historical Center, DANFS Online, s.v. "John Paul Jones" http://www.history.navy.mil/danfs/j3/john_paul_jones.htm.
113. *Ibid.*, 242.
114. *Ibid.*; Milton, *Lincoln's Spymaster*, 48–49.
115. Bulloch, *Secret Service*, I: 242–243, 246–248.
116. Bulloch, *Secret Service*, I: 248; ORN, ser. I, 1: 774.
117. *Ibid.*, 243.
118. Milton, *Lincoln's Spymaster*, 49–50; ORN, ser. I, 1: 400–415. Craven's letter of 4 Aug 1862 reveals the large amount of intelligence he had about the *Alabama*.
119. Bulloch, *Secret Service*, I:, 251–252 (erroneously dated 3 Sep 1862); ORN, ser. I, 1: 775. JDB referred to the passage of confidential messages via Nassau to New York by means of John Fraser and Co., the "Union" branch of Fraser, Trenholm and Co. in Liverpool. This implies a large amount of message traffic used the maritime branch of the "Secret Route," described by Tidwell in *Come Retribution*.
120. ORN, ser. II, 2: 232–233. Porter commanded the Fraser, Trenholm and Co.'s blockade runner, *Merrimac* and later, the *Phantom* for the Confederate Ordnance Department (who had bought the vessel from Fraser, Trenholm and Co. after salt water intrusion ruined the *Merrimac*'s boilers. Porter had to beach the *Phantom* in 1863 and set her afire to prevent her capture by the USS *Connecticut*. See: Howard Michael Madaus, "Small Arms Deliveries Through Wilmington, NC in 1863 and the impact on Confederate Ordnance Supply" *American Society of Arms Collectors Bulletin* 85 (2002): 52–54, http://asoac.org/bulletins/85_madaus_wilmington.pdf.
121. Bulloch, *Secret Service*, I: 253.
122. *Ibid.*, 163–164.
123. ORN, ser. II, 2: 205. Exercising his secretarial privilege, Mallory had named the Confederate raider after his home state, which was a change from the original name he had given to Bulloch: *Manassas*.
124. Bulloch, *Secret Service*, I: 163–164.
125. William S. Hoole, *Four Years in the Confederate Navy: The Career of Captain John Low on the C.S.S. Fingal, Florida, Alabama, Tuscaloosa, and Ajax* (Athens: University of Georgia, 1964), 31. Hoole cites 4 May as the day Maffitt arrived on the former privateer *Gordon* (aka *Theodora*) and that they met 11:00 P.M. that night in the Royal Victoria Hotel.
126. Semmes, *Memoirs of Service Afloat*, 349. Fraser, Trenholm and Co. had used the *Melita* previously, and in Semmes' memoir, he points out that the Isaac brothers now owned her.
127. ORN, ser. I, 1: 685–686.
128. *Ibid.*, 763–764. The *Bahama* had arrived on 25 May 1862, loaded with Confederate war material and two of Semmes' former officers from the *Sumter*, 3rd Lt. John Stribling CSN and Lt. Beckett Howell, CSMC (Marines). Their appearance would have confirmed to US Consul Whiting and official British suspicions that something was afoot in relation to the *Florida*.
129. ORN, ser. I, 1: 771.
130. *Ibid.*; ORN, ser. II, 2: 214–215.
131. John McIntosh Kell, *Recollections of a Naval Life: Including the Cruises of the Confederate States Steamers Sumter and Alabama* (Washington: Neale, 1900), 183.
132. Semmes, *Memoirs of Service Afloat*, 354; Frank L. Owsley, *The* CSS *Florida: Her Building and Operation* (Philadelphia: University of Pennsylvania, 1965). This is still the pre-eminent work on the *Florida*, though works by Robert Thorpe are expected soon that relate to one of the builders, W.C. Miller, and her civilian captain, Duguid.
133. *Ibid.*
134. Bulloch, *Secret Service*, I: 230.
135. Owsley, CSS *Florida*, 25–27.
136. Hoole, *Four Years in the Confederate Navy*, 30–35; U.K. Foreign Office, *The Case of Great Britain as Laid before the Tribunal of Arbitration*, vols. I–III (Washington: GPO, 1872), 301–303; hereafter *CoGB*.
137. *Bahama Herald*, 12 Jul 1862.
138. Bulloch, *Secret Service*, I: 233, ORN, ser. II, 2: 212, Bulloch, *Secret Service*, 2: 218–219, ORN, ser. II, 2: 213–215.
139. Bulloch, *Secret Service*, I: 166.
140. *Ibid.*, 238, 274.
141. JDB received the letter that Lt. Sinclair carried by 8 Jul 1862 as Low and Duguid returned to Liverpool on 20 Jul 1862 onboard the *Minna*. See: Bulloch, *Secret Service*, I: 253 for JDB's typically oblique comments.
142. Bulloch, *Secret Service*, I: 253.
143. Semmes, *Memoirs of Service Afloat*, 402.
144. *Ibid.*, 413.
145. Franklin Buchanan was the ranking Confederate admiral; Semmes was promoted to rear admiral in Feb 1865 and brigadier-general (Artillery) in the Confederate Army in early 1865 after the fall of Richmond, Virginia. See: Warren Spencer, *Raphael Semmes: The Philosophical Mariner* (Tuscaloosa: University of Alabama, 1997), 181–185.
146. Gary McKay, *The Sea King: The Life of James Iredell Waddell* (Edinburgh: Birlinn., 2009). The *Shenandoah* traveled some 58,000 miles in her wartime cruise.
147. ORN, ser. II, 2: 235–239.

148. *Ibid.*
149. ORN, ser. II, 2: 235–239. Given the timing of this letter, Semmes shared the Nassau "scuttlebutt" with JDB, which included information about Maffitt (who was one of those who "abused" by the members of Mallory's Board of 15). Maffitt was probably one of those complainers, who clearly despised Mallory and every thing he did, even though he liked and respected JDB.
150. Bulloch, *Secret Service*, I: 255.
151. Mexico gained independence from Spain in 1821, and had massive debts to France, Spain and England. Sensing a chance to expand his empire, Napoleon III invaded, an event that significantly influenced the international dimensions of the American Civil War. Some 6,500 troops landed at Vera Cruz, and marched toward Mexico City. They were defeated by 4,500 Mexican militia at Puebla on 5 May, thus Mexico's national holiday of Cinco de Mayo. Though Lincoln supported the Mexican government, the French eventually conquered the country, installing Archduke Maximilian as ruler. See: Brian R Hamnett, *A Concise History of Mexico*, 2nd ed. (Cambridge: Cambridge University, 2006), 141–172.
152. George T. Fullam, *Journal of George Townley Fullam: Boarding Officer of the Confederate Sea Raider Alabama*, ed. Charles G. Summersell (Tuscaloosa: University of Alabama, 1973), 11 and Bulloch, *Secret Service*, I: 343–344.
153. Raphael Semmes, *The Log of the Alabama and the Sumter: from the Private Journals of Commander R. Semmes*, et al. (London: Saunders, Otley and Co., 1864).
154. Bulloch, *Secret Service*, I: 255; ORN, ser. II, 2: 783.
155. ORN, ser. I, 1: 783–784.
156. Fullam, *Journal*, 12; Bulloch, *Secret Service*, I, 255.
157. ORN, ser. I, 1: 784 and Semmes, *Memoirs of Service Afloat*, 407.
158. *Ibid.*, 784.
159. *Ibid.*, 785.
160. *Ibid.*
161. *Ibid.*
162. ORN, ser. I, 1: 785; Bulloch, *Secret Service*, I: 256.
163. ORN, ser. II, 2: 257 and ser. I, 1: 776.
164. John J. Hennessy, *Return to Bull Run: The Campaign and Battle of Second Manassas* (Norman: University of Oklahoma Press, 1993).

Chapter 7

1. ORN, ser. II, 2: 183–185. Only one British ship was actually converted, the HMS *Royal Sovereign*.
2. *Ibid.*; Peter Elphick, *Liberty: The Ships That Won the War* (Annapolis: Naval Institute, 2006).
3. Kinnaman, *Most Perfect Cruiser*, 41.
4. Mrs. Hugh McLeod, "The Loss of the Steamer Pulaski," *Georgia Historical Quarterly* 3, no. 1 (Mar 1919): 63–95. Lamar's sister, Rebecca, wrote a poignant story about the sinking that describes the loss of Bulloch's in-laws. Lamar also knew Lt. North, had New York banking interests (Bank of the Republic), was closely connected with John Fraser & Co, and the state of Georgia. He owned a number of blockade runners, and was a partner with the Liverpool-based shipbroker Henry Lafone. See: Wise, *Lifeline of the Confederacy*, 158.
5. Edward K. Haviland, "Early Steam Navigation in China: Hongkong and the Canton River, 1858–1867," *The American Neptune* 24, no. 1 (Jan 1874): 34. Solomon Roosevelt, Jr. (of Roosevelt & Joyce) was the great-grandson of Nicholas and a distant relative of Theodore.
6. U.S. Navy, "Littoral Combat Ships" http://www.navy.mil/navydata/fact_display.asp?cid=4200&tid=1650&ct=4.
7. ORN, ser. II, 2: 183–185; Bennett, *The London Confederates*, 63. Mallory, "had studied his (Coles) views attentively in 1855, and again in 1859" and was well aware of the revolving turret and advanced armor plating. See: ORN, ser. II, vol. 2, 186–187.
8. ORN, ser. II, 2: 185; Spencer, *Confederate Navy*, 49.
9. ORN, ser. II, 2: 192.
10. *Ibid.*, 192–193.
11. *Ibid.*, 238–239.
12. *Ibid.*, 84–85. The British armored batteries were first ordered to the Baltic Sea, but were sent to the Black Sea and arrived too late for the Battle of Kinburn.
13. *NYT*, 16 Aug 1868.
14. Stephen C. Small, "The Ship That Couldn't Be Built," *Naval History* 22, no. 5 (Oct 2008) http://www.usni.org/magazines/navalhistory/2008-10/ship-couldnt-be-built.
15. *Ibid.*
16. *Ibid.*; Naval Historical Center, *DANFS Online*, s.v. "Naugatuck" http://www.history.navy.mil/danfs/n2/naugatuck-i.htm. This small vessel would partially prove Stevens' ideas.
17. Edward M. Steel, Jr., *T. Butler King of Georgia* (Athens: University of Georgia, 1964); U.S. Congress, House of Representatives, *Thomas B. King, H.R. 448, A Bill to provide for the construction of twelve iron war steamers and one iron frigate*, 29th Cong., 1st Sess. May 20th, 1846 http://lcweb2.loc.gov/cgi-bin/ampage?collId=llhb&fileName=029/llhb029.db&recNum=1187; Joseph T. Durkin, *Confederate Navy Chief: Stephen R. Mallory* (Chapel Hill: University of North Carolina, 1954); U.S. Interior Dept., Census Office,. Eighth Census, 1860, Morris Township, Morris County, NJ, series M653, roll: 703, p. 68, s.v. "Capt J. D. Bullock." The dry dock for the Stevens Battery was at Hoboken, NJ. See: *NYT*, 16 Aug 1868.

18. Baxter, *Ironclad Warship*, 110.
19. Walter Brownlee, *Warrior: the First Modern Battleship* (Cambridge: Cambridge University, 1985), 10–52. The HMS *Warrior* is still afloat, has been preserved, and can be visited at the Portsmouth Historic Dockyard.
20. Howard J. Fuller, *Clad in Iron: The American Civil War and the Challenge of British Naval Power* (Westport, CT: Praeger, 2008), 26–34.
21. James L. Nelson, *Reign of Iron: The Story of the First Battling Ironclads* (New York: William Morrow, 2004).
22. Fuller, *Clad in Iron*, 92–93.
23. ORN, ser. I, 1: 776–777; Bulloch, *Secret Service*, I: 254–256.
24. ORN, ser. II, 2: 268.
25. Milton, *Lincoln's Spymaster*, 68–69.
26. *Ibid.*, 79. Adding injury to insult, Dudley reported to Adams on 30 Aug that one of JDB's rams, *No. 294*, had her keel laid in the same stocks as the *Alabama*.
27. ORN, ser. II, 2: 131.
28. *Ibid.*, 269.
29. U.S. Naval Historical Center, "Online Library" s.v. "HMS Agincourt" http://www.history.navy.mil/photos/sh-fornv/uk/uksh-a/aginct68.htm.
30. ORN, ser. II, 2: 274–278; Bulloch, *Secret Service*, I: 391, and II: 248–250.
31. *Ibid.*
32. *Ibid.*
33. *Ibid.*
34. ORN, ser. II, 2: 274–278, Bulloch, *Secret Service*, I: 391 and II: 248–250. After leaving London, Sanders resided in Canada and became involved with the Copperhead and "Peace" movements. Stringer later owned several blockade runners, including the *Atalanta* that was sold to the Confederate Navy and converted into the CSS *Tallahassee*. See: Bennett, *The London Confederates*, 61, 58, 105–106. Stringer also had "unscrupulous" dealings with Huse; U.S. State Dept., "Papers Relating to the Foreign Affairs of the United States," Part II, 38th Cong, 1st Sess. (Washington: GPO, 1864), 1317–1320.
35. Kenneth W. Noe, *Perryville: This Grand Havoc of Battle* (Lexington: University of Kentucky, 2001).
36. ORN, ser. I, 1: 792–793. Semmes' log of the *Alabama* shows that he burned the *Brilliant* on 3 Oct and the *Wave Crest* and *Dunkirk* on 7 Oct. All these vessels were on commonly used routes, e.g., New York–Liverpool, Cardiff-Liverpool, allowing Liverpool, JDB, and insurance agents to receive the news quickly.
37. Milton, *Lincoln's Spymaster*, 79–80.
38. JDB wrote to North from Liverpool on 1 Nov saying that he had been detained in London presumably to see a pediatric doctor since he closed with, "My little child has wholly recovered." See: ORN, ser. II, 2: 288.
39. Martha Stewart Bulloch, letter to Susan Elliott West, Oct 1862, TRC, bMS AM 1785.2 (19), #22.
40. ORN, ser. II, 2: 284–286. Acting British consul to Richmond, Fred J. Cridland, provided the witness statement for Sanders' cotton bond contract.
41. *Ibid.*, 287.
42. *Ibid.*, 289.
43. *Ibid.*, 290–291.
44. *Ibid.*, 291.
45. ORN, ser. II, 2: 291–295, Bulloch, *Secret Service*, I: 291–293 and II: 229.
46. *Ibid.*
47. *Ibid.*
48. *Ibid.*
49. *Ibid.*
50. *Ibid.*
51. *Ibid.*
52. *Ibid.*
53. Martha Stewart Bulloch, letter to Susan Elliott West, 15 Nov 1862, TRC, bMS AM 1785.2 (19), #23.
54. Morgan Dix, *Memoirs of John Adams Dix*, vol. I (New York: Harper & Brothers, 1883), 167, 210, 246; Martha Stewart Bulloch, letter to Susan Elliott West, 26 Feb 1862, TRC. bMS AM 1785.2 (19), #15. Harriott Cross Bulloch related the sad news of her mother's death on Jan 11th in a letter to her stepmother-in-law. It is not apparent that Harriott ever had a close relationship with her father.
55. Corinne Roosevelt Robinson, *My Brother, Theodore Roosevelt* (New York: Charles Scribner's Sons, 31).
56. ORN, ser. II, 2: 345–346; Bulloch, *Secret Service* I: 394–395. JDB, letter to Mallory, 23 Jan 1863, "Send your letters to Mr. James K. Caskie, who has already forwarded you one from me."
57. Dix, *"Memoirs of John Adams Dix*, I: 167, 210, 246.
58. Martha Stewart Bulloch, letter to Susan Elliott West, 2 Dec 1862, TRC, bMS AM 1785.2 (19), #24.
59. ORN, ser. II, 2: 390–391.
60. ORN, ser. I, 1: 689–690; ORN, ser. II, 2: 299–300, 302, 447; Bulloch, *Secret Service*, I: 393.
61. ORN, ser. II, 2: 270; Bulloch, *Secret Service*, II: 260: Naval Historical Center, "Online Library" s.v. "Matthew Fontaine Maury" http://www.history.navy.mil/branches/teach/ends/maury.htm. See: Chester G. Hearn, *Tracks in the Sea: Matthew Fontaine Maury and the Mapping of the Oceans* (New York: International Marine, 2002).
62. Spencer, *Confederate Navy*, 34.
63. ORN, ser. II, 2: 303.

64. ORN, ser. I, 1: 690. Wilson bought the *Sumter* on behalf of Fraser, Trenholm and Co. and renamed it the *Gibraltar*.
65. ORN, ser. II, 2: 306–307. As was the case with most Europeans who became involved on either side of the Civil War, Erlanger was primarily interested in profit, not politics. In Nov 1861, Spence published a cogent argument for disunion of the American republic in a best-selling book that enjoyed numerous printings. See: James Spence, *The American Union*, 3rd ed. (London: Richard Bentley, 1862).
66. Martha Stewart Bulloch, letter to Susan Elliott West, 5 Dec 1862, TRC, bMS AM 1785.2 (19), #25.
67. ORN, ser. II, 2: 309.
68. *Ibid.*, 309–311.
69. *Ibid.*
70. *Ibid.*
71. *Ibid.*
72. *Ibid.*
73. *Ibid.*, 319.
74. *Ibid.*, 322–323.

Chapter 8

1. Edward, T. Cotham, *Battle on the Bay: The Civil War Struggle for Galveston Bay* (Austin: University of Texas, 1998), 124–135.
2. Thomas H. Reilly, *The Taiping Heavenly Kingdom: Rebellion and the Blasphemy of Empire* (Seattle: University of Washington, 2004). Reilly presents a comprehensive review of the "other" great civil war of the nineteenth century.
3. Merli, *Alabama*, 160. The untimely passing of Merli precluded his development of the Chinese effect on the American Civil War, and specifically Southern naval aspirations. Merli's well-researched evidence on this issue deserves additional examination and research, particularly in the context of Southern hopes for a "Trans-Continental Confederacy" as an adaptation of Manifest Destiny.
4. *Ibid.*, 161–162.
5. *Ibid.*, 162. See: Jack J. Gerson, *Horatio Nelson Lay and Sino-British Relations, 1854–1864* (Cambridge: Harvard University Press, 1972), 219, for Hart's proposition of the soon-to-be-named "Lay Flotilla." The fact that Hart's name was not attached to what would become a British diplomatic fiasco benefited his contemporary and historical legacy.
6. Gerson, *Horatio Nelson Lay*, 135.
7. *Ibid.*, 139–152; Bulloch, *Secret Service*, I: 227; ORN, ser. II, 2: 292–293.
8. *Ibid.*, 153.
9. *Ibid.*, 155.
10. *Ibid.*
11. *Ibid.*, 157.
12. *Ibid.*, 160.
13. *Ibid.*, 161, 162; ORN, ser. I, 1: 775–777.
14. *Ibid.*, 161.
15. ORN, ser. II, 2: 330.
16. *Ibid.*, 331.
17. *Ibid.*, 331–332.
18. *Ibid.*
19. *Ibid.*, 337. JDB followed up his letter of 9 Jan with another letter to North on 20 Jan enclosing his official authority for retransfer of the contract and asking if North had contacted Lindsay & Co. for funding (*Ibid.*, 343). Lindsay was a pro–Confederate member of Parliament and ship owner who wrote articles, introduced motions, and even met with Napoleon III four times on behalf of the Confederacy. He and his namesake company invested in the Erlanger loan, proposed similar loans of their own, and owned blockade runners. See: Spencer, *Confederate Navy*, 72; Bennett, *The London Confederates*, 28, 68, 81, 92, 103, 139–142, 148, 156.
20. ORN, ser. II, 2: 342.
21. *Ibid.*, 347.
22. Martha Stewart Bulloch, letter to Susan Elliott West, 30 Jan 1863, TRC, bMS AM 1785.2 (19), #30.
23. Bulloch, *Secret Service*, I: 395; ORN, ser. II, 2: 351. There are slight differences between the two texts; Bulloch's *Secret Service* is cited here.
24. JDB was unaware that Sec. Mallory had just written urging him to go to Paris and implement a building program. Both Mallory and the Confederate commissioner to France, John Slidell, received strong encouragement from members of Napoleon III's government, even though France had issued an even more restrictive neutrality proclamation than did Britain. See: ORN, ser. II, 2: 332–334.
25. See: Tomasz Walczyk, "Lay-Osborn Flotilla" http://oceania.pbworks.com/Lay-Osborn%20Flotilla.
26. ORN, ser. II, 2: 352.
27. *Ibid.*, 359–360.
28. China had no national or naval ensign, which forced Lay to develop one. See: Phil Nelson, *Flags of the World*. "Lay-Osborne Flotilla" http://flagspot.net/flags/cn-lo.html orhttp://www.crwflags.com/FOTW/FLAGS/cn-lo.html for the fascinating history behind this unique naval pennant. Capt. Sherard Osborn's Royal Geographical Society speech

about his "mission" was quoted at length and discussed in the 21 Feb 1863 edition of the *North China Herald*, a publication based in Shanghai.

29. Bulloch, *Secret Service*, II: 12–14. The Laird's *Keangsoo* was launched on 5 Mar, and departed with Capt. Osborn embarked later that month. The Union pressured Russell and the Foreign Office about Confederate efforts to build, buy, or purchase war materiel, but JDB also notes that the "British tradesman was to be left as little hampered as possible." JDB understood that the business of the Empire was, well, business — and foreign policy was an adjunct to that imperative.

30. *Ibid.*, 367. Mallory was correct in his assessment; the torpedo boat CSS *David* successfully attacked the *New Ironsides* in Oct 1863 knocking it out of action for months and nearly sinking the powerful ironclad. See: Robert M.D. Solomon, ed., *The Little David, C.S.S. David: The Story of the First Successful Torpedo Boat* (Colombia, SC: R.L. Bryan, 1970).

31. ORN, ser. II, 2: 366–368.

32. Bulloch, *Secret Service*, I: 396–397. See: ORN, ser. II, 2: 372–373 for a more complete letter than quoted in Bulloch's memoirs. The extract is similar, but JDB's quote may be an extrapolation of a shorter encrypted message. The ORN letter could be JDB's promised full-length letter to Mallory explaining his plan to build a longer, shallower draft ironclad. Contemporary newspapers report that the Lairds rams were the most powerful being built in Britain.

33. ORN, ser. II, 2: 371–372.

34. Merli, *Great Britain and the Confederate Navy*, 163. There is confusion over the precise launch date of the *Alexandra*, with Luraghi citing 7 Apr, and Merli and Milton inferring the same. However, the ship was seized on 5 Apr! It is unlikely that the British authorities would seize the vessel and then allow it to be launched under British government control. JDB says the *Alexandra* was launched about 7 Mar. See: Bulloch, *Secret Service*, I: 330 and 42nd Congress, 2d Session, Senate Ex. Doc. No. 31: GPO, Washington: 1872, 105. JDB's date seems most plausible given the context of Princess Alexandra's arrival at Gravesend on that exact date and the official *Alabama* Claims report that Miller & Sons launched "a new gun-boat, to be called the *Alexandra*" in "early in March, 1863."

35. Milton, *Lincoln's Spymaster*, 80; Baxter, *Ironclad Warship*, 211–220. See: Jules Verne, *A Floating City and The Blockade Runners* (New York: Scribner, Armstrong, 1874) for an entertaining, fact-based novella.

36. Bulloch, *Secret Service*, II: 25; Merli, *Great Britain and the Confederate Navy*, 188–191. North's (*No. 61*) and G.T. Sinclair's (*Canton/Pampero*) ships were under construction in Scotland. Merli summarizes the Slidell-Napoleon III diplomatic relationship.

37. Bulloch, *Secret Service*, II: 25.

38. *Ibid.*, 25–27.

39. Meade, *Judah P. Benjamin*, 73–74, 121; Thomas B. King, *California, the Wonder of the Age: A Book for Everyone Going to, or Having an Interest in That Golden Region* (New York: William Gowans, 1850); Steel, *T. Butler King*, 59–60, 94.

40. Steel, *T. Butler King*, 148.

41. For JDB's thoughts on Mexico, France, the Confederacy, and the Union, See: Bulloch, *Secret Service*, II: 23.

42. Bulloch, *Secret Service*, II: 28.

43. Milton, *Lincoln's Spymaster*, 82–84.

44. *Ibid.*

45. *Ibid.*

46. *Ibid.*, 374–375. In a letter to Mason on 17 Mar, JDB refers to a contract between Mallory and George N. Sanders, another of the agents Mallory sent to acquire ships with no funding. Sanders would later file a self-serving complaint about JDB's supervision of his contracts. See: ORN, ser. II, 2: 470, 577.

47. ORN, ser. II, 2: 397.

48. Milton, *Lincoln's Spymaster*, 85; Spencer, *Confederate Navy*, 98.

49. Spencer, *Confederate Navy*, 98.

50. ORN, ser. II, 2: 397; Spencer, *Confederate Navy*, 98.

51. ORN, ser. II, 2: 445.

52. *Harper's Weekly*, 28 Mar 1863.

53. Milton, *Lincoln's Spymaster*, 83; Douglas H. Maynard, "The Forbes-Aspinwall Mission," *The Mississippi Valley Historical Review* 45, no. 1 (Jun 1958): 72–73, 82.

54. Martha Stewart Bulloch, letters to Susan Elliott West, 15 Nov 1862 and 3 Apr 1863, TRC, bMS AM 1785.2 (19), #23 and 33.

55. Spencer, *Confederate Navy*, 100, 233; David P. Crook, *The North, the South, and the Powers: 1861–1865* (New York: John Wiley and Son, 1974), 294–295. Russell was worried that the fierce Parliamentary debates of 27–28 Mar would require a test legal case. Spencer and Merli disagree in the details of this event, but Russell knew he needed legal clarification on the neutrality laws. Spencer cites a letter from Russell to Palmerston that is incorrectly referenced in Ephraim D. Adams, *Great Britain and the American Civil War*, vol. II (New York: Longmans, Green, and Company, 1925), 135. The letter was written on 3 Sep and not 3 Apr 1863 and refers to JDB's ironclads and not the *Alexandra*. The turning point of British policy was instigated by the *Alexandra* case, but Russell's decision to adopt measures "of policy though not of strict law" were first documented against the rams at Birkenhead.

56. *Ibid.*

57. *Liverpool Journal of Commerce*, 7 Apr 1863 and *NYT*, 22 Apr 1863. Interestingly, the affairs of the Forbes-Aspinwall mission were widely reported in America by then.

58. ORN, ser. II, 2: 403.

59. Spencer, *Confederate Navy*, 93–95.
60. Bulloch, *Secret Service*, 2: 26; ORN, ser. II, 2: 403. McRae would not reach Europe until the first of May 1863.
61. *Ibid.*, 2: 26–29.
62. ORA, ser. IV, 2: 556–557.
63. Milton, *Lincoln's Spymaster*, 83–85; Thomas Sebrell, "Persuading John Bull: The American Civil War Comes to Fleet Street" (PhD. diss., Queen Mary: University of London, 2010), this work is intended for general publication.
64. ORN, ser. II, 2: 375–376. JDB mentions that he had sent a message by Lt. Murdaugh the day before, 15 May 1863, but it was lost to the ORN archives.
65. *Ibid.*
66. *Ibid.*, 423–424.
67. Bulloch, *Secret Service*, I: 400.
68. ORN, ser. II, 2: 375–376, 423–424; Bulloch, *Secret Service*, I: 400–402.
69. Bulloch, *Secret Service*, I: 400–401.
70. ORN, ser. II, 2: 375–376, 423–424; Bulloch, *Secret Service*, I: 400–402.
71. Spencer, *Confederate Navy*, 149–150. France, like Britain, was suffering tremendous unemployment in its textile industry due to the cotton shortage, which created domestic political stresses for Napoleon III as well.
72. *Ibid.*, 153.
73. Ibid; ORN, ser. II, 2: 437.
74. Spencer, *Confederate Navy*, 101.
75. ORN, ser. II, 2: 444–447.
76. *Ibid.* The exact chronology of JDB's information and actions is unclear. In his letter of 30 Jun 1863, he wrote retrospectively, but did not provide dates of occurrence, e.g., when he wrote the Lairds, the Russians approached, or he went to Paris to see Bravay.
77. Bulloch, *Secret Service*, I: 400–403.
78. U.S. Central Intelligence Agency, "Intelligence in the Civil War." This CIA open-source analysis says that Yonge was an "agent" of US Consul Thomas Haines Dudley. While Dudley proclaimed that he had "someone" aboard the *Alabama*, he never asserted that Yonge had become his operative until after he was discharged from the ship.
79. Spencer, *Confederate Navy*, 102–103.
80. Milton, *Lincoln's Spymaster*, 88–89.
81. Spencer, *Confederate Navy*, 102.
82. ORN, ser. II, 2: 444–449. JDB refers to the ownership issue of the *Alexandra* in his second letter written on 30 Jun.
83. ORN, ser. II, 2: 444–447; McPherson, *Battle Cry*, 609, 664–665.
84. Coy F. Cross, II, *Lincoln's Man in Liverpool: Consul Dudley* (DeKalb: Northern Illinois University, 2007), 104–105. Cross cites 18 Jun 1863 as the date JDB signed over the title to Bravay & Co.; ORN, ser. II, 2: 445.
85. *No. 294* was named "*El Tousson*" and *No. 295* "*El Monassir*" to maintain the pretence of Egyptian ownership.
86. ORN, ser. II, 2: 451.
87. *Ibid.*, 449–450. On the same day that JDB wrote to North, North was writing to Mallory that he had been in Paris on 6 Jun to determine the fate of *No. 61*; prior to the *Alexandra* verdict, JDB had recommended selling *No. 61*. Although Bulloch's presence at this meeting is unconfirmed, he was in the Paris area at the time and probably met with Arman, Voruz, North, Huse, and Slidell. North opines that the British government probably would not release the *Alexandra* until Nov 1863, as Lord Chief Baron had applied for a bill of exception against the Court of Exchequer's decision; the British government was already using policy as its guide to implement the Foreign Enlistment Act. See: ORN, ser. II, 2: 450.
88. Cross, *Lincoln's Man*, 104–105; ORN, ser. II, 2: 454.
89. McPherson, *Battle Cry*, 609, 637, 664–665.
90. *Ibid.*
91. Milton, *Lincoln's Spymaster*, 90. See: Thomas Haines Dudley Collection, which has all the affidavits submitted by Yonge, Chapman, Ellis and Russell, as well as others connected with the American counterintelligence effort.
92. ORN, Sr. II, 2: 452–454.
93. *Ibid.*
94. *Ibid.*
95. U.S. Minister to France William Dayton, had heard rumors of Confederate shipbuilding in France, but unlike Adams in London, he had no Dudley to mount a fierce counterintelligence effort. Dayton would die on station on 1 Dec 1864. His replacement, John Bigelow, would write a post-war account and says that he had no substantiated information about JDB's activities until September 1863 — two and one-half months later! See: John Bigelow, *France and the Confederate Navy, 1862–1868: An International Episode* (New York: Harper & Brothers, 1888), 2.
96. ORN, Sr. II, 2: 454.
97. *Ibid.*, 444–447.
98. ORN, ser. II, 2: 455–457.
99. *Ibid.*
100. *Ibid.*
101. *Ibid.*
102. *Ibid.*
103. *Ibid.*

104. *Ibid.* Lt. Commanding James I. Waddell and his executive officer Lt. Whittle of the CSS *Shenandoah* subsequently contemplated this tactic against the city of San Francisco in 1865. See: McKay, *Sea King*, 181–192.
105. ORN, ser. II, 2: 460–461.
106. *Ibid.* These events mark the beginning of tensions between Brazil and the Union, which would nearly start a war in 1864 when the CSS *Florida* was "cut-out" at Bahia by the USS *Wachusett*, commanded by CDR Napoleon Collins. At first, Collins was a national hero, and then court-martialed, but Navy Secretary Gideon Welles set-aside the punishment and promoted him!
107. *Ibid.*
108. *Ibid.*, 462.

Chapter 9

1. ORN, ser. II, 2: 464–468.
2. *Ibid.*, 468–470.
3. *Ibid.*
4. *Ibid.*, 467–468.
5. *Ibid.*, 468–470.
6. *Ibid.*, 471–472.
7. *Ibid.*
8. ORN, ser. II, 2: 471–472.
9. London newspapers reported on Gettysburg as early as 18 Jul, with confirmation of a Union victory by the 22nd. See: Middlesex *Miners' and Workmen's Advocate*, 18 Jul 1863, and *London Nonconformist*, 22 Jul 1863.
10. ORN, ser. II, 2: 472–473.
11. *Ibid.*, 475. JDB says he needed to wade through a "long list of ... dispatches ... in time for Saturday's mail." He typically updated his reports to Mallory just before the departure of the mail ships destined for North America.
12. *Ibid.*, 475–476.
13. *Ibid.*, 475.
14. *Ibid.*, 476–477.
15. *Ibid.*
16. *Ibid.*, 476–478.
17. *Ibid.*
18. *Ibid.*
19. Steven R. Wise, *Gate of Hell, Campaign for Charleston Harbor* (Columbia: University of South Carolina, 1994); U.S. Interior Dept., Battle Summaries, "Port Hudson Battlefield" http://www.nps.gov/history/nr/travel/louisiana/por.htm.
20. Bigelow, *France and the Confederate Navy*, 6–7. This letter is reproduced in French on page 216, forming part of the legal investigation started by Union Minister Bigelow via French lawyer Antoine Pierre Berryer (1790–1869). JDB retained the services of Lt. Robert R. Carter, who would have served under his command in one of the Lairds rams. He needed Carter to meet with the British naval gun maker Blakely so that he might "keep out of sight on the matter." See: ORN, ser. II, 2: 469.
21. Milton, *Lincoln's Spymaster*, 91; Spencer, *Confederate Navy*, 104–119. U.S. Minister Adams and U.S. Consul Dudley had been pressing both Liverpool customs as well as the Foreign Office over the "true" nature of the ownership of *No. 294* and *No. 295* since Jul 1863.
22. Spencer, *Confederate Navy*, 104–107. Sec. Mallory sent Capt. Samuel R. Barron Sr. to Europe, with to the honorary rank of commodore, and orders to take command of one of the Laird rams. Mallory dreamed of an armored Confederate flotilla, comprising *No. 294*, *No. 295*, *No. 61*, Lt. Sinclair's vessel, the two French rams and four corvettes. See: ORN, ser. II, 2: 485–487 for Mallory's orders to Commodore Barron.
23. ORN, ser. II, 2: 485–487.
24. Milton, *Lincoln's Spymaster*, 91; Naval Historical Center, "Online Library" s.v. "HMS Scorpion" http://www.history.navy.mil/photos/sh-fornv/uk/uksh-s/scorpn7.htm.
25. Milton, *Lincoln's Spymaster*, 91, ORN, ser. II, 2: 487–489; Bulloch, *Secret Service*, I: 353–354.
26. ORN, ser. II, 2: 487–489; Bulloch, *Secret Service*, I: 353–354.
27. *Ibid.*
28. *Ibid.*
29. *Ibid.*
30. *Ibid.*
31. Bulloch, *Secret Service*, I: 178–180.
32. *Ibid.*
33. *Ibid.*
34. Milton, *Lincoln's Spymaster*, 91.
35. *Ibid.*
36. Spencer, *Confederate Navy*, 110–111, 233; Crook, *The North, the South, and the Powers*, 294–295; Milton, *Lincoln's Spymaster*, 93.
37. Czar Alexander appeared to be fulfilling de Toqueville's prediction that Russia and America would "rule the

world" as superpowers. Union propagandists believed that Russia fully supported Lincoln's efforts to quell the "rebellious South." When on 11 Sep 1863, a squadron of Imperial Russian warships sailed into New York harbour, the city exploded with joy and British diplomats were worried. The reality of the visit was more related to the Russian admiralty's fear of war over the Polish uprising. They ordered its Baltic and Pacific fleets to neutral ports for protection, thus San Francisco also received a "friendly visit." See: C. Douglas Kroll, *Friends in Peace and War: The Russian Navy's Landmark Visit to Civil War San Francisco* (Washington: Potomac Books, 2006), 16–18; Marshall B. Davidson, "Royal Welcome for the Russian Navy," *American Heritage* 11, no. 4 (Jun 1960): 38–43, 107.

38. Merli, *Great Britain and the Confederate Navy*, 202–208. Merli's meticulous reconstruction of the bureaucratic, political, and legal sides of the issue is still the gold standard of research.
39. Milton, *Lincoln's Spymaster*, 93.
40. Merli, *Great Britain and the Confederate Navy*, 203.
41. Bulloch, *Secret Service*, I: 412–413. JDB's memoirs make a chronological leap from a 9 Jul letter to 1 Oct 1863 regarding the fate of the rams.
42. Merli, *Great Britain and the Confederate Navy*, 202–208.
43. *Ibid.*, 203–204.
44. ORN, ser. II, 2: 494.
45. *Ibid.*, 460. Dudley stated that Maffitt was stepping down as commander of the *Florida* and that Barney was taking over; the agent noted JDB's presence and that repairs would take at least a month.
46. *Ibid.*
47. *Ibid.*, 494–495.
48. *Ibid.*
49. *Ibid.*
50. Merli, *Great Britain and the Confederate Navy*, 207.
51. *Ibid.*, 211.See: Spencer, *Confederate Navy*, 212, for discussion of Palmerston's role.
52. Milton, *Lincoln's Spymaster*, 93.
53. Beckles Willson, *John Slidell and the Confederates in Paris* (New York: Minton, Balch, 1932), 140–141. Bulloch was in France at the time and Willson's anonymous account is entirely credible.
54. ORN, ser. II, 2: 502–503.
55. *Ibid.*
56. Merli, *Great Britain and the Confederate Navy*, 208.
57. ORN, ser. II, 2: 504. It is quite likely that JDB's intelligence network of informers, including his solicitor who maintained contact with Bravay in Paris, notified him of the impending official action.
58. Middlesex *Miner's and Workmen's Advocate*, 17 Oct 1863 (based on reports from the *Liverpool Mercury*). The *Observer* wrote that based on the actions of the *Florida*, the government "could do no less" than hold the rams until they could be thoroughly investigated.
59. ORN, ser. II, 2: 507–511.
60. Phillip Van Doren Stern, *The Confederate Navy: A Pictorial History* (1962; reprint, El Dorado Hills, CA: Da Capo, 1992), 158–161.
61. *Ibid.*
62. ORN, ser. II, 2: 507–511.
63. *Ibid.* In his memoirs, JDB quotes his letter of 20 Oct 1863, but inserts a parenthetical note that the rams were seized on 9 Oct, suggesting that he had timely notification of Palmerston's intentions since they were not physically seized until 15 Oct. See: Bulloch, *Secret Service*, I: 420.
64. Merli, *Great Britain and the Confederate Navy*, 212 (extracted from a letter by Henry Adams, U.S. Minister Adams' son and secretary). See: Massachusetts Historical Society, "Charles Francis Adams," http://www.masshist.org/adams/biographical.cfm, for information on the Adams family.
65. *North China Herald*, 12 Sep 1863.
66. ORN, ser. II, 2: 511–513.
67. *Ibid.*
68. *Ibid.*
69. *Ibid.*
70. *Ibid.*
71. Bigelow, *France and the Confederate Navy*, 1.
72. Bigelow, *France and the Confederate Navy*, 2, 97–99; Willson, *John Slidell*, 134–135. Petermann is also referred to as "Petersmann," "Peterman," or "Trémont." See: Cross, *Lincoln's Man in Liverpool*, 180, and Lynn M. Case and Warren. F. Spencer. *The United States and France: Civil War Diplomacy* (Philadelphia: University of Pennsylvania, 1970), 669ff.
73. Bigelow, *France and the Confederate Navy*, 2–5, 97–99.
74. ORN, ser. II, 2: 526. JDB confirmed that Petermann worked for Voruz, saying, "the confidential clerk has disappeared ... and carried off ... papers relating to the business." See: ORN, ser. II, 2: 463. Voruz had previously referred to "Petersmann" in a letter to his son dated 14 Jul 1863 regarding JDB and his Blakely guns.
75. Bigelow, *France and the Confederate Navy*, 5.
76. *Ibid.*, 6–15.
77. Spencer, *Confederate Navy*, 171.
78. *Ibid.*

79. Peter Davis, "Extracts from the Times Newspaper" http://www.pdavis.nl/Osborn.php. Osborn's memorandum reflects his mandate as a naval officer for Her Majesty's government as specified by the Foreign Office, the Law Office, and the Admiralty.
80. ORN, ser. II, 2: 524–527, Bulloch, *Secret Service*, II: 43.
81. *Ibid.*, 524–527.
82. *Ibid.*, 520–524.
83. *Ibid.* About 3 Nov 1863, the *Pampero* (aka "Sinclair's Ship") was launched into the Clyde at James & George Thomson's Clyde Bank Iron Shipyard, Glasgow.
84. *Ibid.*
85. *Ibid.*
86. *Ibid.*, 524–527; Bulloch, *Secret Service*, II: 38–41.
87. *Ibid.*
88. *Ibid.*
89. *Ibid.*
90. *Ibid.*
91. Spencer, *Confederate Navy*, 170–172. See: Bigelow, *France and the Confederate Navy*, for a lively, though biased, Union view of the contemporary issues facing France. As with Britain, the Union thought they had greater influence than in reality.
92. ORN, ser. II, 524–527; Bulloch, *Secret Service*, II: 38–41.
93. ORN, ser. II, 2: 564.
94. *Ibid.*, 565–566.
95. *Ibid.* Bulloch did not capitalize the title, "lord chief baron," perhaps reflecting his opinion of that official.
96. *Ibid.*
97. Bulloch, *Secret Service*, I: 247.
98. ORN, ser. II, 2: 524–527; Bulloch, *Secret Service*, II: 38–41.
99. ORN, ser. II, 2: 566; *NYT*, 5 Dec 1863; Eller, *Civil War Naval Chronology*, 6: 314. The *Pampero* (aka *Canton* or "Sinclair's ship") was detained around 20 Nov 1863; it was a composite wood and iron steamship, similar to the *Alabama*, built by James and George Thomson's Glasgow shipyard. It would have been commissioned as the CSS *Texas*.
100. Brooke, *Ironclads and Big Guns*, 162.
101. ORN, ser. II, 2: 567–568.
102. *Ibid.*
103. Martha Stewart Bulloch, letters to Susan Elliott West, 28 Oct and 31 Dec 1863, TRC, bMS Am 1875.7(4), #12 and 13.
104. London *Times*, 4 Jan 1864.

Chapter 10

1. Mary B. Chesnut, *A Diary from Dixie*," ed. Isabella D. Martin and Myrta L. Avary (New York: D. Appleton, 1905), 269, 314. Chestnut was the wife of a Confederate Army officer, but did not believe in slavery, though she believed in the right of the Southern states to secede. She only mentioned Semmes after the loss of the CSS *Alabama*.
2. Michael Embree, *Bismarck's First War: The Campaign of Schleswig and Jutland, 1864* (Solihull: Helion, 2007), 18–35.
3. *Ibid.*
4. *Ibid.*, 23–24. Lord Russell attempted to adjudicate the issue between Denmark and Prussia in the spring of 1861 as the American Civil War began.
5. London *Nonconformist*, 6 Jan 1864; *NYT*, 9 Jan 1864. American newspapers, such as the *NYT*, supported a united and stronger Germany.
6. ORN, ser. II, 2: 575–578.
7. On Jan 16th Bismarck demanded that the Danish constitution be dissolved within 48 hours. This was impractical politically and would have destabilized the Denmark. See: Embree, *Bismarck's First War*, 18–50.
8. Spencer, *Confederate Navy*, 172.
9. ORN, ser. II, 2: 586.
10. *Ibid.*, 583.
11. *Ibid.*, 583–586.
12. *Ibid.*, 586.
13. *Ibid.*, 587–588.
14. *Ibid.*, 588.
15. *Ibid.*, 588–590; Bulloch, *Secret Service*, II: 41–43.
16. *Ibid.*
17. Semmes, *Memoirs of Service Afloat*, 663–664; ORN, ser. I, 2: 760; Fullam, *Journal*, 138; David Lyon and Rif Winfield, *The Sail & Steam Navy List: All the Ships of the Royal Navy, 1815–1889* (London: Chatham, 2004), 322. Sir Allen Young achieved fame as an explorer in search of the Northwest Passage and the lost Franklin Expedition.
18. ORN, ser. I, 2: 792.; Fullam, *Journal*, 166; *The Illustrated London News*, vol. 44, no. 1251, 2 Apr 1864.
19. Sir Frederick W.A. Bruce, letter to Earl of Clarendon, 9 Dec 1865, *CoGB*, 819.

20. Merli, *Alabama*, 173–175; Semmes, *Memoirs of Service Afloat*, 709.
21. Embree, *Bismarck's First War*, 136.
22. U.S. Interior Dept., Battle Summaries, "Okolona," http://www.nps.gov/history/hps/ABPP/BATTLES/ms013.htm.
23. Rose O'Neal Greenhow, *European Diary*, Aug 5, 1863, http://www.onealwebsite.com/RebelRose/, 53, 64–66. The Washington socialite Greenhow provided critical intelligence prior to the first Battle of Bull Run. She was caught, imprisoned, and released prior to making her way through the blockade to Europe as a Confederate propaganda agent. There are no other documented interactions between Greenhow and Bulloch, but he likely had a role in her departure from Greenock Scotland on his government-owned blockade runner *Condor*. She left for Wilmington via Halifax on Aug 10th, but came to an unfortunate end when the *Condor* ran aground and she drowned while escaping in a small boat. Her diary was discovered in an archive at the University of North Carolina at Chapel Hill in 1965.
24. Jefferson Davis, *The Papers of Jefferson Davis: October 1863–August 1864*, vol. 10. ed. Lynda Lasswell Crist (Baton Rouge: Louisiana State University, 1999), 246. O'Sullivan coined the term "Manifest Destiny," was U.S. minister to Portugal 1854–1854, and (along with Huse and Hotze) attended the London wedding of the colorful Confederate spy Belle Boyd to former Union Navy Lt. Samuel Hardinge on 25 Aug 1864.
25. ORN, ser. II, 2: 602–603. JDB intended to give Mallory's response to a sympathetic MP, who would introduce Mallory's letter into parliamentary debate by asking if Sir Roundell had received Mallory's response letter; Bulloch would ensure that Sir Roundell also received a copy. If Sir Roundell denied receipt of Mallory's letter, the "Confederate" MP would pounce and embarrass the government, particularly Lord Russell who was despised in Confederate newspapers.
26. Gary D. Joiner, *Through the Howling Wilderness: The 1864 Red River Campaign and Union Failure in the West* (Knoxville: University of Tennessee, 2006), 1–116.
27. ORN, ser. II, 2: 603–605.
28. *Ibid.*, 606–608.
29. *Ibid.*
30. *Ibid.*
31. *Ibid.*, 611–612.
32. *Ibid.*
33. Gert Laursen, Danish Military History, "The Battle of Rügen — March 17th 1864," http://www.milhist.dk/1864/rugen/rugen_uk.htm. The Prussians had lost, but its Austrian ally would later defeat the Danish Navy.
34. Naval Historical Center, *DANFS Online*, http://www.hazegray.org/danfs/csn/g.txt (CSS *Georgia*) and http://www.hazegray.org/danfs/csn/r.txt (CSS *Rappahannock*).
35. ORN, ser. I, 3: 683. Lt. Commanding Fauntleroy of CSS *Rappahannock* (Calais) to Commodore Barron (Paris). Fauntleroy letter reports that JDB would pass through Calais on the way to the "south of France," inferring his destination was Bordeaux, as it was the southernmost port related to Confederate ship builds.
36. ORA, ser. I, 32: 57, Report of Acting Master W. Ferguson aboard the USS *Silver Cloud*, 14 Apr 1864. This is one of many Union reports about the battle.
37. See: Hans Henning Eriksen, "Tabsliste for Kampen den 18 April (1864)" http://www.hheriksen.dk/images/1864tab.jpg (in Danish) for a table of Danish losses.
38. Bulloch, letter to Barron, 29 Apr 1864, Whittle Papers, 2, no. 9, Sargeant Memorial Room, Main Library, Norfolk, VA.
39. Bulloch, *Secret Service*, II: 264; Bulloch, letter to Barron, 3 May 1864, Whittle Papers.
40. Bulloch, letter to Barron, 29 Apr 1864, Whittle Papers, 2, no. 9; Milton, *Lincoln's Spymaster*, 111–112, Bulloch, *Secret Service*, II: 264. The *Georgia's* bill of sale required that she be "dismantled" as a warship. A condition of sale that would have satisfied Lord Russell and the local Customs officials.
41. Bulloch letter to Barron dated 4 May 1864, Whittle Papers, 2; Douglas F. Forrest, *Odyssey in Gray: A Diary of Confederate Service, 1863–1865*, ed. William N. Still, Jr. (Richmond: Virginia State Library, 1979); Spencer, *Confederate Navy*, 173.
42. Forrest, *Diary of Confederate Service*, 176–177. Fauntleroy received a letter directly from Foreign Minister de Lhuys saying that "a Commission of Lawyers has been appointed by the President of the Senate to examine our case." Forrest correctly assessed the probable end of the whole affair by writing that the French intend "to humbug us into submission to further detention."
43. Spencer, *Confederate Navy*, 172–173; ORN, ser. II, 2: 665–668.
44. ORN, ser. II, 2: 653–656, 665–668; Bulloch, letter to Barron, 9 Jun 1864, Whittle Papers, 2, no. 15.
45. ORN, ser. II, 2: 652–653. It's likely that Barron, as senior Navy officer in Europe, intended the ringing endorsement of JDB contained in this letter as confirmation of their positive relationship.
46. *Ibid.*, 653–656. JDB said he would send news of the trial via Henry Hotze, the Swiss-born Confederate propagandist.
47. *Ibid.*
48. *Ibid.*
49. ORN, ser. II, 2: 665–668: Bulloch, *Secret Service*, 2: 55.
50. Spencer, *Confederate Navy*, 174. See: ORN, ser. II, 2: 566 and subsequent messages for the saga of how Thomson's ironclad was sold to the Danish government *before* hostilities broke out with the German Confederation.
51. ORN, Ser. II, 2: 665–668.
52. *Ibid.*, 665–668; Bulloch, *Secret Service*, II: 44–48.

53. ORN, ser. I, 3: 186–187; ORN, ser. II, 2: 682–684; Scharf, *Confederate States Navy*, 803–804; Bulloch, letter to Barron, 29 Apr 1864, Whittle Papers, 2, no. 9; Bulloch, *Secret Service*, II: 264.
54. Spencer, *Raphael Semmes*, 174–175.
55. Bulloch, *Secret Service*, II: 54–55; Willson, *John Slidell*, 146–148. Willson references family descendants of Slidell, relations of the Erlangers, and the papers of Slidell's personal secretary, George Eustis. He uses other un-named "sources" who were intimate with the Confederate scene in Paris. Willson was a well-published historian and commentator of U.S. and British diplomatic history, and a former chief editor of the *Daily Mail*, a leading British newspaper. In World War I he was officer in charge of collecting "media materials" for the British Army and may have been an early member of the British Intelligence service.
56. Stephen Fox, *Wolf of the Deep: Raphael Semmes and the Notorious Confederate Raider* CSS *Alabama* (New York: Knopf, 2007), 227; Bulloch, *Secret Service*, I: 283; Semmes, *Memoirs of Service Afloat*, 786. Irvine was not mentioned as a captive on the *Kearsarge* or rescued by the French, and is assumed to have been on the *Deerhound* with Semmes.
57. ORN, ser. II, 2: 682–684.
58. *Ibid.*
59. *Ibid.*
60. *Ibid.*, 686. JDB erroneously identifies one of the copied messages (dated 10 Jun 1864) as being written from Paris; his letter to Mallory of that date was written from Liverpool prior to his visit to the Cyclops Iron Works and Paris.
61. *Ibid.*
62. *Ibid.*, 689–691.
63. *Ibid.*
64. *Ibid.*, 694–695.
65. *Ibid.*, 816.
66. *Ibid.*, 694–695.
67. *Ibid.*, 710.
68. ORN, ser. II, 3: 1186–1187.
69. ORN, ser. II, 2: 704.
70. *Ibid.*, 709–711.
71. *Ibid.*, 711–712.
72. *Ibid.*, 712–714.
73. *Ibid.*, 504, 707–709; Bulloch, *Secret Service*, 2: 125, 234–235. On her first cruise, the *Sea King* was diverted to New Zealand, arriving in 74 days. She then raced north to Shanghai in only 23 days; including 5 days for coaling stops and was back in Britain 79 days later. It was a thrilling performance in the age of "tea races" when British firms competed to deliver the first tea of the season. See: McKay, *Sea King*, 46–93.
74. ORN, ser. II, 2: 714–715.
75. *Ibid.*, 716–718.
76. *Ibid.* The *Tallahassee* had terrorised the northeast coast of the Union in a dynamic series of raids.
77. Naval Historical Center, *DANFS Online*, s.v. "Tallahassee," http://www.history.navy.mil/danfs/cfa9/tallahassee.htm.
78. ORN, ser. II, 2: 716–718.
79. *Ibid.*
80. ORN, ser. II, 2: 720–722; Bulloch, *Secret Service*, 2: 238–241. Jones, Quiggin & Co. of Liverpool was the prime contractor, but subcontracted the *Deer's* construction to W.H. Potter & Co. of Liverpool, and the *Stag* to Bowdler, Chaffer & Co., of Seacomb, England. The four ships were 230 feet in length with a beam of 26 feet and displacement of 771 tons; the engines were 180hp and their propulsion was by paddle wheel. See: Wise, *Lifeline of the Confederacy*, 290, 295, 315, 321.
81. ORN, ser. II, 2: 720–721. The first runners two were *Rosine* (or *Rosina*) and *Ruby III* by Jones, Quiggin & Co. of Liverpool under contract to John K. Gilliat & Co. See: Wise, *Lifeline of the Confederacy*, 318, 319.
82. *Ibid.*, 721. These ships were the *Lark* and *Wren* built by Laird & Sons for Fraser, Trenholm & Co. length: 210 feet, beam of 23 feet, 120 hp engine, speed over 12 knots. The *Lark* and *Wren* were the last blockade runners to clear a Confederate port (Galveston in May 1865). See: Wise, *Lifeline of the Confederacy*, 275, 308, 327.
83. ORN, ser. II, 2: 720–722; Bulloch, *Secret Service*, 2: 238–241. These ships were the *Albatross* and P*enguin* constructed by Laird & Sons for Fraser, Trenholm & Co. length 240 feet, beam 30 feet, 1,063 tons, 260hp engine. See: Wise, *Lifeline of the Confederacy*, 287, 316.
84. ORN, ser. II, 2: 721; Bennett, *The London Confederates*, 102, 107; Wise, *Lifeline of the Confederacy*, 294, 316, 320–321, 326. Richard Phillips was an intermediary for the *Curlew*; length: 225 feet, beam 24 feet, 645 tons, 160 hp engines. All four ships would remain unfinished when the war came to an end.
85. ORN, ser. II, 2: 717–718, 721, 729; Wise, *Lifeline of the Confederacy*, 310; "Our Official Log," *The Nautical Magazine* 50, no. 2 (Feb 1881): 179; Bennett, *The London Confederates*, 64. Built by John & William Dudgeon, London, the *Louisa Ann Fanny* was named for Louisa Ann Frances, the wife of John Gilliat, the head of J.K. Gilliat & Co.; The *Mary Augusta* was the sister ship of the *Louisa Ann Fanny* and was named for the wife of Algernon Gilliat. Both were 250 feet in length, beam 28, two 130hp engines, and 972 tons. See: Wise, *Lifeline of the Confederacy*, 310–312.
86. ORN, ser. II, 2: pg., 721. These four ships were the *Ajax, Hercules, Adventure,* and *Enterprise* under contract to William Denny & Co., of Dumbarton, Scotland. See: Bulloch, *Secret Service*, 2: 242; ORN, ser. II, 2: 720, 721, 725, 741–742, 767; ORN, ser. I, 3: 721; Wise, *Lifeline of the Confederacy*, 286, 298, 304; Graham, *Clydebuilt*, 165, 191, 194.
87. ORN, ser. II, 2: 723–725; Bulloch, *Secret Service*, 2: 238–241.

88. See: Lancashire OnLine Parish Clerks, "Marriages at St Mary, Liverpool, 1859–1863" http://www.lan-opc.org.uk/Liverpool/Walton/stmary/marriages_1859-1863.html. A witness at the wedding of Charles K. Prioleau and Wright's daughter, Mary Elizabeth, was the U.S. consul at the time (1860), Beverly Tucker, who would go "south" after the beginning of the Civil War and perform curiously "gray" duties for the Confederacy.
89. ORN, ser. II, 2: 723–725; Bulloch, *Secret Service*, 2: 126–127.
90. ORN, ser. II, 2: 723–725.
91. *Ibid*.
92. *Ibid*., 724.
93. *Ibid*., 725; Bulloch, *Secret Service*, 2: 241–243.
94. ORN, ser. II, 2: 726–727.
95. *Ibid*., 728–730.
96. McKay, *Sea King*, 98.
97. *Ibid*., 36–37.
98. ORN, ser. II, 2: 728–730; Carter was the acting master of the USS *Rescue* and Murdaugh was his counterpart on the USS *Advance* with the Grinnell Expedition to the Arctic (1850–51) in search of the Franklin Expedition. Murdaugh befriended the famous Dr. Kane who served as ship's surgeon. See: Kane, *Grinnell Expedition*, 22, 115.
99. *Ibid*.
100. *Ibid*. See: Naval Historical Center, "Online Library" s.v. "Commander Hunter Davidson" http://www.history.navy.mil/photos/pers-us/uspers-d/h-davdsn.htm. Davidson became the Chief of the Argentine Navy's torpedo division 1875, after commanding the Maryland State 'Water Police.' When Davidson resigned to go to Argentina, James Iredell Waddell replaced him. Davidson died in Paraguay in 1913. See: Eduardo C. Gerding, "The Confederate Navy and the Argentine Hydrographic survey: Time of the Spar Torpedo" The *Buenos Aires Herald* (14 Dec 2003) http://www.civilwarhome.com/argentinehydrosurvey.htm for information about Davidson's career in South America.
101. See: U.S. Interior Dept., Battle Summaries, "Chaffin's Farm/New Market Heights," http://www.nps.gov/history/hps/abpp/battles/va075.htm.
102. John T. Mason, "Last of the Confederate Cruisers," *Century Illustrated Magazine* 56 (1898): 600–601.
103. McKay, *Sea King*, 101–102.
104. JDB, letter to Irvine Bulloch, 4 Oct 1864, Confederate Navy Collection, Box: Bulloch, Irvine Stephen, Master, Eleanor S. Brockenbrough Library, The Museum of the Confederacy, Richmond, VA. These were orders for duty on the CSS *Shenandoah* under Lt. Commanding Waddell.
105. Dudley even knew the day the *Laurel* was purchased. See: ORN, ser. I, 3: 343.
106. Milton, *Lincoln's Spymaster*, 112–113; McKay, *Sea King*, 104–106.
107. ORN, ser. I, 3: 10–11.
108. *Ibid*., 749–755.
109. *Ibid*.
110. McKay, *Sea King*, 104–105.
111. ORN, ser. I, 3: 756.
112. *Ibid*., 255. Report of Napoleon Collins to Sec. Gideon Welles, USN.
113. McKay, *Sea King*, 105.
114. ORN, ser. II, 2: 733–734.
115. McKay, *Sea King*, 106; "Memoirs of James Iredell Waddell," ZB files, US Navy Historical Center (Washington, DC).
116. ORN, ser. II, 2: 735–736.
117. *Ibid*.
118. Tidwell, *Come Retribution*, 329, 331; Adam Mayers, *Dixie and the Dominion; Canada, the Confederacy, and the War for the Union* (Toronto: Dundurn, 2003), 159.
119. McKay, *Sea King*, 109–112.
120. ORN, ser. II, 2: 736–737. A Union ship seized the *Georgia* as JDB had predicted.
121. *Ibid*., 738–740.
122. *Ibid*. The forward gun would be a 110-pound Armstrong, mounted on a special pivoting carriage and a 9- or 10-inch gun aft for "crushing work at close quarters."
123. *Ibid*. JDB gave the person's name to Davidson who would reveal it to Mallory.
124. *Ibid*., 741–742.
125. *Ibid*.
126. *Ibid*., 743; JDB met Walker before he left Liverpool for Bermuda via Halifax.
127. McKay, *Sea King*, 116–118; Irvine Bulloch, letter to Martha Stewart Bulloch via Martha Bulloch Roosevelt, 8 Oct 1864, TRC, bMS AM 1834.1 (249), #7.
128. McKay, *Sea King*, 118.
129. JDB, letter to Hotze, 14 Nov 1864, Henry Hotze Papers, AC 3608, Library of Congress; ORN, ser. I, 3: 757–759; Bulloch, *Secret Service*, 2: 141–144. Corbett was acquitted of all charges.
130. *Ibid*. Ramsay, as commander of the *Laurel*, was on his way to run the blockade via Nassau into Charleston where the ship would be renamed the *Confederate States*.
131. Bulloch, letter to Hotze, 14 Nov. 1864, Henry Hotze Papers.
132. ORN, ser. I, 3: 757–759, Bulloch, *Secret Service*, 2: 141–144.
133. Bulloch, letter to Hotze, 22 Nov. 1864, Henry Hotze Papers.

134. ORN, ser. I, 3: 757–759, Bulloch, *Secret Service*, 2: 141–144.
135. See: U.S. Interior Dept., Battle Summaries, http://www.nps.gov/history/hps/abpp/battles/bycampgn.htm#West64.
136. ORN, ser. II, 2: 769.
137. *Ibid.*, 771–772.
138. *Ibid.*, Bennett, *The London Confederates*, 57. President Lincoln issued a Thanksgiving Proclamation the previous month coinciding with George Washington's initial proclamation 75 years earlier that declared the last Thursday of Nov a national day of Thanksgiving; 26 Nov 1863 was the first official U.S. Thanksgiving holiday.
139. ORN, ser. II, 2: 776.
140. Embree, *Bismarck's First War*, 343–344. The Treaty of Vienna ended the war.
141. ORN, ser. II, 2: 738–740.
142. Bulloch, *Secret Service*, 2: 73–74.
143. *Ibid.*, 74–75; ORN, ser. I, 3: 720–724. There is considerable variance among the accounts of how the *Sphinx* got away from Denmark. Due the extreme sensitivity of the operation, JDB and Arman operated "off the books" when possible to preserve operational security.
144. Bulloch, *Secret Service*, 2: 60; Baxter, *Ironclad Warship*, 210–284. See: Fuller, *Clad in Iron* for a good analysis of the Union's largely brown-water monitor program and Britain's seemingly inept efforts to develop turreted armor ships. The Royal Navy actually had more transoceanic or blue-water armored vessels (though not turreted as yet) that were able to strike *everywhere*. The Union Navy, even at the end of the American Civil War was mostly wood-hulled and not until *after* the war did a Union monitor (the USS *Miantonomoh*) cross the Atlantic (1866) and even then she was towed for a considerable time. See: Naval Historical Center, "Online Library," s.v. "*Miantonomoh*" http://www.history.navy.mil/photos/sh-usn/usnsh-m/miantonm.htm.
145. ORN, ser. I, 3: 722.
146. *Ibid.*, 723.
147. *Ibid.*
148. *Ibid.*
149. *Ibid.* Arman received 350,000 francs and Swedish banker Puggard got 80,000 francs.
150. After the American Civil War, Page returned to Argentina, became a cattle farmer, helped create the Argentinean Navy's coastal defenses, and advocated the acquisition of an Ericsson-designed torpedo boat. Page and his family moved to Italy where he died in Rome in 1899. See: Robert A. Brock, ed., "Captain Thomas Jefferson Page, of the C.S. Gunboat Stonewall; Sketch of his life and deeds," *Southern Historical Society Papers* 27 (1899): 220.
151. ORN, ser. I, 3: 719–720.
152. *Ibid.*, 724–725. Bulloch was staying at 5 James Street, S.W. London, where Crenshaw could meet with him if required. Bulloch rarely specified his future locations due to Union-inspired mail tampering.
153. *Ibid.*
154. *Ibid.*, 726.
155. ORN, ser. II, 2: 783–784.
156. *Ibid.*, 783.
157. *Ibid.*, 784–785.
158. *Ibid.*, 785.
159. ORN, ser. I, 3: 728–729.
160. *Ibid.*

Chapter 11

1. *British Standard*, 6 Jan 1865.
2. ORN, ser. I, 3: 726–727; Bulloch, *Secret Service*, 2: 88.
3. *Ibid.*
4. ORN, ser. II, 2: 787–788.
5. *Ibid.*
6. ORN, ser. I, 3: 729.
7. *Ibid.*, 729–730.
8. *Ibid.*, 726–727.
9. *Ibid.* JDB fumed about the presence of the USS *Niagara*, for he encountered several officers from the *Rappahannock* at Calais who not only knew his itinerary, but spoke openly of the *Stonewall*. Then, a letter from Lt. Shryock noted that "the affair is very generally talked about here in Paris." JDB sent a blistering letter to Commodore Barron that those responsible for this gross breach of security should be "forthwith sent out of Europe." See: Bulloch, letter to Shryock, 9 Jan 1865, Whittle Papers, 2, no. 36.
10. Bulloch, *Secret Service*, 2: 89.
11. *London Conformist*, 11 Jan 1865.
12. Bulloch, *Secret Service*, 2: 93.
13. *Ibid.*
14. Chris Michael, *Lelia* (Birkenhead, U.K.: Countryvise, 2004), 71–88, 108.
15. ORN, ser. I, 2: 731–732.
16. *Ibid.*

17. Bulloch, *Secret Service*, 2: 93.
18. *Ibid.*, 93–94.
19. *Ibid.*
20. ORN, ser. II, 2: 790–791. Quinn arrived from Bermuda after working on the double engines that Lt. Carter had sent; his previous assignment was the CSS *Virginia II*. See: ORN, ser. II, 2: 669, 771, and ORN, ser. I, 10: 671.
21. *Ibid.*, 792–793.
22. *Ibid.*, 95.
23. *Ibid.*
24. Bulloch, *Secret Service*, 2: 95–96.
25. Thomas J. Page, "The Career of the Confederate Cruiser Stonewall," *Southern Historical Papers* 7, no. 6 (Jun 1879): 263.
26. *Ibid.* The date of the arrival of the CSS *Stonewall* is extrapolated from Page's account and Hunter Davidson's letter of 6 Feb 1865. See: ORN, ser. I, 3: 733–734.
27. ORN, ser. I, 3: 416–417. There are disparities in Union and Confederate accounts of the chronology of events.
28. *Ibid.*, 735.
29. *Ibid.*, 417–420.
30. *Ibid.* Henri Mercier had just left his post as minister to the U.S. out of frustration with Sec. Seward.
31. *Ibid.*
32. *Ibid.*
33. *Ibid.*, 735.
34. Bulloch, *Secret Service*, 2: 97.
35. ORN, ser. I, 3: 421; Bulloch, *Secret Service*, 2: 97.
36. Bulloch, *Secret Service*, 2: 97.
37. ORN, ser. I, 3: 736.
38. *Ibid.*, 737–739. The *Louisa Ann Fanny* left Victoria Docks on 9 Feb 1865 with 7 passengers, for the CSS *Stonewall*. See: Bennett, *The London Confederates*, 64.
39. *Ibid.*; Lancashire County, England, records, West Derby; Birth Certificate, s.v. "Martha Louisa Bulloch."
40. The officers apparently sent their concerns to Barron just after they arrived in Portugal on 4 Feb. See: Barron, letter to JDB, 10 Feb 1865, and JDB, letter to Barron, 15 Feb 1865, Whittle Papers, 2, no. 38 and 40.
41. JDB, letter to Barron, 15 Feb 1865, Whittle Papers, 2, no. 40.
42. *Ibid.*
43. *Ibid.*
44. *Ibid.*
45. ORN, ser. I, 3: 434–435.
46. ORN, ser. II, 2: 798–799. The *Tuscaloosa* would be turned over to the U.S. Navy at the end of the war.
47. ORN, ser. I, 3: 435; Bulloch, *Secret Service*, 2: 98. Craven's account of the situation is concordant with Carter's, though Craven does not mention the *Sacramento*.
48. ORN, ser. I, 3: 435–436.
49. *Ibid.*, 436.
50. ORN, ser. I, 2: 98.
51. ORN, ser. I, 3: 444, 739–740.
52. Bulloch, *Secret Service*, 2: 268–269.
53. *Ibid.*
54. ORN, ser. I, 3: 821.
55. Bulloch, *Secret Service*, 2: 270; Spencer, *Confederate Navy*, 145–146.
56. *Ibid.*
57. ORN, ser. I, 3: 741; Bulloch, *Secret Service*, 2: 99.
58. ORN, ser. I, 3: 741–743.
59. *Ibid.*
60. *Ibid.*, 743–745.
61. *Ibid.*
62. Forrest, *Diary of Confederate Service*, 292–294; Michael, *Lelia*, 108. Harriott's sister Annette was married to Capt. S. Grosvenor Porter of blockade-running fame, whose sister married TR, Sr.'s brother.
63. ORN, ser. I, 3: 745–747.
64. *Ibid.*
65. John Wilkinson, *The Narrative of a Blockade-Runner* (New York: Sheldon, 1877), 247–251. The aptly named *Chameleon* had been the CSS *Tallahassee*, CSS *Olustee*, and SS *Atalanta*; when handed over to the U.S. in 1866 it would become the *Amelia*, and later the Japanese *Haya Maru*.
66. David Stephen Heidler and Jeanne T. Heidler, eds., *Encyclopedia of the American Civil War: a Political, Social, and Military History* (New York: W.W. Norton, 2000), 67–72, 1709–1711.
67. ORN, ser. II, 2: 810.
68. Mallory remained with the Confederate cabinet to the bitter end, fleeing from Richmond to Georgia, where he finally resigned from the Confederate government. See: Rodman L. Underwood, *Stephen Russell Mallory: A Biography of the Confederate Navy Secretary and United States Senator* (Jefferson, NC: McFarland, 2005).

69. London *Guardian, Watchman and Wesleyan Advertiser, London Nonconformist*, 19 Apr 1865.
70. Bulloch, *Secret Service*, 2: 154–155.
71. *Watchman and Wesleyan Advertiser*, 26 Apr 1865. This paper said the news arrived aboard the *Nova Scotian* via Greencastle.
72. Bulloch, *Secret Service*, 2: 429.
73. Meade, *Judah P. Benjamin*, 317–319. Benjamin attended the last Confederate cabinet meeting in Abbeville, SC, on May 2, 1865, the day Mason wrote his indignant letter. By the time Mathew Fontaine Maury reached Havana, Cuba, Benjamin was on the run in Florida, trying to escape to Nassau and Britain where he arrived on 30 Aug 1865 at the same port Maury departed on the 2nd of May: Southampton.
74. *Ibid.*, 101.
75. *Ibid.*
76. ORN, ser. I, 3: 746.
77. *Ibid.*, 747–748.
78. *Ibid.* Spain did not withdraw belligerent rights until 4 Jun; Great Britain had done the same two days before. See: ORN, ser. I, 3: 552, 578.
79. ORN, ser. I, 3: 747–748.
80. Page, "Career of the Confederate Cruiser Stonewall," 263, 279. Lt. John Low and the CSS *Ajax* returned to Great Britain on 9 Jun 1865.
81. McKay, *Sea King*, 153; ORN, ser. I, 3: 759–760.
82. *London Nonconformist*, 31 May 1865.
83. Bulloch, *Secret Service*, 2: 156.
84. ORN, ser. I, 3: 775.
85. ORN, ser. I, 3: 775–777; Bulloch, *Secret Service*, 2: 156–159.
86. *Ibid.*
87. Bulloch, *Secret Service*, 2: 156–159; ORN, ser. II, 2: 811–812.
88. ORN, ser. I, 3: 777–779.
89. McKay, *Sea King*, 187–192.
90. *Ibid.*, 195–196.
91. *Ibid.*, 200–202.
92. *Ibid.*, 208–210.
93. Andrew C. A. Jampoler, *The Last Lincoln Conspirator* (Annapolis: Naval Institute, 2008), 76.
94. James Murray Mason Papers.
95. McKay, *Sea King*, 212.
96. *Ibid.*
97. Jampoler, *Last Lincoln Conspirator*, 88.
98. ORN, ser. II, 2: 811.
99. *Ibid.*, 214–215.
100. *Ibid.*; ORN, ser. I, 3: 834.
101. See: *Anglo-American Times*, 3 Nov 1865; *The Cork Examiner*, 1 Nov. 1865; *NYT*, 18 and 21 Oct 1865 for passenger lists and arrivals. See: McKay, *Sea King*, 13–16, for Waddell family history.
102. McKay, *Sea King*, 216.
103. ORN, ser. I, 3: 835.
104. *Ibid.*; McKay, *Sea King*, 223.
105. ORN, ser. I, 3: 835; McKay, *Sea King*, 219–223.
106. McKay, *Sea King*, 224–226.
107. Confederate sympathizer Mr. Thwarts owned the *Bee*. See: Cornelius E. Hunt, *Shenandoah, The Last Confederate Cruiser* (New York: George W. Carleton, 1867), 259–261.
108. McKay, *Sea King*, 227.
109. Hunt, *Shenandoah*, 262–263. Hunt's account of the *Shenandoah* cruise has numerous inaccuracies, but this statement is consistent with other accounts. Hunt jumped ship the night before receiving news of the queen's counsel's decision to free the Confederates.
110. Bulloch, *Secret Service*, 2: 174.
111. Angus Curry, *The Officers of the* CSS *Shenandoah* (Gainesville: University of Florida, 2006), 270.
112. Hunt, *Shenandoah*, 261; McKay, *Sea King*, 227.
113. Curry, *Officers of the* CSS *Shenandoah*, 272.
114. McKay, *Sea King*, 228.
115. Prime Minister Palmerston died on 18 Oct 1865, and was succeeded by Lord Russell. Lord Clarendon (a.k.a. George William Frederick Villiers, 4th Earl of Clarendon) assumed the post of British foreign minister. See: *Anglo-American Times*, 30 Dec 1865, which carried twelve full transcripts of letters between Adams and Clarendon from 21 Oct to 11 Dec 1865.
116. *NYT*, 21 Nov 1865. American newspapers learned of the *Shenandoah* surrender on the 19 or 20 Nov 1865; *NYT* ran the story from the 9 Nov 1865 *Liverpool Courier*.
117. Bulloch, *Secret Service*, 2: 186–187; McKay, *Sea King*, 228–229; "Memoirs of James Iredell Waddell."
118. Liverpool Record Office, Register of Baptisms, 1.

Chapter 12

1. Willson, *John Slidell*, 294–296, ORN, ser. II, 2: 811; Meade, *Judah P. Benjamin*, 316–331.
2. The U.S. government filed against Prioleau on 26 Jul 1865 (*U.S. vs. Prioleau*); this was the case of the *Aline*, one of eight Confederate-owned blockade runners with cargoes assigned to Fraser, Trenholm and Co. It was the only one of the eight that cleared the blockade before the end of the war. It had cotton from Galveston that was sold in Havana. The U.S. lost the case, but Prioleau had to file a countersuit to recover some of his money (*Prioleau vs. USA and* President Andrew Johnson, 28 Feb 1866). The other British case was the *U.S. vs.* Wagner (27 Feb 1867) that also ruled against the U.S. In France, the U.S. filed suits against Arman and Voruz that also resulted in rulings against the U.S. See: Charles S. Davis, *Colin J. McRae: Confederate Financial Agent* (Tuscaloosa, AL: Confederate Publishing, 1961), 77–80; Max. A. Robertson and Geoffrey Ellis, eds., *The English Reports, Vice Chancellor's Court*, vol. 71 (Edinburgh: William Green & Sons; London: Stevens & Sons, 1907), 580; U.S. Congress., House, "Fraser, Trenholm & Co.," 39th Cong., 2nd Sess., House, Vol. I, Ex. Doc. 63 (Washington: 1867): 1–51, 434.
3. *The Commonwealth*, 17 Mar 1866.
4. *Galveston Daily News*, 10 Feb 1867. While this reference is for 1867, JDB and Robertson were probably involved in the cotton trading business with Fraser, Trenholm and Co. throughout 1866.
5. McKay, *Sea King*, 231–232.
6. Lawrence James, *The Rise and Fall of the British Empire* (1994; reprint, London: Abacus, 2004), 194–195.
7. U.S. Interior Department, Census Office, Eighth Census, 1860, City of Norfolk, Norfolk County, VA, series M653, roll: 1366, p. 357, s.v. "M. P. Robertson"; ORN, ser. II, 2: 715; *NYT,* 30 Jun 1905; *The Merchant Shippers of London, Liverpool, Manchester, Birmingham, Bristol, and Hull* (London: Straker & Sons, 1868), 103, 243; Truman Abbe and Hubert A. Howson, *Robert Colgate, the Immigrant: A Genealogy of the New York Colgates et al* (New Haven, CT: Tuttle, Moorehouse, & Taylor, 1941), 105, 161–162. Robertson, who was about the same age as Bulloch, arrived in Liverpool in May 1864 and his wife (Annie Thorburn Klein) and two young children followed in Sep. He had worked as a bank teller in Norfolk until the Union occupied the city. He fled to Baltimore in 1862 where he lived until Mar 1864 when Commander James North recommended him to Bulloch.
8. G. C. Boase, *Oxford Dictionary of National Biography*, s.v., "Bruce, Frederick William Adolphus Wright," http://www.oxforddnb.com/index/3/101003730/.
9. Charles C. Beaman, Jr., T*he National and Private 'Alabama Claims' and Their Final and Amicable Settlement* (Washington: W.H. Moore, 1871), 5. Adams, letter to Russell, 20 May 1865.
10. JDB does not give an exact date of this case; however, in Jul 1865 a series of cases were brought against McRae, Fraser, Trenholm and Co., and Charles K. Prioleau. The British courts ruled against the U.S. government. On 28 Feb 1867, the U.S. government sued Wagner, another co-partner of Fraser, Trenholm and Co. See: Davis, *Colin J. McRae*, 77–80.
11. Bulloch, *Secret Service*, 2: 421.
12. *Ibid.*, 421–422.
13. George W. Dalzell, *The Flight from the Flag* (Chapel Hill: University of North Carolina, 1940), 228–229; *Watchman and Wesleyan Advertiser*, 28 Mar 1866. Wilson immediately resold the *Shenandoah* to an agent of the sultan of Zanzibar for a profit of £1000.
14. Eller, *Dictionary of American Naval Fighting Ships*, II: 572.
15. *Anglo-American Times*, 14 Apr 1866.
16. Washington need not have worried about Napoleon III, for Bismarck had the foundering French Empire in its sights; and Napoleon III had ordered home French military units from Mexico. See: Crook, *The North, the South, and The Powers*, 366–367.
17. *Anglo-American Times*, 2 May 1865. The lambasting that Benjamin Disraeli delivered before Parliament is indicative of lingering effects of the American Civil War in Britain.
18. New York Society Library, "New York City Marriage and Death Notices: 1857–1868," http://www.nysoclib.org/king/king3.html. Anna married James K Gracie on 5 Jun 1866.
19. *Illustrated Times*, 16 Jun 1866; Geoffrey Wawro, *The Austro-Prussian War: Austria's War with Prussia and Italy in 1866* (New York: Cambridge University, 1997).
20. *Anglo-American Times*, 2 Jun 1866.
21. London *Guardian*, 11 Jul 1866.
22. *Anglo-American Times,* 4 Aug 1866.
23. *Anglo-American Times*, 28 Jul and 4 Aug 1866.
24. James T. De Kay, *The Rebel Raiders, The Astonishing History of the Confederacy's Secret Navy* (New York: Ballantine Books, 2002), 217.
25. Naval Historical Center, *DANFS Online*, s.v. "Miantonomoh," http://www.history.navy.mil/danfs/m10/miantonomoh-i.htm. The USS *Augusta* towed the ironclad for part of the voyage Halifax to Queenstown for "safety" according to Asst. Sec. of the Navy Gustavus Fox, who was onboard.
26. Adam's first postwar complaint was 18 Nov 1865, only days after the surrender of the *Shenandoah* in Liverpool. See: *CoGB*, 734.
27. Beaman, *Alabama Claims*, 44.
28. *Watchman and Wesleyan Advertiser,* 3 Oct 1863; Meade, *Judah P. Benjamin*, 332–335.
29. *Ibid.* Benjamin's sponsors included Lords Justices Giffard and Turner, Lord Hatherley, and Sir Fitzroy Kelley.
30. Fraser, Trenholm and Co. Papers, Adam Matthew Publications microfilm, B/FT 1/153, 6 Sep 1866 and B/FT 1/154, 25 Sep 1866, Wiltshire, England.

31. Fraser, Trenholm and Co. Papers, B/FT 6/8, 23 Nov 1866.
32. Beaman, *Alabama Claims*, 1–2.
33. *Ibid.*, 44.
34. The inscription says that JDB had the book with him throughout the building of the *Florida, Alabama* etc. See: Marshall University Special Collections, "C.S.S. Alabama; A Virtual Exhibit," http://www.marshall.edu/library/speccoll/virtual_museum/css_alabama/peake_menu.asp.
35. The Sorley advertisement first appeared on 8 Jan 1867 and continued through 28 Feb 1868. Sorley was born in Scotland (1820) and educated in Liverpool. He came to Mobile in 1836 and by 1851, was a Galveston cotton merchant. The blockade runner and former U.S. Revenue Cutter *Dodge*, was renamed in honor of his wife "Mary J. Sorley." Bulloch probably met with Sorley after the war when Sorley escaped to Liverpool, 1865–1867, indicating that Sorley was still residing in Liverpool when this ad first appeared. See: Merrow E. Sorley, *Lewis of Warner Hall: The History of a Family* (1935; reprint, Baltimore: Genealogical Publishing, 2000), 568–569.
36. Bennet Woodcroft, *Subject-Matter Index of Patents Applied for and Patents Granted, for the Year 1866* (London: Commissioners of Patents for Inventions, 1867), 138, 315; Bennet Woodcroft, *Alphabetical Index of Patentees and Applicants for Patents of Invention, for the Year 1867* (London: Commissioners of Patents for Inventions, 1867), 41, 242; Bennet Woodcroft, *Chronological Index of Patents Applied for and Patents Granted, for the Year 1867* (London: Commissioners of Patents for Inventions), 24; U.S. Congress, House of Representatives, *Annual Report of the Commissioner of Patents for the Year 1867*, 40th Cong., 2nd Sess., House Ex. Doc. No. 96, vol. I–II (Washington: GPO, 1868), 1548, #2486 (Cotton Bale Tie. Patented 9 Oct 1866). Wailey had been equally successful with the Patent office in the U.S. with these and other inventions.
37. Beaman, *Alabama Claims*, 4, Stanley, letter to Bruce, 9 Mar 1867.
38. *Ibid.*, 422; U.S. Congress, House of Representatives, "Letter of the Secretary of the Treasury, Recovery of Confederate Property in Europe," 40th Cong., 2nd Sess., vol. 19, House Ex. Doc. No. 304 (Washington: GPO, 1868). Bulloch carefully documented his observations.
39. *Ibid.*, 424–425. These officials may have included McRae (who remained in England until 1867), Caleb Huse (who quickly left for France), James Burton (an Ordnance Bureau purchasing agent), and Norman Walker (the purchasing agent who had arrived from Bermuda in May 1865). Judah Benjamin and Confederate Vice President John Breckinridge (who escaped from Florida with Benjamin) also would have been involved in recovering funds held by Jacob Thompson (the former Confederate commissioner to Canada). James Mason had already departed for Canada in May 1866. See: Bennett, *The London Confederates*, 154–156.
40. Bulloch, *Secret Service*, 2: 426–427.
41. *Ibid.*, 427.
42. Bulloch, letter to Carter, 22 Jul 1868, and dividend payments authorized by Harmood Banner & Son from the estate of Fraser, Trenholm & Co., 14 Dec 1867, 8 Jun 1868, and 22 Dec 1868, Robert R. Carter, Shirley Plantation Collection, 20(1), John D. Rockefeller, Jr. Library, The Colonial Williamsburg Foundation,. The accounting firm of Harmood Banner & Company became one of the twenty-first century's largest accountancy firms, Coopers & Lybrand.
43. *Commercial Daily List*, London, Liverpool, Manchester, and Birmingham, 26 Dec 1866. This recurring advertisement appeared regularly through 20 Jul 1867. The act authorizing the Society was first passed 3 Mar 1866 and re-enacted 29 Jan 29 1867. See: Virginia, General Assembly, *Acts of the General Assembly of the State of Virginia: Passed in 1866–1867* (Richmond: James E. Goode, 1867), 579.
44. De Kay, *Rebel Raiders*, 219.
45. See: U.S. State Dept., "Timeline of U.S. Diplomatic History Purchase of Alaska, 1867," http://web.archive.org/web/20080410122537/http://www.state.gov/r/pa/ho/time/gp/17662.htm; U.S. Library of Congress, "Treaty with Russia for the Purchase of Alaska," http://www.loc.gov/rr/program/bib/ourdocs/Alaska.html.
46. De Kay, *Rebel Raiders*, 219–220.
47. *Ibid.*, 220–221; *NYT*, 22 Nov 1886.
48. Stanley, letters to Thornton, 14, 21, and 30 Mar; *CoGB*, 842, 843–846. Thornton's father was also a British envoy to America from 1800–1804. Sir Frederick Bruce, the previous envoy, died in Boston in 1867, leaving the post without a British diplomat friendly to American interests. See: Sidney Lee, *Dictionary of National Biography*, vol. 56 (London: Smith Elder, 1898), 299; U.K. National Archives, "British Envoys to America, 1791–1891," s.v., "Thornton, Sir Edward" http://yourarchives.nationalarchives.gov.uk/index.php?title=British_Envoys_to_America,_1791-1891#THORNTON.2C_Sir_Edward_.28Jr.29_In_the_U.S.2C_1868-1881.
49. C. Grant Robertson, *Bismarck* (New York: Henry Holt, 1919), 264.
50. *Anglo-American Times*, 8 Aug 1868.
51. Walker, the former Confederate purchasing agent in Bermuda, moved to Liverpool where he, like Bulloch, had a cotton importing business. The Davis family went to Walker's summer home in Wales where they stayed for a considerable period. Walker is probably the "successful businessman" mentioned in the *Anglo-American Times* as having offered Davis a position. See: William J. Cooper, Jr., *Jefferson Davis: American* (New York: Knopf, 2000), 622–623; London *Guardian*, 12 Aug 1868.
52. Stanley, letter to Thornton and Johnson, letter to Lord Stanley, 16 Oct 1868, *CoGB*, 848–850.
53. *Ibid.*, 850–852.
54. *Ibid.*, 852.
55. *Ibid.*
56. London *Times*, 23 Oct 1868.
57. *Dubuque Herald*, 25 Oct 1868.

58. *CoGB*, 853–857.
59. *Ibid.*, 857.
60. George H. Townsend, *The Handbook of the Year 1868* (London: Wyman & Sons, 1869), 245–246.
61. *CoGB*, 857–874.
62. *Ibid.*, 874.
63. *Ibid.*, 875–876.
64. *Ibid.*, 877.
65. *Commercial Daily List,* 1 Jan 1869.
66. U.S. State Dept., "Correspondence Concerning Claims against Great Britain," vol. VI (Washington: GPO, 1871), 182–184. The Fraser, Trenholm & Co. partners of Liverpool included: Dehon Wagner, James Thomas Welsman, William Lee Trenholm, and Charles Kuhn Prioleau until Jul 1864 when George Alfred Trenholm retired; on 1 Jan 1866, John Richardson Armstrong became a partner.
67. R.E. Fulton, ed., *The Commercial Directory and Shippers' Guide*, 3rd ed. (Liverpool: R. E. Fulton, 1871), 98.
68. U.K. Home Office, Public Record Office, London, s.v., "James Dunwoody Bulloch" Ho1/154/6059, Naturalization Application, 16 Jan 1869.
69. *CoGB*, 880–881.

Chapter 13

1. *CoGB*, 885.
2. *Ibid.*, 886; Shine, "A Gallant Little Schooner," 553. Sir Edward transmitted a copy of the "Oregon Complaints" to the Earl of Clarendon on Feb 1st that he received on Feb 15th.
3. *Ibid.*, 887–888.
4. *Ibid.*, 898–801; Charles Francis Adams, Jr., *Charles Francis Adams* (Boston: Houghton Mifflin, 1900), 385.
5. Anna Roosevelt Cowles, letters to Anna Bulloch Gracie, 22 and 24 May 1869, TRC, bMS Am 1785.8(455), #2, 3. The letters and telegrams between Bulloch and Mittie and TR, Sr., that are frequently referenced in family letters during in the period 1866–1869 have not been discovered. These may have been removed by TR or others who would have been concerned about the Roosevelts' politically sensitive support to their unreconstructed Confederate relatives.
6. *NYT,* 13 May 1869. The article provides a listing of the Roosevelt party.
7. Martha Bulloch Roosevelt, letter to Anna Bulloch Gracie, 22 May 1869, TRC, bMS Am 1785.8(455) and Transcripts, early family correspondence to Sep 1869 from Liverpool, #207.
8. Anna Roosevelt Cowles, letters to Anna Bulloch Gracie, 22 and 24 May 1869, TRC, bMS Am 1785.8(455), #2, 3; Summary and biographical note, Robert Hutchison Papers, 1815–1897, Georgia Historical Society. "Clifton" was probably the name of the Bulloch family's farm when they first moved to Roswell.
9. Martha Bulloch Roosevelt, letter to Anna Bulloch Gracie, 2 Jun 1869, TRC, Transcripts early family correspondence #101. Admiral Hornby was one of Britain's most capable seamen, tacticians, diplomatists, and intellectuals. In 1886, he became the principal naval *aide-de-camp* to Queen Victoria and was assigned to the staff of the German emperor Wilhelm II during his visits to England in 1889 and 1890.
10. TR, Sr., letter to Anna Bulloch Gracie, 30 May 1869; TRC, bMS Am 1785.7(36), #1; Theodore Roosevelt, *Theodore Roosevelt's Diaries of Boyhood and Youth* (New York: Charles Scribner's Sons, 1928). 16.
11. *CoGB*, 2, 911; Martha Bulloch Stewart, letter to Anna Bulloch Gracie, 3 Jun 1869, TRC, bMS Am 1875.7(32), #1#1 and Anna Roosevelt Cowles, letters to Anna Bulloch Gracie, 22 and 24 May 1869. TRC, bMS Am 1785.8(455), #2, 3. Mittie refers to the 1st or 2nd of Jun as the departure date from Liverpool.
12. *Ibid.*, 911–913.
13. Morris, *Roosevelt*, 49–51.
14. *Ibid.*
15. *Illustrated Times* of London, 7 Aug 1869. Construction on the Kiel Canal would not begin until 1887 when Alfred Thayer Mahan's best-selling book *The Influence of Sea Power On History* influenced Kaiser Wilhelm II to finance the 8-year project.
16. *Ibid.*
17. Morris, *Roosevelt*, 24–27; *CoGB*, 913–920; *Anglo-American Times*, 2 Oct 1860. Future President of the United States Roosevelt and former President of the Confederate States Davis were in Liverpool at the same time. Davis departed aboard the *Baltimore* from Southampton on Saturday, 2 Oct 1869. U.S. federal charges were dropped against Davis in Feb 1869 while he was in Britain.
18. *CoGB*, 913–920.
19. *Ibid.*, 920–921.
20. *The Edinburgh Evening Courant,* 27 Oct 1869. Viceroy (Khedive) Ismail Pasha ruled Egypt under Ottoman suzerainty suggesting that Prince Louis was observing proper protocol prior to visiting Egypt.
21. *CoGB*, 921,
22. *Ibid.*
23. *Ibid.*, 924–931.
24. James, *Rise and Fall of the British Empire*, 196–197.
25. TR, Sr., letter to Anna Roosevelt Cowles, 22 Nov 1869, TRC, bMS Am 1834.1 (201), #10; Morris, *Roosevelt*, 55–56.

26. *The Edinburgh Evening Courant*, 11 Dec 1869.
27. *CoGB*, 931–932.
28. Morris, *Roosevelt*, 56–57.
29. *Ibid.*
30. *Anglo-American Times*, 6 Aug 1870. Although the article was written several months later, and after the outbreak of hostilities between France and Prussia, it reviews the diplomatic morass the *"Alabama* Claims" process had fallen into by mid-1870.
31. Martha Bulloch Roosevelt, to Anna Cowles, 18 May 1870, TRC, bMS Am 1834.1 (194), #12.
32. *NYT*, 26 May 1870.
33. Geoffrey Wawro, *The Franco-Prussian War* (New York: Cambridge University, 2005), 30–31.
34. *Ibid.*, 32–33.
35. See: University of Cambridge, Alumni Database, s.v., "Villiers, George William Frederick," http://venn.lib.cam.ac.uk/.
36. Michael Howard, *The Franco-Prussian War* (1961; reprint, London: Routledge, 2001), 55–60.
37. *Ibid.*
38. TR, Sr., letter to Anna Roosevelt Cowles, TRC, bMS Am 1834.1 (201), #15.
39. Davis sailed on 10 Aug 1870 and arrived 19 Aug. See: http://www.norwayheritage.com/p_ship.asp?sh=russj.
40. Rice University, "The Papers of Jefferson Davis," http://jeffersondavis.rice.edu/chron.cfm?doc_id=1467.
41. Wawro, *The Franco-Prussian War*, 87–90, 169–185.
42. *Anglo-American Times*, 20 Aug 1870.
43. *The* Portland *Morning Oregonian*, 18 Aug 1870.
44. See: *Anglo-American Times* 8 Aug 1870 for a taste of Motley-bashing.
45. See: U.K. Parliament, "Parliamentary Archives," http://www.parliament.uk/business/publications/parliamentary-archives/.
46. See: Franco-Prussian War, "TimeLine" http://francoprussianwar.com/timeline.htm and Wawro, *Franco-Prussian War*, 228–233, 310 for a concise timeline of the Franco-Prussian War.
47. The Democratic Party told French immigrants that it welcomed the new French Republic. To prevent a wholesale German voter shift to the Republicans, it also congratulated German immigrants for the creation of a unified German nation. New York Republicans would launch Theodore Roosevelt to national prominence, while New York Democrats would do the same for Franklin Delano Roosevelt. See: *Anglo-American Times*, 24 Sep 1870. After Napoleon III's capture at the Battle of Sedan, he would die in exile at Camden Place, Chislehurst, Kent, England, on 9 Jan 1873.
48. London *Guardian*, 28 Sep 1870. The newspaper says Davis had returned after a short visit to Ireland on "Friday" which was 24 Sep. Bulloch also references his "Irish trip" with Davis. See: Bulloch, letter to Davis, 26 Oct 1871, in Jefferson Davis Family Collection at The Museum of the Confederacy, 6.
49. See: Rice University, "The Papers of Jefferson Davis," http://jeffersondavis.rice.edu/Chron.cfm?doc_id=1467.
50. See: Franco-Prussian War, "TimeLine"; Robert M. Citino, *The German Way of War: From the Thirty Years War to the Third Reich* (Lawrence: University of Kansas, 2005). The Germans continuously evolved and adapted tactics from this war against France that the Nazi military applied in World War II.
51. *NYT*, 10 Nov 1870; TR, Sr., letter book, Feb 1869–Jun 1873, TRC, *96M–46 (1), 188, 279.5. "T. Roosevelt (29),""Jas D. Bullock (47) Merchant," and "Miss Roosevelt and maid" arrived in New York City via the SS *Java* on 9 Nov 1870. Bulloch was staying at the Mount Vernon Hotel in Baltimore on 21 Jan 1871. James Waddell also resided in Baltimore and it's probable that they met.
52. TR, Sr., letter book Feb 1869–Jun 1873, TRC, *96M–46 (1) 324, 407.
53. *The Australian and New Zealand Gazette*, 1 Jan 1870.
54. *CoGB*, 937.
55. *Ibid.*, 938.
56. *Ibid.*, 938–939.
57. See: Franco-Prussian War, "TimeLine."
58. *Ibid.*
59. Martha Bulloch Roosevelt, letter to Anna Roosevelt Cowles, 3 Mar 1871, TRC, BMS Am 1834.1(194), #6; TR, Sr., letter book, Feb 1869–Jun 1873, TRC, 96M 46 (1), 324, 450, 471–472. Bulloch could have made an undocumented return to Liverpool sometime between 9 Nov 1970 and Jan 1871. Due to his abrupt departure in Mar 1871, he had to leave the settlement of Captain Fairfax' debt with brother-in-law Roosevelt. It would require all of TR, Sr.'s considerable persuasive skills to get the recalcitrant Fairfax to fulfill his obligation. Seven months later, when Captain Fairfax made the final payment of $150, Roosevelt sardonically commented, "This specimen of human nature forms better than I had expected." See: TR, Sr., letter to Bulloch 10 Nov 1871, TRC, *96M–46 (1), Theodore Roosevelt letter book, Feb 1869–Jun 1873, 476.
60. See: Lancashire County, England, records, West Derby; Waterloo, Death Certificate, s.v., "Henry Dunwoody Bulloch." Henry, aged 9, died *of Scarlatina Anginosa* (scarlet fever). Dr. Edward H. FitzHenry was present at death.
61. *CoGB*, 939.
62. *Ibid.*, 950–952. The U.S. commissioners included: Robert Schenck (Minister Plenipotentiary to Britain), Samuel Nelson (Associate Justice of the U.S. Supreme Court), Ebenezer Hoar of Massachusetts (former Attorney General under Grant) and George H. Williams (Republican Senator from Oregon, pall bearer for Lincoln and future Attorney General under Grant). Hoar addressed the *"Alabama* Claims," while Williams formed the case for fisheries and boundaries.
63. *Ibid.*

64. *CoGB*, 954–964; U.S. Congress, Senate, *The Case of the United States to be Laid before the Tribunal of Arbitration to be Convened in Geneva*, 42nd Cong. 2nd Sess., Senate Ex. Doc. 31 (Washington: GPO, 1872), 11, notes meeting dates of 9, 10, 13 and 14 Mar, then 5, 6, 8, 9, 10, and 12 Apr 1871.

65. U.K. National Archives, Census Returns of England and Wales, 1871, Lancashire, Litherland, Waterloo, class RG10, piece 3838, folio 78, p. 43, GSU roll 841922 "James De Bulloch" and Lancashire, Liverpool, West Derby, Toxteth Park, class RG10, piece 3805. folio 148. p. 10, GSU roll 841907, s.v. "Moses P. Robertson."

66. London *Sun and Central Press*, 17 Apr 1871. The paper quotes from the *Times* of London, but gives no specific reference date.

67. U.S. Congress, Senate, *The Case of the United States*, 13.

68. *Ibid*. Article 14 required each side to provide all commissioners a bound copy of their cases within six months of the exchange of the ratifications; both sides made it, but only just, convening on 15 Dec 1871. Charles F. Adams was appointed via a letter from Grant to Fish on 15 Jul 1871. Grant resisted Adams, questioning his political loyalty and fearing it would cause Britain to walk away from negotiations. See: Ulysses S. Grant, *The Papers of Ulysses S. Grant: June 1, 1871–January 31, 1872*, vol. 22, ed. John Y. Simon (Carbondale: Southern Illinois University, 1998), xxii, 81.

69. JDB, letter to Davis, 26 Oct 1871, Jefferson Davis Family Collection; Harold Lance Bower was the grandson of the founder of Bower & Son, Liverpool cotton brokers and the treasurer of the Liverpool branch of the Royal Life-Boat Institution. See: Thomas Ellison, *The cotton trade of Great Britain: Including a history of the Liverpool cotton market and of the Liverpool Cotton Brokers' Association* (London: Effingham Wilson, 1886), 192, 193; Royal National Life-Boat Institution, The Lifeboat, the Journal of the National Life-Boat Institution 8, 9, and 10 (1873, 1876, and 1879).

70. *NYT*, 6 Dec 1871. George Trenholm retired in July 1864 to become Confederate secretary of treasury.

71. *NYT*, 17 Jun 1868, "The Settlement with Frazer, Trenholm & Co." has a concise description of how the U.S. Dept. of Treasury dealt with this Company.

72. Bulloch, *Secret Service*, 310–313.

73. Grant, letter to Fish, 21 Jul 1871, Grant, *Papers of Ulysses S. Grant*, 79. See: Oxford University, "Oxford Dictionary of National Biography," s.v., "Alexander Cockburn," for more information on Cockburn.

74. *NYT*, 5 Nov 1897.

75. E. Benjamin Andrews, "The Treaty of Washington, 1868–1888," in *History of the United States*, vol. IV (1894; reprint, Washington: Ross & Perry, 2002).

76. De Kay, *Rebel Raiders*, 238–239.

77. Frank Warren Hackett, *Reminiscences of the Geneva Tribunal of Arbitration, 1872, The Alabama Claims* (Boston: Houghton Mifflin, 1911), 90.

78. De Kay, *Rebel Raiders*, 239; Andrews, "The Treaty of Washington."

79. *NYT*, 14 and 16 Dec 1871.

80. *Anglo-American Times*, 27 Jan 1872.

81. *Anglo-American Times*, 9 Mar 1872.

82. *Janesville Gazette*, 22 Jun 1872. The article notes that Nellie Grant was bound for Geneva, as was William Tecumseh Sherman.

83. De Kay, *Rebel Raiders*, 240–241.

84. De Kay, *Rebel Raiders*, 241–242; *NYT*, 23 Jul 1872; Bulloch, *Secret Service*, 2: 399–400. The *NYT* reported on the extraordinary levels of "information blackout" for the Geneva tribunal.

85. *Ibid*.

86. Bulloch, *Secret Service*, 2: 378–402. JDB blasts the failures of the British diplomats and legal experts and much as he does the U.S. government for Britain's penalization before the *Alabama* Claims tribunal.

87. De Kay, *Rebel Raiders*, 244.

88. *The* New York *World*, 9 Sep 1872.

89. *Week's News*, 21 Sep 1872. The phrase, "new order" became a political cliché. The *Alabama* Claims demonstrated that crises could be resolved in an equable manner, a "new order" for the world's nations. Seventy years later, "new order" took on different meaning under the Nazi government of Germany.

90. Bulloch, *Secret Service*, 2: 277–411. JDB spent 134 pages on his *Alabama* Claims rebuttal. Even 8 years later, when he began writing his memoirs, he firmly believed, as did most Britons, that the U.S. should not have been able to force the world's preeminent empire into legal or financial submission.

91. *NYT*, 16 Oct 1872, "Departures for Europe"; *NYT*, 17 Oct 1872; *Week's News*, 19 Oct 1872, "Liverpool dock strike." TR's name is not listed, but he was on the trip as noted in his childhood diaries and family papers.

92. *Anglo-American Times*, 2 Nov 1872, 17; H.W. Brands, *TR, the Last Romantic* (New York: Basic Books, 1997), 32. Young TR's mother and grandmother were ardent Confederate supporters, as was Aunt "Annie" Bulloch — who told him endless stories about Bulloch Hall, its people and events. See: Morris, *Roosevelt*, 8, as an example.

93. Morris, *Roosevelt*, 63.

94. Roosevelt, *Diaries of Boyhood and Youth*, 264–267. Irvine had married the attractive Ella Sears in 1871; they lived near her parents and sister Hattie.

95. London *Sun and Central Press*, 11 Nov 1872.

96. London *Guardian*, 13 Nov 1872. The "jaw-jaw" quote is by Sir Winston Churchill, 1914, uttered for a future war that of course involved the German Empire, World War I. See: Bartleby Bookstore, "Respectfully Quoted," for a compendium of quotes by Churchill.

97. *New York Herald*, 17 Dec 1872; *NYT*, 19 Dec 1872.

98. Morris, *Roosevelt*, 65–66.

99. London *Sun and Central Press,* 26 Mar 1873; James, *Rise and Fall of the British Empire,* 200–202.
100. Morris, *Roosevelt,* 69.
101. Morris, *Roosevelt,* 73; TR, Sr., letters to Martha Bulloch Roosevelt, 7 and 8 Jun 1873, TRC, bMS Am 1785.2 (100), #27 and 28.
102. Morris, *Roosevelt,* 73; TR, Sr., letters to Robertson, Hewitt, and Ashton, 17, 18, and 20 Aug 1873, TRC, *96M–46 (1), TR, Sr., Letter Book, Jun 1873–Jun 1874, 79, 87.
103. Martha Bulloch Roosevelt, letter to TR, Sr., 11 Oct 1873, TRC, bMS Am 1834.1 (194), #57. Bulloch & Robertson's offices were at No. 13 Rumford Street, Liverpool.
104. TR, Sr., letter to Anna Roosevelt Cowles, 18 Oct 1873, TRC, bMS Am 1834.1(201), #47; *NYT,* 6 Nov 1873. The Roosevelts departed for New York City in the SS *Russia* the next Saturday, 25 Oct.
105. Bulloch, *Secret Service,* I: 63; Prefeitura de Petrópolis, "Baron of Mauá—The Empire's most enterprising businessman," http://www.petropolis.rj.gov.br/index.php?url=http%3A//fctpi.petropolis.rj.gov.br/fctpi/modules/xt_con teudo/index.php%3Fid%3D22. In 1870, Ireneo Evangelista de Souza (baron de Mauá) founded the English Amazonas Steam Navigation Company in London providing regular mail and passenger service to Brazil, the United States, and Europe. By 1872, he deployed a telegraph cable linking Brazil with Portugal.
106. *The Hour,* 19 Apr 1873.
107. The Baron de Mauá had twenty-*year* exclusive use for this project. See: London *Sun and Central Press,* 23 Sep 1872.
108. TR, Sr., letter to Hamilton Fish, 1 Nov 1873, TRC, *96M–46 (1), TR, Sr., Letter Book, Jun 1873–Jun 1874, 189–190; *NYT,* 6 Nov 1873.
109. TR, Sr., letter to James K. Gracie, 19 Feb 1874, TRC, *96M–46 (1), TR, Sr., letter book, Jun 1873–Jun 1874, 350; Jefferson Davis, *Jefferson Davis Private Letters, 1823–1889* ed. Hudson Strode (1966; reprint, New York: Da Capo, 1995); Rice University, "The Papers of Jefferson Davis." Davis departed New York City on 25 Jan 1874 and traveled to Paris, London, Scotland, and Germany. On 19 Feb 1874, TR, Sr., made another $500 deposit to Bulloch's account.
110. Bulloch, *Secret Service,* I: 63.
111. Theodore K. Hoppen, *The Mid-Victorian Generation, 1846–1886* (Oxford: Oxford University, 1998).
112. TR, Sr., letters to Navy Dept., Sec. Roberson, Henry Elliott, and Dorr & Co., 23 Jun, 21 and 31 Aug, and 2 Sept 1874 TRC, TR, Sr., letter book, Jun 1874–Feb 1876, 30, 88–89, 102–103, 105–106.
113. TR, Sr. letter to Navy Dept., 6 Oct 1874, TRC, TR, Sr., letter book, Jun 1874–Feb 1876, 161.
114. TR, Sr., letter to Martha Bulloch Roosevelt, 9 Nov 1874, TRC, bMS Am 1785.2 (100), #44.
115. *Ibid.,* 17 Nov 1874, #45.
116. U.S. Treasury Dept., *Decisions of the Comptroller:* 86.
117. TR, Sr., letter to Martha Bulloch Roosevelt, 9 Nov 1874, TRC, bMS Am 1785.2 (100), 27 Nov 1874, #46; *NYT,* 18 Dec 1874.
118. TR, Sr., letter to James King Gracie, 22 Jun 1875, TRC, TR, Sr., letter book, Jun 1874–Feb 1876, 507.
119. New York Society Library, "New York City Marriage and Death Notices: 1857–1868," http://www.nysoclib.org/king/king3.html. Gracie's estate of over $500,000 included bequests of $30,000 to President TR and $10,000 each to Irvine's widow Ella Bulloch and Martha Louise Bulloch, JDB's daughter. See: *NYT,* 4 Dec 1903.
120. Theodore Roosevelt, *Letters from Theodore Roosevelt to Anna R Cowles, 1870 to 1918* (New York: Charles Scribner's Sons, 1924), 13–14.
121. Morris, *Roosevelt,* 87–89.
122. TR, Sr., letters to JDB, and R. J. Cortis, 7 Jul 1877, TRC, TR, Sr., letter book, Feb 1876–Feb 1878, 667 and 668.
123. Morris, *Roosevelt,* 90–92. As JDB and TR, Sr., were long-time friends, it is probable that some conversations took place over the issue of TR's future while JDB was at Oyster Bay.
124. Martha Bulloch Roosevelt, letter to Anna Roosevelt Cowles, 19 Aug 1877, TRC, bMS Am 1834.1 (194), #33; TR, Sr., letter to Anna Roosevelt Cowles, 15 Aug 1877, TRC, bMS Am 1834.1(201), #69; *NYT,* 18 Aug 1877; *Anglo-American Times,* 3 Aug 1877.
125. Morris, *Roosevelt,* 93–94; Brands, *TR,* 78–79.
126. Morris, *Roosevelt,* 70–71.

Chapter 14

1. Sadly, these characterizations are primarily based on references from JDB's future obituaries, which were carried in papers such as the London *Daily Telegraph,* 9 Jan 1901 and the *Savannah Morning News,* 12 Jan 1901.
2. Morris, *Roosevelt,* 139–140; Brands, *TR,* 112.
3. Morris, *Roosevelt,* 123; Brands *TR,* 110, 111.
4. Morris, *Roosevelt,* 128–137; Brands, *TR,* 109–112; Noel F. Busch, *TR, the Story of Theodore Roosevelt* (New York: Reynal, 1963), 34.
5. Morris, *Roosevelt,* 140; Brands, *TR,* 112.
6. *NYT,* 26 Mar 1881.
7. Morris, *Roosevelt,* 140; Brands, *TR,* 112.
8. *NYT,* 12 and 21 May 1881; Morris, *Roosevelt,* 145–146; Brands, *TR,* 115.
9. *Anglo-American Times,* 22 May 1881; U.K. National Archives, Census Returns of England and Wales, 1881, Lancashire, Liverpool, Mount Pleasant, class RG11, piece 3626, folio 56, p. 9, s.v. "James Bullock"; JDB letter to Nannie Hutchison Dawson, 6 Jun 1886, Hutchison-Dawson papers, MS 2226, Georgia Historical Society, Savannah, GA.

10. *NYT,* 19 Jun 1881. The Bulloch-Sears-Roosevelt party departed Liverpool on the *Britannic* on 9 Jun 1881, stopping briefly at Queenstown on Jun 10th.

11. Carlton Putnam, *Theodore Roosevelt, The Formative Years, 1858–1886,* vol. I (New York: Charles Scribner's sons, 1958), 230; Morris, *Roosevelt,* 146, 148, 149; Brands, *TR,* 115–118; Busch, *TR,* 34–35.

12. Kenneth D. Ackerman, *Dark Horse: The Surprise Election and Political Murder of James A. Garfield* (New York: Carroll & Graf, 2004).

13. Morris, *Roosevelt,* 147.

14. Brands, *TR,* 117; Morris, *Roosevelt,* 148–149. Roosevelt related his doubts to his sister Bamie. See: Putnam, *Theodore Roosevelt,* 234–236.

15. Morris, *Roosevelt,* 149; TR letter to Anna Roosevelt Cowles, 14 Sep 1881, TRC, MS Am 1834, #1007; Bulloch, *Secret Service,* 1: 93.

16. TR letter to Anna Roosevelt Cowles, 14 Sep 1881, TRC, MS Am 1834, #1007; Roosevelt, *Letters to Anna R. Cowles,* 50.

17. Bulloch, *Secret Service,* 1: xxxi–xxxii.

18. Robert K. Massie, *Dreadnought* (1991; reprint, London: Vintage Books, 2007), 161–162. Massie notes that of the ironclads that Prussia had before and during the Franco-Prussian War, the *Arminius* was built in England in 1864, the *Friedrich Karl* had been bought from France in 1867 and in 1869, the *König Wilhelm* (a 9,700-ton behemoth) was built in England for the *Kaiserliche Marine.* Bismarck had no inkling of the need for sea power.

19. *Ibid.*, xii–xvii. Massie eloquently summarized British foreign policy as one of "splendid isolation."

20. Thomas Pakenham, *The Scramble for Africa* (1991; reprint, London: Abacus, 2008), 109–122. Otto and Herbert Bismarck had not yet embraced colonialism as a policy for the *Reich,* but they did support any German business or culture that expanded Germany's position in the world. Thus, in South Africa regarding the Transvaal and its Boer population, which was a mix of Dutch and German, German sympathy and business capital was with the Boers, for it created problems for the British Empire.

21. Jean Randier, *La Royale: l'histoire illustrée de la Marine nationale française* (Brest: Editions de la Cite, 1978).

22. David C. Evans and Mark R. Peattie, *Kaigun: Strategy, Tactics, and Technology in the Imperial Japanese Navy* (Annapolis: Naval Institute, 2003), 19.

23. Theodore and Alice departed Liverpool on 24 Sep and arrived in New York on 1 Oct 1881. See: *NYT,* 2 Oct 1881.

24. *NYT,* 28 Dec 1881; *Anglo-American Times,* 3 Feb 1882.

25. Morris, *Roosevelt,* 152–156; Bulloch, *Secret Service,* 1: 93. In his memoirs, JDB says that he worked on "two chapters" in "April–May 1883," and Morris says that *The Naval War of 1812* came out about five months after it was submitted to Putnam, which would have been Apr 1882.

26. Theodore Roosevelt, *The Naval War of 1812,* vol. 1, 3rd ed. (New York: G.P. Putnams' Sons, 1900), 7; Putnam, *Theodore Roosevelt,* 236; TR also thanked Commander Adolf Mensing, formerly of the German Navy; TR's letters contain numerous references to his exchanges with his Bulloch uncles.

27. Massie, *Dreadnought,* 166–167.

28. Bulloch, *Secret Service,* Preface, xxxiii.

29. Brands, *TR,* 188; Morris, *Roosevelt,* 223. The book had "become so exceedingly rare that copies of it are seldom offered for sale." Reprint editions were still in print through 2011. See: Bulloch, *Secret Service* (1884; reprint, New York: Modern Library, 2001), xxv.

30. JDB, letter to Gilmer, 4 May 1883, Museum of the Confederacy, Confederate Navy Collection Box: "Bulloch, James D."

31. Charles Barney Whittelsey, *The Roosevelt Genealogy, 1649–1902* (Hartford: Charles Barney Whittelsey, 1902), 38–40.

32. Mahan was afloat when TR's book appeared; he arrived at the U.S. Naval War College in 1885. See: Robert Seager, *Alfred Thayer Mahan: The Man and His Letters* (Annapolis: Naval Institute, 1977).

33. Busch, *TR,* 44; Putnam, *Theodore Roosevelt,* 308–309; Morris, *Roosevelt,* 198; *NYT,* 25 Feb 1883. In 1874, Sec. Chandler married Lucy Lambert Hale who had been engaged to John Wilkes Booth in 1865.

34. The London *Guardian* newspaper advertisement provides an example in its 3 Oct 1883 edition, 16: "SECRET SERVICE of the CONFEDERATE STATES in EUROPE. By JAMES D. BULLOCH, late Naval Representative of the Confederate States Government in this Country.... 'Full of interest to English sailors, jurists, and statesmen; it abounds with passages which possess equal interest for England and the United States.' *Daily Telegraph.*"

35. *NYT,* 7 Nov 1883.

36. James D. Bulloch, "Building Confederate Vessels in France," *Southern Historical Society Papers* 14 (1886): 454–466.

37. Brands, *TR* , 156–158; Morris, *Roosevelt,* 222–224.

38. Brands, *TR* , 161–162; Morris, *Roosevelt,* 231.

39. *NYT,* 15 Feb 1884; Brands, *TR,* 162–163; Morris, *Roosevelt,* 240–241.

40. JDB, letter to Anna Bulloch Cowles, 14 Feb 1884, TRC, bMS AM 1834, #3. Bulloch's grief is evocative, even for the Victorian era and reveals his shock at the loss of his sister. He referenced a biblical verse: John XIV-18, which in the King James version reads: "I will not leave you comfortless: I will come to you."

41. *NYT,* 11 May 1884.

42. Pakenham, *Scramble for Africa,* 190–191.

43. JDB, letter to Davis, 25 Nov 1884, Jefferson Davis Family Collection, Box 6.

44. *Ibid.*

45. *Ibid.*

46. Brands, *TR,* 182; Morris, *Roosevelt,* 287–290.

47. JDB, letter to Davis, 9 Jan 1885, Jefferson Davis Family Collection, Box 6. Bulloch's appointment would have created a legal conundrum. Bulloch was covered by Pres. Johnson's last general amnesty, but he was a British citizen. Bulloch's appointment would not have survived the political and press uproar.

48. Massie, *Dreadnought*, 85–88; Pakenham, *Scramble for Africa*, 206–14. Bismarck and the German exchequer were burdened with the expense of protectorates in Togo, Cameroon, and Southwest Africa, complicating Bismarck's political control of the *Reichstag*.

49. Brands, *TR*, 193–199; Morris, *Roosevelt*, 312–314.

50. Brands, *TR*, 211–215; Morris, *Roosevelt*, 331–335.

51. *Anglo-American Times,* 4 Jun 1886, 17–18; Maffitt, *Maffitt*, 428.

52. McKay, *Sea King*, 263–266.

53. Alan Bullock and Vincent T. Harlow, *Germany's Colonial Demands* (London: Oxford University, 1939). A wonderful source for the chronology of events regarding the German East African Colony.

54. McKay, *Sea King*, 267–269.

55. Pakenham, *Scramble for Africa*, 294–296.

56. Theodore Roosevelt, *Thomas H. Benton* (Boston: Houghton Mifflin, 899), 234; Morris, *Roosevelt*, 335.

57. Morris, *Roosevelt*, 342–356.

58. *NYT*, 7 Nov 1886; *Anglo-American Times* 19 Nov 1886, 20; Morris, *Roosevelt*, 358–359; Sylvia J. Morris, *Edith Kermit Roosevelt, Portrait of a First Lady* (New York: Coward, McCann, & Geoghegan, 1980), 98–99. Merrifield was one of Roosevelt's ranching partners.

59. *Anglo-American Times*, 19 Nov 1886, 20; Morris, *Roosevelt*, 358–359; Morris, *Edith Kermit Roosevelt*, 98–99. The passenger list has "Miss Roosevelt" and "T. Roosevelt" but no Merrifield.

60. John C. Wilkinson, "The Zanzibar Delimitation Commission 1885–1886," *Geopolitics and International Boundaries* 1, no. 2 (Autumn 1996): 130–135; World at War Timelines Project, "German East Africa" http://www.schudak.de/timelines/germaneastafrica1884-1922.html. See: *Galveston Daily News*, 15 Feb 1887 for a flavor of the newspaper reportage of the time.

61. *NYT*, 28 Mar 1887; Ancestry.com, *United States*; Microfilm serial: *M237*; Microfilm roll: *M237_504*; Line: *23*; pg. 19, List numbers: 845–846.

62. Morris, *Edith Kermit Roosevelt*, 99. Family tradition passed down through the descendants of JDB via his son Stuart Elliott Bulloch, is that JDB's chest of papers reached Australia (where Stuart Elliott immigrated in the early twentieth century) and were burned by Stuart Elliott's wife upon his death, saying, "there were too many secrets." If true, it was a tragic loss. Dr. James Elliott, conversation with author, London, 2010.

63. Morris, *Roosevelt*, 378–381, 387; Morris, *Edith Kermit Roosevelt*, 106–110. The title of TR's opening chapter in *Benton*, "The Spread of the English-Speaking Peoples," shows Roosevelt's acceptance of the "Greater Britain" philosophy and mixed it with "Manifest Destiny" to create an amalgamated view that Anglo-Saxon peoples would expand and bring their language and cultures with them.

64. Massie, *Dreadnought*, 41–44.

65. Toxteth Park Registration District, marriage certificate, Liverpool, Lancashire, s.v., "Maxwell Hyslop Maxwell"; Airgale Pty, "The Descendants of William Hyslop" http://www.airgale.com.au/hyslop/d3.htm for details of the Maxwell family genealogy.

66. Robert Jones, "Bulloch Family Collection," Liverpool, Lancashire, U.K., including photographs and e-mail communications, "King's Rifle Volunteer Brigade, 1882."

67. Passenger list: Year: 1888; Arrival: New York, United States; Microfilm serial: M237; Microfilm roll: M237_518; Line: 11; List number: 488, 18–19; TR letters to Anna Roosevelt Cowles, 20 May and 1 Jul 1888, TRC, bMS 1834 (111–782), #243 and 248.

68. By the first week of Jul 1888, after reviewing the pitiful state of his German Imperial Navy, the Kaiser accepted the resignation of Leo von Caprivi, chief of the Imperial Navy. Kaiser Wilhelm II wanted battleships, not torpedo boats. In an instant, the *Reichstag* found the money for four battleships, rated at 10,000 tons and named *Brandenburg, Kurfürst Friedrich Wilhelm, Worth* and *Weissenburg*. See: Massie, *Dreadnought*, 162–163.

69. Morris, *Roosevelt*, 390–392.

70. *NYT* 2 Sep 1888; Robert Jones, "Bulloch Family Collection."

71. TR letter to Anna Roosevelt Cowles, 20 Nov 1888, TRC, bMS 1834, 260; JDB letter to Nannie Hutchison Dawson, 6 Jun 1886, Hutchison-Dawson papers, MS 2226, Georgia Historical Society, Savannah, GA.

72. Brands, *TR*, 219–220; Morris, *Roosevelt*, 392–393. One of the lobbying targets was former Secretary of State William Evarts, the same person TR, Sr., had lobbied on behalf of JDB's claim against the Navy.

73. John A.C. Gray, *Amerika Samoa*, A History of American Samoa and Its United States Naval Administration (Annapolis: Naval Institute, 1960); Robert Conroy, "Only luck kept the United States from being occupied by Kaiser Wilhelm II's army between 1899 and 1904," Military History 19, no. 18 (Aug 2002); 18.

74. Naval Historical Center, "Online Library," s.v. "Hurricane at Apia, Samoa" http://www.history.navy.mil/photos/events/ev-1880s/ev-1889/sam-hur.htm.

75. John W. Daniel, *Life and Reminiscences of Jefferson Davis* (Baltimore: R.H. Woodward, 1890), 436–440.

76. Massie, *Dreadnought*, 108; London *Local Government Gazette*, 8 Aug 1889.

77. Morris, *Roosevelt*, 410–411; Steel, *T. Butler King*; Massie, *Dreadnought*, 108–109.

78. JDB, letter to Varina H. Davis, 7 Dec 1889, Jefferson Davis Family Collection, Box 30.

79. On 17 Oct 1978, President Jimmy Carter signed a Joint Resolution of the U.S. Senate that restored Jefferson Davis' citizenship.

80. Massie, *Dreadnought*, 92–99, 163. When Admiral Alexander Monts, head of the German Navy, died in Jan 1889, Kaiser Wilhelm II reorganized the command structure of the fleet, alarming the British Royal Navy.
81. TR letters to Anna Roosevelt Cowles, 5 Jan and 10 Apr 1890, TRC, bMS 1834, #272 and 276.
82. U.K. National Archives, Census Returns of England and Wales, 1891, Lancashire, Liverpool, St. Agnes, Toxteth Park, class RG12, piece 2941, folio 5, p. 3, s.v. "James D. Bulloch."
83. Brands, *TR*, 236–238; Morris, *Roosevelt*, 424–425.
84. The most important naval event of 1890 was the appointment of Alfred von Tirpitz as Chief of Staff for the German Baltic Squadron. Tirpitz attended a dinner with Kaiser Wilhelm II who asked about the future course of the *Kaiserliche Marine*. After his superiors waffled, Tirpitz replied succinctly, "Battleships," exactly what the Kaiser wanted to hear. Tirpitz was transferred and promoted. See: Raffael Scheck, "Fleet Building and International Conflicts," at: http://www.colby.edu/personal/r/rmscheck/GermanyB3.html; Massie, *Dreadnought*, 167–168.
85. Naval Historical Center, *DANFS Online*, http://www.hazegray.org/danfs/. See Massie, *Dreadnought*, 164, 231, 256 for examples of Mahan's influence on Kaiser Wilhelm II's views and *Kaiserliche Marine*.
86. JDB, letter to Corinne Roosevelt Robinson, 1 Aug 1893, TRC, bMS Am 1785 (182), #2.
87. Brands, *TR* , 244–249; *New York Sun*, 17 Aug 1891; Morris, *Roosevelt*, 439–443. Bamie and Elliott's family returned to New York on 10 Aug via the SS *La Touraine* from Le Havre. See: Ancestry.com, *1891*; Arrival: *New York, United States*; Microfilm serial: *M237*; Microfilm roll: *M237_573*; Line: *11*; List number: *1201*.
88. Massie, *Dreadnought*, 210–211.
89. Morris, *Roosevelt*, 445; *Anglo-American Times*, 22, 24 and 29 Jan 1892; Ellis Island Foundation, SS *Lahn* manifest, page 740, line 48.
90. Ellis Island Foundation, SS *Teutonic* manifest, page 74, lines 40 and 41; Year: *1892*; Microfilm serial: *M237*; Microfilm roll: *M237_582*; Line: *32*; Page Number: *14*; *NYT*, 9 Mar 1892.
91. Massie, *Dreadnought*, 168–169.
92. *NYT* obituary, 9 Dec 1892; Morris, *Edith Kermit Roosevelt*, 141–142.
93. James King Gracie, letter to Corinne Roosevelt Robinson, 25 Jun 1893, TRC, bMS Am 1785(533), #3; *NYT*, 10 Jun 1893. Anna Bulloch's wealthy husband, James King Gracie, was involved with building New York City's Grand Central Station and canal projects. Upon his death in 1903, Gracie left $30,000 to Teddy Roosevelt, $7,500 to Eleanor Roosevelt, and $10,000 each to Irvine Bulloch's wife Ella and Bulloch's daughter Martha Louise. See: *NYT*, 4 Dec 1903.
94. JDB, letter to Corinne Roosevelt Robinson, 1 Aug 1893, TRC, bMS Am 1785 (182), #1.
95. *Anglo American Times*, 23 Dec 1893, 4; Morris, *Edith Kermit Roosevelt*, 146; Lilian Rixley, *Bamie* (New York: David McKay, 1963), 76.
96. *NYT*, 27 Apr 1894; Peter Karsten, "The Nature of 'Influence': Roosevelt, Mahan and the Concept of Sea Power," *American Quarterly* 23, no. 4 (Oct 1971): 588; ORN Ser. II, 3:18.
97. Massie, *Dreadnought*, 212–230.
98. *Ibid.*
99. Brands, *TR*, 259–260; Morris, *Roosevelt*, 474.
100. JDB, letter to Corinne Roosevelt Robinson, TRC, bMS Am 1785 (182), #2.
101. Brands, *TR*, 265–269; Morris, *Edith Kermit Roosevelt*, 141–142.
102. TR, Sr., had a large family to support and health problems that precluded his fighting in the American Civil War; he "bought" a soldier to replace himself in the Union Army, a common option available to Northern men of means. TR never understood or condoned what he considered to be his father's shirking of patriotic duty.
103. Morris, *Roosevelt*, 476–478, 510. See: *Times* of London, Aug 1895 editions.
104. *Ibid.*, 513.
105. Massie, *Dreadnought*, 220–230. The German consul in to the British Cape Colony had wanted a detachment of German sailors from the German cruisers at Delagoa Bay to "protect" German property and interests against the Jameson raiders. The Royal Navy was recalled before it reached the open Atlantic, but British cruisers continued to shadow the German Indian Ocean cruisers.
106. James, *Rise and Fall of the British Empire*, 260–264.
107. TR letter to Anna Roosevelt Cowles, 3 May 1896, TRC, bMS 1834 (111–782), #507.
108. Brands, *TR*, 304–307; Morris, *Roosevelt*, 540.
109. Morris, *Roosevelt*, 558; TR letters to Anna Roosevelt Cowles, 17 Jan and 3 May 1896, TRC, bMS 1834 (111–782), #493 and #507; Karsten, "The Nature of 'Influence," 588–589.
110. Morris, *Roosevelt*, 559–561.
111. *NYT*, 2 May 1897.
112. Toxteth Park Registration District, Lancashire County, Death Certificate, 3 Jul 1897, s.v., "Harriot Cross Bulloch." According to the death certificate, Harriott died of "peritonitis malignant disease of omentum" with Irvine S. Bulloch in attendance.
113. TR letter to Anna Roosevelt Cowles, 17 Aug 1897, TRC, bMS 1834 (111–782), #558 (on Navy Dept. letterhead); Morris, *Edith Kermit Roosevelt*, 167; Rixley, *Bamie*, 121.
114. Morris, *Roosevelt*, 575–578.
115. *Ibid.*, 569–571; New York *Sun*, 3 Jun 1897, *Herald*, 3 Jun 1897, and London *Times* 8 Apr 1897.
116. Morris, *Roosevelt*, 572–573.
117. *New York World*, "Riots in Havana mean REVOLUTION," 14 Jan 1898; George Dewey, *Autobiography of George Dewey, Admiral of the Navy* (New York: Charles Scribner's Sons, 1913), 167–168; Morris, *Roosevelt* 594–596.

118. John Hohenberg, *Foreign Correspondence: The Great Reporters and Their Times* (1964; reprint, Syracuse: Syracuse University, 1995), 49.
119. Massie, *Dreadnought*, 179.
120. New York *Sun*, 25 Apr 1898.
121. Oscar Alfonso, *Theodore Roosevelt and the Philippines, 1897–1909* (New York: Oriole, 1974).
122. *London and China Telegraph*, 2 May 1898.
123. Morris, *Roosevelt*, 620–631, 639; Morris, *Edith Kermit Roosevelt*, 177. TR's sojourn in San Antonio is commemorated at the historic Menger Hotel where he stayed and drank before, during, and after the war. The families represented among his Rough Rider recruits included Hamilton Fish, Oliver H. Perry, the Astors, and Vanderbilts. See: Docia S. Williams, *The History and Mystery of the Menger Hotel* (Dallas: Republic of Texas, 2000), 187–197.
124. *Times* of London, 15 Jul 1898.
125. Massie, *Dreadnought*, 226–228.
126. Morris, *Roosevelt*, 662, 686–687.
127. Thomas Pakenham, *The Boer War* (New York: Random House, 1979).
128. U.K. British Army, "Life Guards," http://www.army.mod.uk/armoured/regiments/5891.aspx. Named for Bulloch's stepbrother Daniel Stuart Elliott who had died during the Civil War, Stuart was 28 years old in 1899. See: "Roswell Presbyterian Church Cemetery" at http://www.findagrave.com/cgi-bin/fg.cgi?page=cr&GSmpid=46619340&CRid=1985194&pt=Roswell%20Presbyterian%20Church%20Cemetery&.
129. G. Ryden, *The Foreign Policy of the United States in Relation to Samoa* (1933; reprint, New York: Octagon Books, 1975), 571–575; Pakenham, *Boer War*, 729, 732.
130. London *Daily Telegraph*, 9 Jan 1901.

Chapter 15

1. Philip Van Doren Stern, *When the Guns Roared* (Garden City, NY: Doubleday 1965), 247, 248.
2. Fourteen of JDB's supply ships survived the war and 4 of these served in foreign navies (U.S., British, Greek, and Spanish). JDB's blockade runners: *Colonel Lamb* (2 runs, survived, Greek), *Hope* (2 runs, captured; Spanish until 1888), *Ptarmigan* (3 runs, survived, to Argentina as *Pampa*), *Stag* (2 runs, captured, to Argentina thru 1870), *Coquette* (13 runs, survived), *Evelyn* (4 runs, survived), *Falcon* (5 runs, survived), *Lark* (8 runs, survived, until 1895), *Owl* (5 runs, survived), *Wren* (7 runs, survived thru 1884), *Laurel* (also *Shenandoah*'s tender, 2 runs, survived), *Deer* (1 run, captured, renamed *Palmyra* until 1870), *Flamingo* (2 runs, foundered), *Mary Celestia* (7 runs, sunk), *Bat* (USS *Bat*, until 1897), *Condor* (ran aground), *Matilda* (ran aground, most cargo salvaged), *Albatross* (bought by Royal Navy), *Corcovado*, *Curlew*, *Plover*, *Snipe*, and *Widgeon* (all unfinished). Others: *Bermuda* (2 runs in 1861–1862, captured and converted into USS *Bermuda*); *Fingal* (JDB 1 successful run as captain, converted into ironclad CSS *Atlanta*, destroyed). The *Harriet Pinckney* was a tender and supply ship that never ran the blockade, but was sold and survived the war.
3. In addition to the 4 French corvettes, the 9 gunboats were: *Adventure*, *Ajax*, and *Hercules* (Argentina); *Enterprise (II)* and (Brazil); *Louisa Ann Fanny* and *Mary Augusta* (Brazil); *Penguin* (Greece Royal Yacht); *Rosine* (or *Rosina*) and *Ruby III* (Turkey). Bulloch aslo assisted with the gunboats *Alexandra* and *Hawk* that were both converted to merchantmen and sold.
4. Eller, *Dictionary of American Naval Fighting Ships*, vol. VII, 492, 569, 574; Naval Historical Center, "Online Library" s.v. "HMS Scorpion" and "HMS Wivern."
5. See: G. J. A. O'Toole, *Honorable Treachery, A History of U.S. Intelligence* (New York: Atlantic Monthly Press, 1991), 143–145, 152–154.
6. ORN, ser. II, 3: 18.
7. Elliot, J. electronic mail, 15 Nov 2010. The wife of JDB's son Stuart Elliott reportedly burned the family papers after Stuart's death in 1939 in Australia.
8. Theodore Roosevelt, *Theodore Roosevelt, an Autobiography* (1913; reprint, New York: Da Capo, 1985), 12.
9. The dates of JDB's five known postwar visits to the US are: 9 Nov 1870 to 2 Mar 1871, 6–13 Dec 1871, 7 Jul to 18 Aug 1877, 25 Mar to 21 May 1881, and 11 Feb to 9 Mar 1892. He also may have stopped briefly in the U.S. during his several trips to Brazil.
10. *NYT*, 10 Nov 1870; *1870*; Arrival: *New York, United States*; Microfilm serial: *M237*; Microfilm roll: *M237_336*; Line: *32*; List number: *1039*. JDB may have traveled to the U.S. covertly prior to 1870 as TR claimed in his autobiography.
11. Bulloch, *Secret Service*, 193–194.
12. See: Toshi Yoshihara and James R. Holmes, *Red Star Over the Pacific; China's Rise and the Challenge to U.S. Maritime Strategy* (Annapolis: Naval Institute Press, 2010), 30–37, 51–55.

Bibliography

Archives, Official Documents, Unpublished Collections

The Avalon Project. Lillian Goldman Law Library, Yale Law School. http://avalon.law.yale.edu/.
Beard, Robert G. "James Dunwoody Bulloch: Confederate Secret Agent Abroad." Senior thesis, Princeton University, 1950.
Brock Collection. Misc. reel 5071, The Library of Virginia, Richmond, VA.
Canada. Parliament. *Sessional Papers of the Parliament of the Province of Canada, Volume 20, Issue 4.* Quebec: Hunter, Rose, and Lemieux, 1862.
Carter, Robert R. Shirley Plantation Collection, 18: 6 & 7, 20: 1, John D. Rockefeller, Jr. Library, The Colonial Williamsburg Foundation, Williamsburg, VA.
Confederate Navy and Jefferson Davis Family Collection. Eleanor S. Brockenbrough Library, The Museum of the Confederacy, Richmond, VA.
Cross, Osborne. "A report, in the form of a journal, to the quartermaster general, of the march of the regiment of mounted riflemen to Oregon, from May 10 to October 5, 1849." 31st Cong. 2nd Sess., House Ex. Doc. 1, part II, 126–240. Washington: GPO, 1850.
Dudley, Thomas Haines. Collection. Huntingdon Library, San Marino, CA.
Eller, Ernest McNeill, ed. *Civil War Naval Chronology 1861–1865.* Washington: GPO, 1971.
———. *Dictionary of American Naval Fighting Ships.* Vols. I–VIII. Washington: GPO, 1959–1981.
Fenner, Judith Anne. "Confederate Finance Abroad." PhD diss., Rice University, 1969.
Fraser, Trenholm and Co. Papers. Adam Matthew Publications, microfilm, B/FT 1/153, 1/154, 6/8, Wiltshire, England.
Greenhow, Rose O'Neale. European Diary, August 5, 1863 http://www.onealwebsite.com/RebelRose/.
Hotze, Henry. Papers. AC 3608, Library of Congress, Washington, DC.
Huddleston, Connie. "A Social and Economic History of the James Stephens Bulloch Family of Bulloch Hall, Roswell, Georgia." Unpublished manuscript, 2008.
Hutchison-Dawson. Papers. MS 2226. Georgia Historical Society, Savannah, GA.
Jones, Robert. "Bulloch Family Collection." Liverpool, Lancashire, England, including photographs and e-mail communications, "King's Rifle Volunteer Brigade, 1882."
Keaton, Mary Elizabeth. "The Life of Edward Maffitt Anderson." Armstrong State College, Savannah, GA, 29 May 1992.
King, Roswell. Ledgers. Roswell Historical Society and Archives, Roswell, GA.
Lancashire County, England. Records.
Lancashire OnLine Parish Clerks. "Marriages at St Mary, Liverpool, 1859–1863." http://www.lan-opc.org.uk/Liverpool/Walton/stmary/marriages_1859–1863.html.
Liberty County Courthouse. Probate file. Hinesville, Georgia.
Liverpool, England, Record Office. *Register of Baptisms in the Parish of St. John Waterloo, in the County of Lancaster.* London: Shaw & Sons, 1865.
Mariner's Museum. Library. Newport News, VA.
Marshall University Special Collections. "C.S.S. Alabama; A Virtual Exhibit." http://www.marshall.edu/LIBRARY/speccoll/virtual_museum/css_alabama/peake_menu.asp.
Martens, Georg F. et al. *Nouveau Recueil Général des Traités et autres Actes relatifs aux Rapports de Droit international.* 2nd series, vol. XV. Gottingue: G. A. Kaestner, 1857.
Mason, James Murray. Papers. Vol. 8. Library of Congress, Manuscript Division, Washington, DC.
"Memoirs of James Iredell Waddell." ZB Files. U.S. Navy Historical Center, Washington, DC.
North, James. Diary. 1861. James Heyward North Papers 862-z and James Dunwody [sic] Bulloch Papers (#3318-z), Southern Historical Collection, Wilson Library, University of North Carolina, Chapel Hill, NC.

Nuckols, Jack Randall. "A Confederate agent in Europe: the life and career of Commander James Dunwoody Bulloch." Master's thesis, Marshall University, 1982.
Phillips, Ulrich B., ed. "The Correspondence of Robert Toombs, Alexander H. Stephens, and Howell Cobb." IN *Annual Report of the American Historical Association 1911*. Vol. 2. Washington: GPO, 1913.
Prefeitura de Petrópolis. "Baron of Mauá— The Empire's most enterprising businessman." http://www.petropolis.rj.gov.br/index.php?url=http%3A//fctpi.petropolis.rj.gov.br/fctpi/modules/xt_conteudo/index.php%3Fid%3D22.
Reilly, John C., Jr. *The Iron Guns of Willard Park*. Washington: Naval Historical Center, 1991.
Rice University. "The Papers of Jefferson Davis." http://jeffersondavis.rice.edu/index.cfm.
Robertson, Max. A., and Geoffrey Ellis, eds. *The English Reports, Vice Chancellor's Court*. Vol. 71. Edinburgh: William Green & Sons, 1907.
Roosevelt, Theodore. Collection. Houghton Library, Harvard University, Cambridge, MA.
Sebrell, Thomas. "Persuading John Bull: The American Civil War Comes to Fleet Street." PhD. Diss., Queen Mary: University of London, 2010.
Shine, Gregory P. "Sympathy and Prompt Attentions: Fort Vancouver's Relief of the U.S. Schooner Shark on Sept. 13, 1856." In *Campfires & Candlelight Resource Guide 2007*. Washington: National Park Service, 2007.
Toxteth Park, England, Registration District. Marriage certificates.
Tufts University. Perseus Digital Library. "The Daily Dispatch: January 7, 1862." http://www.perseus.tufts.edu/hopper/text;jsessionid=6CFCF08A27D0EF6BA26670F0EEFF6F83?doc=Perseus%3Atext%3A2006.05.0367.
U.K. British Army. "Life Guards." http://www.army.mod.uk/armoured/regiments/5891.aspx.
U.K. Foreign Office. *The Case of Great Britain as Laid before the Tribunal of Arbitration*. Vols. I–III. Washington: GPO, 1872.
U.K. Home Office. Public Record Office. London.
U.K. National Archives. "British Envoys to America, 1791–1891." http://yourarchives.nationalarchives.gov.uk/index.php?title=British_Envoys_to_America.
U.K. National Archives. Census Returns of England and Wales, 1871, Lancashire, Litherland, Waterloo, class RG10, piece 3838, folio 78, p. 43, GSU roll 841922 "James De Bulloch." and Lancashire, Liverpool, West Derby, Toxteth Park, class RG10, piece 3805. folio 148. p. 10, GSU roll 841907, s.v. "Moses P. Robertson."
U.K. National Archives. Census Returns of England and Wales, 1881, Lancashire, Liverpool, Mount Pleasant, class RG11, piece 3626, folio 56, p. 9, s.v. "James Bullock."
U.K. National Archives. Census Returns of England and Wales, 1891, Lancashire, Liverpool, St. Agnes, Toxteth Park, class RG12, piece 2941, folio 5, p. 3, s.v. "James D. Bulloch."
U.K. Parliament. "Parliamentary Archives." http://www.parliament.uk/business/publications/parliamentary-archives/.
U.S. Central Intelligence Agency. "Intelligence in the Civil War, Intelligence Overseas, James Bulloch." https://www.cia.gov/library/publications/additional-publications/civil-war/p31.htm.
U.S. Congress. *Biographical Directory*. http://bioguide.congress.gov/.
U.S. Congress. House of Representatives. *Annual Report of the Commissioner of Patents for the Year 1867*. 40th Cong., 2nd Sess., House Ex. Doc. No. 96. Vols. I–II. Washington: GPO, 1868.
U.S. Congress. House of Representatives. "Fraser, Trenholm & Co." 39th Cong., 2nd Sess., House, Vol. I, Ex. Doc. 63. Washington: GPO, 1867: 1–51.
U.S. Congress. House of Representatives. "Letter of the Secretary of the Treasury, Recovery of Confederate Property in Europe." 40th Cong., 2nd Sess., Vol. 19, House Ex. Doc. No. 304. Washington: GPO, 1868.
U.S. Congress. House of Representatives. "Report of Lieut. Neil M. Howison, United States Navy." 30th Cong., 1st Sess., House Misc. No. 29. Washington: GPO, 1867: 1–36.
U.S. Congress. House of Representatives. "Seizure of the Black Warrior." 33rd Cong., 1st Sess., House Ex. Doc. No. 76, 15 March 1854. Washington: A.O.P. Nicholson, 1854.
U.S. Congress. House of Representatives. *Thomas B. King, H.R. 448, A Bill to provide for the construction of twelve iron war steamers and one iron frigate*. 29th Cong., 1st Sess. 20 May 1846. http://lcweb2.loc.gov/cgi-bin/ampage?collId=llhb&fileName=029/llhb029.db&recNum=1187.
U.S. Congress. Senate. *Annual Report of the Superintendent of the Coast Survey for the Year Ending, Nov. 1851*. 32d Cong., 1st Sess., Senate Ex. Doc. No. 3. (Washington: Robert Armstrong, 1852), 41–42, 118.
U.S. Congress. Senate. *The Case of the United States to be Laid before the Tribunal of Arbitration to be Convened in Geneva*. 42nd Cong., 2nd Sess., Senate Ex. Doc. 31. Washington: GPO, 1872.
U.S. Congress. Senate. *Journal of the Executive Proceedings of the Senate of the United States of America from December 6, 1852 to March 3, 1855 Inclusive*. Vol. IX. 32nd Cong., 2nd Sess. Washington: GPO, 1887.
U.S. Congress. Senate. *Reports of Committee of the Senate of the United States, Senate Rept. 1010*. 53rd Cong., 3rd Sess., Vol. 2. Washington: GPO, 1895.
U.S. Federal Election Commission. "Federal Elections: 1860." Washington: GPO, 1982.
U.S. Interior Department. Battle Summaries. http://www.nps.gov/history/hps/abpp/battles/tvii.htm.
U.S. Interior Department. Census Office. Eighth Census, 1860, City of Philadelphia, Philadelphia County, PA, series M653, roll: 1157, p. 568, s.v. "Dr. H. West."

U.S. Interior Department. Census Office. Eighth Census, 1860, City of Norfolk, Norfolk County, VA, series M653, roll: 1366, p. 357, s.v. "M. P. Robertson."
U.S. Interior Department. Census Office. Eighth Census, 1860, Morris Township, Morris County, NJ, series M653, roll: 703, p. 68, s.v. "Capt J. D. Bullock."
U.S. Interior Department. "Find a Park." http://www.nps.gov/findapark/index.htm.
U.S. Library of Congress. "Abraham Lincoln's Inauguration." http://www.americaslibrary.gov/jb/civil/jb_civil_lincoln2_1.html.
U.S. Library of Congress. "Treaty with Russia for the Purchase of Alaska." http://www.loc.gov/rr/program/bib/ourdocs/Alaska.html.
U.S. Naval Historical Center. "Dictionary of American Fighting Ships." *DANFS Online*. http://www.history.navy.mil/danfs/.
U.S. Naval Historical Center. "Online Library." http://www.history.navy.mil/branches/org11-2.htm.
U.S. Navy. "Littoral Combat Ships." http://www.navy.mil/navydata/fact_display.asp?cid=4200&tid=1650&ct=4.
U.S. Navy Department. *Official Records of the Union and Confederate Navies in the War of the Rebellion*. Series I, Vols. 1–27, and Series II, Vols. 1–3. Washington: GPO, 1894–1921.
U.S. Navy Department. *Register of the Commissioned and Warrant Officers of the Navy of the United States, including Officers of the Marine Corps*. Washington: C. Alexander, 1848, 1849, and 1852.
U.S. State Department. "*Alabama* Claims" http://history.state.gov/milestones/1861–1865/Alabama.
U.S. State Department. "American Consulate in the Azores." http://www.usconsulateazores.pt/HistoryOfTheConsulate.htm.
U.S. State Department. "Correspondence Concerning Claims against Great Britain." Vol. VI. Washington: GPO, 1871.
U.S. State Department. General Records, National Archives. Record Group 59,. Microfilm Publication M1372, 694 rolls, Passport Applications, 1795–1925, s.v. "A. Hutchison" and "J.S. Bulloch."
U.S. State Department. "Papers Relating to the Foreign Affairs of the United States." Part II, 38th Cong, 1st Sess., Washington: GPO, 1864.
U.S. State Department. "Timeline of U.S. Diplomatic History Purchase of Alaska, 1867." http://web.archive.org/web/20080410122537/http://www.state.gov/r/pa/ho/time/gp/17662.htm.
U.S. State Department. "William Henry Seward." http://history.state.gov/departmenthistory/people/seward-william-henry.
U.S. Treasury Department. *Decisions of the Comptroller of the Treasury, containing decisions of Robert B. Bowler, Comptroller, and Edw. A. Bowers, Assistant Comptroller*. Vol. II. Washington: GPO, 1896: 84–89.
U.S. War Department. *The War of the Rebellion: A Compilation of the Official Records of the Union and confederate Armies*. 70 vols. (Ser. I, 1–53; Ser. II, 1–8; Ser. III, 1–5; Ser. IV, 1–6; Ser. 1–3). Washington: GPO, 1880–1901.
University of Glasgow. Archive Services, GUAS Ref: UCS 1, http://www.gla.ac.uk/media/media_60666_en.pdf.
Victoria, Queen. *The Letters of Queen Victoria, Vol. III, 1854–1861*. Edited by Arthur Christopher Benson and Viscount Reginald Esher. London: John Murray, 1907. http://books.google.com/books?id=DB8MAAAAYAAJ&printsec=frontcover#v=onepage&q&f=false !!!
Virginia. General Assembly. *Acts of the General Assembly of the State of Virginia: Passed in 1866–1867*. Richmond: James E. Goode, 1867.
Weed, Thurlow. Papers. Rush Rhees Library, University of Rochester, NY.
Welles, Gideon. *Diary of Gideon Welles: Secretary of the Navy Under Lincoln and Johnson*. Vols. I–III. Edited by Howard K. Beale. New York: Houghton Mifflin, 1911.
West Derby, England, Registration District. Birth certificates.
Whittle Papers. Sargeant Memorial Room, Main Library, Norfolk, VA.
Wilkinson, Martha Allan. "The public career of James Dunwoody Bulloch." Master's thesis, University of Alabama, 1940.
Woodcroft, Bennet. *Alphabetical Index of Patentees and Applicants for Patents of Invention, for the Year 1867*. London: Commissioners of Patents for Inventions, 1868.
_____. *Chronological Index of Patents Applied for and Patents Granted, for the Year 1867*. London: Commissioners of Patents for Inventions, 1868.
_____. *Subject-Matter Index of Patents Applied for and Patents Granted, for the Year 1866*. London: Commissioners of Patents for Inventions, 1867.
Young, Michael T. "A study of the activities of James Dunwoody Bulloch: Confederate naval agent in Great Britain." Master's thesis, University of Nebraska at Omaha, 1968.

Newspapers

Anglo-American Times
The Australian and New Zealand Gazette
Bahama Herald

Charleston Daily Courier
The Charleston Observer
Columbian Museum and Savannah Daily Gazette
Commercial Daily List (London, Liverpool, Manchester, and Birmingham)
Commercial Gazette
The Commonwealth
The Cork Examiner
Daily Alta (California)
Daily Commercial Bulletin (Missouri)
Darien (GA) *Gazette*
Dubuque Herald
The Edinburgh Evening Courant
Galveston Daily News
Harper's Weekly
The Hour
The Illustrated London News
Illustrated Times
Janesville Gazette
Liverpool Journal of Commerce
Liverpool Courier
Liverpool Mercury
London Conformist
London Daily Telegraph
London Guardian
London Local Government Gazette
London Nonconformist
London Sun and Central Press
London Times
Middlesex Miners and Workmen's Advocate
The Milledgeville (GA) *Reflector*
New York Herald
New York Sun
New York Times
New York World
Niles Weekly Register
North China Herald (Shanghai)
Oregon Spectator
The Portland Morning Oregonian
Richmond Daily Dispatch
Richmond Times-Dispatch
Savannah Daily Georgian
Savannah Morning News
Watchman and Wesleyan Advertiser
Week's News

Periodical Articles

Baxter, James P. "The British Government and Neutral Rights, 1861–1865." *American Historical Review* 34, no. 1 (Oct 1928): 9–29.

Brady, Eugene A. "A Reconsideration of the Lancashire 'Cotton Famine.'" *Agricultural History* 37 (Jul 1963): 156–162.

Brock, Robert A., ed., "Captain Thomas Jefferson Page, of the C.S. Gunboat Stonewall; Sketch of his Life and Deeds." *Southern Historical Society Papers* 27 (1899): 219–231.

Bulloch, James D. "Building Confederate Vessels in France." *Southern Historical Society Papers* 14 (1886): 454–465.

Bullock-Willis, Virginia. "James Dunwoody Bulloch." *The Sewanee Review* 34, no. 4 (Oct–Dec 1926): 386–401.

Conroy, Robert. "Only luck kept the United States from being occupied by Kaiser Wilhelm II's army between 1899 and 1904." Military History 19, no. 3 (Aug 2002): 18–22.

Davidson, Marshall B. "Royal Welcome for the Russian Navy." *American Heritage* 11, no. 4 (Jun 1960): 38–43, 107.

Delaney, Norman. "The Strange Occupation of James Bulloch: When Can You Start." *Civil War Times Illustrated* 21(1) (Mar 1982): 18–27.

Haviland, Edward K. "Early Steam Navigation in China: Hongkong and the Canton River, 1858–1867." *The American Neptune* 34, no. 1 (Jan 1974): 17–48.
Howison, Neil M. "Report of Lieutenant Neil M. Howison on Oregon, 1846." *Oregon Historical Quarterly* 14, no. 1 (1913): 1–60.
Hughes, Michael F. "The Personal Observations of a Man of Intelligence: Sir James Fergusson's Visit to North America, 1861." *Civil War History* 45, no. 3 (1999): 238–247.
Janes, Henry Lorenzo. "The Black Warrior Affair." *The American Historical Review* 12 (Jan 1907): 280–298.
Karsten, Peter. "The Nature of 'Influence': Roosevelt, Mahan and the Concept of Sea Power." *American Quarterly* 23, no. 4 (Oct 1971): 585–600.
Loy, Wesley. "10 Rumford Place: Doing Confederate Business in Liverpool." *The South Carolina Historical Magazine* 98, no. 4 (Oct 1997): 349–374.
Madaus, Howard Michael. "Small Arms Deliveries Through Wilmington, NC in 1863 and the Impact on Confederate Ordnance Supply." *American Society of Arms Collectors Bulletin* 85 (2002): 51–58.
Mason, John T. "Last of the Confederate Cruisers." *Century Illustrated Magazine* 56, (1898): 600–610.
Maynard, Douglas H. "The Forbes-Aspinwall Mission." *The Mississippi Valley Historical Review* 45, no. 1 (Jun 1958): 67–89.
McLeod, Mrs. Hugh. "The Loss of the Steamer Pulaski." *Georgia Historical Quarterly* 3, no. 1 (Mar 1919): 63–95.
Menschel, David. "Abolition without Deliverance: The Law of Connecticut Slavery, 1784–1848." *Yale Law Journal* 111, no. 1 (Oct 2001): 183–222.
Nepveux, Ethel S. "Eugene Tessier." *Confederate Historical Association of Belgium News* 34, no. 2 (2006), 61–70.
Noirsain, Serge. "The Blockade Runners of the Confederate Government." *Confederate Historical Association of Belgium News*. http://chab-belgium.com/pdf/english/Blockade%20Runners2.pdf.
"Our Official Log." *The Nautical Magazine* 50, no. 2. (Feb 1881): 175–184.
Owsley, Harriet Chappell. "Henry Shelton Sanford and Federal Surveillance Abroad, 1861–1865." *The Mississippi Valley Historical Review* 48, no. 2 (Sep 1961): 211–228.
Page, Thomas J. "The Career of the Confederate Cruiser Stonewall." *Southern Historical Papers* 7, no. 6 (Jun 1879): 263–280.
Roberts, William P. "James Dunwoody Bulloch and the Confederate Navy." *North Carolina Historical Review* 24, no. 3 (July 1947): 315–366.
Royal National Life-Boat Institution. The Lifeboat, the Journal of the National Life-Boat Institution 8, 9, and 10 (1873, 1876, and 1879).
Shine, Gregory Painter. "A Gallant Little Schooner." *Oregon Historical Quarterly* 109, no. 4 (Winter 2008): 536–565.
Small, Stephen C. "The Ship That Couldn't Be Built." *Naval History* 22, no. 5 (Oct. 2008).
Wilkinson, John. C. "The Zanzibar Delimitation Commission 1885–1886." *Geopolitics and International Boundaries* 1, no. 2 (Autumn 1996): 130–138.

Online Resources

Airgale Pty. "The Descendants of William Hyslop." http://www.airgale.com.au/hyslop/d3.htm.
Aqua Explorers. "The Black Warrior Shipwreck." http://www.aquaexplorers.com/BlackWarrior.htm.
Bartleby Bookstore. "Respectfully Quoted." http://www.bartleby.com.
Boggess, William S. "Minister Solon Borland." http://community-1.webtv.net/billboggess-gray/MINSTERSOLONBORLAND/.
Butler, William M. "Confederate Shipbuilding in England and the Foreign Enlistment Act." 2010 Psi Sigma Journal Special Edition (11 Jun 2010). http://history.unlv.edu/pat/Journal/Entries/2010/6/11_2010_Psi_Sigma_Journal_Special_Edition_files/Butler.pdf.
Cammell Laird. "The History of Cammell Laird." www.cammell-laird.com.
Davis, Peter. "Extracts from the Times Newspaper." http://www.pdavis.nl/Osborn.php.
Ellis Island Foundation. SS Lahn, Feb 08, 1892, page 740, line 48, s.v. "Theo. Roosevelt." http://www.ellisisland.org/default.asp.
Eriksen, Hans Henning. "Tabsliste for Kampen den 18 April (1864)." http://www.hheriksen.dk/images/1864tab.jpg.
Franco-Prussian War. "TimeLine." http://francoprussianwar.com/timeline.htm.
Gerding, Eduardo C. "The Confederate Navy and the Argentine Hydrographic survey: Time of the Spar Torpedo." The Buenos Aires Herald (December 14, 2003). http://www.civilwarhome.com/argentinehydrosurvey.htm.
Hartlepool, This is. "History." http://www.thisishartlepool.co.uk/history/westhartlepool.asp.
Holcomb, Brent. "Senator John Elliott." http://www.quarterman.org/who/senelliott.html.
Kane, Elisha Kent, Historical Society. "Reported Death of Dr. E.K. Kane." http://209.85.229.132/search?q=cache:UkBZtJ7At_IJ:www.ekkane.org/Biographies/Kane%2520Obituary.htm+elisha+kent+kane+returns+1855+new+york+times&cd=3&hl=en&ct=clnk&gl=uk&client=firefox-a.

Laursen, Gert. Danish Military History. "The Battle of Rügen — March 17th 1864." http://www.milhist.dk/1864/rugen/rugen_uk.htm.
Massachusetts Historical Society. "Charles Francis Adams." http://www.masshist.org/adams/biographical.cfm.
Nelson, Phil. *Flags of the World.* "Lay-Osborne Flotilla." http://flagspot.net/flags/cn-lo.html or http://www.crwflags.com/FOTW/FLAGS/cn-lo.html.
New Georgia Encyclopedia. "Bulloch, Archibald." http://www.georgiaencyclopedia.org/nge/Article.jsp?path=/HistoryArchaeology/ColonialEraTrusteePeriod/People-4&id=h-682.
New Georgia Encyclopaedia. "Tybee Island." http://www.georgiaencyclopedia.org/nge/Article.jsp?id=h-2967.
New York Society Library. "New York City Marriage and Death Notices: 1857–1868." http://www.nysoclib.org/king/king3.html.
Ocean Liner Virtual Museum. "Cammell Laird: Shipbuilders to the World (1824–1993). http://www.oceanlinermuseum.co.uk/Cammell%20Laird%20Shipbuilders%20to%20the%20World.htm.
Oxford University. "Oxford Dictionary of National Biography." http://www.oxforddnb.com/index.
Panama Railroad. "The Panama Railroad & the US Mail." http://www.panamarailroad.org/mail.html.
Parker, Randy. "Constitutional Union Party." http://www.ourcampaigns.com/RaceDetail.html?RaceID=58519.
Potash and Company. "Pacific Mail Steam Ship Collection." http://www.potashco.com/potash_2.htm.
Ross, Don. "Era of the Clipper Ships." http://www.eraoftheclipperships.com/.
Roswell Presbyterian Church Cemetery. "Find a Grave." http://www.findagrave.com/cgi-bin/fg.cgi?page=cr&GSmpid=46619340&CRid=1985194&pt=Roswell%20Presbyterian%20Church%20Cemetery&.
Scheck, Raffael. "Fleet Building and International Conflicts." http://www.colby.edu/personal/r/rmscheck/GermanyB3.html.
The Ships List. "Steamships on the Panama Route." http://www.theshipslist.com/ships/descriptions/panamafleet.html.
Tennessee Historical Society. *Tennessee Encyclopedia of History and Culture.* "George Washington Barrow." http://tennesseeencyclopedia.net/imagegallery.php?EntryID=B009.
University of Cambridge. Alumni Database. http://venn.lib.cam.ac.uk.
Vinson, Ron. "List of Merchant Steamboats in NC (1861 to 1880)." http://www.historync.org/NCsteamboatlist1861-1880.htm.
Virtual Museum of the City of San Francisco. "Gold Rush Chronology 1846–1849)." http://www.sfmuseum.com/hist/chron1.html.
Virtualology. *Appletons Encyclopedia.* "Hall of North and South Americans." http://virtualology.com/famousamericans.net/.
Walczyk, Tomasz. "Lay-Osborn Flotilla." http://oceania.pbworks.com/Lay-Osborn%20Flotilla.
World at War Timelines Project. "German East Africa." http://www.schudak.de/timelines/germaneastafrica1884-1922.html.

Published Primary Works

Anderson, Edward C. *Confederate Foreign Agent: The European Diary of Major Edward C. Anderson.* Edited by William S. Hoole. Tuscaloosa, AL: Confederate Publishing, 1976.
Beaman, Charles C., Jr. *The National and Private 'Alabama Claims' and Their Final and Amicable Settlement.* Washington: W. H. Moore, 1871.
Bigelow, John. *France and the Confederate Navy, 1862–1868: An International Episode.* New York: Harper & Brothers, 1888.
Bulloch, James D. *Secret Service of the Confederate States in Europe, or How the Confederate Cruisers were Equipped.* Vols. I & II. New York: G.P. Putnam's Sons, 1884.
_____. *Secret Service of the Confederate States in Europe, or How the Confederate Cruisers were Equipped.* 1884. Reprint. New York: Modern Library, 2001.
Cox, Connie M., and Darlene M. Providence Walsh. *Selected Correspondence of George Hull Camp.* Macon, GA: Indigo Publishing Group, 2008.
Cross, Osborne. *A report, in the form of a journal, to the Quarter-master-General, of the march of the Regiment of Mounted Riflemen to Oregon.* Philadelphia: C. Sherman, 1850.
Davis, Jefferson. *Jefferson Davis Private Letters, 1823–1889.* Edited by Hudson Strode. 1966. Reprint. New York: Da Capo, 1995.
_____. *The Papers of* Jefferson Davis: *October 1863 — August 1864.* Vol. 10. Edited by Lynda Lasswell Crist. Baton Rouge: Louisiana State University, 1999.
Dewey, George. *Autobiography of George Dewey, Admiral of the Navy.* New York: Charles Scribner's Sons, 1913.
Dix, Morgan. *Memoirs of* John Adams Dix. Vol. I. New York: Harper & Brothers, 1883.
Forrest, Douglas F. *Odyssey in Gray, A Diary of Confederate Service, 1863–1865.* Edited by William N. Still, Jr. Richmond: Virginia State Library, 1979.

Fullam, George T. *Journal of George Townley Fullam: Boarding Officer of the Confederate Sea Raider Alabama*. Edited by Charles G. Summersell. Tuscaloosa: University of Alabama, 1973.
Grant, Ulysses S. *The Papers of Ulysses S. Grant: June 1, 1871—January 31, 1872*. Vol. 22. Edited by John Y. Simon. Carbondale: Southern Illinois University, 1998.
Huse, Caleb. *The Supplies for the Confederate Army*. Boston: T.R. Marvin & Son, 1904.
Kell, John McIntosh. *Recollections of a Naval Life: Including the Cruises of the Confederate States Steamers Sumter and Alabama*. Washington: Neale, 1900.
Lincoln, Abraham. *The Collected Works of Abraham Lincoln*. Vol. IV. Edited by Roy P Basler. New Brunswick, NJ: Rutgers University, 1953.
Mars, James. *Life of James Mars, A Slave Born and Sold in Connecticut*. Hartford: Case, Lockwood, 1868.
Merrill, Henry. *The Autobiography of Henry Merrill Industrial Missionary to the South*. Edited by James L. Skinner III. Athens: University of Georgia, 1991.
Richardson, James D. *A Compilation of the Messages and Papers of the Confederacy Including the Diplomatic Correspondence 1861–1865*. Vol. I. Nashville: United States Publishing, 1905.
Robinson, Corinne Roosevelt. *My Brother, Theodore Roosevelt*. New York: Charles Scribner's Sons, 1921.
Roosevelt, Theodore. *Letters from Theodore Roosevelt to Anna R Cowles, 1870 to 1918*. New York: Charles Scribner's Sons, 1924.
_____. *Theodore Roosevelt, an Autobiography*. 1913. Reprint. New York: Da Capo, 1985.
_____. *Theodore Roosevelt's Diaries of Boyhood and Youth*. New York: Charles Scribner's Sons, 1928.
Semmes, Raphael. *Memoirs of Service Afloat, during the War Between the States*. Baltimore: Kelly Piet & Co., 1869.
_____. *The Log of the Alabama and the Sumter: from the Private Journals of Commander R. Semmes et al*. London: Saunders, Otley, 1864.

Published Secondary Works

Abbe, Truman, and Hubert A. Howson. *Robert Colgate, the Immigrant: A Genealogy of the New York Colgates et al*. New Haven, CT: Tuttle, Moorehouse & Taylor, 1941.
Ackerman, Kenneth D. *Dark Horse: The Surprise Election and Political Murder of James A. Garfield*. New York: Carroll & Graf, 2004.
Adams, Charles Francis, Jr., *Charles Francis Adams*. Boston: Houghton Mifflin, 1900.
Adams, Ephraim D. *Great Britain and the American Civil War*. Vols. I–II. New York: Longmans, Green, and Company, 1925.
Alfonso, Oscar. *Theodore Roosevelt and the Philippines, 1897–1909*. New York: Oriole, 1974.
Andrews, E. Benjamin. "The Treaty of Washington, 1868–1888." In *History of the United States*. Vol. IV. 1894. Reprint. Washington: Ross & Perry, 2002.
Barnes, James J., and Patience P. Barnes. *The American Civil War through British Eyes: Vol. 2, April 1862–February 1863*. Kent, OH: Kent State University, 2005.
Baxter, James P. *The Introduction of the Ironclad Warship*. 1933. Reprint. Annapolis: Naval Institute, 2001.
Bennett, John D. *The London Confederates: the Officials, Clergy, Businessmen and Journalists Who Backed the American South during the Civil War*. Jefferson, NC: McFarland, 2007.
Blackbourn, David. *History of Germany, 1790–1918: the Long Nineteenth Century*. 2nd ed. Oxford: Wiley-Blackwell, 2003.
Boaz, Thomas. *Guns for Cotton: England Arms the Confederacy*. Shippensburg, PA: White Mane, 1996.
Bowcock, Andrew. *CSS Alabama: Anatomy of a Raider*. London: Chatham, 2002.
Brands, H.W. *The Age of Gold: The California Gold Rush and the New American Dream*. 2002. Reprint. New York: Anchor, 2004.
_____. *TR, the Last Romantic*. New York: Basic Books, 1997.
Brownell, Henry H. *Lines of Battle*. Boston: Houghton Mifflin, 1912.
_____. *Lyrics of a Day, or Newspaper-Poetry*. New York: Carleton, 1864.
Brownlee, Walter. *Warrior: the First Modern Battleship*. Cambridge: Cambridge University, 1985.
Brooke, John M. *Ironclads and Big Guns of the Confederacy, the Journal and letters of John M. Brooke*. Edited by George M. Brooke, Jr. Columbia: University of South Carolina, 2002.
Bulloch, Joseph G. B. *A Biographical Sketch of the Hon. Archibald Bulloch, President of Georgia, 1776–77*. Privately published, 1900.
_____. *A History and Genealogy of the Habersham Family*. Columbia, SC: R.L. Bryan, 1901.
Bullock, Alan, and Vincent T. Harlow. *Germany's Colonial Demands*. London: Oxford University, 1939.
Busch, Noel F. *TR, the Story of Theodore Roosevelt*. New York: Reynal, 1963.
Butler, Lindley. *Pirates, Privateers and Rebel Raiders of the Carolina Coast*. Chapel Hill: University of North Carolina, 2000.
Caroli, Betty B. *The Roosevelt Women*. New York: Basic Books, 1999.
Caskie, Jacquelin A. *The Caskie Family of Virginia*. Charlottesville: Conway, 1928.

Case, Lynn M., and Warren. F. Spencer. *The United States and France: Civil War Diplomacy*. Philadelphia: University of Pennsylvania, 1970.
Channing, Steven A. *Crisis of Fear: Secession in South Carolina*. New York: W.W. Norton, 1970.
Chesnut, Mary B. *A Diary from Dixie*. Edited by Isabella D. Martin and Myrta Lockett Avary. New York: D. Appleton, 1906.
Cobb, Lyman. *The Reticule and Pocket Companion, or, Miniature Lexicon of the English Language*. New York: Harper & Brothers, 1861.
Coleman, Kenneth, ed. *A History of Georgia*. Athens: University of Georgia, 1991.
Cook, James. *The Governors of Georgia*. Macon, GA: Mercer University, 2005.
Cooper, William J., Jr. *Jefferson Davis: American*. New York: Knopf, 2000.
Cotham, Edward T. *Battle on the Bay: The Civil War Struggle for Galveston Bay*. Austin: University of Texas, 1998.
Crook, David P. *The North, the South, and the Powers: 1861–1865*. New York: John Wiley and Son, 1974.
Cross, Coy F., II. *Lincoln's Man in Liverpool: Consul Dudley*. DeKalb: Northern Illinois University, 2007.
Curry, Angus. *The Officers of the CSS Shenandoah*. Gainesville: University of Florida, 2006.
Dalzell, George W. *The Flight from the Flag*. Chapel Hill: University of North Carolina, 1940.
Dana, Richard H. *To Cuba and Back: A Vacation Voyage*. London: Smith, Elder, 1859.
Daniel, John W. *Life and Reminiscences of Jefferson Davis*. Baltimore: R.H. Woodward, 1890.
Davis, Charles S. *Colin J. McRae: Confederate Financial Agent*. Tuscaloosa, AL: Confederate Publishing, 1961.
Davis, Jefferson. The Rise and Fall of the Confederate Government. 1881. Reprint. New York: Da Capo, 1990.
De Kay, James T. *The Rebel Raiders: The Astonishing History of the Confederacy's Secret Navy*. New York: Ballantine Books, 2002.
De La Pedraja, Rene. *A Historical Dictionary of the U.S. Merchant Marine and Shipping Industry: Since the Introduction of Steam*. Westport, CT: Greenwood, 1994.
Detzer, David. Allegiance: Fort Sumter, Charleston, and the Beginning of the Civil War. San Diego: Harcourt, 2001.
Durkin, Joseph T. *Confederate Navy Chief: Stephen R. Mallory*. Chapel Hill: University of North Carolina, 1954.
Ellis, Edward R. *The Epic of New York City*. 1966. Reprint. New York: Basic Books 2004.
Ellison, Thomas. *The Cotton Trade of Great Britain:* Including a History of the Liverpool Cotton Market and of the Liverpool Cotton Brokers' Association. London: Effingham Wilson, 1886.
Elphick, Peter. *Liberty: The Ships That Won the War*. Annapolis: Naval Institute, 2006.
Embree, Michael. *Bismarck's First War: The Campaign of Schleswig and Jutland, 1864*. Solihull, UK: Helion, 2007.
Evans, David C., and Mark R. Peattie. *Kaigun: Strategy, Tactics, and Technology in the Imperial Japanese Navy, 1887–1941*. Annapolis: Naval Institute, 2003.
Faust, Patricia, ed. *The Historical Times Illustrated Encyclopedia of the Civil War*. New York: Harper and Row, 1986.
Fergusson, Niall. *Empire: How Britain Made the Modern World*. 2003. Reprint. London: Penguin, 2004.
Fuller, Howard J. *Clad in Iron: The American Civil War and the Challenge of British Naval Power*. Westport, CT: Praeger, 2008.
Fulton, R.E., ed., *The Commercial Directory and Shippers' Guide*. 3rd ed. Liverpool: R. E. Fulton, 1871.
Fox, Stephen. *Wolf of the Deep: Raphael Semmes and the Notorious Confederate Raider CSS Alabama*. New York: Knopf, 2007.
Gerson, Jack J. *Horatio Nelson Lay and Sino-British Relations, 1854–1864*. Cambridge: Harvard University, 1972.
Gordon, John S. *A Thread across the Ocean: The Heroic Story of the Transatlantic Cable*. New York: Walker, 2002.
Graham, Eric J. *Clydebuilt: The Blockade Runners of the American Civil War*. Edinburgh: Birlinn, 2005.
Gray, John A.C. *Amerika Samoa;* A History of American Samoa and Its United States Naval Administration. Annapolis: Naval Institute, 1960.
Greene, Jack, and Alessandro Massignani. *Ironclads at War*. Conshohocken, PA: Combined, 1998.
Guggenheim, Harry F. *The United States and Cuba*. 1934. Reprint. New York: Arno, 1970.
Hackett, Frank Warren. *Reminiscences of the Geneva Tribunal of Arbitration, 1872, The Alabama Claims*. Boston: Houghton Mifflin, 1911.
Hamnett, Brian R. *A Concise History of Mexico*. 2nd ed. Cambridge: University of Cambridge, 2006.
Haynes, Sam W., and Christopher Morris, eds. *Manifest Destiny and Empire: American Antebellum Expansionism*. College Station: Texas A&M University, 1997.
Hearn, Chester G. *Admiral David Dixon Porter*. Annapolis: Naval Institute, 1996.
_____. *Gray Raiders of the Sea: How Eight Confederate Warships Destroyed the Union's High Seas Commerce*. Camden, ME: International Marine, 1992.
_____. *Tracks in the Sea: Matthew Fontaine Maury and the Mapping of the Oceans*. New York: International Marine, 2002.
Heidler, David Stephen, and Jeanne T. Heidler, eds., *Encyclopedia of the American Civil War: A Political, Social, and Military History*. New York: W.W. Norton, 2000.

Henderson, Dwight Franklin, ed. *The Private Journal of Georgiana Gholson Walker, 1862–1865: With Selections from the Post-War Years, 1865–1876*. Tuscaloosa, AL: Confederate Publishing, 1963.
Hennessy, John J. *Return to Bull Run: The Campaign and Battle of Second Manassas*. Norman: Oklahoma University, 1999.
Hickey, Donald R. *The War of 1812: A Forgotten Conflict*. Urbana: University of Illinois, 1990.
Hill, Jim Dan. *Sea Dogs of the Sixtie: Farragut and Seven Contemporaries*. Minneapolis: University of Minnesota, 1935.
Hitt, Michael D. *Bulloch Hall*. Roswell, GA: Self-published, 1995.
Hoole, William S. *Four Years in the Confederate Navy: The Career of Captain John Low on the C.S.S. Fingal, Florida, Alabama, Tuscaloosa, and Ajax*. Athens: University of Georgia, 1964.
Hohenberg, John. *Foreign Correspondence: The Great Reporters and Their Times*. 1964. Reprint. Syracuse: Syracuse University, 1995.
Hoppen, K. Theodore. *The Mid-Victorian Generation, 1846–1886*. Oxford: Oxford University, 1998.
Howard, Michael. *The Franco-Prussian War: The German Invasion of France, 1870–1871*. 1961. Reprint. London: Routledge, 2001.
Howarth, Stephen. *To Shining Sea: A History of the United States Navy, 1775–1998*. 1991. Reprint. Norman: University of Oklahoma, 1999.
Hunt, Aurora. *The Army of the Pacific: Its Operations in California etc. 1860–1866*. 1951. Reprint. Mechanicsburg, PA: Stackpole Books, 2004.
Hunt, Cornelius E. *Shenandoah, The Last Confederate Cruiser*. New York: George W. Carleton, 1867.
Hussey, John. *Cruisers, Cotton, and Confederates*. Wirral, UK: Countryvise, 2008.
James, Lawrence. *The Rise and Fall of the British Empire*. 1994. Reprint. London: Abacus, 2004.
James, Wilbur D. *The Confederate Rams at Birkenhead*. Tuscaloosa, AL: Confederate Publishing, 1961.
Jampoler, Andrew C.A. *The Last Lincoln Conspirator*. Annapolis: Naval Institute, 2008.
Johnson, Charles J., Jr. *Mary Telfair: The Life and Legacy of a Nineteenth-Century Woman*. Savannah: Frederic C. Beil, 2002.
Joiner, Gary D. *Through the Howling Wilderness: The 1864 Red River Campaign and Union Failure in the West*. Knoxville: University of Tennessee, 2006.
Jones, Charles C., Jr. *Biographical Sketches of the Delegates from Georgia to the Continental Congress*. 1891. Reprint. Spartanburg, SC: Reprint Co., 1972.
Kane, Elisha Kent. *The U.S. Grinnell Expedition in Search of Sir John Franklin: A Personal Narrative*. New York: Harper & Brothers, 1854.
Kemble, John, H. *The Panama Route 1848–1869*. Berkley: University of California, 1943.
King, Thomas B. *California, the Wonder of the Age: A Book for Everyone Going to, or Having an Interest in That Golden Region*. New York: William Gowans, 1850.
Kinnaman, Joseph. *The Most Perfect Cruiser*. Indianapolis, IN: Dog Ear Publishing, 2009.
Klein, Maury. *Days of Defiance: Sumter, Secession, and the Coming of the Civil War*. 1997. Reprint. New York: Vintage, 1999.
Kroll, C. Douglas. *Friends in Peace and War: The Russian Navy's Landmark Visit to Civil War San Francisco*. Washington: Potomac Books, 2006.
Lee, Sidney. *Dictionary of National Biography*. Vols. 1–63. London: Smith Elder, & Co., 1898.
Lester, Richard I. *Confederate Finance and Purchasing in Great Britain*. Charlottesville: University of Virginia, 1975.
Lyon, David, and Rif Winfield. *The Sail & Steam Navy List: All the Ships of the Royal Navy, 1815–1889*. London: Chatham, 2004.
Maffitt, Emma Martin. *The Life and Services of John Newland Maffitt*. New York: Neale, 1906.
Mahan, Alfred T. *Admiral Farragut*. New York: D. Appleton, 1892.
_____. *The Influence of Sea Power Upon History: 1660–1783*. 1890. Reprint. Boston: Little, Brown, 1918.
Massie, Robert K. *Dreadnought*. 1991. Reprint. London: Vintage Books, 2007.
May, Robert E. *Manifest Destiny's Underworld: Filibustering in Antebellum America*. Chapel Hill: University of North Carolina, 2002.
_____. *The Southern Dream of a Caribbean Empire, 1854–1861*. Baton Rouge: Louisiana State University, 1973.
Mayers, Adam. *Dixie and the Dominion; Canada, the Confederacy, and the War for the Union*. Toronto: Dundurn, 2003.
McBride, William M. *Technological Change and the United States Navy, 1865–1945*. Baltimore: John Hopkins University, 2000.
McCullough, David. *Mornings on Horseback*. New York: Simon and Schuster, 1981.
McGoogan, Ken. *The Race to the Polar Sea: The Heroic Adventures of Elisha Kent Kane*. Berkeley: Counterpoint, 2009.
McKay, Gary. *The Sea King: The Life of James Iredell Waddell*. Edinburgh: Birlinn, 2009.
McPherson, James M. *Battle Cry of Freedom*. 1988. Reprint. London: Penguin, 1990.

Meade, Robert D. *Judah P. Benjamin: Confederate Statesman*. New York: Oxford University, 1943.
The Merchant Shippers of London, Liverpool, Manchester, Birmingham, Bristol, and Hull. London: Straker & Sons, 1868.
Merli, Frank. *Great Britain and the Confederate Navy: 1861–1865*. Bloomington: Indiana University 1970.
_____. *The Alabama, British Neutrality and the American Civil War*. Bloomington: Indiana University, 2004.
Michael, Chris. *Lelia*. Birkenhead, UK: Countryvise Ltd, 2004.
Milton, David H. *Lincoln's Spymaster: Thomas Haines Dudley and the Liverpool Network*. Mechanicsburg, PA: Stackpole Books, 2003.
Monroe, Judy. *The California Gold Rush*. Mankato, MN: Capstone Press, 2002.
Morris, Edmund. *The Rise of Theodore Roosevelt*. New York: Coward, McCann, & Geoghegan, 1979.
Morris, Sylvia J. *Edith Kermit Roosevelt, Portrait of a First Lady*. New York: Coward, McCann, & Geoghegan, 1980.
Morrison, John H. *History of American Steam Navigation*. New York: Stephen Daye, 1958.
Neblett, Thomas R. *Civil War Yacht; Chronicles of the Schooner America*. Mustang, OK: Tate, 2009.
Nelson, James L. *Reign of Iron: The Story of the First Battling Ironclads*. New York: William Morrow, 2004.
Nevins, Allan. *Ordeal of the Union, Volume 4: The Emergence of Lincoln: Prologue to Civil War*. London: Charles Scribner, 1950.
Nepveux, Ethel Trenholm Seabrook. *George Alfred Trenholm and The Company That Went to War*. 2nd Ed. Anderson, SC: Electric City Printing Co., 1994.
Nicolay, John G. and John Hay. *Abraham Lincoln: A History*. 10 vols. New York: Century, 1890.
Niven, John. *Gideon Welles: Lincoln's Secretary of the Navy*. New York: Oxford University, 1973.
Noe, Kenneth W. *Perryville: This Grand Havoc of Battle*. Lexington: University of Kentucky, 2001.
O'Toole, G.J.A. *Honorable Treachery: A History of U.S. Intelligence, Espionage, and Covert Action from the American Revolution to the CIA*. New York: Atlantic Monthly Press, 1991.
Owsley, Frank L., Jr. *The CSS Florida: Her Building and Operation*. Philadelphia: University of Pennsylvania, 1965.
_____. *King Cotton Diplomacy: Foreign Relations of the Confederate States of America*. Chicago: University of Chicago, 1931.
Pakenham, Thomas. *The Boer War*. New York: Random House, 1979.
_____. *The Scramble for Africa: 1876–1912*. 1991. Reprint. London: Abacus, 2001.
Peake, James. *Rudimentary Treatise on Shipbuilding*. London: John Weale, 1859.
Phillimore, Robert. *Commentaries upon International Law*. Vols. I–IV. Philadelphia: T. & J. W. Johnson, 1854, 1855, 1857, 1861.
Pool, William, ed. *Landmarks of Niagara County*. New York: D. Mason, 1897.
Putnam, Carlton. *Theodore Roosevelt: The Formative Years, 1858–1886*. Vol. I. New York: Charles Scribner's Sons, 1958.
Randier, Jean. *La Royale: l'histoire illustrée de la Marine nationale française*. Brest, France: Editions de la Cite, 1978.
Rapier, Regina. *Saga of Felix Senac. Being the Legend and Biography of a Confederate Agent in Europe*. Atlanta: Self-published, 1972.
Reilly, Thomas H. *The Taiping Heavenly Kingdom: Rebellion and the Blasphemy of Empire*. Seattle: University of Washington, 2004.
Rixley, Lilian. *Bamie*. New York: David McKay, 1963.
Robertson, C. Grant. *Bismarck*. New York: Henry Holt, 1919.
Robinson, Corinne Roosevelt. *My Brother, Theodore Roosevelt*. New York: Charles Scribner's Sons, 1921.
Roosevelt, Theodore. *The Naval War of 1812*. Vol. 1, 3rd ed. New York: G.P. Putnams' Sons, 1900.
_____. *Thomas H. Benton*. Boston: Houghton Mifflin, 1899.
Rose, John Holland, et al., eds. *The Cambridge History of the British Empire*. Vol. 7, part 1. Chicago: University of Chicago, 1932.
Ryden, George H. *The Foreign Policy of the United States in Relation to Samoa*. 1933 Reprint. New York: Octagon Books, 1975.
Sawin, Mark M. *Raising Kane: Elisha Kent Kane and the Culture of Fame in Antebellum-America*. Philadelphia: Philosophical Society, 2008.
Scharf, J. Thomas. *History of the Confederate States Navy*. 1887. Reprint. New York: Gramercy, 1996.
Scheina, Robert L. *Latin America's Wars: The Age of the Caudillo: 1791–1899*. Vol. 1. Washington: Brassey's, 2003.
Schlisinger, Galbraith. *Of the People: The 200 Year History of the Democratic Party*. Santa Monica, CA: General, 1992.
Seager, Robert. *Alfred Thayer Mahan: The Man and His Letters*. Annapolis: Naval Institute, 1977.
Settle, Raymond W., ed. *The March of the Mounted Riflemen*. 1940. Reprint. Lincoln: University of Nebraska, 1989.
Silbey, Joel H. *A Respectable Minority: The Democratic Party in the Civil War Era, 1860–1868*. New York: Norton, 1977.

Silverstone, Paul H. *Civil War Navies, 1855–1883*. Annapolis: Naval Institute Press, 2001.
Solomon, Robert, ed. *The Little David, C.S.S. David: The Story of the First Successful Torpedo Boat*. Colombia, SC: R.L. Bryan, 1970.
Sorley, Merrow E. *Lewis of Warner Hall: The History of a Family*. 1935. Reprint. Baltimore: Genealogical Publishing, 2000.
Sowles, Edward A. *History of the St. Albans Raid*. St. Albans: Vermont Historical Society, 1876.
Sparks, Jared, ed. *The American Almanac and Repository of Useful Knowledge for the Year 1842*. Boston: David H. Williams, 1843.
Spence, James. *The American Union: Its Effect on National Character and Policy, With an Inquiry into Secession as a Constitutional Right, and the Causes of the Disruption*. 3rd ed. London: Richard Bentley, 1862.
Spencer, Warren. *The Confederate Navy in Europe*. Tuscaloosa, AL: University of Alabama, 1983.
_____. *Raphael Semmes: The Philosophical Mariner*. Tuscaloosa, AL: University of Alabama, 1997.
Spiller, Roger J., ed. *Oxford Essential Dictionary of the US Military*. New York: Berkley Books, 2001.
Steel, Edward M., Jr. *T. Butler King of Georgia*. Athens: University of Georgia, 1964.
Steiner, Bernard C. History of Slavery in Connecticut. Baltimore: Johns Hopkins University, 1893.
Stevens, William B. *A History of Georgia, from Its First Discovery by Europeans to the Adoption of the Present Constitution in MDCCXCVIII*. Vols. I–II. New York: D. Appleton, 1847.
Stephen, Leslie. *Dictionary of National Biography*. Vol. 7. London: Smith, Elder, 1886.
Stern, Philip Van Doren. *The Confederate Navy: A Pictorial History*. 1962. Reprint. El Dorado Hills, CA: Da Capo, 1992.
_____. *When the Guns Roared*. Garden City, NY: Doubleday, 1965.
Thompson, Samuel Bernard. *Confederate Purchasing Operations Abroad*. Chapel Hill: University of North Carolina, 1935.
Tidwell, William A. *Come Retribution*. Jackson: University of Miss., 1988.
Townsend, George H. *The Handbook of the Year 1868*. London: Wyman & Sons, 1869.
Underwood, Rodman L. *Stephen Russell Mallory: A Biography of the Confederate Navy Secretary and United States Senator*. Jefferson, NC: McFarland, 2005.
Verne, Jules. *A Floating City and The Blockade Runners*. New York: Scribner, Armstrong, 1874.
Waddell, James I. CSS *Shenandoah: The Memoirs of James Iredell Waddell*. Edited by James D. Horan. New York: Crown Publishers, 1960.
Walpole, Sir Spencer. *The Life of Lord John Russell*. Vol. 2. London: Longmans, Green and Co., 1889.
Walther, Eric H. William Lowndes Yancey: The Coming of the Civil War. Chapel Hill: University of North Carolina, 2006.
Waugh, Edwin. *Home-Life of the Lancashire Factory Folk during the Cotton Famine*. 1867. Reprint. Charleston: Bibliobazaar, 2007.
Wawro, Geoffrey. *The Austro-Prussian War: Austria's War with Prussia and Italy in 1866*. New York: Cambridge University, 1996.
_____. *The Franco–Prussian War: The German Conquest of France in 1870–1871*. New York: Cambridge University, 2005.
Whittelsey, Charles Barney. *The Roosevelt Genealogy, 1649–1902*. Hartford: Charles Barney Whittelsey, 1902.
Wilkinson, John. *The Narrative of a Blockade-Runner*. New York: Sheldon, 1877.
Williams, David. The Georgia Gold Rush: Twenty-Niners, Cherokees, and Gold Fever. Columbia, SC: University of South Carolina, 1993.
Williams, Docia S. *The History and Mystery of the Menger Hotel*. Dallas: Republic of Texas, 2000.
Willson, Beckles. *John Slidell and the Confederates in Paris*. New York: Minton, Balch, 1932.
Winks, Robin W. *The Civil War Years: Canada and the United States*. 4th ed. Baltimore: John Hopkins, 1998.
Wise, Steven R. *Gate of Hell, Campaign for Charleston Harbour*. Columbia, SC: University of South Carolina, 1994.
_____. *Lifeline of the Confederacy: Blockade Running During the American Civil War*. Columbia, SC: University of South Carolina, 1988.
Yoshihara, Toshi, and James R. Holmes. *Red Star Over the Pacific: China's Rise and the Challenge to U.S. Maritime Strategy*. Annapolis: Naval Institute Press, 2010.

Index

Accessory Transit Company 26, 293
Adams, Charles F. 54, 66, 71, 74–76, 80–83, 85, 87, 88, 100, 104, 107, 109, 114 115, 118, 121–123, 125, 128, 130, 132, 139–143, 152, 159, 160, 163, 165, 173, 176, 189, 202, 206–208, 212, 214, 215, 217, 219, 220, 227, 228, 237–239, 287, 291, 308, 309, 312, 315, 318–320, 327, 328, 330, 332
Adderley and Co. 72, 85, 290
Adelphi Hotel *see* Liverpool
Adirondacks (NY) 245
SMS *Adler* 261
Admiralty/Royal Navy *see* Great Britain: Admiralty/Royal Navy
USS *Advance* 328
SS *Adventure* 295, 323, 337
Africa 28, 59, 159, 180, 195, 241, 250, 255–259, 266–268, 274, 334, 335; *see also* British Cape Colony; East Africa; German East African colonies
HBM *Agincourt* 101
SS *Agnes E. Fry* 178, 298
SS *Agrippina* 78, 79, 82, 84, 89, 91, 92, 121, 133, 134, 240, 276, 291, 297
CSS *Ajax* 187, 201, 290, 295, 313, 323, 327, 337
Alabama (AL) 25, 31, 304; *see also* Mobile; Montgomery
CSS *Alabama* 1, 5, 46, 48, 49, 51, 56, 64, 68, 71, 74–96, 99, 101, 102, 104, 105, 110, 113–115, 117, 118, 121–123, 128, 133, 134, 140, 150, 152, 153, 155, 158, 159, 163–168, 171, 173, 174, 176, 177, 180, 181, 183, 189, 195, 208, 214, 215, 236, 240, 257, 269, 271, 273, 275, 276, 278, 287–297, 308, 312, 313, 315, 318, 321, 323, 329; *see also Alabama* Claims; *Enrica*; No. 290
Alabama Claims (Geneva Tribunal) 5, 214, 218–223, 225–227, 229–231, 233, 235–243, 251, 255, 278, 281, 287–289, 292, 293, 317, 331, 332

Alabama Steamship Co. 20
Albany (NY) 254, 273
SS *Albatross* 297, 323, 337
Albert, Prince 62–64, 310
Alexander, Czar, II 219, 319
SS *Alexandra* 106, 111, 117–119, 121–123, 125, 127–131, 136, 137, 139, 141, 142, 152, 153, 288, 289, 291, 294, 295, 298, 308, 317, 318, 337
Alger, Russell 271
Alina 180
SS Alliance 298
Alps 228, 229, 248
Amazon River (BR) 243
Amazonas Steam Navigation Company 243, 333
America (yacht) 54, 67; *see also Camilla*
MGP *America* 277, 297
Ammen, Daniel 16, 282, 287
Amoy 154
Amy 298
Anderson, Edward C. 50–60, 64, 67, 68, 287, 308–311
Anderson, Edward Maffitt 59, 63–65, 287, 310
Anderson, George C. 87
Anderson, John 55
Anderson, J.R. 65
Angra Bay (Azores, PO) 91, 185, 189, 298
SS *Annie Childs* 65, 66, 70, 287, 288, 290, 293, 294, 298, 310
Appomattox 199, 212
Arctic (Sea) 27, 177, 204, 290, 291, 324
Argentina (AR) 277, 295, 297, 325; *see also* Bermejo River
SS *Ariel* 214, 297
Arkwright, Capt. W. 104
Arman, Lucien 119–121, 124, 126, 127, 130, 135, 139, 149, 152, 158, 160, 163–170, 182, 183, 189, 193, 287, 289, 291, 318, 325, 328
Armstrong, John R. 223; guns 103, 168, 175, 195, 287, 324, 330
Armstrong, William 170, 179, 180, 183, 287
Arthur, Chester 249

Ascot (UK) 228
Ashton, J. Hubley 242, 243, 333
Aspinwall (PM) 19
Aspinwall, William 120–123, 128, 139, 287–289, 317
Astor, Helen 265, 292
Astor House 33, 289, 306
Astor Library 248
Astoria (OR) 14
Atherton, William 82
Atlanta (GA) 10, 21, 39, 169, 171, 178, 284
CSS *Atlanta* 297
The Atlantic Coast 282, 287
SMS *Augusta* 277, 297
USS *Augusta* 328
Australia (AS) 145, 181, 201, 234, 240, 335, 337
Austria (AU) 63, 155, 157, 228, 229, 248, 264, 322
Azores (PO) 65, 66, 85, 96, 99, 114, 134, 197, 288, 310, 341; *see also* Angra; Monte Brazil; Ponta Delgada; Praya; San Miguel; Terceira
IJN *Azuma* (*Kotetsu*) 263, 295

Babthorp 185, 298
Bache, Alexander D. 303
SS *Badger* 214, 299
SS *Bahama* 73, 80, 85, 86, 88–92, 103, 114, 115, 293, 297, 312, 313
Bahamas (BF) 72, 74, 82, 85, 87, 88, 150, 158, 174, 178, 184, 200, 210, 218, 287, 298; *see also* Nassau
Bahia (BR) 133, 134, 178, 195, 319
Baillie, Thomas 13, 14
Baines, James 208
Ball, Willis 302
Baltic (Sea) 129, 144, 155, 162, 229, 230, 314, 320, 336
Baltimore (MD) 30, 36, 67, 100, 118, 234, 328, 329, 331
SS *Baltimore* 330
Banuelos, Miguel 192
SS *Barcelona* (CSS *Alabama*) 90
Barcroft, William 242, 247
Bard, James 20
Barney, Hiram 47, 287, 292

351

Barney, Joseph N. 144, 287, 295, 320
Barracouta 204, 205
Barron, Samuel 140, 146, 153, 157, 161–164, 166, 168, 171, 175, 182, 184, 185, 192–196, 198, 278, 287, 319, 322, 323, 325, 326
Barron, Samuel, Jr. 185, 188
Barrow, George Washington 39
SS *Bat* 172, 173, 297, 337
Bates, Edward 165
Bavaria 248, 293
Bay of Biscay 189, 191, 194, 197
Bayley, Charles J. 86, 87, 287
Beaufort (SC) 56, 69
Beauregard, Pierre G.T. 33, 48, 213, 261
Bee 207, 327
Belfast (UK) 84
Belgium (BE) 47, 290, 292
Bell, John 30
Belle Isle (FR) 185, 188, 298
Benavides, Antonio 192
Benjamin, Judah P. 7, 24, 37, 39, 41, 42, 120, 169, 200, 210, 211, 214, 215, 217, 218, 223, 255, 257, 266, 267, 287, 290, 307, 327–329
Bent, Silas 257
Benton, Thomas Hart 257–259, 335
Bermejo River (AR) 184
Bermuda (BD) 54–56, 58, 63, 73, 133, 147–150, 154, 158, 168, 172, 174, 178–180, 184, 188, 196, 197, 199, 277, 291, 293, 295, 297, 298, 324, 326, 329
SS *Bermuda* 48–50, 52, 56, 68, 73, 74, 293, 297, 308, 309, 311, 337
USS *Bermuda* 297
Bernard, Montague 236
SS *Bienville* 29–37, 39, 44, 65, 242, 243, 281, 288, 289, 299, 305, 310, 312; USS *Bienville* 35, 65, 310, 312
Bigelow, John 148, 149, 154, 158, 164, 192, 217, 287, 318, 319
Birkenhead (UK) 47, 163, 223, 308, 317
Birmingham (UK) 194, 218
Bismarck, Otto von 63, 111, 113, 123, 129, 144, 155, 162, 213, 219, 220, 229–235, 242, 250, 255–257, 262, 266, 287, 321, 328, 334, 335
HBM *Black Prince* 94
Black Sea 97, 314
CSS *Black Warrior* 297
SS *Black Warrior* 19–22, 24, 25, 32, 172, 201, 299, 304; *Black Warrior* affair 22–24, 32, 77, 267, 281, 291, 292
Black Warrior River 304
Blaine, James G. 256
Blakely guns (Theophilus A.) 67, 139, 297, 311, 319, 320
blockade 26, 40–42, 48, 49, 53, 55, 56, 60, 62, 63, 65, 66, 85, 94, 120, 129, 133, 137, 142, 146, 150, 158, 173, 183, 193, 194, 222, 282, 283
The Blockade and the Cruisers 282, 292
Boers (Boer Wars) 266–268, 274, 334
Bohemia 229, 242
Booth, John Wilkes 178, 200, 204, 279, 280, 291, 308, 334
Borchert, George A. 188
Bordeaux (FR) 119, 120, 126, 134, 135, 143, 144, 148, 150, 151, 158, 162–164, 167–169, 179, 183, 192, 287, 297, 322
Boston (MA) 11, 25, 65, 96, 120, 142, 165, 254, 256, 299, 329
Bower, Harold 237, 332
Boyd, Belle 322
Bravay, Adrien (Company) 126, 128, 129, 132, 136, 139, 143, 144, 146, 148, 157, 158, 160, 161, 169, 287, 290, 318, 320
Brazil (BR) 11, 12, 68, 91, 133, 134, 178, 182, 193–195, 218, 237, 238, 242–244, 267, 277, 288, 289, 292, 295, 297, 299, 319, 333, 337
Breckinridge, John C. 30, 329
Brest (FR) 141, 142, 144, 150, 160, 165, 287, 295
Bright, John 122, 287
Bright's disease 254, 273
Britain (British) *see* England; Great Britain; Scotland; Wales
British Cape Colony 274
British Guyana 268
British North America *see* Canada
Broderick, Richard 76
Brooke, John M. 153, 170, 171, 174, 287
Brooks, William P. 193
Browne, Otis A. 176
Brownell, Henry H. 28, 284, 305
Bruce, Sir Frederick 112, 114, 154, 159, 211, 212, 215, 216, 287, 321, 329
Bryan, William Jennings 274
Buchanan, Franklin 313
Buchanan, James 24, 30
Bull Run, Battle of (Manassas) 48, 322; Second, Battle of 93, 100
HBM *Bulldog* 86, 87, 291
Bulloch, Archibald (JDB's great-grandfather) 5, 7, 8, 287–289, 301, 310
Bulloch, Elizabeth (Lizzie) Euphemia Caskie 16–22, 106, 235, 254, 287, 288, 303
Bulloch, Ella Sears 228, 244, 248, 251, 265, 289, 292, 332, 333, 336
Bulloch, Hester (Hettie) Amarintha Elliott 8, 9, 254, 288
Bulloch, Harriott Foster Cross 26–28, 31, 37, 38, 43, 51, 52, 59, 76, 89, 103, 105, 106, 108, 116, 123, 130, 153, 154, 185, 194, 198, 203, 209, 211, 219, 223, 224, 227–230, 232, 236, 241–245, 251, 259, 263, 265, 269, 287, 288, 292, 309, 315, 326, 336
Bulloch, Henry Dunwody 43, 103, 154, 209, 223, 235, 236, 260, 288, 331
Bulloch, Irvine Stephens 4, 10, 27, 38, 59, 103, 123, 166, 176, 180, 203, 204, 210, 211, 224, 227, 228, 230, 231, 237, 241–244, 247, 248, 251, 253, 254, 265, 273, 287, 288, 307, 308, 323, 324, 332, 336
Bulloch, James (JDB's grandfather) 7
Bulloch, James (JDB's great-great grandfather) 7
Bulloch, James Dunwoody: early years/family 7–10; Confederate secret service 37–209; description 11, 47; Lincoln kidnapping/ assassination 178, 179, 200, 204, 279; merchant career 17–37; post-war career, Bulloch and Robertson 211, 216, 218, 223, 230, 231, 236, 237, 242, 243, 328, 333; rescues Bamie Roosevelt 232–234; rescues Elliott Roosevelt 263, 264; secret service operations 67, 78, 118, 144, 160, 181, 184–187, 238, 278–280; Theodore Roosevelt meetings 227–228, 231, 234, 236, 237, 241, 242, 245, 248–251, 263, 264; U.S. Navy career 10–25; *see also* de Mauá, Baron; *The Secret Service of the Confederate States in Europe, or How the Confederate Cruisers Were Equipped*
Bulloch, James Dunwoody, Jr. 28, 31, 209, 223, 236, 241, 242, 248, 259, 260
Bulloch, James Stephens 8–11, 14–16, 287–289, 252, 253, 302
Bulloch, Jane 7–9, 287, 289, 301
Bulloch, Jessie Hart *see* Maxwell, Jessie Hart Bulloch
Bulloch, John Elliott 9
Bulloch, Martha (Mittie) *see* Roosevelt, Martha (Mittie) Bulloch
Bulloch, Martha Stewart Elliott 9, 10, 15, 16, 27, 37, 38, 54, 103, 105, 106, 108, 116, 123, 154, 180, 287–289, 291, 301, 302, 305, 307, 309, 310, 315–317, 321, 324, 330
Bulloch, Stuart Elliott 123, 209, 223, 236, 241, 269, 274, 288, 335, 337
Bulloch and Robertson *see* Bulloch, James Dunwoody
Bulloch Hall (GA) 2, 3, 10, 11, 15, 16, 21, 171, 284, 291, 293, 302, 332
Burma (BM) 53

Index

Butcher, Matthew J. 78, 80–84, 90–92, 288, 312
Butler, Rhett 284
Butt, Walter R. 118

SS *Cadboro* 14
SS *Cahawba* 20, 25–29, 32, 172, 299, 304, 305
Cairns, Hugh 128, 288, 308
Calais (FR) 126, 162, 163, 168, 188, 322, 325
Calf of Man (UK) 84
California (CA) 14, 17, 18, 27, 28, 112, 120, 204, 234; Gold Rush 15, 18, 19, 26, 29, 280
HBM *Calliope* 261
Camilla 54, 68, 311
Canada 38, 40, 43, 62, 200, 213, 236, 257, 279, 291–294, 297, 308, 315, 329; *see also* Halifax; Montreal; Quebec
Canary Islands (PO) 180, 200
Canton (CH) 95
SS *Canton* 111, 292, 317, 321; *see also* CSS *Pampero*
Cape Clear (EI) 205
Cape Clear (IR) 205
Cape Fear (NC) 16, 289, 298; River 133, 187
Cape Town (SF) 195
Carlsbad (Bohemia) 242
SS *Carnatic* 104
Carow, Edith *see* Roosevelt, Edith Carow
Carter, Jimmy 335
Carter, Robert R. 118, 126, 141, 145, 147, 148, 170, 171, 174, 175, 180, 185, 189, 194, 195, 201, 218, 278, 288, 290, 305, 319, 324, 326, 329
Carter, William F. 161, 189, 193, 288, 297
Caskie, Elizabeth Euphemia *see* Bulloch, Elizabeth (Lizzie) Euphemia Caskie
Caskie, James K. 105, 106, 116, 288, 315
Caskie, John 17, 288, 303
Caskie, Mary Edmonia *see* Hutchison, Mary Edmonia Caskie
Castle Morro (CU) 22, 201
SS *Castor* 134
Catskill Mountains (NY) 253
SS *Cecile* 298
RMS *Celtic* 248
Central Intelligence Agency (CIA) 6, 278, 318
Chagres (PM) 18
SS *Chameleon* 199, 294, 298, 326; *see also* CSS *Tallahassee*
Chapman, George 130, 318
Chapman, Robert T. 107, 115, 288
Charleston (SC) 7, 16, 17, 21, 30, 33, 42, 48, 54, 65, 95, 105, 171, 179, 181, 187, 194, 298, 306, 324
Chase, Salmon P. 30, 32, 33, 120, 122, 288

Chasseloup-Laubat, Justin Napoléon 151, 288
Chatsworth (UK) 228
Chattanooga (TN) 39
Cheops see SMS *Prinz Adalbert*
Cherbourg (FR) 68, 165, 166, 189
Chesapeake Bay (MD) 16, 308
Chesnut, Mary Boykin 155
SS *Chickamauga* 182
Chickamauga, Battle of (AL/TN) 155
China (CH) 27, 39, 59, 89, 95, 111–115, 117, 120, 147, 149, 150, 156, 157, 159, 184, 211, 250, 281, 283, 284, 287, 290, 291, 306, 316; *see also* Hong Kong; Lay-Osborn; Taiping revolt
USS *Chippewa* 115
Christian IX 155
SS *Cicerone* 177
Cincinnati (OH) 38
SS *City of London* 205
SS *City of Richmond* 184, 186, 188–191, 288, 297
Clatsop Spit (OR) 14
Clay, William C. 108
Cleveland, Grover 255, 265, 268
Clifton (farm, GA) 10, 330
Clifton (home, UK) 227, 228
Cobb's Miniature Lexicon (Cobb, Lyman. *The Reticule and Pocket Companion, or, Miniature Lexicon of the English Language*) 42, 78, 307
Cobden, Richard 122, 288
Cochrane's New Anchorage (BF) 85
Cockburn, Alexander 238–240, 288, 332
Coles, Cowper 94, 96, 98, 101, 109, 132, 288, 314
Collier, Robert 80, 81, 207, 288, 312
Collins, Napoleon 176, 178, 194, 288, 319, 324
Collyer, William 19, 305
SS *Colonel Lamb* 297, 337
SS *Columbia* 298
Columbia River (OR) 13, 14, 299
Columbia University (NY) 251
Columbus (GA) 60
SS *Condor* 279, 289, 297, 322, 337
Confederate Secret Service 43, 53, 106, 237
SS *Confederate States* 295, 297, 324; *see also* SS *Laurel*
Confederate States of America (Confederacy, CSA): secession 31, 32, 36, 39, 41, 67, 103, 135, 138, 157, 307, 321; Navy Dept. 40, 42, 46, 72, 74, 94–96, 100, 101, 105, 106, 109, 117, 144, 161, 166–168, 170, 190, 196, 199, 203, 208, 210, 266; Torpedo Service 106, 175, 178, 303; Treasury Dept. 32, 42, 134–138, 146, 150, 153, 188, 190, 199, 212, 293

Conkling, Roscoe 249, 260
Connecticut (CT) 10, 181, 229, 263, 290
USS *Connecticut* 313
Constitutional Union Party 30
SS *Conway* 298
Copenhagen (DA) 182–187, 194
SS *Coquette* 144, 145, 147–149, 167, 170, 288, 297, 337
Corbett, Henry W. 225
Corbett, Julian S. 4
Corbett, Peter S. 177, 180, 181, 288, 324
SS *Corcovado* 297, 337
Corinth, Battle of (MS) 102
SS *Cornubia* 298; USS *Cornubia* 298
Cornwall (UK) 49
Corps Législatif (FR) 232
Cortis, R.J. 245, 333
corvettes (FR) 120, 135, 138, 139, 149, 153, 158, 161, 164, 167, 168, 169, 170, 277, 282, 287, 293, 297, 319; *see also* Bordeaux; Nantes; *Osacca*; *San Francisco*; *Shanghai*; *Yeddo*
SS *Corwin* 36
Costa Rica (CS) 26
cotton 10, 22, 25, 42, 53, 57, 59, 60, 63, 65, 68, 95, 99, 101–103, 106–111, 115, 129, 138, 144, 147, 150, 152, 153, 157, 161, 170–173, 180, 187, 199, 203, 211, 214, 216, 220, 223, 229, 234, 237, 241, 242, 244, 248, 289–293, 298, 311, 315, 318, 328, 329, 332
Coulmiers (FR) 234
Court of the Exchequer 118, 127–130, 161, 318
Cowles, Anna (Bamie) Roosevelt 105, 231–234, 242, 254, 258–260, 262–269, 280, 288, 292, 330, 331, 333–336
Cowles, William Sheffield 265, 268, 269, 288
Craven, Thomas 74, 82, 84, 85, 165, 193, 195–198, 288, 313, 326
Crenshaw, William G. 182, 184, 288, 325
SS *Crescent* 298
Crimean War 97, 98, 218, 222
Crocodile 182, 298
Cross, Annette *see* Porter, Annette Cross
Cross, Osborne 27, 106, 224, 288, 305
Cuba (CU) 18, 19, 22–25, 28, 29, 36, 49, 150, 158, 174, 192, 198, 229, 267–271, 281, 304; *see also* Havana; Santiago
Cuddy, Thomas 189
Cunard line 51, 78, 231, 309, 312
SS *Curlew* 173, 297, 323, 337
Curtis, Richard W. 185, 188

Dabney, Charles 66, 91, 288
Dakota Territory (ND/SD) 254–256, 258, 259, 262

Index

Dallas, George M. 44
Dana, Richard Henry 28, 29, 284, 288
Dannevirke (DA) 157
Danube River 242
SS *Dare* 298
Davidson, Hunter 175, 179, 184, 186, 188–191, 278, 288, 303, 324, 326
Davis, Jefferson 24, 32, 35, 39, 42, 45, 160, 164, 199, 201–204, 219, 229, 232–234, 237, 243, 255–257, 261, 262, 267, 288, 289, 329–335
Davis, Varina 233, 261, 262, 289, 293, 335
Dayton, William L. 145, 149, 151, 152, 158, 164, 168, 182, 287, 289, 318
USS *Decatur* 12, 289, 299, 302
Decie, Henry Edward 68, 311
SS *Deer* 172, 173, 182, 297, 323, 337
Deerhound 166, 290, 323
Delane, John T. 113, 289
USS *Delaware* 12, 299
De Lhuys, Drouhyn 145, 149, 151–153, 157, 158, 162, 164, 170, 192, 290, 322
de Lôme, Henri Dupuy 98
de Mauá, Baron (Ireneo Evangelista de Souza) 242–244, 267, 289, 333
Democratic Party 23, 24, 30, 219, 255–257, 265, 274, 331; Northern Democrats 30; Southern Democrats 23, 24, 30, 257
Denmark 50, 123, 143, 144, 152, 155–158, 160–164, 169, 170, 182, 183, 187, 213, 321, 325; *see also* Copenhagen
Denny, William 174, 297, 323
Derby, 13th Earl of Earl (Smith-Stanley, Edward) 228, 290, 292
Derby, 14th Earl of (Smith-Stanley, Edward George) 50, 160, 214, 221, 222, 228, 229, 292, 309
Derby, 15th Earl of (Lord Stanley) 214–216, 219, 220, 221, 222, 255, 256, 293, 329
Derby Day 228
SS *DeSoto* 29, 243, 299
Detroit (MI) 38, 43
De Veaux, Mary 7, 287, 289
Dewey, George 270–273
SS *Diana* 298
d'Itajuba, Baron (Marcos Antonio de Araujo) 238
Dix, John Adams 105, 106, 289
Dix, Roger Sherman 105
Dobbin, James C. 19
HBM *Donegal* 206, 207, 291
Douglas, Stephen A. 30
Dover (UK) 241
Driving Mist 298
Dublin (EI) 66
Dudley, Thomas H. 64, 66, 70, 71, 74–76, 78–81, 83, 84, 87–89, 100, 102, 103, 107, 109, 114, 118, 119, 121–123, 125–132, 139, 140, 142–144, 148, 154, 175–177, 206–208, 210, 212, 214–216, 219, 237, 289, 293, 311, 312, 315, 318–320, 324
Duguid, James A. 73, 74, 82, 87, 88, 289
Dumbarton (UK) 174, 323
Dungeness (UK) 189
Dunwody, John 9, 289
Dybbøl (DA) 162

East Africa 257
East China Sea 159
SMS *Eber* 261
SS *Economist* (trans-shipper) 73, 289
Edinburgh (UK) 4, 228
Edwards, Samuel Price 83, 85
Egriteria 298
Egypt (EG) 126, 129, 132, 139, 144, 146, 154, 210, 241, 253, 318, 330; *see also* Nile River; Pasha; Suez
Elizabethtown (NJ) 245
Elliott, Corinne Louisa *see* Hutchison, Corinne Louisa Elliott
Elliott, Daniel (Stuart) 54, 105, 123, 288, 289, 337
Elliott, Henry H. 333
Elliott, Hester (Hettie) Amarintha *see* Bulloch, Hester (Hettie) Amarintha Elliott
Elliott, John 8–10, 105, 289, 301
Elliott, Lucy (Lucinda) Ireland Sorrel 105, 289
Elliot, Martha Stewart *see* Bulloch, Martha Stewart Elliott
Ellis, Joseph 130, 318
El Majidi 257, 295; *see also* CSS *Shenandoah*
El Monassir see *No. 295*; CSS *Mississippi*; HBM *Wivern*
El Tousson see *No. 294*; CSS *North Carolina*; HBM *Scorpion*
Emancipation Proclamation 101, 102, 104, 106, 111
SS *Emily II* 298
SS *Emma Henry* 171, 178, 298
SS *Empire State* 36
Ems telegram 232
Enfield Rifles 50
England (UK) 2, 4, 37, 38 43, 45, 47, 49, 50–53, 56, 58, 60, 63–66, 68–70, 73, 82, 86, 88, 89, 92, 97, 101–103, 109, 113, 116, 122–124, 127, 128, 134, 140–142, 144, 145, 147, 148, 154, 157, 160, 165–167, 169, 171, 173, 174, 177–180, 184, 185, 188, 189, 202, 204–210, 213, 223, 227, 228, 233, 238, 241, 243, 255, 258, 264, 265, 267, 274, 278, 280, 281, 284, 287, 289–291, 293, 295, 298, 302, 308, 309, 314, 323, 329–331, 333–335
English Channel 160, 169, 177, 178, 188, 189, 205
SS *Enrica* 76, 78, 91, 287, 288, 290, 295, 312; *see also* CSS *Alabama*
Enterprise 298
CSS *Enterprise II* 297, 323, 337
Ericsson, John 95, 98, 99, 103, 250, 270, 325
USS *Erie* 8, 12, 14, 299
Erlanger, Emile 127, 135, 149, 289, 316
Erlanger and Co. 107, 108, 115, 116, 125, 127, 129, 135, 140, 144, 150, 316; loan/bonds 117, 124
SS *Etruria* 258, 259
SS *Eugenie* 298
Eugénie, Empress 157
Eustis, George 163, 166, 289, 323
Evarts, William M. 238, 242, 243, 281, 289, 335
SS *Evelyn* 297, 337

Fair Head (UK) 84
Fairfax, Donald M. 234, 331
SS *Falcon* 297, 337
Falmouth (UK) 49
Farragut, David Glasgow 12, 284, 289, 299, 302, 305
Fauntleroy, Charles M. 162, 163, 168, 196, 289, 322
Favre, Jules 235
Fawcett, Preston and Company 46, 59, 67, 70, 75, 95, 105, 118, 141, 290, 311
Fayal (Azores, PO) 66
Ferguson, James B. 125, 289
Ferguson, William 322
Ferrol (SP) 191–198
filibusters 26, 36, 126, 267, 280, 293, 299, 305
Fiji 234
SS *Fingal* 52–60, 63–65, 68, 72, 79, 110, 183, 249, 269, 276, 287, 289–293, 297, 309, 337
Finland (FI) 50
First United States Volunteer Calvary *see* Rough Riders
Fish, Hamilton 227, 229–231, 235, 236, 243, 281, 289, 332, 333, 337
SS *Flamingo* 297, 337
Florida (FL) 7, 31, 32, 165, 172, 210, 273, 290, 310, 327, 329
CSS *Florida* 1, 5, 46, 50, 51, 54, 56, 59, 60, 64, 66, 68–78, 80, 82, 85–88, 94–96, 105, 110, 117, 118, 133, 141, 142, 144, 148–151, 160, 161, 165, 170, 174, 177, 178, 181, 183, 185, 188, 189, 193–196, 208, 214, 240, 271, 275, 287–291, 295–297, 306, 308, 311, 313, 319, 320, 329
Forbes, Charles 156, 289
Forbes, John M. 120–123, 125, 128, 287–289, 317
Forbes-Aspinwall mission *see* Aspinwall, William; Forbes, John M.

Forrest, Douglas French 198, 289, 322
Forrest, Nathan Bedford 160
Forster, William 122, 289
Fort Caswell (NC) 133
USS *Fort Donelson* 298
Fort Fisher (NC) 191, 193, 199, 288, 297
Fort Monroe (VA) 95, 105, 106
Fort Pillow (TN) 162
Fort Pulaski (SC) 58, 60
Fort Sumter (SC) 33, 36, 39, 293
Fort Vancouver (OR) 13, 14
Foster, Joseph 26
SS *Fox* 214, 298
Fox, Gustavus 269, 328
Fox, John 35
France (FR) 24, 50, 63, 67, 94, 97, 98, 100, 101, 117–121, 124, 125, 127, 129, 131, 134–140, 142, 145, 146, 148, 151–153, 155, 157–159, 161, 162, 165–167, 169, 176, 182, 183, 186, 187, 201, 205, 213, 219, 220, 228, 229, 231–233, 235, 237, 238, 244, 248, 250, 251, 255, 258, 268, 277, 289–293, 298, 302, 310, 314, 316–318, 320, 321, 328, 329, 331, 334; Navy (*Marine Nationale*) 97, 98, 108, 144, 250; *see also* Belle Isle; Calais; Cherbourg; Coulmiers; Le Harve; Lemans; Nantes; Nice; Paris; Quiberon Bay; Tours; Treaty of Paris; Ushant; Vincennes
Franklin, Benjamin 7, 303
Franklin, John 27, 305, 321, 324
Fraser, John (Company) 48, 85, 313, 314
Fraser, Trenholm and Co. 42, 44, 45–48, 50–52, 54, 55, 60, 64, 66, 67, 70, 72, 73, 77, 89, 99, 103–107, 109, 110, 116–118, 125, 126, 129, 130, 137, 144, 147, 148, 157, 161, 176, 178, 199–201, 203, 208, 210–212, 215–218, 220, 223, 237, 238, 287–291, 293, 294, 297, 198, 307, 310, 313, 316, 323, 328–330
Frederick III 256, 259, 260, 289
Fredericksburg, Battle of (VA) 108
Free Trade Club 253
Freeman, Thomas 207–209
Freemantle, Seaman 57
French, Anthony 216
USS *Fulton* 22
Funchal (PO) 177, 178, 180; *see also* Madeira Islands
HBM *Furious* 113

USS *Galena* 118
USCS *Gallatin* 16, 17, 287, 290, 299
Galt, Francis 86, 88
Galveston (TX) 111, 175, 187, 191, 197, 201, 216, 292, 323, 328, 329
Galveston Bay, Battle of (TX) 111

Garfield, James A. 249
George's Hotel *see* Liverpool
Georgia (GA) 3–5, 7–11, 27, 28, 31, 34, 49, 54, 57, 58, 60, 74, 98, 181, 183, 187, 201, 227, 287, 289, 290, 311, 314, 326; gold belt 10, 15; Hussars 53; *see also* Atlanta; Jonesboro; Marietta; Roswell
CSS *Georgia* 134, 162, 163, 165, 167, 170, 179, 193, 288, 295, 298, 322, 324
SS *Georgia* 17–19, 21, 29, 290, 291, 299, 304
German East African colonies 347, 356
Germany (Federation, *Reich*, GE) 63, 73, 74, 123, 143, 162, 229–232, 237, 242, 250, 251, 256, 261, 264–266, 274, 283, 321, 332–334; Navy 39, 164, 230, 250, 253, 260, 263, 265, 266, 278, 295, 322, 334, 336; *see also* Bismarck, Otto von; Frederick III; Kiel; *Reichstag*; Wilhelm I; Wilhelm II
Gettysburg, Battle of (PA) 111, 129, 130, 132, 137, 139, 319
Gibraltar (UK) 69–71, 74, 76, 82, 106, 107, 115, 116, 263, 288, 298
SS *Gibraltar* 129, 294, 297, 298, 316; *see also* SS *Habana*; CSS *Sumter*
Gilliat, Algernon 173, 289, 323; *see also* J. K. Gilliat & Co.
Gilliat, John K. 173, 289, 323; *see also* J. K. Gilliat & Co.
Gilliat, Louisa Ann 173, 289, 323
Gilliat, Mary Augusta 173, 289, 323
SS *Giraffe* 106, 116, 292, 298
Girard and Co. 101, 104, 194
Gladstone, William 222, 240, 258, 288, 289
Glasgow (UK) 46, 52, 96, 109–111, 136, 137, 144, 145, 153, 158, 170, 178, 180, 187, 211, 234, 297, 298, 309, 321
FNS *Gloire* (*La Gloire*) 67, 98
SMS *Gneiseau* 258
Goderich, Viscount (Robinson, Frederick John) 236
Goldsborough (NC) 59
Goldsborough, Louis M. 58
Goodrich, Caspar 270
SS *Gordon* (privateer) 313
Gordon, Charles "Chinese" 257
Gorringe, Henry H. 253
HBM *Goshawk* 206
Gracie, Anna Bulloch 245, 248, 259, 260, 264, 265, 289, 306, 328, 330
Gracie, James King 213, 234, 243–245, 248, 265, 289, 328, 333, 336
Grand Southern Bazaar *see* Liverpool
Granville, Earl (Leveson-Gower, Granville) 235, 236, 289

Graves, William A. 174, 179, 289
Gravesend (UK) 188, 317
Grand Southern Bazaar (UK) 221, 291
Grand Trunk Railway 43
Grand Vizier of Turkey 230
Great Britain 1, 5, 7, 12, 13, 24, 40, 41, 44, 47, 51, 53, 54, 59, 61, 62, 68, 69, 73, 75–77, 81, 84, 85, 87, 93–95, 97–102, 106, 107, 109, 112–147, 149–153, 155–157, 159–180, 183, 185, 187–189, 192, 194–196, 199, 200, 202–226, 228–244, 247–252, 255–259, 261–268, 270, 273, 274, 276–283, 287–293, 295, 297–299, 301, 305–308, 310–321, 323, 325, 327–332, 334–336; Admiralty/Royal Navy 14, 26, 46, 48, 51, 62, 87, 94, 98, 99, 101, 112–114, 116, 125, 143, 144, 162, 164, 165, 169, 171, 205, 206, 214, 220, 230, 234, 247, 256, 261, 263, 266, 268, 273, 277, 292, 295, 297, 305, 308, 311, 325, 336; Foreign Enlistment Act 41, 45, 80, 81, 86–89, 99, 112, 115, 118, 121–123, 128, 129, 132, 140, 156, 168, 174, 180, 281, 288, 318; Foreign Office 79–82, 84, 112–115, 118, 122, 123, 139, 141, 143–145, 156, 163, 165, 202, 203, 205, 214, 219, 239, 278, 317, 319, 321; Neutrality Act 56, 69, 117, 121, 123, 125, 142, 143, 238, 239, 281; *see also* England; Lancashire; Portsmouth; Scotland; Southampton; Wales
Great Powers 45, 74, 84, 94, 112, 127, 157, 159, 199, 202, 216, 232, 233, 237, 251, 308
SS *Great Western* 238
Greece (Greek, GR) 4, 6, 10, 242, 266, 277, 297
Green, Bennett W. 185
Green, Charles 51, 53, 56, 289, 290, 309, 311
Greenhithe (UK) 188
Greenhow, Rose 160, 279, 289, 297, 322
Greenock (UK) 52, 54
HBM *Greyhound* 87, 290
SS *Greyhound* 298
Greytown (NI) 26
Gueyton, Count de 141
Guiteau, Charles 249
The Gulf and Inland Waters 282, 290
Gulf of Mexico 18, 69, 198, 201, 282, 290
Gulf Stream 25, 57

SS *Habana* 40, 297, 298, 307; *see also* SS *Gibraltar*; CSS *Sumter*
Halifax (Can) 43, 58, 86, 87, 133, 161, 172, 178, 291, 308, 312, 322, 324, 328
Hamel, Felix 79

Index

SS *Hamilton* 302
Hamilton, John 105, 111, 127, 153, 289
Hamlin, Hannibal 30, 289, 306
Hammer, William C. 65, 66
Hammond, Edmund 144, 145, 203
Hampton Roads (VA) 19; Battle of 94, 95, 99, 100
Harding, John 81, 82, 115, 289, 312
Hardinge, Samuel 322
Haro Archipelago (OR/WA) 225
SS *Harriet Pinckney* 298, 337
Harrison, Benjamin 260, 262
Hart, Robert 112, 290, 316
Hartford (CT) 10
USS *Hartford* 305
Harvard University (MA) 2, 4, 244–248, 251, 266
Hatherley, William P. 212, 290, 328
Havana (CU) 18–25, 27, 29–33, 36, 65, 70, 77, 78, 83, 90, 176, 190, 200, 201, 218, 267, 270, 281, 295, 299, 304, 327, 328
Hawaii (HI) 13, 15, 202, 265, 266, 270, 299
SS *Hawk* 295, 298, 337
Hayes, Rutherford B. 245, 249
Hearst, William 270
Heavenly Kingdom *see* Taiping Revolt
Hebrides (UK) 52
Helm, Charles J. 201
Helsingør (DA) 187
SS *Herald I* 298
CSS *Hercules* (CSS *Vicksburg*) 297, 323, 337
SS *Hercules* (tug) 82–84
Heyliger, Thomas 85, 147, 178, 187, 198, 200, 290
Hickley, Henry D. 87, 290
History of the Confederate Navy see Scharf, J. Thomas
Hoare, E.G. 146, 290
Hobson, Charlie L. 198
Holland (Netherlands, NL) 108; *see also* Nieuwe-Diep
Holland, Henry 54, 55
Holstein (region) 123, 155, 156; *see also* Schleswig-Holstein
Holyhead (UK) 54, 55, 66
Hong Kong (CH/UK) 95, 114, 271, 277, 295
SS *Hope* 297, 337
Hotze, Henry 180, 181, 186, 279, 290, 322, 324
Houston, Sam 30
Howell, Becket K. 86
Howison, Neil 13, 14, 290, 303
Howland, Jane 236
Hudson's Bay Company 13, 14
Hull, Frederick S. 45, 46, 217, 237, 290
Hungarian Revolution 50
Hunt, Cornelius 208, 327
Hurr, Major 123
Huse, Caleb 45, 48–54, 67, 68, 70, 73, 85, 125, 287, 289, 290, 308, 311, 315, 318, 322, 329
Hutchison, Corinne Louisa Elliott 9, 10, 16, 288, 290, 302
Hutchison, Mary Edmonia Caskie 10, 288, 290
Hutchison, Nannie Caskie 228, 248, 335
Hutchison, Robert 10, 11, 16, 25, 95, 227, 248, 288, 290, 302

Iberian Peninsula 197, 198
Idaho (ID) 260
India (IN) 50, 112, 159, 267
Indian Ocean 59, 336
The Influence of Sea Power upon History 263
USS *Ino* 74, 311
Ireland (IR) 84, 116, 141, 204, 205, 234, 248, 331, 237; *see also* Dublin; Londonderry; Queenstown
Irish Sea 55, 84, 208
USS *Iroquois* 204
Isabella II, Queen 220, 229
Isthmus of Tehuantepec (MX) 120
Italian Alps 248
Italy (IT) 230, 237, 238, 248, 258, 292, 325; *see also* Palermo

Jackson, Nancy 10, 290
Jameson, Leander 267, 268, 336
Japan (JA) 99, 120, 156, 184, 201, 202, 250, 270, 274, 279, 283, 303, 326; Imperial Navy 39, 250, 256, 263, 278, 295
SS *Japan* 298
SS *Java* 280
J.K. Gilliat and Co. 173, 323
Johannesburg (SF) 266, 267
USS *John Adams* 25
SS *John Fraser* 201
SS *John Randolph* 95, 290
Johnson, Andrew 30, 203, 205, 207, 210, 211, 222, 223, 225, 262, 279, 328, 335
Johnson, Reverdy 219–222, 226–228, 290, 329
Johnson-Clarendon Articles 224–227
Jones, John Paul 71, 84, 198
Jones, Quiggin and Co. 173, 323
Jonesborough (Jonesboro, GA) 171
SS *Julia Usher* 298
Julius, Theodore 105
Jutland, Battle of 95

Kaiser Corp. 95
Kaiserliche Marine see Germany
Kamchatka Peninsula (RS) 201
Kane, Elisha Kent 27, 290, 291, 305, 324
SS *Karnac* (*Karnak*) 29, 78
Karslake, John Burgess 221
Keangsoo 154, 156, 289, 317
Kearny, Lawrence 17, 19

USS *Kearsarge* 74, 166, 168, 293, 295, 323
Kentucky (KY) 62; *see also* Louisville; Perryville
Kettle Hill (CU) 273
Key West (FL) 270, 297
Khartoum (SU) 257
Kiel (GE, Schleswig-Holstein) 155; canal 229, 330
Kilimanjaro (TZ) 257
Kinburn, Battle of (RS) 97, 98, 314
King, Gilbert S. 244
King, Roswell 10, 171, 290
King, Thomas Butler 98, 111, 113, 120, 266, 267, 290
Kinshan 95
IJN *Kotetsu* (*Azuma*) 263, 295
Kriegsmarine see Germany; Navy
Kruger, Peter 266; telegram 268
Kung, Prince 112, 113, 149, 150, 154, 290
Kuril Islands (RS) 201
Kwangtung 159; *see also* Lay-Osborn flotilla

La Coruña (SP) 191, 193, 195, 196
CSS *Lady Davis* 64, 298
SS *Lahn* 264
Laird, Henry 47, 76, 290
Laird, John 47, 95, 127, 135, 143, 221, 290
Laird, John, Jr. 47, 76, 290
Laird, William 47, 76, 290
Laird and Sons (Co. and shipyard) 48, 71, 75, 78, 81, 82, 89, 95, 96, 100–102, 104, 111, 117, 126, 127, 129, 135, 139, 143, 145, 159, 317, 323
Laird rams (ironclads) 85, 99, 102, 110, 116, 117, 126–130, 132, 136, 139–141, 143–149, 152, 157, 158, 164, 167, 170, 192, 196, 218, 214, 221, 256, 263, 267, 277, 287, 288, 290, 308, 317–319
Lake Como (AU) 248
Lake Erie (Can/US) 43, 178
Lamar, Gazaway Bugg 95, 290, 314
Lamar, Lucius 255, 257, 290
Lancashire (UK) 63, 100, 214
SS *Lark* 214, 297, 323, 337
Las Desertas (Madeira, PO) 180
SS *Laurel* 176–178, 180, 240, 290, 295, 297, 324, 337
Law, George 19, 290, 304
Lay, Horatio Nelson 112–115, 149, 290, 316
Lay-Osborn (affair, flotilla) 114–118, 120, 122, 128, 129, 143, 147, 150, 154, 156, 159, 211, 281, 287, 289–292, 316
Laynard, Austin H. 143
Leamington (UK) 76, 210, 290
Lee, Alice *see* Roosevelt, Alice Lee
Lee, Baby Alice *see* Longworth, Alice Roosevelt
Lee, Robert Edward 127, 130, 132, 133, 155, 199, 200, 203, 204, 212, 213, 275, 282

Lees, John Campbell 88
Le Havre (FR) 120, 150, 336
SS *Lelia* 189, 198
Lemans (FR) 235
Le Mat revolvers 101, 103
Lenox Plate Glass 228
USS *Lexington* 15, 16, 299, 303
Liberty County (GA) 9
Liberty Party 7
Liberty ships 95
SS *Lilian* 298
Lincoln, Abraham 3, 27, 30–33, 36, 39–42, 45, 50, 62, 74, 85 94, 100, 121, 125, 127, 129, 160–162, 222, 255, 289, 307, 314, 320, 325; assassination/kidnap 102, 178, 200, 203–205, 208, 262, 279, 280, 291–293, 331; *see also* Emancipation Proclamation
Lindsay, William S. *see* William S. Lindsay (and Co.)
Lisbon (PO) 192, 193, 197, 198
Littoral Combat Ship (LCS) 96
Liverpool (UK) 4, 27, 37, 38, 43–49, 51–54, 59, 63–73, 75–90, 92, 95, 96, 100–108, 110, 111, 113, 114, 116–124, 126–128, 130, 131, 133, 134, 136, 137, 139, 141–145, 147, 148, 150, 153, 154, 156–158, 160–163, 165, 166, 169–171, 173–178, 180–183, 185, 187, 189, 190, 193, 194, 196, 198–209, 211–219, 221, 223–228, 230–232, 234, 236, 237, 240–249, 251, 255–261, 263–265, 269, 274, 279–281, 283, 284, 287–293, 298, 307–309, 311–315, 317, 319, 323, 324, 328–334; Adelphi Hotel 213, 219, 227; Bank of Liverpool 218; #76–77 Canning Street 4, 242, 274; Chapel St. 204; Dale St. 207; Exchange 213; George's Hotel 207; Grand Southern Bazaar 221, 291; #63 Irbey Terrace 246; #2 Marine Terrace 52; North Docks 249; Rock Ferry 206; #10 Rumford Place 84, 114, 128, 130, 141, 176, 198, 204, 211, 218; #13 Rumford St. 218, 333; Sailor's Home 208; St. Agnes Church 259; #30 Sydenham Ave. 263, 269; Toxteth 246, 259, 269, 274; Upper Parliament St. 246, 248; Woodside Landing 83
Livingston, Crocheron and Co. 20, 33, 34, 36, 37; *see also* SS *Black Warrior*; SS *Cahawba*
Lloyds (shipping co.) 66, 75, 173, 181
Lodge, Henry Cabot 260, 268, 270, 274
London (UK) 4, 37, 42, 44, 48–51, 53, 67, 69–72, 75, 76, 78, 80–83, 85, 86, 92, 94, 100, 102, 103, 106, 107, 113, 115, 119, 121, 122, 125–128, 130, 140–143, 146, 153, 154, 156, 160, 162, 166, 168, 173, 176, 177, 182, 184–186, 188, 200, 205, 206, 210, 215, 218, 219, 221, 223, 225, 227, 228, 233, 236, 241, 243, 248, 257–259, 265, 268, 274, 279, 288–292, 294, 308, 315, 318, 319, 322, 333; Hanover Square 258; Haymarket Theatre 309; High Holborn 177; #5 James St. 184, 325; London Armory Co. 104; #6 Oxford St. 67; Portland Place 44; Queen's Stables 67; #37 Russell Square 70; St. George's Church 258
Londonderry (UK) 43, 308
Long, John D. 269–271
Long Island (NY) 245, 253, 259
Longworth, Alice Roosevelt 254, 259
Louis-Napoléon Bonaparte *see* Napoléon
Louis of Hesse 230
SS *Louisa Ann Fanny* 173, 174, 193, 194, 288, 289, 297, 323, 326, 337
Louisiana (LA) 24, 28, 31, 161, 289, 292; Louisiana Board of War 34, 35, 39; *see also* Plaquamene
CSS *Louisiana* 287, 297
Louisville (KY) 39, 42
Low, Andrew 51–53, 56, 76, 289, 290, 309, 311
Low, Harriet 76, 290
Low, John 53, 55, 59, 63, 65, 72, 74, 77, 82, 85, 88, 158, 187, 195, 201, 273, 289, 290, 295, 309, 311, 313, 327
SS *Lucania* 265
Lumpkin, Wilson 11, 302
Lynchburg (VA) 199, 259, 260

MacDonald, John 236
Madame Tussauds Wax Works (UK) 67
Madeira Islands (PO) 104, 179, 180, 187; *see also* Funchal
Madison (NJ) 180
Madonna 298
Madrid (SP) 24, 191, 192, 195
Maffitt, Eugene Anderson 63–65, 290, 310
Maffitt, John Newland 16, 17, 64, 72–74, 80, 85–88, 107, 141, 142, 144, 148, 151, 165, 175, 196, 257, 278, 287, 290, 295, 299, 310, 311, 313, 314, 320
Magruder, John B. 111
Maguire, Matthew 76, 290, 312
Mahan, Alfred Thayer 4, 6, 252, 253, 263, 265, 268, 270, 271, 282, 283, 290, 293, 330, 334, 336
Maine (ME) 59, 289; *see also* Portland
USS *Maine* 270, 271
Makin, John 56–58
Malacca Strait 159

Mallory, Stephen 36, 37, 39–42, 48, 50–54, 56, 58–60, 64, 65, 67–72, 75–81, 85, 86, 89, 94–109, 115–118, 121, 122, 126, 129–142, 144–148, 150–154, 158, 160, 161, 164–175, 178–182, 184, 185, 188, 190, 193, 194, 199, 200, 278, 179, 288, 290, 291, 307–319, 322–324, 326
CSS *Manassas see* CSS *Florida*
Manifest Destiny 13, 26, 36, 218, 257, 259, 261, 262, 265, 266, 269, 270, 281, 316, 322, 325
Manila Bay (RP) 273
Mann, Dudley 42, 44, 51, 53, 67, 69, 70, 290, 294, 307
Maori (NZ) 62
Maria 298
Marie Victoria 178
Marietta (GA) 21
Marine Nationale see France: Navy
Marine Society of the City of New York 28
Mars, James 10, 302
Martha's Vineyard (MA) 17
Martin, Patrick C. 178, 179, 200, 204, 279, 291
SS *Mary Ann* 298
SS *Mary Augusta* 173, 174, 289, 297, 323, 337
SS *Mary Celestia* 297, 337
Maryland (MD) 36, 132, 178, 279, 324; *see also* Baltimore
SS *Maryland* 297
Mason, James M. 24, 62, 76, 92, 99, 106, 113, 115–117, 126, 137, 146, 157, 160, 164, 166, 176, 199, 200, 202–205, 210, 278, 291, 292, 294, 312, 317, 327, 329
Massachusetts (MA) 16, 155, 221, 225, 242, 331
Matamoros (MX) 176
Mathews, Lloyd 257
SS *Matilda* 297, 337
Maury, Matthew Fontaine 106, 107, 109, 121, 125, 134, 147, 151, 162, 163, 168, 174, 184, 185, 196, 200, 201, 291, 298, 303, 327; *see also* CSS *Georgia*; mine warfare (torpedoes); CSS *Rappahannock*
Maury, William L. 291
Maximilian I 289, 314
Maxwell, Jessie Hart Bulloch 28, 103, 209, 223, 236, 241, 259, 260, 265, 266, 269, 274, 291
Maxwell, Maxwell Hyslop 259, 262, 263, 265, 269, 274, 291, 335
Mazeline 150
McDowell, Irvin 48
McDowell, Robert 161
McGowan, John 19
McKean, William Wister 58
McKillop, Henry F. 86, 87, 291
McKinley, William 268–270, 274
McMillan, Lewis 204
McNair, Angus 58, 291

McQueen, Alexander 78, 82, 84, 91, 133, 134, 291
McRae, Colin J. 124, 134, 136, 141, 146, 150, 151, 153, 161, 167–169, 184, 190, 208, 212, 278, 281, 291, 318, 328, 329
Mediterranean Sea 12, 28, 73, 241, 299
SS *Melita* 73, 76, 85, 298, 313
Mercier, Henri 192, 326
SS Merrimac 299, 313
USS *Merrimack* see CSS *Virginia*
Mersey River (UK) 74, 82, 83, 88, 90, 114, 119, 140, 143, 163, 165, 176, 189, 205–208, 227, 260, 308
Mersey Steel and Ironworks (UK) 102, 108
Metropolitan Club 269
Mexico (MX) 13–15, 36, 90, 120, 124, 129, 152, 153, 157, 158, 160, 161, 164, 176, 201, 213, 280, 289, 290, 292, 314, 317, 328; *see also* War with Mexico
USS *Miantonomoh* 214, 325, 328
Miller and Sons (W.C.) 2, 46, 51, 70, 75, 118, 141, 291, 308, 313
Mine warfare (torpedoes) 106, 107, 168, 170, 175, 178, 180, 182, 185, 196–198, 200, 201, 251, 271, 288, 291, 298, 299, 303, 324; torpedo boat(s) 171, 174, 179, 185, 190, 250, 251, 282, 289, 303, 317, 325, 335
SS *Minna* 88, 289, 313
Minnesota (MN) 93
Mississippi (MS) 24, 31, 102; *see also* Oklona; Tupelo; Vicksburg
CSS *Mississippi* (French corvette) 287, 295; *see also* SMS *Augusta*
CSS *Mississippi* (Laird ram) 103, 295; *see also* Laird rams; HMB *Wivern*
Mississippi River 35, 69, 129, 130, 132, 133, 139, 162, 175, 191, 283
Mobile (AL) 20–22, 24, 25, 141, 169, 299, 304, 305, 329
Mobile Bay, Battle of (AL) 169, 305
HBM *Modeste* 13
Moelfra Bay (UK) 82–84
USS *Mohican* 134, 159
USS *Monitor* 94, 95, 98, 99
Monte Brazil (Azores, PO) 91
Montgomery (AL) 21, 32, 35, 37, 39, 41, 42, 67, 273
Montreal (Can) 43, 178, 308
USCS *Morris* 16, 290, 299
Morris, Charles (Commodore) 28, 302
Morris, Charles Manigault 31, 291, 295, 306
Morristown (NJ) 28
Morse, Freeman H. 37, 121, 176, 212, 216, 217, 291, 306, 308
Motley, John Lothrop 228–231, 233, 291, 331
Moville (EI) 204

Murdaugh, William 137, 175, 196, 278, 290, 291, 305, 318, 324
Mystic (CT) 229

Nagasaki (JA) 202
Nantes (FR) 123, 124, 126, 127, 135, 136, 139, 143, 148, 158, 161, 163, 165, 167, 169, 293, 297
Nantucket (MA) 16
Napoléon III 63, 94, 97–99, 101, 119, 120, 123, 124, 127, 129, 143–146, 149, 152, 153, 157, 158, 160, 163–165, 168, 170, 176, 182, 201, 211, 213, 219, 220, 229, 231, 232, 234, 290, 291, 314, 316–318, 328, 331
Nashville (TN) 39, 307
CSS *Nashville* 55, 56, 60, 69, 130, 289, 290
Nassau (BF) 54–56, 65, 70, 72–74, 76, 79, 85–89, 105, 185, 187, 197–200, 290, 291, 293, 298, 312–314, 324, 327
The Naval War of 1812 248, 251, 253, 268, 282
New Brighton (UK) 83
USS *New Ironsides* 118, 171, 317
New Jersey (NJ) 2, 27, 37, 98, 307; *see also* Elizabethtown; Madison; Morristown
New Orleans (LA) 18, 25–27, 29, 31–33, 35, 39, 40, 44, 69, 120, 132, 161, 216, 243, 290, 299, 304, 305, 307
New York (NY) 3, 9, 19, 134, 184, 256, 269, 270, 273, 289, 292, 331; Adjutant General, New York National Guard 270; Collector of Customs 245, 249; *see also* Albany; Catskill Mountains; Niagara Falls; Saratoga Springs
New York and Alabama Steamship Company 20
New York & New Orleans Steamship Company 25, 243, 304
New York Central Railroad 38
New York City (NY) 3, 11, 15, 16, 18–22, 24–34, 36–39, 43, 44, 47, 51, 52, 54, 59, 65, 67, 75, 85, 95, 96, 98, 105, 108, 116, 120, 123, 142, 196, 207, 213, 215, 223, 225, 227, 228, 231, 232, 234, 236–239, 241–245, 248, 249, 251, 254, 256, 258–260, 264–268, 280, 287–289, 299, 302, 304, 305, 307–309, 311–314, 320, 331, 333, 334, 336; Beach St. 25; Central Park 105, 247, 253; #28 East 20th St. 305; Harrison St. 20; Manhattan 18; North River 20, 25; Pier #27 25; Port Authority 20; Robinson St. 25; Wall Street 95; West 21st St. 28; #6 West 57th St. 247
New Zealand (NZ) 62, 234; Maori Revolt 62

Newcastle-upon-Tyne (UK) 179, 287
Newhaven (UK) 205
Newport (RI) 263
Newport News (VA) 20, 312
USS *Niagara* 165, 177, 178, 186, 188, 193, 195–197, 288, 325
Niagara Falls (NY) 38
Niagara Falls Bridge Co. 28, 293
Nicaragua (NI) 25, 26, 124, 267, 299, 305
Nice (FR) 123
Nieuwe-Diep (NL) 185
Niger (NG) 255
Nile River (EG) 242
USS *Nipsic* 261
Norfolk (VA) 2, 11, 12, 95, 299, 304; Navy yard/base 1, 99; *see also* Hampton Roads
North, James H. 51, 54, 64, 66–72, 74–80, 86, 88, 96, 97, 100, 103, 104, 106, 108–111, 115–117, 121, 123–125, 130, 136–139, 144–149, 151, 153, 158, 164, 168–170, 180, 182, 291, 293, 307, 308, 311, 312, 314–318, 328; *No. 61* (North's ironclad) 97, 100, 103, 106, 108–110, 115–117, 124, 136, 138, 139, 144, 146, 148, 151, 153, 158, 169, 170, 317–319
SS *North American* 44, 308
North Atlantic 52, 66, 171, 187, 189; USN squadron 230
North Carolina (NC) 10, 16, 66, 302; *see also* Goldsborough; Wilmington
CSS *North Carolina* 103, 295; *see also* Laird rams; HBM *Scorpion*
SS *North Carolina* 65
North Dakota (ND) 262; *see also* Dakota Territory
North Pacific 170, 173, 175, 177, 199, 204, 240
Northcote, Stafford 236
Northern Democrats *see* Democratic Party
No. 61 see North, James H., ironclad
No. 290 71, 74–76, 295, 312; *see also* CSS *Alabama*

Oblates of Mary Immaculate (UK) 204
Official Records of the Union and Confederate Navies in the War of the Rebellion 53, 166, 181, 252, 266, 278, 279, 283, 301
O'Hara, Scarlett 284
USS *Ohio* 303
Oklona (MS) 160
SMS *Olga* 261
Olmstead, Charles 58
Ontario (Can) 43
Oregon (OR) 13, 18, 225, 233, 280, 299, 305, 330, 331; Oregon Treaty 13; *see also* Clatsop Spit
Oregon City (OR) 13

Index

SS *Oreto* see CSS *Florida*
SS *Orizaba* 26
Orton Point (NC) 65
CSS *Osacca* 287, 297
Osborn, Sherard 113, 114, 147, 150, 154, 156, 159, 288, 291, 316, 317, 321; *see also* Lay-Osborn
Ostend (BE, Affair, Manifesto) 24, 290, 292
O'Sullivan, John L. 160, 322
Ottoman Empire (sultan) 97, 230, 330
SS *Owl* 168, 170, 172, 173, 214, 290, 297, 337
Oyster Bay (NY) 245, 253, 259, 266, 268, 333

Pacific Mail Steamship Service 18
Pacific Ocean 59, 120, 124, 204, 257, 260, 266; U.S. Pacific fleet/squadron 12, 14, 15, 280, 299; *see also* North and South Pacific
Page, Thomas Jefferson 118, 184–201, 278, 291, 325, 326
Palermo (IT) 73, 74
Palliser, John 161
Palmer, Roundell 82, 128, 160, 207, 291
Palmerston, Lord Henry 49, 63, 100, 102, 112, 113, 121–123, 128, 129, 140, 142–144, 156, 288, 291, 308, 317
SS *Pampero* (*Canton*, Sinclair's ship) 111, 151, 153, 292, 317, 319–321, 327
Panama (PM) 29; canal 120, 283, 290; railroad 290, 304; *see also* Aspinwall; Chagres
Paovitch, Noel 228
Paraguay River (PA) 184
Paris (FR) 68, 101, 107, 118, 120, 122–128, 130, 131, 134–136, 142–146, 148–153, 157, 158, 160, 161, 163–166, 168, 169, 175, 182, 185, 192–196, 209, 210, 216, 217, 222, 230–233, 235, 244, 255, 264, 279, 287, 289, 290, 292, 316; *see also* Treaty of Paris
Pasha of Egypt 126, 129, 132, 139, 144, 330
Paynter, James 206, 207, 291
Peake, James P. *see Rudimentary Treatise of Shipbuilding*
Pearson, Chief Engineer 193
Peck, Penn 48, 49
Pegram, Robert 55, 56, 59, 69, 291, 311
SS *Penguin* 214, 297, 323, 337
USS *Pennsylvania* 12, 299
Perez and Co. (SP) 194
Pernambuco (BR) 242
Perrin, Eugene 223, 291
USS *Perry* 45
Perry, Horatio J. 74, 192
Perry, Matthew C. 12, 303
Perry, Oliver Hazard 337
Perryville, Battle of (KY) 102
SS *Persia* 51

Peru (PE) 12, 229, 293, 297; Navy 277, 297
SS *Peruvian* 204
Petermann (Peterman, Trémont) 148, 149, 151, 320
Petersburg (VA) 167, 169, 176, 199
Petin, Godot and Co. 150
Pezuela, Marquis de la 22, 23
SS *Phantom* 123, 298, 313
Philadelphia (PA) 15, 27, 28, 37, 38, 103, 105, 123, 227, 293, 305; Naval shipyard 12
Phillimore, Sir Robert 207, 291
HBM *Philomel* 46, 51, 308
Pickering, Charles W. 74
Pierce, Franklin 23
Pirate (piracy) 26, 45, 52, 75, 88, 112, 184, 200–202, 204, 207, 208, 226, 281
Pittsburgh (PA) 38, 39
Plaquamene (LA) 27
SS *Plover* 173, 297, 337
Poland (PL) 111, 143
Pollack, Jonathan F. 129
Pollaky, Ignatius 54, 291
Ponta Delgada (Azores, PO) 104
Port Royal (SC) 58, 62, 65, 196, 198
Portballintrae (UK) 84
Porter, Annette Cross 27, 85, 224, 288, 291, 292, 326
Porter, David Dixon 17, 18; Cuban incident 19, 21, 291, 299
Porter, John L. 100, 291
Porter, Seth Grosvenor 27, 85, 288, 291, 313, 326
Portland (ME) 142
Portrush (UK) 84
USS *Portsmouth* 303
Portsmouth (NH) 133, 134; Naval base/shipyard 133, 234
Portsmouth (UK) 115, 315
Portugal (PO) 160, 165, 192, 241, 322, 326; *see also* Azores; Lisbon; Madiera Islands
USS *Potomac* 11, 299
Potomac River (VA) 1, 133
Praya (Azores, PO) 55, 82, 84
SS *Presto* 298
Pretoria (SF) 274
Prince of Wales 249, 261, 308
Princess of Wales 106
SMS *Prinz Adalbert* (ex–*Cheops*) 220, 256, 263, 278, 295
SMS *Prinz Adalbert* (*II*) 258
Prioleau, Charles K. 2, 45, 48, 51, 54, 64, 65, 68–70, 99, 106, 117, 125, 137, 147, 173, 183, 199, 210, 211, 214–217, 219, 281, 291, 294, 307, 324, 328, 330
Prussia 50, 63, 111, 113, 143, 152, 153, 155–157, 162–165, 169, 170, 182, 213, 214, 219, 220, 228–234, 250, 277, 278, 287, 293, 295, 297, 321, 322, 331, 334
SS *Ptarmigan* 297, 337
Puggard, Rudolph 183, 186, 291, 325

SS *Pulaski* 16, 95, 290, 302, 314
Putnam, George Haven 252
Putnam, G.P. 251, 252, 334

Quangtung see *Kwang-tung*
Quebec (Can) 43, 44, 219
Queenstown (EI) 66, 205, 245, 328, 334
Quiberon Bay (FR) 185, 188, 189, 190
Quinn, Michael 190, 291, 326

Ramsay, John F. 177, 178, 180, 181, 324
CSS *Rappahannock* 162, 163, 166, 168, 188, 189, 192, 194, 196, 198, 240, 289, 291, 295, 298, 322, 325
Rathlin Island (UK) 84
Red River Campaign (LA/TX) 161, 322
FNS *Redoutable* 250
Reichstag 271, 335
Rennie, William 145, 170, 173, 181
RMS *Republic* 248
Republican Party 30, 219, 256, 258, 264, 267–269, 273, 274, 331
USS *Rescue* 324
Rhode Island (RI) 36, 263, 270
Rhodes, Cecil 266, 267
Richmond (VA) 2, 17, 19, 21–22, 27, 30, 50, 51, 56, 58, 59, 64, 69, 70, 102, 103, 106–108, 116, 118, 124, 133–135, 137–140, 152, 153, 169, 170, 174, 176, 179, 182, 184, 185, 190, 194, 196, 199, 203, 303, 304, 310, 312, 313, 315, 326
Rio de Janeiro (BR) 15
Rising Sun 90
Rivière, Henri A. de 135, 182–184, 186, 187, 191, 291
Roberson, Henry E. 243, 333
SS *Robert E. Lee* 298; *see also* SS *Giraffe*
Robert Gilfillan 69
Robertson, A.F. 218
Robertson, George C. 290
Robertson, Moses P. 170, 182, 183, 210, 211, 216, 218, 223, 230, 231, 236, 237, 242, 243, 291, 328, 333
Robertson, William H. 22, 291
Robinson, Corinne Roosevelt 248, 254, 265–267, 291, 292, 315, 336
Robinson, John F. *see* Goderich
Rock Channel (UK) 83
Rock Ferry *see* Liverpool
Roosevelt, Alice (baby) Lee *see* Longworth Alice Roosevelt
Roosevelt, Alice Lee 247–249, 251, 253–255, 259, 292, 334
Roosevelt, Anna Eleanor 263–265, 292, 336
Roosevelt, Anna Hall 263–265
Roosevelt, Corinne *see* Robinson, Corinne Roosevelt

Roosevelt, Cornelius Van Schaack, Jr. 27, 29, 288, 292
Roosevelt, Edith Carow 244, 245, 247, 256, 258–260, 263, 267, 292
Roosevelt, Elliott 244, 253, 263–267, 269, 292, 336
Roosevelt, James A. 47, 287, 292, 308
Roosevelt, Martha (Mittie) Bulloch 3, 10, 15, 19, 21, 25, 28, 37, 38, 105, 180, 227, 228, 231, 233, 234, 241, 242, 244, 245, 251, 253–255, 265, 267, 269, 284, 285, 288, 291–293, 304, 308, 309, 330
Roosevelt, Silas Weir 15, 25, 38
Roosevelt, Theodore 1–5, 28, 37, 105, 167, 227–231, 241, 245, 247, 251, 252, 254, 256, 258–273, 274, 277–283, 285, 290–293, 301, 305, 330, 333–337
Roosevelt, Theodore, Sr. 3, 10, 15, 19–21, 25, 27, 35, 38, 54, 105, 106, 228, 230, 231, 233, 234, 236, 241–245, 249, 281, 284, 288, 289, 291, 292, 301, 304, 305, 308, 309, 318, 326, 330, 331, 333, 335, 336
Roosevelt and Joyce (NY) 95, 314
SS *Rosine* (*Rosina*) 297, 323, 337
Rost, Pierre 68, 292
Roswell (GA) 2, 3, 10–12, 15, 16, 21, 171, 288, 290, 330; Roswell Presbyterian Church 16, 105
Rough Riders 271, 273, 281, 337
Royal Hotel (UK) 54
Royal Navy *see* Great Britain: Admiralty/Royal Navy
Royal Victoria Hotel (BF) 87
SS *Ruby* (*I, II, III*) 185, 297, 298, 323, 337
Rudimentary Treatise of Shipbuilding 46, 216
Rumford (Place/St.) *see* Liverpool
SS *Runber* 182, 185, 298
Russell, Lord John 62, 63, 71, 79, 81, 100, 102, 112–114, 117, 118, 122, 123, 128, 129, 139–145, 147, 149, 150, 152, 156, 159, 162, 163, 165, 173, 202, 203, 206, 207, 214, 220, 288, 292, 312, 317, 321, 322, 327, 328
Russell, William Hayden 130, 318
Russia (RS) 97–100, 111, 126, 128, 129, 143, 144, 153, 155, 156, 201, 203, 214, 218, 219, 222, 255, 279, 290, 318, 319; Russian fleet 97, 320
SS *Russia* 231, 232, 234, 237, 239, 241, 242, 244, 333

Sabine Pass (TX) 133
USS *Sacramento* 177, 178, 192, 195–197, 288, 326
Sagamore Hill (NY) 260, 268
St. Agnes Church *see* Liverpool
St. Georges (BD) 56

St. George's Channel (UK) 205
St. George's Church (UK) 258
USS *Saint Marys* 204
St. Thomas (VQ) 194
Samoa (WS) 234, 260, 261, 274, 335
Samuda brothers 94
San Antonio (TX) 273, 337
Sanders, George N. 102, 153, 211, 292, 299, 319, 320
Sandwich Islands (HI) *see* Hawaii
Sanford, Henry S. 47, 50, 54, 144, 291, 292, 308
San Francisco (CA) 14, 15, 120, 203, 204, 225, 299, 319, 320
SS *San Francisco* 297
USS *San Jacinto* 62
San Juan de Nicaragua (NI) 25, 299
San Juan Hill (CU) 24, 273
San Juan Island (OR/WA) 220, 236
San Miguel (Azores, PO) 191
São Paulo Railway Company (BR) 243
USS *Saranac* 204
Saratoga Springs (NY) 16
Savannah (GA) 5, 7–10, 16, 31, 49, 50, 53, 55–60, 62–65, 67, 69, 72, 73, 79, 95, 110, 120, 181, 183, 185, 188, 254, 273, 287, 290, 293, 311
Savannah (privateer) 45
SS *Savannah* 8
SS *Savannah* (blockade runner) 297, 299
USS *Savannah* 49
Savannah River (GA) 49, 57, 58, 60, 64, 65
Savoy (FR) 123
Saxony (GE) 63
Scharf, J. Thomas 12
Schaumburg, Bartholomew von 305
Schaumburg, Louisa von 27
Schenck, James F. 14, 292, 303
Schenck, Robert 237, 239, 241, 243, 292, 331
Schenck, Woddhull Smith 14, 292
Schleswig 213
Schleswig-Holstein 123, 155, 158, 161, 162, 182, 213
Sclopis, Count Frederic de 238, 240, 292
HBM *Scorpion* 256, 277, 295; *see also* Laird Rams; CSS *North Carolina*
SS *Scotia* 213, 227
Scotland (UK) 7, 52, 53, 58, 78, 130, 173, 228, 236, 248, 265, 288, 291, 292, 317, 322, 323, 329
SS *Sea King* 2, 145, 170, 171, 173, 174, 176–181, 188, 288, 294, 323; *see also* CSS *Shenandoah*
Sea of Azov 98
Sea of Okhotsk 203
Seacombe (UK) 82, 323

Sears, Harriet 248, 298
Sears, Henry B. 228, 242, 292
The Secret Service of the Confederate States in Europe, or How the Confederate Cruisers Were Equipped 249, 252, 253, 255
Selby Town (UK) 273
Sellar, John A. 223, 292
Seminole War 39
Semmes, Raphael 40, 69–71, 76, 77, 79, 80, 82, 84–92, 99, 103, 105, 106, 128, 133, 134, 139, 154, 155, 158, 159, 163, 165, 166, 175, 195, 198, 207, 257, 273, 278, 290, 292, 295, 298, 307, 311–315, 321, 323
Seward, William H. 30, 37, 38, 47, 56, 58, 62, 85, 103, 108, 132, 162, 196, 202, 211, 212, 214, 222, 226, 227, 262, 292, 306, 308, 311
Shanghai (CH) 147, 159, 202, 317, 323
SS *Shanghai* 297
USS *Shark* 12–14, 225, 237, 280, 288, 290, 292, 299
CSS *Shenandoah* 1, 2, 5, 89, 156, 174–177, 179–183, 185, 192, 199, 201–210, 212, 214, 240, 257, 271, 273, 275, 287, 288, 291, 293–297, 305, 313, 319, 324, 327, 328
Shenandoah Valley (VA) 74
Sheridan, Phillip H. 74
Sherman, William T. 3, 74, 171, 178, 181, 183, 185, 187, 191, 196, 197, 201, 332
Shirley Plantation (VA) 218; *see also* Carter, Robert R.
Shryock, George S. 188, 189, 292, 325
Sibley, Henry Hopkins 120
Siccardi 55
USS *Silver Cloud* 322
Simon's Town (SF) 159
Sinclair, Arthur 189, 292
Sinclair, George T. 60, 64, 79, 80, 86, 89, 101, 111, 151, 153, 292
Sinope, Battle of (TU) 97, 98
Sioux Nation 93
slaves (slavery) 9, 10, 23, 24, 26, 30, 33, 34, 44, 101, 102, 111, 122, 187, 212, 225, 262, 290, 293, 321
Slidell, John 24, 62, 113, 118–120, 122, 123, 125–127, 130, 138, 139, 146, 148, 149, 152, 157, 160, 161, 163, 164, 166–169, 193, 196, 210, 257, 266, 289, 292, 292, 294, 316–318, 323
Smith, L.W. 32
Smith, William S. 160
Smith-Stanley, Edward *see* Derby, Earl (13th)
Smith-Stanley, Edward George *see* Derby, Earl (14th)
Smithville (NC) 133
SS *Snipe* 173, 297, 337

Index

Soley, James 266, 282, 283, 292
Somerset, Lord Edward 113, 292
Sorley, James 216, 292, 329
Soulé, Pierre 24, 292, 304, 307; *see also* Ostend Manifesto
South Africa (SF) 266–268, 274, 334; *see also* Cape Town; Simon's Town
South America 12, 156, 185, 205, 243, 253, 267, 268, 280, 324
South Atlantic 89
South Carolina (SC) 7, 30, 31, 33, 56, 58, 62, 65, 168, 185, 237, 299
South Dakota (SD) 262
South Pacific 176, 234, 250
Southampton (UK) 82, 83, 165, 166, 194, 211, 229, 264, 293, 327, 330
USS *Southampton* 303
Southern Democrats 23, 24, 30, 257
Spain (SP) 22–24, 36, 74, 76, 90, 191–197, 201, 219, 220, 229, 267–271, 281, 292, 297, 304, 314, 327; Spanish Navy 29, 191, 193, 201, 270–273, 283, 297, 298
Spence, James 107–109, 116, 125, 130, 139, 219, 223, 293, 316
SS *Sphinx see* CSS *Stonewall*
Sprague, Horatio J. 74
Spring-Rice, Cecil Arthur 258
Springfield (IL) 30
Squarey, Andrew T. 80, 121, 293
SS *Stag* 172, 173, 178, 297, 323, 337
Stämpfli, Jacob 238
Stanley, Lord *see* Derby, Earl (15th)
Stanton, Edward 37, 38, 47, 99, 108
HBM *Steady* 46
Stephens, Alexander H. 202
Stevens, Edwin and Robert (brothers, battery) 87, 98, 119, 132, 293, 314
Stewart, Martha *see* Bulloch, Martha Stewart
Stobo, Rev. Archibald 7, 299, 293
Stobo, Jean 7, 287, 288, 293
Stoeckel, Eduard de 218
CSS *Stonewall* 1, 155, 183–201, 218, 220, 256, 263, 277–279, 287, 288, 291–293, 295, 297, 325–327
SMS *Stosch* 258
Strait of Gibraltar 263
Stringer, Edgar P. 102, 110, 153, 293, 315
Suez (EG) 154; canal 230, 263
CSS *Sumter* 40, 69, 70, 76, 79, 82, 85, 86, 88, 106, 107, 115–117, 192, 288, 290, 294, 295, 297, 298, 307, 312, 313, 316; *see also* SS *Gibraltar*
Surigao Strait 95
Surratt, John H. 200, 204, 205, 279, 293
SS *Susan Bierne* 178, 180, 182, 298

Swartwout, Samuel 17
Sweden (SW) 99, 155, 156, 163, 164, 183
Switzerland (SZ) 220, 232, 237–239

Taiping Revolt (CH) 112, 120, 294, 316
Takeaki, Enomoto 250
CSS *Tallahassee* 171, 173, 182, 212, 298, 299, 315, 323, 326; *see also* SS *Chameleon*
Tampa (FL) 273
SS *Tartar* 178, 297; *see also* SS *Wren*
Tattnall, Josiah 31, 58, 60, 293, 306
telegraph 4, 21, 23, 30, 35, 38, 39, 41, 43, 58, 64, 128, 142, 150, 154, 185, 186, 188, 189, 194, 195, 198, 210, 219, 222, 225, 226, 234, 243, 245, 254, 257, 258, 260, 268, 305, 307, 333
Tenerife (Canary Is., PO) 180
Tennant, G. B. 168
Tennessee (TN) 39, 62, 307
Terceira (Azores, PO) 55, 89–91, 185
Tessier, Eugene 48, 49, 73, 88, 91, 163–165, 167, 191, 193, 194, 197, 293
Tetley, Ellen 236
SS *Teutonic* 264, 267
Texan Star 159
Texas (TX) 30, 36, 45, 111, 120, 133, 161, 172, 197, 198, 200, 201, 273, 297, 321
Thames River (UK) 176–178, 186, 188
Thomas Hart Benton 257
Thornton, Edward, Jr. 219, 221, 222, 225, 230, 235, 329
Tidball, Edward 168
Tiernan, Miss 108
Tipping and Lawden 194
Tirpitz, Alfred 251, 265, 271, 293, 336
Tonawanda 105
USS *Topeka* 269
Topete, Juan Bautiste 219
Tours (FR) 123
Tower House (NJ) 180
Toxteth (UK) 246, 259, 269, 274; *see also* Liverpool
Trafalgar, Battle of 250
Transvaal Republic (SF) 268, 274, 334
Treaty of Paris (1856) 41, 42, 222, 230
Treaty of Vienna (1865) 182, 325
Tremlett, Francis 166, 293
Trenholm, George A. 188, 223, 237, 287, 293, 330, 332; *see also* Fraser, Trenholm and Co.
Trenholm, William 237, 330
HMS *Trent* 62, 85, 113, 115, 125; *Trent* affair 291, 292, 294
USS *Trenton* 261
Tryom 298

Turkey (TU) 144, 230, 242; Navy 97, 277, 297
CSS *Tuscaloosa* 158, 195, 290, 313, 326
USS *Tuscarora* 74, 82–85, 116, 288, 311
Tybee Island (GA) 17, 60

United Kingdom *see* England; Great Britain; Scotland; Wales
USS *United States* 11, 299
United States Coast Survey (USCS) 14–17, 28, 57, 72, 257, 282, 299, 303; *see also* USCS *Gallatin*; USCS *Morris*
United States Navy (USN): Asiatic Fleet 270; Asst. Sec. of the Navy (Fox, Roosevelt, Soley) 5, 268, 269, 283, 328; Naval Academy 175, 266, 268; Naval War College (CT) 263, 270; North Atlantic Squadron 270; *Official Records of the Union and Confederate Navies in the War of the Rebellion* 252; Secretary of the Navy (Dobbin, Fox, Long, Roberson, Welles) 18, 19, 33, 35, 47, 49, 56, 59, 85, 99, 103, 108, 120, 122, 132, 159, 165, 176, 195, 196, 243, 269–271, 288, 293, 304, 319
Upton, George 225, 226
Upton, Otto 88
Ushant (FR) 185

Valparaiso (CI) 15
USS *Vandalia* 261
Vanderbilt, Cornelius 26, 293, 337
Venezuela (VE) 267, 268, 297
Vice-Admiralty Court (UK): Halifax (Can) 87, 291; Nassau (BF) 87, 88
Vicksburg (MS) 122, 129, 130, 132, 133, 137, 146
CSS *Vicksburg* 297
Victoria, Queen 41, 50, 62–64, 112, 220, 237, 256, 257, 261, 262, 268, 289, 290, 293, 307, 308, 310, 330
Vienna (AU) 229, 263, 264; Vienna International Exposition 241–243
Vincennes (FR) 68
Vincent, Count Benedetti 232
Virginia (VA) 8, 16, 45, 48, 53, 133, 191, 199, 213, 218, 260, 288, 291, 298, 299; *see also* Lynchburg; Norfolk; Petersburg; Richmond
CSS *Virginia* 94, 95, 99, 293, 310
CSS *Virginia* 139; *see also No. 61*
CSS *Virginia II* 326
Voruz, Jean 124, 127, 135, 139, 143, 145, 148, 149, 151, 152, 160, 168, 291, 293, 318, 320, 328

USS *Wabash* 60
USS *Wachusett* 176, 178, 288, 319

Waddell, James Iredell 118, 175–179, 181, 199, 201–208, 257, 273, 278, 293, 295, 319, 324, 327, 331
Wailey, Charles W. 216, 329
Wales (UK) 54, 83, 142, 273, 329; see also Prince of Wales; Princess of Wales
Walker, Norman S. 180, 188, 219, 220, 293, 324, 329
Walker, William 26, 293, 305
Wall Street 95
War with Great Britain (War of 1812) 66
War with Mexico 13, 15, 27, 280, 290
USS *Warren* 14–16, 299, 303
HBM *Warrior* 94, 98, 311, 315
Washington (WA) 13, 225, 262
USCS *Washington* 17, 299
Washington, George 325
Washington DC 1, 12, 13, 16, 17, 29, 31, 32, 36, 93, 99, 100, 133, 200, 201, 211, 219, 221–223, 225, 230, 231, 235, 266, 267, 269, 270, 311, 322
Washington Treaty (1871) 237
SS *Wasp* 214, 299
USS *Wateree* 204
Waterloo (UK) 66, 72, 89, 114, 126, 130, 145, 198, 227, 232, 236, 247, 263; #2 Marine Terrace 52; St. John Church 209; #30 Sydenham Ave. 263, 269; #3 Willington St. 52, 194, 211
Welles, Gideon 33, 35, 47, 49, 56, 58, 85, 99, 103, 108, 120, 122, 132, 159, 165, 176, 195–196, 288, 293, 319

West, Hilborne 15, 27, 37, 38, 245, 292, 293, 303, 307
West, Susan (Susy) Elliott 9, 10, 15, 27, 38, 103, 105, 106, 116, 123, 245, 288, 293, 302, 305, 307, 309, 310, 315–317, 321
West Hartlepool 48–50
West Indies 73, 125, 291
Whampoa (CH) 95
Wharncliffe, Lord and Lady 221, 291, 293
Whig Party 30, 301
SS *Whisper* 182, 299
White, Hollis 37–40, 43, 293, 307
White House (US) 262
White Star line (UK) 248, 264
Whitehall (UK) 125
Whiting, Samuel 85, 87, 88, 293, 313
Whitney, Charles A. 26
Whittle, William C. 59, 118, 130, 132–134, 138–140, 146, 175, 177, 207, 208, 293, 313
Whitworth gun 103, 106, 174
SS *Widgeon* 173, 297, 337
Wilding, Henry 47, 293, 308, 309
Wilhelm I 63, 123, 129, 144, 155, 161, 162, 213, 220, 231, 232, 235, 250, 255, 256, 259, 293
Wilhelm II 256, 260–265, 267, 268, 289, 290, 293, 330, 335, 336; Crown Prince William 259, 260
Wilhelmshaven (GE) 250
Wilkes, Ashley 284
Wilkes, Charles 62, 85, 125, 294
Wilkinson, John 199, 294
Willamette River (OR) 13

William S. Lindsay (and Co.) 116, 211, 216, 290
Williams, Geroge H. 331
Williamson, William P. 179
Wilmington (DE) 16
Wilmington (NC) 59, 65, 133, 140, 171, 172, 174, 175, 179, 183, 187, 191, 313, 322
Wilmington Island (SC) 60
Wilson, James A.K. 107, 294, 316, 328
Wilson, James Harrison 267
Wilson, Nathaniel I. 212
Windsor (Can) 43
The Winning of the West 259–261
Winslow, John A. 166, 293
HBM *Wivern* 256, 277, 288, 295; see also Laird Rams; CSS *Mississippi*
Wood's Hotel (UK) 177
Woodside Landing see Liverpool
Woolwich Royal Arsenal (UK) 68
SS *Wren* 178, 297, 323, 337
Wright, Richard 173, 176–178, 294, 324

Xiuchuan, Hong 112, 294

Yancey, William Lowndes 42, 44, 67, 290, 294
SS *Yangtze* 297
Yangtze River (CH) 112
Yeddo 168, 170, 287, 297
Yonge, Clarence R. 63–65, 82, 84, 90, 91, 128–130, 148, 294, 318
Yorktown 75

Zanzibar 257, 258, 295, 328

www.ingramcontent.com/pod-product-compliance
Lightning Source LLC
Chambersburg PA
CBHW081536300426
44116CB00015B/2649